Handbook of
ADOPTION

DEDICATIONS

RAFAEL A. JAVIER

To all those who gave me a better appreciation of the adoption experience in all its complexity. To my nephew, Bill (Sasha) Homolka, who made me an adopted uncle and to Jenna Stern, who not only enriched the life of her adopted mother (my neighbor and colleague), but mine as well. I also dedicate this book to my friend and colleague, Dale Hahn, whose willingness to share her personal journey of her adoption experience had a profound impact on me. Finally, I dedicate this book to all the members of the adoption triad.

AMANDA BADEN

I'd like to dedicate this book and all of the work that went into it to my parents, Leon and Marianne Baden, my sister, Rebecca Baden-Eberwein, and my loving husband, Michael Glicksman. They are both the source of my strength and my inspiration for the work that I do in adoption.

FRANK A. BIAFORA

To LeaAnn, the woman who, during the creation of this book, started out as my best friend and became my bride by the end. You were my strength and my sounding board throughout this entire process.

ALINA CAMACHO-GINGERICH

I would like to dedicate this book to my mother, Dr. Daria Rivero, who many years after her death continues to be my inspiration; to my husband, Willard; and my children, Tanya and Daniel, for their love and support in all my endeavors.

Handbook of
ADOPTION

Implications for Researchers, Practitioners, and Families

Rafael A. Javier
St. John's University

Amanda L. Baden
Montclair State University

Frank A. Biafora
St. John's University

Alina Camacho-Gingerich
St. John's University

Preface by David Brodzinsky

SAGE Publications
Thousand Oaks ▪ London ▪ New Delhi

KH

For information:

Sage Publications, Inc.
2455 Teller Road
Thousand Oaks, California 91320
E-mail: order@sagepub.com

Sage Publications Ltd.
1 Oliver's Yard
55 City Road
London EC1Y 1SP
United Kingdom

Sage Publications India Pvt. Ltd.
B-42, Panchsheel Enclave
Post Box 4109
New Delhi 110 017 India

Printed in the United States of America.

Library of Congress Cataloging-in-Publication Data

Handbook of adoption : implications for researchers, practitioners, and families / edited by Rafael A. Javier . . . [et al.].
  p. cm.
Includes bibliographical references and index.
ISBN 1-4129-2750-1 or 978-1-4129-2750-5 (cloth)
ISBN 1-4129-2751-X or 978-1-4129-2751-2 (pbk.)
1. Adoption. 2. Adoption—Research. I. Javier, Rafael Art.

HV875.J38 2007
362.734—dc22   2006025203

This book is printed on acid-free paper.

06 07 08 09 10   10 9 8 7 6 5 4 3 2 1

Acquiring Editor:	Kassie Graves
Editorial Assistant:	Veronica Novak
Project Editor:	Astrid Virding
Copyeditor:	Quads
Typesetter:	C&M Digitals (P) Ltd.
Proofreader:	Scott Oney
Indexer:	Kathy Paparchontis
Cover Designer:	Janet Foulger

9/19/07.

Contents

List of Figures and Tables

Acknowledgments

Writing a book of this nature always entails working with a variety of individuals whose contributions to the final product are unmistakably evident throughout the process in various ways; it involves establishing a common vision and making necessary compromises to ensure the timely completion of the book, without compromising in quality and depth. It also involves from the very beginning a clear recognition that the task could not be accomplished without the active participation of each of those who contributed to the book. For it was not only the creative process involved in writing this book that was crucial in its creation but the establishment of the necessary working relationships with a group of already accomplished colleagues who shared a great deal of passion for the subject matter that we all decided to tackle as editors and contributors to the book. Indeed, each editor and contributor brought to bear his or her expertise and passion to ensure, at the end, not only that the book was high in caliber of contents and comprehensiveness but also that it reflected the excitement and dynamism that guided us as we prepared it. So, the first thanks go to my esteemed colleague Amanda Baden for her hard work and leadership and to Frank Biafora and Alina Camacho-Gingerich for the many rich discussions, the gives-and-takes, and the long and arduous hours we spent together. Thank you for a job well done and for the great deal of respect and appreciation for one another's contributions you exhibited throughout the process. Thank you for making the preparation of this comprehensive handbook of adoption such a wonderful and rewarding journey. It is certainly a testimony of your commitment to making adoption an important topic of discussion for academics, professionals and members of the triad. Thank you also to all the contributors for your dedication and for working so closely with us in meeting deadlines, your timely responses to our many suggestions for corrections to your manuscripts, and so on. You certainly made the book possible. THANK YOU!

We also extend our great appreciation to Cathy Lancellotti, who provided important assistance in the initial stage of the book's preparation, and to Margaret Cashin for her willingness to gather important data that were incorporated in some of the chapters of the book and her consistent and appreciated support throughout the process. The assistance provided by Louis Mora, Jennifer Salhanny, and Lorie Blas, students at St. John's University, is also recognized. They worked behind the scenes, doing the necessary research and preparing the bibliography.

In addition to those acknowledged above, I, Amanda Baden, would like to thank my colleagues at Montclair State University, especially Dr. Muninder Ahluwalia for her support and for her willingness to review drafts of chapters and provide helpful feedback. I'd also like to thank my graduate assistants, Laura Thomas and Miryam Kass, for their hard work and dedication. Their efforts and contribution are greatly appreciated. I'd also like to thank Carla Vale, a student worker who also assisted with organization for this project. Last, I'd like to thank Dr. Robbie J. Steward, one of my coauthors as well as a mentor who led me to this work and supported me throughout.

I, Frank Biafora, would also like to extend my appreciation to those who made the preparation of our book possible, but particularly my coeditors and contributors. A special thanks go particularly to my graduate assistant, Mr. Christopher Coes, who came in early, stayed late, and entertained my telephone calls on the weekends as I was working on different manuscripts. And, a very warm heartfelt thank you to my wife, LeaAnn, who provided hours of thoughtful feedback and editing throughout the writing of this book.

I, Alina Camacho-Gingerich, also join my colleagues in recognizing the tremendous assistance we received from so many people as we worked in the different stages of the book preparation. I would like to thank, first of all, my coeditors, Drs. Rafael Javier, Frank Biafora, and Amanda Baden, for the countless hours of shared work and input; to all the authors for their valuable contributions; and, last but not least, my graduate research assistant, Julisa Sime, for her help in various tasks related to this book.

Finally, we recognize that without the initial contact made by Bruce Kellogg to St. John's University requesting that the school find a way to address adoption issues, the book would not have been possible. Thus, our thanks to Bruce for his encouragement and dedication over the years and to all those who actively participated in the initial organization and early publications on adoption, particularly Douglas Henderson and B. J. Lifton. Finally, we would also like to extend our appreciation to Art Pomponio, Veronica Novak, and Kassie Graves from Sage for their guidance and support throughout our journey.

Foreword

DAVID BRODZINSKY

Rutgers University

Evan B. Donaldson Adoption Institute

Adoption touches the lives of millions of Americans and is now viewed by most individuals as an estimable means of family formation (Evan B. Donaldson Adoption Institute, 2002). Over the past three decades, however, the nature of adoption has changed dramatically (Brooks, Simmel, Wind, & Barth, 2005). The stereotype of the infertile couple adopting a same-race, newborn baby and having little or no information about, or contact with, the child's birth family is rapidly giving way to a much more complex and diverse form of family life. For example, as the availability of adoptable babies declined in the second half of the 20th century, individuals seeking to adopt began to turn their attention to older children living in foster care, as well as children born in foreign countries. In many cases, these children were of a different race or ethnic background from the adoptive parents and had special medical, psychological, or educational needs. In addition, during this period, the field of adoption moved decidedly toward increased openness, with adoption agencies sharing more information with adoptive parents about the child's birth history and/or facilitating open placements in which there is some form of direct contact between adoptive- and birth-family members.

As adoption has become more visible in society, as well as more complex in its nature, it has begun to capture the interest of both academic researchers and the mental health community. Behavior geneticists, for example, have become interested in adoption because it provides them with a means of understanding the unique influence of nature versus nurture in the growth and development of the human being (Plomin, 2004; Wadsworth, Corley, Plomin, Hewitt, & DeFries, 2006). Developmental researchers, on the other hand, are interested in adopted individuals because their diverse, and sometimes adverse, early histories offer insights into the role prenatal and postnatal experiences play for different developmental pathways (Gunnar & Kertes, 2005; Rutter, 2005). Finally, mental health practitioners have become increasingly interested in the unique psychodynamics and adjustment patterns of adopted individuals and their families (Brodzinsky, Smith, & Brodzinsky, 1998; Reitz & Watson, 1992). Issues related to separation and loss, trauma, attachment disruption, and conflicted identity, all of which are viewed as core components of the adoption experience, have raised concerns among many clinicians about the psychological risks associated with adoption.

Most of the early research on adoption was quite narrow in focus and suffered from serious methodological limitations (Brodzinsky et al., 1998). For example, the research was primarily descriptive and cross-sectional in nature, with small convenience samples, and typically examined the relative adjustment of adopted versus nonadopted individuals.

Although the bulk of this research suggested that adopted children were more likely to manifest behavioral and emotional problems than their nonadopted age-mates, what was often overlooked was the fact that the vast majority of adopted individuals were well within the normal range of adjustment (Brodzinsky & Palacios, 2005; Brodzinsky et al., 1998). Furthermore, other research pointed out that the practice of adoption could be viewed as a protective factor in the lives of children, especially for those living in institutions or foster care, as well as those whose biological parents were neglectful or abusive (Brodzinsky & Pinderhughes, 2002; Hoksbergen, 1999).

Recently, several noticeable and important changes have emerged in the adoption field (Palacios & Brodzinsky, 2005). First, research has become much more theory-driven than in the past. This change reflects the desire not only to document adjustment patterns in adoption but to understand them more fully. Genetic theory, neurobiological risk theory, attachment theory, stress and coping theory, social role theory, family systems theory, cognitive-developmental theory, and communication theory, among others, all have been used by different investigators to explain various aspects of adoption adjustment. Although offering valuable insights into children's adjustment to adoption, each of these theories fails to capture the richness and diversity of adoptive family dynamics. As Palacios and Brodzinsky (2005) noted, "Understanding contemporary adoption as a developing, multisystemic experience necessitates a more complex representation than most theoretical models have provided to date" (p. 259).

A second change that has occurred in the field is the shift from looking primarily at the relative risk associated with adoption status to examining individual, family, and systemic processes accounting for the variability in adoption adjustment throughout the developing years. This trend is providing important information on the adjustment of adopted individuals in response to both normative-developmental and family life cycle tasks, as well as those unique to adoption (e.g., the adoption revelation process, the meaning of being adopted to the child, identification with two sets of parents, coping with adoption-related loss, contact with birth-family members, etc.). Related to this trend is the shift from a psychopathological perspective on adoption to one that focuses on issues of resilience. The stereotype of adoption as inherently associated with an array of psychological problems has given way to a more balanced perspective in which adoption also is viewed as a potential benefit for children whose early histories are replete with biological and/or social adversity. In addition, there is greater interest today among adoption researchers in identifying those factors, both internal and external to the child, that facilitate healthier coping with adoption-related stress.

Recent investigators also have sought to overcome the methodological problems of past adoption research associated with the use of small, convenience samples as well as cross-sectional designs. In the past decade, a number of researchers have turned to national database survey data as a means of gathering more representative information on adopted children and their families. Furthermore, a number of longitudinal investigations on adoption adjustment also have been published during this time period. These efforts have significantly bolstered our knowledge of adoption practice and adoptive family life.

Finally, the shift toward greater openness in adoption also has been paralleled by a growing interest in examining the impact of contact with the birth family on adopted children and their families, as well as the influence of greater communication openness on adoption triad members (Brodzinsky, 2005, in press; Wrobel, Kohler, Grotevant, & McRoy, 2003). This change represents a significant step toward bridging the gap between research and adoption practice.

Yet for all the changes that have taken place in the field of adoption over the past few decades, it still remains a significantly underresearched area of inquiry. In addition, adoption practice, as a whole, has not been adequately informed by the findings of this growing body of data. Fortunately, more and more empirical investigators, from a variety of disciplines, are turning their attention to the field of adoption. In many cases, these individuals have a strong interest in the practical implications of their work. The current *Handbook of Adoption*, edited by Rafael Javier, Amanda Baden, Frank Biafora, and Alina Camacho-Gingerich, is in keeping with this new trend. The editors have pulled together a talented group of researchers and practitioners, some of whom have a long association with the field of adoption, and others of whom are relatively new to the field. The chapters authored by these individuals cover a wide range of important, and in some cases cutting-edge, topics. They offer the reader a roadmap to unraveling some of the complexities associated with the practice of adoption as well as of adoptive family life. However, what is most valuable about the *Handbook*, in my opinion, in addition to the up-to-date review of the literature, is the effort made by most of the contributors to address practical concerns. In developing their volume, the editors chose wisely and ensured that a wide range of practice-related issues were included. For example, several chapters discuss the importance of training and educating mental health professionals for adoption therapy competence. Others explore a variety of assessment and treatment issues in working clinically with adoption triad members. In addition, the implications of research for social casework practice also are considered by a number of the authors.

In their introductory chapter, the editors invite the reader to take a journey with them, to explore the many issues associated with adoption in an open and frank manner. It is an invitation well worth accepting. The reader will encounter a wealth of information about adoption written by knowledgeable and experienced researchers and adoption professionals. The editors and contributors to the *Handbook of Adoption* should be commended for providing the adoption community with an invaluable resource on the psychology of adoption.

REFERENCES

Brodzinsky, D. M. (2005). Reconceptualizing openness in adoption: Implications for theory, research, and practice. In D. Brodzinsky & J. Palacios (Eds.), *Psychological issues in adoption: Research and practice* (pp. 145–166). Westport, CT: Praeger.

Brodzinsky, D. M. (in press). Family structural openness and communication openness as predictors in the adjustment of adopted children. *Adoption Quarterly*.

Brodzinsky, D. M., & Palacios, J. (Eds.). (2005). *Psychological issues in adoption: Research and practice*. Westport, CT: Praeger.

Brodzinsky, D. M., & Pinderhughes, E. E. (2002). Parenting and child development in adoptive families. In M. H. Bornstein (Ed.), *Handbook of parenting: Vol. 1. Children and parenting* (pp. 279–311). Mahwah, NJ: Lawrence Erlbaum.

Brodzinsky, D. M., Smith, D. W., & Brodzinsky, A. B. (1998). *Children's adjustment to adoption: Developmental and clinical issues*. Thousand Oaks, CA: Sage.

Brooks, D., Simmel, C., Wind, L., & Barth, R. P. (2005). Contemporary adoption in the United States: Implications for the next wave of adoption theory, research, and practice. In D. Brodzinsky & J. Palacios (Eds.), *Psychological issues in adoption: Research and practice* (pp. 1–25). Westport, CT: Praeger.

Evan B. Donaldson Adoption Institute. (2002). *2002 National Adoption Attitudes Survey*. Harris Interactive. Retrieved August 3, 2006, from www.adoptioninstitute.org/survey/Adoption Attitudes Survey

Gunnar, M. R., & Kertes, D. A. (2005). Prenatal and postnatal risks to neurobiological development in internationally adopted children. In D. Brodzinsky & J. Palacios (Eds.), *Psychological issues in adoption: Research and practice* (pp. 47–65). Westport, CT: Praeger.

Hoksbergen, R. A. C. (1999). The importance of adoption for nurturing and enhancing the emotional and intellectual potential of children. *Adoption Quarterly, 3*, 29–42.

Palacios, J., & Brodzinsky, D. M. (2005). Recent changes and future directions for adoption research. In D. Brodzinsky & J. Palacios (Eds.), *Psychological issues in adoption: Research and practice* (pp. 257–268). Westport, CT: Praeger.

Plomin, R. (2004). Genetics and developmental psychology. *Merrill-Palmer Quarterly, 50*, 341–352.

Reitz, M., & Watson, K. W. (1992). *Adoption and the family system*. New York: Guilford Press.

Rutter, M. (2005). Adverse preadoption experiences and psychological outcomes. In D. Brodzinsky & J. Palacios (Eds.), *Psychological issues in adoption: Research and practice* (pp. 67–92). Westport, CT: Praeger.

Wadsworth, S. J., Corley, R., Plomin, R., Hewitt, J. K., & DeFries, J. C. (2006). Genetic and environmental influences on continuity and change in reading achievement in the Colorado Adoption Project. In A. C. Huston & M. N. Ripke (Eds.), *Developmental contexts in middle childhood: Bridges to adolescence and adulthood* (pp. 87–106). New York: Cambridge University Press.

Wrobel, G. M., Kohler, J. K., Grotevant, H. D., & McRoy, R. G. (2003). The family adoption communication model (FAC): Identifying pathways of adoption-related communication. *Adoption Quarterly*, 7, 53–84.

Breaking the Seal

1

Taking Adoption Issues to the Academic and Professional Communities

RAFAEL A. JAVIER

St. John's University

AMANDA L. BADEN

Montclair State University

FRANK A. BIAFORA

St. John's University

ALINA CAMACHO-GINGERICH

St. John's University

DOUGLAS B. HENDERSON

University of Wisconsin–Stevens Point

A doption has a long history in human civilization, with clear reference to its existence as far back as biblical time. The adoption triad, which consists of birth parents, adoptive parents, and adopted persons, can be readily identified within these biblical stories. For example, one is reminded of the story of Moses who was adopted by the Pharaoh and almost became the heir to the throne until he abdicated to return to the people he came from and felt greatest affinity to, the Hebrews. His was technically a closed adoption, since there was no reference to his awareness, while growing up, of his biological family until later in life when he decided to search for his birth identity and birth family. His search was precipitated by his unexplained feelings of empathy when seeing a Hebrew woman about to be crushed by one of the block-columns that was being positioned for the construction of the temple. His decision to search for his birth identity resulted in his losing the connection with and protection of his adoptive parents and set the stage for the show-down between him and his adoptive brother, Ramsey.

The most famous and complicated biblical adoption story is the one of Jesus, who was adopted by Joseph the Carpenter after having been conceived mysteriously in the body of a virgin, Mary. In the eyes of many, Joseph was the biological father and the legal husband of Mary, although Joseph knew that Jesus was not his creation and was his adopted child (Gardner, 1995). Joseph's son was known as Jesus of Nazareth so that the issue of the last name was bypassed. That was not the case, however, for many during the Romans' time, in which the issue of the preservation of the family's name was the primary reason for adoption. In fact, adoption was used as an effective way to ensure the continuation of the family's name in families of the nobility when they were unable to engender a progenitor or their sons were unfit to inherit (Encyclopedia of Adoption, 2006). This practice extended to the emperors, resulting in a number of Roman emperors and high officials who were adopted during their adolescence or adulthood. Children from less well-to-do families were adopted into families with better means, immediately acquiring the new family's name with full right of heritage. It was expected that all family ties with birth families were to be permanently severed. This was not unique to the Romans, as this practice was also found in the Chinese Qing Dynasty, India, and Hawaiian royal families (Chinese Qing Dynasty, 2006; Hawaiian Royal Families, 2006; India Princely States, 2006).

Adoptions have taken place throughout history in various forms, where children end up being raised at some point in their lives by people other than their birth parents. It was even present at the very beginning of the birth of the United States as a nation. In fact, many adopted triad members have led notable and illustrious lives. Well-known and admired adoptees include leaders (e.g., Catherine I, Crazy Horse, John Hancock, William Jefferson Clinton), artists (e.g., Gian Giacomo Caprotti), performers (e.g., John Lennon, Ella Fitzgerald, Faith Hill, Willie Nelson), writers (e.g., Truman Capote, Edgar Allen Poe, Charles Dickens), actors (e.g., Jack Nicholson, Ray Liotta, Gary Coleman, Ingrid Bergman), athletes (e.g., Greg Louganis, Scott Hamilton, Dan O'Brien), and business owners (e.g., Dave Thomas, Steven Jobs) (Dever & Dever, 1992; Freedman, 1996; Goldman, 1996; Longworth, 1973; Petre, 1991; Plimpton, 1997; Terrill, 1994; Tyler, 1998).

The list above includes famous people from the adoption triad (birth parents, adoptive parents, and adoptees). Those listed led prominent lives in history and were largely power-ful and accomplished in their lives. However, other stories and representations of adopted persons also exist—those for whom their adoption may have been used as a partial explanation for their criminal and pathological behavior. For example, Lyle and Erik Menendez were adoptees who became infamous for killing their adoptive parents and reinforcing Kirschner's (1990) "adopted child syndrome" that has reinforced the stigma surrounding adoption. In fact, Kirschner built his theory in his 1978 paper on David Berkowitz, the ser-ial killer known as the Son of Sam, who was adopted as an infant. These and similar stories have contributed to both a glorification and a condemnation of adoption, leaving many without any clear picture of the true nature of adoption. The stigmatization of adoption has created a society of people who may end up having a stereotypical view of adoption, in which each part of the triad reenacts the scenes from history, and each is infused with attributes that reflect their role. For example, the birth parents who died tragically or were unknown or uncaring, the damaged and wounded adoptees whose bad luck and bad birth will reveal themselves in some unwanted way, and the heroic and suffering adoptive parents who sought to rescue unwanted children. With these images and with the roles already ingrained in the consciousness of society, how can we adequately begin to understand and address the needs of the adoption triad? In particular, how will clinicians, whose role it is to intervene and assist those affected by adoption, be prepared to help, and be effective and competent in their treatment?

To begin to assist the adoption triad, these tainted images and ideas of adoption and the stigma that accompanies them must be unraveled and replaced with accurate, unbiased, and useful knowledge that both acknowledges the potential issues and tolerates the ambiguity of differing outcomes within this population. It is our hope that this *Handbook* will assist triad members, their families, clinicians, laypeople, and anyone interested in adoption in their efforts to approach the members of the adoption triad with the respect and understanding that they deserve, while simultaneously recognizing the complexity of the experiences that adopted people and their two sets of parents have in this world that operates on assumptions of a genetic and biological heritage.

The questions regarding the forces responsible for creating the necessary conditions to have children available for adoption are complex and multifaceted, as are the consequences. This has been clearly delineated in the different parts included in this book. The book has been divided into nine parts specifically designed to cover critical issues in the adoption experience, from a review of the major theoretical, historical, and research issues to specific discussions on assessment and treatment issues with members of the adoption triad. The first part is meant as a foundation to address historical and theoretical issues to provide the reader with a comprehensive review of the adoption landscape from past to present and to set the stage for the other parts in the book. Thus, chapters by Esposito and Biafora (Chapter 2), Biafora and Esposito (Chapter 3), and Freundlich (Chapter 4) provide excellent discussions on the history of adoption in general and, particularly, in North America. They also place special emphasis on identifying the social, political, and economic forces that have accompanied the adoption experience throughout history and resulted in the enactment of the many laws influencing adoption practice. These are considered foundation chapters because they provide readers with important information to help them understand the state of adoption in today's society and gain the necessary appreciation of the complexity of the adoption experience and the historical antecedents to the current historical, political, and legal forces that are guiding the current debate on the adoption experience. As discussed further below, other parts include discussions on issues pertaining to transracial adoption, special issues in adoption (i.e., foster care, single parents, special needs, etc.), training and education issues, relevant research findings in adoption, assessment and treatment issues, and finally, samples of how the adoption experience can provide unique dynamism to the creative process. Each part has a part-specific introduction (or preface) in which a series of learning goals are listed to guide the reading of the different chapters in that part. A list of resources covering topics discussed in the book is included at the end of the book. You will also find in most of the chapters a list of reflection questions that can be used, by those using the book as a textbook, to guide the learning of the subject. Thus, readers are strongly encouraged to use the reflection questions to guide their reading of the different chapters. They are also encouraged to look at the preface of each part where specific learning goals are listed and the resource list at the end of the book, if they are interested in additional information about the topic.

THE CURRENT STATE OF AFFAIRS

Given the longevity of adoption throughout history, including North American history, and the prevalence of adoption in the United States and other parts of the world, how are we to understand that adoption issues still remain largely unaddressed and off the radar in terms of interest to the professional and academic disciplines? How is it possible that training programs that prepare professionals for human services do not systematically include discussions on adoption issues, as suggested by Post (2000) and Henderson (2000)? It is, indeed, truly perplexing that even after so many generations of families have been directly or indirectly involved with and affected by the adoption experience, our understanding remains so rudimentary. The fact that many adoptive triad members still feel that the complexities of adoption are not fully understood by the professional community not only is unfortunate but leaves many adoptees and their families at a loss as to where to go to address unanswered questions. This ignorance may be responsible for the lack of systematic research on the issues in behavioral science and the lack of clear and useful training and treatment guidelines for those involved in the evaluation and treatment of adoptive triad members.

FUNDAMENTAL ISSUES IN ADOPTION

Attachment Issues and Identity Formation

There are a number of fundamental issues that are in need of more systematic attention from behavioral scientists and practitioners alike. Children are adopted at different stages in their developmental trajectory, and yet an empirically validated and comprehensive model documenting the psychosocial life span development of adoptees does not yet exist. How do these children develop bonding and attachment, their self-identities, their views of the world, their relationships with others, their sense of belonging, and so on, in the context of their adoption experience, are questions that have largely eluded the scientific community. We know from the work of Freud (1896, 1905), Sullivan (1953), Piaget (1995), Erickson (1950, 1982), Mahler, Pine, and Bergman (1975), and Stern (1985) that individuals' basic identity, personality, values, and belief systems, their assumptions concerning causality, time, space, and human nature, as well as culturally specific styles of relating and moral standing are developed during the formative years and in relationship with their human and ecological environments (Dana, 1993; Javier, 1996; Javier & Rendon, 1995; Javier & Yussef, 1998). For adoptees, this environment includes birth parents, membership in an extended family system, geographical and environmental landscapes, genetic and familial heritage, culture, traditions, customs, and language. These authors provide a vivid description of this development where the child is initially in a totally dependent relationship with those he or she relies on for care and comfort. As the child's brain capacity grows more sophisticated, the child's ability to organize its experience with itself and others also becomes more sophisticated. It is in this context that the child learns to handle tension and anxiety, develops a language to communicate, develops categories of emotions, and develops "a relatively enduring pattern of experience of the self as a unique, coherent, entity over time" (Moore & Fine, 1991, as cited in Herron, 1998, p. 321). This sense of self-identity becomes consolidated later in life during the critical adolescent period (Erickson, 1950, 1982) when the child normally challenges and questions many of the assumptions that have guided his or her belief system and values, and that up to that point were accepted without much question. Because of the vulnerability of the child's cognitive and emotional condition during the formative years, this development could be derailed by obstacles in the child's environment. When adoption enters this developmental trajectory, what happens to the child's sense of identity when removed from his or her birth environment early in life and adopted into another environment? And what happens when this new environment also involves different cultural norms, race relationships, and language? What happens to the sense of identity when adoption occurs later in development, during the adolescent years, or when the adopted adolescent who was adopted in childhood is unable to reconcile the discrepancy of race/cultural differences with the adoptive family or the information made available about his or her origin? These are just some of the incredibly complex questions ably addressed in Part II of this book by McGinn (Chapter 5), Grotevant, Dunbar, Kohler, and Lash Esau (Chapter 6), and Baden and Steward (Chapter 7).

Beginning with the work of Spitz (1946) investigating the deaths of many of the British infants raised in institutions in World War II, and accelerating in the 1980s, psychologists have studied the concepts of attachment and bonding as they relate to several aspects of the developing child. Our understanding of the sensory and cognitive capabilities of the infant has expanded rapidly and now includes knowledge of these processes in the fetus as well. With this new knowledge, we have reevaluated the effects of adoption, especially in terms of the environment of the prenatal child. It has been suggested that adoption affects the experience of separation from the birth mother and the early postnatal environment, including possible foster or institutional placements prior to adoption (Henderson, 2000).

Nydam (1999), Verrier (1993), and Verny and Kelly (1981) are but three of the many authors who have written about how the infant destined to be adopted, experiences pre- and postnatal life differently than the infant who will remain with the birth family. Emphasizing the importance of early attachment and bonding, Nydam (1999) calls for specific and separate discussions of the relinquishment experience and of its effects on adoption triad members.

McGinn's contribution in Chapter 5 is particularly relevant in this context because it includes a comprehensive discussion of attachment and "attachment derailment" and the consequences of these issues throughout the adoptee's life span, including their effect on adoptees' capacity to develop meaningful relationships. Anchoring his chapter in the work of John Bowlby, Erik Erickson, and Margaret Mahler, McGinn provides an informative discussion on some of the potential obstacles and challenges for adopted persons in the context of their developmental trajectory.

In the final analysis, a self-identity that emerges as a result of all these different cultural, racial, and ethnic influences can only result in the development of what Herron (1998) referred to as "ethnic identity," which goes through the same basic four stages of development (i.e., identity diffusion, identity foreclosure, moratorium, and finally identity achieved). Only when the individual reaches the stage of "identity achieved" is a secure sense of self assumed to have developed. The work of Grotevant et al. in Chapter 6 provides relevant empirical support to the crucial importance of an identity formation for the adoptees that includes the adoption experience, or what they referred to as "adoptive identity." These authors emphasize the iterative and integrative nature of the identity development process for the adoptee rather than a linear one. According to these authors, the major task of identity development in the context of the adoption experience "involves 'coming to terms' with oneself in the context of the family and culture into which one has been adopted." This is the case because most aspects of adoption include things that the adopted person has not chosen. The process of coming to terms is a progressive one and includes *unexamined identity, limited identity, unsettled identity,* and *integrated identity.* Thus, the highest level of identity formation will be one where the individual has managed to integrate all his or her experiences as an adoptive person in ways that promote sound mental health and a good level of functional adaptation.

Baden and Steward in Chapter 7 take the issue of identity to the next level by suggesting a comprehensive model that explains a variety of possible identities when dealing with transracial adoption. According to their model, 16 different identities are possible depending on the degrees to which the adoptee has "knowledge of, awareness of, competence within, and comfort with their own racial group's culture, their parents' racial group's culture, and multiple cultures." These authors highlight other models of identity formation found in the literature, such as Helms's People of Color Racial Identity Model, and make a convincing argument as to how these models are insufficient in explaining the full experience of the adopted person. Theirs, although still largely a theoretical model, is the first Cultural-Racial Identity Model to recognize and separate cultural identity and racial identity as two different and interrelated identities, making different and, at times, competing demands on the individual's identity formation.

Although these chapters are challenging to absorb, given the advanced theoretical assumptions they use, we encourage the reader to become familiar with the work of these important authors since they provide the most comprehensive explanation of the different challenges likely to affect adoptees in various ways.

Impact of Transracial Adoption on Triad Members

What is clear, however, is that throughout history there have been recurrent forces around the world, precipitated by war conflicts, natural disasters, and socioeconomic and political forces, that have forced the displacement of many individuals from their families and countries (Holt, 2006; Rippley, 2005), leaving many without any family ties. Most recently, we see this in the Middle East conflicts, the genocides in many African nations, the continuous slaughter of innocent people in the Darfur region of Sudan, Africa AIDS epidemics, the Southeast Asia Tsunami disaster, and the Hurricane Katrina disaster in New Orleans (Gibbs, 2005; Holt, 2006; Sachs, 2005), which have left many children without birth parents, abandoned, in the care of other family members, or in orphanages. In terms of sociopolitical forces having a direct impact on adoption, particularly international adoption, we see also how poverty, governmental policies restricting the number of children within families (e.g., China), and gender preferences based on Confucian principles (e.g., China and India) can lead to abortions, abandonments, and relinquishments, as discussed by Baden in Chapter 8 of Part III of this volume.

Thus, it is clear that adoption has permeated and continues to permeate and penetrate our history and society. Indeed, one is now highly likely to encounter someone who is an adoptive triad member, whether an adoptee, an adoptive parent, or a birth parent. According to some estimates, between 40 million (Henderson, 2000) and 100 million (www.adoptioninformationinstitute.org) Americans are directly affected by adoption in very fundamental ways. And these adoptees come from many parts of the world, particularly from several countries in South and Central America, Korea, China, and Russia, as discussed by Baden (Chapter 8), Camacho-Gingerich, Branco-Rodriguez, Pitteri and Javier (Chapter 10), and McGinnis (Chapter 11). Thus, questions such as what are the psychological, socioeconomic, sociopolitical, and legal challenges facing adopted persons, birth parents, and adoptive parents become even more complex when considering the different cultural, racial, sociopolitical, ecological, and linguistic backgrounds that triad members may bring to the adoption equation. The ramifications of these factors cannot be underestimated considering that approximately 8% of all adoptions are transracial and that the numbers of international adoptions have more than doubled from 1992 to 1999 (Baden, 2002).

Thus, we decided to dedicate a whole part (Part III) to the exploration of issues related to transracial and cross-cultural adoptions. In this context, we include a contribution from Baden (Chapter 8), who provides an important discussion of the Chinese American experience for Chinese adoptees and examines the attitudes toward domestic versus international adoption in China, governmental policies affecting a gender differential, and attitudes with regard to who ends up being placed in adoption. The resulting stigmatization in both China and the host country, in this case the United States, continues to be a challenge for adoptive families and adopted persons. The clinical implications of these attitudes, perceptions, motivations, and their impact on adoptees are also seriously examined.

Roorda's contribution in Chapter 9 adds another crucial component to the discussion, by focusing on the challenges normally faced by African American and biracial children adopted by White parents. These types of adoptions have a long history of controversy here in the United States, with clear opposition by the National Association of Black Social Workers Associations. She examined research findings that attempted to study the effect of these types of adoptions on these children's self-esteem, identity formation, and racial group identity. The author concluded that under the right conditions, transracial adoption can be a good thing.

The contributions by Camacho-Gingerich et al. (Chapter 10) and McGinnis (Chapter 11) examine the experience of two other cultural/linguistic groups with a solid representation in adoption triads. We are referring to adoptions from Latin America and Korea. What comes across from these chapters is the need to look at these different cultural adoption groups as unique and as representing unique adjustment challenges. The fact that adoptees coming from these groups present clearly distinguishable phenotype features and skin color, and that the groups from which they come have their own unique values, cultures, customs, worldviews, and languages, creates the necessary conditions for identity, cultural, and linguistic clashes when these children are adopted by families from other racial, cultural, and linguistic backgrounds. These clashes become particularly evident during the adolescent years. These are the issues extensively addressed by Camacho-Gingerich, Branco-Rodriguez, Pitteri, and Javier, who examine the political and socioeconomic conditions of a Latin American group (Argentinean) that tend to influence the extent to which national (domestic) and international adoptions are encouraged. Using a group of Colombian adoptees, these authors also examine the kind of adjustment challenges that Latin American adoptees are likely to face once adopted internationally. McGinnis, on the other hand, offers an excellent historical review of the Korean experience over the last 50 years with emphasis on the kinds of issues still affecting these adoptees today. Of great importance to consider with regard to the Argentinian situation is the fact that that country is not a signature to the Hague Convention and thus making irrelevant to the Argentinian children and parents a series of rules and procedures that have been established to ensure proper protection of children for adoption in the international arena. Although we appreciate the rationale as to the Argentina's reluctance to be part of the Hague Convention agreement, mostly based on the serious abuses committed during the military regime with regard to children being snatched from families (who were later killed) to be given to members of the ruling class that were unable to conceive, the fact is that by not being part of the international efforts to protect children that are adopted, it may encourage adoptions of Argentinian children through informal and, perhaps, illegal means. At the end, it provides Argentinian children being adopted and their families less legal protection and oversight, which is paradoxically what Argentina is attempted to avoid by refusing to sign on to the Hague Convention.

Consequences of Open or Closed Adoption

The consequences of open or closed adoption and the interrelated subject of "search" and "reunion" issues, as related to adoptive triad members or children in permanent foster care, have yet to be empirically and systematically examined, and few models have been presented or agreed on by the adoption community. For the three sides of the adoption triad, the process of adoption has been viewed by many as a "win-win-win" situation. The birth parents "won" by being freed of child care responsibilities for which they were told they were unprepared. Adoptees "won" by being placed in a better home than the one their birth family could have provided, and adoptees were also sheltered from the negative stereotype of illegitimacy. Adoptive parents "won" by being able to raise the child. The story of an adoption was believed to end with the phrase "and the baby was adopted," much as other stories end with the phrase "and they lived happily ever after." In the traditional view, adoptions did end with everyone involved living happily ever after and never looking back. The adoptee and adoptive parents were believed to have spent their lives as a family indistinguishable from any other family, and the birth mother (and birth father if he was involved) were assumed to have returned to pick up their lives again.

The more contemporary and realistic view of adoption, however, is that every adoption represents both gains and losses, and that adoption is a multigenerational and ongoing process, which only begins with the discovery of an unplanned pregnancy and which permanently affects the lives of all involved. We know that the story of an adoption does not "end" the day the parents and their new child walk out of court as a legal family and the birth parents become legally childless.

A similar process occurs in the foster care triad (birth parents, foster care parents, and foster care child) where the child is removed from the home environment to protect him or her from emotional and physical danger, "for the best interest of the child." But members of the triad are then confronted with a series of challenges, particularly when the child begins to ask serious questions, such as "Why was I taken from my home?" "Why don't my parents love me enough to stop taking drugs?" "Why can't I be with family members?" "Was it something about me?" The complication for an untrained eye is that these questions are not always verbalized in this manner, but they are present in the form of behavioral difficulties at school and at home, learning problems, substance abuse, gang involvement, and so on.

Adoptive and foster care children and parents are at a tremendous disadvantage when they are not provided with much information (as in closed adoption) about the physical health of the child and family medical history, especially when dealing with a child with special needs. The consequences for the integrity of the reconstituted family and the physical and emotional health of the child cannot be overemphasized. Sooner or later, adopted or foster care children demand (especially during adolescence) to know, "Where did I come from?" "Why am I living here?" "Why is my skin color different from that of my adoptive parents?" "Why do I feel different from my adoptive siblings?" and a host of other questions. The extent to which answers to these questions are forthcoming will provide the necessary ingredient for children to come to terms with their past and look to the future with a strong and integrated sense of self.

Driven by the need to address these types of questions more specifically, the editors of this volume decided to dedicate a part to special issues in adoption (Part IV). The part begins with a chapter by McRoy, Grotevant, Ayers-Lopez, and Henney (Chapter 12) in which the authors address issues surrounding open adoptions. Using data from a longitudinal outcome study, these authors engaged in a critical discussion regarding the benefits and complications of open adoption. According to these authors, it is a complex dance in which the roles and needs of the participants change over time. It requires that each member of the triad redefine the boundary of what constitutes family and the self within that family. At some point, a balance has to be struck that allows the adoptive or foster family to develop its own identity separate and apart from the birth parent's identity. It is this dance and a description of the consequences of different kinds of communications possible among the members of the triad that is the main subject of this chapter.

The chapter by Pakizegi (Chapter 13) addresses the poignant issue of single parents by choice who become involved in adoption and foster care. She suggests that delays in preparation for child rearing and increases in infertility are two reasons why single adoptive parents should be examined given the increase in their numbers. The personal struggle facing these individuals (women and men), including the stigma associated with the assumption that these individuals were unable to find suitable partners and/or unable to conceive, could prove to be quite challenging to each member of these newly constituted families. Pakizegi calls for a more systematic study of what distinguishes these single individuals who decide to adopt from single women and men who decide not to adopt. Similarly, she calls for more research on how single-parents in adoptive families manage to navigate their lives successfully in the midst of the stigma and on what distinguishes those who decide to adopt one child versus those who decide to adopt more than one. It is clear that these alternative family structures are challenging the notions of the traditional family, and Pakizegi invites the reader to wrestle with the issue head-on because this is an increasing reality in the adoption community.

In the next chapter (Chapter 14), Keagy and Rall address an important topic often associated with anxiety and concern for adoptive families and adoption professionals: children with "special needs." Adoptable children who, due to medical issues or other special circumstances at the time of adoption (i.e., children previously abused and neglected, with attachment difficulties and serious behavioral problems, or with genetically based physical illness), are in need of more intense professional interventions are a population that must be considered when working with the adoption triad. They are considered children with special needs because they require special attention. But the parents may be ill-prepared for the time, emotional, and financial commitments required of them to appropriately care for a child with special needs.

The authors place a great deal of emphasis on the importance of open communication about the child's condition and the need to offer preparatory programs for these parents and for postadoption services. It is their contention that the greatest obstacle in being able to address the special needs of an adopted child is the kinds of expectations the adoptive family have due to the lack of information they received about the true condition of the child. Thus, adequate preparation, education, establishing appropriate expectations, the need of continuing to monitor parental stress, availability of counseling for members of the triad, and availability of respite care and support groups for the parents are some of the major mechanisms proposed by these authors to ensure positive adoption outcomes in these situations.

The question of the special challenges that gay, lesbian, and bisexual (GLB) adoptive families have to face in many parts of society is aptly addressed by Boyer in Chapter 15 on the double stigma GLB adoptive family members face. The fact that these individuals belong to an already stigmatized group, with implicit and explicit negative social attitudes, leaves these individuals with inconsistent legal protection at best or, at worst, totally absent protection. Despite the shortcomings in the law and in response to increased opportunities for adopting domestically and internationally, GLB adoptive families are testing the "adoption waters" and demanding to be counted as legitimate families. The implications of these types of adoptions are enormous not only with regard to the redefinition of what constitutes a family, as addressed by Pakizegi in Chapter 13, but also with regard to the issues addressed in Chapters 5 through 7 in this book pertaining to identify formation, self-definition, view of the world, view of relationships, and the like. Much needs to be known about the mechanisms that may be needed to help members of these types of families, already suffering the burden of being stigmatized by society, to be able to successfully negotiate the hostile environment so as to encourage a psychologically healthy outcome for those involved. The challenge is for the professional community that is often called on to address issues affecting these individuals to overcome their own prejudice. The author addresses this and other related treatment issues well in the chapter. Finally, the author provides an excellent examination of the many issues likely to arise in gay and lesbian adoptions and invites the readers to become familiar with them and actively involved in changing the stigmatization and discrimination prevailing in the current environment.

The chapter by Doyle (Chapter 16) is an important one because it forces the reader to recognize the similarities between issues in the traditional adoption experience and the foster care situation. The differences, however, are evident, particularly with regard to the impact of lack of permanency in the foster care home environment. Nevertheless, foster children and foster parents are forced to confront crucial questions pertaining to identity, self-definition, sense of security, and self-esteem in the context of the foster environment. The possibility for emotional derailment partly precipitated by the instability of the home environment is clearly described by Doyle in the various case presentations she offers throughout her chapter. Also discussed in the chapter are the challenges associated with situations where there are cultural and ethnic differences between the foster child and the foster family. Finally, her discussion of the history and governmental policies that guide this practice is very instructive even for those with professional experience with this population of children.

Many of the central questions that we have covered in the previous chapters, related to identity formation, self-esteem, worldview, issues of attachment and separation, development of meaningful relations, and so on, take center stage in the school setting. It is in this context that many of the most crucial personal battles are fought, because curiosity from peers about their looks, skin color, ethnic makeup, and so on may elicit confusion, frustration, and isolation, which, according to Fishman and Harrington (Chapter 17), "can turn into increased aggression, oppositional behavior, uncommunicativeness, depression, and self-image problems." Once the adopted child is in this whirlwind of emotion, school performance is likely to suffer, and so too the general attitude about school; hence, our decision to dedicate a chapter to address school issues more directly. This struggle may become more intense and emotionally debilitating in cases where the child's adoption experience is characterized by secrecy or paucity of information (as in closed adoption), thereby leaving the adoptee unable to find answers to his or her many questions. The authors take particular care to address the various ways in which school lessons and assignments can be redesigned such that they could be more sensitive to adoptees' experiences. Specific recommendations are provided in this regard.

CHALLENGES TO THE ACADEMIC AND PROFESSIONAL COMMUNITIES

It is clear from our discussion that the adoption experience affects every member of the triad in very fundamental ways, from attachment and identity development, to the concept of family, to relationships with peers and romantic relations. Different stages of development call for the consolidation and resolution of these various challenges (as discussed in previous chapters); and to the extent to which each member of the triad is able to find an acceptable solution to the various challenges, a cohesive and integrated self-definition for the adopted child and the adoptive and birth families will be possible. But one of the greatest obstacles in finding solutions to these dilemmas is the level of awareness the academic and professional communities have about issues of adoption and how adoption affects the triad members in fundamental ways, as amply discussed in Chapters 19 and 20 in Part V, 21 through 24 in Part VI, and 25 through 31 in Part VII of this volume. According to Porch (Chapter 19), Sass and Henderson (Chapter 20), and Henderson (Chapter 25), the current state of affairs is such that many adoptive families have to see up to 10 therapists before finding one who understands their unique circumstances, if they find one at all, or these families find themselves in the position of teaching the therapist about the most basic issues of adoption (Casey Family Services, 2002; Sass, Webster, & Henderson, 2000).

These authors provide a comprehensive examination of this issue, presenting data recently collected, and discuss some of the attempts made by the professional community to bridge the gap. In this context, Henderson, Sass, and Carlson (Chapter 24) present data on how the paucity of information received by both the adoptees and adoptive parents at placement, and the lack of information given to the birth mothers and adoptees about the nature of the postadoption experiences that they are more likely to endure, render the members of the triad ill-prepared to face the intensity of feelings associated with the adoption experience. They found that 55% of adoptees and 86% of birth parents in their sample experienced mental health or emotional problems related to adoption. With the tremendous consequences to the psychological survival of individuals, why are we still in such a state of affairs where secrecy or paucity of information is more the norm than the exception when it comes to adoption issues? Henderson (Chapter 25) provides an excellent discussion of the possible reasons for the current state of affairs in that regard and examines the various obstacles that need to be overcome to change the present course. Pavao's chapter (Chapter 18) is also particularly relevant in this regard, in that it provides a treatment model (Pavao's brief long-term therapy model) that allows for the kinds of issues discussed by Henderson et al. (Chapter 24), Henderson (Chapter 25), Freundlich (Chapter 21), Carr (Chapter 22), Baden (Chapter 23), and others to be addressed. It has been found to be very effective in addressing the complexity of adoption issues with members of the triad. It is an inclusive, intergenerational, developmental, and systemic approach that seeks to normalize the stages of development. It includes many extended family members (including birth parents and grandparents) because this model is particularly sensitive to the complexity and multilayer aspects of the kind of influences the adopted child is likely to experience. Finally, the model is based on a comprehensive examination of the adoption experience and the need to maintain an open discussion of issues of relinquishment, loss, grief, search, and reunion, as well as the need to institute psychoeducational interventions in potential adoptive families. It is clear, however, that only when the academic community takes up the issue of adoption as a systematic focus of academic endeavor will more comprehensive treatment and assessment models be possible. The call for a more systematic inclusion of adoption-related issues in the curriculum as an essential part of the training of future professionals is clearly evident in these and other chapters in this book.

Freundlich's critical examination of the emerging research contributions in Chapter 21 provides important suggestions to guide future research initiatives. She acknowledges the importance of the increasing amount of research on issues such as the impact of relinquishment, search and reunion, and open versus closed adoption on birth mothers, adopted children, and adoptive families (see McRoy et al., in Chapter 12 of this volume), particularly of middle-class and White women. (See Carr's contribution in this regard, in Chapter 22 of this volume, where she discusses the factors that tend to influence the extent to which Caucasian birth mothers will develop a personally fulfilling life, postrelinquishment.) Unfortunately, not much is known about the effects of the psychological and social ramifications of these issues on birth mothers in other countries and from different social and cultural backgrounds.

According to Freundlich (Chapter 21), what is also missing from the current research literature is an examination of the role of birth fathers in the adoption experience. Birth fathers have suffered from a number of stereotypical assumptions (e.g., that they are uninvolved and uninterested in the adoption experience, including search and reunion, loss, grieving, etc.). Leaving the birth fathers out of the adoption equation paints a very incomplete picture of the adoption experience, with major consequences for the psychological lives of many adoptees. Freundlich points out the need to focus more research attention on the impact of adoption on children adopted at older ages, the impact of the adoption qualification process on the adoption experience, and the determination of who should or should not be permitted to adopt. According to Porch (Chapter 19), it is more likely that children adopted from foster care are older, from racial minority populations, and adopted by parents with lower socioeconomic means. An examination of the reason(s) for this phenomenon could provide important information to help us develop better models that address the issue of foster care adoption more effectively in the future. According to Freundlich, the fact that so little is known about foster care adoption, and the impact of openness on the members of the adoption foster care triad, reflects the overarching need for greater research emphasis on the adoption of older children with histories of abuse and/or neglect.

The important work of Baden (Chapter 23) on issues related to identity and psychological adjustment within the context of culture and race and the work of Henderson et al. (Chapter 24) are two good examples of how research data can assist us in understanding the complexity of the adoption experience. Using the Cultural-Racial Identity Model discussed by Baden and Steward in Chapter 7, the authors were able to examine variations in the potential cultural-racial identities that transracial adoptees are able to report. By refining more carefully the different ways in which adoptees may be affected by their cultural and ethnic backgrounds and the different and multiple identities that may be formed, a more refined approach to intervention for these individuals may be possible.

Assessing the Mental Health Needs of Triad Members

Considering the multiplicity of emotional challenges members of the triad go through from the time the birth mothers consider relinquishing the child for adoption and the adoptive parents consider the creation of their family through adoption, to the developmental questions adopted children have to face as they go through the different stages of their lives from infancy (with questions about bonding and attachment issues) to adolescence (with questions about identity development, self-definition, and self-esteem) to adulthood (with questions about the ability to develop meaningful and romantic relationship with others), these individuals have to come to terms with these challenges and develop a cohesive and integrated sense of themselves as individuals and as adoptive families or relinquishing parents. Much is at stake as the adoption experience reverberates throughout their lives and influences them and the people they come into contact with in very fundamental ways.

Because of these inherent challenges, questions have been raised as to whether adoptees and other members of the triad are more prone to mental illnesses and to psychological and behavioral problems. Are adoptees more likely to suffer from attachment disorders and have difficulty developing relationships? What are the central treatment issues professionals should keep in mind in assessing and treating members of the triad? At what point is it appropriate to search for and reunite with the birth parents? These are some of the questions that have been addressed by a number of prominent scholars and clinicians over the last few years, including B. J. Lifton, Ron Nydam, Joyce Pavao, David Brodzinsky, Ruth McRoy, Harold Grotevant, Nancy Verrier, Doug Henderson, Christopher Deeg, Amanda Baden, and Rene Hoksbergen, to name a few. We have included the contributions of many of these individuals in Part VII of this book, because they have provided important answers to these questions, enriched our understanding, and substantially increased our knowledge of issues affecting the adoption community. What comes across from the work of these authors is that it is important to recognize that although the issues raised before, such as bonding and attachment problems, issues of loss, grief, and identity, and self-esteem problems, are central and fundamental issues to be addressed in assessing and treating adoptees, this does not suggest that adoption, in and of itself, is toxic to one's mental health. What is toxic, these authors argue, is the veil of secrecy and the paucity of information given to triad members about the challenges likely to emerge in the adoption experience. Such a practice has deprived the adoptee of the necessary information to come to terms with his or her unique situation of having been relinquished by one family and adopted by another, of having to process two family histories into his or her personal narrative, and, in the case of international adoption, to come to terms with two or more cultural and ethnic backgrounds. Thus, the reader is encouraged to examine the work by Henderson (Chapter 25), who addresses the issue "Why has the mental health community been silent on adoption issues?" and the chapter by Lifton (Chapter 26), which provides an excellent discussion on the concept of cumulative and multiple adoption traumas adoptees need to work through in their process of self-identity development. Hoksbergen and Laak's contribution (Chapter 30) provides important empirical data on the extent to which adoptees are more likely to suffer from reactive attachment disorders, including in adulthood. Baden and Wiley's contribution (Chapter 27) pays particular attention to the clinical symptoms birth parents are likely to experience, including unresolved grief related to the relinquishing experience, isolation, difficulty with future relations, and trauma. Concerned with the long-term reverberations of the issue of relinquishment and loss in the psychological development of adoptees, Nydam (Chapter 28) uses psychoanalytic formulations to provide a vivid description of the intense internal struggle of the adoptees and offers recommendations to clinicians that will help ensure that these issues are not overlooked in their clinical practice. Thus, issues of mourning the loss of the birth parents, the common struggles that adoptee have with identity, the challenges of bonding when early trust is broken, challenges with sustaining intimacy often faced by many adult adoptees, the resolution of the fantasies about birth parents and birth families, are some of the issues discussed in this chapter. Also using a psychoanalytic framework, Deeg's (Chapter 29) and Zuckerman and Buchsbaum's (Chapter 31) chapters provide further descriptions of the inner world of the adoptee, including the different parental representations (biological and adoptive parents) that adopted persons need to reconcile. Deeg places particular emphasis on presenting a theoretical model to explain the genesis of these representations and the various defensive constellations that tend to show up in the treatment situation. In this context, he discusses various transference/countertransference dyads that echo the adoptee's unique intrapsychic exigencies. He also explores the relation of the adopted self with the biological parents and how that relation is a critical determinant in the development of meaningful relationships with self and others (object relations) and the formation of identity. A central challenge to clinicians is how to help adoptees come to terms with transference material that incorporates two sets of self/parent representations. Zuckerman and Buchsbaum's chapter not only provides additional theoretical discussions on the clinical issues affecting adoptees but also presents a clinical situation to bring the point home more poignantly.

CONCLUSION

An emerging theme in the work of all these authors is that adoptees are no more likely to suffer from mental disorders than are others; rather, the psychological challenges they face are enormous, which requires the scientific and professional communities to be more involved in providing answers to these questions. As demonstrated by the chapter on poetic reflections and other creative processes (Chapter 32), with the work of poets Penny Partridge and Christian Langworthy, and writer Sarah Saffian, we recognize that adoption could have a wonderful and powerful effect on the creative process. That these writers are able to flourish and become different kinds of writers as a result of their adoption experience and of coming to terms with the many challenges associated with being adopted is eloquently and ably discussed by Alina Camacho-Gingerich in her preface. In this context, Camacho-Gingerich delineates, in her convincing presentation, the subtle and profound ways in which adoption issues appear in the different writings included in this book. How the creative process can become derailed when the creative person is saddled with emotional turmoil and unresolved self-identity questions is amply described in the psychoanalytic literature (Kavaler-Adler, 1993).

Thus, we are left with the question of where we can go from here and what the future of adoption is. These questions are addressed more directly in the concluding chapter (Chapter 33), where we make some suggestions and recommendations in this regard. What is clear is that we need to break the seal of secrecy such that open and frank discussions of issues likely to affect the triad members are possible so as to give fair opportunities to adopted individuals to come to terms with their various challenges. It is the purpose of this book to offer readers a wide range of topics about the adoption experience today and to bring together the most influential voices in the adoption experience so as to provide a foundation for further discussions. Let this book serve as an invitation to come with us on a journey where, at the end of the day, our understanding of all facets of the adoption experience is improved and new models of research and treatment emerge in this context.

Good luck and happy trails!

REFERENCES

Baden, A. (2002). The psychological adjustment of transracial adoptees: An application of the Cultural-Racial Identity Model. *Journal of Social Distress and the Homeless, 11*(2), 167–191.

Casey Family Services. (2002). *Strengthening families and communities: An approach to post-adoption services*. Retrieved August 19, 2006, from http://cpexpress.acf.hhs.gov/index.cfm?issue_id=2002-2004&articule_id=430

Chinese Qing Dynasty 1644–1911. (2006). Retrieved May 10, 2006, from http://famous.adoption.com/chinese-qing-dynasty.html

Dana, R. H. (1993). *Multicultural assessment perspectives for professional psychology*. Boston: Allyn & Bacon.

Dever, M., & Dever, A. (1992). *Relative origins: Famous foster and adopted people*. Portland, OR: National Book.

Encyclopedia of Adoption. (2006). Retrieved May 2, 2006, from http://encyclopedia.adoption.com/intro/introduction/2.html

Erickson, E. H. (1950). *Childhood and society*. New York: Norton.

Erickson, E. H. (1982). *The life cycle completed: A review*. New York: Norton.

Freedman, R. (1996). *The life and death of Crazy Horse*. New York: Holiday House.

Freud, S. (1896). The etiology of hysteria. *Standard Edition, 3,* 189–221.

Freud, S. (1905). Three essays on the theory of sexuality. *Standard Edition, 23,* 255–269.

Gardner, P. (Ed.). (1995). *Complete who's who in the Bible*. London: Harper Collins Religious.

Gibbs, N. (2005, September 12). New Orleans lives by the water and fights it. *Time-Special Report*, pp. 44–49.

Goldman, M. S. (1996). *Crazy Horse: War chief of the Oglala Sioux*. New York: Franklyn Watts.

Hawaiian Royal Families 18th-21st Centuries. (2006). Retrieved May 10, 2006, from http://famous .adoption.com/famous/hawaiian-royal-families.html

Henderson, D. B. (2000). Adoption issues in perspective: An introduction to the special issue. *Journal of Social Distress and the Homeless, 9*, 261–272.

Herron, W. (1998). Development of the ethnic identity. In R. A. Javier & W. G. Herron (Eds.), *Personality development and psychotherapy in our diverse society: A source book* (pp. 319–333). Northvale, NJ: Jason Aronson.

Holt, J. (2006, March 12). Math murders. *The New York Times Magazine*, Section 6, pp. 11–12.

India Princely States. (2006). Retrieved May 10, 2006, from http://famous.adoption.com/famous/ India-princely-states.html

Javier, R. A. (1996). In search of repressed memories in bilingual individuals. In R. P. Foster, M. Moskowitz, & R. A. Javier (Eds.), *Reaching across boundaries of culture and class: Widening the scope of psychotherapy* (pp. 225–241). Northvale, NJ: Jason Aronson.

Javier, R. A., & Rendon, M. (1995). The ethnic unconscious and its role in transference, resistance and countertransference: An introduction. *Psychoanalytic Psychology, 12*, 513–520.

Javier, R. A., & Yussef, M. (1998). A Latino perspective on the role of ethnicity in the development of moral values. In R. A. Javier & W. G. Herron (Eds.), *Personality development and psychotherapy in our diverse society: A source book* (pp. 366–382). Northvale, NJ: Jason Aronson.

Kavaler-Adler, S. (1993). *The compulsion to create: Women writers and their demon lovers*. New York: Routledge.

Kirschner, D. (1978). "Son of Sam" and the adopted child syndrome. *Adelphi University Society for Psychoanalysis & Psychotherapy Newsletter*, 7–9.

Kirschner, D. (1990). The adopted child syndrome: Considerations for psychotherapy. *Psychotherapy in Private Practice, 8*, 93–100.

Longworth, P. (1973). *The three empresses: Catherine I, Anne and Elizabeth of Russia*. New York: Holt, Rinehart & Winston.

Mahler, M. S., Pine, F., & Bergman, A. (1975). *The psychological birth of the human infant*. New York: Basic Books.

Nydam, R. (1999). *Adoptees come of age*. Louisville, KY: Westminster John Knox.

Petre, F. L. (1991). *Napoleon & Archduke Charles: A history of the Franco-Austrian Campaign in the Valley of the Danube in 1809*. London: Greenhill Books.

Piaget, J. (1995). *The language and thought of the child*. Cleveland, OH: Meridian Books.

Plimpton, G. (1997). *Truman Capote: In which various friends, enemies, acquaintances and detractors recall his turbulent career*. New York: Nan A. Talese.

Post, D. E. (2000). Adoption in clinical psychology: A review of the absence, ramification, and recommendations for change. *Journal of Social Distress and the Homeless, 9*(4), 361–372.

Rippley, A. (2005, September 2). An American tragedy: How did this happen? *Time*, pp. 54–59.

Sachs, J. (2005, March 14). The end of poverty. *Time* (Exclusive book excerpt), pp. 42–54.

Sass, D. A., Webster, J., & Henderson, D. B. (2000, April). *Triad members' experiences in therapy*. Paper presented at the meeting of the American Adoption Congress, Nashville, TN.

Spitz, R. A. (1946). Anaclitic depression: An inquiry into the genesis of psychiatric conditions in early childhood, II. *Psychoanalytic Study of the Child, 2*, 313–342.

Stern, D. N. (1985). *The interpersonal world of the infant*. New York: Basic Books.

Sullivan, H. S. (1953). *The interpersonal theory of psychiatry*. New York: Norton.

Terrill, M. (1994). *Steve McQueen: Portrait of an American rebel*. New York: D. I. Fine.

Tyler, G. (Ed.). (1998). *Encyclopedia of Virginia biography*. Baltimore: Genealogical.

Verny, T., & Kelly, J. (1981). *The secret life of the unborn child*. New York: Dell.

Verrier, N. (1993). *The primal wound*. Baltimore: Gateway Press.

Foundation

Preface

FRANK A. BIAFORA

St. John's University

This opening section of *The Handbook of Adoption: Implications for Researchers, Practitioners, and Families* is designed to provide readers with an overview of adoption in the United States from three complementary analytic approaches: (1) a sociological analysis, (2) a statistical trend analysis, and (3) a legal history analysis. The editors believe that it is important that a broader history and foundation of the subject be recounted before venturing into more specific issues of assessment, treatment, training, and research. In Chapter 2, "Toward a Sociology of Adoption: Historical Deconstruction," Dawn Esposito and Frank Biafora take readers on an interrelated cultural-political-religious-economic journey through America's adoption past. These authors, both university professors of sociology, deconstruct adoption as they guide readers through a Colonial period, an industrial revolution and urbanization movement, two world wars, a civil rights movement, and a gender revolution. We are reminded that adoption is not merely a formal legal transaction between members of a triad; rather, it is part and parcel of a complex and ever-changing cultural tapestry, one which earlier witnessed children and adolescents being scattered about the country on orphan trains in an effort to instill a wholesome—that is, Protestant, midwestern—ethic. To be sure, this sociological recounting is filled with many ironic cross-products inclusive of prejudice and compassion, fear and love, and discrimination and generosity.

In Chapter 3, "Adoption Data and Statistical Trends," Biafora and Esposito present a summary of existing adoption data and statistics dating back to key research studies originating over half a century ago. The authors offer a review of the various statistical methodologies currently in use by adoption researchers today. Some readers may be surprised to learn that the recording of all finalized adoptions is not mandated by a governing body and, as such, a large number of completed adoptions go unrecognized and undocumented. Lacking any single, comprehensive database, those interested in exploring adoption statistics must piece together disparate data sources in an effort to come up with reliable estimates of total adoption activity. This chapter presents a balance of domestic and international adoption trends.

The final chapter in this section is written by one of the most highly respected scholar-practitioners within the adoption community, Madelyn Freundlich. Her chapter "A Legal History of Adoption and Ongoing Legal Challenges" offers an expert recounting of major legal developments in adoption law both domestically and internationally. Freundlich, a lawyer and social worker, reminds us that adoption policymakers, building on the Constitutional concepts of individual rights and liberty, have tended to gravitate toward Roman law rather than English common law because of provisions guaranteeing inheritance to legally adopted heirs, not just to kin bonded by blood ties. In this chapter, readers are able to trace the origin and evolution of several important themes common to the adoption literature, including the "best interest of the child" principle, confidentiality of birth records, postadoption rights, matching, and the rights of birth fathers, to name but a few. Some readers will be surprised at the wide variations and inconsistencies that remain between states despite efforts to unify state adoption statues.

LEARNING GOALS

These authors had specific learning goals in mind as they approached their respective chapters. Below are some learning objectives we encourage our readers to consider as they delve into this foundational section.

- To trace the history of adoption from a critical sociological perspective. Technically, adoption is a legal act of human transfer at a specific point in time. But adoption is also a social construction having gone through many cultural revisions since the founding of the 13 colonies.

- To explore the origin of adoption in the United States as an early source of cheap labor and indentured servitude.

- To trace the evolution of transracial adoption and to expose the often neglected concerns within the African American community regarding the adoption of Black children by non-Black families.

- To trace the major statistical trends in the three major sources of adoption—that is, domestic foster care, domestic private, and international adoption.

- To trace the history of major adoption data-gathering tools—NCSC, AFCARS, and population surveys.

- To understand the strengths and weaknesses in the various data-gathering methodologies.

- To highlight the changing order of the 10 most common sending countries of international children over a 10-year period.

- To develop an understanding of the origins of adoption law in the United States and the legal developments leading to the current structure of adoption law.

- To identify areas in which adoption law is continuing to evolve.

- To develop an appreciation of the complexity of adoption law.

Toward a Sociology of Adoption

2

Historical Deconstruction

DAWN ESPOSITO

St. John's University

FRANK A. BIAFORA

St. John's University

CHAPTER OVERVIEW

This chapter explores adoption with the aid of a wide-angle, sociological lens. With a few important exceptions (Berebitsky, 2002; Fiegelman & Silverman, 1983; Fisher, 2003; Pertman, 2000), the current, growing body of scholarly literature presents adoption and related practices of temporary foster care from the epistemological position of individual actors in a related triad (i.e., adopted persons, adoptive parents, and biological parents). While important and necessary, explored in this way, our current tapestry of knowledge is framed and informed primarily by the research and expertise of psychiatrists, psychologists, social workers, and adoption professionals, many of whom have contributed to this *Handbook*. Fisher (2003) reminds us, however, that because these studies so often use clinical populations or personal experiences, they are more likely to focus on the occasional pathological aspects of adoption and of the cognitive/developmental aspects of adoption on individual actors. Viewed in this manner, adoption "is" an experience worthy of study. Our position, however, was to move away from this trend and instead follow Wegar's (1997) suggestion to examine adoption "as" an American experience from a sociological vantage point.

The authors of this chapter have not forgotten that at the core of adoption is the desire to create a family, however broadly defined. Historically, the image of the typical American family, especially the White Anglo family, has been of a rather fixed, nuclear unit. Interestingly, adoption has been a social force that has helped at once to maintain tradition as well as to shatter it; the married heterosexual couple who find they cannot have a biological child can still create, through adoption, their nuclear "family," just as the homosexual couple can create a family of their own. Adoption has stretched the view of the American family as a conventional model of a racially homogeneous and heterosexual nuclear unit (Berebitsky, 2002).

When viewed from within a sociological paradigm, the history of adoption emerges as more than a one-sided story with more than just a few stakeholders. A surface view of adoption is one of kindness, justice, and hope for children in need of a loving home and of adults in need of a child to love. But this is certainly not the whole picture. This chapter explores the charitable as well as the surreptitious sides of adoption, with its policies that have been handcrafted to maintain a specified social order. We openly claim at the outset that our starting bias is a sociological one; that underlying America's story of adoption is a complex posturing of social, cultural, political, economic, and religious forces in a continual convergence and struggle. Simply stated, adoption is socially constructed.

SOCIOLOGICAL HISTORY OF ADOPTION IN THE UNITED STATES

Adoption is a social practice, a solution to a social problem, and an act of making a family at a particular moment in time. Like all social practices, adoption is intertwined with the production of social order. Adoption is also a public phenomenon determined by social and cultural forces that transcend individual actors. As a practice, it has always been determined by a general social, ideological discussion of the construction and meaning of the family, motherhood, biological kinship, race, social class, poverty, the citizen, and his or her responsibility to the social whole. As Berebitsky (2002) has claimed, "adoption is a public site to thrash out meanings" (p. 3). Importantly, adoption is a means of providing a permanent home for a child without one. The tension between children's needs and social forces permeates the history of adoption. The discourse on adoption is an evolving one, yet when read across its history certain tendencies emerge, which have direct bearing on the present day. The story that follows is both old and new at the same time.

Colonial Times (1750–1800)

Adoption began as an informal practice during the formative years of the United States. Carp's (2004) research on the colonial period found "dependent children, those from the poor or working classes, some of whom were orphaned some not, were often placed out as apprentices" (p. 3) in cross-generational families based on a loose connection to biological kinship. What today would be likened to foster care in some respects was, in fact, a practice of indentured servitude where children were thought of as an available source of labor. The creation of these "families" was often based on economic rather than emotional ties. Since the prevailing explanation for dependency in this period was a failure to adhere to a strong work ethic, the placed children were expected to gain from this experience and be reformed in the process. The possibilities for abuse were built into the system itself. By 1800, however, public outcry was such that the practice of indentured servitude was abandoned. A close cousin to indentured servitude would again resurface but with more religious and moral overtones at the height of the great Irish immigration.

The beginnings of a more modern framework for adoption and child placement began with the founding of the orphan asylums, usually by reformed-minded women. As Porter (2004) notes, "The founders saw both the children and their relatives as blameless victims of misfortune and were sympathetic rather than judgmental" (p. 31). One of the more hopeful policies of the orphanages during this time was to place children where possible with biological kin, anticipating a return to their birth families. But as Porter's research demonstrates, relatives were not always a reliable source of support; some were too poor and others continued the practice of indentured servitude. Problems of abuse and the return of children to the orphanages were common among the orphaned, and many would never again unite with their birth families.

The failure of birth parents to adequately care for their children is a familiar story and has become a central factor in the modern move toward early termination of parental rights and permanency. Berebitsky (2002) highlights the fact that "the language of the market . . . represent(s) one of the significant frames through which Americans saw adoption" (p. 4) in this period. Despite the privileging of the emotional role of the family in the contemporary public discourse on adoption, the economic character should not be overlooked. Children currently in need of adoption tend to come from poor or otherwise distressed families; the system of foster care, with built-in financial incentives, has evolved as one solution to address the large numbers of children without stable homes as well as to satisfy our nation's desire to support the cultural notions of a traditional family.

The Early Asylums (1800–1840)

The practice of child placement was an evolving one. When placing children with relatives failed, the asylum directors began to place them in wealthy families. The assumption was that the skills and values that these families transmitted would enable the children to transcend, as they reached adulthood, the impoverishment experienced in their birth families. But again, the more common experience was one of servitude to the family. This forced the asylum directors to turn to middle-class families, making no distinction between those families with or without children. Porter (2004) suggests that this be seen as a solution to their conflict between "empathy and opportunity. . . . The adopted child would be treated and educated like a member of the family" (p. 36). The child's physical and emotional needs would be served, and her parents would consider themselves amply repaid by the pleasure of having a complete family. The specificity of the gendered pronoun is appropriate since "young, appealing and usually female" children were wanted. Asylum records of this period indicate that

> the typical child left the asylum at age seven or eight, too old to be an adorable toddler but old enough to have a known character, young enough to benefit from a middle-class education but not too young to be helpful in the household. (p. 38)

Placement in a middle-class family, at least at this point in time, was an ideal not often achieved, although it would be in a later period. The children were more often than not adopted by relatives or nonrelatives of roughly the same class position. Porter (2004) has uncovered evidence to indicate that "20% of adopted children had negative family experiences," which led asylum managers to conclude that adoption "could never replace the natural home" (p. 38). This position, given full expression in the Victorian ideology's reverence for the family and shared by early-20th-century professional social workers, represents a tension in adoption discourse. The ideological assumption of the superiority of the biological family is a shadow haunting the valorization of the intentionally constructed family. This shadowing is conveyed through phrases that appear in the professional and academic literature related to types of families being constructed: "just like your own"; "better than nothing"; "the best or good enough"; and, in reference to adoption by single women during the Progressive Era, "left-over woman, left-over child."

The Orphan Trains 1850: Placing Out

Great forces of social change swept the country in the mid-19th century. The economic shift from agrarian to factory production, urbanization, and large-scale immigration resulted in considerable increases in urban and rural poverty. Unstable work, crowded living conditions, and cultural, racial, and religious diversity posed a new array of problems never before confronted in modern cities. In response to the failure of informal social controls, reformers first turned to large-scale safety valves and institutions such as outdoor relief, public almshouses, and private orphanages to reduce the cost to the state. These institutions, intended to reform and educate paupers, were expensive and failed. Levels of poverty and child relinquishment were not abated. Some social reformers, influenced by child development theory, turned to "God's orphanage"—that is, the family, emphasizing its "ability to produce at little expense sociable, independent, and industrious citizens" (Berebitsky, 2002, p. 5). The New York Children's Aid Society (CAS), founded in 1853 by Charles Loring Brace, a Baptist Minister, social worker, and author of the "Dangerous Classes of New York" (1872), was a leading force in a renewed movement toward home placement. During the next 40 years, Brace and his like-minded Protestant reformers placed out 84,000 children, transporting them on "orphan trains" from the eastern city slums to families in the Midwest, locations where labor was in short supply. The trains would stop en route and the children were *put up* on platforms for locals to see, a term still in use today in modern adoption language. Despite the fact that many of these children were not adopted, scholars point to the orphan trains as the impetus behind the nation's first adoption statutes, which "(made) a public record of private adoption agreements (that were) analogous to recording a deed for a piece of land" (Berebitsky, 2002, p. 5).

Brace's placing out program began shortly after the codification of the "best interests of the child" standard in the 1840s, which became the guide for child custody decisions. This welfare doctrine stipulated that young or sickly children be "placed out" in the custody of a woman, that older boys be placed in the custody of a man, that a child's formed ties of affection be recognized, and that an older child's wishes be taken into account when making a decision. These principles became embedded in the 1851 Massachusetts Adoption Act, the first adoption law in the country, which came to serve as a model for other states. The Massachusetts Adoption Act gave courts the power to sever legal bonds between biological parents and their children and gave judges the responsibility to determine whether adoptive parents were "fit and proper." The Act made it legally possible for the state to create families. This new state power was reaffirmed in 1853 when the Pennsylvania Adoption Act mandated that "courts were to be satisfied that the welfare of such child will be promoted by such an adoption" (Carp, 2004, pp. 5–6). The opposition between the claims of birth parents and the state's power to sever parental rights instituted in this period reverberate in the 1997 Social Welfare Reform legislation, which will be discussed below.

While Brace's intentions may have been noble, his actions reflect a deep-seated classist and nativist framework that have functioned as a subtext in the history of adoption. As Pfeffer (2004) has noted, "Brace did not attempt to support the youngster's natural families . . . instead, he preferred breaking up poor biological families to 'save' the children. Brace also didn't investigate the receiving homes either before or after placement" (p. 102). The majority of the children Brace placed in Protestant homes were from Irish Catholic and other immigrant families. He distrusted immigrant culture, seeing in it patterns of behavior and expectation that led to impoverishment. As Gutman (1976) points out, this belief is similar to that held by the dominant culture in regard to the African American family immediately after emancipation; scholars such as Patton (2000) and Day (1979) argue that it is being played out in the contemporary debate as well. Brace was certain that exposure to the American work ethic, thought to be found only in Protestant families, would rescue the children from repeating the lives of their parents. He expected the children to receive care and moral instruction in return for their labor. As Berebitsky (2002) suggests, "Brace also hoped that the children would be treated as members of the family, a goal that was often achieved and, on a few occasions, legally formalized" (p. 42). The reality was that many of the children were not adoptable. Scholars report that at least half of those on the orphan trains, some taken without parental permission, had at least one living parent and either returned to their families or struck out on their own after their period of indenture was over (Berebitsky, 2002; Pfeffer, 2004).

It would be a mistake to understand Brace's placing out model as simply grounded in the labor potential of children, however. His model incorporated a new cultural emphasis on "nurturing" as a mechanism for child development. Nurturing was held up as the corrective to biological deficiencies. Shifting theoretical and political evaluations of the potential and limits of both biology and nurture influence evolving adoption practices from this period on.

Response to Brace: Catholic and Jewish Agencies

Brace's practice of placing children in Protestant homes engendered a quick response in the Catholic and Jewish communities and earned Brace a reputation as more of a child stealer than child saver. Each group, fearing the assimilation of their children, developed an alternative for taking care of the homeless children in their communities. Lay male Catholic activists, following the second wave of Irish immigration in 1848 and 1849, founded the Chicago conference of the St. Vincent DePaul Society in 1857. Supported by the Sisters of Charity of St. Vincent, this became the principal Catholic response. As Pfeffer (2004) notes, Catholics understood religion as

> something more than an external value to children, but rather [as] an obligation basic to their nature. Committed to the basic principle that Catholic children placed for adoption could have their total needs met only in Catholic adoptive homes, in 1881 Catholics established a home for foundlings and pregnant, unmarried women and their infants, St. Vincent's Infant Asylum. (p. 104)

Catholic families were sought for the children, but since many of the children were half orphans, and thus not adoptable, keeping the children in the institutions was a common occurrence. The staff, mostly nuns, took on the responsibility of religious training.

The Jewish community established local institutions with a focus on family services grounded in tradition. Pfeffer (2004) points out that while legal adoption did not exist in Jewish law, "The caring for a dependent child who does not have a biological relationship with one's family, is very much a part of Jewish tradition" (p. 107). Jewish families were sought for first placement, but advocates of the homes also believed that institutional care was a practical necessity under difficult conditions existing at the time. Most children remained in the institutions. But by the mid-1890s, Jewish philanthropists, influenced by scientific studies attributing the high death rate of institutionalized infants to the "lack of mother's milk and love," established the Jewish Home Finding Society of Chicago. This organization was formed to help mothers keep their children at home while also arranging for adoptions when home care was not possible.

African Americans were another group experiencing severe economic hardship during this period. As Berebitsky (2002) and others have noted, as a marginalized group without a strong political or social voice during this time, African American communities tended to hold to the tradition of kinship care or "informal adoption" for orphaned and needy Black children, a custom that originated in Africa, continued and was adapted in slavery, and persists to this day. From its inception, then, adoption was a process typically involving the placement and selection of White infants and young children with White families. Records indicate that the "earliest known adoptions of Black children by Whites occurred in the late 1940s and early 1950s. But these were very few" (Day, 1979, p. 92). Despite the historical practice of taking in distantly related or nonrelated children in the Black community, Black families have historically been excluded from consideration by adoption agencies seeking placement for children of any race. The racist attitudes motivating these patterns have been a persistent presence in the history of adoption. They would remain unchallenged as long as a supply of White infants and children was available.

Victorian Era (1850–1900)

The economic, political, and social shifts during the rise of industrialization had a tremendous impact on the development of the middle-class nuclear family. Husbands entered the labor market, while wives assumed responsibility in the domestic sphere. The cult of true womanhood established a maternal identity at the core of femininity. Families were centered on the emotional connection between members and sustained through the nurturing sustenance of women. The family became a private entity separated from the larger social community. This shift, especially the socially ascribed role of mother, had a tremendous impact on the future of adoption. The discourse in the field began to focus on the mother as biological caregiver, and attention was brought to bear on illegitimacy. The Catholic position, that unwed mothers keep their babies, was shared by other religiously affiliated service agencies. Salvation Army homes required prospective residents to sign a contract promising to keep their children (Berebitsky, 2002, p. 31). The ideological assumption was that women could be saved from moral depravity only through the assumption of their maternal role.

By the turn of the 20th century, professional social workers asserted increasing influence in child welfare agencies. "The casework method endeavored to help individuals adjust to their environment by attempting to treat each family or individual as a unique problem and discover the data pertinent to that particular family's history" (Pfeffer, 2004, p. 108). In practice, this meant keeping poor families intact and unwed mothers and their children together. Child health was also reflected in this position as

> the infant mortality rate of illegitimate children was almost three times that of children of legitimate birth . . . [K]eeping the child supplied with an abundance of mother's milk proved the most effective way to lower the death rate. (Berebitsky, 2002, p. 32)

Interestingly, adopters were less concerned with the legitimacy of a potential child than were the caseworkers. Most children in public and private child welfare systems had at least one parent unknown to the agencies who was, thus, potentially able to reclaim his or her child. As we will see, this would be just one of the times when the interests of adopters and the policies of adoption professionals would come into conflict. Couples interested in adoption just wanted a child, but the position taken by social workers limited the number of available children. The conflict between social workers and families seeking adoption over the profession's valorization of biological motherhood was reinforced in the culture at large. As Berebitsky (2002) reports,

> The dominant culture's idealization of mothers generally equated motherhood with biology, not nurturance. Because they had not given birth, adoptive mothers found themselves on the edges of the culture's ideal . . . [A]doptive mothers (and their advocates) argued for a definition of motherhood that would legitimate their identity as real mothers . . . [T]hey made their claim by showing how their motherhood fit with tenets of the ideal that were not dependent on a blood tie or physical maternity. (p. 76)

In the first two decades of the century, adoptive mothers, possessing exceptional maternal instincts, were represented as rescuers of cast-off children. After 1920, representations highlighted the conscious choice adoptive mothers were making and thus their exceptional preparedness for motherhood. These constructions made room for the potential of single women to adopt, and some did for a brief period. The current acceptance of foster care and single-woman adoption is grounded in this logic. This logic moved the notion of the ideal mother beyond blood ties to those of care and commitment; it modified the notion of instinct. This shift in the ideology makes a connection between the role of woman/mother and her responsibility as a citizen. Native-born, middle-class women had a duty to raise their own children and also the children of mothers not up to the task. As noted in a story in the *Delineator* (see Berebitsky, 2002, p. 80), a popular magazine that featured a save-the-children campaign of the period, "Adoption was a means to Americanize children and maintain Anglo-Saxon values." While motherhood was looked to as the means for producing the right kind of citizen, it also made women into the right kind of citizen. Another commentator in the *Delineator* wrote "that without a child to love, a woman could become a danger to society, her heart the 'breeding place for dragons and other things unnatural.'"

Progressive Era: Save-the-Child Campaign (1900–1920)

The *Delineator*'s campaign was grounded in the social climate of the Progressive Era (1900–1920). The social and economic conditions resulting from industrialization had a tremendous negative impact on the poor, the massive numbers of recent immigrants, and African Americans. The conditions of their lives were perceived to be a threat to social order; their families were judged to be lacking in the skills and ambition that the changing American landscape required for success. This led to intervention strategies on both the public and private levels. The discourse on the family in this period was set by a 1909 White House conference at which President Theodore Roosevelt endorsed home care. His position reflected the belief, shared by many social reformers of the day, that the American family's capacity to mold citizens was the highest achievement of civilization. "Both the future of the nation and the future of the species seemed to balance on the ability of native-born White women to raise children with middle-class standards of self-sufficiency, moral uprightness and Protestant sobriety" (Hart, 2004, p. 142). It was believed that the children of the poor could be saved only if severed from the corrupting influences of their families. Poor parents may have been guided by this belief as well. Adoption records of the period indicate that

> men and women relinquished when adoption seemed the only way for their children to have decent lives. Women relinquished to spare children abuse, provide them protection, food and appropriate shelter. Men relinquished, so their children could receive consistent, caring female nurturing. Young women relinquished to avoid social sanctions against illegitimacy and hopeless poverty. (Hart, 2004, p. 145)

Scientific knowledge became a transcendent public discourse in the late 1920s and would become an avenue for positioning debate in future discussions of adoption. Science was offered as a corrective to the notion of maternal common sense. This added to the legitimacy of adoptive mothers; if biological mothers needed to be educated, physical birth no longer mattered. Although it seems logical that scientific mothering could be adopted by both married and single women, by this point in time, single women were no longer considered fit for motherhood. This represented a turnaround from thinking that prevailed only a few years earlier. Married women were favored because of their perceived celibacy and commitment to traditional gender roles in a nuclear family setting. A number of women reformers in the Progressive Era, motivated by personal and intellectual reasons, adopted children and raised them within support networks that included their female partners.

By 1930, public discourse had shifted; adoption by single women was framed as a challenge to the normative family. This reemphasis on the nuclear family was fueled by the increasing influence of psychoanalytic theory in social work practice, which emphasized the importance of fathers in children's lives and the leadership role social workers assumed in agencies involved in adoption. Women's sexuality came increasingly under scrutiny, and lesbianism, identified as deviant sexuality, was constituted as a danger to the healthy psychological development of children. The exclusion of single women from adoptions continued through the 1950s. While demand for children exceeded the supply, single women were seen as depriving married couples of the children they desired. Maternal status, once dependent simply on being a woman, now depended on occupying the combined roles of mother and wife. It has been argued that the exclusion of single women from adopting during this transitional era caused adoption to lose its potential to "radically expand the culture's definition of the family" (Berebitsky, 2004, p. 127). We will have to wait and see if the gradual move in present-day adoption practices to allow for adoptions by single women and men and gay and lesbian couples will make a radical redefinition realizable.

Social Work Era (1930–1960)

The 1930s saw the highest point of voluntary childlessness among married couples in the United States. The economic collapse during the Depression led to an increase in the number of applicants to child placement agencies. Social workers instituted the practice of "matching" children and parents. They evaluated a child's heredity through extensive background investigation and intelligence testing. Social workers asserted that they could find a child who "might have been born to you." "Children could fit their adoptive homes in physical characteristics, intellectual capacities, temperament and religious and ethnic affiliation. The policy of matching assumed that this affinity would lead to easier assimilation" (Hart, 2004, p. 157). Social workers believed that this practice was in the best interest of the child as well as the family. They had a model of the best, most suitable family in mind, and, while single women were certain to be excluded, now certain heterosexual nuclear families were unfit as well. Parents had to prove their psychological fitness; their "natural desire" to have a child was scrutinized.

> Social workers wanted adoptive homes in which husband and wife, according to the marital ideals of the time, enjoyed a healthy sex life, supported their partner's dreams, and accepted their socially prescribed gender role. A strong marriage . . . provided the most solid basis for a successful adoption. (Hart, 2004, p. 152)

Infertility, long considered to be the purist motive for adoption in the culture at large, came under scrutiny as a possible "neurotic basis for childlessness." The expertise of the social worker was relied on to assess whether a couple's infertility was perhaps a result of the wife's rejection of her ascribed feminine role. Since the intention of such careful matching was the creation of a nuclear family that would appear to be natural, it was essential that the woman be ready to fulfill her duties as a homemaker and mother. The practice of matching extended to older couples, who, while denied infants, were able to adopt older children. This practice would become particularly beneficial as the supply of available infants toward the conclusion of World War II began its decline.

The shortage of infants precipitated a change in the social evaluation of illegitimacy. Psychiatric social work redefined the White unwed mother as

> neurotic and therefore unfit as a parent . . . [T]he experts maintained that illegitimacy had little to do with sex and much to do with psychological sickness. Social workers encouraged these "sick" unwed mothers to give their children up for adoption; in cases in which an unwed mother wished to keep her child, the encouragement could turn into coercion. (Hart, 2004, p. 154)

While this practice pitted the unwed White woman and her married, childless counterpart against each other, the potential for each of these women to reach the ideal of womanhood depended on the other. Each of them could become married with children. As Day (1979) has argued, unwed Black women, often turned away from private adoption agencies, were forced to turn to public agencies and the state-run foster care system. The supply of Black infants also was in decline, but since the image of the family social workers looked to for placement tended to be White, a supply of older Black children remained in the foster care system.

From the postwar period through the 1960s, adoption policies and practices developed in response to an unprecedented increase in requests for healthy White infants from infertile White, middle-class, heterosexual married couples (Ladner, 1977). This practice was rooted in an ideology that naturalized and normalized the state's reproduction of White nuclear families. The practice rendered the sexual deviance of White unwed mothers and infertile White couples invisible. As a consequence, the system's resources were devoted to the placement of healthy White babies, neglecting the placement of Black children. Despite claims that the system was "color-blind," a racial ideology was nevertheless present. Patton (2000) points out that "Black women were often turned away from adoption agencies because there was no 'market' for their children" (p. 46).

The 1970s: Transracial Adoption

By the early 1970s, when there was no longer a supply of White babies, any aversion to race mixing had to be abandoned; transracial placements had to be made. Since the number of White children placed in Black homes during this period was negligible, transracial adoption then and now must be seen as the adoption of Black children by White families. While there may have been initial reluctance on the part of social workers to transracial placements, a number of factors led to the increasing reliance on it. Critics such as Patton (2000) and her colleagues have characterized this practice as "an extension of the White man's burden of civilizing the [impoverished urban] native" (p. 5). The tensions surrounding the practice have come to dominate the terrain of adoption ever since. It seems that "when it comes to transracial adoption," argues Patton (2000), "questions of socialization and race are inseparable" (p. 159).

Scholars point to several primary reasons to explain the decreased supply of babies that began in the 1970s, including the legalization of abortion, a shift in cultural attitudes toward illegitimacy, the increasing use of contraception, later onset of marriage, and the modern view of "woman" in greater control of her own body and destiny. The effects of the shift to more open thinking about legitimacy would be gradual, but the result was inevitable; more single women began keeping their babies. Although the supply of White babies was most affected, the number of Black babies diminished as well. Older Black children, however, were still in abundant supply. Day (1979), relying on data reported by the Child Welfare League of America, found that,

> in 1969, shortly before the change in the legal status of abortion, a survey of 240 adoption agencies revealed there were only 39 non-White homes approved for every 100 non-White children. . . . In 1975, a smaller survey . . . showed an improvement . . . [T]here were 85 Black homes approved for every 100 Black children reported as needing adoptive placement . . . [I]n 1975, a total of 57 agencies accepted for adoption 533 Black children for whom they did not find adoptive homes. (p. 5)

Black children were increasingly adopted by White adults, and transracial families became much more prevalent across America.

Black Social Worker Response to Transracial Adoption

The number of transracial adoptions from the mid-1960s through the early 1970s is estimated at 15,000 (Day, 1979). The parents and professionals in support of these adoptions saw them as promoting color blindness, but critics claimed they were a form of cultural genocide. In 1972, the National Association of Black Social Workers (NABSW) took the following position:

> Black children should be placed only with Black families whether in foster care or for adoption. Black children belong physically, psychologically and culturally in Black families in order that they receive the total sense of themselves and develop a sound projection of their future. Human beings are products of their environment and develop their sense of values, attitudes, and self-concept within their own family structures. Black children in White homes are cut off from the healthy development of themselves as Black people. (Day, 1979, p. 98)

A heated public debate ensued. The central questions for Black social workers at this time were whether White parents were capable of providing the foundations of African American culture and history or instilling in their Black children the survival skills necessary in a racially divided and unequal nation. The protest by the association was motivated by a concern for the futures of Black children as well as a desire to strengthen the Black family. But at the same time, it was a protest against "state-sanctioned regulations determining which families African American children would become part of, and thus be socialized by" (Patton, 2000, p. 3). Critics of the association's position argued that it would negatively affect Black children in the system, denying them loving homes.

National survey data from this period raise questions regarding the active search for Black families for the children in the system. Surveys in 1973 and 1974 found that Black children accounted for about 20% of all children adopted and 40% of all children waiting for adoption (Day, 1979). The evidence does seem to indicate that Black families, even when willing to adopt, were discouraged by adoption agencies. Despite the body of literature written by social work practitioners involved in Black adoptions, agencies relied on studies indicating that the Black middle class either wasn't interested in adoption or did not adopt, but because the number of Black middle-class families was small, there was little impact on the number of children in need. In her comparative study of adoption agencies, Day (1979) identified a number of practices that discouraged Black families from adopting. These included the following: (1) The White middle-class standard of a working father and stay-at-home mother used by many agencies denied the economic reality of stable working-class Black families looking to adopt, (2) the failure to have evening hours and the insistence on a home visit during the day denied this reality as well, and (3) communication problems between the social worker and the client also negatively affected the agency's decision to place children with Black families. Moreover, family placement professionals judged parenting capacity by the applicants' ability to "stick it out" through a difficult adoption process. The tendency on the part of Black families to not persist because they were discouraged was interpreted negatively by the social workers, and, as such, they would often turn instead to those who were seen as more persistent and, by extension, more suited to care for children—that is, White parents.

Implicit in the position taken by the NABSW is the understanding that the welfare system socially constructs the family and identity of adoptees. Given the evidence that Black families were being discouraged by adoption agencies, and the historical failure to place White children with Black families, their concern had merit. It echoes in today's public discourse as well.

> Public discourse has typically asked: Should White parents be allowed to adopt Black children? In light of the intersecting issues of gender, poverty, and race we must broaden the question now to ask: How do so many Black children become (placed in foster care) and available for adoption? (Patton, 2000, p. 17)

Social Welfare Reform of the 1990s

By this time, most of the children in the public child welfare system had been removed from low-income families. Poor families, already involved in the social welfare system and possessing attributes that Solinger has defined as "social demerits," are subjected to more scrutiny and, thus, are more vulnerable to charges of abuse or neglect (Patton, 2000, p. 122). Many of these families are headed by single Black mothers. Long a subject of public and intellectual discourse, the single Black mother and her children have been viewed as a threat to social order (Moynihan, 1965). Federal welfare reform policies instituted in this period must be seen as a corrective response to this perceived threat.

The Personal Responsibility and Work Opportunity Reconciliation Act (welfare reform) and the Small Business Job Protection Act (minimum wage law) signed by President Clinton in 1996 were intended to address this threat. Together, they provide a modern framework for the regulation of the reproductive capacity of poor women and the socialization of their children as productive citizens. The welfare reform legislation

> placed a five year limit on benefits, required able-bodied adults to work after two years, required minors to be enrolled in school and living at home or with a responsible adult, required unwed mothers to cooperate in identifying paternity, disallowed support to anyone convicted of a felony drug charge, and denied benefits to legal immigrants. (Patton, 2000, p. 161)

The minimum wage law provided a $5,000 to $6,000 tax credit to families that adopt, removed all restrictions on transracial placements, and prohibited the use of race in considering child placement in adoption. The 1995 draft of the Personal Responsibility Act included a provision for removing restrictions on transracial adoption. That it was contained in a section called "Reducing Illegitimacy" demonstrates what the real threat was perceived to be. The section enumerated a long list of "negative consequences of out-of-wedlock birth on the mother, the child, the family and society." It included the following statements: "Children of teenage single parents have lower cognitive scores, lower educational aspirations and a greater likelihood of becoming teenage parents themselves. Areas with higher percentages of single-parent households have higher rates of violent crime" (see Patton, 2000, p. 23). The underlying logic motivating the adoption trains of the 1850s is in play here as well. Poor families, incapable of taking care of their children, relinquish their responsibility to the state, in this case the foster care system. Welfare reform and transracial adoption were intended to remedy the state's growing foster care burden.

Public discourse of the 1990s, grounded in empirical evidence, suggested that Black children remained in foster care because of institutionalized racist policies that opposed racial mixing. Debate centered on comments suggesting that while Black families were not seeking to adopt, White families were both willing and able. Interracial adoptions were depicted in positive terms; the suggestion that children could be deprived of their culture was dismissed. A longitudinal study conducted by Simon and Alstein (see Patton, 2000, p. 142) was used to support the conclusion that transracial adoptees were well-adjusted. There was little discussion of the impact on mothers whose children were being permanently taken from them. Instead, the discourse promoted "color-blind" transracial adoptions as the solution to problems in the child welfare system.

Social critics, not necessarily opposed to transracial adoptions, have insisted that "color-blind" policies are implicated in racist ideology and practices. Barbara Katz Rothman (2005), in her recent autoethnography, describes her experience raising her adopted Black daughter, acknowledging that

> I profit from American racism . . . [W]e have enough racism so that it is Black babies and children that disproportionately are up for adoption, and White families that disproportionately have the wherewithal to adopt—and enough racism that it is hard to imagine the circumstances in which a Black family would/could adopt a White baby. (p. 10)

Arguments in favor of the welfare reform policies, such as the one made by Batholet (see Patton, 2000, p. 143), "promote a narrative of Black family pathology and White family values." Black children, failed by their families, need White families to save them.

It is too early to know if current policies will have their intended effect and reduce the number of Black children lumped into a category of "special need" foster care, many of whom have not been adopted because of the intersection of race, age, disability, and status as a member of a sibling group. Those who have been in the system for a number of years are likely to have been placed in a number of different foster homes. There is ample evidence that these are the conditions that lead to social and emotional problems and deviancy and contribute to a cycle of poverty (Day, 1979). Federal policy outlined by the Adoption and Safe Families Act of 1997, mandating the speedy removal of children and terminating parental rights after a little more than 1 year of temporary placement in the foster care system, is more likely to increase the supply of babies and young children who have always been more readily adopted. Critics of the new federal policy raise questions about the control it places on poor and Black women's bodies and the shift in economic costs from the state to individual families.

> A lot of what adoption is about is poverty; a lack of access to contraception and abortion, a lack of access to the resources to raise children. And a lot of what poverty is about in America is racism. It's not just that people of color are more likely to be poor. It's also that poor people of color lack the resources to overcome racial discrimination, find themselves powerless before the state. Race and poverty play out together to push/pull Black children out of Black homes. (Rothman, 2005, p. 18)

Further Comment on Transracial Families

Scholars and practitioners have made suggestions regarding the screening of White applicants when considering the placement of Black children. Joyce Ladner (1977) suggested in a
study of transracial adoption that

> only those parents who are able to accept and live with differences should be allowed
> to adopt. Agencies should reject any would-be parent who engages in denial involv-
> ing the child's color, hair texture, biological parentage, or any overt or latent char-
> acteristic. (p. 113)

A Black child should be the couple's first choice, not settled on when a White child is unavailable. It's preferable if they live in an integrated neighborhood; their child won't bear the added
burden of being the lone Black. Ladner (1977) cautions that "the adoption should not be done
to prove a point, such as demonstrate independence from the parents' families, the couple's
liberalism, or whatever" (p. 245). Patton's more recent study (2000) of transracial adoptees
suggests that families should "be conscientious about exposing their children to their cultural
patterns of origin" (p. 13). She found that both international and Black adoptees felt compelled
as adults to explore their cultural origins. Ladner's observation that for many White families,
adopting Black children was "an expression of their commitment to the philosophy of the
'brotherhood of man'" (p. 92), is echoed in Rothman's observation that transracial adoption
reflects a vision of the world. "Taking a child marked as one thing and raising it in a family
marked as another, is to weave together the two communities" (p. 150). She emphasizes that
"the deepest connections are created, not born . . . the deepest human connections are formed
in mundane acts . . . in the work of nurturance" (p. 136).

Despite the repeated scholarly finding that "within Black civil society, notions of interpersonal relations forged during slavery endured—such as equating family with extended
family, of treating community as family" (Collins, 2000, p. 53), Black families have largely
been ignored by adoption agencies. Ladner (1977) is just one of the scholars to observe that
"a narrowly drawn White, middle-class, Christian, suburban, nuclear family came to be seen
as the ideal and only 'legitimate' form of family" (p. 56). Challenges to this ideological construct emanated from the civil rights movement of the 1960s. In some cases, federal funds
were used to set up programs intended to involve Black families in the formal adoption
process. One of the most successful programs, Homes for Black Children in Detroit, can be
looked to as a model. Recognizing the economic reality of most Black families, the "question of whether a couple is financially able to care for a child (was) based on how that family
use(d) its resources" (Day, 1979, p. 124). Some children were placed in families where the
parents had grade school educations, and recognizing employment patterns determined by a
stratified labor market, including the employment of Black women, frequent changes in jobs
by Black men were not taken as an indication of instability. Yet the following observation
by Rothman (2005) deserves consideration:

> As much as the Black community stands with open arms, absorbing as many of those
> babies and children it can, the same poverty that pushes all those babies and children
> into the adoption stream ensures that there won't be enough Black homes to take them
> all. (p. 18)

Current welfare reform policies look to encourage permanent adoption of those children
already in foster care while at the same time only guaranteeing that those numbers will
increase. The likely increase in the pattern of Black children being adopted into White
families as the model for "color-blind" placement replicates as well as challenges racist practices that have long existed throughout the history of adoption in America.

ADDITIONAL SOCIOLOGICAL OBSERVATIONS: INTERNATIONAL AND GAY AND LESBIAN ADOPTIONS

International Adoption

Families formed by adopting from outside U.S. borders clearly challenge the hegemonic notion that biological ties make a family. Occasionally, these families are distinctly interracial in the American sense of Black and White; more often the families are multicultural. Race morphs into culture or ethnicity and the children have an "almost Whiteness" appearance. The first international adoptions began immediately after World War II and involved Japanese children. Korean and Vietnamese children were adopted following those wars, although the numbers of Vietnamese children have since declined. It seems that Americans turn most often to countries of eastern Europe, Asia, Latin America, and the Caribbean for adoptable children. Rothman (2005) suggests that "it is not only the availability and almost-Whiteness of the children that draws Americans to international adoption, it is also the almost complete erasure of the mother" (p. 46). There has always been a preference for infants on the part of White adoptive families; international adoptions make this preference realizable. And while the language of market consumption could and has been used to describe international adoption practices, the families that form themselves convey an ethos of value. In some cases, baby girls in China being the most obvious, the children being adopted are devalued in their countries of origin; here they are cherished and loved.

Gay and Lesbian Adoption

Single women have always figured in the history of adoption. Some of these women were then, as many are today, lesbians who did not reveal their sexual identity; their challenge to the heteronormative nuclear family was private. A more vocal and public challenge is being made by today's lesbian and gay movement. Same-sex couples create legally viable two-parent families through adoption. But as Dalton (2001) notes,

> The adoption system . . . has a long history of dividing adoption petitioners into two mutually exclusive categories: married couples and single individuals. Within this system, married couples create two-parent families by adopting children jointly, while single adults create single-parent families by adopting individually. (p. 205)

There is no provision in the legal tradition's adoption model for unmarried couples to adopt a child jointly. This has led gay and lesbian couples to turn to what has been labeled "second-parent" adoptions. This procedure allows a parent to extend his or her parental right to another adult. It was intended for heterosexual couples raising children from previous marriages and requires that the biological mother or father relinquish his or her rights. Gay men and women seeking to adopt their partners' children from previous heterosexual marriages have not met with much success going this route. More successful arguments have been made via discourse over what is ultimately in the best interest of the child—permanent placement into a loving nontraditional family or continued limbo and aging out in foster arrangements. The use of second-parent adoptions as a legal challenge is more likely if the child is conceived outside the context of heterosexuality (artificial insemination, sperm bank). It requires that the couple convince the court that the proposed adoption is both in the best interest of their child and permissible under that state's law. As Bernstein and Reimann (2001) report, the economic level of the couple, in those cases that have been favorably disposed, is the most important determinant of the outcome (p. 435). While this legal strategy exists in principal, the practice is limited. About half the states as of this writing have ruled against second-parent adoptions by homosexual couples (Bushlow, 2004). It is reasonable to conclude that, at this time, despite some change, the middle-class heterosexual nuclear family is still the normative model privileged in legal adoption practices. Yet the challenge gay families present, no matter how they are formed, to the heterosexual, nuclear norm is unmistakable.

CONCLUSION

Sociological analysis is intended to reveal the general tendencies and contradictions surrounding a social practice. The above discussion has identified a number of dichotomies inherent in the historical development of adoption such as blood ties/bonds of caring, ideal mother/loving woman, married couple/single person, heterosexual family/gay family, color-blind/nativist. These dichotomies inform present-day adoption practices just as they have done for previous generations. The struggle to define the family and the best interests of children goes on. Ordinary people in their everyday lives make the struggle. Prospective adoptive families have continuously struggled to get the children they want; ultimately these are the people defining what a family is. To say that structural racism has influenced adoption policies and practices does not mean that families seeking specific children are racist. Most remain, as they always have been, motivated by their desire to have and raise a child, often initially one who resembles themselves. One of the defining characteristics of the adoption revolution, exclaims Pertman (2000), is "the realization of the truth" (p. 71). Whether adoption is domestic interracial, international transracial, or by a gay parent, the messages of tolerance and acceptance are coming through loud and clear and adoption is leading the charge. Some might say that adoption is itself cracking the walls of prejudice and providing a living history lesson to be learned and shared. We hope so. Lessons learned from these experiences can and should be used as guides for all families and all persons wishing to create a family of their own.

REFLECTION QUESTIONS

1. What impact did the Industrial Revolution have on the family and, by extension, on the attitudes toward adoption and adoption practices in the United States?

2. What were the concerns of the religious community and their responses to Brace's orphan trains?

3. Prior to the 1960s, the number of White babies available for adoption was significantly larger than it is today. What social forces may help to account for the drop in adoptable White infants over the past 40 years?

4. What concerns do members of the African American professional community have about non-Black families adopting African American children?

REFERENCES

Berebitsky, J. (2002). *Like our very own: Adoption and the changing culture of motherhood 1851–1950*. Kansas City: University of Kansas.

Berebitsky, J. (2004). Rescue a child and save the nation: The social construction of adoption in the delineator, 1907–1911. In E. W. Carp (Ed.), *Adoption in America* (pp. 124–139). Ann Arbor: University of Michigan.

Bernstein, M., & Reimann, R. (Eds.). (2001). *Queer families queer politics: Challenging culture and the state.* New York: Columbia.

Brace, C. L. (1872). *The dangerous classes of New York and twenty years' work among them.* New York: Wynkoop & Hallenbeck.

Bushlow, A. (2004). *Gay and lesbian second parent adoptions.* New York: National Resource Center for Foster Care and Permanency Planning, Hunter College School of Social Work.

Carp, E. W. (Ed.). (2004). *Adoption in America.* Ann Arbor: University of Michigan.

Collins, P. H. (2000). *Black feminist thought.* New York: Routledge.

Dalton, S. (2001). Protecting our parent-child relationships: Understanding the strengths and weaknesses of second-parent adoption. In Bernstein & Reimann (Eds.), *Queer families queer politics* (pp. 201–220). New York: Columbia.

Day, D. (1979). *The adoption of Black children.* Lexington, MA: Lexington Books.

Fiegelman, W., & Silverman, A. (1983). *Chosen children: New patterns of adoptive relationships.* New York: Praeger.

Fisher, A. P. (2003). Still "Not quite as good as your own?" Toward a sociology of adoption. *Annual Review of Sociology, 29,* 335–361.

Gutman, H. (1976). *The Black family in slavery and freedom, 1750–1925.* New York: Pantheon Books.

Hart, P. S. (2004). A nation's need for adoption and competing realities: The Washington Children's Home Society, 1895–1915. In E. W. Carp (Ed.), *Adoption in America* (pp. 140–159). Ann Arbor: University of Michigan.

Ladner, J. (1977). *Mixed families: Adopting across racial boundaries.* Garden City, NY: Doubleday.

Moynihan, D. P. (1965). *The Negro family: The case for national action.* Washington, DC: U.S. Department of Labor.

Patton, S. (2000). *Birth marks transracial adoption in contemporary America.* New York: New York University Press.

Pertman, A. (2000). *Adoption nation.* New York: Basic Books.

Pfeffer, P. F. (2004). A historical comparison of Catholic and Jewish adoption practices in Chicago, 1833–1933. In E. W. Carp (Ed.), *Adoption in America* (pp. 101–123). Ann Arbor: University of Michigan.

Porter, S. (2004). A good home: Indenture and adoption in nineteenth-century orphanages. In E. W. Carp (Ed.), *Adoption in America* (pp. 27–50). Ann Arbor: University of Michigan.

Rothman, B. K. (2005). *Weaving a family: Untangling race and adoption.* Boston: Beacon.

Wegar, K. (1997). In search of bad mothers: Social constructions of birth and adoptive motherhood. *Women's Studies International Forum, 20*(1), 77–86.

Adoption Data and Statistical Trends

3

FRANK A. BIAFORA

St. John's University

DAWN ESPOSITO

St. John's University

SOURCES OF ADOPTION DATA

There has never been a single, comprehensive, and continuous national data collection effort to capture information on all adoption activity in the 50 states of the United States and its territories. For the most part, what we know of the extent of formal adoption practices, whether public or private, domestic or international, derives from a combination of disparate data sources often pieced together and often estimated. The lack of a complete and consistent database is not surprising, argues Pertman (2000), considering that

> generations of secrecy have prevented us from knowing just how widespread [adoption] has become. The subject has been considered off-limits for so long, both by individuals and by society as a whole . . . that determining how many triad members there are—or have been—would require sorting through the individual finalization records of every courthouse in every city and town in every state. (pp. 8–9)

Adoption data that are available vary in terms of purpose, reliability, and length of recording. The most common sources of adoption statistics today include (1) state court records of adoption filings and dispositions, (2) national foster care records compiled from state public welfare divisions, (3) U.S. State Department records of issued international visas, (4) vital records of birth certificates, and (5) general population surveys, including the U.S. Census. The first three of these capture information related to formally recognized adoptions, whereas population surveys remain the primary sources for providing information on the extent of informal caregiving, adoption demand, and adoption-seeking behaviors. State bureaus of vital records have also been an important resource in keeping track of reissued birth certificates.

Each of these data sources, coupled with recent advances in electronic data-gathering technologies, has made numerical compilation of adoption activity more possible than ever before. The best estimates today suggest that about 125,000 adoptions occur each year (U.S. Department of Health and Human Services, 2004), that 2% of all children residing in the United States are adopted, and that as many as 4% of all families in the United States have an officially recognized adopted child (Child Welfare League of America [CWLA], 2005). Moreover, when these formal counts are coupled with statistical estimates of undocumented kinship care and informal adoption, some researchers suggest that as many as 7% of all children in the United States currently reside in some form of substitute/adoptive relationship (Testa & Falconnier, 1998). Most recent estimates from the U.S. Census put the total numbers of adopted children under the age of 18 at 1.6 million (Kreider, 2003), with as many as 6 million adoptees of all ages residing in the United States (Pertman, 2000).

While some success has been made in the area of data collection and dissemination, there is still much room for improvement. What might be considered a recent success in this area can be traced to three, if not more, sources, among which are federal adoption legislation and mandates, a growing awareness as a function of adoption institutes and national organizations, and an expanding interest in adoption by academic institutions and legal scholars. Additionally, the U.S. Department of Health and Human Services, Administration for Children and Families, has carved out funding for the National Adoption Information Clearinghouse (NAIC). The NAIC serves professionals, policymakers, and citizens by synthesizing data and providing information on adoption research and statistics. However, there is some concern that these recent investments in data gathering and reporting may be short-lived because of mounting federal and state budget deficits (McFarland, 2003). In times of budget downturns, many of the agencies currently responsible for data gathering may find it difficult to continue to collect and maintain critical data on the characteristics of adoption.

Limited Private Adoption Data

Throughout the past 60 years, various divisions and offices within the federal government have played an important role in capturing basic statistical information on national adoption activity, with most success coming in the form of tracking public agency and international adoptions. Very little progress has been made by federal authorities in capturing consistent and reliable data on the extent of formal adoptions processed privately or independently through adoption mediators. This latter point is particularly significant when one considers that until only recently (i.e., about the time states were to receive financial incentives for adoption placements—see the section describing the Adoption and Foster Care Analysis and Reporting System [AFCARS] below) the number of private adoptions have far outpaced the number of public welfare adoptions (Flango & Flango, 1995). It is through private adoption agencies that a majority of healthy infants and children are placed. The general lack of voluntary cooperation by private adoption agencies to engage in statistical reporting is not surprising for two reasons. The first relates to the fact that there are no incentives (or punishments) for private agencies to report information to outside sources (McFarland, 2003). A second reason is more a comedy of errors, suggests a report by the U.S. Department of Health and Human Services (2004), in that "some private agencies assume that these data are already captured by public agencies, who in turn are often under the impression that private agencies keep comprehensive information on their own adoptions" (p. 16). As is commonly found throughout the adoption literature as well as with the data trends (including those presented in this chapter), data analysts have, out of necessity, "backed out" the counts of private agency adoptions by subtracting from state court reports the numbers of completed public adoptions and international adoptions, thereby leaving estimates of remaining private, kinship, and tribal adoption activity (U.S. Department of Health and Human Services, 2004).

National Center for Social Statistics (NCSS)

Annually between 1957 and 1975, the federal government worked with state-run agencies on a voluntary basis to capture basic summary information on finalized adoptions using data primarily from state court records (Maza, 1984; Stolley, 1993). Coordinated by the Children's Bureau and the National Center for Social Statistics (NCSS), adoption cases, both public and private, were collected and compiled, offering legislators and human services personnel for the first time longitudinal estimates of national adoption trends. Early in this process, less than one half the states participated in the annual survey. By 1966, all 50 states participated in the NCSS data-gathering effort. A summary report published by the Administration for Children, Youth and Families (Maza, 1984) remains one of the most widely referenced, estimating that the total numbers of domestic adoptions doubled from about 50,000 in 1944 to 100,000 by 1950, reaching a peak of about 175,000 by 1970 (see Figure 3.1).

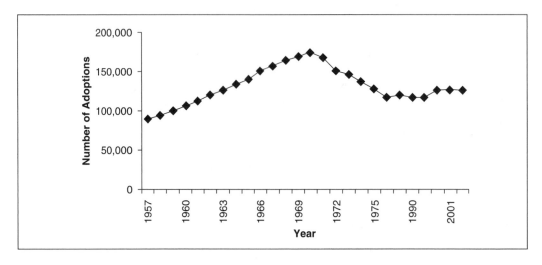

Figure 3.1   Estimated Number of Total Adoptions (1957–2001)

SOURCES: The 1957 to 1975 estimates are from National Center for Social Statistics reports (Maza, 1984); the 1987 to 1992 estimates are from Voluntary Cooperative Information System reports (Flango & Flango, 1995); and the 2000 to 2001 estimates are from National Center for State Courts (U.S. Department of Health and Human Services, 2004).

NCSC, AFCARS, and International Visas

When the NCSS was dissolved in 1975, with it went any serious effort for several years to secure national adoption information on a systematic basis. Despite further limited attempts by the federal government to track national adoption trends through special project grants and a voluntary reporting survey, commonly known as the VCIS (Voluntary Cooperative Information System), administered for a brief time by the American Public Welfare Association (see Stolley, 1993), those interested in monitoring adoption trends would have to wait several years before reliable data would again became available from two important but unrelated sources: (1) the not-for-profit National Center for State Courts (NCSC—not to be confused with the NCSS) Adoption Technical Assistance Project, and (2) the national Adoption and Foster Care Analysis and Reporting System (AFCARS). Both the NCSC and the AFCARS have since become the authoritative resources for general adoption statistics.

The NCSC has collected and compiled data on the total number of public and private adoptions processed through the courts by calendar year since 1987 (Flango, 1990; Flango & Flango, 1995). The NCSC organized in 1971 at the request of then chief justice Warren Burger, who argued for the creation of a central information and technical clearinghouse that could serve state court representatives (see www.ncsconline.org). Because adoption is a process that requires court action, the NCSC was in a good position to develop a recording protocol, making it possible for state courts to systematically report out on basic adoption activity, regardless of whether the adoption had originated through a private or public agency. Two central pieces of information have customarily been obtained and reported by the NCSC project—counts of adoption petitions filed with the courts and the number of cases disposed. Unfortunately, no other detailed information is captured at this time. As such, the NCSC is unable to discern the race, age, gender, or special needs of the adopted person or any relevant information regarding the birth or adoptive parents. While the filed court records may in fact capture these data, currently there exists no systematic data-gathering effort by the NCSC to extract them. Despite these limitations, the courts remain perhaps the single best source for total numbers of adoptions in the states.

AFCARS emerged originally under the 1986 federal mandate (Title IV-E, Section 479 of the Social Security Act, as amended by Pub. L. No. 99-509, Section 9443 of the Omnibus Budget Reconciliation Act) and was later enhanced as part of the 1997 Adoption Incentive Program (also known as the Adoption Bonus Program) under Pub. L. No. 105–89, the Adoption and Safe Families Act (ASFA) (Maza, 2000; U.S. Department of Health and Human Services, 2004). AFCARS represents the intersection of several major trends in federal and state child welfare programming, namely, outcome-based accountability and the shift toward "early permanency" over "family reunification" as part of the "best interest of the child" philosophy (Maza, 2000, p. 445). Under the direction of President Clinton in 1996, the secretary of the U.S. Department of Health and Human Services was charged with developing and implementing a strategy that would achieve permanency more quickly for children in out-of-home care and have as its specific target a doubling in the number of adoptions, from 27,000 to 54,000 annually. All this came together under ASFA, which established Section 473A of the Social Security Act. As part of this federal directive, Congress authorized a financial rewarding mechanism to states to be eligible to receive an annual "bonus" of up to $4,000 for each adoption finalized, with an additional $2,000 for special needs adoptions (Title IV-E, Adoption Assistance agreement), over an established baseline number (see U.S. House of Representatives, 2004, for the most recent explanation of the financial award structure and baseline methodology). This legislation authorized the AFCARS as the sole electronic platform for capturing case-specific public adoption data and for determining state incentive funds. AFCARS is also the only database that currently collects summary data on the characteristics of all triad members. The reporting of other adoptions such as those through independent or private agencies is only encouraged but not required. Failure to report AFCARS data or failure to report data that meets with quality check standards results in financial penalties to the states (Maza, 2000).

Last, the U.S. State Department's Office of Children's Issues and the Office of Immigration Statistics within the Office of Homeland Security records and publishes data on the number of international visas issued to immigrant orphan children adopted from abroad (U.S. Department of State, 2005). Inasmuch as the adoption takes place outside of the United States, the visa becomes the principal document for federal/state documentation and statistical recording. States are not required to document or keep data on intercountry adoptions. Although many new parents may, for added protection, "readopt" in state courts once on U.S. soil, such action is not required. Up-to-date international adoption figures and highlights can be found on the State Department's homepage (http://travel.state.gov/family).

Population Surveys

Before concluding this section, it is important to make mention of a supplemental source of data that has become increasingly important for discerning the current state of adoption practices and attitudes, namely local/state and national population-based surveys. One of the most ambitious and largest remains the National Survey of Family Growth (NSFG), a periodic survey of diverse women aged 15 to 44 designed to provide national information related to fertility, family formation attitudes, and direct measures of adoption demand and adoption-seeking behaviors (Testa & Falconnier, 1998). Other national surveys such as the Current Population Survey (CPS) and the Survey of Income and Program Participation

Sources of Adoption

After the total number of adoptions, one of the most commonly asked questions relates to the auspices of adoption placement. For decades, the prevalence of adoptions from public foster care has lagged far behind private/independent adoptions (U.S. Department of Health and Human Services, 2004). More recent evidence demonstrates the beginning of a trend whereby private domestic adoptions have become comparatively less common. Figure 3.3 offers a snapshot of adoption activity at two points in time, 1992 and 2001. Included in these data compiled and published by the National Clearinghouse are the estimated percentages of the three most common sources of adoption—public, private, and international (U.S. Department of Health and Human Services, 2004).

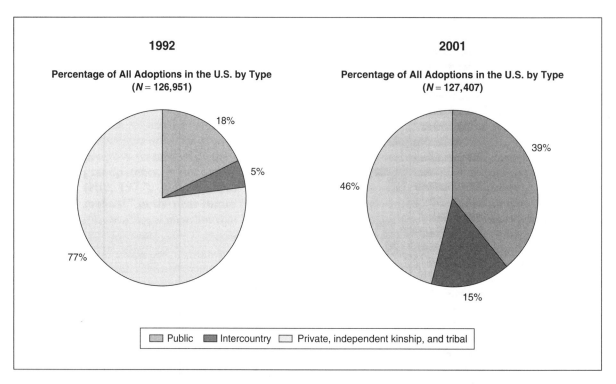

Figure 3.3   Percentage of All Adoptions in the United States by Type

SOURCE: Re-created from U.S. Department of Health and Human Services (2004).

Each of these years saw approximately the same number of recorded adoptions at about 127,000, a figure that has remained relatively constant since the mid-1970s. In 1992, adoptions originating from private/independent sources accounted for more than three quarters of all adoptions compared with only 18% from public and 5% from international sources. In 2001, the prevalence of private/independent adoptions dropped in proportion to the others, accounting for less than one half of all adoptions, whereas public adoptions grew to account for nearly 40%, a relative increase of about 117% from the previous decade. Intercountry adoptions also grew in popularity, as shown by these data, increasing from 5% to 15% of all adoptions.

It should be noted again that these statistical trends are based on national estimates and that the prevalence of public agency adoptions as a percentage of total adoptions varies considerably by state. As an example of interstate disparity, public adoption accounted for about 82% of adoptions in Illinois (67% in Iowa and 66% in Oklahoma) in 2000, whereas only 10% of all adoptions in Alabama were from a public source (13% in Wyoming and 16% in Tennessee) (U.S. Department of Health and Human Services, 2004).

It has been suggested that recent increases in public foster care adoption is traceable to the ASFA of 1997 in which the "best interest of the child" is to be achieved by terminating parental rights within mandated time frames to speed the process of adoption, authorizing financial incentives to states, to increase the number of completed adoptions, and encouraging "concurrent" or sequential planning, a process whereby adoption placement workers work toward reunification while at the same time establishing a contingency plan (Evan B. Donaldson Adoption Institute, 2002; Fisher, 2003; Schene, 2001; Zamostny, O'Brien, Baden, & O'Leary Wiley, 2003). Others point out that the growth in public adoption began well in advance of ASFA (Cole & Donely, 1990). In fact, the number of completed adoptions nearly doubled from about 25,000 in 1995 to about 47,000 in 1999 (Wulczyn & Hislop, 2002). No matter on which side of the debate one stands, the fact remains that a greater proportion of children under state care are being placed into permanent family relationships than ever before.

The National Adoption and Foster Care Analysis and Reporting System offers a more detailed analysis of foster care activity and characteristics of triad members than previously available. Findings from the most recent 5 years (1999–2003) of continuous data collection and reporting offer a closer glimpse of this population. The number of eligible, cleared children "waiting" for adoption remained well over 100,000 nationally from 1999 to 2000 (U.S. Department of Health and Human Services, 2005). Of the 567,000 children in active foster care in 1999, 131,000 (23%) were waiting and eligible to be adopted. By 2003, the number of active foster care children had dropped to 523,000, but those on the waiting list still accounted for about 23% (118,000) of all children in the public foster care system. Over this same 5-year period, the percentage of children adopted from the waiting lists was 36% in 1999 (47,000 of 131,000) and 42% in 2003 (49,000 of 118,000). Conversely, about one half of the children eligible for adoption at the end of fiscal year 2003 remained without a permanent home.

Boys and girls are equally likely to be adopted from foster care. Gender parity tends to also hold in public adoption cases but not in international adoption, as females account for 63% of all out-of-country adoptions. Of the 297,000 children who entered foster care in 2003, 46% were White, 27% Black, and 17% Hispanic. A majority of children (47%) adopted from foster care were very young, ranging in age from 1 to 5; another 30% were ages 6 to 10. The average age was 7. In terms of the relationship of the adoptive parents to the child prior to the adoption, a majority of children adopted from the state welfare system in 2003 went home to foster parents (62%) a relative (23%), or a nonrelative (15%).

International Adoption

At any given moment, an estimated 100 million children located around the world have no available caregivers (Child Welfare League, 2003). A joint report by the United Nations and United Nations International Children's Emergency Fund (now United Nations Children's Fund) (2002) estimates that the numbers of children with no parental care may be as high as 65 million in Asia, followed by Africa (34 million) and Latin America and the Caribbean (8 million). The causes are many, but a majority of these children are the product of civil war, overpopulation, famine, poverty, abandonment, or as is the case in China, a devaluation of girls. The United States remains, by far, the primary receiving nation of orphaned children, followed distantly by other Western nations, including France, Canada, and Germany. Of the 40,000 or more international adoptions that are estimated to have taken place worldwide in 2004, more than one half ($N = 22,884$) were adopted by U.S. families (U.S. Department of State, 2005). Pertman (2000) points out that given the fact that the United States is a nation of immigrants, "it's not an accident that Americans adopt more children than do the inhabitants of the rest of the planet combined" (p. 68).

Over the past quarter century, there has been a surge in international adoptions by American families. Available data demonstrate that a total of 174,395 foreign children were adopted between 1994 and 2004, a 175% increase in just one decade, as verified by immigrant visa records maintained by the U.S. Department of State (2005). Figure 3.4 offers a histogram demonstrating the significant growth in international adoption activity. Going back to 1989 figures, 8,102 international orphan visas were issued compared with 22,884 in 2004. With respect to the gender of the child, a majority of international children adopted into the United States are female (e.g., 63% in 2001); clearly, this is a direct result of the fact that nearly all the children adopted from Mainland China, the largest of the sending nations, is female. For the remaining nations of origin, the gender disparity is nonexistent (CWLA, 2003).

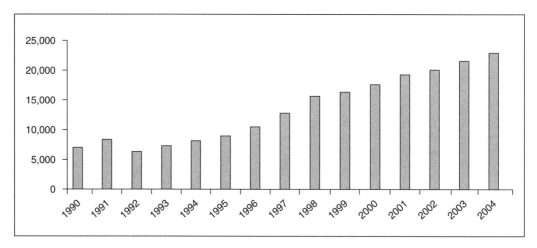

Figure 3.4   International Adoption (1990–2004): Immigrant Visas Issued to Orphans

SOURCE: U.S. Department of State (2005).

The ordering of the 10 most common sending nations changes rather frequently. This is typically in direct relation to the political climate of the time, for example, reflecting nationalism and pride as much as anything else, argues Pertman (2000), which in turn spills over into wavering adoption policies. The Department of State maintains an up-to-date Web site, where interested parties can turn to determine the specific adoption policies of each sender nation. Here is but one example in just a 10-year period (1994–2004):

	1994			*2004*	
No.	*Country*	*Visas Issued*		*Country*	*Visas Issued*
1.	South Korea	1,795		Mainland China	7,044
2.	Russia	1,530		Russia	5,865
3.	China	787		Guatemala	3,264
4.	Paraguay	483		South Korea	1,716
5.	Guatemala	436		Kazakhstan	826
6.	India	412		Ukraine	723
7.	Colombia	351		India	406
8.	Philippines	314		Haiti	356
9.	Vietnam	220		Ethiopia	289
10.	Romania	199		Colombia	287

International adoption is viewed often as a first choice among middle-class working adults, over natural childbirth or domestic adoption. One important and obvious observation in modern patterns is that American families are actively seeking to adopt children who are racially and culturally different from themselves. The rise in international adoption seeking may also be correlated with the strong possibility of locating and adopting an infant. In 2001, only 2% of the children adopted from the public welfare system were less than 1 year of age, whereas 44% of all internationally adopted children were less than 1 year. Another reason for the recent momentum may be traced to more humanitarian reasons, a sense of obligation to support children in the aftermath of the U.S.-led military involvement in South-east Asia, that is, Korea and Vietnam. Powerful images of orphaned and abandoned children were brought into the homes of mainstream America in the form of evening news, daily papers, and weekly magazines. Moving images of Operation Babylift during the Vietnam War in 1975 left not only indelible images but also dreams in the minds of many for the first time of adopting and raising an international child. International alliances and shared policy documents have also continued to take shape and lay a framework for international cooperation. Some of the most important have included the 1957 International Conference on Intercountry Adoptions, the 1959 United Nations Assembly Declaration of the Rights of the Child, the 1961 Immigration and Nationality Act, and the 1999 Hague Convention.

While many adoption experts see the positive sides of internationalization, some researchers have described the challenging conditions confronted by a growing number of international orphans, particularly those who are a bit older and have spent long periods of time in decaying institutions and who have been exposed to adverse conditions. In a recent report published by the Institute of Child Development at the University of Minnesota, Gunnar, Bruce, and Grotevant (2000) call for greater awareness and research that will help families and policymakers better understand the physical, cognitive, and behavioral consequences of maternal deprivation, malnutrition, starvation, stimulus privation, and unsanitary conditions in institutionalized settings. While many children are incredibly resilient and demonstrate remarkable recovery and growth after adoption, oftentimes, as these authors note, the problems are so serious that they can easily overwhelm the adoptive families mentally and financially. Too often, children's records in the nation of origin are unavailable, incorrect, or falsified (Gunnar et al., 2000).

In reaction to the growing demand for international babies, a number of adoption service organizations and private attorneys have emerged to offer specialized services for prospective parents. While many of these have been motivated principally by compassion and altruism, one adoption expert cautions us that a growing number have joined the business to make a quick buck from "the misery of destitute children and infertile adults" (Pertman, 2000, p. 74). Adoptive parents are coming together in greater numbers and sharing critical information in parent support groups as well as staying connected and informed through digital networks. To be certain, the computer, Internet technology, and dedicated software packages have radically altered many aspects of the adoption process, from exposing could-be parents to photos of available children as close as their nearest state-run foster care agency to as far away as China, India, and member nations of the former Soviet Union. Additionally, in terms of tracking adoption data, recent advances in electronic data entry and database technology offer the potential for adoption experts to stay on top of statistical trends as they unfold. Ultimately, adoption statistics are only as reliable as the source of data itself. As the saying goes, among statisticians when referring to the reliability of data sources, "garbage in, garbage out." We are encouraged by the possibility that in the years to come, footnotes describing the cautions of missing and estimated data will no longer be necessary.

REFLECTION QUESTIONS

1. What are the strengths and weaknesses of the three primary sources of adoption statistics available today—NCSC, AFCARS, and population surveys?

2. Of the three most common sources of adoption data—that is, public foster care, international adoption, and domestic private adoption, the least reliable and least valid in terms of statistics remains domestic private adoption. Why is this?

3. How do random population surveys further our understanding of adoption?

REFERENCES

Child Welfare League of America. (2003). International adoption: Trends and issues. *CWLA November Issue Briefs*. Retrieved August 11, 2006, from http://ndas.cwla.org

Child Welfare League of America. (2005). *Adoption fact sheet*. Retrieved January 15, 2006, from http://cwla.org/programs/adoption/adoptionfactsheet.htm

Cole, E., & Donely, K. (1990). History, values and placement policy issues. In D. Brodzinsky & M. Schechter (Eds.), *The psychology of adoption* (pp. 273–294). New York: Oxford University Press.

Evan B. Donaldson Adoption Institute. (2002). *Fact overview*. Retrieved January 15, 2006, from www.adoptioninstitute.org/factoverview.html

Fisher, A. (2003). Still not quite as good as having your own? Toward a sociology of adoption. *Annual Review of Sociology, 29*, 335–360.

Flango, V. (1990). Agency and private adoptions, by state. *Child Welfare, 69*(3), 263–275.

Flango, E., & Flango, C. (1995). How many children were adopted in 1992? *Child Welfare, 74*, 1018–1032.

Gunnar, M., Bruce, J., & Grotevant, H. (2000). International adoption of institutionally reared children: Research and policy. *Development and Psychopathology, 12*, 677–693.

Hill, R. (1977). *Informal adoption among black families*. Washington, DC: National Urban League.

Kreider, R. (2003). Adopted children and stepchildren, 2000. *Census 2000, special reports*. Washington, DC: U.S. Bureau of Census.

Lenzini, L., & Russo, G. (2004). *Family ties*. Special report published by the Children and Family Research Center at the School of Social Work, University of Illinois at Urbana, Champaign. Retrieved January 15, 2006, from www.fosteringresults.org

Maza, P. (1984). Adoption trends: 1944–1975. *Child welfare research notes, No. 9*. Washington, DC: Administration for Children, Youth and Families.

Maza, P. (2000). Using administrative data to reward agency performance: The case of the federal adoption incentive program. *Child Welfare, 79*(5), 444–456.

McFarland, M. (2003). Adoption trends in 2003: A deficiency of information. *National Center for State Courts Documents*. Retrieved August 11, 2006, from www.ncsconline.org/WC/Publications/KIS_Adopt_Trends03.pdf

Pertman, A. (2000). *Adoption nation: How the adoption revolution is transforming America*. New York: Basic Books.

Schene, P. (2001). Implementing concurrent planning. In B. Sparks (Ed.), *A handbook for child welfare administrators*. National Child Welfare Resource Center, University of Southern Maine, Portland.

Stolley, K. (1993). Statistics on adoption in the United States. *The Future of Children, 3*(1), 26–42.

Testa, M., & Falconnier, K. (1998). *Improving data collection on adoption and relinquishment of children in the National Survey of Family Growth*. Chicago: School of Social Service Administration (Report to the Centers for Disease Control and Prevention, U.S. Department of Health and Human Services).

United Nations Children's Fund. (2002). *Children on the brink 2002: A joint report on orphan estimates and program strategies from USAID, UNICEF and UNAIDS*. Washington, DC: TvT Associates. Retrieved January 15, 2006, from www.dec.org/pdf_docs/PNACP860.pdf

U.S. Department of Health and Human Services. (2004). *How many children were adopted in 2000 and 2001?* Washington, DC: National Adoption Information Clearinghouse.

U.S. Department of Health and Human Services. (2005). *AFSCARS report No. 10.* Retrieved May 1, 2006, from www.acf.hhs.gov/programs/cb

U.S. Department of State. (2005). *Immigrant visas issued to orphans coming the the U.S.: Top countries of origin.* Retrieved January 7, 2006, from http://travel.state.gov/family/adoption/stats/stats_451.html

U.S. House of Representatives, Committee on Ways and Means. (2004). *Title IV Adoption Assistance Program* (available in the *2004 Green Book*). Washington, DC: Government Printing Office.

Wulczyn, F., & Hislop, K. (2002). *Growth in adoption population.* University of Chicago, Chapin Hall Center for Children, Discussion Papers. Retrieved April 5, 2006, from http://aspe.hhs.gov/hsp/fostercare-issues02/adoption/index.htm

Zamostny, K. P., O'Brien, K. M., Baden, A. L., & Wiley, M. O. (2003). The practice of adoption history, trends, and social context. *The Counseling Psychologist, 31*(6), 651–678.

A Legal History of Adoption and Ongoing Legal Challenges

4

MADELYN FREUNDLICH

Child Welfare Consultant, Excal Consulting Partners LLC, New York

Adoption is both a social and a legal process. The legal process of adoption in the United States has evolved over time from a largely informal process to a process that is now regulated by states and the federal government and that is internationally regulated by the Hague Convention on Intercountry Adoption. Both domestically and internationally, there have been significant developments in adoption law. Nonetheless, challenges remain regarding many aspects of adoption law. This chapter briefly examines the major legal developments in adoption in the United States and the areas in which law continues to evolve. A legal history timeline is presented at the end of this chapter. Readers may find this visual a helpful guide as they move through this chapter.

ORIGINS OF ADOPTION LAW IN THE UNITED STATES: COLONIAL TIMES THROUGH THE LATE 1800S

Adoption laws in the United States may be seen as having stronger roots in Roman law antecedents than in English common law principles (Huard, 1956). Under English common law, adoption was not formally recognized, whereas under Roman law, adoption was used for inheritance purposes. Under Roman law, families that lacked a male offspring were permitted to bring male strangers, typically adults, into their households and designate these individuals as their lawful heirs (Hollinger, 2002a). These adopted individuals then became members of their new families with no ties to their birth families. The goal of adoption in Roman society was to continue family lines, thereby principally serving the interests of the adoptive families (Kempin, 1963). The adopted adult, however, benefited through receipt of his adoptive family's property and status (Kempin, 1963).

English common law, by contrast, did not embrace adoption, largely owing to the strong English commitment to blood lineage as the basis for differentiating class and social status (Presser, 1971). Nonetheless, English courts recognized "quasi-adoption" arrangements that later influenced the development of adoption law in the United States. These arrangements included wardships and guardianships designed to protect or provide support for orphaned children, apprenticeships to provide children with a trade, and other arrangements intended to discipline or otherwise train the children of families who were subject to the English poor laws (Hollinger, 2002a).

Because the social climate in the United States differed significantly from that of the United Kingdom, adoption law developed in a very different environment. The absence of a formal class structure in the United States and the widespread pursuit of social and economic mobility allowed for a broader acceptance of the "taking in" of children. In the 1880s, religious and moral concerns regarding the welfare of children and economic interests merged in the United States, and efforts were initiated to find ways to support dependent children beyond the poorhouse or apprenticeships for learning a trade (Leiby, 1978). As concerns about the welfare of children coincided with the interests of some adults in bringing unrelated children into their homes, the first state statutes appeared that legitimated the many informal transfers of parental rights that had been occurring since the colonial era (Hollinger, 2002a).

The adoption statutes that appeared in the 1850s and 1860s in the United States, however, did not establish adoption as a legal relationship. Instead, they simply recognized the informal transfers of children to relatives or strangers by poor parents or by institutions that had assumed responsibility for the care of children (Hollinger, 2002a). These arrangements typically involved agreements that the child would provide farm or domestic services for the family and that the family would support and educate the child and include the child as an heir to the family's property. Without a formal will that designated the child as an heir, however, informally adopted children had no legal claim to the deceased adult's estate. As the number of informal adoptions increased, the number of probate court disputes increased as well, leading to efforts to provide for the legal recognition of adoptive relationships (Presser, 1971). Because interest was primarily on property ownership, the inheritance rights of adopted children were the focal point of these early adoption statutes (Cahn & Hollinger, 2004).

Several states enacted adoption statutes in the mid-1800s, including Mississippi (1846), Texas (1850), and Massachusetts (1851). Some of these statutes merely provided a procedure for recording private agreements, focusing on the "adoption" of an individual child through legislative petitions (Cahn, 2003). The Massachusetts statute, however, established the principle of judicial oversight of adoption and, as such, is considered the first modern adoption statute. The Massachusetts statute provided that an individual adopted through judicial proceedings was a child of the adoptive parents "to all intents and purposes," and it provided that the child was entitled both to parental support until he reached the age of majority and to a share of the parent's estate (Presser, 1971). The statute also contained provisions that were forerunners of modern adoption law: a requirement of written consent of the child's parent(s), a requirement of consent of the child if he or she was 14 years of age or older, the necessity of joining the adopter's spouse as a party to the adoption, the need for the judge to assess the suitability of the prospective adopters, and the termination of the biological parent's rights and responsibilities for the child (Cahn, 2003; Hollinger, 2002a). Later, California (1872) and New York (1873) enacted adoption statutes that contained similar provisions. These laws, although not specifically grounded on the needs and interests of the child, set the stage for the later development of the principle of "best interest of the child" (Grossberg, 1985; Peck, 1925).

The Continuing Evolution of Adoption Statutes: 1850 Through the 1930s

Between 1850 and the 1930s, formal adoptions began to take place, although in a social and economic climate that differed greatly from the current adoption environment. During this era, many of the children who were likely to be "adopted" resided in publicly supported institutions that were empowered to "bind out" indigent children to unrelated families through indenture or "adoption" (Cahn, 2003; Ross, 2004). It was within this context that state statutes were enacted. These statutes, however, broadly incorporated certain concepts in elementary form that more fully characterize adoption law and practice today: the concept of parental consent to adoption, recognition of the principle of "best interest of the child," the relationship between the child and the biological family after adoption, the status of adoption records, and the nature of adoptive relationships (Grossberg, 1985; Leiby, 1978).

The adoption statutes during this period recognized the need for parental consent but did not specify when consent should be given or how. There were few procedures in place to ensure that parental consent was informed and voluntary, and parents were rarely represented by attorneys. When children were born to single mothers, only the mothers were required to consent to the adoption. Unmarried fathers played no role in adoption unless they were themselves adopting the child, or in a very rare case, they formally legitimated the child. Some statutes dispensed with parental consent under certain conditions: The parent had abandoned the child, was mentally ill, had maltreated the child, or was "morally depraved" (Hollinger, 2002a). In many cases, adoptive parents simply represented these facts to courts that accepted the explanation of abandonment, parental death, or incapacity without further inquiry. Procedures for review of parental consent were even more minimal when institutions placed children for adoption. Negative societal views of poor parents who placed their children in institutions as morally and personally lacking enabled institutions to elude judicial scrutiny of the adoption arrangements for children placed in these facilities (Ross, 2004). During this period, state statutes did not address the rights of birth parents to revoke consent to adoption or to reclaim their children from the institutions in which they had placed them. Few parents attempted to do either, as most lacked the resources or knowledge to regain custody of their children (Peck, 1925).

With regard to the concept of "best interest of the child," state statutes enacted during this period generally required that adoptive parents be determined to be suitable and that the "moral and temporal" interests of the child be served through adoption (Hollinger, 2002a). These requirements typically existed more in form than in substance. Suitability of the adoptive parents, if addressed at all, largely was a question of the prospective adoptive family's financial means, and the "best interest" of the child was principally viewed in economic terms. The one noneconomic criterion that factored into placement decision making was the religion of the child and the adoptive family (Hollinger, 2002a). The religion of many children, however, was not known, and consequently, the preference for same-religion adoptive parents usually translated into an institution's or agency's preference for families of the same religion as the religious affiliation of the institution or agency (Hollinger, 2002a). During this period, judicial oversight of the suitability of adoptive parents, whether determined on economic or other grounds, was largely "ministerial" rather than "judicial," with the proceedings simply validating an already accomplished transfer of the child to the family (Parker, 1927). In the case of institutions and other child-placing agencies, the routine placement of children with families continued with little judicial oversight.

The latitude of child-placing agencies during this era is illustrated by the freedom with which Charles Loring Brace of the Children's Aid Society gathered up children he described as "street Arabs" from the streets of New York City and dispatched them via "orphan trains" to the Midwest and West to provide agricultural and other labor for families who took in the children (Brace, 1872; Ross, 2004). These children were rarely formally adopted by their "adoptive" families, and there was little, if any, court oversight of this practice (Hollinger, 2002a; Ross, 2004). In the early 1900s, social reformers such as Julia Lathrop (who became the first director of the U.S. Children's Bureau) attacked the orphan train movement and the failure of the society to screen the families with whom children were placed and monitor the welfare of these children after families took them in (Folks, 1902). As criticisms mounted and efforts intensified to create the forerunner of modern foster care, the practice of "boarding out" the orphan train practice eventually came to a close (Folks, 1902).

Although the statutes during this time period allowed children to be adopted by families selected by birth parents or by child-placing agencies, they did not penalize the practice of placing children for profit or the placing of children without a judicial proceeding, nor did they address the activities of unlicensed agencies in placing children for adoption (Hollinger, 2002a). Baby-selling scams, as well as questionable placements of children with families as laborers, were well-known, but the law did not respond either to punish the individuals and agencies engaging in these practices or to attempt to prevent such activities in the future (Hollinger, 2002a).

This era also saw growing attention to, but continuing ambiguity about, the nature of the ongoing relationship between the child and his or her biological family. The concept of exclusivity—that is, that adoption ends all ties between the birth family and the child and the adoptive family becomes the child's family—was not fully embraced. Under the law, for example, adopted children could inherit from their birth parents if the birth parent died intestate. There continued to be disputes as to whether a child was the child of the adoptive family "for all intents and purposes" in connection with distribution of the adoptive parent's property at time of death. Similarly, courts were divided as to whether, if the adoptive family became destitute, the birth parents could be required to support the child whom they had placed for adoption. As late as the 1930s, in about half of the states, there was uncertainty about the child support obligations of birth parents under these circumstances (Hollinger, 2002a).

The statutes enacted during this era did not provide for the confidentiality of adoption records. Adopted persons could readily obtain their original birth certificates if they existed. To the extent that information about an adoption was protected, barriers to information access were designed to maintain the privacy of the arrangement from the public, not to shield adoption information from the parties to the adoption (Samuels, 2001). If information was not shared among the parties to the adoption, it was usually the result of incomplete records. By the 1930s, however, confidentiality provisions had begun to be included in some states' adoption statutes (Samuels, 2001). Before 1930, for example, birth certificates were not amended when a child was adopted; during the 1930s, states began to provide new birth certificates for children, substituting the adoptive parents' names for birth parents' names (Samuels, 2004). Paralleling this legal development were changes in the practice of some child-placing agencies, both reputable and not reputable, with regard to information access. With increasing frequency, it was reported that agencies threatened single pregnant women that their privacy regarding their pregnancies would not be honored unless they placed their babies for adoption (Hollinger, 2002a). At the same time, it was reported that agencies promised prospective adoptive parents that their identities would be withheld to attract families to child-placement agencies and away from the direct placement of children by their birth parents (Hollinger, 2002a). These practices, though of concern, did not trigger a legal response.

Finally, the statutes during this era were not clear about the duration of an adoption. Although adoption was presumably permanent, many statutes allowed adoptions to be overturned on a number of grounds: for example, if the adoptive parents did not support the child, if the child was "unruly" or "willfully disobedient," or if the adoptee became insane or epileptic as a result of factors that existed before the adoption but which were not communicated to the adoptive family (Zainaldin, 1979). The New York State statute, for example, provided that adoptions could be annulled for "any misdemeanor or ill behavior" on the part of the child, a provision that reflected the prevailing legal ambivalence about the actual permanency of adoption (Hollinger, 2002a).

The Development of the Modern Statutory Framework for Adoption: 1930s to Present

Beginning in the 1930s, adoption law began to emerge in fuller form. By this point in time, adoption had become a more broadly accepted form of family formation, and the courts and social workers had come to recognize the need to work cooperatively to ensure that adoptions were properly arranged (Hollinger, 2002a). The concept of "best interest of the child" broadened beyond economic well-being to include social and psychological

significant paternal interest in his child, denying the right to consent or withhold consent to an adoption violated his equal protection rights.

Finally, in 1983, in *Lehr v. Robertson*, the Court examined the new statutory scheme enacted by New York State after *Caban v. Mohammed*, and held that the unmarried father had failed to meet any of the statutory provisions that would render him eligible for notice of an adoption proceeding. His name was not recorded on the child's birth certificate, he had not lived with the mother and child after the child's birth, and he had not offered marriage to the mother. The court held that the "mere existence of a biological link does not merit equivalent constitutional protection" as that provided to unmarried fathers who had a "developed" relationship with and "full commitment" to their children (463 U.S. at 262).

Since these cases were decided, most states have amended their statutes to accord greater recognition to the rights of birth fathers. Because the Court has ruled on the rights of birth fathers in only five cases, none of which involved the adoption of a newborn or the adoption of a child by a party other than a stepparent, however, there continue to be many unanswered questions regarding the legal rights and responsibilities of unmarried fathers. These questions include the status of an unmarried father of a newborn placed for adoption, the rights of fathers whose efforts to have a relationship with their children have been thwarted by the birth mother or the adoption agency, and the rights of unmarried fathers who receive no notice of the child's birth.

Federal Law and the Adoption of Children in Foster Care. Since the late 1970s, federal law has recognized the value of adoption for children in foster care and has addressed various aspects of adoption practice on behalf of children in the custody of states' foster care systems. The provisions of federal law that address adoption issues, however, have taken a variety of forms (Garrison, 1996).

In 1978, Congress enacted the Indian Child Welfare Act (ICWA), the first major federal law that addressed adoption. ICWA was enacted following a series of congressional hearings that documented the pervasive, unwarranted removals of Native American children from Native families and tribes, the serious psychological and social consequences for Native children and families as a result of these practices, and the near decimation of some tribes as a result of these removals (Freundlich, 2000). Of great concern to tribal communities and to Congress were the large numbers of Native children being freed for adoption and placed with non-Native families (Indian Child Welfare Act, Section 1901). ICWA, in making clear that priority was to be placed on a Native American child's cultural heritage and tribal identity, created an adoption placement hierarchy: A child is first to be placed with a member of the child's extended family, second with another member of the child's tribe, and third, with another Native family (Indian Child Welfare Act, Section 1915(a)). A court, however, may override the statutory placement hierarchy on a showing of "good cause" (Indian Child Welfare Act, Section 1915).

Two years later, in 1980, Congress enacted comprehensive federal legislation on foster care and adoption, the Adoption Assistance and Child Welfare Act (Pub. L. No. 96-272). That law created a far more intensive federal role in the delivery of foster care and adoption services than had previously been the case. Permanency for children in foster care became a federal public policy goal, and adoption was expressly recognized in the statute as a permanency option for children in foster care who could not be reunited with their birth families. Federal supports for adoption were created, taking the form of federal matching funds for adoption subsidies for children who met financial eligibility criteria and had "special needs" (U.S. House of Representatives, 2003).

Fourteen years passed before Congress again addressed adoption through major legislation. In 1994, Congress enacted the Multiethnic Placement Act (MEPA), which legislatively defined the role of race, color, and national origin in decisions regarding children's adoptive placements. In a highly volatile political environment, MEPA represented a compromise between those who argued that race should not be a factor in children's placements with adoptive families and those who argued that race was a critical factor in determining the best interests of children placed for adoption. MEPA stated that race could be one factor in decisions regarding adoptive families for children, but not the determinative factor. It further required that states diligently recruit adoptive families who represented the racial and ethnic backgrounds of children in foster care who were waiting for adoptive families (Courtney, 1997).

In 2 short years, MEPA was amended by the Interethnic Placement Act (IEPA) of 1996 (Hollinger, 2004c). IEPA established new prohibitions on adoptive placement decision making by states and other entities that provide foster care or adoption services and receive federal funds. IEPA prohibited states and other entities from delaying or denying a child's foster care or adoptive placement on the basis of the child's or prospective parent's race, color, or national origin, and it prohibited agencies from denying any individual the opportunity to become a foster or adoptive parent on the basis of the prospective parent's or the child's race, color, or national origin. Under IEPA, race and ethnicity were not to be used in making adoptive placements except in a "few specific cases" when the child's best interests "may require attention to racial or ethnic factors" (Hollinger, 2004c, p. 190). Under IEPA, the mandate on states with regard to the diligent recruitment of foster and adoptive parents who reflect children's racial and ethnic backgrounds continued.

In the same year, 1996, as part of the Small Business Protection Act, Congress created an adoption tax credit for families whose adopted children qualify as dependents (Hampton, 2002). Subsequently amended by the Hope for Children Act of 2001, the tax credit, as of this writing, permits families to obtain a tax credit for "qualifying expenses" for adoption (such as fees paid to an adoption agency, travel expenses, court costs, and attorney fees) up to $10,000. When families adopt children with "special needs" from foster care, they may claim the full $10,000 tax credit, regardless of whether they have qualifying expenses. An additional change allowed families whose employers have an adoption assistance program to use payment and reimbursements through those programs to exclude up to $10,000 from their gross income (Hampton, 2002).

One year later, in 1997, Congress again enacted broad adoption legislation, passing the Adoption and Safe Families Act (ASFA, Pub. L. No. 105-89). This law made fundamental changes in Pub. L. No. 96-272 with regard to adoption, including the imposition of time frames within which petitions to terminate parental rights must be filed on behalf of children in foster care; the creation of adoption incentive payments to states that increase the number of adoptions of children in foster care over established baselines; and the extension of children's eligibility for adoption subsidies when their adoptive parents die. ASFA has been consistently viewed as a major catalyst in the increase in the number of adoptions of children in foster care (Gendell, 2001; Wulczyn, 2002).

It is unclear to what extent Congress will continue to act in the area of adoption. In recent congressional sessions, bills have been introduced to, among other matters, change the eligibility and/or financing structure for the federal adoption assistance program. These proposals have generated significant debate, and the course of future congressional action is unclear.

Better Coordination of State-to-State Adoption Activities

A second area of legal development has been the regulation of interjurisdictional adoptive placements. In the 1950s, attention focused on children's placements with adoptive families across state lines. That practice, which was wholly unregulated at the time, generated concerns about the safety and well-being of children adopted through such arrangements. In the absence of any structure to regulate interjurisdictional adoptions, there were no assurances that the interests of children, their birth parents, or their adoptive families were protected. In particular, there were concerns about placements of children in foster care across state lines as it had become apparent that some states were attempting to avoid their legal and financial responsibilities for children by, according to some commentators, "dumping" children into other states (Wendell & Rosenbaum, 1995, p. 3-A-1). Concerns about these practices led to the development of the Interstate Compact on the Placement of Children

(ICPC), which created a legal structure to govern interjurisdictional foster care and adoptive placements of children (Freundlich, 1997).

The ICPC was designed to ensure the safety and well-being of children placed across state lines and to promote appropriate jurisdictional arrangements for those children's care (Secretariat to the Association of Administrators of the Interstate Compact on the Placement of Children, 1990). As a compact, it provided a legal framework to which states could voluntarily become parties (Freundlich, 1997). Almost all northeastern states became parties to the ICPC in the early 1960s (Wendell & Rosenbaum, 1995). Between the early 1970s and the mid-1980s, almost all other states became parties to the ICPC (Wendell & Rosenbaum, 1995). Although many benefits of the ICPC were realized over the ensuing decades, the limitations of ICPC also became more apparent, particularly with regard to the long delays in processing interstate adoptive placement requests, uncertainties as to the types of cases that were subject to the ICPC, and little by way of legal enforcement when adoption agencies or independent practitioners violated ICPC provisions (Freundlich, 1997).

In 2004, the American Public Human Service Association, which serves as administrator for the ICPC, initiated, with the collaboration of the 50 states, a revision of the ICPC to address the major barriers to interstate foster care and adoption practice. Through the revision process, a host of issues were identified regarding the most effective legal framework for regulating interstate adoptions—issues that include the types of adoptions that the ICPC should regulate and the appropriate approach when the ICPC is violated. The revised ICPC was issued in 2006 and is currently being reviewed by states for enactment.

Regulation of International Adoption

Regulation of international adoption is a third area of continuing legal development. In 1990, the Hague Conference on Private International Law began work on a multinational treaty on intercountry adoption. In 1993, 55 countries, including the United States, signed the resulting Hague Convention on Intercountry Adoption (Hollinger, 2002b). The Convention has three primary objectives: (1) to ensure that international adoptions take place in the best interest of children and with respect for children's fundamental rights as recognized by international law; (2) to prevent the abduction, trafficking, and sale of children; and (3) to ensure the recognition of adoptions in countries that ratify the Convention and follow its provisions (Hague Convention on Intercountry Adoption, Article 1). The Convention establishes minimum standards and procedures for international adoptions between countries that have ratified the Convention, including assurances that children are free for adoption and have been appropriately separated from their birth parents (Article 4); adoptive parents have been determined to be "eligible and suited to adopt" (Article 5); and each country has a central authority that oversees international adoption and takes "all appropriate measures to prevent improper gain in connection with an adoption and to deter all practices contrary to the objects of the Convention" (Article 8).

In 2000, the United States enacted the Intercountry Adoption Act (IAA) to complete its ratification and implementation of the Convention. The IAA designated the U.S. Department of State as the central authority for the United States and put into place mandates designed to ensure fairness and protection of the rights of birth parents, children, and adoptive families; eliminate fraud and abuse in the international adoption process; and streamline the international adoption process (Hollinger, 2002b). The essential remaining step in the full ratification and implementation of the Convention by the United States, however, is the completion of implementing regulations by the Department of State. That process, which began with the issuance of draft regulations for public comment in 2003, continues as of this writing and is not expected to be completed until 2006 at the earliest (U.S. Department of State, 2005). This process has been significantly delayed as a result of conflicts between adoption agencies and consumer groups about the allocation of risks and costs of international adoption (Hollinger, 2002b). It remains unclear how the United

States will proceed with ratification and full implementation of the Convention and the extent to which it will, through regulation, address some of the thorniest problems affecting international adoption.

Clarification of Postadoption Rights and Responsibilities

Postadoption rights and responsibilities are issues that have generated considerable interest and advocacy. In the 1970s, adoptees filed constitutional challenges to sealed records laws, asserting that these laws violated the rights of adopted individuals to obtain personal information (Samuels, 2004). These court challenges failed, but in a few states (Tennessee, Oregon, Alabama, and New Hampshire), state laws were changed in the 1990s through legislative action or referendum to permit adopted persons' access to their original birth certificates or their adoption records (Samuels, 2004). Most states, however, have demonstrated considerable caution in opening adoption records (Samuels, 2004). Although advocacy has continued to amend state statutes to provide adopted adults with access to their original birth certificates and adoption records, these efforts have encountered significant resistance.

Despite the general reticence to allow access to adoption records on completed adoptions, states have evidenced a growing acknowledgment of the general benefit of greater openness in adoptions. Since the mid-1990s, states have enacted statutes to legally support planned openness in adoption as compatible with the established legal framework of adoption (Hollinger, 2004a). By 2003, more than 20 states had laws in place to permit postadoption contact agreements between adoptive families and children's biological parents and, in some cases, other members of the child's biological family. Although there is variation among these statutes, they are uniform in requiring that all postadoption contact agreements be approved by the court during adoption proceedings, in making the agreements enforceable after the adoption is finalized, and in clarifying that the existence of or disputes about the agreement do not affect the validity and finality of the adoption (Hollinger, 2004a). It can be expected that the law will continue to support planned openness in adoption given changes in adoption practices regarding openness and the relative success of postadoption contact statutes in the states that have already enacted these provisions.

Paralleling legal developments regarding access to identifying information about other members of the adoption triad were judicial and statutory developments regarding access to nonidentifying information. In 1986, the first "wrongful adoption" lawsuit was decided, a case in which adoptive parents asserted that their adoption agency had failed to disclose known health and other background information about their child prior to the adoption. In *Burr v. Board of County Commissioners*, an Ohio court recognized for the first time the right of adoptive parents to sue for monetary damages when adoption agencies have misled them about their child's background; they moved forward with the adoption without this information; and they subsequently experienced economic and emotional harm in attempting to meet the needs of their adopted child (Freundlich & Peterson, 1998). In subsequent years, courts in a number of other states also recognized "wrongful adoption" as a legal cause of action. Beginning in the mid-1980s, most states also moved to enact statutes mandating that background information about children be disclosed to prospective adoptive parents. These statutes and court decisions have led to significant changes in adoption agencies' practices related to information disclosure (Freundlich & Peterson, 1998).

The Rights of Nontraditional Families to Adopt

One of the most controversial legal issues in the current legal environment is the right of lesbian and gay couples to legitimize and protect their relationships with children whom they wish to adopt. Increasingly, legal focus is being placed on second or co-parent

REFERENCES

Armstrong v. Manzo, 380 U.S. 545, 85 S. Ct. 1187, 14 L. Ed. 2d 62 (1965).

Brace, C. L. (1872). *The dangerous classes of New York and twenty years work among them.* New York: Wynkoop & Hallenbeck. (Reprint Montclair, NJ: P. Smith, 1967)

Burr v. Board of County Commissioners, 23 Ohio St. 3d 69, 491 N.E.2d 1101 (1986).

Caban v. Mohammed, 441 U.S. 380, 99 S. Ct. 1760, 69 L. Ed. 2d 297 (1979).

Cahn, N. R. (2003). Perfect substitutes or the real thing? *Duke Law Journal, 39–47 (Public Law Research Paper No. 61).*

Cahn, N. R., & Hollinger, J. H. (2004). Adoptees' inheritance rights. In N. R. Cahn & J. H. Hollinger (Eds.), *Family by law: An adoption reader* (pp. 78–79). New York: New York University Press.

Courtney, M. E. (1997). The politics and realities of transracial adoption. *Child Welfare, 76*(6), 749–779.

Folks, H. (1902). *The care of destitute, neglected and delinquent children.* New York: Macmillan.

Freundlich, M. (1997). Reforming the Interstate Compact on the Placement of Children: A new framework for interstate adoption. *University of Pennsylvania Journal of Law and Social Change, 4*(1), 15–54.

Freundlich, M. (2000). *The role of race, color and national origin in adoption.* Washington, DC: CWLA Press.

Freundlich, M., & Peterson, L. (1998). *Wrongful adoption: Law, policy, and practice.* Washington, DC: CWLA Press.

Garrison, M. (1996). Parents' rights and children's interests: The case of the foster child. *New York University Review of Law and Social Change, 22,* 371–393.

Gendell, S. (2001). In search of permanency: A reflection on the first three years of the Adoption and Safe Families Act. *Family Court Review, 3925–3942.*

Grossberg, M. (1985). *Governing the hearth: Law and family in nineteenth century America.* Chapel Hill: University of North Carolina Press.

Hampton, L. P. (2002). The aftermath of adoption: The economic consequences: Support, inheritance, taxes. In J. H. Hollinger (Ed.), *Adoption law and practice* (Vol. 3, pp. 12-1 through 12-96). New York: Matthew Bender.

Hollinger, J. H. (1995). Adoption law. *Future of Adoption, 3*(1), 43–61.

Hollinger, J. H. (2002a). Introduction to adoption law and practice. In J. H. Hollinger (Ed.), *Adoption law and practice* (Vol. 1, pp. 1-1 through 1-84). New York: Matthew Bender.

Hollinger, J. H. (2002b). Intercountry adoption: Legal requirements and practical considerations. In J. H. Hollinger (Ed.), *Adoption law and practice* (Vol. 3, pp. 11-1 through 11-72). New York: Matthew Bender.

Hollinger, J. H. (2004a). Overview of legal status of post-adoption contact agreements. In N. R. Cahn & J. H. Hollinger (Eds.), *Families by law: An adoption reader* (pp. 159–162). New York: New York University Press.

Hollinger, J. H. (2004b). Second parent adoptions protect children with two mothers or two fathers. In N. R. Cahn & J. H. Hollinger (Eds.), *Families by law: An adoption reader* (pp. 235–238). New York: New York University Press.

Hollinger, J. H. (2004c). The what and why of Multiethnic Placement Act. In N. R. Cahn & J. H. Hollinger (Eds.), *Families by law: An adoption reader* (pp. 189–193). New York: New York University Press.

Huard, L. A. (1956). The law of adoption: Ancient and modern. *Vanderbilt Law Review, 9*(23), 743–758.

Kempin, F. G. (1963). *Legal history: Law and social change.* Englewood Cliffs, NJ: Prentice Hall.

Lehr v. Robertson, 463 U.S. 248, 103 S. Ct. 2985, 71 L.Ed. 614 (1983).

Leiby, L. (1978). *A history of social welfare and social work in the United States.* New York: Columbia University Press.

Meyer, D. D. (1999). Family ties: Solving the constitutional dilemma of the faultless father. *Arizona Law Review, 41,* 753–780.

Parker, I. R. (1927). *Fit and proper? A study of legal adoption in Massachusetts.* Boston: Church Home Society.

Peck, E. F. (1925). *Adoption laws in the United States.* Publication No. 148. Washington, DC: U.S. Department of Labor, Children's Bureau, Government Printing Office.

Presser, S. B. (1971). The historical background of the American law of adoption. *Journal of Family Law, 11,* 446–461.

Quillon v. Walcott, 434 U.S. 246, 98 S. Ct. 549, 54 L.Ed. 511 (1978).

Ross, C. J. (2004). Society's children: The care of indigent youngsters in New York City, 1875–1903. In N. R. Cahn & J. H. Hollinger (Eds.), *Families by law: An adoption reader* (pp. 11–18). New York: New York University Press.

Samuels, E. J. (2001). The idea of adoption: An inquiry into the history of adult adoptee access to birth records. *Rutgers Law Review, 53,* 367–392.

Samuels, E. J. (2004). The idea of adoption: An inquiry into the history of adult adoptee access to birth records. In N. R. Cahn & J. H. Hollinger (Eds.), *Families by law: An adoption reader* (pp. 136–141). New York: New York University Press.

Secretariat to the Association of Administrators of the Interstate Compact on the Placement of Children. (1990). *Guide to the Interstate Compact on the Placement of Children.* Washington, DC: American Public Human Service Association.

Stanley v. Illinois, 405 U.S. 645, 92 S. Ct. 1208, 31 L. Ed. 2d 551 (1972).

U.S. Department of State. (2005). International adoption: Hague implementation. Retrieved August 7, 2006, from http://www.state.gov/r/pa/prs/ps/2006/61274.htm

U.S. House of Representatives, Committee on Ways and Means. (2003). *The green book.* Washington, DC: Government Printing Office.

Wendell, M., & Rosenbaum, B. (1995). Interstate adoptions: The Interstate Compact on the Placement of Children. In J. H. Hollinger (Ed.), *Adoption law and practice* (Vol. 1, pp. 3-A-1 through 3-A-34). New York: Matthew Bender.

Wulczyn, F. (2002). *Adoption dynamics: The impact of the Adoption and Safe Families Act.* Washington, DC: U.S. Department of Health and Human Services.

Zainaldin, J. (1979). The emergence of a modern family law: Child custody, adoption, and the courts, 1796–1851. *Northwestern University Law Review, 72,* 1038–1089.

Zelizer, V. (1985). *Pricing the priceless child.* Princeton, NJ: Princeton University Press.

chapter provides relevant empirical support to the crucial importance of an identity formation (adoptive identity) for the adoptees.

Finally, Baden and Steward, in "The Cultural-Racial Identity Model: A Theoretical Framework for Studying Transracial Adoptees" (Chapter 7), take the discussion on identity to the next level by suggesting a new model for understanding and depicting the unique identity experiences of those reared in racially and/or culturally integrated families. The model accounts for heterogeneity within groups defined by their racially integrated families. For the purpose of describing and presenting the model, it was applied to the unique experiences of transracial adoptees. The model allows distinctions to be made between racial identity and cultural identity. These distinctions comprise 16 proposed identities of transracial adoptees and are made up of the degrees to which they have knowledge of, awareness of, competence within, and comfort with their own racial group's culture, their parents' racial group's culture, and multiple cultures as well as the degree to which they are comfortable with their racial group membership and with those belonging to their own racial group, their parents' racial group, and multiple racial groups. A model for understanding the role of parents, extended families, and social and environmental contexts is also presented as a guide for demonstrating the factors affecting the cultural-racial identities of transracial adoptees or others from racially and/or culturally integrated families.

LEARNING GOALS

We hope that in reading the contributions in this part, the readers will

- become acquainted with the developmental challenges often faced by adoptees;
- become sensitive to the long-term intrapsychic repercussions of relinquishment and adoption in the context of the models of Bowlby, Erikson, and Mahler;
- gain clarity into adoption-related development issues by reviewing case study scenarios;
- be able to define and contextualize the meaning of "adoptive identity";
- be able to identify how adoptive identity development is embedded within three contexts: intrapsychic, the family environment, and contexts beyond the family (including culture and history); and
- be able to develop strategies, approaches, and resources that will be useful to professionals working with adopted children and adolescents around identity issues; also, we expect that readers who are nonadoptees will gain an empathic understanding of adoptive experience by imagining themselves as a person who has been relinquished and adopted.

Developmental Challenges for Adoptees Across the Life Cycle

5

MICHAEL F. McGINN

Freeport, New York, Public Schools

Adoptees face challenges becoming part of a new family in the context of separation from the biological family. To see adoption as a simple variation on the typical manner in which families are formed is to miss the complexity surrounding the processes of relinquishment and adoption.

As Brodzinsky, Smith, and Brodzinsky (1998) point out, overall adoption statistics are difficult to come by as national data have not been systematically collected for some time. States are not required to record or report the number of private, domestic adoptions, although international adoption statistics are reported. The Evan B. Donaldson Adoption Institute (1997) estimates that there are 1.5 million adopted children in the United States—that is, more than 2% of American children. When other members of the "adoption triad" (birth and adoptive parents) are added to these numbers, as well as extended birth and adoptive families and all those who will become connected to adoptees during their lives (e.g., adoptees' spouses, children, grandchildren), the percentage of persons touched by adoption grows considerably. The Evan B. Donaldson Adoption Institute's 1997 Public Opinion Benchmark Survey found that 58% of Americans know an adoptee, have adopted a child, or have relinquished a child for adoption.

Of children who are adopted in the United States, slightly more than half are adopted by birth-family members, often referred to as "kinship adoptions," while the remainder are adopted by persons to whom they are not biologically related (Brodzinsky et al., 1998). Kinship adoptive parents have often become so reluctantly as a result of their own personal losses such as the death or inability of the child's birth parents (e.g., their own child or sibling) to raise the child. The circumstances preceding relinquishment are often tragic and sometimes include the trauma(s) of neglect, abuse, or other mistreatment. In nonkinship adoptions, parents often adopt due to infertility, which carries its own issues of shame, sadness, and loss. The process of attempting to conceive a child and failing, often repeatedly, can be a lengthy and traumatic one for couples who ultimately choose adoption to create their families. These circumstances can put considerable strain on the couple as well as on each individual parent. In most cases, then, although it may not be the case for single, gay, or lesbian persons, adoption situations are not the first-choice route to parenthood. As Russell (1996) has noted, "People do not expect to grow up, get married, and adopt a child" (p. 35). The adopted child therefore arrives into what is sometimes a setting of mourning as well as celebration.

Furthermore, adoptees themselves are often burdened by a lack of background information. As Russell (1996) pointed out, adoptees are the only Americans prohibited by law from seeing their original birth certificates. Instead, modified birth certificates are often created, with the adoptive parents listed as the birth parents, forcing adoptees to live "as if" they are part of a biologically unrelated family (Lifton, 1979, p. 14). While this has changed in some states, it is still the national norm. Accordingly, lacking historical information, an adoptee's history begins with himself or herself. He or she loses not only the birth parents but also all the information about the birth parents, birth kin, racial identity, medical history, and other basic existential information which nonadoptees take for granted. All this secrecy and deception contributes to what has been described as a sense of "genealogical bewilderment" in the adoptee (Sants, 1964).

PRENATAL AND PERINATAL ADOPTEE EXPERIENCE

Maternal Stress and the Physiology of the Prenatal Environment

As Ingersoll (1997) pointed out,

> Most adopted children . . . are born to young, unmarried mothers, a group who often do not receive adequate prenatal care. . . . Teenage pregnancies are also associated with low birth weight, which in turn is associated with behavioral and emotional problems in childhood. (p. 63)

Furthermore, mothers who experience an unplanned pregnancy often undergo great psychological stress. Emotional factors such as heightened, sustained anxiety are known to have many physiological effects. Just as unhealthy lifestyle factors, such as smoking and poor nutrition, are known to be risk factors for developing fetuses, psychological stress may also negatively affect the developing fetus.

Thus, the mother who is young, stressed, and without optimal prenatal care, as is often the case with birth mothers who relinquish a child, carries her child in a suboptimal in utero environment.

From Prenatal to Perinatal

While often seen as a "win-win-win" situation for all members of the adoption triad, relinquishment and adoption also entail losses for all parties. As Verrier (1993) pointed out, even in the most ideal circumstance, the adoptee feels the loss of the birth mother, the birth parents feel the loss of their child, and the adoptive parents feel the loss of their fertility and genetic continuity. This foundation of loss, as described by Kirk (1964), contributes to the unique psychodynamics of adoptees, which Jones (1997) suggested includes "issues of loss, separation, abandonment, trust, betrayal, rejection, worth and identity" (p. 64).

The lack of appreciation of the gravity of loss for a neonate adoptee underestimates the significance of the in utero experience. During gestation, a developing fetus hears its mother's voice, experiences her biological rhythms, and indeed shares her very existence in a most literal way. Verny and Kelly (1981) described the experience thus:

> (The pre-natal bonding experience is) . . . at least as complex, graded and subtle as the bonding that occurs after birth. . . . His (the neonate's) ability to respond to his mother's hugs, stroking, looks and other cues is based on his long acquaintance with her prior to birth. Sensing his mother's body and eye language is not very challenging to a creature who has honed his cue-reading skills in utero on the far more difficult task of learning to respond to her mind. (pp. 75–76)

Brodzinsky et al. (1998) also emphasized the inevitability of adoptee loss, regardless of age at placement:

> For later placed children, the loss of family . . . connections is overt, often acute, and sometimes traumatic. In contrast, for children placed as infants, loss is of necessity more covert, emerging slowly as the youngster begins to understand the magnitude of what has happened. (p. 98)

So, even for an adoptee relinquished straight into the arms of the adoptive parents, the bond that has developed in utero with the birth mother is abruptly severed. The sudden loss of that familiar voice, smell, pattern of movement, and so on does not go unnoticed. Rather, the adoptee is aware of the disruption in the continuum of care. Even the most sensitive and skilled new caretaker will not be the person to whom the neonate has become accustomed in utero. Verrier (1993) characterized this separation as a "primal wound":

> When this natural evolution (from conception to care) is interrupted by postnatal separation from the biological mother, the resultant experience of abandonment and loss is indelibly imprinted upon the unconscious minds of these children, causing that which I call the "primal wound." (p. 1)

Russell (1996) adds a note of irony when applying this to questions regarding disclosure of adoptive status: "Adoptive parents may find it reassuring to realize that, on some level, adoptees already know they were adopted. They were there."

Even in infant adoption, then, adoptees enter a family in which the preplacement circumstances may have been less than optimal and with the trauma resulting from the abrupt severing of the only relationship they have ever known, the in utero relationship with the birth mother. Furthermore, an adoptive mother is at a disadvantage from the start as she has not had the benefit of the 40 weeks of in utero bonding to help her and her child become attuned to one another.

Adoptees subsequently face unique challenges in forming secure attachment relationships with their adoptive parents due to the resonance of this "primal wound" experience. If insecure in their parental attachment, some suggest they may later have additional difficulty intrapsychically separating from their parents in childhood, and later separating both intrapsychically and physically in adolescence and adulthood. Having once experienced parental loss, or abandonment, as it may be perceived, adoptees may be particularly fearful of and sensitive to the possibility of other losses, and this may hamper separation. Trust issues are both the cause and effect of these attachment challenges, for as Russell (1996) suggested, "If an infant is separated from the only mother it has known for nine months, it will be more difficult for that child to establish trust" (p. 66). Furthermore, the experience of growing up in an environment in which secrets are kept or deceptions perpetrated (i.e., when adoptees are denied historical information or given false information, such as modified birth certificates) can impede the development of trust.

ATTACHMENT DEFINED AND ITS FUNCTIONS

Attachment is a term used to refer to close, enduring, emotionally based interpersonal relationships. While attachment relationships exist between dyads of many kinds (e.g., spousal attachment, sibling attachment), the term in the present context refers to both the relationship between children and their parents or caregivers and the process by which these relationships develop.

John Bowlby (1977) saw attachment as an affectional tie with a preferred individual who is seen as stronger and wiser. He defined attachment behavior as "any form of behavior that results in a person attaining proximity to some other clearly identified individual who is conceived as better able to cope with the world" (Bowlby, 1980, p. 203). Mary Ainsworth and her colleagues (Ainsworth, Blehar, Waters, & Wall, 1978) stressed the security aspect of attachment and coined the term *secure base* to describe what an infant should experience in a healthy attachment relationship.

Writing on attachment issues more recently, Melina (1998) echoed Ainsworth's basic definition:

> Attachment . . . is a reciprocal process between a parent and child. . . . It is the development of a mutual feeling that the other is irreplaceable. . . . Attachment . . . develops as the child learns that he can count on his parents to meet his physical and emotional needs. (p. 62)

Levy (2000) stressed reciprocity in parent/child attachment:

> Attachment . . . is not something that parents do to their children; rather it is something that children and parents create together in an ongoing reciprocal relationship. . . . [I]t is a "mutual regulatory system" with the baby and caregiver influencing one another over time. (p. 6)

Bayless (1989) characterized this reciprocal relationship as a "cycle of need." For example,

> a cycle of need is initiated by the infant when they express hunger by fussing or crying. If the parent responds to the need by picking up the child while fixing the bottle, by holding the child while warming the bottle and by continuing to hold, stroke and talk to the baby during feeding, the cycle will continue as the baby responds by relaxing, smiling and cuddling. (p. 5)

Bayless asserts that after the cycle has been completed successfully several times, "the child will become positively attached to the person completing the cycle" (p. 5). Fahlberg (1991), who termed this the "arousal-relaxation cycle," concluded, "Repeated successful completion of this cycle helps the child to develop trust, security and to become attached to his primary caregiver" (p. 34).

Case Study: Marta

Marta's birth mother, Angela, was 15 when she became aware of her pregnancy. It was unplanned, and Angela was scared and nervous, and she kept it a secret as long as possible. She did not attend to her nutritional needs and did not receive standard prenatal care as a result. Marta was born at 34 weeks' gestation well below normal birth weight and remained hospitalized for a short period during which she had very limited physical contact with Angela. Eventually she was deemed strong enough to be sent home to live with Angela and her parents, Marta's grandparents. Angela was reluctant to handle the frail infant, and despite her best intentions, she lacked the emotional maturity and parenting skills to care for Marta in a reliable, consistent manner. She was not educated as to the need for consistent eye contact and reciprocal play. Marta's schedule was erratic, and Angela either rushed to fill any possible need (she was not skilled at determining Marta's needs accurately) when Marta fussed or did not step forward to relieve Marta's distress if she was too tired or engaged in other activities. Angela's parents were not comfortable with becoming grandparents so much sooner than they had hoped, both worked, and Angela attended school as often as possible, so Marta's caretakers changed several times per day. As Marta progressed toward and passed her first birthday, other relatives began to observe that she was not hitting her developmental milestones (crawling, sitting up, babbling, standing, etc.) as they would have expected. She was wary of anyone she did not see regularly and seemed oblivious to opportunities for play with other children. She became increasingly difficult to comfort when frustrated and often looked to the side or over the heads of those who sought to interact with her.

ATTACHMENT'S LIFELONG REVERBERATIONS

For Bowlby (1977), the primary survival function of early attachment behavior is for the infant to secure the caregiver's nurturance and attention, so that the helpless infant will have its needs met. Furthermore, he proposed that "working models," or sets of internal representations about self and others, are formed as a by-product of the early attachment relationship with primary caregivers. These consist of sets of expectations and beliefs about whether caretakers are loving, responsive, and reliable, and whether the self is worthy of love, care, and attention. These determine to a large extent how an individual anticipates and construes self and others in interpersonal relationships. Bowlby (1979) warned that children whose basic needs have not been met consistently, and who therefore are not securely attached, might respond to the world either by shrinking away from it or by doing battle with it. Randolph (1994) similarly cautioned,

> A failure on the part of the mother to provide consistent reciprocal interactions with her infant during the first year of life can have serious lifelong consequences. . . . He may develop attachment problems where he finds it hard to form close relationships with others, or where he is indiscriminately friendly with strangers. . . . Or he may develop the most severe form of attachment disruption, Attachment Disorder. (p. 5)

Attachment is not an all-or-nothing phenomenon. Theorists and researchers have developed categories to describe the quality and level of individuals' attachment "styles." For example, Ainsworth and Wittig (1969) categorized infants as securely attached, insecurely attached/avoidant, or insecurely attached/ambivalent, depending on their responses to the comings and goings of their mothers in an experimental situation. More recently, Main and Goldwyn (1985) developed the Adult Attachment Interview and categorized participants, in their recollections and descriptions of their early relationships with their parents, as secure-coherent, insecure-dismissing, or insecure-preoccupied. It is important to be mindful of Melina's (1998) words: "Attachment is a continuum, with securely attached children at one end, completely unattached children at the other, and the vast majority somewhere in between" (p. 79).

Where a child will fall on this continuum is greatly affected by the circumstances of relinquishment/placement and the consistency and reciprocity in the relationship with the permanent caregivers.

When relinquishment occurs at birth and a child is placed directly into a permanent adoptive home, the repercussions of prenatal physiological stressors, the "primal wound," and the disadvantage for the mother/child dyad in becoming attuned to one another's cues due to the lack of prenatal bonding all may still come into play and contribute to challenges in forming a secure attachment. In less ideal circumstances, such as when a child has been relinquished after experiencing poor or inconsistent care with the birth parent, and/or where the child has experienced multiple placements, the challenges are even greater. A child who has experienced unreliable, chaotic, neglectful, or inconsistent care cannot readily come to trust even the most well-intentioned, competent new caregiver.

Attachment is the early keystone on which other developmental tasks rest. A child who experiences consistent, reliable caretaking will feel secure and think that the world is a safe, benign place to explore. The child's tasks of gaining control of its body (grasping, walking, smiling), making appropriate eye contact, learning to regulate its emotions, developing language—all these can best be attempted in the context of a safe, reciprocal relationship with a primary caretaker. Similarly, these developmental tasks can be more difficult to achieve for a child who is not securely attached. These tasks are subject to delays if the primary task, attachment, is impeded in some way.

Some writers on the topic of adoption believe that, in the long term, adoptees' attachment outcomes do not differ substantially from those of nonadoptees. Fahlberg (1991), for example, believes that the development of attachment after birth proceeds in a nearly identical manner whether or not an infant is genetically connected to the parent, despite the severing of prenatal bonds. Melina (1998) believes that birth parents may have an advantage, due in part to the innate in utero bonding discussed above, but that attachment in adoptive families generally is as strong as in birth families: "Intellectually, we know that natural childbirth, rooming-in and breast feeding are helpful but not necessary for attachment. Adoptive parents and their children . . . form attachments as successfully as do biological families" (p. 60). Bayless (1989) echoes this view: "The most important element in developing healthy attachment is neither blood ties nor the gender of the caretaker, but the nature of the relationship of this person to this child" (p. 3).

The limited amount of empirical research that has focused on adoptee attachment has yielded conflicting results. On the one hand, Brodzinsky et al. (1998) reported that the quality of mother/infant attachment in the middle-class families with same-race adopted infants he studied was comparable to that of mother/infant attachment in nonadoptive families. Furthermore, Juffer and Rosenboom (1997) found that internationally adopted infants displayed secure attachment relationships at rates comparable to nonadoptees. On the other hand, Horlacher (1989) found that adopted adolescents scored significantly lower on measures of reciprocity than nonadoptees, suggesting attachment impairment, and Fischman (1995) found that adopted adults were more insecurely attached, with increased feelings of abandonment and sensitivity to issues of object loss, than nonadoptees. However, Fischman also found that, when adoptees who had searched for birth parents were separated from those who had not searched, nonsearch adoptees did not differ from nonadoptees in terms of object relations and attachment. Thus, whether the views of Fahlberg (1991), Melina (1998), Bayless (1989), and others that adoptees do not ultimately differ from nonadoptees in terms of long-term attachment outcomes are supported by empirical research depends on which of the limited number of research studies one considers, and how one interprets their findings.

In all cases, an appreciation of the impact of the child's preadoptive experiences and an understanding of the need for attachment building (i.e., understanding that love alone is often not enough) will improve the chances of achieving healthy attachment outcomes for all children placed in adoptive homes.

Attachment Begets Trust, and Trust Is Necessary for Attachment

The word *trust* comes up frequently in the adoption literature, often in conjunction with discussion of attachment, as is evident from the foregoing discussion. Referencing the ramifications of the "primal wound," Verrier (1993) proposed that "the child's experience of abandonment causes him to mistrust the permanence of the present caretaker and to defend against further loss by distancing himself from her" (p. 66). Russell (1996) suggested, "If the infant is separated from the only mother it has known for nine months, it will be more difficult for the child to establish trust" (p. 66).

Trust is portrayed as an essential for the development of healthy attachments. Conversely, healthy attachment is seen as necessary for the development of a sense of trust. Thus, trust and attachment are often portrayed as opposite sides of the same coin: Trust allows for attachment, and attachment begets trust.

In addition to its generic meaning of confidence in the reliability and honesty of another, "trust" is also the positive component of the basic trust versus basic mistrust stage of Eriksons's (1968) model of development. In each of Erikson's eight stages of psychosocial development, the individual wrestles with the polar opposite constructs which define the stage. In basic trust versus basic mistrust, the first of the psychosocial stages, which occurs from infancy to about 18 months, Erikson proposed that the mother's consistent meeting of the child's needs leads to the infant feeling a sense of continuity, security, and trust:

> After emerging from the comfort of the uterus, the parents' ability to regularly meet (the child's) needs leads to trust and the expectancy of needs being met. . . . Mothers create a sense of trust in their children by that kind of administration which in its quality combines sensitive care of the baby's individual needs and a firm sense of personal trustworthiness. . . . [T]his forms the basis in the child for a sense of being "all right," of being oneself. (p. 249)

Brodzinsky and Schechter (1990) applied Erikson's basic trust versus basic mistrust directly to adoptees. They proposed that the most salient psychosocial task confronting an infant is the development of a basic sense of trust, and that in adoptive families, this is complicated by several factors, such as, of course, the separation from the birth mother. Verrier (1993) proposes that adoptees, due to the "primal wound" of mother loss, have difficulties in basic trust versus basic mistrust: "The loss of the mother disallows the achievement of basic trust, the first milestone in the healthy development of a human being" (p. 36). Verrier also proposes that these early trust issues may have long-term consequences: "The lack of trust is demonstrated over and over again in the adoptees' relationships throughout their lives" (p. 60). Weider (1977) too felt that early trust difficulties will have an impact on adoptees' future relationships: "Adoptees have difficulty trusting her [the adoptive mother] . . . or others who come to represent her" (p. 17).

Erikson (1968) himself characterized the development of trust as a crucial foundation for the child's first social achievement, separation from the mother, the intrapsychic process that Mahler, Pine, and Bergman (1975) termed *separation-individuation*.

STEPPING OUT IN THE WORLD

Separation-Individuation, Adoption, and Trust

Mahler et al. (1975) described the developmental process of separation-individuation that occurs from approximately birth to 36 months as the child's emergence from a symbiotic fusion with the mother (separation) and the assumption of his or her own individual characteristics (individuation).

Mahler et al.'s (1975) model describes a multiphase intrapsychic process:

The Separation-Individuation Process

1. Normal autistic phase   Birth to 4 weeks
2. Symbiotic phase   4 to 20 weeks
3. Separation-Individuation Proper

   Differentiation subphase   5 to 10 months
   Practicing subphase   10 to 16 months
   Rapprochement subphase   16 to 24 months
   Object constancy subphase   24 to 36 months

During the normal autistic phase, the neonate is still half asleep. The major developmental task is to achieve homeostatic equilibrium. In the symbiotic phase, now more awake, the neonate functions "symbiotically" as if fused to the mother, not consciously perceiving or appreciating their separateness.

As noted earlier, however, trauma can result from the abrupt physical removal of neonates from the birth mothers who have carried them, and neonates are aware of this break. Applying this to adoptee separation-individuation, Verrier (1993) commented,

> An uninterrupted continuum of being, within the matrix of the mother, is necessary for the infant to experience a rightness or wholeness of self from which to begin his separation or individuation process. The continuity and quality of this primal relationship is crucial, because it may set the tone for all subsequent relationships. (p. 29)

Even the adoptee relinquished at birth, then, carries the vestiges of this trauma into the normal autistic and symbiotic phases.

In differentiation, the first subphase of separation-individuation proper, the infant hatches from the autistic shell and engages in comparative scanning—that is, the infant begins to be aware of what is and what is not "mother." It is here, when the infant is first aware that there is anything other than mother, that *stranger anxiety* can appear. Mahler et al. (1975) suggested that in children whose basic trust has been less than optimal, abrupt changes to acute stranger anxiety may occur. With this assertion, Mahler et al. directly related trust, the sine qua non of Erikson's model, to separation-individuation.

Logically, it is reasonable to assume that less than optimal attachment (or, the other side of the coin, less than optimal basic trust) will contribute to difficulties in separation-individuation. A healthy attachment provides the "secure base" Ainsworth et al. (1978) spoke of, away from which the toddler, physically and intrapsychically, separates. The more problematic the relationship with the foundation, or the weaker the trust in the base, the more difficult the process of moving away from it (i.e., separating) will be.

In the practicing subphase, at 10 to 16 months, toddlers gain a deeper understanding of separateness because of the achievement of locomotion. It is in this stage that *separation anxiety* appears. Given all the challenges outlined above, this anxiety may be more intense for adoptees than for other toddlers. So, for those with less than optimal attachment and lingering trust concerns, both stranger anxiety and separation anxiety may be more intense and stressful.

During rapprochement, toddlers are ambivalent in their desire for separateness. They may seek to reconcile the gap of which they are increasingly aware by engaging in clinging behavior, by running away from and then back to mother, and/or by bringing objects to their mother for the dyad to share together. For adoptees who are aware that they have already been separated from a primary object in a most literal and permanent way, this ambivalence in rapprochement may be heightened. Separateness may seem very dangerous.

In object constancy, toddlers internalize a coherent image of mother as, ideally, a reliable object. The experiences of the mother who comforts and provides for them is integrated with that of the mother who is sometimes absent or frustrates them as being one person, one good object. Adoptees may engage in aggravated "splitting," seeing an object as either all good or all bad, due to their dichotomous experience of dual parentage, and may therefore have greater difficulty than nonadoptees in achieving object constancy in their internalization of a coherent image of their parents.

Although the initial separation-individuation process was proposed by Mahler et al. (1975) to occur from birth to age 3 years, these authors also emphasized that new phases of the life cycle see derivatives of the earlier separation-individuation process. The degree to which an individual has successfully completed the separation-individuation process in the first 3 years of life will affect his later functioning. Verrier (1993) cautioned, "(for adoptees) separating seems to be an even greater problem than attaching. Once a relationship is established, many adoptees do not want to separate, even when the relationship proves unsatisfactory" (p. 90).

Adoptees in the Phallic and Latency Stages

It has been suggested that the adoptee may have more difficulty in resolving the Oedipus and Elektra complexes of the phallic stage of Sigmund Freud's (1909) psychosexual development model, since the parent-child relationship is not a biological one and, therefore, the "incest barrier" that helps to speed the resolution of these complexes does not apply in as clear a fashion in adoptive families.

Many writers have discussed the latency stage adoptee's unique experience of the "family romance" fantasy. This common reverie of the school-age child involves daydreaming about having different, perhaps royal or "superhero" lineage, and fantasizing that one has somehow been kidnapped or stolen by one's caretakers. They may fantasize about rescue and reunion with their rightful parents. As Sorosky, Baran, and Pannor (1978) stated, "The adopted child in fact has two sets of parents. He/she cannot use the 'family romance' as a game as the biological born child, because for him/her it is real" (p. 99). Furthermore, especially during times of stress in the adoptive family, adoptees may intrapsychically "split" their parents into the "all good" birth parents, about whom they fantasize in the family romance, and the "all bad" adoptive parents who are treating them so badly. So, dual parentage can present particular challenges in the achievement of Mahler's "object constancy," as well as complicate "family romance" reveries.

ADOLESCENCE AND THE ADOPTEE

Fahlberg (1991) described the adolescent separation-individuation process as follows:

> The primary psychological tasks of adolescence echo the tasks of years one to five. The young person must once again psychologically separate, this time from the family, finding his place in society as a whole, rather than solely as a member of the family. (p. 107)

The adopted teen must separate from two sets of parents, one of which may be like ghost figures in his life. Separation may reactivate feelings of rejection, and independence may feel like abandonment. Again, separation may feel very dangerous.

A reworking of attachment issues is another task of adolescence. Kaplan (1984) described it thus: "The adolescent is like a mourner. . . . What the adolescent is losing, and what is so difficult to relinquish, are the passionate attachments to the parents" (p. 19).

Accordingly, when faced with the adoption-related challenges of letting go of attachments and separating into the larger society, as Sorosky et al. (1978) stated, "Adolescence is an especially difficult period for adoptees and their parents. . . . Adoptees appear to be particularly susceptible to the development of identity confusion" (pp. 105–110). Indeed, the penultimate adolescent question "Who am I?" is not so easily answered for persons intimately connected to two families, especially as they often lack birth-family information and may experience "genealogical bewilderment" (Sants, 1964) as a consequence. Brodzinsky, Schechter, and Henig (1992) proposed that "when adopted adolescents ask themselves 'Who am I?', they are really asking a two-part question. They must discover not only who they are, but who they are in relation to adoption" (p. 103).

Without a doubt, as identity formation goes hand in hand with the second separation-individuation and the shifting of attachments in adolescence, all these processes can be more complicated for adopted adolescents, as they are for adopted infants and toddlers.

Adoptive parents, too, can have difficulty with adolescent separation-individuation. As Pavao (1998) stated, "In many . . . families, not only do the kids have problems with loss and ending, but so do the parents" (p. 79). Adoptive parents sometimes fear that their teen, now old enough to do so without their help or approval, may search for birth parents and reenter their lives, perhaps even choosing the birth family over the adoptive family. These fears may be especially pronounced if there is significant conflict in the family, and thus adoptive parents may consciously or unconsciously thwart normal adolescent separation efforts because they, too, can fear abandonment, this time of the parent by the child.

Case Study: Thomas

Thomas was born to an impoverished Eastern European family and given the name Jacek. After struggling for several months to find the means to adequately provide for him, his birth parents relinquished him for adoption and he was placed in a relatively modern, well-run institution. He remained institutionalized and received passable institutional care while his waiting adoptive parents in the United States worked with their attorney and the government bureaucracy. When he was just under 1 year old, his adoptive parents flew to his birth country to bring him back to the United States. They renamed him Thomas. He had heard very little English spoken, and his adoptive parents did not speak or understand his native language.

Despite the challenges inherent in this scenario, Jacek/Thomas adjusted quickly to his new life. His adoptive parents were dedicated, well-versed in techniques to help speed the parent/child attachment, and very responsive to his needs. The trio became attuned to one another in short order. Though he exhibited several developmental delays, especially in the area of language development, Thomas soon caught up with his peers and developed age-appropriate skills.

As Thomas's parents prepared him for prekindergarten, he became more clingy and nervous and was easily unnerved by his parents' departures. He stammered occasionally and had occasional bed-wetting incidents. He was often hypervigilant and extremely driven to please, yet he occasionally threw tantrums which were followed by periods of sobbing.

GROWTH, LOSS, AND ADOLESCENCE

Loss is inherent in all development. As a new self emerges, the old self is given up, or lost. In adolescence, childhood is lost. Such inherent developmental losses, as described by Pavao (1998), are *maturational*, as opposed to *situational* losses, such as the objective and tangible losses of people in one's life. Normal maturational losses can be more difficult to work through for individuals with significant histories of situational losses. Adoptive families' histories are rife with situational losses, and their legacy can therefore complicate the maturational losses of adolescence, for the children and the parents. As Pavao (1998) stated,

> For . . . adopted adolescents who have issues of loss and of disconnection, leaving home is extremely difficult. . . . Applying to college, moving away from home, beginning a family, carry with them strong and serious issues. (pp. 69–75)

As such, an adoptee's journey through adolescence, including a revival of separation-individuation issues, a shifting of attachments, and the struggle for identity, may be more stressful than a nonadoptee's, as all entail maturational loss, and loss is a core issue for adoptees.

ARE ADOPTEES "AT RISK"?

It is reasonable to ask whether adoptees, given all of the above, as a group, experience more psychological difficulties than nonadoptees. Sorosky, Baran, and Pannor (1975) suggest that indeed adoptees are more vulnerable than the population at large because of the greater likelihood of encountering difficulties in the working through of the psychosexual, psychosocial, and psychohistorical aspects of personality development. Lifton (1994) described a set of traits and behaviors in the adoptees with whom she works, which she says result from "cumulative adoption trauma" (p. 7)—that is, the extra layer of losses and developmental challenges faced by adoptees. Kirschner (1990) suggested that the experience of loss and other facets of adoptive experience could create what he termed an "adopted child syndrome," characterized by personality and behavioral features such as impulsivity, low frustration tolerance, manipulativeness, and a deceptive charm that covers over a shallowness of attachment (p. 93).

Adoptees' Overall Representation in Mental Health Settings

One way to assess whether adoptees are at elevated psychological risk is to consider the numbers of adoptees seeking mental health treatment relative to their prevalence in the general population. As Brodzinsky et al. (1998) stated, "Research has consistently shown that adopted children are over-represented in both outpatient and inpatient mental health settings" (p. 35). Indeed, statistics suggest that 5% to 15% of the American children brought for treatment in clinical settings are adoptees (Brinich, 1980; Brodzinsky et al., 1998). In one early study, Schechter (1960) reported that 13% of the children in his private practice were adopted. In summarizing his review of many studies of psychological risk in nonkinship adoptees, Brodzinsky et al. (1998) concluded, "The proportion of adopted children in outpatient clinical settings is between 3 and 13%, with a conservative mid-range estimate of 4 to 5%—at least twice what one would expect given their representation in the general population" (p. 35).

Methodological Problems in Research on "Adoptees"

One must interpret this apparent overrepresentation with caution. First, in some statistical analyses, all adoptees are grouped together regardless of prenatal experience, preadoptive experience, age at adoption, and other factors. This is problematic for many reasons.

As was noted earlier, children ultimately placed for adoption are often the products of stressed pregnancies. Furthermore, their birth mothers are often young women with limited access to quality prenatal care. Thus, inadequate prenatal care and a stressed in utero environment may result in children being born prematurely, with low birth weight, and so on. These factors sometimes contribute to temperament difficulties, the need for neonatal medical treatment, and other complications such as learning deficits. These may account for some of the apparent overrepresentation of adoptees in clinical settings, rather than adoption itself per se.

Additionally, regardless of prenatal experience, children who were placed for adoption subsequent to such traumas as abuse, neglect, and parental death are not merely "adoptees" but also children who were the victims of abuse, neglect, parental death, and so on. Therefore, it is misleading to include them in an "adoptee" group for the purposes of determining the percentages of adoptees in clinical populations just as it is misleading to include as "adoptees" children who were born prematurely, requiring intensive neonatal care, and so on, who happen to also ultimately be adopted. The roots of their mental health difficulties may have little if anything to do with adoption. It is often the circumstances preceding the relinquishment, or that influence a birth parent's decision to relinquish, that account for the difficulties seen in some adoptees, not adoption itself.

In addition to these basic methodological problems, it has also been suggested that adoptive parents are quicker to seek care for their children than nonadoptive parents. Brodzinsky et al. (1998) suggest that this may be due to adoptive parents' "greater vigilance regarding potential psychological problems in their children resulting from working with . . . mental health professionals during the pre-placement period" (p. 36). In a study of 88 adopted and nonadopted children presented for therapeutic treatment, Cohen, Coyne, and Duvall (1993) found that the families of the nonadopted children tended to experience greater dysfunction prior to referral than the adoptive families—that is, the adoptive families did not wait as long as the nonadoptive families to seek treatment. Consequently, clinical settings may see disproportionate numbers of adoptees. Furthermore, as McRoy, Grotevant, and Zurcher (1988) point out, compared with the general population, adoptive parents tend to be socioeconomically advantaged. In Ingersoll's (1997) words, "Since adoptive parents are more affluent and better educated than parents in the general population, they are, therefore, in a better position to recognize psychiatric problems and to obtain appropriate treatment" (p. 59). Thus, one must be mindful that adoptive parents, as a group, may be hypervigilant and bring children for treatment more quickly, and they may be better equipped socioeconomically to readily secure mental health treatment, than nonadoptive parents.

Therefore, while it is reasonable that adoptees may be at somewhat greater psychological risk than nonadoptees, given the extra layer of developmental challenges they face, the statistics that suggest that adoptees experience psychological problems at minimally twice the rate of nonadoptees must be viewed with caution. As Ingersoll (1997) warns,

> Parents and professionals alike should eschew the simplistic assumption that psychological problems in adopted children are primarily attributable to the fact of adoption, per se. . . . Parents and professionals alike . . . may overlook problems which exist independent of the fact of adoption. (p. 66)

Symptomatology in Adopted Children and Adolescents

As empirical research yields murky results regarding the degree of overrepresentation of adoptees in clinical settings, and methodological questions exist, one should also view empirical studies of symptomatology characteristically manifested by adoptees with a critical eye. For example, Silver (1989) found increased rates of academic problems and learning disabilities among adopted children. However, Wadsworth, DeFries, and Fulker (1993) found little or no evidence of increased rates of learning problems in infant-placed adoptees. Some research suggests that adoptees are more prone to display symptoms of Attention Deficit-Hyperactivity Disorder than nonadoptees (Dickson, Heffron, & Parker, 1990). Furthermore, some research found indications of increased rates of conduct disorders in adopted children and adolescents (Kotsopoulos, Walker, Copping, Cote, & Stavrakai, 1993). However, Goldberg and Wolkind (1992) found significant differences in conduct problems only in adopted girls compared with nonadopted girls, with no differences between adopted and nonadopted boys. Still other studies found no differences whatsoever in conduct problems between adopted and nonadopted youth, male or female, in clinical settings (Dickson et al., 1990; Rogeness, Hoppe, Macedo, Fischer, & Harris, 1988). On the other hand, in his meta-analysis of adoption studies, Wierzbicki (1993) found not only that adoptees tend to display significantly more externalizing disorders than nonadoptees, but also that adopted adolescents tended to have a larger effect size than nonadopted children for both internalizing and externalizing disorders. In a longitudinal study, Fergusson, Lynskey, and Horwood (1995) studied 1,265 children in adoptive two-parent, biological two-parent, and biological single-parent homes. They found that the adoptee group experienced greater family stability and better mother-child interaction than children in the other types of homes. However, they also found that the adoptees exhibited conduct disorders, juvenile delinquency, and substance abuse at significantly higher rates than children raised in biological two-parent families but at lower rates than children raised in single-parent families.

So, while adopted children and adolescents are overrepresented to some degree in clinical populations, the empirical research literature does not consistently suggest that adoptees experience greater rates of specific psychological problems. Given the contradictory results of even just the few research results listed here, it is best to be mindful of the caution urged by Brodzinsky et al. (1998): "Whether adopted children are seen as at risk psychologically depends on the body of research that is examined" (p. 43).

FROM ADOLESCENCE TO YOUNG ADULTHOOD AND BEYOND

Given this extra layer of developmental challenges in attachment, separation-individuation, developing trust, resolution of psychosexual conflicts (oedipal issues, family romance confusion), identity formation, and other unique facets of adoptive experience, many have suggested that adoptees may be impaired in their ability to establish and maintain satisfying interpersonal relationships in adulthood. Russell (1996) opined, "It is typically the more intimate level of relationship that is difficult for adoptees" (p. 65). On adoptee identity formation and intimacy, Pavao (1998) suggests, "Intimacy? It takes knowing who you are to know who you can be with another" (p. 90).

Theory and research have consistently suggested a positive correlation between early attachment experiences and long-term outcomes for all individuals along a number of dimensions. Bowlby (1979) believed that "there is a strong causal relationship between an individuals's experience with his parents and his later capacity to make affectional bonds" (p. 135).

Empirical data on attachment outcomes in adolescents and adults is mixed. Armsden and Greenberg (1987a, 1987b) found that adolescents' self-reports of secure attachment to parents positively correlated with self-esteem and negatively correlated with depression and anger. Homann (1997) found adolescent depression to be correlated with insecurity in maternal attachment. Sroufe (1983), reporting on his longitudinal research, asserted that children securely attached as infants were more resilient, independent, compliant, empathic, and socially competent in later life, with greater self-esteem than children who were insecurely attached as infants. Turkisher (1993) found that self-reports of secure attachment positively correlated with self-esteem and subjective well-being in young adults. Bradford and Lyddon (1993) found a significant negative correlation between self-reports of strong parental attachment and overall psychological distress in college students. Levy (2000), after an extensive review of attachment literature, summarized his findings:

Numerous longitudinal studies have demonstrated that securely attached infants and toddlers do better in later life regarding: self-esteem, independence and autonomy, enduring friendships, trust and intimacy, positive relationships with parents and other authority figures, impulse control, empathy and compassion, resilience in the face of adversity, school success, and future marital and family relations. (p. 7)

Investigating the literature on adult attachment outcomes and the quality of intimate romantic relationships specifically, Mikulincer, Florian, Cowan, and Cowan (2002) assert,

Attachment studies have consistently reported that persons differing in attachment style vary in a) the likelihood of being involved in long term couple relationships, and b) the vulnerability of these relationships to disruption. . . . More securely attached persons have been found among seriously committed dating relationships or married couples than in samples of single individuals. (p. 410)

Furthermore, "Secure persons, as compared with insecure persons, a) are more likely to be involved in long term couple relationships, b) have more stable couple relationships, and c) suffer fewer difficulties and/or disruptions in the relationship" (p. 411). Kirkpatrick and Hazan (1994) found that the relationships of secure persons were more likely to be intact after 4 years than were those of insecure persons.

These few examples from the research literature are typical in that they find early attachment experience as predictive of later satisfaction in intimate relationships. As discussed, research on long-term adoptee attachment outcomes is limited, and research on adoptee functioning and satisfaction in intimate adult relationships is more limited still. Logically, however, if we accept the premise that adoptees face more challenges in forming secure attachments in infancy, childhood, and adolescence, it follows that adoptees are more likely to face further challenges in forming and maintaining satisfying intimate relationships later in life. That this has not yet been sufficiently supported by empirical study does not negate the validity of the premise.

CONCLUSIONS

Adoptees are relinquished by birth mothers in whose bodies they have live for 40 weeks, and with whom they have formed a bond that cannot be replicated. They are placed, sometimes immediately, sometimes after an extra-uterine relationship with birth kin, sometimes after numerous foster placements, sometimes after suffering abuse or neglect, with adoptive parents who seek to raise them and create a family that is as like a birth family as possible. Regardless of the specifics, the child nonetheless experiences this separation from her birth mother as a trauma and often has little information about her heritage.

These experiences may complicate the individual's developmental journey. In Erikson's psychosocial model, the development of trust in the basic trust versus mistrust stage can be hampered due to the initial separation from the birth parent and other factors adoptees experience. Adoptees may have difficulty asserting themselves in later stages, due to fears of abandonment and feelings of indebtedness. Furthermore, adoptees may develop negative self-images as they compare their families with other families, and see some family systems as all good and others as all bad due to "splitting." In adolescence, adoptees may have greater difficulty creating a solid identity and defining their roles. They may also have greater difficulty separating from their families than do nonadoptees. All these factors can culminate in adoptees having difficulties in creating satisfying, intimate interpersonal relationships in adulthood, and/or in severing unsatisfying relationships.

It is hoped that an increased understanding of the characteristics of adoptive experience will aid adoptees and adoptive families in overcoming the obstacles—some inevitable and some self-inflicted—which relinquishment and adoption can place in the path of healthy individual and family development.

IMPLICATIONS FOR ADOPTIVE PARENTS AND BIRTH PARENTS

This chapter has focused on the needs and characteristics of adopted persons. Inherently, much of what is written here is relevant to adoptive parents, as a huge proportion of the materials presented here centers on the nature of the adoptee/adoptive parent relationship, and how this can help or hinder the adoptee in his or her journey to face challenges unique to those who have been relinquished by birth parents.

Adoptive parents will of course wish to avail themselves of the many publications, from books to magazines to newsletters, which are available to them. Furthermore, adoptive parents may wish to join with and learn from others by becoming involved with organizations such as the Adoptive Parents' Committee, with chapters throughout most of the United States. Adoptive parents may wish to participate in research activities such that academics and clinicians can better collect data that helps to further put the puzzle together, for the benefit of themselves and their children.

Adoptive parents should inform themselves as to how and why traditional parenting techniques may be ineffective, even counterproductive, when parenting the child who has a history of poor, chaotic, or inconsistent attachment relationships. Techniques based on the presumption that children trust and want to please their parents may not work with a child with a history of insecure or severed attachments. These parents need to avail themselves of all resources available to them. If times get tough with a youngster, these parents should be mindful of their own needs, including their need for rest/respite and their need for humor. Furthermore, asking for help is often the surest, least stressful way to overcome an obstacle.

For birth parents, this chapter may cause alarm. However, it should do the opposite. Birth parents should understand that, with the myriad resources and ever-growing body of knowledge out there, children they have relinquished have a better chance of successfully meeting their unique challenges than ever before. The odds that an adoptive family, armed with truth and knowledge about what is normative in adoptee development, what can be avoided and what is inevitable, what is realistic and what is naive/misguided, can help the child of any birth parent to thrive, should be of some comfort to a birth parent who worries. The delineation here of obstacles and challenges and pitfalls and possible negative outcomes that the relinquished child may face just demonstrates that many people out there are knowledgeable, concerned, and competent to understand and address their birth child's special needs.

REFLECTION QUESTIONS

1. How might knowing that those who raised me are not biologically related to me change my relationship with them? How might it change my image of myself? How might it affect my willingness to enter into close relationships with others?

2. Can I imagine that I was relinquished (or "given up") by those persons who feature prominently in my earliest childhood memories? How would my relationship with my current caregivers/parents differ if I had conscious memories of early experiences with other caregivers/parents?

3. From Pavao (1998): "What would it be like if you did not know another human being *on this earth* who was related to you?" (p. 65)

REFERENCES

Ainsworth, M. D. S., Blehar, M. C., Waters, E., & Wall, S. (1978). *Patterns of attachment: A psychological study of the strange situation.* Hillsdale, NJ: Lawrence Erlbaum.

Ainsworth, M. D. S., & Wittig, B. (1969). Attachment and exploratory behavior of one-year-olds in a strange situation. In B. M. Foss (Ed.), *Determinants of infant behavior, IV* (pp. 113–136). New York: Wiley.

Armsden, G. C., & Greenberg, M. T. (1987a). The inventory of parent and peer attachment: Individual differences and their relationship to psychological well-being in adolescence. *Journal of Youth and Adolescence, 16*(5), 427–454.

Armsden, G. C., & Greenberg, M. T. (1987b). The inventory of parent and peer attachment: Relationships to well-being in adolescence. *Journal of Youth and Adolescence, 18,* 683–692.

Bayless, L. (1989). *Assessing attachment, separation and loss.* Atlanta, GA: Child Welfare Institute.

Bowlby, J. (1977). The making and breaking of affectional bonds: I. Aetiology and psychopathology in the light of attachment theory. *British Journal of Psychiatry, 70,* 201–210.

Bowlby, J. (1979). *The making and breaking of affectional bonds.* London: Tavistock.

Bowlby, J. (1980). *Attachment and loss.* New York: Basic Books.

Bradford, E., & Lyddon, W. J. (1993). Current parental attachment: Its relation to perceived psychological distress and relationship satisfaction in college students. *Journal of College Student Development, 34,* 256–260.

Brinich, P. (1980). Some potential effects of adoption on self and object representations. In A. Solnit & R. Eissler (Eds.), *The psychoanalytic study of the child* (pp. 107–131). New Haven, CT: Yale University Press.

Brodzinsky, D. M., & Schechter, M. D. (Eds.). (1990). *The psychology of adoption.* New York: Oxford University Press.

Brodzinsky, D. M., Schechter, M. D., & Henig, R. M. (1992). *Being adopted: The lifelong search for self.* New York: Doubleday.

Brodzinsky, D. M., Smith, D. W., & Brodzinsky, A. B. (1998). *Children's adjustment to adoption: Developmental and clinical issues.* Thousand Oaks, CA: Sage.

Cohen, N. J., Coyne, J. C., & Duvall, J. (1993). Adopted and biological children in the clinic: Family, parental and child characteristics. *Journal of Child Psychology and Psychiatry and Allied Disciplines, 34*(4), 545–562.

Dickson, L. R., Heffron, W. M., & Parker, C. (1990). Children from disrupted and adoptive homes on an inpatient unit. *American Journal of Orthopsychiatry, 60,* 594–602.

Erikson, E. (1968). *Identity: Youth and crisis.* New York: Norton.

Evan B. Donaldson Adoption Institute. (1997). Benchmark Survey.

Fahlberg, V. (1991). *A child's journey through placement.* Indianapolis, IN: Perspectives Press.

Fergusson, D. M., Lynskey, M., & Horwood, L. J. (1995). The adolescent outcome of adoption: A 16-year longitudinal study. *Journal of Child Psychology and Psychiatry and Allied Disciplines, 36*(4), 597–615.

Fischman, D. (1995). *Assessment of object relations and attachment capacity in adult adoptees.* Doctoral dissertation, Adelphi University, Garden City, NY.

Freud, S. (1909). Family romances. *Standard Edition, 9,* 235–241.

Goldberg, D., & Wolkind, S. N. (1992). Patterns of psychiatric disorder in adopted girls. *Journal of Child Psychology and Psychiatry, 33,* 935–940.

Homann, E. (1997, April). *Attachment and affect regulation in depressed mothers and their adolescent daughters.* Paper presented at the biennial meeting of the Society for Research in Child Development, Washington, DC.

Horlacher, L. J. (1989). *Attachment impairment: A comparison of adopted and non-adopted adolescents in therapy and those not in therapy.* Doctoral dissertation, United States International University.

Ingersoll, B. D. (1997). Psychiatric disorders among adopted children: A review and commentary. *Adoption Quarterly, 1*(1), 57–73.

Jones, A. (1997). Issues relevant to therapy with adoptees. *Psychotherapy, 34*(1), 64–68.

Juffer, F., & Rosenboom, L. (1997). Infant-mother attachment of internationally adopted children in the Netherlands. *Journal of Behavioral Development, 20*(1), 93–107.

Kaplan, L. J. (1984). *Adolescence: The farewell to childhood.* New York: Simon & Schuster.

Kirk, H. D. (1964). *Shared fate.* New York: Free Press.

Kirkpatrick, L. A., & Hazan, C. (1994). Attachment styles and close relationships: A four-year prospective study. *Personal Relationships, 1,* 123–142.

Kirschner, D. (1990). The adopted child syndrome: Considerations for psychotherapy. *Psychotherapy in Private Practice, 8,* 93–100.

Kotsopoulos, S., Walker, S., Copping, W., Cote, A., & Stavrakai, C. (1993). A psychiatric follow-up study of adoptees. *Canadian Journal of Psychiatry, 38,* 391–396.

Levy, T. (Ed.). (2000). *Handbook of attachment interventions.* San Diego: Academic Press.

Lifton, B. J. (1979). *Lost and found.* New York: Dial.

Lifton, B. J. (1994). *Journey of the adopted self.* New York: Basic Books.

Mahler, M. S., Pine, F., & Bergman, A. (1975). *The psychological birth of the infant.* New York: Basic Books.

Main, M., & Goldwyn, R. (1985). *Adult attachment interview, scoring and classification manual.* Unpublished manuscript, University of California at Berkeley.

McRoy, R. G., Grotevant, H. D., & Zurcher, L. A. (1988). *Emotional disturbance in adopted adolescents.* New York: Praeger.

Melina, L. R. (1998). *Raising adopted children.* New York: Harper.

Mikulincer, M., Florian, V., Cowan, P. A., & Cowan, C. P. (2002). Attachment security in couple relationships: A systemic model and its implications for family dynamics. *Family Process, 41*(3), 405–434.

Pavao, J. M. (1998). *The family of adoption.* Boston: Beacon Press.

Randolph, E. (1994). *Children who shock and surprise: A guide to attachment disorder.* Salt Lake City, UT: RFR Publications.

Rogeness, G. A., Hoppe, S. K., Macedo, C. A., Fischer, C., & Harris, W. R. (1988). Psychopathology in hospitalized adopted children. *Journal of the American Academy of Child and Adolescent Psychiatry, 27,* 628–631.

Russell, M. (1996). *Adoption wisdom.* Santa Monica, CA: Broken Branch.

Sants, H. J. (1964). Genealogical bewilderment in children with substitute parents. *British Journal of Medical Psychology, 37,* 133–141.

Schechter, M. D. (1960). Observations on adopted children. *Archives of General Psychiatry, 3,* 21–32.

Silver, L. B. (1989). Frequency of adoption in children and adolescents with learning disabilities. *Journal of Learning Disabilities, 22,* 10–14.

Sorosky, A. D., Baran, A., & Pannor, R. (1975). Identity conflicts in adoptees. *American Journal of Orthopsychiatry, 45*(1), 18–27.

Sorosky, A. D., Baran, A., & Pannor, R. (1978). *The adoption triangle.* San Antonio, TX: Corona.

Sroufe, L. A. (1983). Infant-caregiver attachment and patterns of adaptation in preschool: The roots of maladaptation and competence. In M. Perlmutter (Ed.), *Minnesota symposia on child psychology: Vol. 16. Development and policy concerning children with special needs* (pp. 41–83). Hilldale, NJ: Lawrence Erlbaum.

Turkisher, T. (1993). *Attachment style, self-esteem and subjective well-being among late adolescents.* Doctoral Research Project, Pace University, New York.

Verny, T., & Kelly, J. (1981). *The secret life of the unborn child.* New York: Dell.

Verrier, N. W. (1993). *The primal wound: Understanding the adopted child.* Baltimore: Gateway.

Wadsworth, S. J., DeFries, J. C., & Fulker, D. W. (1993). Cognitive abilities of children at 7 and 12 years of age in the Colorado Adoption Project. *Journal of Learning Disabilities, 26,* 611–615.

Weider, H. (1977). On being told of adoption. *Psychoanalytic Quarterly, 46,* 1–22.

Wierzbicki, M. (1993). Psychological adjustment of adoptees: A meta-analysis. *Journal of Clinical Child Psychology, 22,* 447–454.

Adoptive Identity

6

How Contexts Within and Beyond the Family Shape Developmental Pathways

HAROLD D. GROTEVANT

University of Minnesota

NORA DUNBAR

University of Minnesota

JULIE K. KOHLER

Public Interest Projects, New York City

AMY M. LASH ESAU

Northwestern College, St. Paul, Minnesota

AUTHORS' NOTE: The authors wish to acknowledge the National Institute of Child Health and Human Development, National Science Foundation, William T. Grant Foundation, and Minnesota Agricultural Experiment Station for research support during the time this chapter was prepared. The authors also thank Ruth G. McRoy, Co-principal Investigator on the Minnesota/Texas Adoption Research Project. The authors especially thank the adolescents who participated in their research and whose reflections and insights have taught them a great deal about identity development. All case studies in the chapter were drawn from interviews conducted with adolescents participating in Wave II of the Minnesota-Texas Adoption Research Project, their longitudinal research project on openness in adoption. Unless otherwise stated, all names and identifying circumstances have been changed to protect confidentiality.

Portions of this chapter are reproduced from the following paper: Grotevant, H. D., Dunbar, N., Kohler, J. K., & Esau, A. M. L. (2000). Adoptive identity: How contexts within and beyond the family shape developmental pathways. *Family Relations, 49,* 379–387. Copyrighted 2000 by the National Council on Family Relations, 3989 Central Ave, NE, Suite 550, Minneapolis, MN 55421. Reprinted with permission.

When I was a child, probably the thing that consumed my childhood the most, I guess, like what I thought about a lot was, was being adopted. I think that, like at some point, the child needs like, even to find out that they're bad or they died, or whatever—they need to know that just to have that sense of closure. (female, age 18)

I guess like the big thing is similarities, because I guess growing up in a family it's hard when everybody's like—like my mom's family looks a lot alike and I don't look like any of them. And, you know, they'll say, "So and so looks like so and so" and it's really hard. But you know when you see the pictures then you can say, "Well, who do you think I look more like?" Or, this is when my birthfather would write me a letter and something would sound like me and I'd say that and I'd say, "Well, oh, this is where I get this from." That's, I think, the part that interests me the most about it. It's just discovering why I am the way I am." (female, age 18)

I seem to have a compelling need to know my own story. It is a story that I should not be excluded from since it is at least partly mine, and it seems vaguely tragic and somehow unjust that it remains unknown to me. (Andersen, 1988, p. 18)

The three statements above illustrate adopted persons' attempts to probe their adoptive identities—the answer to the question, "Who am I as an adopted person?" The question of identity has been of great interest in the social sciences for several decades (see Bosma, Graafsma, Grotevant, & deLevita, 1994; Erikson, 1950, 1968). For persons who were adopted, this question adds layers of complexity because they have different parents of birth and rearing and because the knowledge of their biological heritage may be incomplete.

In this chapter, we begin by discussing how identity has been shaped by recent social changes and then explore the meaning of adoptive identity and its developmental course. We focus on three contexts of development: intrapsychic, the family environment, and contexts beyond the family, including relationships with friends, connection to community, and culture. We conclude with implications for practice with adoptive families.

DEFINING AND CONTEXTUALIZING ADOPTIVE IDENTITY

Interest in the identity of adopted persons has arisen from several directions. First, because of the growing popular American interest in "roots" and genealogy and the emphasis on blood ties in families, adoptees themselves have expressed the need and desire to know their biological origins. These needs are articulately expressed in the three quotes that began this chapter. Second, advances in medicine and genetics have made the general public increasingly aware of inherited conditions and have stimulated adopted persons to learn more about medical or genetic risks they might carry. Finally, reports of higher levels of behavioral problems among adopted adolescents compared with nonadopted adolescents (for reviews, see Haugaard, 1998; Ingersoll, 1997) caused clinicians and social scientists to wonder whether such problems might be due to underlying confusion about identity, given the complexities mentioned above. Several studies compared identity in adopted and nonadopted adolescents (e.g., Benson, Sharma, & Roehlkepartain, 1994; Hoopes, Sherman, Lawder, Andrews, & Lower, 1970; Stein & Hoopes, 1985) and found little or no difference between the groups. However, these studies looked at identity in a global way rather than one's sense of identity as an adopted person, which we call *adoptive identity*.

Adoptive identity cannot be understood without placing it in the context of societal attitudes toward kinship. Social scientists such as Schneider (1980), Bernardes (1985), and Wegar (1997) have argued that dominant Western society bases kinship ties primarily, if not exclusively, on blood relations. This puts adopted persons in an awkward position, since their familial ties are grounded in social relations rather than biology. "Adoptees are marginalized compared to the dominating kinship narrative. In this narrative the rootmetaphor 'common blood' is given special meaning and attention and adoptees discuss their own identity along lines informed by the rootmetaphor" (Cristensen, 1999, p. 153).

Adoptive identity development concerns how the individual constructs meaning about his or her adoption. From Erikson's (1959, 1968) extensive writings about identity and our own synthesis of this area of scholarship (e.g., Graafsma, Bosma, Grotevant, & deLevita, 1994), we have identified three aspects of identity that are particularly important: self-definition, coherence of personality, and sense of continuity over time (Grotevant, 1997). First, identity refers to self-definition, the set of characteristics by which one identifies oneself and by which individuals are recognized by others within a particular social and historical context. Second, it refers to the person's subjective sense of coherence of personality or how the various aspects of one's identity fit together. Third, identity refers to one's sense of continuity over time, linking past, present, and future, and, across place, linking multiple contexts and relationships (e.g., Cooper, 1999). Identity connects personality, subjective awareness, relationships, and external context. Thus, the essence of identity is *self-in-context*.

Identity development, a lifelong process, involves a dynamic tension between something considered core and something considered context to that core (Graafsma et al., 1994). "Attunement between these two guarantees the sameness or continuity over time that we think of as identity" (p. 163). We can think of adoptive identity as involving three levels: an intrapsychic component, a component involving relationships within the family, and a component involving the social world beyond the family. The negotiation between core and context can be seen at the intersection of each of these three levels. At the intersection of the intrapsychic and family levels, adolescents strive to make meaning of their situation while negotiating their differences from and similarities to members of their family, including adoptive and birth-family members. The physical and psychological presence or absence of the relevant network members determines the nature of social interactions the adolescent will have (Fravel, 1995). Identity work occurs when the fit between core (intrapsychic sense of self) and family context is explored, evaluated, or challenged (Graafsma et al., 1994; Grotevant, 1987).

The component of identity development involving family relationships is embedded within broader social contexts that include the adolescent's friends, school, community, and culture. What was context at a lower level (family relationships) becomes core at the next higher level, which in turn interacts with the next level of context—social relations and institutions outside the family. For example, the numerous ways in which changes in societal attitudes toward families, secrecy, and sexuality have changed the context in which adoptive relationships are played out illustrate a link between core and context in which identity development is experienced.

Yngveson (1999) commented that "adoption transgresses our notions about identity," implying that the journey of identity development is complex and potentially problematic for adopted persons. In the sections that follow, we examine how the intrapsychic component, family relationships, and social worlds outside the family influence adoptive identity development. As a heuristic, it is useful to discuss each core/context component and related processes separately. However, this is admittedly artificial as all parts and processes are interrelated and work together to contribute to the process of identity development.

Intrapsychic Component of Adoptive Identity

I think that I am who I am because, not just because of, you know, my family who raised me, or, you know, because of the two people that made me, you know. I think it's a combination of all that. Being able to know all of them has really helped me to just, you know, become who I am. (female, age 18)

The intrapsychic component refers to the cognitive and affective processes involved in constructing one's adoptive identity; an outcome of this process is shown in the quote above from a young woman of 18. The intrapsychic component of adoptive identity is grounded in the theoretical work of Erikson (1968) and the identity status research of Marcia and others (for a review, see Marcia, Waterman, Matteson, Archer, & Orlofsky, 1993). In this literature, the developmental processes involving exploration and consideration of possible futures in a given identity domain, and commitment to a specific future, are highlighted. For example, a young adult who considered numerous occupational futures before settling into a career in public service would be considered identity achieved, in contrast to a person who chose such a career pathway by default (i.e., a foreclosed identity).

Whether the identity statuses form a developmental sequence from less mature to more mature has been hotly debated (see van Hoof, 1999; Waterman, 1999). The literature may be equivocal because the "maturity" of a particular identity status must be judged with respect to the person's context. For example, a foreclosed identity might be very adaptive for a person whose living circumstances dictated that putting bread on the table was more important than self-actualization (Grotevant & Cooper, 1988). Our view of identity development is that it is an iterative and integrative process rather than a linear one (Grotevant, 1987; Marcia, 1993).

The identity domains studied by Marcia and colleagues well into the 1990s typically concerned aspects of identity over which one has some degree of choice, such as occupation, religion, political values, and ideas about relationships (for reviews, see Marcia, 1980; Marcia et al., 1993). Since that time, there has been interest in understanding identity development concerning issues about which one has no choice or which are assigned to an individual—for example, gender, ethnicity, sexual orientation, and adoptive status (Grotevant, 1992). Because most aspects of adoption do not concern things that the person has chosen, the task of identity involves "coming to terms" with oneself in the context of the family and culture into which one has been adopted (Grotevant, 1997). Although most children are not involved in the choice to be adopted, children do nevertheless influence the extent of disclosure of information shared and the contact with their birth families through communicative interchanges with their adoptive parents (e.g., Wrobel, Kohler, Grotevant, & McRoy, 1998). Although the identity task may be more complex for adopted than nonadopted persons, this does not imply that there is anything pathological about it.

The importance or prominence of adoptive identity differs across individuals. While some individuals engage in a great deal of intense reflective thinking about their status as adopted persons and the meaning that identity holds for them, others devote relatively little thought to the identity and its meaning. This range in behavior falls along a continuum of *salience* of adoption. At one end of the continuum, adolescents show little or no interest in exploring aspects of adoptive identity. At the other end of the continuum lies preoccupation, in which adoptive identity is the organizing theme of the person's identity and consumes considerable psychological and emotional energy. Toward the middle of this continuum, we find adoptees for whom adoptive identity is meaningful, yet balanced with other aspects of their identity (Grotevant, Dunbar, & Kohler, 1999).

The concept of preoccupation parallels early research on searching, in that it assesses the intense curiosity some adopted persons may have about their biological heritage and birth parents or their desire to synthesize their dual identities. However, unlike searching, preoccupation is thought to more aptly capture the "identity work" that occurs across levels of openness. In other words, intense curiosity about one's identity as an adopted person is not an inherent by-product of confidential adoptions. Preoccupation with adoption may look qualitatively different in mediated or fully disclosed adoptions from how it does in confidential adoptions (Dunbar, Kohler, van Dulmen, Grotevant, & McRoy, 2000; Kohler, Grotevant, & McRoy, 2002). The following example of preoccupation highlights its intrapsychic and relational aspects.

In her narrative, Melanie reveals a high preoccupation with her adoption, especially in her desire to search for her birthparents. She reports that meeting her birthmother is a "lifetime dream." She often thinks about her birthmother and even daydreams of looking in old high school yearbooks to see if she can identify her. Melanie states that she is more interested in meeting her birthmother than her birthfather. She relates this feeling to her closeness with her adoptive father and her feelings of distance from her adoptive mother, sensing that she is perhaps more in need of a "mother figure." Melanie talks with her adoptive parents about her adoption, asking them for more information about her birthmother and reminding them how close she is to the age when she can look in her file at the agency. Although she strongly wishes for contact with her birthparents, she says she would understand if they didn't search for her because it would be "a hard memory to bring back." (female, age 17)

Gender may add a layer of complexity to the development of adoptive identity. Although minimal gender differences have been found in identity formation in domains involving vocation, religion, and politics (Grotevant & Thorbecke, 1982), identity development in relational domains (sex roles, relationships) appears to be more complex for girls (Archer, 1992). Whereas boys seem to focus their exploration on aspects of identity having to do with school and work, girls tend to integrate aspirations and goals across more areas of life at the same time (Meeus, Iedema, Helsen, & Vollebergh, 1999). Adoptive identity provides adolescents with another relational identity to integrate along with other areas of life. The identity literature suggests that girls will achieve such integration more readily than boys (Kroger, 1997). If and when boys try to integrate their adoptive identity with other important aspects of their lives, they may encounter more difficulty than girls do because they have had less experience integrating relational and social identities in general.

Although the identity status literature has yielded many important insights since its beginnings in 1966, it has not satisfactorily dealt with the issue of identity integration (Grotevant, 1997; van Hoof, 1999). In an attempt to understand identity in a more integrated way, scholars have turned to a narrative approach as another way of understanding how one's intrapsychic sense of being an adopted person is woven into the larger fabric of one's life (e.g., Grotevant, 1993; McAdams, 1988). Narrative psychology focuses on meaning-making—how it is that our story helps us make sense of how and where we fit in the world. The developmental process can be seen in the growing sense of coherence in the person's adoption narrative. Understanding of this intrapsychic developmental process also requires knowledge of the degree of exploration that it has been given, the relational contexts in which it has been considered, the salience of adoptive identity to the person, the positive and negative affect associated with it, and its integration into a larger sense of identity.

Dunbar and colleagues on the Minnesota-Texas Adoption Research Project (Dunbar, 2003; Dunbar & Grotevant, 2004) analyzed the interviews of 145 adolescents (mean age 15.6 years) who were adopted as infants by same-race parents. Four subgroups were identified. Adolescents with *unexamined identity* had not thought much about adoption issues and reported that these issues were not very central in their lives. They simply didn't think about adoption very much, and their discussions were neither particularly positive nor negative in tone. Adolescents with *limited identity* had begun to explore their ideas about adoption. They did show evidence of talking about adoption with their friends and answering people's questions about adoption, but adoption was still not particularly central in their lives, and they reported that they did not think about it very much.

In contrast, adolescents with *unsettled identity* had thought about adoption quite a bit, had explored its meaning in their lives, and felt that it was very significant for them. They also had moderate to high degrees of negative affect associated with adoption, sometimes involving anger or resentment toward their birth parents or adoptive parents, or sometimes feeling bothered that there were things about their past that they did not know. Many felt "different" from their adoptive families. Those who had contact with their birth parents tended to be dissatisfied with the contact, typically wanting to have more than they had at present, but feeling that they were unable to bring about the additional contact (Mendenhall, Berge, Wrobel, Grotevant, & McRoy, 2004). Adolescents in this group conveyed the impression that they were trying to sort out their feelings about adoption, but that it was a difficult process.

Adolescents with *integrated identity* had also thought a great deal about adoption. They felt clear and resolved about its meaning in their lives, and their discussions about adoption were couched in generally positive terms. They generally viewed themselves as fortunate, and they felt that their family situations were positive. They looked on their birth parents with sympathy, compassion, and understanding.

Although these four identity profiles are very different from each other, they should be viewed as snapshots in time rather than endpoints, since identity development during adolescence is fluid. We do not believe that one of these identity patterns is "healthier" than another, especially during adolescence. Different adolescents will explore adoption with different levels of intensity on their own timetables. By young adulthood, the time of the next follow-up study currently under way, we expect that many more of these adopted persons will have developed an integrated sense of identity.

Relational Contexts Within Families

Adoptive identity is negotiated and enacted in relational contexts within families. Adoptive families vary in degree of openness with birth-family members, ranging from adoptions that are confidential, to those that are mediated and include the exchange of nonidentifying information, to those that are open. These different openness configurations present different relational contexts in which adoptive identity development occurs.

For most children adopted as infants, the developmental process follows a fairly predictable pathway. The early socialization process for adopted children typically engages the child with a family adoption story or narrative (Brodzinsky, Lang, & Smith, 1995). The story, which usually contains information about birth parents and circumstances surrounding adoption, communicates the "facts" that the adoptive parents wish to disclose at that time as well as subtle cues about the child's birth parents and their circumstances that will influence his or her developing narrative. In the early years, the family serves as a source of interpretation for the child through stories, songs, written material, and social affiliations. The family narrative is influenced by what adoption professionals have told the parents about "revelation": what should be told, how much, and when. The family's comfort with acknowledging that adoptive parenting is inherently different from biological parenting (e.g., Kirk, 1981), and their comfort with discussing adoption, is also part of the context.

The family narrative may come into question in several ways. If the child were not told of the adoption, the discovery could be very traumatic (e.g., Fisher, 1973). The child may have been raised to think of adoption in a neutral way (just another way to build a family), but other children who tease or misunderstand what adoption is about may challenge this view. As abstract reasoning capabilities develop during adolescence, the child comes to understand all the legal, societal, relational, and sexual meanings involved in adoption (Brodzinsky, Singer, & Braff, 1984). The normal questioning associated with this time period may extend to questioning the motives of the child's birth parents or adoptive parents and may lead the adolescent to realize that there is another component of his or her identity that will have to be worked through and integrated into a larger whole (see Grotevant, 1997).

Adoption often becomes "visible" within families because of real or perceived differences in physical appearance, abilities, or personality. Within biologically related families, differences are frequently attributed to heredity; if there is no one in the immediate family whom the child resembles, the similarity may be attributed to an extended family member—"Oh, your temperament is just like your Uncle Harry's." In adoptive families, differences are obviously not due to heredity from the adoptive parents or extended family. When nothing is known about the child's birth parents, attributions are sometimes still made to hypothesized characteristics of birth-family members—"Your mother must have had hair just like that." Children who are adopted internationally or transracially are, almost by definition, different in physical appearance from the members of their adoptive families.

How families deal with difference plays an important role in adoptive identity development. Kaye (1990) examined discourse processes in families considered "high distinguishing" (i.e., emphasizing the difference between adoptive and biological status) and "low distinguishing" (rejecting the difference between the two). Examining transcripts of family discussions, Kaye asked whether the adolescent's freedom to express feelings about adoption that were different from his or her parents might be related to the adoptee's identity formation. Such a hypothesis is reasonable, given research with nonadoptive families demonstrating the link between family discourse and adolescent identity exploration (Grotevant & Cooper, 1985). Kaye found that the high and low extremes of distinguishing were associated with family problems and low self-esteem, both of which may have consequences for identity development. This finding is congruent with the assertions of Brodzinsky (1993) that either denial or insistence of difference may be problematic for adoptive families.

Even in the absence of information about or contact with birth parents, adolescents will construct a narrative, although it may not be as coherent as one based on real people and events (Grotevant, Fravel, Gorall, & Piper, 1999). During this phase of narrative construction, the adolescent's sense of adoptive identity may become much more important and central than other aspects of identity. Other domains may await some resolution of adoptive identity before they can be undertaken. One strategy adolescents in confidential adoptions may use is to contemplate or initiate searches for birth parents to synthesize their dual identities—as a birth child of unknown birth parents and an adopted child of their adoptive parents—and establish a sense of continuity in their lives (Stein & Hoopes, 1985). The following case example from our research illustrates how meeting her birth father had a significant influence on a young woman's adoptive identity development.

Case Study

There were so many questions I had that no one could answer, I mean, my parents didn't know. No one knew. And, I just would sit and think about it all the time. And I'd think of different, you know, scenarios, and by the time I got done thinking I was so confused I didn't know what to do, and, no one was there to talk to me about it because I didn't know anyone else who was adopted, I mean my mom was always there, but it's different. As soon as I met [my birthfather] it was like, I knew who I was, and I don't know why that had anything to do with it, but, it was like, I was more focused on me. . . . *I didn't actually feel a part of the [adoptive] family until I met my biological parents, and then it was like, I knew myself more* [emphasis added]. So I became my own person. But I don't, I don't know why that had such an impact on me. But it, it just did. And it was like I could become me, after meeting someone else. (female, age 18)

An increasing number of infant adoptions are open from the beginning, as birth mothers may choose the parents to adopt their children, and the adoptive parents may be present at the birth. Such an arrangement implies that the adoptive parents have already made a decision that their family's boundaries extend beyond their household. Even if the parties do not plan extensive contact postplacement, they know each other and know how to contact each other. There is no pretense of the child's "passing" as a biological child of the adoptive parents. In fact, the act of choosing an open adoption implies an acceptance of differentness within the adoptive kinship network (adopted child, adoptive-family members, and birth-family members).

The family narrative into which the child is socialized may be co-constructed by the members of the adoptive kinship network. Co-construction of the narrative is more likely and perhaps more challenging in the context of an open adoption, because there are more relational contexts or relationships in which to construct an identity. Although all family relationships present opportunities for secrets and conflicts to occur, the nature of open adoptions reduces the likelihood of secrets related to the circumstances of adoption, since the relevant parties are known to each other. Although there may be fewer secrets about biology or heritage in open adoptions, this does not mean that all the children's questions are answered. An open adoption does not make the child immune to the questioning that is inherent in adolescence. In fact, we have found that all adopted children are curious about their birth families; but that children in different openness arrangements are curious about different things (Grotevant & McRoy, 1998).

In adoptions involving mediated or direct contact, a significant predictor of the child's socioemotional development (measured during middle childhood) is the collaboration of the adoptive parents and birth-family members toward the child's best interest (Grotevant, Ross, Marchel, & McRoy, 1999). These results suggest that collaboration in relationships may be one benchmark for successful adaptation in adoptions involving contact. This finding is similar to the current findings about postdivorce relationships (e.g., Hetherington, 1999). Children thrive best when the adults are able to have a civil, reasonable relationship with each other, and when they recognize that the children's best interests come first. The degree of collaboration among the adults in the child's adoption will serve as input to the process of adoptive identity development, in that it has to do with the child's primary relationships and how those individuals think about and portray adoption to the child.

Interaction With Contexts Outside the Family

Adoptive identity also involves interaction beyond the family. Yngveson (1999) has suggested that adoptive identity is more about movement and tension than it is about self-sameness. For example, she noted that an Ethiopian young adult who had been adopted into Sweden as a young child may feel more Ethiopian (than Swedish) when in Sweden, yet more Swedish when in Ethiopia—thereby exemplifying the dynamic tension between self and context. March (1994, 1995) has argued that the process of social interaction may make adoptees feel disconnected from others because others define them as "different" based on their adoptive status. In this view, the presence or absence of autobiographical information affects how the adoptee will present himself or herself in social interaction, thereby eliciting different responses from social partners. In some cases, lack of information led adoptees to experience "a sense of uncertainty over the authenticity of the identity that they had presented" to others (March, 1994, p. 219). Thus, the definitions of others, formed through social interaction, play an important role in the development of identity.

Adopting children across racial or national lines makes families bicultural or multicultural. The racial and cultural mix of the family's community will determine whether their status is a source of visible difference or not. Depending on the community context, adopted children may experience a whole range of reactions, from open arms to teasing and denigration. The "fit" of the adoptive family with its community context will have an impact on the identity development of its children. For example, Cheri Register, an American parent of two daughters adopted from Korea, wrote a book about her experience with family-community fit titled Are Those Kids Really Yours? (Register, 1991). The title echoed the many encounters she had had with strangers in the grocery store, airport, and neighborhood. It speaks to the issue of self in context—not only the child's identity but also the identity of the whole family. Lee (2003) has underscored the salience of this dilemma, labeling it the "transracial adoption paradox." For children adopted by White parents across racial or ethnic lines, the child or adolescent may be viewed by the larger society as an ethnic minority or a person of color. However, they may be perceived by some (and perhaps by themselves) as members of the majority culture, since they were adopted into a White family and grew up in that context. The sometimes contradictory experiences that can arise in this situation have implications for the developing sense of identity in adolescents and young adults.

Even if children adopted transracially or internationally are accepted in their community, they may encounter challenges to their emerging sense of identity if they move into a dramatically different context. For example, a Korean child adopted into a rural community may be well-liked and well-accepted; however, if the child attends college in a large multicultural urban area, others may respond socially in ways that challenge his or her identity (Meier, 1999). Through social interaction, adopted adolescents may begin to identify or align themselves with ethnic groups to which their adoptive parents may not belong. Adolescents may also seek out adoption-related groups and affiliation with the "adoption community" when they move into contexts where their adoptive status or family and community membership is questioned. The availability of numerous adoption-related Web sites and Internet chat rooms has made it possible for adolescents to participate in this exploration separately from their family, yet before they leave home.

If the child was adopted transracially or internationally, is there a community of like individuals with whom the child (and perhaps the family) can identify and interact? The availability of the community itself is only one piece of the puzzle; the child must be interested in interacting in this way, and the community itself must be welcoming. For example, because there are so many Korean adoptees in Minnesota, there are Korean culture camps offered in the summer for internationally adopted children. Although many children love them and benefit from them, there are other children who want nothing to do with them. Similarly, members of the child's ethnic community may not be interested in interacting with the adopted child, who is different from them as well as from his or her adoptive parents (Meier, 1998).

CONCLUSIONS

Several contexts of adoptive identity development have been explored in this chapter: intrapsychic, relationships within the family, and connections beyond the family, to friends, neighborhood, community, and culture. Although it was argued that adoption itself presents adolescents with a number of complexities that demand integration into their emerging sense of self, we also showed that children with different adoption arrangements have different resources and challenges with which to work in the identity development process.

Multiple and complex factors, stemming from different sources, influence adoptive identity development. Some are related to early experience, some are related to the fit of the child within the family and the surrounding community, and some are due to societal attitudes about adoption in general or specific types of adoption. Taken together, they underscore the challenges associated with integrating one's sense of self as an adopted person with other significant domains of identity.

Although a clearer picture of adoptive identity is emerging through recent research advances, much remains to be understood. The diversity of situations experienced by adopted children and adoptive parents will provide adoption researchers rich opportunities for further understanding the complexity and intricacy of adoptive identity development. This approach will also be relevant for understanding identity integration in the case of other "assigned" identities, such as gender, ethnicity, and sexual orientation.

IMPLICATIONS FOR RESEARCH AND THEORY

Although Erikson's (1968) theory of identity has been central to the emerging understanding of adoptive identity, further theoretical work is needed to clarify the links connecting adoption as an assigned identity, other domains of identity that involve choice (e.g., occupation, values), and the social contexts in which this developmental process takes place. This chapter is a first step in this direction. To our knowledge, the only measure specifically designed to assess adoptive identity is the interview developed by our research team and its accompanying codebook (Grotevant, Dunbar, et al., 1999). The interview takes a narrative approach to understanding identity and evaluates the following aspects of adoptive identity: depth of exploration, valence of affect, salience, relationship connections, and four aspects of narrative coherence (internal consistency, organization, flexibility, and congruence between affect and content). It is hoped that this chapter will stimulate further theoretical and methodological advances in understanding adoptive identity.

Best Practices for Professionals Working With Adopted Persons

This discussion of adoptive identity development suggests a number of specific implications for professionals who work with adopted persons and their families.

1. Overall, we recommend that professionals be aware of the tremendous variation in adolescents' individual cognitive processes and in the resources—within both the family and the larger community—that adolescents have available to them as they construct a sense of themselves as adopted individuals.

2. Practitioners working with adopted adolescents should be particularly aware of how different adolescents perceive their adoptive identity as being more or less salient to their overall sense of self and that these degrees of salience may hold implications for other activities in adolescents' lives (initiating a search for birth parents, deciding on an adoption-related career, etc.). They should also attend to adolescents' personal perceptions of adoption-related "stigma" and the resources they have to deal with such feelings. They should be cognizant of the different levels of access to background or biographical identity information that adopted adolescents may have, due to the nature of their adoption (international vs. domestic, confidential vs. mediated or fully disclosed) and the dynamics in the adoptive family (e.g., the degree to which adoption is discussed within the adoptive family).

3. Because of the existence of these differences, professionals working with adopted adolescents should be careful to avoid a "one-size-fits-all" approach. In any group of adopted adolescents, school personnel or other professionals might find adoptees in each of the four identity categories described above. Although it may be extremely useful to connect some internationally adopted youth with organized cultural resources, such as cultural camps or agency programs, not all youth may be comfortable with these activities. Searching may be a necessary activity for some adolescents to feel "complete" but irrelevant to others. Since there is no single course for adoptive identity development, educational and clinical interventions should be carefully designed with adolescents' individual characteristics and specific family and community contexts in mind.

4. Despite the need for individually tailored interventions, some basic guidelines may be useful to family professionals in their work with adopted adolescents and adoptive families (for further discussion, see Wrobel, Hendrickson, & Grotevant, 2006). For example, it is important for professionals to use language respectful of adoption and its participants. It is preferable to say "birth mother" rather than "natural mother," to avoid suggesting that there is something "unnatural" about adoptive mothering. Teachers and family life educators should develop curricula respectful of adopted children. It should not be assumed that children adopted from other countries are experts on their home countries or necessarily want to become experts. Family trees, autobiographies, and studies of genetics should be done in such a way that the assignment can be completed by all students, and so that adopted children do not feel singled out. Professionals should familiarize themselves with adoption issues by reading first-person accounts and the research literature. Informed professionals will, in turn, be able to help combat uninformed stereotypes, expectations, or attitudes. Finally, professionals can be attuned to the issues adopted adolescents might be considering (searching, connecting with a home country, etc.) and be prepared to listen and provide a safe climate in which they can consider options.

REFLECTION QUESTIONS

1. Why might adopted adolescents show different patterns of identity development, and what factors might stimulate movement from one pattern to another?

2. How can adults who have contact with adopted children and adolescents identify and support the needs that such children and youth might have?

3. What impact do changes in society's attitudes about adoption and the meaning of family have on young people's identity development process? What will the situation look like in the year 2030?

4. We often think of identity as something that is worked out during adolescence. In what ways is identity development a lifelong process?

REFERENCES

Andersen, R. S. (1988). Why adoptees search: Motives and more. *Child Welfare, 67,* 15–19.

Archer, S. L. (1992). A feminist's approach to identity research. In G. R. Adams, R. Montemayor, & T. P. Gullota (Eds.), *Advances in adolescent development: Adolescent identity formation* (Vol. 4, pp. 25–49). Newbury Park, CA: Sage.

Benson, P. L., Sharma, A. R., & Roehlkepartain, E. C. (1994). *Growing up adopted: A portrait of adolescents and their families.* Minneapolis, MN: Search Institute.

Bernardes, J. (1985). "Family ideology": Identification and exploration. *Sociological Review, 33,* 275–297.

Bosma, H. A., Graafsma, T. L. G., Grotevant, H. D., & deLevita, D. J. (1994). *Identity and development: An interdisciplinary approach.* Thousand Oaks, CA: Sage.

Brodzinsky, D. M. (1993). Long-term outcome in adoption. *The Future of Children, 11,* 153–166.

Brodzinsky, D. M., Lang, R., & Smith, D. W. (1995). Parenting adopted children. In M. Bornstein (Ed.), *Handbook of parenting: Vol. 3. Status and social conditions of parenting* (pp. 209–232). Mahwah, NJ: Lawrence Erlbaum.

Brodzinsky, D. M., Singer, L. M., & Braff, A. M. (1984). Children's understanding of adoption. *Child Development, 55,* 869–878.

Cooper, C. R. (1999). Multiple selves, multiple worlds: Cultural perspectives on individuality and connectedness in adolescent development. In A. Masten (Ed.), *Cultural processes in child development: The Minnesota Symposia on Child Psychology* (Vol. 29, pp. 25–58). Mahwah, NJ: Lawrence Erlbaum.

Cristensen, I. B. (1999). Is blood thicker than water? In A.-L. Rygvold, M. Dalen, & B. Saetersdal (Eds.), *Mine–yours–ours–and theirs: Adoption, changing kinship and family patterns* (pp. 147–155). Oslo, Norway: University of Oslo.

Dunbar, N. D. (2003). *Typologies of adolescent adoptive identity: The influence of family context and relationships.* Unpublished doctoral dissertation, University of Minnesota, St. Paul, MN.

Dunbar, N., & Grotevant, H. D. (2004). Adoption narratives: The construction of adoptive identity during adolescence. In M. W. Pratt & B. H. Fiese (Eds.), *Family stories and the life course: Across time and generations* (pp. 135–161). Mahwah, NJ: Lawrence Erlbaum.

Dunbar, N., Kohler, J. K., van Dulmen, M. H. M., Grotevant, H. D., & McRoy, R. G. (2000). *Why adoption does and doesn't matter: Factors predicting adoptive identity salience.* Paper presented at the biennial meeting of the Society for Research on Adolescence, Chicago.

Erikson, E. H. (1950). *Childhood and society.* New York: Norton.

Erikson, E. H. (1959). *Identity and the life cycle.* New York: Norton.

Erikson, E. H. (1968). *Identity: Youth and crisis.* New York: Norton.

Fisher, F. (1973). *In search of Anna Fisher.* New York: Ballantine Books.

Fravel, D. L. (1995). *Boundary ambiguity perceptions of adoptive parents experiencing various levels of openness in adoption*. Unpublished doctoral dissertation, University of Minnesota, St. Paul, MN.

Graafsma, T. L. G., Bosma, H. A., Grotevant, H. D., & deLevita, D. J. (1994). Identity and development: An interdisciplinary view. In H. A. Bosma, T. L. G. Graafsma, H. D. Grotevant, & D. J. deLevita (Eds.), *Identity and development: An interdisciplinary approach* (pp. 159–174). Thousand Oaks, CA: Sage.

Grotevant, H. D. (1987). Toward a process model of identity formation. *Journal of Adolescent Research, 2*, 203–222.

Grotevant, H. D. (1992). Assigned and chosen identity components: A process perspective on their integration. In G. R. Adams, R. Montemayor, & T. Gulotta (Eds.), *Advances in adolescent development* (Vol. 4, pp. 73–90). Newbury Park, CA: Sage.

Grotevant, H. D. (1993). The integrative nature of identity: Bringing the soloists to sing in the choir. In J. Kroger (Ed.), *Discussions on ego identity* (pp. 121–146). Hillsdale, NJ: Lawrence Erlbaum.

Grotevant, H. D. (1997). Coming to terms with adoption: The construction of identity from adolescence into adulthood. *Adoption Quarterly, 1*(1), 3–27.

Grotevant, H. D., & Cooper, C. R. (1985). Patterns of interaction in family relationships and the development of identity exploration in adolescence. *Child Development, 56*, 415–428.

Grotevant, H. D., & Cooper, C. R. (1988). The role of family experience in career exploration: A life-span perspective. In P. Baltes, R. M. Lerner, & D. Featherman (Eds.), *Life-span development and behavior* (Vol. 8, pp. 231–258). Hillsdale, NJ: Lawrence Erlbaum.

Grotevant, H. D., Dunbar, N., & Kohler, J. K. (1999). *Manual for coding identity in adopted adolescents*. Unpublished manuscript, University of Minnesota, Minnesota-Texas Adoption Research Project.

Grotevant, H. D., Fravel, D. L., Gorall, D., & Piper, J. (1999). Narratives of adoptive parents: Perspectives from individual and couple interviews. In B. H. Fiese, A. J. Sameroff, H. D. Grotevant, F. S. Wamboldt, S. Dickstein, & D. L. Fravel (Eds.), *The stories that families tell: Narrative coherence, narrative style, and relationship beliefs* (pp. 69–83). *Monographs of the Society for Research in Child Development, 64*(2, Serial No. 257).

Grotevant, H. D., & McRoy, R. G. (1998). *Openness in adoption: Exploring family connections*. Thousand Oaks, CA: Sage.

Grotevant, H. D., Ross, N. M., Marchel, M. A., & McRoy, R. G. (1999). Adaptive behavior in adopted children: Predictors from early risk, collaboration in relationships within the adoptive kinship network, and openness arrangements. *Journal of Adolescent Research, 14*, 231–247.

Grotevant, H. D., & Thorbecke, W. L. (1982). Sex differences in styles of occupational identity formation in late adolescence. *Developmental Psychology, 18*, 396–405.

Haugaard, J. (1998). Is adoption a risk factor for the development of adjustment problems? *Clinical Psychology Review, 18*, 47–69.

Hetherington, E. M. (1999). Social capital and the development of youth from nondivorced, divorced, and remarried families. In W. A. Collins & B. Laursen (Eds.), *Relationships as developmental contexts: The Minnesota Symposia on Child Psychology* (Vol. 30, pp. 177–210). Mahwah, NJ: Lawrence Erlbaum.

Hoopes, J. L., Sherman, E. A., Lawder, E. A., Andrews, R. G., & Lower, K. D. (1970). *A follow-up study of adoptions: Vol. 2. Post placement functioning of adopted children*. New York: Child Welfare League of America.

Ingersoll, B. D. (1997). Psychiatric disorders among adopted children: A review and commentary. *Adoption Quarterly, 1*(1), 57–74.

Kaye, K. (1990). Acknowledgment or rejection of differences? In D. M. Brodzinsky & M. D. Schechter (Eds.), *The psychology of adoption* (pp. 121–143). New York: Oxford University Press.

Kirk, D. H. (1981). *Adoptive kinship: A modern institution in need of reform*. Toronto, Ontario, Canada: Butterworth.

Kohler, J. K., Grotevant, H. D., & McRoy, R. G. (2002). Adopted adolescents' preoccupation with adoption: Impact of adoptive family dynamics. *Journal of Marriage and the Family, 64*, 93–104.

Kroger, J. (1997). Gender and identity: The interaction of structure, content, and context. *Sex Roles, 36*, 747–770.

Lee, R. M. (2003). The transracial adoption paradox: History, research, and counseling implications of cultural socialization. *The Counseling Psychologist, 31,* 711–744.

March, K. (1994). Needing to know: Adoptees search for self completion. In M. L. Dietz, R. Prus, & W. Shaffir (Eds.), *Doing everyday life: Ethnography as human lived experience* (pp. 213–226). Mississaugua, Ontario, Canada: Copp Clark Longman.

March, K. (1995). Perception of adoption as social stigma: Motivation for search and reunion. *Journal of Marriage and the Family, 57,* 653–660.

Marcia, J. E. (1980). Identity in adolescence. In J. Adelson (Ed.), *Handbook of adolescent psychology.* New York: Wiley.

Marcia, J. E. (1993). The status of the statuses: Research review. In J. E. Marcia, A. S. Waterman, D. R. Matteson, S. L. Archer, & J. L. Orlofsky (Eds.), *Ego identity: A handbook for psychosocial research* (pp. 22–41). New York: Springer-Verlag.

Marcia, J. E., Waterman, A. S., Matteson, D. R., Archer, S. L., & Orlofsky, J. L. (Eds.). (1993). *Ego identity: A handbook for psychosocial research.* New York: Springer-Verlag.

McAdams, D. P. (1988). *Power, intimacy, and the life story: Personological inquiries into identity.* New York: Guilford.

Meeus, W., Iedema, J., Helsen, M., & Vollebergh, W. (1999). Patterns of adolescent identity development: Review of literature and longitudinal analysis. *Developmental Review, 19,* 419–461.

Meier, D. I. (1998). *Loss and reclaimed lives: Cultural identity and place in Korean American intercountry adoptees.* Unpublished doctoral dissertation, Department of Geography, University of Minnesota, Minneapolis, MN.

Meier, D. I. (1999). Cultural identity and place in adult Korean-American intercountry adoptees. *Adoption Quarterly, 3*(1), 15–48.

Mendenhall, T., Berge, J. M., Wrobel, G. M., Grotevant, H. D., & McRoy, R. G. (2004). Adolescents' satisfaction with contact in adoption. *Child and Adolescent Social Work Journal, 21,* 175–190.

Register, C. (1991). *Are those kids really yours? American families with children adopted from other countries.* New York: Free Press.

Schneider, D. M. (1980). *American kinship: A cultural account.* Chicago: University of Chicago Press.

Stein, L. M., & Hoopes, J. L. (1985). *Identity formation in the adopted adolescent.* New York: Child Welfare League of America.

Van Hoof, A. (1999). The identity status field re-reviewed: An update of unresolved and neglected issues with a view on some alternative hypotheses. *Developmental Review, 19,* 497–556.

Waterman, A. S. (1999). Identity, the identity statuses, and identity status development: A contemporary statement. *Developmental Review, 19,* 591–621.

Wegar, K. (1997). *Adoption, identity, and kinship: The debate over sealed records.* New Haven, CT: Yale University Press.

Wrobel, G. M., Hendrickson, Z., & Grotevant, H. D. (2006). Adoption. In G. G. Bear & K. M. Minke (Eds.), *Children's needs: Vol. 3. Development, problems, and alternatives* (pp. 675–688). Washington, DC: National Association of School Psychologists.

Wrobel, G. M., Kohler, J. K., Grotevant, H. D., & McRoy, R. G. (1998). Factors related to patterns of information exchange between adoptive parents and children in mediated adoptions. *Journal of Applied Developmental Psychology, 19,* 641–657.

Yngveson, B. (1999, May). *Geographies of identity in transnational adoption.* Paper presented at the conference Mine, Yours, Ours, & Theirs: Adoption and Changing Kinship and Family Patterns, Oslo, Norway.

The Cultural-Racial Identity Model

7

A Theoretical Framework for Studying Transracial Adoptees

AMANDA L. BADEN

Montclair State University

ROBBIE J. STEWARD

Michigan State University

Multiracial children, transracial adoptees, and foster children in families wherein more than one racial or cultural heritage exists have a unique experience inside and outside the home that is distinctly different from children being raised in racially and culturally homogeneous families. Because healthy development of these children is contingent on their effective management of diversity-related issues both inside and outside of the home, psychologists and counselors must be prepared to accurately assess and develop appropriate strategies for intervention when psychological and emotional dilemmas become evident within these households.

Although there are increasing numbers of racially mixed families within general society, psychologists' examination of the experiences of racially integrated family systems remains limited. To better inform the practice of psychotherapy with these individuals, guidelines for addressing the effects of racial integration within families must be developed. With this goal in mind, the Cultural-Racial Identity Development Model (Baden & Steward, 2000; Steward & Baden, 1995) was developed. This model addresses the compelling roles of both race and culture within families where racial homogeneity does *not* exist. The Cultural-Racial Identity Model serves as a framework for understanding and working with members of racially integrated families by attending to racial and cultural differences among parents and children and

SOURCE: Portions of this chapter have been previously published in "A framework for use with racially and culturally integrated families: The cultural-racial identity model," in *Journal of Social Distress and the Homeless*, 9(4) and "The psychological adjustment of transracial adoptees: An application of the cultural-racial identity model type," in *Journal of Social Distress and the Homeless*, 11(2). Reprinted with permission of Springer Science and Business Media.

by considering the impact that the experiences and the attitudes of parents, peers, extended family, social support networks, and the larger community have on child development. The Cultural-Racial Identity Development Model was the first comprehensive guide for practitioners' use with racially and culturally integrated families. This chapter focuses on explaining the Cultural-Racial Identity Model when used with transracial and international adoption. In this chapter, we review the need for a systematic means for understanding the identity experiences of transracial adoptees, describe the terminology used to understand transracial adoption, explain the framework used in the model, and discuss clinical applications of this model.

Definitions: An Introduction to Transracial Adoption

Transracial adoption refers to the adoption of infants or children by parents of a different race (Evan B. Donaldson Adoption Institute, 2005). *International adoption*, in which citizens from the United States (for example) adopt infants or children from other countries, is in some cases transracial but in almost all cases transcultural (or between cultures) (Zamostny, O'Brien, Baden, & Wiley, 2003). Thus, transracial adoption subsumes aspects of international adoption such that the adoptions involve racial and ethnic differences that are often determined by physical features. For the purposes of this chapter, transracial adoption will refer to all adoptions, both domestic (within the United States) and international (between the United States and foreign countries), that involve adoption across racial lines.

Race, as commonly defined, refers to heritage with a group based on geography and a common set of physical characteristics as manifested in traits transmitted via genetics such as skin color, hair texture and color, and facial features (Hays, 2001). *Ethnicity*, on the other hand, refers to dimensions of characteristics that are transmitted via socialization (Helms & Talleyrand, 1997) and to ancestry via shared biological history, values, customs, and individual and group identity (Hays, 2001). Finally, *culture* refers to traditions, history, beliefs, practices, and values that are passed from generation to generation via perception, beliefs, evaluation, communication, and action (Hays, 2001). Language, holidays, and religious beliefs can be shared elements that represent culture.

To comprehensively address transracial and international adoption, issues related to the psychosocial task of identity formation must also be defined. The construct of identity can be traced back to the Eriksonian concept of personal identity (Erikson, 1968) and was originally associated with the adolescent struggle for identity or the struggle to gain knowledge of self, others, and the self in relation to others (Erikson, 1980). During this struggle, individuals work to negotiate the ego identity versus identity diffusion crisis so that they can achieve an integrated identity. Marcia (1966, 1980) extended Erikson's work to include a model that depicted four potential identity statuses that can describe individuals at various points in the process of identity formation. In addition to providing a delineated pathway along which identity might be charted, Marcia's work suggested that identity formation consists of a process and that the pathway is not necessarily linear using stages but may instead be statuses that define a point in time in an individual's life. Although Erikson's work proposed that identity formation was a task for adolescence, contemporary thought supports the notion that identity formation is a lifelong task (Greve, Rothermund, & Wentura, 2005; Honess & Yardley, 1987; Marcia, 1987).

Over time, identity was applied to areas in psychosocial development far beyond vocational aspirations. In fact, given Erikson's (1968) emphasis on the impact of the environment and the context in which an individual matures, identity as a construct was well suited for its application to issues surrounding race, ethnicity, and culture.

To adequately address the identity experiences of transracial and international adoptees, questions of race, ethnicity, and culture as well as racial, ethnic, and cultural identity must be included. Unfortunately, the definitions used when referring to racial, ethnic, and/or cultural identity have not been consistent throughout the literature. For example, researchers have used the term *racial identity* in their research when they are actually measuring aspects of racial labeling, racial group preferences, racial and ethnic categorizations, and acculturation (e.g., Andujo,

1988; Johnson, Shireman, & Watson, 1987; McRoy, Zurcher, Lauderdale, & Anderson, 1982, 1984; Shireman & Johnson, 1985, 1986; Zastrow, 1977). Fortunately, within the past 20 years, leaders in counseling psychology have clarified the concepts by further delineating how this component (racial identity) of individuals' psychosocial identity formation can be defined (Atkinson, Morten, & Sue, 1998; Benson, Sharma, & Roehlkepartain, 1994; Cross, 1978; Cross, Parham, & Helms, 1991; Helms, 1990). Based on their work, racial identity has been consistently defined as the quality of one's identification with one's racial group and the psychological and internalized effects of race-based messages garnered from society and from one's reference group (Helms, 1990; Helms & Cook, 1999). *Ethnic identity* has also been inconsistently defined in the literature (Phinney, 1990); however, a widely accepted definition incorporates individuals' self-label, sense of belonging, attitudes toward their own ethnic group, and involvement in ethnic group social and cultural practice (Phinney, 1990). Last, the definition for cultural identity has also been subject to shifts in focus from terminology mirroring acculturation to that involving individuals' relationships to their reference group. Typically, *cultural identity* has been defined as the culture with which one identifies as shown through knowledge, behaviors, and beliefs. More recently, Germain (2004) defined cultural identity as involving the process of "self-awareness achieved either through the collective experience within a membership group or the individual perception as we compare ourselves to a reference group" (p. 134).

Adoption Across Race and Culture

Adoption was informally practiced throughout the history of civilization but was formalized in the 1800s to provide a means for placing orphaned children with couples or families wanting or needing children (Zamostny et al., 2003). However, according to the modern history of transracial and international adoption as documented by Lee (2003), the Indian Adoption Project (removing American Indian children from reservations to be adopted into mainstream American families) and the Korean War orphans (children orphaned by the war or biracial children fathered by military soldiers and Korean mothers were adopted by American families) mark the beginning of modern transracial and international transracial adoption to the United States, respectively. In the early 1970s, transracial adoption was criticized for its potentially damaging effects on children (National Association of Black Social Workers, 1972), and transracial adoption placements became much less frequent, especially domestic transracial adoptions. After a series of studies were conducted to disprove the criticisms of transracial adoptions, legislation was passed that allowed resurgence in transracial adoption placements (e.g., the Multiethnic Placement Act of 1994). Today, transracial adoption has become an increasingly popular option for those wishing to adopt given widespread attention to new sources of infants available for adoption (e.g., China, Russia, Guatemala) (Child Welfare League of America [CWLA], 2003).

Clearly, despite concerns about the viability of transracial and international adoption, children have continued to be placed transracially and internationally, and many have grown into adulthood. Surprisingly little information about effective psychotherapeutic models and methods is available for this unique population, but much attention has been focused on the impact of transracial adoptive families. Researchers have begun to address these questions, but the most prominent issues that continue to deserve more attention include the following: (1) the effects of transracial and international adoption on the adoptees' adjustment (e.g., Baden, 2002; Cederblad, Höök, Irhammar, & Mercke, 1999; DeBerry, Scarr, & Weinberg, 1996; Sharma, McGue, & Benson, 1998; Silverman & Feigelman, 1981, 1990; Vroegh, 1997; Wickes & Slate, 1997; Yoon, 2001; Zastrow, 1977); (2) the effects of transracial and international adoption on the adoptees' racial and cultural identities (e.g., Baden, 2002; Brooks & Barth, 1999; Feigelman, 2000; Johnson et al., 1987; Shireman & Johnson, 1986); (3) techniques for raising and treating transracial adoptees (e.g., Bradley & Hawkins-Leon, 2002; Helwig & Ruthven, 1990; Jones, 1997; Lee, 2003; Liow, 1994; Rickard Liow, 1994); and (4) the ways that transracial and international adoptees identify culturally, racially, and ethnically (Baden & Steward, 2000; Bagley, 1992; Grotevant, 1987; Hollingsworth, 1998; McRoy et al., 1984).

In this chapter, the model that we propose goes beyond the question of differences between transracial adoptees and same-race adoptees or nonadoptees and instead addresses the differences or heterogeneity that exists within the group of transracial adoptees. The racial differences between adoptive parents and their adopted children necessitate attention to the experiences of these families whether or not they are affected by these differences. Historically, these differences were expected to cause problematic "racial identity" formation and adjustment issues (National Association of Black Social Workers, 1972). Subsequent research has worked to clarify these concerns, and legislation (e.g., Multiethnic Placement Act of 1994 and Interethnic Placement Act of 1996) has prevented restrictions in adoptive placements based on these concerns. Assumptions about the impact of racial differences on adjustment have continued to suggest that racial differences may be the primary predictor of adjustment, and little attention has been given to the parenting issues that affect adjustment. Just as differences in racial oppression experiences between parents and children may have an impact, so may the manner in which adoptive parents address (or fail to address) adoption-related issues, racial issues, behavioral problems, and many other concerns. Essentially, the discourse around the impact of transracial adoption must become more complex and multifaceted.

To begin this work, Baden and Steward (2000) introduced the Cultural-Racial Identity Model to address the more complex status of transracial adoptees' identities. They attempted to remedy the inconsistency that exists in definitions for constructs such as racial identity. For example, frequently, studies purporting to examine racial identity tended to investigate only the racial group preferences and objective racial self-identification of transracial adoptees and not their racial identity development (e.g., McRoy et al., 1984; Shireman & Johnson, 1986). These studies conceptualized racial identity as being the racial group (e.g., Black, White, Korean, Native American) to which the adoptees felt they belonged. This conceptualization of racial identity appears to be based on the acknowledgment or recognition of racial group membership rather than on feelings about, attitudes toward, knowledge of, competence within, or comfort with one's racial group. Thus, these other conceptualizations of racial identity may actually contain information about the identities sanctioned by society rather than the actual identities of transracial adoptees.

To implement these suggestions for future research on transracial adoption, a guideline for observing and systematizing the study of transracial adoptees is needed. The Cultural-Racial Identity Model addresses potential variation in identity statuses of transracial adoptees. These identity statuses differ from previous models of identity, racial identity, and ethnic identity because of the distinction made between culture and race in the model. This distinction is vital given the mismatch that can occur for transracial adoptees between their physical appearance (i.e., their race) and their cultural practices. Moreover, although we chose to call this model the Cultural-Racial Identity Model, we chose to use the terms *culture* and *race* rather than *culture* and *ethnicity* for specific reasons. When we speak about race, we are actually referring to the sociocultural construction of race, or sociorace (Helms & Talleyrand, 1997), rather than the more traditional scientific classification or biological construction of race. In essence, ethnicity actually bridges aspects of both race and culture but does not allow for clear distinctions between both of them (Helms & Talleyrand, 1997). As a result, when examining the experiences of transracial adoptees, we believe that culture and race more clearly maintain the distinctions that we find vital to understanding their experience. Furthermore, use solely of the term *ethnicity* can be problematic given the ease with which individuals may choose to use the term *ethnicity* as an excuse to focus on the more familiar and less threatening concepts of culture and cultural activities as opposed to the very important, sometimes uncomfortable, and clearly socially constructed meanings that accompany race (Helms & Talleyrand, 1997).

Theoretical Bases for the Cultural-Racial Identity Model

Identity Formation in Adoptees. As noted above, the process of identity formation is lifelong and for adoptees is clearly complicated by the issues associated with the seven core issues of adoption (Silverstein & Kaplan, 1988), namely loss, rejection, guilt and shame, grief, identity, intimacy, and mastery/control. Identity is one of those core issues and lies at the heart of much of the work in adoption. LeVine and Sallee (1990) theorized that adoptees must work to accept their adoptive status, and if they develop a clear understanding of the impact and meaning of their adoption, they will experience greater levels of adjustment. They also advocated that clinicians learn to distinguish between adoption-related issues (e.g., loss and belonging) and family dynamic issues (e.g., parenting). LeVine and Sallee depicted the process of acceptance of adoption as having five phases: (1) *Phase I* or preawareness, (2) *Phase II* or dim awareness of a special state, (3) *Phase III* or cognitive integration of biological and social differences, (4) *Phase IV* or identity crisis of the adopted adolescent, and (5) *Phase V* or concomitant acceptance of the biological and adoptive family. Clearly, this model suggests that adoptees become aware of their adoptive status and reach a cognitive awareness of their unique biological and social status as adoptees before they work on identity issues or get "1) a conscious sense of their individual uniqueness; 2) an unconscious striving for continuity of experience; and 3) a solidarity with group ideals" (p. 223). LeVine and Sallee theorized that adoptees' attempts at achieving continuity with their past and solidarity with the group are more difficult, and their questions about their biological roots are most salient for them. These difficulties coupled with such early childhood traumas as abuse, neglect, and poor parental bonding may make adoptees more vulnerable to maladjustment, particularly in the form of narcissistic personality disorders. LeVine and Sallee also listed signs of maladjustment according to the phase of adjustment of the adoptees. Some examples are being unresponsive to adults, language deficits, rage, inappropriate affect, splitting, active rejecting of adoptive family, and emerging personality disorders.

Another model of identity for adopted individuals was proffered by Grotevant (1997). To gain a sense of their origins, adopted persons seek a sense of heritage and origins that are part of an adoptee's identity. Although early conceptualizations considered identity development a task for adolescence, it is now recognized as a lifelong process (Grotevant, 1997). A more comprehensive adoptee identity framework was built on Grotevant's (1987) developmental and multilevel process model of identity formation for all adolescents and was applied specifically to adopted individuals (Grotevant, 1997). Grotevant described the three aspects of identity most salient for adoptees as follows: (1) self-definition (the characteristics by which one is recognized as he or she self-defines within his or her historical context); (2) coherence of personality (the subjective experience of the ways in which various facets of one's personality fit together); and (3) sense of continuity over time (the connections between past, present, and future that traverse place and connect relationships and contexts). These three aspects of identity were labeled the "self-in-context" (Grotevant, Dunbar, Kohler, & Esau, 2000) and consist of three levels: intrapsychic, family relationships, and the social world beyond the family. The primary task of identity for an adopted person was described as "'coming to terms' with oneself in the context of the family and culture into which one has been adopted" (Grotevant et al., 2000, p. 383).

Similarly, Dunbar and Grotevant (2004) used a narrative approach to empirically explore Grotevant's (1997) identity statuses and found four adoptive identity types among their 145 adolescent adoptees: (1) *unexamined identity*, where the adoptees had not thought about adoption issues, responded with low emotion, and reflected no salience of the adoptive identity; (2) *limited identity*, where the adoptees were willing to think about and discuss adoption but did not view it as a prominent concern in their lives as reflected by their low depth of exploration, low salience of adoptive identity, moderate positive affect, and minimal negative affect; (3) *unsettled identity*, where the adoptees reported moderate salience of their adoptive identity, were moderately involved in thinking about their adoptive identities, and yet described low to moderate positive affect and moderate to moderate/strong negative affect; and (4) *integrated identity*, where most of the adoptees were moderately or greatly exploring their adoptive identities, saw their adoptive identities as significant, and reported substantial moderate to strong positive affect and low to minimal negative affect.

Thus, the adoption literature has not reached a consensus on the impact of adoption on identity. To answer this question, researchers must more clearly define the constructs of adoptee identity and operationalize it. Although identity is assumed by most of the adoption literature to be more complex for adoptees (Grotevant, 1997; Grotevant et al., 2000; Hoopes, 1990; Stein & Hoopes, 1985), the empirical literature has been slow to systematically address these assumptions. The literature has noted such concerns as the "adopted child syndrome" (Kirschner, 1990) and even included attention to the externalizing behaviors of adopted persons (e.g., Brodzinsky, Smith, & Brodzinsky, 1998; Miller, Fan, Christensen, Grotevant, & van Dulmen, 2000; Wierzbicki, 1993), but the empirical literature has not yet adequately explored identity development. In fact, Wilson (2004) suggested that methodological constraints such as the heterogeneity of the adopted population, lack of suitable comparison groups, and within-group differences might also explain the mixed findings.

Identity Formation in Racial Ethnic Minorities. As noted above, although racial and ethnic identities were defined by psychologists, examinations of racial and ethnic identities across disciplines have not consistently used those definitions or the measures such as the multigroup ethnic identity measure (Phinney, 1992) to operationalize those definitions. More recent empirical research has used qualitative research designs to examine racial, ethnic, and cultural identity (e.g., Friedlander, 1999; Huh, 1997; Westhues & Cohen, 1998), but researchers have not structured their findings according to any consistent or comprehensive model of racial identity. Interestingly, in these studies, questions of acculturation to Korean and American cultures, for example, and ethnic group pride were included in the structured interview protocols. Thus, researchers who examined the impact of transracial and international adoption designed studies that reflected their view of racial and ethnic identity as being highly similar to the models of racial identity as depicted in the models initially introduced by William Cross (1971), Janet Helms (1990), and Atkinson, Morten, and Sue (1993). Common to these models of racial identity is the premise that psychological adjustment and self-concept may, to a degree, depend on the racial identity of the individual. Individuals in particular stages or having particular statuses of development are believed to have poorer adjustment and poorer self-concepts. The parallel between this belief and that found in Erikson's (1968) theory is evident.

Relationship Between Racial Identity and Eriksonian Theory. As discussed above, the construct of racial identity has been defined in numerous ways across different disciplines. However, within the field of psychology, one theorist is largely credited with its development (Cross, 1971, 1978) and others with its expansion and refinement to other racial groups. Also, Janet Helms's work on racial identity has led the field in more recent decades (Helms, 1990, 1995). Their work built on and advanced the ideas of Erik Erikson regarding the sociocultural influences on identity (Erikson, 1968). Essentially, Helms (1990) described racial identity as being composed of a combination of personal identity (one's feelings and attitudes about oneself), reference group orientation (degree to which one's thoughts, feelings, and behaviors are based on the values, ideologies, etc., of a particular racial group), and ascribed identity (one's overt and expressed affiliation with a particular racial group). Helms and Cross (Cross, 1971, 1978) also posited that racial identity is related to psychological types or statuses that develop in response to racism, oppression, and other racial information in society and that at various stages or times in individuals' lives, different people and institutions are influential in the development of racial identity. For example, during early childhood and infancy, parents and adult authority figures are most influential on racial identity, whereas peers or cohort and nonfamilial social institutions (e.g., school, media) are more influential during late childhood and adolescence. Models of racial identity are essentially similar and typically include several stages or statuses of development in which people go from a state of unawareness of race through embracing their own culture exclusively and then on to a commitment to advocating for all oppressed groups and eliminating oppression. For example, Helms's (1995) People of Color

Racial Identity Model has the following six statuses: (1) conformity, where the individual identifies with Whites, rejects his or her own racial group, and denies the importance of race; (2) dissonance, where the individual experiences racial confusion and a disruption in his or her views of the world; (3) immersion, where the individual shifts idealization to his or her own racial group and denigrates Whites and where the individual replaces negative or missing information about his or her own group with positive information; (4) emersion, where the individual feels solidarity, a sense of community, and feelings of comfort with his or her own racial group and when surrounded by that group; (5) internalization, where the individual has pride in his or her own racial group and is also able to critically and objectively analyze racial issues and respond to those from his or her own group and the White dominant group; and (6) integrative awareness, where the individual has positive views of his or her own racial group and racial self, is able to recognize and resist racism and oppression, and has cognitive complexity around race so that the individual can value his or her own and other racial groups.

As these models depict, culture and race affect individuals' experiences, identity, and development across multiple domains. Individuals from ethnic minority groups, or people of color (POC), must negotiate additional complexity in their identity formation given that their process of identity formation includes multiple sources of identification, including their own racial and ethnic group as well as the dominant, mainstream White racial group (Phinney & Rosenthal, 1992). Phinney and Rosenthal (1992) identified differences between the dominant culture and adolescents' cultures of origin as primary factors in adolescents' abilities to integrate ethnic identity into self-identity. They also posited that a positively valued ethnic identity is necessary for the construction of a positive and stable self-identity (as described by Erikson, 1968).

The role of culture in identity has been more complicated. Although the literature frequently refers to the construct of cultural identity (e.g., Atkinson & Gim, 1989), a comprehensive and cohesive definition is difficult to determine. As with the terminology for race, culture, and ethnicity, cultural identity and racial identity are often used interchangeably. More purposeful definitions for cultural identity were offered by Dalal (1999), who loosely defined cultural identity as a subjective sense of belonging to a group of people based on one's "cultural home." Jensen (2003) further delineated cultural identity as being formed by endorsing a worldview (e.g., beliefs about human nature, relationships, and moral and religious values) and a set of behavioral practices (e.g., behaviors related to traditions, food, dressing, and recreation) that bond people within a community. Whaley (1993) reviewed the literature on cultural identity formation for African American children and found that interactions among cultural factors, cognitive-developmental processes, and social experiences determine identity formation. Whaley argued that young children (between ages 2 and 6) have not reached cognitive developmental stages at which they can accurately racially self-identify. Thus, racial awareness and cultural identity increase with each successive stage in Piagetian cognitive-developmental theory. Ultimately, the importance of cultural identity in racial ethnic minority adolescents varies according to "the degree of identification with their ethnic/racial group, level of self-exploration and self-awareness, and cross-cultural social experiences" (p. 414). Whaley also found that children's self-esteem was affected by the degree to which children feel *competent* in areas that they value and by the level of regard or support they perceive from significant others. Thus, personal efficacy, or competence, is likely to be relevant to the identity formation of adolescents.

Identity Formation in Transracial Adoptees. One of the early attempts at understanding the identity experiences of transracial adoptees was offered by Falk (1970) and Zastrow (1977), who predicted that Black children would learn the special meanings and value of being Black in America through their birth parents and their community. When Black children are reared in White families, they also learn the values and meanings of their White middle-class families. Zastrow poignantly described two potential outcomes for transracial adoptees' identity experiences:

At some point the TRA [transracially adopted] child will cast off the protectiveness of the family of orientation and establish his more-or-less independent identity in the community of his choosing. If in this new circumstance he finds himself forced into situations where he is identified stereotypically and he is without prior experience in coping with them, he may face an identity crisis. . . . His identity will be with the white world while others assume that his identity is with the black world. His rearing establishes the white world as his referent, and his new peers demand that his referent be the minority world. (p. 57)

Clearly, Zastrow anticipated the need for a more detailed understanding of identity for transracial adoptees. He believed that adoptive parents could provide the necessary guidance and affection for transracial adoptees to develop a positive self-concept and the social and interpersonal skills needed to successfully cope with the environment. Furthermore, exposure to the history and culture of the transracial adoptee's birth culture and racial group should help transracial adoptees obtain more information regarding the meanings and values associated with their birth culture and race.

Another conceptualization of the racial identity of transracial adoptees was proposed by Loenen and Hoksbergen (1986), who addressed attachment relations and identity issues in intercountry adoptees in The Netherlands. Although they perceived similarities between transracial adoptees in The Netherlands and those in the United Kingdom, they, like other researchers, questioned the notion of a "single identity." Instead of a single identity, they advocated for terms such as *situational identity* and *identity options*. Loenen and Hoksbergen stated,

A black youngster living in a white family and in a predominantly white society needs to be appreciated and accepted for having a range of identities which are more or less salient in different contexts at different times in his or her life-cycle. He or she needs to be encouraged and assisted to develop his or her black identity in a situation which may deny or discourage it. (pp. 25–26)

However, they cited the lack of "relevant" Black communities in The Netherlands as complicating this process.

Huh (1997) studied 40 internationally adopted Korean children and their 30 families to determine their ethnic identity process. She found that Korean adoptees' attitudes toward their birth culture and ethnic group membership fit into a developmental model. From the ages of 4 to 6 years, the adoptees reported a pseudo-understanding of adoption, noticed physical differences between themselves and their parents, desired physical similarity with parents, and denied the importance of ethnic identity. Children from 7 to 8 years of age acknowledged their adoption and understood it, could identify their own and others' ethnicities, and either favored Korean culture (if their family valued Korean culture) or showed no interest (if they had no exposure to Korean culture). During the period from ages 9 to 11, adoptees tended to question about and grieve for their birth parents, accepted the differences between themselves and their parents and others, and were proud of the differences, but some children were apathetic about their ethnicity and identified as "American" or "human." In the last stage studied, adoptees from ages 12 to 14 typically asked fewer questions about birth parents (they felt they had all the information they were likely to receive), were focused on their friends, and worked to integrate their Korean ethnicity and their American cultural values into their identity. Huh also identified four attitudes that Korean adoptees were likely to express toward their culture and ethnicity throughout their lives and which will likely change continuously. These attitudes are "(1) denial of importance of ethnic identity; (2) disfavor toward both Korean and American cultures; (3) apathy toward Korean culture and assimilative attitude toward American culture; (4) affection for both Korean and American cultures" (Huh, 1997, p. iii).

The research on racial, ethnic, and cultural identity of transracial adoptees supports the need to better understand the process of identity formation for this population. Furthermore, theoretical and political links between healthy or positive racial identities and adjustment and self-esteem were made, but mixed support for their predictions has been found (Lee, 2003). Tizard and Phoenix (1995) critiqued the evidence regarding the relationship between self-esteem and racial identity and found that despite the theorized dependence of self-esteem on racial identity, few studies have assessed both constructs in the same children. They questioned assumptions regarding the "inextricable link" between self-esteem and racial identity and suggested an alternative theory in which self-esteem and other aspects of mental health are developed primarily in the context of individuals' most salient and important relationships (i.e., as children, these relationships are within the family). Racial identity in Black children, for example, although influenced by the family, would develop through their relationships with the dominant/White culture. In this conceptualization of racial identity, Black children, regardless of their adoption status, may hold some negative feelings about their racial identity but still maintain healthy self-esteem and adjustment. On the other hand, those with poor family relationships, but with high or positive racial identities, may still have low self-esteem and poor psychological adjustment.

Tizard and Phoenix (1995) shared the view of Steward and Baden (1995) regarding assumptions of homogeneity within cultures and racial groups. Advocating a "positive" Black identity as if it were a commonly shared state disregards the vast differences among people of African descent. Tizard and Phoenix acknowledged the problematic nature of children misidentifying themselves (i.e., believing they look White or are White when they are not), but they made distinctions between a self-identification problem and an identity problem. They also suggested that racial identity be considered using a frame borrowed from gender identity conceptualizations as follows: (1) the degree to which individuals' identity is based on perceived similarities between themselves and others in the group, (2) the extent of awareness of a common fate, and (3) the degree to which membership in the group is central to the ways individuals think of themselves.

Recent conceptualizations of identity depart from Erikson's (1968) conception of identity as a task for adolescence and instead recognize it as a lifelong process (Grotevant, 1997). Similarly, Helms (1990) considered racial identity development to take place and change continuously throughout one's life span; however, transracial adoption researchers have frequently attempted to measure racial identity in adoptees before they are developmentally prepared to struggle with issues of race and identity. Hollingsworth's (1998) results demonstrating that "racial/ethnic identity may decrease as transracial/transethnic adoptees become older" (p. 314) also call for a better understanding of the effects of age on transracial adoptees' identity. Perhaps transracial adoptees begin the process of racial identity formation at a later age, or perhaps Hollingsworth (1998) depicts transracial adoptees' racial identity at the height of their struggle (i.e., adoptees in the studies that Hollingsworth analyzed all had average ages less than 18 years). Bagley (1992) described identity formation as a long-term process and cautioned that "uncertainty and unhappiness at one point in a child or adolescent's development may simply be a transient phenomenon as the individual copes with certain problems in the formation of personal identity, at different points in the life cycle" (p. 101). Based on this reasoning, Bagley advised against studies of adoptees before the crucial phase of adolescence because of their tendency to be misleading, and he suggested final assessments of adoptions when adoptees are young adults.

THE CULTURAL-RACIAL IDENTITY MODEL

Rationale for Developing the Model

The racial, ethnic, and cultural identities of transracial adoptees have been the focus of much of the attention and criticisms of transracial adoption (e.g., CWLA, 2003; National

Association of Black Social Workers, 1972). The empirical literature addressing transracial adoption has primarily examined its effects on the adoptees' racial identity, self-esteem, and psychological adjustment. However, despite all the evidence showing similar levels of adjustment and self-esteem between transracial adoptees and intraracial adoptees (e.g., Andujo, 1988; Benson et al., 1994; Cederblad et al., 1999; McRoy et al., 1982, 1984; Silverman & Feigelman, 1981; Simon & Altstein, 1987), the practice of transracial adoption continues to be debated and controversial (Bradley & Hawkins-Leon, 2002). Baden and Steward (Baden & Steward, 1997, 2000; Steward & Baden, 1995) viewed this controversy as resulting from a lack of theory conceptualizing the unique experiences of transracial adoptees, especially their racial identity and cultural identity. They also critiqued existing theories of racial identity (e.g., Helms, 1995) and found that they were not applicable for transracial adoptees because of the inherent racial differences that exist between transracial adoptive parents and transracial adoptees. Although it is widely recognized that the experiences of transracial adoptees differ from those of intraracial (same-race) adoptees and of nonadoptees, prior to the Cultural-Racial Identity Model (Baden & Steward, 2000; Steward & Baden, 1995), no systematic means for depicting that experience existed.

The Cultural-Racial Identity Model was also developed in response to the critiques of transracial and international adoption research. For example, Tizard's (1991) review of international adoption research indicated that the majority of studies did not examine the degree to which adoptees endorse a mixed cultural identity; rather, these studies had transracial adoptees choose between their adopted and birth cultures as the only viable options with which they could have identified. This limitation in racial and cultural identity research for transracial adoptees is confounded by the paucity of research that compared immigrant children raised by their birth parents with transracial adoptees. Without such comparisons, a clear understanding regarding the degree to which "the identity conflicts of the intercountry adoptees stem from living in a white culture, rather than with white parents *per se*" (p. 754) cannot be accurately understood. Given that racial identity involves feelings of affiliation and pride in one's racial group, a systematic means for reflecting the impact that the transracial and international adoptees' experiences (e.g., growing up in a racially mixed family and choosing racial and cultural self-identifiers) might have on their racial and cultural identity is greatly needed (Trolley, 1994–1995). Trolley sought the identification of variables "which promote pride in one's native culture and how the benefits of both cultures can be integrated" (p. 261).

To accurately capture the racial and cultural identity processes for transracial adoptees, clinicians and researchers must recognize that despite the presence of some similarities between biracial or multiracial nonadoptees and transracial adoptees, some substantial differences exist between the groups. Although parallels can be discerned between these groups, we believe that the state of being adopted further complicates and qualitatively alters the experiences of transracial adoptees. The Cultural-Racial Identity Model can describe the identity experiences of nonadoptees raised in racially mixed families, but a clear understanding of the impact of adoption on their experiences must be incorporated. In fact, findings regarding identity for biracial young adults indicated a nonlinear journey toward racial identity and the need for different conceptualizations of racial identity—some identified as Black and some as White, but most preferred an interracial identity if given the option (Brown, 1995). Of particular interest for the Cultural-Racial Identity Model was the finding that biracial individuals reported differing public and private identities. This compartmentalization seemed to evolve due to the desire to maintain their interracial self-perception while simultaneously attempting to adhere to social expectations that they ignore their White backgrounds (Brown, 1995). Biracial adults' conforming behavior appeared to be both a coping mechanism (resulting from families' conditioning and from societal expectations) and a conscious and often sudden decision when their interracial or White self-perceptions were criticized. Predictors of racial identity were cited as (1) messages from family or friends regarding racial group membership, (2) acceptance by Blacks within their social networks, (3) racial status laws, (4) contact with various racial groups, (5) exposure to both Black and White cultures, and (6) physical appearance or phenotype. According to Brown (1995), these results reflected the emotional cost of having a White identity for biracial adults, the societal pressure for them to identify as Black, diminished identity conflict with an interracial identity, and lack of institutional recognition of an interracial identity.

As Brown's research reflects, the process of racial identity formation for biracial adults already has multiple complications, yet the component of adoption status was not even added to this process. To add all these components into one model, we must account for the impact of having two parents who are racially different from their child or children (Tizard & Phoenix, 1995), transracial adoptees who may also be adopted internationally (Meier, 1999), transracial adoptees who are also multiracial (Simon & Roorda, 2000), and transracial adoptees who may have little if any contact with their birth culture or people from their own racial group (Huh, 1997).

Description of the Cultural-Racial Identity Model

The Cultural-Racial Identity Model (Baden & Steward, 2000; Steward & Baden, 1995) consists of two axes: the Cultural Identity Axis and the Racial Identity Axis. The final model combines these two axes into a single model and a single graphic representation. This final model consists of 16 potential cultural-racial identities. Before describing the final model, the two axes will be presented.

Baden and Steward separated culture from race (i.e., unlike previous models of racial identity and ethnic identity) by creating two dimensions: racial identity and ethnic identity. As described above, they defined culture as consisting of the traditions, history, beliefs, practices, languages, and values passed between generations. Relying on the vast amounts of literature describing various cultures in the United States and abroad, Baden and Steward acknowledged that the racial groups and ethnic groups living in the United States have differing sets of customs, beliefs, languages, and so on (i.e., cultures) that are associated with those racial and ethnic groups. For example, Chinese Americans tend to endorse particular values, beliefs, and the like that compose the Chinese American culture. Similarly, African Americans tend to possess a culture unique to their racial group. Although Baden and Steward acknowledged that individuals belonging to these racial groups do not necessarily endorse all the cultural values, practices, beliefs, and so on, associated with these groups, a culture common to African Americans and Chinese Americans and other racial ethnic groups does exist in the United States. However, in the case of transracial adoptees, the adoptees are from a different racial group than their adoptive parents and can potentially endorse a cultural identity that could be associated with their country of origin or racial ethnic group (i.e., hereafter referred to as birth culture) or with their adoptive parents' racial ethnic group or some other group(s) altogether. Thus, at least two different racial groups as well as two different cultures can be represented within transracially adopting families. For this reason, Baden and Steward developed the *cultural identity axis* to represent four possible combinations of cultural endorsement.

The Cultural-Identity Axis has two dimensions: (1) *adoptee culture dimension*, or the degree to which transracial adoptees identify with their birth culture (i.e., if the adoptee is Korean, to what degree does the adoptee identify with Korean culture) and (2) *parental culture dimension*, or the degree to which transracial adoptees identify with their adoptive parents' racial group's culture (i.e., because most transracially adopting parents are White, to what degree does the adoptee identify with White culture).

Transracial adoptees' levels of identification with a culture or cultures are determined by their levels of *knowledge*, *awareness*, *competence*, and *comfort* with their birth culture, the culture of their parents' racial group, or the cultures of multiple racial groups or no cultural group affiliation. Four types of cultural identities (e.g., Bicultural Identity, Pro-Self Cultural Identity, Pro-Parent Cultural Identity, and Culturally Undifferentiated Identity) can result based on transracial adoptees' level of identification with two dimensions (the Parental Culture Dimension and Adoptee Culture Dimension). For example, transracial adoptees identifying more highly with their adoptive parents' racial groups' culture (i.e., the White culture) would be high on the Parental Culture Dimension and low on the Adoptee Culture Dimension; thus, the adoptees would have Pro-Parent Cultural Identities. This identity may have similarities to the conformity status of the POC Racial Identity Model (Helms, 1995). Transracial adoptees identifying more highly with their birth culture than with the culture of their adoptive parents would be low on the Parental Culture Dimension and high on the Adoptee Culture Dimension; thus, they would have Pro-Self Cultural Identities. Such an identity may mirror the immersion and emersion racial identity statuses of the POC Racial Identity Model (Helms, 1995). A graphic representation of the Cultural Identity Axis is depicted in Figure 7.1.

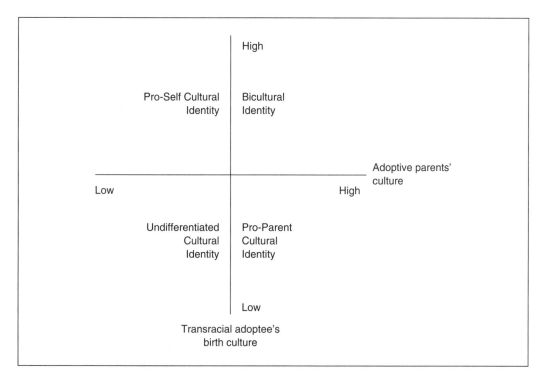

Figure 7.1   Cultural Identity Axis

In transracially adopting families, racial differences also exist among family members. Steward and Baden viewed these differences as affecting both racial/ethnic self-identification and the allegiances and friendships of transracial adoptees. Using the definition of race as noted above, racial groups were defined using heritage based on geography and physical characteristics as well as by incorporating affiliations and social relations with others from the same or different races. Research and theory suggest that transracial adoptees may make decisions about their racial group membership based on societal pressures (Brown, 1995; Huh, 1997; Lee, 2003) and the degree to which they have an achieved racial or ethnic identity (Phinney & Rosenthal, 1992). Choosing racial and ethnic self-labels or self-descriptors may also be influenced by the transracial adoptees' feelings about and affiliation toward their racial group. Labels chosen that do not "match" one's appearance, heritage, and birth origins have been used to warn the transracial and international adoptive community about the importance of "healthy" racial identity. Like the biracial adults in Brown's (1995) study and the transracial adoptees in Tizard's (1991) review of international adoption research, Steward and Baden chose to view "mislabeling" as indicative of racial identity status rather than as symptomatic of an unhealthy identity.

To account for varying racial ethnic self-identifications of transracial adoptees and for the role of allegiances and friendships in transracial adoptees' experiences, Stewart and Baden developed the *Racial Identity Axis* in the Cultural-Racial Identity Model. The Racial Identity Axis has two dimensions: (1) *Adoptee Race Dimension*, or the degree to which transracial adoptees identify with their own racial group (i.e., if the adoptee is African American, to what degree does the adoptee identify with African Americans) and (2) *Parental Race Dimension*, or the degree to which transracial adoptees identify with their adoptive parents' racial group (i.e., because most transracially adopting parents are White, this dimension involves the degree to which the adoptee identifies with Whites).

Transracial adoptees' levels of identification with a racial group are determined by assessing the degree to which the adoptees self-identify as belonging to their own racial group or their parents' racial group. They also consist of the adoptees' comfort level with people from their own racial group and their adoptive parents' racial group. The transracial adoptees' comfort level with different racial groups involves their allegiances to those racial groups and the friendships they have with members belonging to different racial groups. In other words, these racial identities are determined according to the degree to which transracial adoptees (1) accurately identify their own racial group membership, (2) are comfortable with their racial group membership, and (3) are comfortable with people from their racial group, from their parents' racial group, or from multiple different racial groups. Four racial identities are possible: Biracial Identity, Pro-Self Racial Identity, Pro-Parent Racial Identity, and Racially Undifferentiated Identity (see Figure 7.2).

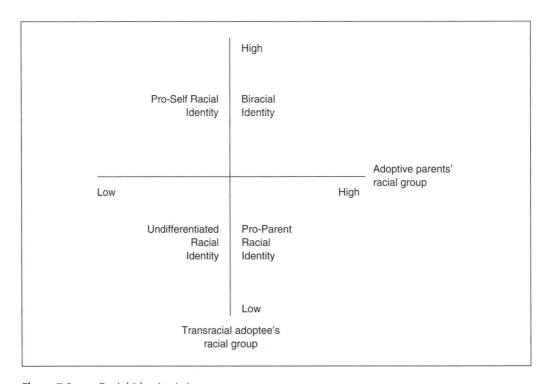

Figure 7.2   Racial Identity Axis

The final model combines the Cultural Identity Axis and the Racial Identity Axis into a single model. The Cultural-Racial Identity Model represents the pairing of each of the four types of possible cultural identities, as in Figure 7.1, with each of the four types of possible racial identities, as in Figure 7.2. The resulting model has 16 identity statuses to describe the identities of transracial adoptees. These identity statuses can be seen in Figure 7.3.

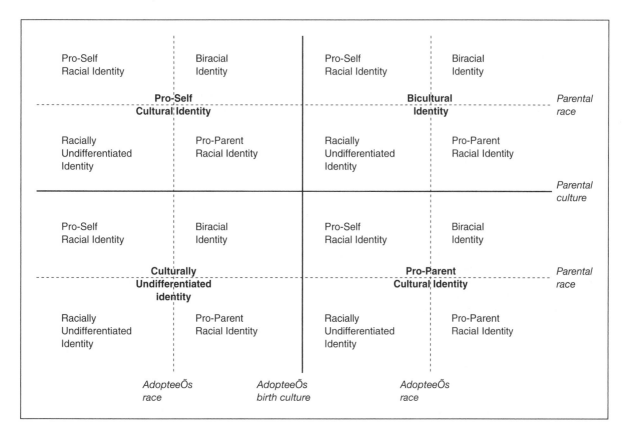

Figure 7.3   The Cultural-Racial Identity Model

To better describe how transracial adoptees develop characteristics of each of the 16 cultural-racial identities and what may affect transracial adoptees' progression through and entrance into each of the identities, descriptions of environmental or contextual factors likely to affect the identities of transracial adoptees were formulated (see Figure 7.4).

The Cultural-Racial Identity Model provided a description of the potential identities of transracial adoptees, but Baden and Steward (1997) also sought to more fully depict the types of family and social rearing environments that might lead to the various cultural-racial identities. They developed a graphic representation that reflected some of the choices that adoptive parents make regarding how and whether they will address racial and cultural issues (Lee, 2003) and how they will frame the relationships in adoption (Kirk, 1964). That is, Baden and Steward sought to depict the contextual and familial situations, attitudes, and characteristics that would produce transracial adoptees from each of the 16 potential cultural-racial identities in the Cultural-Racial Identity Model.

Essentially, Baden and Steward (1997) posited that "parental attitudes and beliefs that either *affirm* or *discount* the transracial adoptees' culture and racial group membership" (p. 10) would influence the development of the various cultural-racial identities. Their concept of affirming or discounting culture, race, or adoption is mirrored in adoption literature. David Kirk (1964) reflected on the "shared fate" or the inherent differences that exist between adoptive parents and their adopted children. He advocated for acknowledging differences rather than rejecting differences as a means for more effective parenting, authenticity, and adjustment. Similarly, building on the concept of cultural socialization in the literature, Lee (2003) identified strategies that transracial adoptive parents may use to cope with racial differences and to promote or hinder racial and cultural identity development. He identified four strategies: (1) cultural assimilation (deny or downplay racial and

Pro-Self Cultural Identity—Pro-Self Racial Identity

High in knowledge, awareness, competence, and comfort in the culture of their own racial ethnic group and feel most comfortable with individuals of their own racial ethnic group. May have been raised in a neighborhood in which the adoptee's racial group's culture predominated. May have rejected their adoptive parents' culture and may feel like an outsider in their parents' culture due to negative experiences in their parents' culture or due to perceived pressure from members of their own racial ethnic group.

Pro-Self Cultural Identity—Biracial Identity

High in knowledge, awareness, competence, and comfort in the culture of their own racial ethnic group and feel most comfortable with individuals of either own racial ethnic group or parents' racial ethnic group. May have been raised in a neighborhood in which the adoptee's racial group's culture predominated, but were exposed to many members of their parents' racial group and role models from both their own racial group and their parents' racial group.

Pro-Self Cultural Identity—Racially Undifferentiated Identity

High in knowledge, awareness, competence, and comfort in the culture of their own racial ethnic group and feel most comfortable with individuals of multiple racial ethnic groups. May have been raised in a neighborhood in which the adoptee's racial group's culture predominated. May have been exposed to members of multiple racial ethnic groups and to role models from multiple racial ethnic groups. A "human" identity may have been endorsed by parents.

Pro-Self Cultural Identity—Pro-Parent Racial Identity

High in knowledge, awareness, competence, and comfort in the culture of their own racial ethnic group and feel most comfortable with individuals of their parents' racial ethnic group. May have been raised in a neighborhood in which the adoptee's racial group's culture predominated. May not be visibly racially different from their adoptive parents' appearance and/or may have had negative experiences with individuals of their own racial ethnic group (e.g., perceived rejection due to visible differences or due to transracial adoption status). May have been exposed to members and/or role models of their parents' racial ethnic group.

Culturally Undifferentiated—Pro-Self Racial Identity

Not afliated primarily with either their own or their parents' racial ethnic groups' cultures. Instead, they are high in their knowledge, awareness, competence, and comfort in multiple cultures, including their own and their parents' racial ethnic groups as well as other racial ethnic groups. Feel most comfortable with individuals of their own racial ethnic group. May have been raised in a neighborhood in which multiple racial groups' cultures were represented. May have been exposed primarily to members of the adoptee's racial ethnic groups and to role models from the adoptee's racial ethnic group. May have rejected their adoptive parents' culture and may feel like an outsider in their parents' culture due to negative experiences in their parents' culture or due to perceived pressure from members of their own racial ethnic group.

Culturally Undifferentiated—Biracial Identity

Not afliated primarily with either their own or their parents' racial ethnic groups' cultures. Instead, they are high in their knowledge, awareness, competence, and comfort in multiple cultures, including their own and their parents' racial ethnic groups as well as other racial ethnic groups. Feel most comfortable with individuals of both their own and their parents' racial ethnic groups. May have been raised in a neighborhood in which multiple racial groups' cultures were represented. May have been exposed primarily to members of both the adoptee's and the parents' racial ethnic groups and to role models from both of those groups.

Culturally Undifferentiated—Racially Undifferentiated Identity

Not afliated primarily with either their own or their parents' racial ethnic groups' cultures. Instead, they are high in their knowledge, awareness, competence, and comfort in multiple cultures including their own and their parents' racial ethnic groups as well as other racial ethnic groups. Feel most comfortable with individuals of multiple racial ethnic groups. May have been raised in a neighborhood in which multiple racial groups' cultures were represented. May have been exposed to members of multiple racial ethnic groups and to role models from multiple racial ethnic groups. A "human" identity may have been endorsed by parents.

Culturally Undifferentiated—Pro-Parent Racial Identity

Not afliated primarily with either their own or their parents' racial ethnic groups' cultures. Instead, they are high in their knowledge, awareness, competence, and comfort in multiple cultures including their own and their parents' racial ethnic groups as well as other racial ethnic groups. Feel most comfortable with individuals of their parents' racial ethnic group. May have been raised in a neighborhood in which multiple racial groups' cultures were represented. May not be visibly racially different from their adoptive parents' appearance and/or may have had negative experiences with individuals of their own racial ethnic group (e.g., perceived rejection due to visible differences or due to transracial adoption status). May have been exposed to members and/or role models of their parents' racial ethnic group.

Figure 7.4   Depictions of the 16 Cells of the Cultural-Racial Identity Model

Bicultural—Pro-Self Racial Identity

High in knowledge, awareness, competence, and comfort in the cultures of both their own and their parents' racial ethnic groups and feel most comfortable with individuals of their own racial ethnic group. May have been raised in a neighborhood in which both the adoptee's and the parents' racial groups' cultures predominated. Although competent and knowledgeable in birth and adoptive parents' cultures, may prefer to associate with individuals from their own racial group due to real, perceived, or developmental pressures from members of their own racial ethnic group and due to discomfort with individuals from other racial groups, particularly the dominant White racial group.

Bicultural—Biracial Identity

High in knowledge, awareness, competence, and comfort in the culture of both their own and their parents' racial ethnic groups and feel most comfortable with individuals of either their own racial ethnic group or their parents' racial ethnic group. May have been raised in a neighborhood in which both the adoptee's and the parents' racial groups' cultures predominated and were exposed to many members of their parents' racial group and role models from both their own racial group and their parents' racial group.

Bicultural—Racially Undifferentiated Identity

High in knowledge, awareness, competence, and comfort in the culture of both their own and their parents' racial ethnic groups and feel most comfortable with individuals of multiple racial ethnic groups. May have been raised in a neighborhood in which both the adoptees' and the parents' racial groups' cultures predominated. May have been exposed to members of multiple racial ethnic groups and to role models from multiple racial ethnic groups. A "human" identity may have been endorsed by parents.

Bicultural—Pro-Parent Racial Identity

High in knowledge, awareness, competence, and comfort in the culture of both their own and their parents' racial ethnic groups and feel most comfortable with individuals of their parents' racial ethnic group. May have been raised in a neighborhood in which both the adoptee's and the parents' racial groups' cultures predominated. May not be visibly racially different from their adoptive parents' appearance and/or may have had negative experiences with individuals of their own racial ethnic group (e.g., perceived rejection due to visible differences or due to transracial adoption status). May have been exposed to members and/or role models of their parents' racial ethnic group.

Pro-Parent Cultural Identity—Pro-Self Racial Identity

High in knowledge, awareness, competence, and comfort in the culture of their parents' racial ethnic group but feel most comfortable with individuals of their own racial ethnic group. May have been raised in a neighborhood in which the parents' racial group's culture predominated. May have rejected their adoptive parents' culture and may feel like an outsider in their parents' culture due to negative experiences in their parents' culture or due to perceived pressure from members of their own racial ethnic group.

Pro-Parent Cultural Identity—Biracial Identity

High in knowledge, awareness, competence, and comfort in the culture of their parents' racial ethnic group and feel most comfortable with individuals of either their own racial ethnic group or their parents' racial ethnic group. May have been raised in a neighborhood in which the parents' racial group's culture predominated. Were exposed to many members of their parents' racial group and role models from both their own racial group and their parents' racial group.

Pro-Parent Cultural Identity—Racially Undifferentiated Identity

High in knowledge, awareness, competence, and comfort in the culture of their parents' racial ethnic group and feel most comfortable with individuals of multiple racial ethnic groups. May have been raised in a neighborhood in which the adoptee's racial group's culture predominated. May have been exposed to members of multiple racial ethnic groups and to role models from multiple racial ethnic groups. A "human" identity may have been endorsed by parents.

Pro-Parent Cultural Identity—Pro-Parent Racial Identity

High in knowledge, awareness, competence, and comfort in the culture of their parents' racial ethnic group and feel most comfortable with individuals of their parents' racial ethnic group. May have been raised in a neighborhood in which the parents' racial group's culture predominated. May not be visibly racially different from their adoptive parents' appearance and/or may have had negative experiences with individuals of their own racial ethnic group (e.g., perceived rejection due to visible differences or due to transracial adoption status). May have been exposed to members and/or role models of their parents' racial ethnic group.

Figure 7.4 (Continued)

cultural experiences), (2) enculturation (exert effort to teach children about birth culture), (3) racial inculcation (actively teach coping skills for dealing with racism and discrimination), and (4) child choice (provide opportunities but adjust based on child's wishes).

Baden and Steward's (1997) framework for understanding the influence of parental attitudes and characteristics on transracial adoptees' cultural and racial identities suggests that the degree to which parents, extended family, and the environment affirm (i.e., acknowledge, accept, approve of, reflect/mirror) transracial adoptees' race and ethnicity and their birth cultures will influence their identity formation and status. Similarly, discounting (i.e., decreased emphasis, lack of interest in, lack of acceptance of, lack of presence in life) transracial adoptees' race and ethnicity and birth culture will be likely to affect their identity formation and status. Figure 7.5 depicts the affirming and discounting factors to indicate that the environments in which transracial adoptees are raised can (1) either affirm or discount the adoptive parents' culture and/or racial group membership, (2) either affirm or discount the transracial adoptee's birth culture and/or race, or (3) have some combination of affirming and discounting the adoptive parents' and transracial adoptee's cultures and racial groups. Baden and Steward (1997) cautioned that the attitudes and characteristics in this framework were not likely to be due to explicit/intentional efforts, behaviors, beliefs, and the like, nor did they necessarily result from inadvertent or unintentional efforts, behaviors, beliefs, and the like. Rather than attempting to predict how active or passive adoptive parents may be in the transmission of these attitudes to transracial adoptees, Baden and Steward instead warned that the child-rearing context (including extended family, schools, teachers, community leaders, and peers) may also contribute to affirming or discounting contexts.

		Parent	
		Affirming	**Discounting**
Child	**Affirming**	Parent affirming – child affirming	Parent discounting – child affirming
	Discounting	Parent affirming – child discounting	Parent discounting – child discounting

Figure 7.5 Parental Attitudes and Characteristics Model for Affirming/Discounting Environments

As noted above, the attitudes and characteristics that lead to an affirming or discounting environment may be explicit, intentional, active efforts or they may be inadvertent, unintentional, passive messages. For example, parents may intentionally or inadvertently promote or expose transracial adoptees to attitudes and contexts that are prejudiced toward or discriminatory toward the adoptee's racial or cultural group. In this case, the context in which the adoptees were reared may affirm the parents' racial and cultural groups and discount the adoptee's racial and cultural groups. Furthermore, although parents serve as the primary source for conveying attitudes and for creating the child-rearing context, transracial adoptees may also be affected by other aspects of their context as well. For example, schools, teachers, community leaders, and peers may contribute to the creation of the contexts to be described. Although this model does not account for the degree of intentionality of the attitudes and resulting contexts that adoptive parents provide, the degree of intentionality is an area to which clinical attention should be paid.

Transracial adoptees raised in a *parent affirming-child affirming* context were likely to have peers and role models from both their own racial group and that of their adoptive parents. The environment may contain images, attitudes, role models, friends, and extended family who are affirming and supportive of the adoptive parents' racial and cultural groups as well as of the transracial adoptee's racial and cultural groups. The predominant attitude in this category is acceptance of both racial and cultural groups. If not mediated by exposure to knowledge highlighting different racial histories and past and current attitudes of racism, a potential drawback to this attitude is the possibility of denial of the racial climate and the conflicts regarding race and culture in this country.

A *parent discounting-child affirming* context is likely to result when the adoptive parents focus on the racial group and culture of the transracial adoptee to the extent that they may disregard or neglect to account for their own racial and cultural group. The role models to whom the transracial adoptee has been exposed may result in the approval of the transracial adoptee's racial group and the culture of his or her racial group. With or without intending to do so, the adoptive parents may minimize the role of their racial and cultural group, which, ironically, is often the dominant White middle class. In this case, adoptive parents may minimize or fail to account for the power and impact of those of their own racial and cultural group in their environment. The adoptee may be exposed to positive role models from his or her racial group and be exposed to role models from the dominant group that were framed as somewhat ineffectual or insignificant. The predominant attitude shown is acceptance and approval of the transracial adoptee's racial group and birth culture and discounting or minimization of the adoptive parents' racial group. The drawback to this attitude may be in the failure to acknowledge and present positive role models from the dominant race and culture so that the adoptee may engage in a dichotomous belief system about race and may assume discrimination and oppression when there is none.

A *parent affirming-child discounting* context may be due to adoptive parents who are preoccupied and focused on their own racial and cultural group to such a degree that they may disregard that of the transracial adoptee. Positive role models for the adoptee may tend to represent the parental racial and cultural group without equal or similar attention given to role models from the transracial adoptee's race and birth culture. The adoptive parents may have little interaction with and/or knowledge of the transracial adoptee's race or birth culture, thus resulting in an exposure bias toward their own racial and cultural group. The predominant attitude may be acceptance and approval of the parental culture without attention or exposure to the role of the transracial adoptee's racial group membership and the culture of his or her racial group. This attitude may impede the transracial adoptee by failing to recognize, affirm, and accept individuals physically similar to the adoptee. Although this may be unintentional, it may convey a disrespect for or dislike of those similar to the adoptee and may cause an identity confusion that is difficult to resolve. Again, a dichotomous belief system is likely to result.

Transracial adoptees reared in a *parent discounting-child discounting* environment may endorse a "human race" or a "color-blind" society and attitude as healthiest, so the adoptive parents may not attend to the racial and cultural groups of both the parents and the transracial adoptee. Instead, they endorse a disposition attesting to the equality of all races without attention to or preference for any in particular. Positive role models may be from multiple racial groups, including parental and adoptee's racial and cultural groups, but when exposure to the role models occurs, the race and culture of the role models may not be addressed and attributions for success and health may be made to other characteristics or attitudes. The predominant attitude could be one of attributing importance, power, success, and happiness to individual characteristics not based on race or culture. This attitude has considerable appeal, but the danger may be similar to that found in the parent affirming-child affirming attitudes—denial. The parents and adoptees may be unrealistic about discrimination and oppression and fail to understand the dynamics in society based on racial and cultural group membership.

Other factors likely to have an impact on the cultural and racial identities of transracial adoptees are the attitudes and degree of emotional support given by the community (schools, social agencies, teachers, peers) and extended family members, including grandparents of the transracial adoptee. Finally, the support networks established by the adoptive parents may affect the adoptee. These factors will influence identity due to their status as alternative sources of feedback for adoptees and the level of influence they may exert on parental and adoptees' attitudes and beliefs.

CONCLUSION

The Cultural-Racial Identity Model is the first theoretical model to separate cultural identity and racial identity. The implications for its use are vast and point to the need for the empirical validation of the model. Its use with the populations already identified in this chapter must also be empirically validated.

Following empirical validation, the Cultural-Racial Identity Model will be a comprehensive framework for researchers to use with individuals raised in racially integrated families. The model can also serve as a guide for transracial adoptees and adoptive parents to better understand and guide their life experiences. Furthermore, psychotherapeutic practitioners can use the model as a guide for determining the counseling needs of those raised in racially integrated families, particularly as they differ from the needs of individuals raised in same-race households. The information to be gleaned from the use of this model as a framework for research and practice will allow those from racially integrated families to be better served and for their unique experiences to be addressed appropriately and comprehensively.

The Cultural-Racial Identity Model represents an important step in addressing the needs of individuals who have multiple identities with which to describe themselves. The strength of the model is in its willingness to account for heterogeneity within groups that have previously been studied without respect for the uniqueness within these populations. With the information gleaned from the application of the Cultural-Racial Identity Model to groups such as transracial adoptees and biracial individuals, psychologists, social workers, adoption workers, and others in the helping professions will be better prepared to address the adjustment, identity, and self-esteem problems that have been of such concern to opponents and proponents of transracial adoption alike.

REFLECTION QUESTIONS

1. When considering identity formation for adoptees, how would you try to integrate adoption identity issues with cultural and racial identity issues? Why?

2. How would a domestic transracial adoptee (e.g., African American child adopted by White parents) identify differently from an international adoptee (e.g., Korean child adopted by White parents)? Why?

3. How would a transracial adoptee who was reared in a parent affirming-child discounting environment identify on the Cultural-Racial Identity Model? Why?

REFERENCES

Andujo, E. (1988). Ethnic identity of transethnically adopted Hispanic adolescents. *Social Work, 33*(6), 531–535.

Atkinson, D. R., & Gim, R. H. (1989). Asian-American cultural identity and attitudes toward mental health services. *Journal of Counseling Psychology, 36*(2), 209–212.

Atkinson, D. R., Morten, G., & Sue, D. W. (1993). *Counseling American minorities: A cross-cultural perspective* (4th ed.). Madison, WI: Brown & Benchmark/Wm. C. Brown.

Atkinson, D. R., Morten, G., & Sue, D. W. (1998). *Counseling American minorities* (5th ed.). New York: McGraw-Hill.

Baden, A. L. (2002). The psychological adjustment of transracial adoptees: An application of the Cultural-Racial Identity Model. *Journal of Social Distress & the Homeless, 11*(2), 167–191.

Baden, A. L., & Steward, R. J. (1997, February). *The role of parents and family in the psychological adjustment of transracial adoptees: Implications for the Cultural-Racial Identity Model for transracial adoptees.* Paper presented at the Fourteenth Annual Teachers College Roundtable on Cross-Cultural Psychology and Education, Teachers College, New York.

Baden, A. L., & Steward, R. J. (2000). A framework for use with racially and culturally integrated families: The Cultural-Racial Identity Model as applied to transracial adoption. *Journal of Social Distress & the Homeless, 9*(4), 309–337.

Bagley, C. (1992). The psychology of adoption: Case studies of national and international adoptions. *Bulletin of the Hong Kong Psychological Society, 28,* 95–115.

Benson, P. L., Sharma, A. R., & Roehlkepartain, E. C. (1994). *Growing up adopted.* Minneapolis, MN: Search Institute.

Bradley, C., & Hawkins-Leon, C. G. (2002). The transracial adoption debate: Counseling and legal implications. *Journal of Counseling & Development, 80*(4), 433–440.

Brodzinsky, D. M., Smith, D. W., & Brodzinsky, A. B. (1998). *Children's adjustment to adoption: Developmental and clinical issues.* Thousand Oaks, CA: Sage.

Brooks, D., & Barth, R. P. (1999). Adult transracial and inracial adoptees: Effects of race, gender, adoptive family structure, and placement history on adjustment outcomes. *American Journal of Orthopsychiatry, 69*(1), 87–99.

Brown, U. M. (1995). Black/White interracial young adults: Quest for a racial identity. *American Journal of Orthopsychiatry, 65*(1), 125–130.

Cederblad, M., Höök, B., Irhammar, M., & Mercke, A.-M. (1999). Mental health in international adoptees as teenagers and young adults: An epidemiological study. *Journal of Child Psychology & Psychiatry, 40*(8), 1239–1248.

Child Welfare League of America. (2003). *International adoption: Trends and issues.* Retrieved August 5, 2005, from http://ndas.cwla.org/include/text/IssueBrief_International_Adoption_FINAL.pdf

Cross, W. E. (1971, July). The Negro-to-Black conversion experience. *Black World,* pp. 13–27.

Cross, W. E. (1978). The Thomas and Cross models of psychological nigrescence: A review. *Journal of Black Psychology, 5*(1), 13–31.

Cross, W. E., Jr., Parham, T. A., & Helms, J. E. (1991). The stages of Black identity development: Nigrescence models. In R. L. Jones (Ed.), *Black psychology* (3rd ed., pp. 319–338). Berkeley, CA: Cobb & Henry.

Dalal, F. (1999). The meaning of boundaries and barriers in the development of cultural identity and between cultures. *Psychodynamic Counselling, 5*(2), 161–171.

DeBerry, K. M., Scarr, S., & Weinberg, R. (1996). Family racial socialization and ecological competence: Longitudinal assessments of African-American transracial adoptees. *Child Development, 67*(5), 2375–2399.

Dunbar, N., & Grotevant, H. D. (2004). Adoption narratives: The construction of adoptive identity during adolescence. In M. W. Pratt & B. H. Fiese (Eds.), *Family stories and the life course: Across time and generations* (pp. 135–161). Mahwah, NJ: Lawrence Erlbaum.

Erikson, E. H. (1968). *Identity: Youth and crisis.* Oxford: Norton.

Erikson, E. H. (1980). *Identity and the life cycle.* New York: Norton.

Evan B. Donaldson Adoption Institute. (2005). *Overview of adoption in the United States.* Retrieved August 18, 2005, from http://www.adoptioninstitute.org/FactOverview.html#head

Falk, L. (1970). A comparative study of transracial and inracial adoptions. *Child Welfare, 49,* 82–88.

Feigelman, W. (2000). Adjustments of transracially and intracially adopted young adults. *Child & Adolescent Social Work Journal, 17*(3), 165–183.

Friedlander, M. L. (1999). Ethnic identity development of internationally adopted children and adolescents: Implications for family therapists. *Journal of Marital & Family Therapy, 25*(1), 43–60.

Germain, E. R. (2004). Culture or race? Phenotype and cultural identity development in minority Australian adolescents. *Australian Psychologist, 39*(2), 134–142.

Greve, W., Rothermund, K., & Wentura, D. (Eds.). (2005). *The adaptive self: Personal continuity and intentional self-development.* Ashland, OH: Hogrefe & Huber.

Grotevant, H. D. (1987). Toward a process model of identity formation. *Journal of Adolescent Research, 2*(3), 203–222.

Grotevant, H. D. (1997). Coming to terms with adoption: The construction of identity from adolescence into adulthood. *Adoption Quarterly, 1*(1), 3–27.

Grotevant, H. D., Dunbar, N., Kohler, J. K., & Esau, A. M. L. (2000). Adoptive identity: How contexts within and beyond the family shape developmental pathways. *Family Relations: Interdisciplinary Journal of Applied Family Studies, 49*(4), 379–387.

Hays, P. A. (2001). Seeing the forest and the trees: The complexities of culture in practice. In P. A. Hays (Ed.), *Addressing cultural complexities in practice: A framework for clinicians and counselors* (pp. 3–16). Washington, DC: American Psychological Association.

Helms, J. E. (1990). *Black and White racial identity: Theory, research, and practice.* New York: Greenwood Press.

Helms, J. E. (1995). An update of Helms's white and people of color racial identity models. In J. G. Ponterotto & J. M. Casas (Eds.), *Handbook of multicultural counseling* (pp. 181–198). Thousand Oaks, CA: Sage.

Helms, J. E., & Cook, D. A. (1999). *Using race and culture in counseling and psychotherapy: Theory and process.* Needham Heights, MA: Allyn & Bacon.

Helms, J. E., & Talleyrand, R. M. (1997). Race is not ethnicity. *American Psychologist, 52*(11), 1246–1247.

Helwig, A. A., & Ruthven, D. H. (1990). Psychological ramifications of adoption and implications for counseling. *Journal of Mental Health Counseling, 12*(1), 24–37.

Hollingsworth, L. D. (1998). Adoptee dissimilarity from the adoptive family: Clinical practice and research implications. *Child & Adolescent Social Work Journal, 15*(4), 303–319.

Honess, T., & Yardley, K. (Eds.). (1987). *Self and identity: Perspectives across the lifespan.* New York: Routledge.

Hoopes, J. L. (1990). Adoption and identity formation. In D. M. Brodzinsky & M. D. Schechter (Eds.), *Psychology of adoption* (pp. 144–166). London: Oxford University Press.

Huh, N. S. (1997). Korean children's ethnic identity formation and understanding of adoption. *Dissertation Abstracts International Section A: Humanities & Social Sciences, 58*(2), 586.

Jensen, L. A. (2003). Coming of age in a multicultural world: Globalization and adolescent cultural identity formation. *Applied Developmental Science, 7*(3), 189–196.

Johnson, P. R., Shireman, J. F., & Watson, K. W. (1987). Transracial adoption and the development of Black identity at age eight. *Child Welfare, 66*(1), 45–55.

Jones, A. (1997). Issues relevant to therapy with adoptees. *Psychotherapy: Theory, Research, Practice, Training, 34*(1), 64–68.

Kirk, H. D. (1964). *Shared fate: A theory of adoption and mental health.* New York: Free Press.

Kirschner, D. (1990). The adopted child syndrome: Considerations for psychotherapy. *Psychotherapy in Private Practice, 8*(3), 93–100.

Lee, R. M. (2003). The transracial adoption paradox: History, research, and counseling implications of cultural socialization. *The Counseling Psychologist, 31*(6), 711–744.

LeVine, E. S., & Sallee, A. L. (1990). Critical phases among adoptees and their families: Implications for therapy. *Child & Adolescent Social Work Journal, 7*(3), 217–232.

Liow, S. J. R. (1994). Transracial adoption: Questions on heritage for parents, children and counsellors. *Counselling Psychology Quarterly, 7*(4), 375–384.

Loenen, A., & Hoksbergen, R. (1986). Inter-country adoption: The Netherlands: Attachment relations and identity. *Adoption & Fostering, 10*(2), 22–26.

Marcia, J. E. (1966). Development and validation of ego-identity status. *Journal of Personality & Social Psychology, 3*(5), 551–558.

Marcia, J. E. (1980). Identity in adolescence. In J. Adelson (Ed.), *Handbook of adolescent psychology* (pp. 159–187). Toronto, Ontario, Canada: Wiley.

Marcia, J. E. (1987). The identity status approach to the study of ego identity development. In T. Honess & K. Yardley (Eds.), *Self and identity: Perspectives across the lifespan* (pp. 161–171). New York: Routledge.

McRoy, R. G., Zurcher, L. A., Lauderdale, M. L., & Anderson, R. (1984). The identity of transracial adoptees. *Social Casework, 65*(1), 34–39.

McRoy, R. G., Zurcher, L. A., Lauderdale, M. L., & Anderson, R. (1982). Self-esteem and racial identity in transracial and inracial adoptees. *Social Work, 27*(6), 522–526.

Meier, D. I. (1999). Cultural identity and place in adult Korean-American intercountry adoptees. *Adoption Quarterly, 3*(1), 15–48.

Miller, B. C., Fan, X., Christensen, M., Grotevant, H. D., & van Dulmen, M. (2000). Comparisons of adopted and nonadopted adolescents in a large, nationally representative sample. *Child Development, 71*(5), 1458–1473.

National Association of Black Social Workers. (1972). *NABSW opposes transracial adoption* (Report). New York: National Association of Black Social Workers.

Phinney, J. S. (1990). Ethnic identity in adolescents and adults: Review of research. *Psychological Bulletin, 108*(3), 499–514.

Phinney, J. S. (1992). The multigroup ethnic identity measure: A new scale for use with diverse groups. *Journal of Adolescent Research, 7*(2), 156–176.

Phinney, J. S., & Rosenthal, D. A. (1992). Ethnic identity in adolescence: Process, context, and outcome. In G. R. Adams & T. P. Gullotta (Eds.), *Adolescent identity formation* (pp. 145–172). Thousand Oaks, CA: Sage.

Rickard Liow, S. J. (1994). Transracial adoption: Questions on heritage for parents, children and counsellors. *Counselling Psychology Quarterly, 7*(4), 375–384.

Sharma, A. R., McGue, M. K., & Benson, P. L. (1998). The psychological adjustment of United States adopted adolescents and their nonadopted siblings. *Child Development, 69*(3), 791–802.

Shireman, J. F., & Johnson, P. R. (1985). Single-parent adoptions: A longitudinal study. *Children & Youth Services Review, 7*(4), 321–334.

Shireman, J. F., & Johnson, P. R. (1986). A longitudinal study of Black adoptions: Single parent, transracial, and traditional. *Social Work, 31*(3), 172–176.

Silverman, A. R., & Feigelman, W. (1981). The adjustment of Black children adopted by White families. *Social Casework: The Journal of Contemporary Social Work, 62*, 529–536.

Silverman, A. R., & Feigelman, W. (1990). Adjustment in interracial adoptees: An overview. In D. M. Brodzinsky & M. D. Schechter (Eds.), *Psychology of adoption* (pp. 187–200). London: Oxford University Press.

Silverstein, D. N., & Kaplan, S. (1988). Lifelong issues in adoption. In K. T. L. Coleman, H. Hornby, & C. Boggis (Eds.), *Working with older adoptees: A source book of innovative models* (pp. 45–53). Portland: University of Southern Maine.

Simon, R. J., & Altstein, H. (1987). *Transracial adoptees and their families: A study of identity and commitment*. New York: Praeger.

Simon, R. J., & Roorda, R. M. (2000). *In their own voices: Transracial adoptees tell their stories*. New York: Columbia University Press.

Stein, L. M., & Hoopes, J. L. (1985). *Identity formation in the adopted adolescent*. New York: Child Welfare League of America.

Steward, R. J., & Baden, A. L. (1995). *The Cultural-Racial Identity Model: Understanding the racial identity and cultural identity development of transracial adoptees* (Report No. UD030908). East Lansing: Michigan State University. (ERIC Document Reproduction Service No. ED395076)

Tizard, B. (1991). Intercountry adoption: A review of the evidence. *Journal of Child Psychology & Psychiatry, 32*(5), 743–756.

Tizard, B., & Phoenix, A. (1995). The identity of mixed parentage adolescents. *Journal of Child Psychology & Psychiatry, 36*(8), 1399–1410.

Trolley, B. C. (1994–1995). Grief issues and positive aspects associated with international adoption. *Omega: Journal of Death & Dying, 30*(4), 257–268.

Vroegh, K. S. (1997). Transracial adoptees: Developmental status after 17 years. *American Journal of Orthopsychiatry, 67*(4), 568–575.

Westhues, A., & Cohen, J. S. (1998). Ethnic and racial identity of internationally adopted adolescents and young adults: Some issues in relation to children's rights. *Adoption Quarterly, 1*(4), 33–55.

Whaley, A. L. (1993). Self-esteem, cultural identity, and psychosocial adjustment in African American children. *Journal of Black Psychology, 19*(4), 406–422.

Wickes, K. L., & Slate, J. R. (1997). Transracial adoption of Koreans: A preliminary study of adjustment. *International Journal for the Advancement of Counselling, 19*(2), 187–195.

Wierzbicki, M. (1993). Psychological adjustment of adoptees: A meta-analysis. *Journal of Clinical Child Psychology, 22*(4), 447–454.

Wilson, S. L. (2004). A current review of adoption research: Exploring individual differences in adjustment. *Children & Youth Services Review, 26*(8), 687–696.

Yoon, D. P. (2001). Causal modeling predicting psychological adjustment of Korean-born adolescent adoptees. *Journal of Human Behavior in the Social Environment, 3*(3), 65–82.

Zamostny, K. P., O'Brien, K. M., Baden, A. L., & Wiley, M. O. (2003). The practice of adoption history, trends, and social context. *The Counseling Psychologist, 31*(6), 651–678.

Zastrow, C. H. (1977). *Outcome of Black children-White parents transracial adoptions.* San Francisco: R & E Research Associates.

Transracial and International Adoption

Preface

AMANDA L. BADEN

Montclair State University

This part of *The Handbook of Adoption: Implications for Researchers, Practitioners, and Families* examines the visible or "conspicuous" adoptions that have come to reflect the 21st century's face of adoption. Racial, cultural, and ethnic differences within adoptive families have become more prevalent and prominent in the adoption world within the past 50-plus years. In the United States, transracial adoption, which can be either domestic (adoptions of children by families within the children's country of birth) or international (adoptions of children by parents across national borders), refers to placing children with parents from a different racial or ethnic group. Since its inception as an adoption practice, the impact of transracial adoptive placements has been scrutinized, and questions have been raised about the long-term outcomes for transracial adoptees and for the communities and countries from which they come. The chapters in this part address these issues both broadly, as they pertain to the practice of transracial adoption, and more specifically, focusing on transracial and international adoptions from some specific countries.

To begin the discourse on transracial and international adoption, Chapter 8 in this part, by Amanda Baden, "Putting Culture Into Context: The Impact of Attitudes Toward the Adoption for Chinese Adoptees," focuses on the clinical and intrapersonal impact that the histories of adoption in both the country of birth and the country of adoption may have on adopted persons. In particular, the impact of the circumstances and attitudes that surround the adoptions of Chinese children by American citizens is examined by considering how Chinese adoptees in the United States may be affected by the ways in which they perceive Chinese culture and attitudes toward adoption. To explore this relationship, an examination of the cultural belief systems, social and political climates (including legislation), and the economic and familial support systems that exist currently and at the time of relinquishment in the adoptees' birth countries is conducted. To further contextualize their adoption circumstances, attitudes of Chinese and American people toward the relinquishment of children, adoption domestically and internationally, and transracial adoption were discussed. Using a case study of Chinese adoption, I also explored the clinical and intrapersonal implications for Chinese transracial adoptees that these contextual issues may present for families and adoptees.

As Esposito and Biafora reported in Chapter 2, the history of transracial adoption in the United States grew and evolved around the legal placement of Black and biracial children into White families. Although this has been a controversial topic in the United States for over 30 years, in Chapter 9, titled "Moving Beyond the Controversy of the Transracial Adoption of Black and Biracial Children," Rhonda Roorda presents a compelling argument for addressing the needs of Black and biracial individuals who were transracially adopted. Roorda also covers the detailed history of transracial adoption policy, examines the current public adoption law, and discusses the potential implications for social work professionals and transracial adoptive families. Chapter 9 also draws on the findings from work Roorda did with Rita Simon (2000) in their book, *In Their Own Voices: Transracial Adoptees Tell Their Stories,* which documented the personal accounts of 24 Black and biracial adult trans-racial adoptees who discussed their complex experiences in grappling with their racial iden-tity and self-esteem within their adoptive families and in American society. Last, Roorda explores strategies to further strengthen the self-identity and cultural mobility of Black and biracial adoptees.

In Chapter 10 in this part, "International Adoption of Latin American Children: Psychological Adjustment, Cultural and Legal Issues," Alina Camacho-Gingerich, Susan Branco-Rodriguez, Raul Ernesto Pitteri, and Rafael Javier expand the discussion of transra-cial and international adoption by examining adoptions of Latin American children by White American families. They examine the adoptions of Latino children with the recogni-tion that some of these children are racially different and visibly appear to be so (i.e., they are transracially adopted), whereas other Latino children may fall into the White racial group (i.e., they are not transracially adopted but are internationally adopted). Given the recognition that these children have birth heritages and cultures that differ from their adop-tive parents' cultures and heritages, transcultural adoption issues must be addressed.

The final chapter in this part, "From the Ashes of War: Lessons From 50 Years of Korean International Adoption," provides an excellent introduction to the history and path of international adoption as led by Korean adoptees. Hollee McGinnis, in this chapter, gives a thorough overview of the historical, social, cultural, and political forces that shaped the development of international adoption in South Korea over the past 50 years, including the contributions of adult adopted Koreans to the field in the past 25 years. Her chapter examines the lessons that can be learned from the Korean adoption experience and the particular effects of geopolitics, policies, and the media on practice, and argues that the future continuation of international adoption practice is not assured.

LEARNING GOALS

As noted earlier in this book, the authors proposed specific learning goals as they approached their respective chapters. Below are some learning objectives we encourage our readers to consider as they delve into this part on transracial and international adoption.

- To address the attitudes toward and practice of domestic and international adoption, with particular attention to China and the United States.
- To discuss information that Chinese adoptees seek and receive about their adoptions and how that may affect their adjustment, identity, and connection to their birth culture.
- To review case studies of transracial and international adoptees to the United States to illustrate the potential challenges and strengths of these adopted persons.

- To advocate for the importance of addressing race and identity for transracial adoptees.
- To review and critique the evidence and research that assessed the outcomes for transracial adoption.
- To present findings from a series of personal interviews with adult transracial adoptees.
- To make recommendations for the healthy development of identity for Black and biracial transracial adoptees.
- To present an overview of the historical, social, cultural, and political forces that have shaped international adoptions from South Korea since the 1950s.
- To trace three primary factors as promoting international adoption: GI babies, the shift from humanitarian aid to supply and demand, and developing politics and ideology.
- To present the experiences of Korean adult adoptees and their recommendations for improved adjustment based on race, culture, ethnicity, and identity.

Putting Culture Into Context

8

The Impact of Attitudes Toward the Adoption of Chinese Adoptees

AMANDA L. BADEN

Montclair State University

The practice of placing orphaned or abandoned children transracially and internationally has been the subject of scrutiny in the United States and Europe for the past 35 years. As a result of the concern expressed over the outcomes of these placements, clinicians, researchers, and child policy professionals sought to determine the "best interests of the child" by conducting research to assess the adjustment and psychological impact of adoption on children and adolescents adopted transracially and internationally. However, despite investigating variables affecting adoptees such as racial and ethnic identity (e.g., Andujo, 1988; Huh, 1997; McRoy, Zurcher, Lauderdale, & Anderson, 1984; Shireman & Johnson, 1986), psychological adjustment (e.g., Cederblad, Höök, Irhammar, & Mercke, 1999), school achievement (e.g., Brodzinsky & Steiger, 1991; Liu, Wyshak, & Larsen, 2004), and attachment (Smith & Sherwen, 1988; Steele, Hodges, Kaniuk, Hillman, & Henderson, 2003; Ward & Lewko, 1987), questions remain about what shapes the experiences of transracial and international adoptees. One factor of great interest to many adopted persons, clinicians, and researchers involves the circumstances surrounding relinquished and orphaned children in their countries of origin. The circumstances surrounding relinquishment and subsequent international adoptions are often more complex than a single policy or rule can describe, and they often encompass both the reasons that may be given for relinquishment (e.g., individual, family, community, social, economic, and governmental factors) and the climate or atmosphere in which those relinquishments are made (e.g., social stigma, racial purity, social dictates). Thus, both the reasons for relinquishment and the climate in which it occurred are likely to affect adoptees' attitudes toward their countries of origin and their fellow ethnic group members. This in turn may affect the adoptees' feelings of belongingness and affiliation with their ethnic group. To better understand the circumstances, given that the ways in which adoptees make sense of the reasons and judge the climate within their countries of origin may affect adopted children's adjustment, attachment, self-esteem, and identity, an examination of the cultural belief systems, social and political climates, and economic and familial support systems that exist currently and that existed at the time of relinquishment in the adoptees' birth countries is warranted.

As the statistics reported later in this chapter reflect, China is the leading country of origin of children adopted internationally for the past 6 years. China has also had the distinction of being the most populous country in the world (Central Intelligence Agency, 2006), and that dominance is reflected in the population of Asians in the United States. The 2000 U.S. Census reported that of the 11.9 million Asians residing in the United States, 20%, or 2.7 million, are of Chinese heritage (Barnes & Bennett, 2002). In fact, the largest Asian group in the United States is composed of those ethnically Chinese. As more Chinese children are adopted from China by families who are not ethnically Chinese (the vast majority of the adoptive parents), a greater understanding of the impact of cultural attitudes toward relinquishment and adoption is needed to best inform adoption professionals, train adoption competent therapists, prepare adoptive parents, and treat the adoptees themselves.

This chapter will briefly review the documented historical and contextual perspectives on transracial and international adoption (TIA) for China. From that perspective, the attitudes of Chinese people toward relinquishment of children, adoption domestically and internationally, and transracial adoption will be discussed. Comparisons and contrasts of attitudes in the United States toward these same issues (e.g., relinquishment and adoption placements) will be addressed. Finally, a case study example will be given and discussed.

CURRENT STATUS OF INTERNATIONAL ADOPTIONS

Since international adoptions were initially practiced following World War I, the processes by which children born abroad were then adopted by American families have changed drastically. With changes in international adoptions as formalized via the Hague Convention, no longer can children simply be "baby lifted" without more stringent legal and personal protections in place. But who is being internationally adopted? How many orphans are there abroad? These questions have frequently been addressed by governmental agencies such as the Child Welfare League of America (CWLA; 2003), who estimated that more than 100 million children in Asia (65 million), Africa (34 million), and Latin America and the Caribbean (8 million) remain orphans and need caregivers. (Note: Orphaned children in Europe are not included in this number.) Clearly, with so many children needing families, some examination of the factors leading to their orphan status and their likelihood of being adopted must be examined.

To understand who is getting adopted by American families, one need only review the U.S. Department of State's (2006) report on the numbers of immigrant visas issued for orphans born abroad. Recent statistics reflect that in 2005, when 21,968 children were adopted internationally, the highest number of children came from the People's Republic of China (PRC; 7,906 children), with 36% of all international adoptions. Table 8.1 summarizes the immigrant visas issued by the United States for children born abroad and reflects that in 2005, the majority of orphaned children being adopted to the United States came primarily from Asia (50.8%) and from Eastern Europe (25.4%).

The number of immigrant visas issued to orphans adopted by Americans indicates that despite the large numbers of international adoptions by American parents and by other countries (e.g., Canada, the United Kingdom, Ireland, the Netherlands), millions of children still likely need adoptive placements. However, the wide availability of orphaned infants and toddlers in foreign countries and the perceived unlikelihood that foreign birth parents will seek reunions or rescind their decisions, combined with rising infertility rates in the United States, decreased stigma for single parenthood, effective contraception, and legalized abortion have steadily increased the number of transracial adoptions in the United States.

Table 8.1	Immigration Visas Issued to Orphans From the U.S. State Department by Year			
Rank for Countries of Origin	2005	2004	2003	2002
1	People's Republic of China (7,906)	People's Republic of China (7,044)	People's Republic of China (6,859)	People's Republic of China (5,053)
2	Russian Federation (4,639)	Russian Federation (5,865)	Russian Federation (5,209)	Russian Federation (4,939)
3	Guatemala (3,783)	Guatemala (3,264)	Guatemala (2,328)	Guatemala (2,219)
4	South Korea (1,630)	South Korea (1,716)	South Korea (1,790)	South Korea (1,779)
5	Ukraine (821)	Kazakhstan (826)	Kazakhstan (825)	Ukraine (1,106)
6	Kazakhstan (755)	Ukraine (723)	Ukraine (702)	Kazakhstan (819)
7	Ethiopia (441)	India (406)	India (472)	Vietnam (766)
8	India (323)	Haiti (356)	Vietnam (382)	India (466)
9	Colombia (291)	Ethiopia (289)	Colombia (272)	Colombia (334)
10	Philippines (271)	Colombia (287)	Haiti (250)	Bulgaria (260)
11	Haiti (231)	Belarus (202)	Philippines (214)	Cambodia (254)
12	Liberia (182)	Philippines (196)	Romania (200)	Philippines (221)
13	Taiwan (141)	Bulgaria (110)	Bulgaria (198)	Haiti (187)
14	Mexico (98)	Poland (102)	Belarus (191)	Belarus (169)
15	Poland and Thailand (both 73)	Mexico (89)	Ethiopia (135)	Romania (168)
16	Brazil (66)	Liberia (86)	Cambodia (124)	Ethiopia (105)
17	Nigeria (65)	Nepal (73)	Poland (97), Nepal (73)	Poland (101)
18	Jamaica (63)	Nigeria (71)	Thailand (72)	Thailand (67)
19	Nepal (62)	Thailand and Brazil (both 69)	Azerbaijan (62)	Peru (65)
20	Moldova (54)	Romania (57)	Mexico (61)	Mexico (61)
Total	21,968	21,900	20,516	19,139

SOURCE: U.S. Department of State (2006).

HISTORICAL PERSPECTIVES

Although a complete history of TIA is beyond the scope of this chapter, the literature contains numerous depictions of both transracial and international adoption's history (e.g., Lee, 2003; Wilkinson, 1995; Zamostny, O'Brien, Baden, & Wiley, 2003). As Baden and Steward (Chapter 7) and Roorda (Chapter 9) described, the concerns in the 1970s in the United States centered on domestic transracial adoptions. A report of the National Association of Black Social Workers (NABSW; 1972) and the Indian Child Welfare Act (ICWA) of 1978 (Simon & Alstein, 2000) identified their fears regarding the impact of transracial placements; they predicted difficulties with racial identity and adjustment and expressed concern about the impact of transracial placements on the Black and American Indian communities, referring to the practice as "cultural genocide" (NABSW, 1972).

With respect to international/intercountry adoption, criticisms have referred to this practice as the "ultimate expression of American Imperialism" (Ryan, 1983, p. 51) and a "new form of colonialism" (Tizard, 1991, p. 746). For more than 50 years, children have been placed both internationally and transracially in the United States, starting with the relinquishment of Korean children during and following the Korean War (Kim, 1978; Wilkinson, 1995). Within the past 30 years, even more countries have placed children in the United States. In fact, many of the children currently available for international adoption were not orphaned through wars or disasters but were relinquished due to poverty, social ostracism (e.g., biracial children), or population control mandates (Bartholet, 1993; Wilkinson, 1995). A more detailed history of Korean adoption, by McGinnis, can be found in Chapter 11.

Federal legislation, the Multiethnic Placement Act (MEPA), was implemented in 1994 and further refined in 1996 through the Interethnic Placement Act (IEPA), to attenuate the controversy around transracial placements and to provide guidelines for federally funded adoption agencies. With the goal of protecting children and parents around the world and preventing child trafficking and abuse, the Hague Convention on Protection of Children and Cooperation in Respect of Intercountry Adoption was introduced at the United Nations in 1993 and has since been ratified by 67 countries (Hague Conference on Private International Law, 2005). Only three countries that are member states of the Hague Conference (the United States, the Russian Federation, and Ireland) have yet to ratify the Hague Convention and thereby make the conditions of the Convention legally binding. In the United States, the Intercountry Adoption Act of 2000 was passed as a measure to ratify the Hague Convention, but as of November 2005, formal processes to fully ratify the Convention were designed but not yet enacted (U.S. Department of State, 2006).

Despite new policies that permit and support both international adoption and transracial adoption (which, by definition, can also be international—see Chapter 7), these placements continue to foster controversy politically, socially, and psychologically. To better understand the dynamics that occur in TIAs, the influence that culture has on attitudes toward adoption and the practice of adoption can begin to help clarify the questions, create bridges for understanding and serving these individuals and their families, and demystify the issues surrounding TIA.

Some primary areas to consider when assessing individual, community, and social attitudes toward TIA include (1) the stigma associated with adoption for both domestic and international adoptions; (2) the stigma associated with single parenthood, relinquishment, and gender of the child; and (3) the social, political, and economic contexts in which children are relinquished, abandoned, and orphaned.

CURRENT PERSPECTIVES: RELINQUISHMENT ABROAD

The policies that have shaped the status of adoption abroad have resulted from a wide array of events, including international conflicts, civil wars, AIDS epidemics, population control, social constraints, and of course, poverty. These events encompass social, political, and economic factors that have clearly had a far-reaching impact on adoption practice and mechanisms as well as on attitudes toward adoption. The perspectives that nations, governments, society, and people form about adoption domestically and internationally have power far beyond the adoption agency. Within the adoption constellation, birth parents, adoptive parents, and adopted persons are often exposed to those messages (e.g., adoption is a "second best" way to form a family, China does not value females) so that they may in turn be influenced by them and possibly even internalize them before ever exposing them to scrutiny. Additional perspectives on TIA can be found by examining the social structure of various countries. Social structures within countries have direct effects on the family unit, and these structures are often influenced by attitudes and beliefs that encompass national pride (e.g., racial and ethnic homogeneity), cultural values (e.g., Confucian ideals and teachings), and religion (e.g., Christianity). Thus, social norms as evidenced by family structure, family rules, and cultural values provide insight into cultural perspectives on adoption in adoptees' countries of origin. To gain awareness of a multifaceted perspective, the countries from which children were adopted and the countries to which they were adopted can serve as foundations for this exploration. In this chapter, the social structure and norms in China as well as those in the United States may provide substantial insight into some of the challenges and successes that Chinese adoptees in the United States may encounter.

Relinquishment, abandonment, and deaths of caregivers are the three primary means by which children both in the United States and abroad become orphaned and available for adoption. Various political, social, and economic factors have been cited as leading to the availability of these children (Rojewski, Shapiro, & Shapiro, 2000). Interestingly, when making attributions for relinquishment domestically (i.e., children born to American people and relinquished in the United States), individuals may cite teen pregnancies, poverty, religion, drug dependence, or the challenges of single parenting as reasons. However, when making attributions for relinquishment in international adoption, individuals may tend to assume homogeneity in both the foreign people and in the explanations given for relinquishment—that is, they may cite a single reason or two to explain decisions to relinquish rather than examine the complexity of adoption in other countries and cultures. Adoption researchers and policymakers worked to educate the public to be aware of the plight of families in the nations that provide the most frequent source of adoptable children internationally—China (the PRC) and Russia. The reasons for the availability may be simply stated as "the one-child policy" in China (Johnson, 2004) or the political and economic unrest and the resultant poverty found in Russia (Homestudies and Adoption Placement Services [HAPS], n.d.). Regardless of the simplicity with which these reasons are cited, the impact of these and other more complex and variable reasons found for relinquishment is likely to be significant in the transracially and internationally adopted child, adolescent, or adult.

The explanations that are "used," "found," or even "given" for relinquishment abroad basically constitute the frame through which researchers, practitioners, adoption triad members, and society view the culture of a given country. Thus if China has been "framed" as abandoning female infants in favor of male infants due to a one-child policy, the influence of that perception on how families and children adopted from China relate to China is likely to be substantial. But what will that influence be? In essence, answers to a series of questions such as the following will likely assist in assessing this influence: (1) How do people in the United States view international adoption and international adoptees? (2) How do individuals in China view international adoption and international adoptees? (3) How do Americans and people in other countries view international versus domestic adoption? (4) How are international adoptees affected by these views?

To begin to answer these questions, this chapter will focus on the policies, economics, social structure, and international adoption from the PRC. As the leading source of children adopted internationally to the United States, China represents this dilemma well. Chinese children adopted transracially by White American parents represent the largest portion of these international adoptions, thus making them transracial and international adoptees.

The Case of Chinese Adoptions: The People's Republic of China

Given the 50-plus years of international adoptions from South Korea to the United States, examinations of Chinese adoptions typically draw on the history of South Korean adoptions, the experiences of and outcomes for adult Korean adoptees, and the social and political climate surrounding these adoptions.

Relinquishment in South Korea

Comparisons made between international adoptions from Korea and China are complex, given the differing circumstances surrounding relinquishment (e.g., reasons given for relinquishment, adoption plans, abandonment, governmental policies regarding relinquishment). For example, a South Korean birth mother who was living in an unwed mothers' home was encouraged to write the letter below to her unborn child by the social workers in the home.

> *Seoul, South Korea*
>
> *My baby, what can I say to you. . . . I fear that you will not believe what I have to say. I do hope that you will believe me when I say that I love you, my daughter. I know that no matter what I say I cannot be forgiven, but I hope that you will come to understand me a little.*
>
> *My baby, when you grow up you may ask why your mother gave you up for adoption abroad. You may think that if you had grown up in Korea and had been adopted by a Korean family, you would not have gone through so much hardship. However, when I was faced with the decision of giving you up for adoption I believed that you would be better off in a country where you would be given an equal chance.*
>
> *The reason I did not give you up for domestic adoption was that children adopted in Korea, even if they are not born out of wedlock, are discriminated against and looked down upon. Even if your adoptive parents tried to keep the fact of your adoption a secret, eventually it would be revealed. When I considered how you would be shocked when you found out too late that you had been adopted, I had to decide that it would be best for you to be adopted abroad.*
>
> *My baby, if you understand me a little, I hope that you will realize that I want you to love your adoptive parents. Even though I am your biological mother, I could not provide you with the loving environment that you need. I admit that I was irresponsible. Your adoptive parents, even though they are not your biological parents, will care for you with all the love and attention they can give . . . I will never forget you but I will always pray for you. My love for you will continually grow.*
>
> *I love you.*
>
> *From your loving mother* (Dorow, 1999, pp. 44–45; reprinted by permission of Yeong & Yeong Book Company.)

When reading this letter, it is important to remember that birth mothers in China do not relinquish their children while living with other women making similar decisions or while under the care of a social worker. In fact, most of the circumstances surrounding the relinquishment of children differ between South Korean birth mothers and Chinese birth mothers (in the PRC). However, as McGinnis (Chapter 11) described, some similarities can be found if the history of adoption (30 to 50 years ago) in Korea is considered. Despite those similarities, adoption from South Korea within the past 25 years has been quite different. Another letter contains the following paragraph.

> *I reproached myself for being so bad, and cried with my heart aching and tearing apart. I thought about raising you by myself, but it would be hard, especially in Korea where the Confucian ideas are deeply rooted in society. So I decided to send you to good parents who could make you happy. I was in agony and despair, but now I have decided to live just praying for you.* (Dorow, 1999, pp. 19–20)

These letters reflect the cultural climate that exists in Korea and other countries where single parenthood and birth by an unwed mother is socially unacceptable. Other letters reflect the desire for reunions with their relinquished children ("Even though I wish to meet you someday, it is up to you" [Dorow, 1999, p. 38]) and demonstrate that such reunions may be possible despite popular belief that birth parents in these countries will not seek such reunions.

One area not fully elucidated in the research on international adoption includes the need for understanding the cultural, political, and social reasons for relinquishing children in countries outside the United States as well as the psychological impact of those reasons on birth parents. For example, on a visit to South Korea, the author visited Ae Ran Won, a home in Seoul for unwed birth mothers who were relinquishing their children for adoption both internationally and domestically. The birth mothers expressed deep regret, sorrow, and shame for their decision but felt they had few options for their survival. Given the social stigma, poverty, social structure of Korean society, and lack of social support, the women felt that they had no choice but to relinquish their child. Without the father of the child to affirm paternity and thereby enable the child to be legally registered, the child would have no status in Korean society and could not legally attend Korean schools or have a future free from poverty. Furthermore, unwed, Korean single mothers would face severe moral stigma and social disenfranchisement as a result of their status (Kim & Davis, 2003).

Relinquishment in China

Political, social, and economic reasons affecting the relinquishment or abandonment of infants in China should also be further understood. Johnson, Banghan, and Liyao (1998) detailed the misunderstandings in China's infamous one-child policy and explained the gender bias toward female abandonment as follows:

> Sons are necessary to continue the patrilineal family line and all that this stands for in the family-centered culture and religious life of rural China. Most importantly, sons are permanent members of their father's family and are still the major source of support for elderly parents in old age since rural China, outside of a few wealthy suburban areas, lacks a social security system. Daughters "marry away" and join their husband's family, where they are obligated to support his parents. The main problem with daughters is that they "belong to other people." (p. 475)

Johnson et al. (1998) also described the double bind that birth parents face if they have a child that forces them over their quota of one in urban areas and two in rural areas (if the first is a girl). Voluntary relinquishment of a child is illegal and does not exist. Abandonment of children carries with it stiff financial penalties, if one is caught, that are similar to fines imposed by the Chinese government for "overquota" children (approximately a year's income), in addition to mandatory sterilization for the mothers. Thus, families already struggling to survive must choose between even more severe poverty to keep the child and risking abandonment without being caught.

Chang (2003) described the origins of the infamous "one-child policy" as tied to Mao Zedong's (aka Tse-tung) belief that birth control was a form of genocide and the Deng administration's creation of that policy to control the exploding population in China. In exchange for adherence to the policy, families received better government benefits, whereas violation of the policy resulted in heavy fines. The long social history of Chinese women as childbearers, whose worth was measured on their ability to produce sons and care for their families (Lee, 1997), was difficult to change with governmental policies, so Chinese couples resorted to hiding daughters with relatives, abandonment, and even infanticide (Chang, 2003). When abandonment was chosen, couples often cited the pressure from the government and their hopes to recover their daughters at some point (Johnson, 2004). For example, one couple wrote,

> This baby girl was born on 1992 at 5:30 A.M. and is now 100 days old. . . . She is in good health and has never suffered any illness. Because of the current political situation and heavy pressures that are too difficult to explain, we, who were her parents for these first days, cannot continue taking care of her. We can only hope that in this world there is a kind-hearted person who will care for her. Thank you.
>
> In regret and shame, your father and mother. (Johnson, 2004, p. 75)

In essence, due to the illegality of relinquishing children for adoption, the social, cultural, and familial pressure to produce a male heir, and government birth-planning policies, the abandonment of infant girls was described by Johnson (2004) as reflecting a continuum of care in adoption planning. That is, many instances of female infant abandonment might be appropriately viewed as ranging from abandonment while hoping for the best to carefully developing what might be considered an alternative adoption plan. The Chinese couples that Johnson and her colleagues interviewed reported choosing crowded areas where the children would be likely to be found, doorsteps of families who were childless or had only sons, or other towns or places where they could see their children found yet stay anonymous and undetected.

Although a continuum certainly exists among the forethought and planning that went into the relinquishment, the choices made by birth parents in China who willfully violated birth-planning policies and abandoned their children must be examined as it affects Chinese adoptees and their families. The reality of relinquishment in China and the culture of abandonment are likely to become very powerful elements of Chinese adoptees' conceptions of their adoptions.

Attitudes Toward Domestic Versus International Adoption in China

Orphaned children in China have historically been cared for in orphanages and have, throughout China's history, been adopted domestically. Although Confucian principles may be interpreted as emphasizing bloodlines and adoption only within those bounds, Johnson (2004) reported that many strains of Confucianism allow and support adoption across bloodlines as well as preferences for adopting nonrelatives due to the perceived permanency and lack of interference from birth families. In fact, Johnson's (2004) research in China and the Chinese governmental policies regulating domestic adoptions revealed that Chinese citizens do adopt children domestically. Johnson reported that most of the orphaned children who were formally adopted throughout the past 50 years were adopted by childless couples, often peasants from the countryside. Johnson described the cultural expectation and the resultant pressure from society that married couples have children (whether by birth or adoption) as being of vital importance and as an obligation in the culture. Foundlings, as abandoned infants are often called, who were placed on the doorsteps of specific families that relinquishing parents believed were in the position to adopt, were often adopted either formally or informally by the families who "found" the children, at a rate of about 23% (86 of 370 cases of females) (Johnson, 2004). In fact, many of the families who adopted foundlings were considered "chaoboa," or overquota adopters, and they defy the common stereotype that only international adopters want these "lost daughters of China" (Johnson, 2004, p. 159).

Interestingly, adoption has yet to be fully destigmatized in Chinese society. Many adoptive families hide the adoption status from their children, and for many years couples with children were routinely banned from adopting because politicians feared that adopted children would be treated differently and with less privilege than their nonadopted siblings (Johnson, 2004). Despite the stigma, however, Johnson (2004) reported that "contemporary adoptive parents routinely insist that adopted children have the same status as birth children and are raised and treated 'as if born to' the parents" (p. 141). The support for and practice of domestic adoption within China reinforces the contention that domestic adoption can and would be practiced widely in China, given the legal statutes allowing these adoptions. However, the one-child policy continues to limit this practice.

A major factor that depicts the attitudes of Chinese people toward adoption, however, has frequently been tied to gender and the place of males and females in the strict patrilineal society of China. In China, bloodlines follow the males and sons care for parents in their old age. Thus, in an orphanage in Wuhan, Johnson (2004) reported that very few male children were relinquished and those that were, either healthy or with disabilities, were typically adopted immediately. Female infants, on the other hand, accounted for almost all the orphaned children. Despite the documented disparities in the number of abandoned male versus female children, for many years prior to the more strictly enforced population control policies, many orphaned female infants were adopted. Females were often adopted because of the scarcity of infant boys available for adoption.

The patrilineal society that seems to support and sustain the preference for males over females has led to great confusion as well as problematic assumptions about the character of the Chinese people and the values in Chinese culture. Families have asked, "How could they abandon those children?" Children have asked, "Don't they like girls?" The assumptions have oversimplified the availability of children in China as being related only to the one-child policy and to the character of a nation of people who seem to devalue females. Yet little, if any, attention was given to the growing segment of the Chinese adoptive parents who adopted foundlings or abandoned children domestically within China. These families have routinely been overlooked, and international adopters have been characterized as the primary means for reducing the number of orphans in China (Johnson, 2004).

With all the attention focused on the abandonment of children and the limitations surrounding the domestic adoptions of these orphans, the literature has yet to examine the attitudes that Chinese citizens and Chinese Americans have toward the international adoptions of these Chinese children. Anecdotal evidence from families seen in therapy or in adoption workshops by the author paints a picture in which Chinese people in the United States refer to the adopted Chinese girls as "lucky" and thank the adoptive parents for raising them. In essence, families have reported reactions that suggest Chinese people in the United States may view these children as Chinese citizens in the care of these American adoptive families, who must ensure that they preserve their ties to the Chinese culture and community. Furthermore, no evidence of international adoption of children from foreign nations to China (the PRC) was located, so Chinese citizens' attitudes toward the adoption of non-Chinese children to Chinese families could not be explored. Clearly, research on the attitudes of the Chinese community both within the PRC and in the United States deserves more systematic attention and understanding to fully account for their impact on adoptees' conceptions of their adoption history and experiences.

Attitudes Toward Domestic Versus International Adoption in the United States

The history of adoption in the United States, as noted above, is complex. Domestic adoption has been practiced in the United States both formally and informally throughout its history. From the orphan trains to expensive private adoptions, American couples have historically turned to adoption for various reasons (e.g., infertility, the desire to parent, altruism for orphaned children). However, as fewer healthy, White infants became available for adoption due to lowered voluntary relinquishment rates (Child Welfare Information Gateway, 2005) but more infertile White couples sought children, domestic and international transracial adoptions became alternative solutions (Zamostny, O'Brien, et al., 2003).

In the United States, domestic transracial adoptions have been controversial and complex. With respect to transracial adoption, the heterogeneity within the American population, the long history of controversy regarding transracial adoption within the United States (see Chapters 7 and 10), and the racial and ethnic composition of the children available for adoption all play vital roles in shaping the attitudes toward domestic transracial adoption. As the data from the U.S. Census of 2000 (Grieco & Cassidy, 2001) reflect, in 2000 the United States was composed of approximately 281,421,906 individuals. As shown in Table 8.2, 75.1% described themselves as White (69.1% as White, non-Hispanic and 12.5% as primarily White and Hispanic), 12.3% as Black or African American, 0.9% as American Indian or Alaskan Native, 3.6% as Asian, 0.1% as Native Hawaiian or other Pacific Islander, 5.5% as from some other race, and 2.4% as having two or more races. Interestingly, although White non-Hispanics dominate the population in the United States, the racial composition of the children available for domestic adoption via public agencies depicts very different proportions.

As of September 30, 2004, 119,000 children were in foster care and were waiting to be adopted (U.S. Department of Health and Human Services, 2005). Of those children, 37%

Table 8.2   Race/Ethnicity Reported on U.S. Census of 2000 and the Adoption and Foster Care Analysis and Reporting System for Fiscal Year (FY) 2003

Race/Ethnicity	U.S. Population During Census of 2000	Children in Foster Care Awaiting Adoption (FY 2003)		Children Adopted From Public Foster Care (FY 2004)	
Non-Hispanic	87.5%	102,450	86%	42,220	84%
White	69.1%	43,820	37%	20,940	42%
Black or African American	12.3%	47,630	40%	16,570	33%
Asian	3.6%	510	0%	320	1%
American Indian or Alaskan Native	0.9%	2,190	2%	700	1%
Hawaiian Native or Pacific Islander	0.1%	340	0%	130	0%
Some other race	5.5%		N/A		
Unknown/unable to determine	N/A	4,240	4%	1,370	3%
Two or more races	2.4%	3,720	3%	2,190	4%
Hispanic	12.5%	16,210	14%	7,900	16%
White and Hispanic	6%	N/A	N/A	N/A	N/A
Black or African and Hispanic	0.3%	N/A	N/A	N/A	N/A
Asian and Hispanic	0.1%	N/A	N/A	N/A	N/A
Some other race and Hispanic	5.3%	N/A	N/A	N/A	N/A
Two or more races and Hispanic	0.8%	N/A	N/A	N/A	N/A

NOTE: Percentages given reflect the percentages of the total population or sample reported. N/A = not applicable; information not reported.

were White and non-Hispanic, 14% were Hispanic, 40% were Black and non-Hispanic, 2% were American Indian and non-Hispanic, 0% were Asian and non-Hispanic, 0% were Native Hawaiian or other Pacific Islander and non-Hispanic, 4% were unknown or unable to determine, and 3% were described as having two or more races that were non-Hispanic. These figures reflect that children of color were disproportionately available for adoption as compared with their proportions within the U.S. population. However, the White children who were adopted during that same fiscal year were again somewhat disproportionately placed into adoptive homes. That is, although fewer White children than Black children were available for placement in 2003, more (47.79% of those available) were placed into adoptive homes than were Black children (only 34.79% of those available). This observation, in combination with reports of Black and biracial children being adopted in increasingly large numbers to Canada and to European countries, raises questions regarding the attitudes of American couples to domestic transracial adoptions. Although legislation has cleared transracial placements of children of color with White families, the data presented above paint a very different picture that suggests a need for more exploration regarding preferences for children available through foster care. Attitudes toward domestic transracial adoption have shown support for the practice of transracial adoption (Whatley, Jahangardi, Ross, & Knox, 2003), yet the prevalence of international adoptions in the face of so many waiting children in the United States urges a greater understanding of these dynamics. Perhaps the complicated family histories, the remnants of the cautions against adopting biracial and African American children (i.e., warnings from the NABSW), racial preferences and cultural biases, fears regarding permanency of placements, altruistic attitudes toward other countries, or the desire for infants might begin to explain some of these observations.

With respect to international adoption, Americans have been adopting internationally since after World War I. Since that time, hundreds of thousands of children born abroad have been adopted to the United States by American couples seeking children. In fact, the CWLA (2003) estimated that within the past 30 years, more than 250,000 foreign-born children had been adopted to the United States by American parents. However, the circumstances under which these children were internationally adopted varied based on the social and political climate of the time. Social and moral constraints on unwed mothers and single parents in the United States have lessened in the past 50 years, birthrates in the United States have decreased, and the rates of infertility have increased (Chang, 2003; Zamostny, O'Brien, et al., 2003), and these changes have led to an increased interest in international adoption. Furthermore, adoptee and birth-parent activism that challenged closed birth records and adoption secrecy and that normalized birth-parent searches led to greater openness in adoption (Zamostny, O'Brien, et al., 2003). A few highly publicized cases of adoptions where birth parents challenged the final relinquishment or changed their minds also contributed to the interest in international adoptions, which have often been referred to as more permanent adoptions where birth families were not likely to contest the adoption. Interestingly, out of 79 adoptive parents who responded to a survey by Rojewski (2005) and had adopted children from China, 12 parents chose China as the country from which they would adopt due to concerns about U.S. adoption laws, and an additional 9 parents chose China due to the assurance that there would be no potential parental claims on the child in the future.

Despite the long history of both domestic and international adoption in the United States, the stigma of adoption (March, 1995; Miall, 1987; Zamostny, Wiley, O'Brien, Lee, & Baden, 2003) has been an ongoing challenge for adoptive families and adopted persons. Attitudes toward adoption frequently reflect the stigma that may be both American and universal. For example, Miall (1987) reported that 71 involuntarily childless women shared their beliefs regarding societal perceptions of adoption as indicating that biological ties are vital for love and bonding, bonding and love via adoption is "second best," adopted children are "second rate" due to their unknown biological history, and adoptive parents are not viewed as "real parents" to their adopted children. Clearly, although there is greater awareness of the stigma surrounding adoption, it is yet to be eliminated.

Comparisons and Contrasts in History and Attitudes: China and the United States

As noted above, domestic adoption in China differs in the visibility of the adoptions and, clearly, the regulations that exist on adopting domestically. In both cases, families who would like to adopt domestically have difficulties, but the difficulties in the United States tend to be more related to availability of infants, especially White infants, and the concerns about permanency or problems when adopting domestically. Chinese families struggle due to governmental policies that bind families interested in domestic adoption based on population control policies (Johnson, 2004). Both countries struggle with issues of stigma, and both countries have past histories where adoption was seen as not serving the "best interests" of the children being adopted. Other differences have been rooted in social issues such as poverty and economic power. The relative wealth and prosperity of the American people as a whole in comparison with the Chinese families both relinquishing and adopting is a striking contrast. In 2005, the average per capita income for Americans was $41,800, whereas for Chinese from the PRC it was $6,200 (Central Intelligence Agency, 2006). Families in the United States have no restrictions on the number of children they can parent, and they have demonstrated their ability to financially support international adoption placements.

In contrast, Chinese families who would parent more children have governmental restrictions that limit their family size and economics that limit their ability to adopt internationally.

As is widely reported in the media and in popular culture, China has found itself in a position where gender preferences have led to a much skewed distribution of orphaned girls versus boys with far greater numbers of orphaned girls. The centuries-old tradition of needing male heirs for security and bloodlines can be found, to varying degrees, in both the United States and China. Both societies typically follow a patriarchal line for families; however, the greater degree of poverty in China in conjunction with mandates on family size may have complicated this similarity so that differences between the two countries have developed and emphasized the gender preference. That is, children abandoned and orphaned in China may not be as readily adopted domestically due to stringent regulations on family size even through adoption (Johnson, 2004), and more children are abandoned and orphaned due to those same regulations on family size. Although no clear formula can be derived from the circumstances that account for the values, laws, and social structure, it is clear that the United States and China have as many similarities as they have differences. However, the negative conceptualization of the attitudes, values, and practices of each country may fail to acknowledge these similarities. In fact, the negative stereotypes of the Chinese character that exist in the United States today (Chang, 2003) are likely to affect the manner in which Chinese adoptees conceptualize themselves and their identities and how they incorporate their understanding of their history into their lives.

Clinical Implications: Attitudes, Perceptions, Motivations, and Their Impact on Adoptees

Given all the complexities involved in TIAs and the subsequent attitudes that exist in China and the United States, Chinese adoptees are likely to be affected by (1) the perceptions they have about the status of adoption both in their country of origin and in the country to which they were adopted, (2) the way adoptees relate to their birth culture and their adopted culture, (3) the information they receive about their adoptions (e.g., demographics), and (4) their assessment of the information they receive. As argued above, the perceptions that Chinese adoptees have about Chinese and American attitudes both toward adoption and toward them as adoptees may have a substantial impact on this assessment.

The information that Chinese adoptees receive about their adoption includes, but is not limited to, the following: (1) why they were relinquished (e.g., unwed mother, birth-planning policies, death of family members), (2) when they were relinquished (e.g., age and date if known, immediately after birth or following some extended period of time), (3) how they were relinquished (e.g., "abandoned" or "placed where he or she would be found"), (4) where they were relinquished (e.g., train station, hospital, street), (5) where they lived and with whom after they were relinquished (e.g., orphanage, foster care, Ahma or caregiver in China), (6) who relinquished them (e.g., married couple, single woman, other descriptors of birth families), (7) why they were adopted (e.g., adoptive parents were infertile, wanted to help needy children, wanted to become parents), (8) when they were adopted into the family (e.g., the date often called their Gotcha Day, Adoption Day, Family Day, or Special Day), (9) who chose to adopt them (e.g., mom wanted to adopt, dad was cautious); (10) what they were named prior to adoption (e.g., their given Chinese names), (11) what place they fill in their adoptive families (e.g., only adoptee, older sister), and (12) what physical, social, and/or emotional characteristics described them as infants and made them both able to be relinquished and able to be adopted. In addition to this information, Chinese adoptees may seek and receive information about Chinese culture and may apply that information to fill in gaps in their understanding or even to replace information that they may doubt or question. Thus, the content of adoptees' stories as well as the manner in which the stories are told may powerfully affect Chinese adoptees' self-concept, identity, self-esteem, and connection to their country and culture of origin. The effective clinical treatment of Chinese adoptees necessitates the consideration of the various facets of information that a Chinese adoptee may receive about his or her adoption.

Case Study

Presenting Issues: Lily, a 12-year-old girl adopted from China by Caucasian American parents, had been asking questions about her adoption and was expressing anger, social withdrawal, and discomfort with her appearance. Lily was resisting attending school and was complaining of hating her "slanty" eyes. Lily's mother contacted the agency that they used to adopt for a referral.

Preadoptive Background: Lily was born in the Anhui Province in China and was abandoned outside of a hospital when she was 3 days old. A note was pinned to her shirt that gave her birth date as November 4, 1993. The orphanage director named her Mei Lin, and she was raised by orphanage care workers and "grandmas" (nonrelated, retired care workers). Mei Lin was placed with her adoptive parents, John and Anne O'Neill, when she was 11 months old. Mei Lin was small for her age and malnourished but otherwise healthy. The O'Neills returned with Mei Lin to their home in a suburb of New York City and renamed her Lily.

Adoptive Background: John O'Neill, a 49-year-old White American man of Irish and British descent, and Anne O'Neill, a 47-year-old White American woman of English, Welsh, and Irish descent, were married for 5 years when they adopted Lily. John is a lawyer and Anne is a writer. They have no other children, and both were previously married and divorced. They received treatments for infertility and decided to adopt from China when conception seemed unlikely. Growing up, Lily had playgroups with both adopted (many Chinese adopted) and nonadopted children (primarily White, middle-class children). Lily knew many families like hers.

Treatment Issues: After developing rapport and trust with Lily, the therapist's questions about Lily's classes at school revealed that her teacher in social studies had just covered a unit on China and the culture. The teacher described birth-planning policies as a means for decreasing the population in China and taught them about Confucius and the importance of male heirs and filial piety. When Lily went home, she searched the Internet and read more about adoption from China. Lily had always known that most of the other adoptees from China were girls, but the explanations she had received tended to be unclear. As Lily read more and remembered conversations she had heard, she recalled hearing that in China, girls were "just thrown away." She struggled with her competing feelings: Chinese people are "heartless" and "cruel," yet she herself was Chinese and did not believe that about herself. Lily also thought that Chinese men and boys must be "mean" because she had met very few and she deduced that they must not like girls because they only wanted boys in their families. She did not like the preference that seemed to exist for boys. The therapist began discussing Lily's perceptions of her birth country, and Lily was able to articulate her until then unspoken fear of Chinese people. Through the psychoeducational use of books and films, Lily began to develop a more realistic and factual understanding of Chinese culture. As therapy progressed, Lily began to discuss her worries about her birth family, their poverty, and whether they thought about her. She was just beginning to process some emotions about her adoption but was more focused on correcting some of the negative stereotypes about Chinese people and about her birth parents that she had grown up hearing. Lily became interested in learning more about Chinese culture, but she wanted to know what people believed and valued instead of just about clothes, food, dances, and celebrations. The therapist worked with the family to introduce them to opportunities where they could meet some Chinese American people (families including adults and teens) and begin to replace stereotypes about China with real information. The therapist explored Lily's negative perceptions about her appearance and helped her and her parents to understand how she had internalized negative judgments and stereotypes about China and Chinese people. Using this multicultural model for increasing awareness and self-acceptance enabled Lily and her parents to become aware of the oppression and racism that Lily had experienced. Lily's parents participated in an awareness workshop on White Racial Awareness and became invested in finding Chinese American mentors for Lily who could help support her and guide her to more effectively cope with discrimination, develop more positive models of Chinese people and culture, and increase her self-esteem and pride in being Chinese American.

As the case study above illustrates, adoptees' perceptions and beliefs about their adoptions may significantly affect their adjustment. Those perceptions and beliefs are affected by what adoptees know about their adoptions as well as the cultural context from which they came (China) and into which they were adopted (middle-class American). Although this case is just one example of how their perceptions can affect the way adoptees process their experiences, it reflects the complexity that clinicians who work with adoptees must be prepared to examine.

RESEARCH AND FUTURE IMPLICATIONS

This chapter reflects the need for increased study of the cultural context into which international transracial adoptees are adopted. The cultural context discussed in this chapter is based on Chinese adoptions, but no empirical validation of these observations about society and about clinical practice has been done. To prepare adoption workers, agency professionals, mental health workers, and families to assist Chinese adoptees in their adjustment and negotiation of their cultural and racial identities, more work in this area should be conducted. Qualitative research with Chinese adoptees using the Cultural-Racial Identity Model (Baden & Steward, 2000) may help clarify their experiences and help contextualize their integration of American and Chinese cultures, attitudes toward adoption, and racial identification.

Other gaps in our understanding of international adoption include the cultural contexts that exist within other leading countries from which children have been internationally adopted. For example, as Table 8.1 shows, the Russia Federation, Guatemala, South Korea, and Kazakhstan all have histories and attitudes toward adoption that have not been sufficiently explored. The international adoptees from these countries will seek and need assistance in clarifying and contextualizing their adoptions, so research in these areas is vital.

REFLECTION QUESTIONS

1. What might Chinese adoptees internalize about Chinese people and culture? How could that affect them?

2. How does knowing about adoption attitudes in the United States and in China affect the Chinese adoptees?

3. Why might Chinese children or teens develop negative perceptions of their birth culture and ethnic group?

REFERENCES

Andujo, E. (1988). Ethnic identity of transethnically adopted Hispanic adolescents. *Social Work*, 33(6), 531–535.

Baden, A. L., & Steward, R. J. (2000). A framework for use with racially and culturally integrated families: The Cultural-Racial Identity Model as applied to transracial adoption. *Journal of Social Distress & the Homeless, 9*(4), 309–337.

Barnes, J. S., & Bennett, C. E. (2002, February). *The Asian population: 2000.* Retrieved April 10, 2006, from www.aasc.ucla.edu/cic/data/c2kbr01-16.pdf

Bartholet, E. (1993). International adoption: Current status and future prospects. *Future of Children, 3*(1), 89–103.

Brodzinsky, D. M., & Steiger, C. (1991). Prevalence of adoptees among special education populations. *Journal of Learning Disabilities, 24*(8), 484–489.

Cederblad, M., Höök, B., Irhammar, M., & Mercke, A.-M. (1999). Mental health in international adoptees as teenagers and young adults: An epidemiological study. *Journal of Child Psychology & Psychiatry, 40*(8), 1239–1248.

Central Intelligence Agency. (2006). *The world factbook.* Retrieved February 12, 2006, from https://www.cia.gov/cia/publications/factbook/rankorder/2004rank.html

Chang, I. (2003). *The Chinese in America: A narrative history.* New York: Penguin Books.

Child Welfare Information Gateway. (2005). *Voluntary relinquishment for adoption: Numbers and trends.* Retrieved August 14, 2006, from http://www.childwelfare.gov/pubs/s_place.cfm

Child Welfare League of America. (2003). *International Adoption: Trends and Issues.* Retrieved August 5, 2005, from http://ndas.cwla.org/include/text/IssueBrief_International_Adoption_FINAL.pdf

Dorow, S. (Ed.). (1999). *I wish for you a beautiful life: Letters from the Korean birth mothers of Ae Ran Won to their children.* St. Paul, MN: Yeong & Yeong.

Grieco, E. M., & Cassidy, R. C. (2001). *Overview of race and Hispanic origin: Census 2000 brief.* Retrieved April 10, 2006, from www.census.gov/prod/2001pubs/c2kbr01-1.pdf

Hague Conference on Private International Law. (2005). *33: Convention of 29 May 1993 on protection of children and co-operation in respect of intercountry adoption.* Retrieved November 21, 2005, from http://hcch.e-vision.nl/index_en.php?act=conventions.text&cid=69

Homestudies and Adoption Placement Services [HAPS]. (n.d.). *Information for prospective parents: Russian Federation.* Retrieved December 20, 2005, from http://haps.org/rusppinfo.html

Huh, N. S. (1997). Korean children's ethnic identity formation and understanding of adoption. *Dissertation Abstracts International Section A: Humanities & Social Sciences, 58*(2), 586.

Johnson, K. A. (2004). *Wanting a daughter, needing a son: Abandonment, adoption, and orphanage care in China.* St. Paul, MN: Yeong & Yeong.

Johnson, K. A., Banghan, H., & Liyao, W. (1998). Infant abandonment and adoption in China. *Population and Development Review, 24*(3), 469-510.

Kim, D. S. (1978). Issues in transracial and transcultural adoption. *Social Casework, 59,* 447–486.

Kim, E., & Davis, K. (2003). Conceptualizing unmarried motherhood in South Korea: The role of patriarchy and Confucianism in the lives of women. *Journal of Social Work Research and Evaluation, 4*(1), 107–120.

Lee, E. (1997). Overview: The assessment and treatment of Asian American families. In E. Lee (Ed.), *Working with Asian Americans* (pp. 3–36). New York: Guilford Press.

Lee, R. M. (2003). The transracial adoption paradox: History, research, and counseling implications of cultural socialization. *The Counseling Psychologist, 31*(6), 711–744.

Liu, J., Wyshak, G., & Larsen, U. (2004). Physical well-being and school enrollment: A comparison of adopted and biological children in one-child families in China. *Social Science & Medicine, 59*(3), 609–623.

March, K. (1995). Perception of adoption as social stigma: Motivation for search and reunion. *Journal of Marriage & the Family, 57*(3), 653–660.

McRoy, R. G., Zurcher, L. A., Lauderdale, M. L., & Anderson, R. E. (1984). The identity of transracial adoptees. *Social Casework, 65*(1), 34–39.

Miall, C. E. (1987). The stigma of adoptive parent status: Perceptions of community attitudes toward adoption and the experience of informal social sanctioning. *Family Relations: Journal of Applied Family & Child Studies, 36*(1), 34–39.

National Association of Black Social Workers. (1972). *NABSW opposes transracial adoption* (Report). New York: Author.

Rojewski, J. W. (2005). A typical American family? How adoptive families acknowledge and incorporate Chinese cultural heritage in their lives. *Child & Adolescent Social Work Journal, 22*(2), 133–164.

Rojewski, J. W., Shapiro, M. S., & Shapiro, M. (2000). Parental assessment of behavior in Chinese adoptees during early childhood. *Child Psychiatry & Human Development, 31*(1), 79–96.

Ryan, A. S. (1983). Intercountry adoption and policy issues. *Journal of Children in Contemporary Society, 15*(3), 49–60.

Shireman, J. F., & Johnson, P. R. (1986). A longitudinal study of Black adoptions: Single parent, transracial, and traditional. *Social Work, 31*(3), 172–176.

Simon, R. J., & Alstein, H. (2000). *Adoption across borders: Serving the children in transracial and intercountry adoptions.* New York: Rowman & Littlefield.

Smith, D. W., & Sherwen, L. N. (1988). The bonding process between mothers and their adopted children. In E. J. Anthony & C. Chiland (Eds.), *Child in his family, Vol. 8: Perilous development: Child raising and identity formation under stress* (pp. 105–115). Oxford, UK: Wiley.

Steele, M., Hodges, J., Kaniuk, J., Hillman, S., & Henderson, K. (2003). Attachment representations and adoption: Associations between maternal states of mind and emotion narratives in previously maltreated children. *Journal of Child Psychotherapy, 29*(2), 187–205.

Tizard, B. (1991). Intercountry adoption: A review of the evidence. *Journal of Child Psychology & Psychiatry, 32*(5), 743–756.

U.S. Department of Health and Human Services. (2005, April). *The AFCARS Report: Preliminary FY 2003 estimates as of April 2005 (10).* Retrieved February 6, 2006, from www.acf.hhs.gov/programs/cb/stats_research/afcars/tar/report10.pdf

U.S. Department of State. (2006). *Immigrant visas issued to orphans coming to the U.S.* Retrieved February 4, 2006, from http://travel.state.gov/family/adoption/stats/stats_451.html

Ward, M., & Lewko, J. H. (1987). Adolescents in families adopting older children: Implications for service. *Child Welfare, 66*(6), 539–547.

Whatley, M., Jahangardi, J. N., Ross, R., & Knox, D. (2003). College student attitudes toward transracial adoption. *College Student Journal, 37*(3), 323–326.

Wilkinson, H. S. (1995). Psycholegal process and issues in international adoption. *American Journal of Family Therapy, 23*(2), 173–183.

Zamostny, K. P., O'Brien, K. M., Baden, A. L., & Wiley, M. O. (2003). The practice of adoption history, trends, and social context. *The Counseling Psychologist, 31*(6), 651–678.

Zamostny, K. P., Wiley, M. O., O'Brien, K. M., Lee, R. M., & Baden, A. L. (2003). Breaking the silence: Advancing knowledge about adoption for counseling psychologists. *The Counseling Psychologist, 31*(6), 647–650.

Moving Beyond the Controversy of the Transracial Adoption of Black and Biracial Children

9

RHONDA M. ROORDA

Transracial Adoption Advocate

What are the implications for children who are adopted by parents who are racially and ethnically different? Do these children grow up to be psychologically healthy, and with which ethnic group will they identify? Will these children be able to function in dual societies when they become adults? Does race even matter? These are vital questions and concerns that have spawned intense discussion in the public arena and among social work professionals, political organizations, scholars, and families for more than three decades.

The issue of transracial adoption, particularly the adoption of Black and Biracial children into White homes in this nation, is a fascinating subject. The issue ignites great curiosity about the development of adoptees in this situation and the responsibilities and roles of the adoptive parents, siblings, the extended family, and the community in guiding transracially adopted children into healthy adulthoods. This type of adoption brings the issues of race, identity, love, belonging, forgiveness, and racial reconciliation into the forefront for adoptees and their adoptive families.

In recent years, transracial adoptees who were adopted in infancy or early childhood have come into adulthood and have generated numerous contributions to our understanding of the outcomes of transracial adoption. Through the personal accounts of adult transracial adoptees and via books, films, and scholarly work done by transracial adoptees or other adoption triad members, the knowledge, awareness, and familiarity with the issues linked to transracial adoption have grown substantially, but much more territory must still be covered. Transracial adoption and its attendant results and impacts must be studied and be viewed as a priority in academia and within our social structures for the sake of those who are directly involved—the transracial adoptive families and children.

This chapter will examine some of the groundbreaking research and critical thought at the heart of the transracial adoption controversy, which centers primarily on the identity formation of Black and Biracial children adopted by White parents. From that premise, the findings reflected in the book *In Their Own Voices: Transracial Adoptees Tell Their Stories* (Simon & Roorda, 2000), which featured firsthand accounts about the experiences of Black and Biracial adoptees, will be explored. What do the findings reflected in that book and the impact of the transracial adoption controversy mean for Black and Biracial children adopted by White parents today? One useful way to answer this is to extract key information from these "pioneers" of the 1970s and 1980s who set the stage for the discussion and exploration of the study of domestic transracial adoptions to occur. Another way is to listen to the stories of those adoptees struggling with their identity and to learn from them. Using the perspectives offered in both the empirical and personal literature, researchers, practitioners, and leaders in ethnically diverse communities can better assist adoptive parents in creating strategic avenues through which transracial adoptees (children, adolescents, and adults) can most effectively develop a knowledge base that enables them to embrace their ethnic heritage(s) and communities, their adoptive families, and most important, themselves. This chapter aims to serve as a critical review of the literature and theory relevant to transracial adoption and as a practical resource for adoptive parents and those who are affected by and, in turn, affect the lives of transracial adoptees so that they can develop psychologically, culturally, and spiritually. Research, theory, and practice as well as my own experience as an adoptee and with adult adoptees tell me that we must possess a greater understanding of the issues that have an impact on transracial adoptees to promote their development into dynamic citizens able to move into racially, ethnically, economically, and socially diverse worlds. Finally, this chapter will consider where we go from here. It should be a call to action and is targeted at adult adoptees, parents, mental health professionals, clergy, policymakers, scholars, and the general public.

LESSONS LEARNED: THE VIEWPOINT OF A TRANSRACIALLY ADOPTED ADULT

As an African American woman, adopted across the color line, whose identity was significantly influenced by her genetic makeup, foster care, and her own journey of transracial adoption, I recognize and appreciate the complexities and challenges inherent in finding a balance within oneself. I have worked to reconcile the true value of "who I am" as a person in my own skin with my unique talents and abilities, to learn and incorporate my ethnic heritage, and to value the love I have for my adoptive family. I've done all this while nurturing the love I've developed for myself amid a society that too often defines the limits of a person based on race. The level of self-confidence and the development of my identity were truly contingent on my honoring all of who I am. This is hard work, and at moments I feel as though I am walking a tightrope ready to go off balance. Yet I have seen excellent examples of balance, through my own adoptive experiences as well as through listening to adoptive families throughout the country. Many parents are raising children of color cross-culturally and are successfully creating bridges into their children's ethnic communities—efforts that are clearly in the best interests of their child and his or her blended family. This investment proves to yield unbelievable dividends. In cases like these, I see transracial adoption as a viable option for building families. I believe this choice must be viewed realistically, as a long-term commitment that requires awareness, intentionality, planning, flexibility, and humility on the part of adoptive parents, (biological) siblings, and adoptees. It also requires the guidance obtained through good and inclusive research on transracial adoption and through comprehensive training/counseling for adoptive families conducted by social work and mental health professionals.

Every child needs and deserves to be loved, to have shelter and nourishment. Every child deserves to grow roots in a family. But how do White adoptive parents raise Black and Biracial children to be culturally/racially confident and psychologically strong? The response to this question should expand the meaning of love to include empowering transracial adoptees to be able to successfully navigate and feel comfortable in different worlds simultaneously.

Transracial adoptees should be raised not only to be comfortable in their adoptive homes but also to be able to enter and thrive in a society that still perceives/judges individuals and their abilities on the basis of their skin color. Given this reality, the manner in which transracial adoptees choose to address the bias and complexities of racial relations will influence how they negotiate who they are, their personal/professional relationships and their worldview, and ultimately their success. Therefore, providing transracial adoptees early on in their lives with the tools that will teach them to value who they are as adoptees and persons with a rich cultural heritage is, in addition to love, essential.

When I think about identity, race, and culture, I compare it to a poetic jazz improvisation composed of unique and colorful sounds, all playing significant parts that ironically rely on each other but ultimately transform each other. To me, the beauty of a jazz and poetry ensemble is that it cannot be fully felt or appreciated in isolation. It needs to be heard in its entirety. African American writer Mari Evans (1992) wrote about the role of African American poetry, and she described poetry as being traditionally the essence of a people's culture that showcases who they are, what they feel, and how they view their surroundings. She stated:

> We are the sum and substance of all that is past. Racial and ethnic identities and histories have significantly shaped the climate in which we presently move, determining not only how we appear physically, but why we live as we do and, most importantly, why we think as we do. (p. 644)

Mari Evans continued by saying, "who we are, then, becomes a complexity of past and present, and when we go in search of ourselves, we often find the keys to ourselves in the poetry that reflects the culture of our people" (p. 644).

My story and the stories of other transracial adoptees are intertwined in a mosaic that includes the poetic voices inside each of us, in concert with the beat of our racial/ethnic histories, and the "chord" that is instrumental in binding us to our adoptive families. For that reason, I believe that social work professionals, policymakers, and researchers who seek to determine the ways in which White adoptive parents can successfully raise Black and Biracial children will find that their answer lies in seeking a qualitative and holistic approach in research and practice centered on these adoptees, their experiences, and the relationship they (and their adoptive families) have with members in their ethnic communities. If the hope is to promote healthy self-identities and self-esteem among Black and Biracial transracial adoptees, it seems that instead of quantitative research, a qualitative and inclusive methodology may prove to be a more flexible and effective approach for exploring the impact of transracial adoption on the identities of these adoptees in the long term.

History of the Transracial Adoption Controversy

To get to the heart of the transracial adoption controversy, it is crucial to go back to the early 1960s to fully comprehend the tone and content that shaped the fears and concerns about Black and Biracial children being raised by White parents. The practice of transracial adoption would change the trajectory and the rhythm in which these children struggled for their identities. In the 1960s during the Civil Rights Movement, society became aware of the acute needs of parentless Black children in America. Because of the increasing number of organized groups committed to meeting the needs of these children, public and private agencies began to feel pressured to permit adoption placements with White adults (Kennedy, 2003). By the late 1960s, the opinion of many progressive adoption professionals and agencies regarding adhering to a strict race-matching policy in placing available children shifted and became open to transracial placements, as reflected in the Child Welfare League of America (CWLA) Standards for Adoption Service in 1968 (Macaulay & Macaulay, 1978).

In fact, Kennedy (2003) observed that the CWLA changed its viewpoint both to advocate for transracial placements and to be mindful that problems did not arise with transracial placements. Subsequently, in 1971, there was a surge in transracial adoption placements of Black and Biracial children into White homes in the United States (Simon, Altstein, & Melli, 1994). While the numbers of same-race and transracial adoptions that occurred annually prior to 1975 are difficult to determine accurately due to incomplete data obtained by the U.S. government, it is estimated that approximately 12,000 Black children from 1968 to 1975 were placed with White families (Simon et al., 1994). Within this 7-year period, the greatest number of Black children to be transracially adopted (2,574) were adopted in 1971 (Simon et al., 1994); as a result, this became the turning point when the controversy regarding placing Black children into White homes was publicly raised.

Deeply concerned about the loss of Black children from their communities, the Black community mobilized to reclaim its children (Townsend, 1995). Fueled largely by the National Association of Black Social Workers (NABSW), opposition against the transracial adoption policy heightened. The controversy was further augmented and garnered national attention when in 1972, at the national conference of the NABSW, its president, William T. Merritt, announced on the record that "Black children should be placed only with Black families, whether in foster care or for adoption" (NABSW, as cited in Simon et al., 1994). The following excerpt taken from his speech embodied the tone and concern for the identity of Black children who were removed from their cultural heritage.

> Black children belong physically, psychologically and culturally in Black families in order that they receive the total sense of themselves and develop a sound projection of their future. . . . Black children in White homes are cut off from the healthy development of themselves as Black people. The socialization process for every child begins at birth. Included in the socialization process is the child's cultural heritage which is an important segment of the total process. This must begin at the earliest moment; otherwise our children will not have the background and knowledge which is necessary to survive in a racist society. This is impossible if the child is placed with White parents in a White environment. . . . We [the members of the NABSW] have committed ourselves to go back to our communities and work to end this particular form of genocide [transracial adoption]. (Simon et al., 1994, p. 40)

Also, during that same period, Leon Chestang (1972) became interested in the phenomenon of transracial adoption and its effects on the identities of Black and Biracial children. He recognized the dilemma that accompanies Biracial adoption and posed a series of critical questions to White parents who had adopted transracially or who were considering adopting a Black. He argued that transracial adoptive parents must consider (a) what they are "getting into" (p. 104), (b) whether they see their decision to adopt as humanitarian and without consequences, (c) whether they have considered the response or condemnation of friends and family, (d) whether they have thought about the personal consequences for their transracially adopted children, (e) whether they can relate to their children's needs, and (f) whether the families are trying to work through their own or through society's problems via the transracial adoption. Essentially, Chestang described the problems that Black children raised by White families are likely to experience and the outcomes of these adoptions. He predicted that, should these children survive, they have the potential to become catalysts for change in society (Chestang, 1972).

In response to the deep-seated concerns for these transracially adopted children expressed by those like Chestang and the NABSW, researchers and professionals primarily in the field of social work and child development set out to explore the legitimacy of such claims. Much of their work in the 1970s and 1980s was empirical in nature and looked at the extent to which Black/Biracial children adapted to their White adoptive families (compared with Black children adopted into Black families and White children adopted into White families). Their work also attempted to measure whether these children had a healthy sense of racial self-identity. A few landmark studies set the course for this exploration.

In 1977, Charles Zastrow, a doctoral student, compared the responses of 44 White couples who adopted a Black child with 44 White couples who adopted a White child. All these couples lived in Wisconsin and were grouped according to the age of their children and the socioeconomic status of the adoptive parents. All the children were reported to be preschoolers. In his work, Zastrow set out to measure the degree of satisfaction and difficulties both groups encountered with their adoptive placements. Data were obtained through in-home interviews with the adoptive parents and by reviewing the agency adoptive record material on these families. The outcome assessment of the study was then determined by the parents' overall satisfaction with their adoptive experience. The results reported cited that the outcomes of the transracial adoption placements were as successful as the inracial placements (Zastrow, 1977). On a subtle but important note, many of the transracial adoptive parents in the study indicated that they opted to become "color-blind" and accept their child as an individual who is a member of their family (Zastrow, 1977, p. 81).

Ruth McRoy, Louis Zurcher, Michael Lauderdale, and Rosalie Anderson conducted exploratory studies in which they examined the self-esteem and racial identity of Black transracial adoptees compared with Black inracial adoptees (McRoy et al., 1982) and assessed the adoptees' racial identities based on their adoptive parents' perceptions of their children's attitude toward their racial background (McRoy et al., 1984). In both studies, respondents—30 parents and 30 adoptees of at least 10 years of age in each study set— were selected from the Southwest, Midwest, and Upper Midwest regions of the United States and were identified through adoptive parents' groups and adoption agencies (McRoy et al., 1982, 1984). Teams of Black and White researchers interviewed parents and children.

In their 1982 study, McRoy and colleagues found that while the Black parents who adopted Black children lived in predominately Black communities (70%) and the majority of White parents who adopted Black children resided in predominately White communities (87%), the adoptees in both groups still exhibited similar levels of self-esteem, believing that they were persons of value (McRoy et al., 1982). Their findings suggested that these adoptees possessed healthy and positive feelings of self-regard regardless of the race of their adoptive parents. Yet when these same researchers looked at the racial identity of the Black transracial adoptees, their data revealed a correlation between (a) the perceptions the parents had of their children's identities and the communities in which they lived and (b) their children's perceptions of their own identities (McRoy et al., 1984). For example, those transracial adoptees whose families lived in a racially integrated community and who were exposed to people physically resembling themselves tended to identify themselves as Black persons and inwardly adopted positive self-images of their blackness (McRoy et al., 1984). But those adoptees who were raised separate from their ethnic communities tended to develop stereotyped impressions of Blacks and believed that they were advantaged by being in White families rather than in Black families. Interestingly, those children of color who were segregated from their ethnic communities (as occurred for the majority of the transracial adoptees in the study) felt an acute feeling of differentness. To compensate for this alienation, they tended to dismiss the importance of their racial identity and heritage and acted like their White peers and family members so as to appear normal.

Another landmark study, conducted by Joan Shireman and Penny Johnson (1986), was designed to measure the racial identity of 26 Black transracial adoptees whose parents were White compared (and studied separately) with that of 27 inracial Black adoptees from Black adoptive families; all were studied at preschool age (4 years old) and at 8 years of age and were living with their families in Chicago. The researchers used the well-known Clark and Clark Doll Test to determine how each of these children viewed themselves racially. At the first time point (age 4), they found that 71% of the transracially adopted children identified themselves as Black compared with 53% for the inracially adopted Black children. At age 8, equal percentages of both groups of children identified themselves as Black and displayed positive images of their blackness. Inherent in the report of Shireman and Johnson and contrary to the expectations of opponents to transracial adoption was the underlying message that Black transracial adoptees developed and maintained their positive racial identity despite living in predominately White communities. In essence, based on the results of their 4-year longitudinal study that found only a small but insignificant difference between the ways in which Black transracial and inracial adoptees viewed their racial identities, Shireman and Johnson concluded that adoption, including transracial adoption, is a good solution for children and families.

In an anticipated report, Rita J. Simon, Howard Altstein, and Marygold S. Melli (1994) published *The Case for Transracial Adoption* and announced the findings of their 20-year longitudinal study that attempted to answer the question of whether transracial adoption is in the best interests of the child. From 1971 to 1991, Simon and colleagues initially surveyed 206 transracial adoptive families with White parents in the Midwest. Unlike in the studies discussed earlier, Simon et al. interviewed families with adopted Black children as well as families who adopted other children of color, including Korean and Native American adoptees. They examined how relationships developed, particularly between the adoptive parents and the adoptees, and how parents' perceptions of their adopted children's racial identities varied over time. The report conveyed a positive message for White, prospective, adoptive parents and policymakers—transracial adoption was assessed as a viable option for children and families. Simon et al. concluded that during adolescence and adulthood, the transracial adoptees in their study were aware of and comfortable with their Black racial identity. These authors clearly advocated transracial adoption and asked policymakers and adoption professionals to provide permanent homes for children in foster care regardless of race.

Critique of the Empirical Research

The discussion and controversy surrounding transracial adoption is likely to be affected by the individual's connection to transracial adoption. For example, whether individuals are White adoptive parents in the process of caring for their Black/Biracial child, African American grandparents who informally adopted and fear the loss of Black children to the White community, or transracial adoptees in search of their identity, the lenses through which participants view their realities are important and valid to the discussion of transracial adoption. Sadly, these different viewpoints seldom get discussed on one stage because they appear polarized and on opposite sides of the abyss. Researchers and professionals in the field of child welfare would be remiss were they to fail to attend to those affected by transracial adoption. They must study this phenomenon from a multidimensional perspective to provide more enlightenment on how to assist adoptive parents in raising their Black/Biracial transracially adopted children to value themselves and how to most effectively navigate Black, Biracial, and White worlds as individuals and as persons of color.

But what are the implications of transracial adoption on the adoptees? The empirical studies highlighted in this chapter reflect the history and spirit of the core research that has been done on the transracial adoption of Black and Biracial children by White parents. The empirical literature has reported findings that suggest that children of color generally adapted to their White adoptive families and their predominately White surroundings (Zastrow, 1977); these transracial adoptees possessed a healthy sense of who they are (McRoy et al., 1982) and were aware and proud (to varying degrees) of their Black identities (Shireman & Johnson, 1986; Simon et al., 1994). Furthermore, they were expected to grow into well-adjusted members of society (Simon et al., 1994). While some of the research cautiously expresses concern about the potential identity development conflicts that may arise among Black/Biracial transracial adoptees living in predominately White settings (McRoy et al., 1982, 1984), the consensus of the empirical research was that Black children in the United States had adequate adjustment and racial identity (Alexander & Curtis, 1996). Love was assumed to be enough when raising these children regardless of race or ethnicity (Simon et al., 1994). Interestingly, the ages at which the children were studied, the lack of examination of transracial adoptees during adulthood, and other methodological issues, although noted in some reviews of the literature (Hollingsworth, 1997), have not diminished the impact of these findings. However, the perspective that love is sufficient must be further examined.

Certainly, the research conducted on transracial adoption is useful in several ways. First, it brought attention and resources to learning, in greater depth, about the effects this type of adoption had on families and adoptees over time. It also sought to find value in transracial adoption as an opportunity to provide permanent placements for children in need of homes. As an African American transracial adoptee, I am particularly attentive to the studies that home in on the identity development of children of color adopted by White parents, which in the majority of cases have been within predominately White communities, schools, and places of worship. These landmark studies suggest that most, if not all, transracial adoptees seem, at the point at which the particular study was conducted, to have the ability to successfully adapt to and identify with their adoptive families. Also, these children seemingly possess the inner ability to reciprocate the love their adoptive parents and siblings have for them, transcending the color line.

However, these landmark studies were limited in several important ways. First, they relied primarily on childhood to make their assessments, and racial identity was only studied during childhood, whereas researchers have recognized that racial identity is more crucial and of primary concern during late adolescence and adulthood (Baden & Steward, 2000). Second, this empirical research, which set the framework for this discussion on transracial adoption at a practical level, is by nature designed primarily for the benefit and reassurance of White adoptive parents (and other interested parties in support of the transracial adoption policy). They effectively give White adoptive parents a "stamp of approval" that transracial adoption has been proven to be in the best interests of the child without even considering or thinking about the adults these adopted children become and without fully challenging these same parents and holding them accountable for considering and incorporating the racial and ethnic richness their adoptive children bring into the fabric of their family. These studies make it much easier for parents, educators, and society to minimize (a) the racial and physical differences between White parents and their transracially adopted children and (b) any potential conflicts that could arise as transracial adoptees attempt to negotiate their racial identities by believing in the "color-blind" perspective or the denial of differences method (e.g., they see adoptive children the same way as they see all children). On the contrary, this message says families do not have to change their lifestyles or priorities as a family to assist their children of color in developing their racial identity because they do not view the children's racial identity as important and because they are uncomfortable with all these issues.

Another possible unintended consequence of the traditional empirical research is that it could influence how the identity development of Black and Biracial transracial adoptees is understood and viewed. The design of the bulk of the research essentially measures the level of these children's racial identity and self-esteem within a narrowly defined concept which consists of (a) how these children view themselves and (b) how their adoptive parents (who may assume theirs is a "color-blind" philosophy) view their transracially adopted children, solely within the confines of their adoptive families and within what the parents perceive to be a safe, nonthreatening environment. This research bias may mistakenly be used as an excuse to avoid learning about the racial identity components that are part of their children's lives; instead, they believe that racial realization is static or fixed (e.g., "My child is an individual who is happy and happens to be Black, end of story"). Furthermore, the framework and methodology of these studies considerably limited transracial adoptees' ability to (a) freely provide responses to research questions, (b) raise questions about their racial identity outside the comfort zone of their adoptive parents, or (c) share experiences that surpassed or were beyond the understanding, expectations, and biases of the researchers. According to my conversations with more than 45 young adult transracial adoptees from various racial and ethnic groups throughout this country, I found that it was challenging for a significant number of these adoptees to become adequately comfortable and self-confident enough to explore and nurture their racial identities. They expressed fear that they would compromise the "unspoken" boundaries within their families or potentially, in the adoptees' minds, jeopardize the love their adoptive families had for them (personal communication, 1999–2005).

To move beyond the limited confines of previous research and perceptions is an integral component of learning more about raising successful and competent Black and Biracial transracial adoptees. Ideally, the insight gained from future transracial adoption research will examine the identity development of transracial adoptees within the context of their relationships with their adoptive families, the adoptees' racial and ethnic communities, and the larger society. This research can create an intended consequence of empowering these adoptees to feel secure in their multifaceted realities and to be continuously curious and interested in refining their racial identities.

Federal Legislation

A significant addition to the discussion on transracial adoption was the introduction of two complementary pieces of federal legislation enacted in 1994 and 1996 based largely on the transracial adoption research conducted by social scientists in the 1970s and 1980s; in effect, these two pieces of legislation changed the face of the national policy on adoption from strictly upholding same-race placements to accepting transracial placements (Alexander & Curtis, 1996). Authored by former Senator Howard M. Metzenbaum (D-Ohio) out of the need to address the plight confronting many children, especially the disproportionate numbers of children of color waiting and available to be adopted in the U.S. child welfare system, the Multiethnic Placement Act of 1994 (MEPA; 1994) was passed by the 104th Congress and signed into law by President Clinton. MEPA was designed to prohibit agencies (those managing foster care/adoption placements and receiving federal assistance) from delaying and denying the placement of children based solely on the race or national origin of the adoptive or foster parents or the children involved (Part E, Subpart 1). However, the vague language inherent in the MEPA statute created confusion among child welfare agencies and practitioners regarding the implementation guidelines in the law, so Congress passed an amendment, the 1996 Interethnic Adoption Provision Act (IEPA; 1996), to strengthen the initial intent of MEPA (Fenster, 2002).

The effect of MEPA and IEPA made it clear that same-race foster care and adoption placements would *no longer be legal* except in those cases in which it was specifically justified by the needs and best interests of the child (Fenster, 2002). In other words, if there is a Black child available for adoption, and a qualified White couple (or parent) that meets its needs is available and willing to adopt this child, under the MEPA/IEPA statutes, an adoption plan must be made for both the child and the parent(s) expeditiously. The agency or case worker cannot stall placement indefinitely in anticipation of a potential Black couple (or parent) to provide a home for the child. Although race cannot be a factor in determining placements for a child in the majority of cases, the hope of MEPA/IEPA, as outlined in its implementation guidelines, is to encourage agencies to be creative and aggressive in their recruitment efforts to find a more ethnically/racially diverse pool of parental applicants who reflect the ethnic and racial diversity of the children in the system and who are willing to foster and adopt these children (Hollinger & The ABA Center on Children and the Law National Resource Center on Legal and Courts Issues, 1998).

How MEPA/IEPA will play out in the following years and whether these two pieces of legislation in conjunction with good child welfare practice will drastically reduce the number of children in the system by moving them into viable permanent homes is still uncertain. According to the U.S. Department of Health and Human Services and the Administration for Children and Families (Children's Bureau, 2004), the estimated number of children in foster care from 1999 to 2003 slightly but steadily decreased from 567,000 children in 1999 to 523,000 children in 2003, a 7.8% (roughly 44,000 children) drop over a 5-year period. We can only hope that the trend will continue and that the displaced children in the child welfare system of the United States will be expeditiously granted loving, supportive, and permanent homes. The next step for those children of color who are placed in transracial adoptive homes is learning to address the complexities of their identity living within White families. The pressing issue then becomes how social work practitioners, mental health professionals, and parents can assist these children in this effort.

Complexities of Identity: Beyond Adjustment

The fact remains that MEPA/IEPA constitute the law, but ultimately how that law is carried out is based on how case workers and agency professionals interpret the law as well as their attitudes toward these laws. In a recent study, Fenster (2002) surveyed 363 social workers (158 African American and 205 Caucasian), who were categorized based on their identification as members of either the National Association of Social Workers (NASW) or the NABSW, throughout the United States about their attitudes toward transracial adoption—in this case, Black children being adopted by White parents. The goal of the study was to determine whether social workers generally favored transracial adoption as a social policy and if social workers were divided by race in their views about transracial adoption. Interestingly, although the study did not indicate how many of the Black (or White) social workers were in a position to make placement decisions within their agencies, the results did show that the race of the respondents was a dividing factor in how these social workers viewed transracial adoption; Black social workers who identified more strongly with their ethnic group were more opposed to transracial adoption (Fenster, 2002). Thus, as these findings indicate, NABSW members (given the position of the NABSW in 1972) were less supportive of transracial adoption placements than were nonmembers (Fenster, 2002). Fenster concluded that, on average, the respondents had positive feelings about the transracial adoption policy, but only 43.5% of the social workers surveyed in this study were Black (Fenster, 2002). What does this mean for Black children placed by White social workers into White homes? Will these social workers be more inclined to help prepare White parents to raise children of color by exposing these children to their cultural heritage and the rich Black experience, while also appropriately and creatively operating within compliance of the MEPA/IEPA statutes? Or will these same social workers, out of fear of potential lawsuits or personal discomfort, choose to achieve the easier task of not educating the parents about the racial/cultural sensitivities that may confront the family?

It can be argued that the case against transracial adoption articulated by the NABSW and other opponents of transracial adoption over the past 35 years has not been supported within academia or in the halls of Congress because it has not been sustained by empirical data (Altstein, 2006; Turner & Taylor, 1996). In spite of the failure to meet academic criteria, there is immeasurable value that can be obtained by extracting firsthand knowledge from the Black community on the issue of transracial adoption and the transracial adoptees who have lived transracial adoption.

Truly, it proves to be easy for transracial adoptees, in the short term, to deny their Blackness, especially when issues of racism, inequality, and injustice test "minority groups." It is also easy for transracial adoptees, in the short term, to be unresponsive to the challenges that affect Black America. Clearly, more work must be done by adoptive families and adoptees to incorporate the values of African American history and experiences within the core values of the family structure so that these transracial adoptees can authentically identify and become comfortable with the development of their identities both within their homes and within society. To support these goals, those in the Black community, whether they are leaders or citizens, cannot stand on the sidelines indifferent to learning more about transracial adoption and to building relationships with Black and Biracial adoptees and their families.

Transracial adoptees need the Black community and the Black community needs transracial adoptees for the long term to promote a cohesive future. As some of the interviews collected by Simon and Roorda (2000) reflect, it is clear that White adoptive families need the Black community. All must hold each other accountable and do what is difficult and responsible for the integrity of the families, research, and society.

The Significance of Overcoming Racial Stereotypes: My Journey

When I was about 12 years old, my adoptive family and I had recently moved to the city of Takoma Park, Maryland, a predominately Black neighborhood. We lived on the top of the hill in a geodesic dome. During that time, my brother and I worked for the *Washington Post* delivering newspapers. Our paper route was located in the adjacent neighborhoods. The challenge for me, especially on Saturday mornings when I needed to walk down our street to get to my route, was to avoid the Black males in our neighborhood because I felt that they might harm me. I thought I was good at avoiding them. I could usually dodge them from a distance. I willingly walked a mile or more out of my way so that I would not come in contact with these Black males. One particular morning, I happened to walk down the street as usual but I did not notice the young Black man in front of me until I could feel his breath on my face. In a panic, I dropped my bag and my cart and ran up the street to my home. I was so shaken up by what seemed to me his invasion of my world that I vomited in the bathroom.

It was at that poignant moment I knew that I had a deep fear of Black of males that had the potential to paralyze me. Even though I lived in a Black neighborhood, I had allowed myself to insulate my world with primarily White friends, who attended the same private Christian elementary school that I did, as well as friends from church. I had absorbed the values, the experiences, and the stereotypes about people of color from the perspective of White mainstream America, from the other side of the abyss, without questioning if any of those values/experiences conflicted with who I truly was. Although I was an African American, I had no understanding about how people of color were judged and ill-treated simply from a quick and casual observation. This man, this Black man, who was in front of me that Saturday morning, had simply said hello, and I had reacted to him as if I had seen him premiere on the nightly news as a criminal who had just been arrested for a horrible crime! I was Black, yet I sat in the same living room with my family and took in the same images over the television airwaves of news broadcast stories, ads, and drama series that negatively portrayed Black people. My family was not aware that these images struck me in a more personal and negative way than it had appeared to them, and they did not provide commentary about these media "realities." Equally unenlightened, neither did I seek to aggressively find positive images of people who looked like me. I was too ready to digest the prepackaged images that were delivered to me by the television tube and other media, in part because I was more concerned about not causing waves in my family; the result was that my self-identity was harmed and slowly sacrificed. To attempt to reconcile these disparate realities, I sadly overcompensated and rationalized to myself on the surface that I was far removed from these poor images of Black Americans I saw portrayed on television and in print media.

Obviously, these images set the trajectory of how I responded to Black males in society and how mainstream America has pigeonholed this segment of the population. Nevertheless, because of that morning walk on the streets of Takoma Park, Maryland, I realized that my journey would be longer and more complicated than just my need to overcome my fear of Black men. I came to a committed awareness that for me to succeed in achieving my unique purpose, I needed to develop, one step at a time, more quality relationships with people of color based on their character instead of a 30-second sound bite on the nightly news. I would also have to eradicate the shallow and stereotypical images in my mind of persons of color by replacing those images with more informed images of people who looked like me and were making lasting contributions to humankind. This challenge led me to reflect on myself as an adoptee, as a Black female, and as someone who was and is blessed with God-given and genetically ingrained gifts and talents. Out of that process, through lonely moments, tears, anguish, and triumph, a book was birthed; my painful labor helped to deliver a broader and deeper understanding of how race and identity have an impact on the transracial adoptee.

Identity: In the Voices of Adult Transracial Adoptees

In the spring of 2000, with the support of transracial adoptees, adoptive parents, adoption groups, politicians, leaders, and caring people in the Black and White communities, and those in the social work and law professions, *In Their Own Voices: Transracial Adoptees Tell Their Stories* (Simon & Roorda, 2000) was published. This book used a narrative format and primarily provided a forum for young adult Black and Biracial adoptees to discuss in their own words, and in their own rhythm and style, their experiences of being raised transracially adopted. This text presented the history and legal status of transracial adoption as well as the controversy surrounding the issue. Those represented in the book are now young adults. The project brought together the prolific scholar Rita J. Simon and her colleagues (also scholars in transracial adoption) with the improvisational-like stories of adoptees who were living lives shaped by transracial adoption. The project results were indispensable and provided a more informed insider's understanding of how to most effectively raise psychologically strong and culturally confident Black and Biracial children adopted transracially.

Simon and Roorda (2000) wanted to go behind the scenes in the lives of Black and Biracial adoptees around the country and see (1) if they experienced similar (or different) challenges/successes throughout their lives, particularly when moving into arenas of higher education, career, dating, and home ownership; (2) how they developed their identities and attempted to juggle their divergent worlds; and finally, (3) whether they believed that "love was enough," based on their experiences as children of color adopted by White parents. As an adoptee, I believed early on that there was a depth and complexity within me that reached far beyond the scope of research models, mail questionnaires/surveys, and focus groups used in the traditional studies identified earlier in this chapter. While those parameters are valuable in giving clinical researchers a "snapshot in time" to assess the general thoughts and behavior of the respondents, they do not show the mental, emotional, or physical progression required for individuals to get to a certain point in their journey under their unique circumstances. We sought the stories of these adoptees that we believed could only be obtained by connecting as adult adoptees (Roorda and the interviewees).

The stories from the adult adoptees interviewed by Simon and Roorda (2000) revealed several interesting points. First, a reoccurring theme among most of the adoptees was that they expressed feelings of sincere love and loyalty toward their adoptive parents and their appreciation for having the opportunity to grow within a family through adoption. Second, the adoptees in this book identified with and embodied key character-building values taught to them by their adoptive parents, which clearly contributed to their inner confidence. These values included love, trust, honesty, and respect for one another, hard work, and education. Tage Larsen, who is a professional classical trumpet player and at the time of this interview was playing in the President's Own U.S. Marine Band, said that his parents taught him to "work hard and stay focused and determined" (Simon & Roorda, 2000, p. 252).

There should be no question after reading *In Their Own Voices* that the love, stability, and care provided by the majority of the adoptive parents to their Black and Biracial adult children, particularly during their childhood and adolescent years, was immeasurable and contributed to building a strong foundation for the adoptees. Yet what emerged from this project that was not emphasized in previous studies was the fact that love, while essential to the development of a healthy self-esteem and identity, was not enough when raising children of color who have been adopted by White parents. In fact, race and ethnicity do substantially matter in the fundamental healthy upbringing of transracial adoptees. This realization was especially clear to many of the adoptees as they entered into society as adults. There is a point, it seems, where the perceptions of society toward Black and Biracial adoptees living within their White families converged with society's perceptions of other Black Americans. Obviously, as children adopted transracially become adolescents and then adults, they are eventually viewed and judged through society's eyes using the same lens as they do for other African Americans. We see race and ethnicity issues moving to the forefront even more as adult transracial adoptees marry Black and White spouses, parent children of color, work in corporate America, or attend higher education institutions. I believe that some transracial adoptees do perceive themselves to be capable and even confident. However, in my opinion, far too many (based on this project and meeting more than 100 adult adoptees of color in this country) unfortunately left their adoptive families without an adequate plan or knowledge/experience base to strategically negotiate the new societal terrain away from their "safe" adoptive family structure.

"Aaliyah," who was born and raised in the predominately White environment near Grand Rapids, Michigan, struggled throughout her adolescence and into adulthood with low self-esteem and feelings of differentness from her adoptive family. She found herself desperately seeking answers from within the "city," at times putting herself in harm's way physically and psychologically. In her search for identity and happiness, she described herself as "going this way and that way and not knowing which way to turn" (Simon & Roorda, 2000, p. 193). While wanting to remain close to her adoptive parents, she acknowledged in the interview that there began to be a growing racial and cultural divide between the three of them. She stated,

> I feel like we're [her adoptive parents] totally different. Since I've grown up from a teenager to an adult, I've changed a lot because I've lived in the city and have seen that side now. I lean toward that. I don't think my parents ever really liked my boyfriend (who's from the city). They thought all the decisions I made were wrong. (Simon & Roorda, 2000, p. 185)

Aaliyah struggled with not wanting to lose her parents' love and the values they taught her yet having an unexplainable need to explore her Black identity. Her search, which turned out to be both aimless and harmful to her at the point of the interview, kept her stuck, unable to navigate her course effectively in the Black community (or in the White community). The result has been that she is unable to truly achieve her potential because she has lost her inner compass and confidence. Unlike Aaliyah, Seth Himrod, who was raised in Evanston, Illinois, had parents who were more educated about the difficulties of race. At the time I interviewed him, he was a stockbroker and a single father living next door to his adoptive parents. And while Seth personified a good and honest man with a high caliber of professionalism, his parents' best efforts could not shield him from the harsh realities of society, he explained:

> As I got older, I stopped being this cute little boy and others perceived me as this Black teenager and a menace to society. Apparently, I was liable to rape, kill, or whatever. I got pulled over by the cops; I got slammed against the wall with a flashlight up in my face. Questions were thrown at me, like what am I doing? Where am I going? You fit the description; come over here, we got to talk to you. Those things are what anger me. The fact that I was able to go to my dad and see his pain and outrage, the same way as I was feeling even though he never experienced it, was a support system for me. He never had a cop do that to him. Instead of asking me what I was doing, he'd tell me I should be upset about what happened. (Simon & Roorda, 2000, p. 296)

Raised in a predominately White suburb of Chicago, cut off from her ethnic community of origin, Rachel is an adult adoptee who is supportive of transracial adoption, but who carried a lingering sentiment throughout the interview of sadness and confusion. She believes that this was, in large part, because she did not know about her ethnic heritage. Because of this growing sense of insecurity, she ended up having difficulties with fitting in physically within the White community and also being totally comfortable in the Black community. When asked about her views regarding White parents adopting Black children, she said,

> I think they [White adoptive parents] need to make sure that the children stay in touch with their roots. It's essential that they know the history and background of their people. I feel as though I've lost touch with who I am. (Simon & Roorda, 2000, p. 157)

As advice for adoptive parents raising Black and Biracial children as well as other adoptees, Simon and Roorda (2000) indicated that it was helpful to them as children when they and their family members were exposed to the African American community through the friendships made through church, school, and support groups. Also, opportunities where the family as a unit could naturally discuss and celebrate adoption through "life books" and other celebratory events had a positive impact. Sadly, what was missing for most of the adoptees interviewed in this book were Black and Biracial role models and mentors in the lives of these individuals, leading up to and into their adult years. Why is that important? Because too many of these adoptees were disillusioned when they entered the "real" world, and this was magnified by not having the depth of understanding about how to maneuver in life with dark skin. And far too many believed that once they recognized they needed the Black community or that they shared a common bond, the Black community in general would be immediately receptive to them rather than suspicious of them. There are cultural differences among Black/Biracial children raised in White homes versus those Black children raised in same-race homes; it takes someone familiar with both perspectives to patiently share their knowledge, love, and time with the other about the world in which they live. Transracial adoption is still a controversial subject, and the act requires conscientious effort toward and long-term focus on building stepping-stones for these children and their adoptive families as a unit. We must look beyond the immediate comfort of these children's families to the long-term outcomes of these children's lives as adults, their belief systems, and their interactions (or lack thereof) with their ethnic communities.

Many possibilities and outcomes are achievable by families who transracially adopt children. For those gains to be realized, families must heed the lessons learned from pioneers (critics, researchers, adoptive parents, adoptees) who first ventured on this journey and apply these lessons to making blended families more dynamic. Are adoptees and adoptive families willing to grab hold of these opportunities and blessings and move beyond the controversy associated with transracial adoption? I know that adoptive parents and children have the will, commitment, and perseverance within them not only to move beyond survival but also to flourish and be successful.

To plan for the future, transracial adoptive families should create a strategic "Multicultural Adoption Plan" (MAP) for the long-term enrichment of each family member, particularly the adoptive child. The goal of this MAP is for the adoptive family to become knowledgeable about and comfortable with the adopted child's racial/ethnic heritage and adoption experiences. With the whole family's involvement in learning about and understanding the important and necessary steps that transracially adopted children need to take, the children will have greater support in their efforts to develop healthier racial identities and senses of self. The ultimate hope, of course, is that with this caring support, adoptive children will flourish and fulfill their unique purpose in society. In the following section I give an example of one such plan. This MAP outline comes from my personal adoption experience and from listening to many adoptive parents/children across the country.

A MULTICULTURAL ADOPTION PLAN

Strengthening the Heart and Mind of the Adoptive Parent: Preparing to Embrace Your Child of Color

The successful adoption of children of color by White parents requires those parents to be willing to experience the close encounters with racism that their children—and they as parents—will have and to be prepared to talk to their children about them. Ultimately, they need to examine their own identities as White people, going beyond the idea of raising a child of color in a White family to a new understanding of themselves and their children as members of a multiracial family (Tatum, 1997, p. 190).

• *Examine reasons for choosing to adopt transracially:* Are the adoptive parents committed to raising their adopted children into adulthood with the goal of maintaining a lasting and respectful relationship with their Black/Biracial children even if their child ultimately decides to closely identify with the African American community?

• *What are their views of the adopted children's ethnic communities of origin?* Do the adoptive parents hold views of superiority, inferiority, or equality toward their adopted children's ethnic communities compared with the White community? Whatever the adoptive parents' views, children will see the truth. Will adoptive parents realistically put their children's best interests first, even if they have not yet become entirely comfortable in associating with those from their children's ethnic/cultural heritage?

• *Build up the reservoir of knowledge regarding the transracial adoptees' ethnic/cultural heritage and adoption:* Read! Read! Read! Become educated about racial issues, the history of African Americans in this country, and the sometimes difficult losses that are also a part of the adoption story.

• *Plan to raise children of color by assessing the community, relationships, and resources of the adoptive parents:* Examine the current situation of the adoptive family. Encourage the adoptive parents to be reflective and examine themselves to ensure that a social agenda was not part of the reason they wished to transracially adopt. Be sure that the reasons for adopting are to form families and are not related to altruistic causes. Consider whether there are African Americans in the community/place of worship/place of work into which the children will be adopted. Have the adoptive families established any genuine relationships with African Americans, or do they have any African American friends/acquaintances? Begin building safe, nurturing environments for the transracial adoptees to insure that they are comfortable with people who look like they do.

• *Develop smart support systems for the adoptive family in this transracial adoption experience:* To be helpful to transracial adoptees, families need to locate and create a network of support persons/systems that will help guide them in this transracial adoption process. Do not put the burden on the children—the parents' job is to teach and comfort their children in times of difficulty. Children should not be the primary resource for parents about race, nor should their role be to comfort their parents regarding any discomfort they might have about race.

Creating a Solid Foundation for Children to Begin Developing Stepping-Stones to Healthy Levels of Self-Esteem

• *Embrace children's emotional, physical, and spiritual identity and bring it into your family:* Spirituality anchors racial identity, providing hope and purpose. When teaching children to tap into this source, their religious and moral values are nurtured. Children learn that to be Black and to be able to survive requires a hard-won, tenacious resistance of the psyche—a resistance that recognizes the interdependency of African Americans on each other, on the history that shaped our (African American) faith, and on faith itself. For resisters resist with the body, mind, and spirit (Ward, 2000, p. 257).

• *Share with children their adoption story:* Do this using age-appropriate language and honoring children and their need to be loved. Revisit the children's story over time as questions may change. Some of these questions are as follows:
1. Where do I come from?
2. Who am I?

3. Where do I belong?

- *Listen to children.*
- *Advocate on behalf of these children at home, at school, and in the community.*
- *Expand the worldview of the family: Explore possibilities!*

REFLECTION QUESTIONS

1. In what ways can African American and White scholars collaborate on future research projects on race, identity, and adoption?

2. As researchers, therapists, and parents interested in transracial adoption, have you examined your own thoughts about your views toward different ethnic/racial groups and about the inherent complexities for the transracial adoptee in confronting issues of loss, identity, self-esteem, and love, living in paradoxical realities?

3. What relationship-building strategies can your agency develop that will create linkages in racial/ethnic communities for reciprocal educational, recruitment, and support purposes?

4. What resources are available in your adoption agency, counseling center, or home that address the subjects of adoption, transracial adoption, and race/culture?

5. How can more attention be focused on data and information organizations to develop a universal database tracking transracial adoptive families and adoptees for more comprehensive research conducted on this important issue?

6. For parents: Beyond the cuteness of your child or even the cause for why you adopted your child, are you committed to encourage your child to embrace his or her racial heritage and identity and work diligently to uphold that commitment even when your child grows to become a Black/Biracial man or Black/Biracial woman in this country?

7. As it relates to transracial adoption, when one looks at the decision-making roles in foster care and adoption agencies, academic institutions, clinical centers, and political arenas, are there African American and other persons of color present at the table?

REFERENCES

Alexander, R., Jr., & Curtis, C. M. (1996). A review of empirical research involving the transracial adoption of African American children. *Journal of Black Psychology, 22*(2), 223–235.

Altstein, H. (2006). Race need not be an issue in adoption: More matches possible if we stop talking about race. *HoustonChronicle.com*. Retrieved January 28, 2006, from www.chron.com/cs/CDA/printstory.mpl/editorial/outlook/3619130

Baden, A. L., & Steward, R. J. (2000). A framework for use with racially and culturally integrated families: The cultural-racial identity model as applied to transracial adoption. *Journal of Social Distress & the Homeless, 9*(4), 309–337.

Chestang, L. (1972). The dilemma of Biracial adoption. *Social Work, 17,* 100–105.

Children's Bureau, Administration for Children and Families, HHS (AFCARS Data). (2004). *Trends in foster care and adoption.* Retrieved November 10, 2005, from www.acf.dhhs.gov

Evans, M. (1992). *Contemporary poetry, African American literature: Voices in a tradition.* Orlando, FL: Holt, Rinehart & Winston.

Fenster, J. (2002). Transracial adoption in Black and White: A survey of social worker attitudes. *Adoption Quarterly, 5*(4), 33–58.

Hollinger, J. H., & the ABA Center on Children and the Law National Resource Center on Legal and Courts Issues. (1998). *A guide to the Multiethnic Placement Act of 1994 as amended by the interethnic provisions of 1996.* Retrieved February 1, 2001, from www.acf.dhhs.gov

Hollingsworth, L. D. (1997). Effect of transracial/transethnic adoption on children's racial and ethnic identity and self-esteem: A meta-analytic review. *Marriage & Family Review, 25*(1), 99–130.

Interethnic Adoption Provision Act of 1996. (1996). P.L. 104-188, Title I. Section 1808(c), 110 Stat. 1904.

Kennedy, R. (2003). *Interracial intimacies: Sex, marriage, identity, and adoption.* New York: Pantheon Books.

Macaulay, J., & Macaulay, S. (1978). Adoption for Black children: A case study of expert discretion. *Research in Law and Sociology, 1,* 265–318.

McRoy, R., Zurcher, L. A., Lauderdale, M. L., & Anderson, R. N. (1982). Self-esteem and racial identity in transracial and inracial adoptees. *Social Work, 27,* 522–526.

McRoy, R., Zurcher, L. A., Lauderdale, M. L., & Anderson, R. N. (1984). The identity of transracial adoptees. *Social Case Work, 65,* 34–39.

Multiethnic Placement Act of 1994. (1994). P.L. 103-382 Sections 551–553; 108 Stat. 3518.

Shireman, J. F., & Johnson, P. R. (1986). A longitudinal study of Black adoptions: Single parent, transracial, and traditional. *Social Work, 31,* 172–176.

Simon, R., Altstein, H., & Melli, M. (1994). *The case for transracial adoption.* Washington, DC: American University Press.

Simon, R. J., & Roorda, R. M. (2000). *In their own voices: Transracial adoptees tell their stories.* New York: Columbia University Press.

Tatum, B. (1997). *Why are all the Black kids sitting together in the cafeteria.* New York: Basic Books.

Townsend, J. T. (1995). Reclaiming self-determination: A call for intraracial adoption. *Duke Journal of Gender Law & Policy,* 1–16. Retrieved October 16, 2005, from www.puaf.umd.edu/puaf650-Fullinwider/Transracial%20Adoption-Townsend.htm

Turner, S., & Taylor, J. (1996). Underexplored issues in transracial adoption. *Journal of Black Psychology, 22*(2), 262–265.

Ward, J. (2000). *The skin we're in: Teaching our children to be emotionally strong, socially smart and spiritually connected.* New York: Free Press.

Zastrow, C. (1977). *Outcome of Black children: White parents, transracial adoptions.* San Francisco: R&E Research Associates.

International Adoption of Latin American Children

10

Psychological Adjustment, Cultural, and Legal Issues

ALINA CAMACHO-GINGERICH

St. John's University

SUSAN BRANCO-RODRIGUEZ

Virginia Polytecnic Institute and State University

RAÚL ERNESTO PITTERI

University Cuenca del Plata, Corrientes, Argentina

RAFAEL A. JAVIER

St. John's University

I n the United States, as well as in several other countries, the practice of adopting children from foreign countries emerged in the post–World War II period (Lovelock, 2000; McRoy, 1991; Weil, 1984) as a response to the needs of the displaced children of Europe

AUTHORS' NOTE: Raúl Ernesto Pitteri acknowledges that his participation in this chapter has been possible thanks to the academic agreement between St. John's University CLACS and the University of Cuenca del Plata, Argentina.

during and after the war. The first provision for intercountry adoption into the United States was President Truman's directive of December 22, 1945, which allowed for the migration of refugees and minors not accompanied by family members (Lovelock, 2000). The children came primarily from Poland, Czechoslovakia, Hungary, and Germany. The responsibility for caring for these children fell on both the federal government and private agencies. Some of the younger children were adopted by citizens of the United States.

By the 1950s, international adoption of children became an established practice. Since then, the availability of children from other nations for adoption has always been shaped by political unrest, civil wars, natural disasters, and domestic family policies in the Third World countries. The practice of international adoption of children has been conceptualized as having occurred in two waves (Alstein & Simon, 1991; Lovelock, 2000; Westhues & Cohen, 1998). The first wave, from the end of World War II to the mid-1970s, was considered a mostly humanitarian response to children in need of families from poor and war-torn countries. The second wave, from the 1970s to the present, although also inspired by the desire to provide a nurturing family environment for children from poor countries in political turmoil, was also driven by falling fertility rates and the diminishing supply of healthy Caucasian infants available for adoption domestically.

As the demand for healthy Caucasian infants exceeded the availability domestically, prospective parents in the United States increasingly turned to international adoption. However, there were no legislative provisions in place to facilitate this process (Carlson, 1988; Forbes & Weiss, 1985; Lovelock, 2000). The U.S. military intervention in Asia prompted the United States in 1953 to institute special provisions to facilitate military and government employees stationed in Korea to adopt Korean orphans (Carlson, 1988; Lovelock, 2000). The Refugee Act of 1953 was the first legislation to explicitly address international adoption and the demands of prospective parents domestically. This act, geared at citizens fleeing the Eastern Block countries, also allowed 4,000 special nonquota visas for orphans (Forbes & Weiss, 1985). For the first time, prospective parents in the United States had a nonrestrictive international adoption immigration policy available to them (Lovelock, 2000). Between 1954 and 1958, when this act expired, about 10,000 children were adopted from abroad by families in the United States. Many of these children were from Germany, Japan, and Korea, adopted by military personnel stationed in those countries (Lovelock, 2000; Pettis, 1958).

Permanent provisions for the international adoption of children in the United States were not made until 1961 with the passing of the Immigration and Nationality Act of that year (Carlson, 1988). In the 1960s, international adoption became more frequent, and by the 1970s, it was a fully accepted way to complete a family. The vast majority of these adoptions were interracial (Tristeliotis, 1991). By the mid-1970s, the Latin American and Caribbean nations had become significant sources for U.S. parents looking to adopt children. These adoptions represent the turning point from the first wave of migration of children to the second wave (Lovelock, 2000). The main motivation for prospective parents in these cases was infertility and the inability to adopt domestically. Different from previous international adoptions, these adoptions were not associated with U.S. military involvement or any international political conflict. Many of these adoptions were interracial, and of children unknown to the prospective adoptive parents (Hoksbergen, 1986; Lovelock, 2000).

In the late 1980s and 1990s, Latin America continued to be a significant region for parents looking to adopt children. With the increased demand came more opportunities for corruption. In many cases, large amounts of money were paid by prospective parents to intermediaries who controlled the supply. These intermediaries pressured poor women to put up their babies for adoption. Black markets became common in some Latin American countries as well as in Asia. A few sensationalized reports of "baby farms" emerged in Honduras, Brazil, Peru, and Sri Lanka, among other places (Lovelock, 2000). It seemed that the welfare of the children to be adopted was at best secondary; nobody seemed to care about the biological or adoptive parents. The Latin American nations involved responded in some cases by attempting to regulate the international adoptions; in other cases, they prohibited these adoptions until some measures were taken that allowed these countries to supervise and regulate the adoptions.

Responding to these abuses, the Organization of American States attempted to introduce some uniformity in the adoption of Latin American children (Lovelock, 2000). The Inter-American Convention on Conflicts of Laws Concerning the Adoption of Minors of 1984 tried to define questions of applicable law and jurisdiction (Carro, 1994; Lovelock, 2000). The Inter-American Convention on International Traffic in Minors, adopted in Mexico, DF, on March 18, 1994. It tried to reconcile regional laws on adoption with international conventions on the protection of minors internationally. It was an attempt to meet the requirements of the UN Convention of the Rights of the Child adopted by the UN General Assembly in November of 1989 (Carro, 1994; Lovelock, 2000). All these measures were intended to address the abuses in the adoption of children from Latin America. Although these measures were a good start, most experts believe abuses continue to take place, especially with independent adoptions, the most prevalent form of international adoption in the United States (Lovelock, 2000). The needs and the well-being of the child to be adopted as well as those of the biological family should be of paramount importance. In the United States there was no policy that protected the welfare of the child migrating for adoption until the recommendations of international conventions of 1993.

PSYCHOLOGICAL AND MENTAL HEALTH ISSUES FOR ADOPTEES IN INTERNATIONAL ADOPTION

In 2004, more than 22,000 children became sons and daughters of U.S. citizens through inter-country adoption (*Encyclopedia of Adoption*, 2006). Since 1971, more than a quarter million international adoptees (INAs) have been adopted in the United States. As indicated earlier, these children arrived and continue to arrive from countries such as China, Russia, Guatemala, India, and Colombia, to name a few. Restrictions in adoption laws in some of the Latin American countries, such as Argentina, had made it more difficult to adopt from these countries (Puhl, 1999), and hence, the number of adoptees from these countries are low. As the INA population grows, the need to explore and examine the unique challenges that members of this group face as they develop throughout their life span has become more poignant.

Much of the current research on INAs tends to focus on adolescent identity development and grief and loss issues. It is clear that adoptive parents will be in a much better position to address issues that are likely to emerge in their adopted children if they acquire a better understanding of common developmental issues their INA children are likely to encounter as they progress in their developmental trajectory in the new country. Mental health practitioners, too, must become knowledgeable of typical challenges encountered by the INA, particularly during adolescence and young adulthood, to provide appropriate and efficacious services. This chapter will present a review of current INA research with regard to adjustment issues and will review some of the legal restrictions that countries such as Argentina have in place and that affect the extent to which INA adoption from these countries is possible. All the literature cited contains Central/South American adoptees in their samples and, thus, allows us to gain some general understanding of the international adoption experience in Latino children. The chapter will then describe a small focused group study that one of the authors of this chapter conducted with adult Colombian adoptees to identify factors that they found helpful in their development.

Challenges in Identity Development in International Adoption

Erik Erikson (1968, 1980), well-known for his human development theory and also an adoptee, spent a great deal of his professional life explaining the different challenges the individual tends to face as he or she progresses through his or her developmental path. It was his belief that the extent of success at a specific developmental stage was a function of the success of the previous stage. Focusing specifically on the period of adolescence, he believed that the central issue to be resolved is the issue of ego identity versus identity confusion. He defined identity as a subjective sense of self that remains stable over time and that is validated and shared by others and that defines the quality of one's relationships with the world. The question is how these issues played out in adoptees, especially in those coming from another country. We believe that during adolescence and young adulthood, INAs encounter a unique situation where challenges to identity development are particularly poignant. Since international adoption requires the adopted child to leave his or her country of origin and to acquire a new culture and language, part of the process of identity development involves coming to terms with what it means to lose one's connection to one's biological heritage and birth country. For those adopted by parents from different ethnic and racial groups, it also involves coming to terms with their ethnic and racial dissimilarity to their adoptive families. In most nonadoptive families, adolescents incorporate their family of origin's history, culture, race, and ethnicity into their own identity schema, giving them an important point of reference for personal meaning. In the case of the INA, the adolescent does not have access to such identifying information and could experience what Brodzinsky (1987) calls "genealogical bewilderment." According to Brodzinsky, this term is used to describe confusion, uncertainty, and disconnection to one's biological origins. Additionally, INAs who are ethnically and racially dissimilar from their adoptive families may potentially experience more distress during identity development because of the additional challenges with which they have to come to terms.

Mental Health Issues in INAs

Many INA adolescents experience increased mental health concerns and adjustment difficulties. One study in Sweden (Hjern, Lindblad, & Vinnerljung, 2002), the home of the largest INA population in Europe, compared INAs (11,320) with a general population group (85,419) as well as an immigrant group (94,006) using data from the country's national register. Additionally, they analyzed separately a sibling group (2,342) who were children with one or more biological parents with an INA sibling group. They found that INAs were referred to child and adolescent psychiatric clinics at a higher rate than nonadopted children. However, these authors emphasized the need for caution about these findings because the above average referral rates could be more of a product of "active help seeking parents" (p. 444) than chronic mental illness. Even with this consideration, they found that adolescent INAs were three to four times more likely to have serious mental health problems, such as suicide, suicide attempts, and psychiatric admissions, than the general population group. Furthermore, adolescent INAs examined in this study were five times more likely to commit crimes than the nonadopted population with similar socioeconomic backgrounds.

In contrast, another smaller Swedish adoption study (Cederblad, Hook, Irhammer, & Mercke, 1999) compared 211 INA adolescents to 187 Swedish-born adolescents. They found INAs exhibited no significant differences in mental health compared with the Swedish-born group of similar age and socioeconomic background. Some of the INAs in this study reported experiencing teasing about their physical appearances and being treated as immigrants. However, no significant difference was found between groups regarding identity confusion, as measured by clinical interviews and self-report checklists. Interestingly enough, 90% of the INAs identified themselves as Swedish and 70% reported no connection to their birth country.

Similar findings were also reported by another study in Canada of INAs that yielded no significant results to directly correlate maladjustment to international adoptive status. Adolescent and young adult INAs from several countries were interviewed to assess their level of family integration, self-esteem, acceptance by peers, and ethnic and racial identity (Westhues & Cohen, 1998). The researchers described this INA sample as "a well-adjusted group" (p. 129). Although the majority of INAs reported feeling comfortable with their ethnic identity, most reported experiencing racial and or ethnic slurs by peers or others. Such incidents included the following: peers refusing to play with them, bullying, staring from adults, and stereotypical assumptions made by others. Over half (59.8%) strongly agreed with the statement, "Some people would argue that visible minority children in this country face a lot of discrimination" (p. 128). The researchers concluded that discrimination and racism could potentially be a damaging factor to healthy INA development in Canada.

These findings notwithstanding, other research in different countries confirms previous findings about negative outcomes in INA development. In a Dutch study (Verhulst & Versluis-den-Bieman, 1995), for instance, 1,538 INAs were studied to determine, among other things, the developmental pattern of problem behaviors from middle childhood through adolescence. They found that INAs who scored high on the Child Behavior Checklist (CBCL) at ages 11 to 14 continued to do so when they were 14 to 17. Some even exhibited increased problematic behaviors. Overall, the INA group, when compared with nonadopted populations of the same age, demonstrated an increase of maladaptive adjustment during adolescence. The researchers emphasized that they could not "conclude that differences in ethnicity between the parent and the INA" (p. 155) were responsible for the increased maladjustment scores. However, they did consider ethnic and racial dissimilarity to the adoptive family to be an important factor in increased maladaptive behaviors with regard to experiencing racism and difficulty constructing an ethnic identity.

One of the few studies of identity development and adjustment among Latino adoptees in the United States indicated that those adoptees raised by ethnically similar adoptive parents fared better than those raised by ethnically dissimilar parents. Andujo (1988) examined the self-esteem and identity development among Mexican American adopted adolescents. She compared one group of 30 adoptees with Mexican American adoptive parents and one group of 30 with Caucasian adoptive parents in an attempt to discern differences in development. She found that the adoptees with Caucasian adoptive parents presented with differences in identity and physical self-concept and were less likely to identify themselves as Mexican Americans. Andujo hypothesized that adoptees with Mexican American parents will be better prepared to manage and cope with ethnic and racial discrimination based on learning from their parents' experiences.

Andujo's study remains relevant despite the fact that the adoptive sample could be considered more a domestic sample than an INA sample. Most INAs tend to be of minorities adopted into Caucasian families. Andujo states, "Once the adoptees are beyond the confines of their immediate families, they will experience the same interactive threats all minorities experience in society, and ultimately will experience some role confusion" (1988, p. 534). This is the same issue that was raised in the Canadian study that found that INAs suffered racial and/or ethnic discrimination. As suggested by Brodzinsky (1987), experiencing prejudice can create adjustment problems. Such incidents are often not reported by the INA to adoptive parents, and when they are, they are frequently minimized, possibly out of parents' feeling helpless to effectively offer guidance in these situations (Andujo, 1988). Myrna Friedlander (1999), a family therapist, expresses similar concern about young adult INAs encountering racism and warns that the adolescent/young adult is "part of two cultures but feels alienated by both" (p. 564).

LEGAL COMPLICATIONS: THE ARGENTINA CASE

Adopting children from Latin American countries into the United States and other countries is full of complications, particularly precipitated by the increased concern that the financial gains to those involved in facilitating the adoption transactions tend to encourage questionable and criminal practices with less concern for the well-being of the child and the birth parents (Chavanneau, 1977; Videla, 1997). Some of the countries have even placed morato-ria on international adoptions because of these abuses, while others, such as Argentina, have not only refused to adhere to international adoption procedures (Di Lella, 1997; Meeting on the Rights of Children, 1995, Commission No. 2) but have refused to sign on agreements with other countries to facilitate international adoption of their children. In the case of Argentina, part of the reason for this reluctance is the belief that domestic adoptions should take prece-dence over international ones and the fact that it is difficult to monitor the quality of the adoption experience in the international arena. This is not to say that there are not children who are taken out of the country to be adopted abroad, but when it happens, it takes place outside the legal framework (Vidal, 2005).

Adoption in Argentina has changed significantly in the last 10 years, concerning both its legal and social aspects (Giberti & Chavanneau de Gore, 1991). The Argentine government has provided a regulated framework within which adoptions are to take place, but it is often transgressed (Family Court Cases at the province of Chaco, 2005). These legal measures have the child's best interests at heart, but more often than not the slowness of the process and the relatively easy way "to get a child" outside the established legal system tend to seri-ously harm the chances of registered couples who wish to become adoptive parents follow-ing the legal route. The fact of the matter is that legal adoptions in Argentina are not a private contract between parties but a matter of state and can only be granted by a compe-tent judge in the matter (Oppenheim, 1999). These procedures are followed to protect the best interests of the child.

In the last few years, the existence of this legal procedure has intensified the conflict with individuals who make a profit out of providing children for adoption clandestinely (Puhl, 1999); it has also come into conflict with the custom, deeply rooted in cultural practice, by which a birth mother (usually extremely poor) would leave her child with a family (often belonging to a higher social class) who wished to adopt (Family Court Cases at the province of Chaco, 2005). Such a practice is discouraged to safeguard the child from falling into the hands of unscrupulous and unknown people. The fear is that the birth mother, when not driven by monetary gain, is often under duress because of the inherent social inequality (Chavanneau, 1977; Videla, 1997). Thus, guided by the need to protect the best interest of the child, the Argentinian legal system has delineated clear sets of procedures that anyone interested in adoption is expected to follow.

- First, it is mandatory for adoptive parents to sign up in the Registry of Adoptions.

- Those wishing to adopt must satisfy a series of requirements, such as a psychological evaluation and home study assessment performed by a psychologist and social worker pro-vided by the court (Adoption Law No. 24779).

- Once these requirements are satisfied, when there is a child potentially available for adoption, the adopting parents are called from a numerical waiting list where they have been placed.

The term *potentially available for adoption* is not to be confused with a *needy child*. Not all needy children are available for adoption, but only those termed in *abandoned condi-tions*. These children have spent most of their lives in institutions because their birth parents were either unable to provide adequate care or have not as yet relinquished their parental rights (Puhl, 1999). The sooner this fact is known by the Family Court, the faster a decision can be made about adoption, so that these children don't have to extend their stay at institutions unnecessarily. It is a well-known fact that the older the child, the harder his chances for adoption (Family Court Cases at the province of Chaco, 2005). The only time children are put up for adoption at once is when there are clear signs that they have suffered from various forms of neglect and abuse. The easiest but less frequent situation is presented when the birth mothers themselves voluntarily come to the court and offer their child up for adoption.

Additional Mechanisms to Ensure Adequate Protection of the Child's Rights

There are other characteristics pertaining to the Adoption Law in Argentina that are important to emphasize because they are specifically designed to offer the best protection of the child's rights.

• The adoptive parents are expected to commit themselves to tell the child his or her real life story and to help the child get to know his or her background and origin so as to be able to develop his or her personal narrative. Indeed, the importance of making sure that the child was not deceived was an important consideration when laying the foundations for the Adoption Law (Adoption Law No. 24.777)

• The law requires a postplacement supervision, normally a 6-month period, which is expected to begin as soon as the child is placed in the adoptive family's care. This includes home visits to supervise how the adoptive parents and child develop family ties. These visits are more frequent and of the utmost importance in adoptions of children older than 2 years of age since bonding is not always easy for either side (Giberti, 1997).

• The law makes provision to ensure the rights of the adopted child, when he or she is of age, to have access to his or her adoption file and find out about his or her birth parents or siblings. This amendment was made in 1997, and it is still being debated since the long-term effect of this measure is yet unknown (Di Lella, 1997).

The emphasis of the law on the right to self-identity of the adopted child could be seen as a residue or a social defence mechanism arising from the bloodshed years of the 1970s. The military regime in power at the time organized the systematic disappearance of adults and the illegal misappropriation of young children after the murder-disappearance of their parents (conclusions and recomendations from the meeting on "The Right of Children in the New Constitution").

International Versus Domestic Adoption

There are poignant questions regarding international adoptions that are of great concern for those interested in making sure that children going into international adoption are properly cared for. Thus, questions such as the following arise:

• Who will evaluate the adoptive parents?

• How will this be done?

• Who will control postplacement supervision? Should the role of the countries "exporting-sending" these children abroad be limited to merely handing them over and waiving their rights or should their own laws be applied?

These issues are particularly complex when these children are no longer infants.

The feelings of loss and cross-cultural issues the child will likely face require supervision that cannot be easily handled by the adopted child's native country alone (Giberti, 1997). One of the main reasons why international adoptions have not been legalized in Argentina is because a large number of domestic adoptive parents are on a waiting list (National and Provincial Adoption Registry). In the Province of Chaco, for instance, with an estimated population of 1 million people, there are currently 90 adoptive parents who have signed up at the Adoption Registry waiting for a child (Family Court at the Adoption Registry Chaco Province). According to some statistics, there are about 220 additional registered adoptive parents from different parts of the country, including Buenos Aires (Family Court at the

Adoption Registry Chaco Province), and some adoptive parents have already been to different registries throughout the country. Since the year 2000, the Province of Chaco instituted a Single Registry of Adoptions and has recorded close to 300 adoptions, an average of 60 per year (Family Court at the Adoption Registry Chaco Province).

Again, it is important to keep in mind that a large number of children are adopted outside the legal process (mainly by people not entered in the Registry of Adoptions) for clear financial gain for those who facilitate the transaction. They are often adopted by foreigners who are prepared to pay a large sum of money (Vidal, 2005). If we take into consideration the fee for international adoptions (between $15,000 and $20,000) that foreign adoptive parents are willing to pay and compare it with the average yearly salary of an Argentine citizen ($3,000), it is easy to see how this might come about.

It is not uncommon to see foreign couples traveling throughout the northeastern part of Argentina looking for children to adopt. The reason for seeking children for adoption from that part of the country may be that many of the Europeans that immigrated to Argentina through the 1960s were Eastern European, and they settled in the provinces of Misiones and Chaco. This is a way to increase the likelihood that the child adopted will come from an Eastern European background and thus be closer to the parents' preferred race.

ASSESSING FACTORS AFFECTING IDENTITY DEVELOPMENT IN LATINO ADOPTEES

Since many of the international Latino adoptees tend to come from countries with different ethnic and cultural configurations, international Latino adoptees are often faced with serious challenges as to how to define themselves in this cultural context. It is clear that research findings lead toward the belief that racial and ethnic issues play a role in INA identity development (Verhulst & Versluis-den Bieman, 1995). What is not clear is what sort of experiences can be helpful in helping the adoptees develop a sense of belonging and personal centeredness as they try to adjust to a new family and new country with different cultural and linguistic demands. The need to identify what experiences are perceived by the adoptees as helpful or unhelpful in contributing to developmental adjustment is of paramount importance.

In an attempt to find some possible answers to this question, one of the authors of this chapter asked a series of questions to a group of Colombian adoptees in the form of a focus group and more in-depth individual interviews. Both the focus group and individual interviews reported similar themes in positive factors that enhanced their adjustment as Colombian adoptees. These factors primarily revolved around feeling accepted by the Latino community at large. Many found association with other Latino groups as helpful in fostering identity development and a feeling of inclusion. Some group members indicated that relationships with other Colombian adoptees helped in normalizing their self-perceptions through sharing common thoughts, feelings, and life stories. Additionally, important to note is that all 12 participants in the focus group described themselves as Latino/Hispanic or Colombian. This suggests that even though most were raised by Caucasian families, they perceive themselves to be ethnically or racially different.

It is not surprising that factors identified as not helpful were nearly the opposite of those found helpful in adjustment. The two most commonly reported unhelpful experiences, perceived rejection or exclusion by the Latino/Colombian community and experiencing racism, both reflect current research findings in Canada, Europe, and the United States that describe experiencing racism or prejudice as contributors to maladjustment (Verhulst & Versluis-den Bieman, 1995). Some reported feeling isolated and rejected from other Latino communities because of language inabilities, being perceived as "White" by other Latinos, and feeling shamed by negative stereotypes of their country of origin. It should be noted that three of the five interview respondents were raised in homogeneous Caucasian communities and all three reported feeling uncomfortable initially when encountering Latino people because of their unfamiliarity with the culture.

IMPLICATIONS FOR ADOPTIVE PARENTS AND PROFESSIONALS

Regarding advice to parents and professionals, respondents emphasized the importance of prospective adoptive parents accepting the child's birth country and birth family and demonstrating acceptance of these aspects. Some of those interviewed in our study suggested *learning Spanish, visiting the country,* and *learning about its history and culture* as important in becoming more prepared to address issues of INAs. Many felt that preadoptive screening via the home study process should include mandatory workshops on INA development. Several stressed that individual INA testimonials would also greatly benefit potential adoptive parents. Some emphasized the need for pre-, post-, and lifelong adoption counseling to address common concerns that both INAs and adoptive parents encounter. Counseling during adolescence "when identity development becomes so important" was also suggested.

CONCLUSION

INAs and their families are a growing population in the United States. The Immigration and Naturalization Service reports that in 2004 more than 22,884 international children were adopted by United States citizens (U.S. Department of State, 2005). Of this number, 3,729 were adopted from Latin American countries such as Guatemala, Colombia, Mexico, and Brazil. Legal restrictions in some Latin American countries have made international adoption problematic, thus contributing to the illegal and unregulated adoption of children from these countries.

Of importance in this regard is the fact that Argentina is not a signature to the Hague Convention and thus making irrelevant to Argentinian children and parents a series of rules and procedures that have been established to ensure proper protection of children for adoption in the international arena. In this chapter, we sought to develop a descriptive analysis of the adaptive factors that shape international adoption by using data obtained from a sample of Colombian adoptees as an example. The chapter offers specific recommendations as to how adoptive parents and mental health professionals can better support INAs in their developmental adjustment efforts.

BEST PRACTICE

It is evident that identity development, particularly during adolescence and young adulthood, is a crucial time when INAs may need additional family and possibly professional support to assist in adaptive adjustment. Based on the issues raised in this chapter and findings discussed earlier, the following best practices apply:

• Latino adoptive INA families should consider residence in an area with a Latino presence, hence facilitating easier access to and participation in the culture.

• Latino adoptive INA parents should actively seek organizations or groups with other Latino INA families in an effort for their children to connect with others with a similar background.

• Latino adoptive INA parents need education, guidance, and support on managing and responding to racism or prejudice that may be experienced by their children.

• Mental health professionals should normalize and validate difficulties faced by Latino INAs during adolescence and young adulthood while educating their families on this developmental stage and offering recommendations on how to be supportive to their children during this developmental stage.

• In places where the possibility for abuse and misappropriation of children by groups guided by financial gains exists, it will be important to create not-for-profit organizations with the specific task of helping to develop a better and more organized and centralized control mechanism regarding the children available for adoption so that they will not fall prey to illegal adoptions. This may not only shorten domestic waiting lists but also result in developing a mechanism to facilitate and open up the possibility for international adoptions.

REFLECTION QUESTIONS

1. What differences can be found between the adoption proceedings in Latin American countries and the United States? Mention advantages and disadvantages.

2. Do you think that adoptions that take place through child placement agencies promote unequal or equal chances in developing countries?

3. How do you think parents could be helpful when adolescent Latino INAs experience racism in their community, at school, or with relatives?

3. What are potential barriers to identity development in Latino INAs?

4. How can mental health professionals best serve the individual Latino INA and his or her family?

REFERENCES

Alstein, H., & Simon, R. J. (1991). *Intercountry adoption: A multinational perspective.* New York: Praeger.

Andujo, E. (1988). Ethnic identity of transethnically adopted Hispanic adolescents. *Social Work, 33*(6), 531–535.

Brodzinsky, D. M. (1987). Adjustment to adoption: A psychosocial perspective. *Clinical Psychology Review, 7,* 25–47.

Brodzinsky, D. M., Smith, D. W., & Brodzinsky, A. B. (1998). Children's adjustment to adoption: Developmental and clinical issues. *Developmental Clinical Psychology and Psychiatry, 38,* 1–141.

Carlson, R. R. (1988). Transnational adoption of children. *Tulsa Law Journal, 23*(3), 317–377.

Carro, J. L. (1994). Regulation of intercountry adoption: Can the abuses come to an end? *Hastings International and Comparative Law Review, 18*(1), 121–155.

Cederblad, M., Hook, B., Irhammar, M., & Mercke, A. (1999). Mental health in international adoptees as teenagers and young adults: An epidemiological study. *Journal of Child Psychology and Psychiatry, 408*(8), 1239–1248.

Chavanneau, S. (1977). Women who give up their children (Mujeres que entregan a sus hijos). *Psychology Today Journal, Buenos Aires (Buenos Aires, en Revista Actualidad Psicológica), 22*(241), 11–13.

Di Lella, P. (1997). Reforms on the new adoption law (Reformas en la nueva ley de adopción). *Student Center Law Journal, Buenos Aires* (Revista Jurídica del Centro de Estudiantes).

Encyclopedia of adoption. (2006). Retrieved May 2, 2006, from http://encyclopedia.adoption.com/intro/introduction/2.html

Erikson, E. H. (1968). *Identity: Youth and crisis.* New York: Norton.

Erikson, E. H. (1980). *Identity and the life cycle.* New York: Norton.

Forbes, S. S., & Weiss, P. (1985). Unaccompanied refugee children: The evolution of U.S. policies, 1939–1984. *Migration News, 3,* 3–36.

Friedlander, M. L. (1999). Ethnic identity development of internationally adopted children and adolescents: Implications for family therapist. *Journal of Marital and Family Therapy, 25*(1), 563–580.

Giberti, E. (1997). The adoption of older children. *Psychology Today Journal, Buenos Aires, 22*(241), 2–6.

Giberti, E., & Chavanneau de Gore, S. (1991). A historical version. In *Adoption and silences.* Buenos Aires, Argentina: Sudamericana.

Hjern, A., Lindblad, F., & Vinnerljung, B. (2002). Suicide, psychiatric illness, and social maladjustment in intercountry adoptees in Sweden: A cohort study. *The Lancet, 10*(360), 443–456.

Hoksbergen, R. A. C. (Ed.). (1986). *Adoption in world wide perspective: A review of programs, policies and legislation in countries.* Lisse, The Netherlands: Swets & Zeitlinger.

Lovelock, K. (2000). Intercountry adoption as a migration practice: A comparative analysis of intercountry adoption and immigration policy and practice in the United States, Canada and New Zealand in the post WWII period. *International Migration Review, 34*(3), 907–949.

McRoy, R. G. (1991). Significance of ethnic and racial identity in intercountry adoption within the United States. *Adoption and Fostering, 15*(4), 53–61.

Meeting on the Rights of Children in the New Constitution. (1995). *Conclusions and recommendations* (Commission Nos. 1 and 2), Law School, Buenos Aires University.

Oppenheim, R. (1999). Adoption: From the law to the practice. *Family and Adoption Journal, Buenos Aires* (published in Adoptare Foundation, No. 1).

Pettis, S. T. (1958). Effect of adoption of foreign children on U.S. adoption standards and practices. *Child Welfare,* 27–33.

Puhl, S. (1999). *Adoption: Legal and psychological considerations.* Buenos Aires, Argentina: Buenos Aires University, Psychology Student Center Publication.

Tristeliotis, J. (1991). Intercountry adoption: A brief overview of the research evidence. *Adoption and Fostering, 15*(4), 47–52.

U.S. Department of State. (2005). Immigrant visas issued to orphans coming to the U.S. Retrieved September 14, 2005, from http://travel.state.gov/family/adoption/stats/stats

Verhulst, F. C., & Versluis-den Bieman, J. M. (1995). Developmental course of problem behavior in adolescent adoptees. *Journal of the American Academy of Child and Adolescent Psychiatry, 34*(2), 151–159.

Vidal, D. (2005). The Noruegian conexión. *Digital Magazine of Culture (Sitio al Margen).* www.almargen.com.ar

Videla, M. (1997). Mothers for rent and the differences with adoptions. *Psychology Today Journal, Buenos Aires, 22*(24), 7–10.

Weil, R. H. (1984). International adoptions: The quiet migration. *International Migration Review, 18,* 276–293.

Westhues, A., & Cohen, J. (1998). The adjustment of intercountry adoptees in Canada. *Children and Youth Services Review, 20*(1–2), 115–134.

From the Ashes of War

11

Lessons From 50 Years of Korean International Adoption

HOLLEE A. McGINNIS

Evan B. Donaldson Adoption Institute, New York

On January 13, 1903, the first Korean immigrants to the United States arrived in Honolulu, Hawaii, on the *SS Gaelic*. In commemoration, President Bush issued a proclamation declaring January 13, 2003, as the Centennial of Korean Immigration to the United States, commencing yearlong activities to celebrate the contributions of Korean immigrants and their descendents over the past 100 years (Office of the Press Secretary, 2003). Since the Korean War (1950–1953), more than 1 million South Korean nationals have emigrated abroad, of whom a significant fraction—15%—have been children adopted by families overseas. According to official statistics from the Korean Ministry of Health and Welfare, between 1953 and 2004 a total of 156,242 South Korean children were sent to predominately Western nations for adoption, although it has been estimated that this total may be closer to 200,000 children, including unaccounted-for private adoptions. Of this total, 104,319 were adopted by American citizens, constituting 1 out of 10 Korean Americans, and 42,231 were adopted into European families, half of whom were placed in Sweden, Norway, and Denmark (Hubinette, 2005).

The Korean-born children who emigrated overseas for the purposes of international adoption in the immediate aftermath of the Korean War were pioneers in a new form of international child welfare. Although the first international adoptions occurred in response to the aftermath of the Second World War and consisted mostly of children from ravaged European nations and, some children from Japan, as well as children orphaned by the civil war in Greece (Freundlich & Lieberthal, 2000; Riley, 1997), the adoption of children from South Korea initiated the large-scale practice of international adoption known today. Since 1971, more than a quarter million children have been adopted from overseas by American families (Evan B. Donaldson Adoption Institute, 2001), and in the last decade the number of foreign-born children entering the United States for adoption has nearly tripled, from 7,093 children in 1990 to an estimated 22,728 children in 2005 (U.S. State Department, 2006b).[1]

Currently, the practice of international adoption involves the transfer of an estimated 20,000 to 30,000 children from more than 50 countries annually, with the United States receiving the largest number of the world's children (Lovelock, 2000; Masson, 2001). Although official statistics are not available, the United States also sends an estimated 500 children annually for overseas adoption to other Western nations (Smolowe & Blackman, 1994; Stahl, 2005). South Korea has the longest running international adoption program and has sent more children overseas for adoption than any other country in the world to date, since the mid-1990s, mainland China and Russia have surpassed South Korea in the total number of children received per year. South Korea, however, remains one of the top four sending countries to the United States, along with mainland China, Russia, and Guatemala, averaging 1,700 to 2,000 children annually (U.S. State Department, 2006b).

Today, the first generation of internationally adopted Korean children has reached adulthood, and research has generally found that the majority of them have faired well (Feigelman, 2000; Feigelman & Silverman, 1984; Tizard, 1991). Many of these pioneers of international adoption, the vast majority of whom were adopted by Caucasian parents and raised in transracial families, have prospered to become healthy, contributing members of their society, but for many this came at a cost. In the past 25 years, adult Korean adoptees have returned to South Korea to experience their birth culture or search for their birth families and have articulated the need for postadoption services that address issues of identity, race, and culture. Others have formed organizations and associations to share their experiences and provide support, and many are imparting their wisdom—through books, film, music, and art—to the next generation of international adoptees and their multiethnic families (Hubinette, 2005; McGinnis, 2003).

The experiences of this first cohort of international adoptees and the evolution of practice within South Korea provide powerful lessons and reflect current controversies that continue to influence international adoption practice. The following is an overview of the historical, social, cultural, and political forces that shaped the development of international adoption in South Korea over the past 50 years, including the contributions of adult adopted Koreans to the field. This chapter will also discuss the lessons that can be learned from the Korean adoption experience and the particular role of geopolitics, policies, and the media in practice, and argues that the future continuation of the practice of international adoption is not assured.

"GI BABIES"

There can be little denying the toll of war on Korea's children. In 1951, one year into the war, there were already 100,000 orphaned children, and by 1954, one year after the war had ended, a total of 2 million children under the age of 18 had been displaced (Hubinette, 2004). In response to the plight of Korea's children, Western relief organizations set up orphanages and hospitals, evacuated children to safety, and established practices, including sponsorship, foster care, and adoption. Some of the orphaned children had already been taken in by soldiers on military bases as regimental mascots, houseboys, or interpreters, with some informally adopted before the end of the war (Hubinette, 2004). In addition, thousands of children born to Korean mothers and Western military fathers serving under the United Nations auspices during the war faced an uncertain future in a country obsessed with notions of blood purity. Many of these children, referred to as *Amerasian* or *GI babies*, were stigmatized by their mixed-race status and illegitimate births and consequently abandoned by both parents (Freundlich & Lieberthal, 2000).

The plight of Korea's mixed-race orphans was disseminated through Western media raising awareness of their situation. The Nobel and Pulitzer Prize winning author Pearl S. Buck was one of the most vocal supporters of Americans adopting Amerasian children abandoned after the Korean War. She had herself adopted seven mixed-race children from China through her agency, Welcome House, established in 1949 to place Amerasian children from

China and Japan (Hubinette, 2005). The Christian relief organization World Vision created a documentary on the situation of mixed-race Korean war orphans, which toured America in 1954 and inspired one farmer and his wife, Harry and Bertha Holt from Oregon, to adopt eight children (Hubinette, 2005). The Holts' efforts inspired others to adopt, and in 1956 Harry and Bertha Holt founded what is known today as Holt International Children's Services, a leading agency in international adoption placements; the Holts would also be instrumental in establishing permanent legislation to permit international adoption placements. In the years immediately following the war, from 1953 to 1959, 2,899 Korean children, the majority of whom were mixed-race war orphans, were adopted overseas (Hubinette, 2005).

At the end of the Korean War and the division of the country at the 38th parallel, North Korea also faced the problem of thousands of orphaned children. The communist state response was to designate these orphans as national heroes, establishing special orphanages and schools to help orphans advance in society and encouraging domestic adoption. More recently, information has revealed that during the war North Korea also sent war orphans overseas to various Communist countries, including Romania, Poland, Hungary, Czechoslovakia, Bulgaria, Mongolia, China, and Russia (Hubinette, 2002/2003). Some scholars argue that a cold war mentality and anti-Communist foreign policy contributed to the motivation by Americans to "rescue" the mixed-race orphans in South Korea as well; in addition, Christianity, missionary work, and religion played important roles in initiating international adoption from Korea on a mass scale, as many of the relief organizations establishing orphanages and arranging adoptions were Christian (Hubinette, 2005).

In Korea, children who were orphaned were traditionally taken care of by the extended family, with the first Western-style orphanages introduced by missionaries in the late 19th century (Hubinette, 2004). Although the Western practice of adoption by nonrelatives through an agency was generally not practiced, cultural beliefs rooted in the Neo-Confucian doctrine since the 17th century recognized adoption for the purposes of inheritance and continuation of paternal lineage, although adoption was generally viewed unfavorably (Kim, 2004). After the Korean War, cultural beliefs in ethnic homogeneity, discrimination toward children born out of wedlock, postwar chaos, poverty, social upheaval, and the decline of traditional Korean society contributed to the continuation of intercountry adoption practices. Close political and economic ties forged after the Korean War between the United States and South Korea facilitated the growth of international adoptions between the two nations and the practice's eventual establishment as an important component of South Korean social policy for orphaned and abandoned children (Sarri, Baik, & Bombyk, 1998).

FROM HUMANITARIAN AID TO "SUPPLY AND DEMAND"

In the decades following the Korean War, international adoption continued to expand in response to changing economic, social, and political realities. The nation faced problems of massive poverty, overpopulation, and child abandonment as it began a process of transformation from an agrarian society into a modern, industrial nation. Massive internal migration (between 1967 and 1976, 6.7 million people migrated from rural areas to cities), urbanization, and economic instability eroded traditional family structures and supports. Industrialization led to the abandonment of children born to young unmarried women recruited to work in new factories, and thousands of other children were abandoned due to urban poverty, family breakup, disability, neglect, and prostitution (Hubinette, 2005). Cultural attitudes contributed to the abandonment of children, including a pervasive stigma regarding adoption, cultural preference for boys, and a belief that abandoning a child would provide a better future, as well as nominal government support for single mothers and limited legal rights for women (Freundlich & Lieberthal, 2000; Kim, 2004). Under the Family Law of 1960, which codified patriarchal Neo-Confucian beliefs into modern law, a child was legally considered the father's property, and women had no rights to inheritance or custody of a child; the law would not be revised until 1991 (Kim, 2004).

In addition, governmental policies supported the practice of international adoptions as a means of addressing the problem of overpopulation and integrated the practice into national family planning and emigration programs (Hubinette, 2005). The national family planning measures, implemented during the military dictatorships under Park Chung Hee (1961–1979) and Chun Doo Hwan (1981–1987), included a one-child policy, sex education, contraception, legalized abortion (in 1973), and economic incentives to reduce family size, as well as overseas adoption (Hubinette, 2005; Sarri et al., 1998). The government also encouraged emigration, which resulted in the migration of 1 million Koreans overseas for work as cheap laborers, international adoption, and international marriage (Hubinette, 2005). By the end of the 1960s, the majority of children being sent overseas for adoption were no longer mixed-race war orphans but abandoned ethnic Korean children, the preponderance being girls (Hubinette, 2005). During the 1970s and mid-1980s, most of the children relinquished for intercountry adoption were born to young, unmarried, middle-class mothers; since the 1990s, the absolute majority of children sent abroad have been born to young, single mothers who enter homes for unwed mothers and make adoption plans (Hubinette, 2005; Rahn, 2005).

At the same time, by the early 1970s, South Korea's international adoption program was gaining popularity among Western nations, who perceived the practice to be highly successful and who were also experiencing cultural and societal changes. The advent of effective contraception, legalized abortion, weakening of cultural taboos regarding unmarried mothers, and government support for single parenthood, as well as the strengthening of women's rights in the 1970s, contributed to a decline in the number of White, healthy infants available for adoption as more mothers chose to parent (Lovelock, 2000; Masson, 2001; Vonk, Simms, & Nackerud, 1999). At the same time, fertility rates in Western nations began to drop while attitudes toward adoption became more liberalized. In the United States, adoption agencies began to shed traditional notions of physically "matching" children with adoptive parents, and transracial adoption became a new option. In addition, a growing number of socially progressive middle-class couples saw adoption as a way of expanding their families without contributing to population growth, and adopting across race as a demonstration of social tolerance (Benet, 1976). As a result of opposition to domestic transracial adoptions of Black children into White homes, many of the predominately Caucasian, middle-class and upper-class parents seeking to adopt saw a new option in international adoption (Lovelock, 2000; Vonk et al., 1999).

Thus, some scholars (Alstein & Simon, 1991; Lovelock, 2000) have distinguished two waves in the development of international adoption. Although both waves were motivated by humanitarian concerns, the first wave, which lasted until the mid-1970s, has been characterized by the need to find families for children; the second wave, shaped by falling fertility rates and scarcity of infants for domestic adoption in the United States and other Western nations, has been characterized by the demand for children. The latter development of international adoption has thus been characterized by the "language of economics" and transformed what had initially been intended as a humanitarian measure meant to provide one of several child welfare options for a child in need of out-of-home care into—in certain cases—a lucrative commercial business (United Nations Children's Fund International Child Development Centre, 1998, p. 3). The second wave of international adoption has also been distinguished by the development of international declarations and conventions in the 1980s and 1990s to address the protection and rights of children involved in international adoption.

DEVELOPING POLITICS AND POLICIES

The United States lacked a permanent policy to permit international adoptions until 1961. Early legislation provided temporary provisions for the immigration of certain groups of refugees and set strict quotas. The first formal international adoptions from South Korea occurred in 1953 when the U.S. Congress passed the Refugee Relief Act granting 4,000 special nonquota visas for orphans to enter the United States for adoption (Lovelock, 2000). In 1957, Congress passed the Orphan Eligibility Clause of the Immigration and Nationality Act, which replaced the Refugee Relief Act and allowed the continuation of international adoption practice. In 1961, the Orphan Clause was adopted as an amendment to the Immigration and Nationality Act, firmly establishing international adoption permanently in U.S. law (Lovelock, 2000). The South Korean government formally set up an overseas adoption program in 1954, with a presidential order establishing Children Placement Services (presently Social Welfare Society) for the purpose of placing mixed-race children with families in the United States and Europe through proxy adoption (Freundlich & Lieberthal, 2000). A legal and permanent framework for international adoption in South Korea would not be established until 1961 with the passage of the Orphan Adoption Special Law (Sarri et al., 1998). The law continued to evolve and in 1966 was amended to allow only licensed agencies, working with Western counterparts, to conduct international adoptions.

The decades of the 1970s and 1980s, during which South Korea would be ruled by military dictatorships, were also the decades in which the largest number of Korean children were sent overseas for adoption, with the number peaking at 6,597 children in 1976 and reaching an all-time high of 8,837 children in 1985 (Hubinette, 2004). At the same time, in these decades, the South Korean government would twice attempt to stop overseas adoption practice. In response to North Korea's public accusations of South Korea's "export" of babies for profit, the South Korean government revised its adoption law in 1976 and enacted the Five Year Plan for Adoption and Foster Care (1976–1981), aimed at reducing international adoptions (except for mixed-race and disabled children) and increasing domestic adoptions, with the eventual phasing out of international adoptions by 1981 (Sarri et al., 1998). Changes in the adoption law included restricting the number of receiving countries to 11, requiring adoption agencies in South Korea to be run by Koreans, and limiting the number of agencies that could conduct international adoptions to four: Social Welfare Society, Holt Children's Services, Korea Social Services, and Eastern Child Welfare Society (Hubinette, 2005).

By the early 1980s, this policy was abandoned as a result of the government's failure to significantly increase the number of domestic adoptions. In 1981, the government reversed its policy and expanded international adoptions by incorporating them as part of an emigration and "good-will ambassador" policy to foster ties with Western allies (Sarri et al., 1998). However, in the face of massive international criticism in Western media of South Korea's adoption practices during the 1988 Olympic Games in Seoul, this policy was overturned. In addition, reports in the early 1980s of trafficking, corruption, and agencies hastily sending children not available for adoption overseas (which ended the practice of sending abandoned children for international adoption) led the government, in 1989, to enact a policy that would terminate international adoptions by 1996, except for mixed-race or disabled children, and provide tax incentives to promote domestic adoption (Hubinette, 2005; Sarri et al., 1998).

In 1994, with continuing low rates of domestic adoption, this policy would be abandoned again. In 1996, the South Korean government revised its adoption law to what is currently known as the Special Law on Adoption Promotion and Procedure. The new law called for an annual decrease in international adoptions by 3% to 5%, with an eventual phasing out by 2015; two small revisions to the law were made in 1999 and 2000 (Hubinette, 2005). Since then the number of children sent overseas for adoption has hovered around 2,000 children annually, except during the Asian economic crisis (1997–1999), when international adoptions increased slightly to 2,400 "IMF orphans" (Hubinette, 2005). The South Korean government has continued to try to promote domestic adoptions. In 2005, the government designated May 11 as National Adoption Day, and in March 2006, the government was considering financial aid for adoptive parents (Bae, 2005; Lee, 2006). Despite these efforts, of the 9,420 children available for adoption in 2005, 1,461 were adopted domestically while 2,001 children were adopted overseas (Lee, 2006).

By the late 1980s and early 1990s, awareness of corruption in international adoption practice, including black markets, stories of baby farms, and poor women being coerced into relinquishing their children, drove an interest in developing international instruments to protect children involved in international adoption and address abuses (Lovelock, 2000). In this climate, the Hague Convention on Protection of Children and Co-operation in Respect of Intercountry Adoption (hereafter referred to as the Hague Convention) and its Recommendation on Displaced Children was convened and adopted on May 29, 1993, and entered into force on May 1, 1995 (Hague Conference on Private International Law, 1993). The Hague Convention was created to establish a legal framework for the arrangement and formalization of international adoptions through a system of national central authorities. In addition, the Hague Convention reinforced the importance of adoptions being arranged in the best interests of the child and with respect for his or her fundamental rights, while acknowledging international adoption as offering a permanent family to a child "for whom a suitable family cannot be found in his or her State of origin" (Hague Conference on Private International Law, 1993, Preamble).

The Hague Convention is limited in that it is not an international criminal code but rather only a secure framework that works against abuse indirectly (Masson, 2001). In addition, the Hague Convention only applies to contracting states, although in 2000 a recommendation was adopted to encourage the application of its standards and safeguards to all international adoptions, including those countries that had not joined the Convention. As of January 2006, 68 countries have joined the convention, including mainland China, which ratified the convention in 2005 (Hague Conference on Private International Law, 2005). The United States was an original signatory to the Hague Convention in 1994, and in 2000 the U.S. Congress passed the Intercountry Adoption Act of 2000 (IAA) to authorize the ratification of the Hague Convention once preparations for its implementation had been established. In February 2006, the final regulations for implementation needed for ratification were published, and it is estimated that the Hague Convention will be in force in the United States by 2007 (U.S. State Department, 2006a). South Korea has not signed the Hague Convention, although in 2005 the government was evaluating possible adoption (Bae, 2005).

ADULT ADOPTEE EXPERIENCES

The first generation of Korean-born, adult, adopted people began to return to their birth country by the late 1970s as participants in motherland tours organized by adoption agencies and associations in South Korea, or independently (Hubinette, 2005). By the end of the 1980s, advertisements submitted by adopted Koreans searching for birth parents began to appear in the South Korean media, and by the 1990s a Korean television show to assist adoptees in finding birth families had developed (Hubinette, 2005). Since the late 1980s, myriad services have sprung up in the United States in response to the maturation of the first generation of international adoptees, including the development of culture camps for internationally adopted youth. The adult adopted Korean community continued to evolve throughout the 1990s, facilitated by the advent of the Internet, as formal and informal associations developed throughout the United States, Europe, and South Korea, where some adopted Koreans were choosing to live permanently.

The realization of a distinct adopted Korean community culminated in a 3-day conference held in September 1999 in Washington, D.C. The Gathering of the First Generation of Adult Korean Adoptees (hereafter known as the Gathering), sponsored by Holt International Children's Services, the New York-based adult adoptee organization Also-Known-As, the Korea Society, and the Evan B. Donaldson Adoption Institute, brought together nearly 400 adults adopted from Korea between 1955 and 1985, representing more than 30 U.S. states and several European countries, for the first time (Freundlich & Lieberthal, 2000). This conference was unique in its purpose to provide an opportunity for the first generation of adopted Koreans to share their experiences and connect as a community. Participants discussed (in small groups based on birth years) topics such as memories of Korea and arrival at their new home, impact of early experiences on adoptees' lives, discrimination, identity, dating and relationships, feelings toward Korea, search and reunion, and perceptions of adoption (Freundlich & Lieberthal, 2000). To gain greater insight into the experiences of adult adopted Koreans, the Evan B. Donaldson Adoption Institute surveyed participants and published one of the first reports to examine international adoption from the adult adopted person's perspective. This conference was covered widely by both U.S. and South Korean media, propelling recognition of these pioneers in international adoption.

At the same time, the South Korean government under the presidency of Kim Dae Jung (1998–2003) took a strong interest in adoption and vastly increased awareness and support for adopted Koreans. President Kim Dae Jung, whose democratic election marked the first peaceful transfer of power in South Korean history, had met overseas adopted Koreans during his time in exile as an opposition leader. In his inaugural address, in early 1998, he stated that international adoption would be one of the main issues during his presidency and 8 months later invited a group of 29 adopted Koreans from eight nations to the presidential Blue House in Seoul (Hubinette, 2005). During this meeting in October 1998, the president formally apologized on behalf of the nation for sending so many children abroad for adoption and encouraged adoptees to take pride in their Korean roots while remaining loyal citizens of their adoptive nations (Savasta, 1999).

At the Gathering, First Lady Lee Hee-ho wrote a letter and recorded a video welcome to greet the participants. In her welcome address, she reiterated the president's view of adopted Koreans being unique bridges between South Korea and Western nations, and members of the larger overseas Korean community (Hubinette, 2005). Efforts to include adopted Koreans as part of South Korea's diaspora included the creation of the F-4 Visa for overseas adopted Koreans in 1999, which allowed them, as well as other overseas Koreans, to legally reside and work in South Korea indefinitely (Global Overseas Adoptee Link, 2001). Since 1999, numerous organizations in South Korea have developed programs for adopted Koreans to help them embrace their cultural roots, including motherland visits, guest houses, language programs, and searches for birth families (Hubinette, 2005). In 1993, the Ministry of Health and Welfare began to track the number of adopted Koreans returning to visit their adoption agencies in South Korea; this number has more than doubled from 1,236 visitors in 1993 to 2,760 visitors in 2001 (Hubinette, 2004).

Since the Gathering, adopted Koreans in the United States have continued to meet at "mini-gatherings" throughout the country, new organizations of adopted Koreans have sprung up, and a plethora of Web sites now connect adopted Koreans throughout the world. A second gathering, organized by adopted Korean associations in Europe, took place in Oslo, Norway, in July 2001, and in 2004 a third gathering of adopted Koreans was organized in Seoul, South Korea; a fourth gathering is also being planned for Seoul in 2007, sponsored by the newly formed International Korean Adoptee Associations network. In addition, adopted Koreans are collaborating with internationally adopted adults from Vietnam, the Philippines, India, and Colombia, and some have formed mentorship programs for internationally adopted youth, particularly the thousands of girls adopted from mainland China since the 1990s.

Some adopted Koreans are now scholars, contributing to the growing body of research on international adoption, while others have written memoirs and anthologies and made documentaries and films expressing the challenge of balancing identities—one by birth and the other by adoption—and the paradoxical losses and gains inherent in adoption. When the first adopted Koreans were sent overseas 50 years ago, most adoption professionals assumed those children would never return to their country of birth or be interested in their countries of origin. Today, most adoption practitioners know that this is not true, and many parents adopting today are encouraged to maintain connections to their adopted child's birth culture.

The formation of a community of internationally adopted adults is also a unique evolution of international adoption, demonstrating how adopted adults are not passive recipients but active agents. Over the past 50 years, adopted adults and their families are bending traditional notions of family, ethnicity, and race to accommodate their unique experience, and transforming the societies in which they live.

LESSONS LEARNED

International adoption in South Korea began in the ashes of war, reflecting the geopolitical nature of international adoption and ties to wars, disasters, political and economic crises, and social upheavals. The effort to adopt Amerasian children born to U.S. military fathers and Vietnamese mothers would be echoed in the aftermath of the Vietnam War. Economic crises and civil wars resulted in many children from Latin America being adopted in the 1970s, and, with the fall of the Iron Curtain and massive media attention to the plight of children in former Soviet states, such as Romania, in the late 1980s, many children from Central and Eastern Europe were adopted overseas (McGinnis, 2005). Most recently, overpopulation in mainland China, a cultural preference for boys, and a "one-child" policy have contributed to the availability and adoption of thousands of abandoned Chinese girls overseas since the 1990s.

The Korean international adoption experience also reflects many of the factors that continue to contribute to the development of this practice in sending countries, including poverty, social and economic collapse, cultural stigma toward illegitimate births, racial and gender prejudices, disruption of traditional extended families, overpopulation, limited rights for women, and lack of a developed social welfare system to support families, resulting in few alternatives besides the abandonment of a child. Similarly, factors contributing to the growth in Korean adoptions in the 1970s continue to be reasons for there being "demand" for international adoption by Western nations, including declining fertility rates, fewer infants available for domestic adoptions, postponement of childbirth and marriage, destigmatization of single motherhood, and equality of rights for women. In addition, the Internet and proliferation of adoptive parent organizations have facilitated information sharing about adopting internationally (Masson, 2001).

The history of adoptions from South Korea also shows the susceptibility of international adoption to changes in governmental policies and negative media attention. Although the United States has passed, legislation to make it easier for children who have been adopted overseas to become naturalized citizens (Child Citizenship Act of 2000, Pub. L. No. 106-395) and other legislation to provide a tax credit to any parent who adopts (Economic Growth and Tax Relief Reconciliation Act of 2001, Pub. L. No. 107-16), recently, other nations have begun to restrict the practice. In January 2005, Russia passed a law that extends, from 3 to 6 months, the time orphans must be on the federal data bank before they are eligible for international adoption; and after the untimely death of an adopted Russian child at the hands of his American mother in May 2005, politicians have called for even tighter regulations (McGinnis, 2005; Sector, 2005).

The European Union (EU) has required nations to "outlaw intercountry adoption as a condition for joining" (Bartholet, 2005, p. 10). In response, Romania enacted a law in 2004 eliminating international adoption (except for adoption by children's grandparents), which left approximately 1,700 international adoption cases that had begun to be processed before the ban in limbo (U.S. State Department, 2005). Reports of baby trafficking in mainland China in early February 2006 were swiftly crushed by the government, which was quick to assure that none of those children had been involved in overseas placements with American families (Associated Press, 2006). An all-time high of 7,906 Chinese children adopted by U.S. families in 2005 (U.S. State Department, 2006b) was, coupled with the pending 2008 Summer Olympics in Beijing and stories of child trafficking parallel to those arising during the 1988 Olympics in Seoul; but only time will tell if this will have any impact on China's international adoption policy.

Over the last half century, international adoption has become a multinational and multi-million-dollar industry, but considerable controversy remains regarding its practice, which leaves its future uncertain. Opponents of international adoption argue that the practice exploits impoverished nations, robs children of the opportunity to be raised in their community of origin and of their identity, takes away resources that could be used to improve the lives of a larger number of children, and contributes to the problem of abduction, coercion, and trafficking of children (Masson, 2001). Supporters of international adoption counter that the practice benefits children by removing them from the detrimental effects of growing up in institutional settings or on the streets by providing permanent families; helps children who might otherwise be marginalized in their societies as a result of illegitimacy, disability, or racial/ethnic difference; and provides children with families, in a context where there is little evidence that the elimination or restriction of international adoptions would remove the problems of poverty that contribute to the abandonment of children (Bartholet, 2005).

Thus, much has to be learned still about the implications of the practice of international adoption, so policies can be developed that reflect not only its impact on the lives of adopted individuals and their families but also its ramifications in society in both sending and receiving countries. The experience of adopted Koreans already provides some lessons on the impact of international adoption on race, culture, ethnicity, identity, and family and also the lifelong experience of adoption; however, research examining their experiences as adults and their effect on American society is limited. In addition, balancing the need to respect a child's right to his or her ethnic identity and, religious and cultural background against the known detrimental effects caused by early deprivation of primary caregivers (as a result of institutional care, or multiple caregivers in foster care) is a challenge for all those interested in the welfare and protection of children.

What is evident is the great need to find families for children. According to a 2004 UNICEF report, an estimated 143 million orphans from birth to 17 years of age around the world are in need of care (UNICEF, 2004). International adoptions will never be able to provide all of those millions of children with homes and, in some cases, may not be in a child's best interest. However, understanding the evolution of international adoption in South Korea can provide invaluable insights for the development of international adoption practices and their role in providing one of several options for children in need of out-of-home care. In addition, understanding the experiences of the first generation of internationally adopted adults—including the benefits and trade-offs—would turn the focus in the field to finding out what is truly in a child's best interest from the perspective of those who are supposed to be the beneficiaries of the practice.

NOTE

1. U.S. State Department data on international adoptions are based on the number of immigrant visas issued to U.S. citizens for orphans from other countries within a given federal fiscal year (October 1 to September 30) and reflect a child's immigration and not adoption. Although the visa records are relatively reliable, the year a visa was issued does not necessarily reflect the year an adoption was finalized, depending on the type of visa that was issued: IR3 visas are issued for orphans whose adoptions are finalized within their birth country prior to immigrating to the United States and IR4 visas are issued for orphans whose adoptions are finalized within U.S. state courts after they have immigrated to the United States. The regulations in the birth country determine the kind of visa issued.

REFERENCES

Alstein, H., & Simon, R. J. (1991). *Intercountry adoption: A multinational perspective*. New York: Praeger.

Associated Press. (2006, March 17). *No babies in trafficking case sent to US: China*. Retrieved March 25, 2006, from www.chinadaily.com.cn/english/doc/2006-03/17/content_542254.htm

Bae, Keun-min. (2005, March 22). May 11 designated as Adoption Day. *Korea Times*. Retrieved March 23, 2005, from http://times.hankooki.com/lpage/200503/kt2005032215342910220.htm

Bartholet, E. (2005). International adoption. In Lora Askeland (Ed.), *Children and youth in adoption, orphanages, and foster care: A historical handbook and guide*. Westport, CT: Greenwood.

Benet, M. K. (1976). *The politics of adoption*. New York: Free Press.

Evan B. Donaldson Adoption Institute. (2001). *International adoption facts*. Retrieved February 12, 2006, from www.adoptioninstitute.org/research/internationaladoption.php

Feigelman, W. (2000). Adjustments of transracially and inracially adopted young adults. *Child and Adolescent Social Work Journal, 17*, 165–183.

Feigelman, W., & Silverman, A. (1984). The long-term effects of transracial adoption. *Social Service Review, 58*, 588–602.

Freundlich, M., & Lieberthal, J. K. (2000, June). Korean adoptees perception of international adoption. *Evan B. Donaldson Adoption Institute: New York*. Retrieved March 6, 2003, from www.adoption institute.org/proed/korfindings.html

Global Overseas Adoptee Link. (2001). *F-4 visa*. Retrieved March 15, 2006, from http://goal.or.kr/english/guide/f4.htm

Hague Conference on Private International Law. (1993, May 29). *Convention on protection of children and co-operation in respect of intercountry adoption*. Retrieved February 15, 2006, from http://hcch.e-vision.nl/index_en.php?act=conventions.text&cid=69

Hague Conference on Private International Law. (2005, September 16). *China joins The Hague Intercountry Adoption Convention: Over 200 experts from 66 nations meet at The Hague to discuss the protection of children in intercountry adoption*. Retrieved September 25, 2005, from http://hcch.e-vision.nl/index_en.php?act=events.details&year=2005&varevent=110&zoek=intercountry%20adoption

Hubinette, Tobias. (2002/2003, Winter). North Korea and adoption. *Korean Quarterly, 5*(2), 24–25.

Hubinette, Tobias. (2004). *Demographic information and Korean adoption history: Guide to Korea for overseas adopted Koreans*. Seoul, South Korea: Overseas Koreans Foundation.

Hubinette, Tobias. (2005). *Comforting an orphaned nation: Representations of international adoption and adopted Koreans in Korean popular culture*. Unpublished doctoral dissertation, Stockholm University Department of Oriental Languages, Stockholm, Sweden.

Kim, E. (2004). *Adoption in Korea, then and now: Guide to Korea for overseas adopted Koreans*. Seoul, South Korea: Overseas Koreans Foundation.

Lee, Jin-woo. (2006, March 17). Foster parents to get 2 million won for adoption. *Korea Times*. Retrieved March 25, 2006, from http://times.hankooki.com/lpage/nation/200603/kt2006031717574611970.htm

Lovelock, K. (2000). Intercountry adoption as a migratory practice: A comparative analysis of intercountry adoption and immigration policy and practice in the United States, Canada, and New Zealand in the post W.W. II period. *International Migration Review, 34*(3), 907–923.

Masson, J. (2001). Intercountry adoption: A global problem or a global solution? *Journal of International Affairs, 55*(1), 141–146.

McGinnis, H. (2003). Adult Korean intercountry adoptees: A resource for adoption practice. *Columbia University Journal of Student Social Work, 1*(1), 8–14.

McGinnis, H. (2005). *Intercountry adoption in emergencies: The tsunami orphans*. New York: Evan B. Donaldson Adoption Institute.

Office of the Press Secretary. (2003, January 13). *The centennial of Korean immigration to the United States: A proclamation by the President of the United States of America*. Retrieved January 16, 2006, from www.whitehouse.gov/news/releases/2003/01/20030113-4.html

Rahn, K. (2005, March 1). Single mothers face discrimination. *Korea Times*. Retrieved March 23, 2005, from http://times.hankooki.com/lpage/200503/kt2005030118042110230.htm

Riley, N. (1997). American adoptions of Chinese girls: The socio-political matrices of individual decisions. *Women's Studies International Forum, 20*(1), 87–102.

Sarri, R. C., Baik, Y., & Bombyk, M. (1998). Goal displacement and dependency in South Korean-United States intercountry adoption. *Children and Youth Services Review, 20*(1–2), 87–114.

Savasta, P. (1999, January). Adoption news: President Kim Dae Jung's address to overseas adoptees. *Transcultured Magazine, 1*(2), 20.

Sector, C. (2005, May 17). Boy's death may halt U.S. adoptions from Russia. *ABC Online*. Retrieved May 26, 2005, from http://abcnews.go.com/International/US/story?id=755137&page=1

Smolowe, J., & Blackman, A. (1994, August 22). Babies for export. *Time*, pp. 64–65.

Stahl, L. (2005, February 13). Born in the USA; United States exporting Black infants for adoption in Canada and other countries. In Don Hewitt (Producer), *60 Minutes*. New York: CBS.

Tizard, B. (1991). Intercountry adoption: A review of the evidence. *Journal of Child Psychology and Psychiatry, 32*, 743–756.

UNICEF. (2004). *Children on the Brink 2004 Report*. Retrieved January 2005, from www.unicef .org/publications/index_22212.html

United Nations Children's Fund International Child Development Centre. (1998, December). *Innocenti digest 4: Intercountry adoption*. Florence, Italy: Author. Retrieved November 9, 2002, from www.unicef-icdc.org

U.S. State Department. (2005, December 16). *U.S. backs European request for Romanian adoptions to proceed*. Retrieved December 23, 2005, from http://usinfo.state.gov/xarchives/display.html?p= washfile-english&y=2005&m=December&x=20051216170414mvyelwarc0.8375666&t=livefeeds/ wf-latest.html

U.S. State Department. (2006a, February 15). *The Hague Convention on intercountry adoption: Accreditation/approval regulations published in the Federal Register*. Retrieved February 24, 2006, from www.state.gov/r/pa/prs/ps/2006/61272.htm

U.S. State Department. (2006b). *Immigrant visas issued to orphans coming to the US*. Retrieved February 6, 2006, from http://travel.state.gov/family/adoption/stats/stats_451.html

Vonk, M., Simms, P., & Nackerud, L. (1999). Political and personal aspects of intercountry adoption of Chinese children in the United States. *Families in Society: The Journal of Contemporary Human Services, 80*(5), 496–505.

Special Issues in Adoption

Preface

AMANDA L. BADEN

Montclair State University

This section of *The Handbook of Adoption: Implications for Researchers, Practitioners, and Families* presents special topics in adoption that deserve attention but have not yet reached wider attention in the literature. The six chapters included in this part continue to answer the question of who adopts and who is adopted, but these questions are expanded to include an understanding of the conditions under which individuals are adopted and how these conditions may play out in early environmental situations. We open this part with a chapter by Ruth McRoy, Harold Grotevant, Susan Ayers-Lopez, and Susan Henney titled "Open Adoptions: Longitudinal Outcomes for the Adoption Triad." This chapter begins to address open adoption—a form of adoption that presents alternatives to the more traditionally closed adoption system. Open adoption refers to adoptions that permit various levels of contact between birth and adoptive families throughout the life span of the adoptee, and the contact can range from full disclosure and personal meetings to exchanging information and pictures only. Because the life course of an open adoption has been minimally addressed in the adoption literature, McRoy and her colleagues described various types of open adoption and some background on this form of adoption. Using data from a longitudinal study, they examined the outcomes found for varying degrees of openness in adoption for birth mothers, adoptive parents, and adopted children. They looked at satisfactions and dissatisfactions with varying degrees of contact, changes in openness and relationships over time, and the impact of openness on the socioemotional adjustment of adopted children. This chapter shares interview data from adoptive families, their adopted children, and birth mothers who placed children for adoption 12 to 20 years ago. They also analyzed the data both quantitatively and qualitatively, resulting in a unique picture of the course of their adoption openness. McRoy and her colleagues also discuss the implications of this study for clinical practice, policy, and research.

In "Single-Parent Adoptions and Clinical Implications" (Chapter 13), Behnaz Pakizegi presents an overview of issues found in single-parent led adoptive families. She notes the increasing numbers of adoptive families led by single parents and begins her chapter with a deconstruction of the stigma that adoptive families, single-parent led families, and ultimately single-parent led adoptive families experience. Pakizegi works to clarify myths about these families by reviewing existing research studies. Overall, she notes that family process and functioning have been found to be more important than family structure for single-parent led adoptive families. She also notes methodological limitations and the gaps in the literature on adolescent and adult children from single-parent led adoptive families. Pakizegi notes that the stigma these families face and the increasing research on adoptions pointing to some important clinical issues suggest that new research is needed on single adoptive parents. In this chapter, implications of the findings on stigma and of the characteristics of these families for clinical work with child and adult members of single-parent led adoptive families are discussed and illustrated through critical case studies. Pakizegi also conducts critical analyses of the "second best" status of single parenthood and adoption and of the "loss" theory for clinicians' successful work with these families.

Elizabeth Keagy and Barbara Rall, in "The Special Needs of Special-Needs Adoptees and Their Families" (Chapter 14), amply address adoptive families of children with special needs. Their chapter outlines the unique challenges faced by these families such as previous abuse and neglect, attachment difficulties, and behavioral problems. They review effective pre- and post-adoption services designed to meet the needs of these families, and they include adequate preparation, education, and information, establishing appropriate expectations, monitoring parental stress, counseling services, respite care, and support groups. Case studies illustrate their concerns and treatment strategies. Keagy and Rall also suggest that accessible and available services can help to minimize adoption disruption and ensure positive adoption outcomes.

Lesbian and gay adoptive families are addressed in Chapter 15 by Carol Boyer. This chapter, "Double Stigma: The Impact of Adoption Issues on Lesbian and Gay Adoptive Parents," acknowledges that although adoptive families face unique concerns that are intrinsic to their nonbiological status, lesbian and gay adoptive families encounter these same issues, but their experience of them is different due to their membership in an already-stigmatized group. In addition, lesbian and gay adoptive families encounter issues that heterosexual adoptive families do not, such as negative social attitudes toward lesbian and gay parenting, ambivalent attitudes toward gays and lesbians among adoption professionals, and inconsistent—or sometimes absent—legal protections. This chapter examines the literature pertaining to these issues and the impact they have on the adoption experience for lesbians and gay men. Implications for clinical practice will be discussed as well as possible avenues of future research.

Kathleen Doyle considers "The Importance of Kinship Relationships for Children in Foster Care" in Chapter 16. Doyle argues that the relationships in the foster care setting among foster families, children, and their biological families are critical to children's development of identity, self-esteem, and successful maturation. In this chapter, Doyle examines some of the critical similarities and differences between children in foster care and those adopted. Doyle suggests that one of the primary challenges to foster caregivers and policymakers in the 21st century is to incorporate an understanding of the history of foster care and its successes and failures to effectively assist these children and families.

The final chapter in this section examines an area that is of great importance although not well studied. Francine Fishman and Elliotte Sue Harrington's "School Issues and Adoption: Academic Considerations and Adaptation" (Chapter 17) does a thorough job of examining the issues that arise for adoptees and adoptive families during the school-age years. This chapter considers the educational and school-related issues that may be related to the adoption status of children. Fishman and Harrington address the following topics: developmental ages and stages through adolescence; adoption-related implications for school and school-based issues; the impact of adoption on school performance; school interventions; IQ and environment; considerations of race, culture, and ethnic identity; and special education issues. Fishman and Harrington use vignettes and case studies throughout the chapter to illustrate common topic-related concerns.

LEARNING GOALS

Each of these authors had in mind specific learning goals as they approached their respective chapters. Below are some general learning objectives for this part that we encourage our readers to consider as they delve into this foundational section.

- To explore the service needs of families with evolving openness in adoption.
- To explore the impact of openness on the socioemotional adjustment of the adopted child.
- To understand the additional layers of stigma and challenge that single-parent led adoptive families experience.
- To understand the outcomes and developmental issues for adopted children and their parents found for single-parent led adoptive families.
- To address the clinical issues and strategies useful for working with single-parent led adoptive families.
- To reach an understanding that the severance of kinship, either through legal procedures or placement strategies, has a profound impact on the personal identity and future of the child in foster care, often superseding other traumatic events in the child's life.
- To recognize that the attitudes, beliefs, and emotional reactions of foster parents and important others (teachers, caseworkers, peers) toward the biological parents of children in foster care can affect these children in significant ways (self-esteem, self-worth, desire for relationship with biological parents, etc.).
- To develop an understanding of the origins of adoption law in the United States and the legal developments leading to the current structure of adoption law.
- To address and appreciate the complexity and ongoing evolution of adoption law in the United States as it affects children in foster care.
- To understand what motivates behavior difficulties in special-needs adoptees and how parents can cope more effectively.
- To become familiar with the aspects associated with special-needs adoptions.
- To learn about essential pre- and postadoption services that can ensure positive adoption outcomes.
- To understand LGB families as a multicultural minority and the ways in which their experience of forming family differs from that of the majority.
- To assist readers in examining their own alignment with mainstream U.S. culture with respect to marrying and forming families.
- To assist readers in exploring the assumptions and biases they may hold.
- To understand how the concept of stigma can affect alternative families—particularly alternative families of color—on multiple levels.
- To understand the educational and school-related issues that school-age adopted children experience during major developmental periods.
- To assist educators, parents, clinicians, and adoption professionals in appropriately recognizing adoption issues as they may arise within educational settings.
- To consider how factors like school assignments and assessment can be sensitive to and appropriate for issues related to adoption, including transracial and international adoptive backgrounds of students.

Open Adoptions

12

Longitudinal Outcomes for the Adoption Triad

RUTH G. McROY

University of Texas at Austin

HAROLD D. GROTEVANT

University of Minnesota

SUSAN AYERS-LOPEZ

University of Texas at Austin

SUSAN M. HENNEY

University of Houston–Downtown

Openness in adoption can be broadly defined as a purposeful act of contact or communication between adoptive parents, adopted persons, and birth families. Openness in an adoption can begin at any time prior to placement or after placement. It may vary in form and may include sharing information, gifts, letters, phone calls, and so on. In addition, it may vary in terms of frequency and who initiates and is

AUTHORS' NOTE: This chapter is an adaptation of two previously published chapters with permission of the publisher, British Association for Adoption and Fostering (BAAF). The excerpted materials were published in the following edited book: Neil, B. & Howe, D. (Eds.). (2004). *Contact in permanent placements: Research, theory, and practice*. London: British Association for Adoption and Fostering. Authors and titles of the original published chapters in the BAAF book were as follows: Grotevant, Harold D., McRoy, Ruth G., and Ayers-Lopez, Susan. (2004). "Contact after adoption: Outcomes for infant placements in the USA" (pp. 7–25). Henney, Susan M., Ayers-Lopez, Susan, McRoy, Ruth G., and Grotevant, Harold D. (2004). "A longitudinal perspective on changes in adoption openness: The birth mother story" (pp. 26–45).

involved in the contact (Frasch, Brooks, & Barth, 2000; Grotevant & McRoy, 1998). It may also vary in terms of the duration of the exchange because at times contact may cease for a period of time and in other openness arrangements contact is ongoing.

Contact between members of a child's adoptive family and birth family is becoming a significant issue to consider in adoption planning. Early debates focused on whether contact was "good" or "bad" overall. The dialogue has now shifted to ask more subtle questions about what type of contact might be advisable, for whom, and when. For example, the act of communication in open adoptions may, for some birthmothers, unlock a satisfying and mutually agreeable long-term relationship with the adoptive family. For others, the communication is equally satisfying but is of short duration and is used to fill a void of knowledge about the adopted child. Still other birthmothers yearn for communication, but have none, and are dissatisfied with their lack of knowledge about the child or relationship with the adoptive family. The factors leading to satisfaction and dissatisfaction with adoption openness, or the lack thereof, are as varied as the life experiences of those involved in the adoption.

We have been following 190 adoptive families and 169 birthmothers since the mid-1980s (McRoy, Grotevant, & White, 1988; Grotevant & McRoy, 1998), when adoption agencies in the United States began offering options that included contact between members of the child's families of adoption and birth. The children were voluntarily placed for adoption by their birthmothers in the late 1970s to early 1980s. The mean age of placement was 4 weeks (range: immediately after birth to 44 weeks). Ninety percent of the children were placed by 9 weeks. Because of this restricted range, age of placement was not an important contributing factor to child outcomes and will not be discussed further in this chapter.

Adoptive families and birthmothers were recruited through 35 private adoption agencies across all regions of the United States. The sample intentionally did not include transracial, international, or special-needs placements so that the clearest possible conclusions about openness could be drawn. Families and birthmothers were first interviewed between 1987 and 1992, when the children were between 4 and 12 years of age (mean age = 7.8 years) and again between 1995 and 2000, when the children were adolescents (mean age 15.7 years). For a more detailed description of the entire sample, see Grotevant and McRoy (1997, 1998).

The sample included 190 adoptive fathers, 190 adoptive mothers, 171 adopted children, and 169 birthmothers at Wave 1 (W1). Seventy-seven of these families were in "corresponding sets" or kinship networks, in which we interviewed the adoptive parents, child placed for adoption, and the child's birthmother. Almost all families were White, and all placements were within-race. At Wave 2 (W2), the longitudinal sample included at least one member of 177 of the originally participating 190 adoptive families (173 adoptive mothers, 162 adoptive fathers, 156 adopted adolescents), and 127 of the original 169 birthmothers.

In this research, openness is conceptualized as a spectrum involving differing degrees and modes of contact and communication between adoptive family members and the child's birth parent(s). Families from across the full range of openness participated. Four major categories were used to differentiate among levels of openness:

- *confidential* adoptions, in which no information was shared between birth and adoptive parents after 6 months postplacement (at W1: $n = 62$ adoptive families, 52 birthmothers; at W2: $n = 51$ adoptive families, 31 birthmothers);
- *mediated stopped* adoptions, in which information was transmitted between adoptive parents and birthmothers by agency caseworkers, but the information sharing had stopped by the time we interviewed the participants (at W1: $n = 17$ adoptive families, 18 birthmothers; at W2: $n = 31$ adoptive families, 29 birthmothers);
- *ongoing mediated* adoptions, in which indirect exchange of letters, pictures, or gifts was mediated by the agency and was continuing (at W1: $n = 52$ adoptive families, 58 birthmothers; at W2: $n = 19$ adoptive families, 23 birthmothers); and
- *fully disclosed* adoptions, in which direct sharing of information occurred between the adoptive parents and the birth mother, usually accompanied by face-to-face meetings.

For 57 adoptive families and 41 birthmothers, this contact was *ongoing* at the time of the interview; for 2 adoptive families, the contact had ceased and the parties did not intend to resume contact (*stopped*). At W2, there were 67 adoptive families and 43 birthmothers with ongoing fully disclosed arrangements as well as 9 adoptive families and 1 birth mother with fully disclosed adoptions in which contact had stopped. The frequency and intensity of contact in the fully disclosed adoptions ranged quite widely, from occasional letters or phone calls to several meetings per year. The exchange of phone calls, letters, and holiday and birthday gifts was more typical. When the adoptive family lived far away from the birth mother, visits were less frequent, although letters and phone calls may have been exchanged more frequently. In some cases, contact with the birth mother was infrequent, but there was more contact with other members of her extended family.

The project has studied changing family relationships within the context of changing social policies and practices. (For details about changing adoption agency practices that occurred during the study, see Henney, Onken, McRoy, & Grotevant, 1998; Henney, McRoy, Ayers-Lopez, & Grotevant, 2003.) It is the largest study involving personal interviews and standardized questionnaires with adoptive parents, birth parents, and adopted children experiencing a range of postadoption contact and followed longitudinally.

STUDY METHODOLOGY

At W1, adoptive families were interviewed in their homes in one session that lasted 3 to 4 hours. The session included separate interviews with each parent and the target adopted child as well as a joint couples' interview with the adoptive parents. Several questionnaires were administered, including the Understanding of Adoption Scale (Brodzinsky, Singer, & Braff, 1984), Self-Perception Scale for Children (Harter, 1985), and Child Adaptive Behavior Inventory (CABI; Miller, 1987). Eight years later, at W2, participants were once again interviewed in their homes. The session lasted 4 to 5 hours and included individual interviews with each parent and the target adopted child as well as a family interaction task. Several questionnaires were also administered, including the Child Behavior Checklist (CBCL; Achenbach & Edelbrock, 1983), Youth Self-Report (YSR; Achenbach & Edelbrock, 1987), and Brief Symptom Inventory (BSI; Derogatis, 1993).

At both waves, birthmothers were interviewed by phone using a structured interview schedule and were administered several standardized questionnaires. The four major topics assessed in the interview included (1) birthmothers' adjustment to the adoption decision, (2) changes in openness, (3) relationship with the adoptive parents, and (4) relationship with the adopted adolescent. In reference to openness, each birth mother described, via a structured openness checklist, the degree to which there has been identified or nonidentified information sharing and contact between the birth mother and the adoptive parents and/or the adopted child.

At W2, 1995 to 2000, 127 birthmothers from the original sample participated again. The average age of the birthmothers at the W2 interview was 35.42 years (ranging from 29 to 54). The birthmothers' average family income was about $30,000 per year, with a range of less than $3,000 to more than $50,000. Slightly more than a third of birthmother participants had family incomes greater than $50,000. birthmothers reported an average of 14.16 years of education (e.g., between 2 and 3 years of college), ranging from 10 to 20 years of education. One hundred and twenty-three birthmothers (98%) were White/Caucasian, two (2%) were Hispanic/Mexican American, and 1 (1%) was Black/African American. Eighty-four birthmothers (66%) were married, 25 (20%) divorced, and 18 (14%) single.

Table 12.1	Nine-Category Openness Definitions
Category	*Definition*
Confidential	No information is shared between triad members beyond 6 months postplacement. Any information shared before 6 months is nonidentified.
Confidential with updates	Information is given to update agency files after placement, and this information is not necessarily intended for current transmission.
Mediated stopped	Any contact has stopped for at least 1 year past the point when it normally should have occurred. Before the stop, all contact was arranged through the agency or agency personnel and occurred beyond 6 months after placement. Information shared was intended for the other party and was perceived as received.
Mediated stopped with updates	All criteria for mediated stopped adoptions are met, plus file updates have occurred at the agency.
Mediated paused	Contact has occurred through the agency, but there has been a temporary cessation of a regular pattern of contact without an agreement or a conscious decision to stop.
Mediated ongoing	Contact is occurring through the agency. Contact could be reciprocal or one way only. The party sending believes the information is being received, and the party receiving believes it was transmitted with the other party's knowledge and approval.
Fully disclosed stopped	The parties have shared identifying information and/or contact directly, without agency mediation. The same rules for stopped contact that apply to mediated cases apply here.
Fully disclosed paused	The parties have shared identifying information and/or contact directly without agency mediation. The same rules for paused contact that apply to mediated cases apply here.
Fully disclosed ongoing	The parties have shared identifying information and/or contact directly without agency mediation. The same rules for ongoing contact that apply to mediated cases apply here.

SOURCE: From B. Neil & D. Howe (Eds.) (2004), *Contact in permanent placements: Research, theory, and practice.* London: British Association for Adoption and Fostering.

The birthmother interview was coded using several discrete and qualitative codes to achieve different levels of specificity as to the nature of the openness arrangement and changes in openness. The most detailed code is the openness changes code, wherein information from the interview was used to create a list of each change that occurred in the adoption arrangement from the time of the placement through the W2 interview. These openness changes included changes in frequency, category, persons involved in contact, and so on. Each change was then rated as an increase, decrease, mixed (an aspect of openness increased and another decreased simultaneously), or stable (not technically an increase or decrease) openness change.

Each birth mother was also assigned a specific, descriptive nine-category openness code for both W1 and W2, the primary purpose of which is to allow descriptive analysis of birthmothers' openness situations. The definitions provided in Table 12.1 are standard across all triad members. Finally, the broadest conceptualization of openness is represented by a four-category openness code. This code represents a reduction of the nine-category openness code for the purpose of statistical analysis.

This chapter provides a summary of the key findings concerning outcomes for the birth parents, adoptive parents, adopted children, and adolescents. The issues to be discussed include changes in openness, impact of openness on the socioemotional adjustment of the adopted child, collaboration in relationships in the adoptive kinship network, and satisfactions and dissatisfactions with contact.

Changes in Birthmothers' Openness Arrangement Over Time

Using a broad conceptualization of openness, birthmothers experienced changes in openness from W1 to W2. These changes were primarily experienced by the birthmothers who were in ongoing mediated adoptions at W1. Of the 44 birthmothers involved in an ongoing mediated adoption at W1, 52.3% had experienced an increase to fully disclosed or a decrease to mediated stopped adoption at W2. Using only the four-category code, only 8.7% of those involved in a confidential adoption had experienced a change in openness category to mediated or fully disclosed adoption, and one birth mother involved in a mediated stopped adoption had resumed contact so her adoption changed to the ongoing mediated category.

The more descriptive nine-category openness classification of the 127 reparticipating birthmothers is presented in Table 12.2. Overall, 50 of the 127 birthmothers (39.4%) in our sample experienced a change in openness category from W1 to W2. Of these birthmothers, 29 (58%) experienced an increase in openness and 21 (42%) experienced a decrease in openness. Most increases were from confidential to confidential with updates (41.4% of increases) or from ongoing mediated to ongoing fully disclosed (31% of increases). Most decreases were from ongoing mediated to mediated stopped (52.4% of decreases) or from ongoing mediated to mediated paused (28.6% of decreases).

Fluctuations in Contact for Birthmothers With Experiences of Openness

As the analysis of birthmothers' openness in adoption progressed, it became clear that changes in openness category did not tell the full story of the course of birthmothers' openness over time. Many birthmothers who had contact at W2 or had contact sometime between W1 and W2 had experienced fluctuations in that contact. Fluctuations in contact are conceptualized as changes in frequency, person(s) contacted, or mode of contact (i.e., beginning phone calls in an already fully disclosed adoption) and can be within-category increases in contact, decreases in contact, mixed, or stable.

Of the 58 birthmothers in mediated and fully disclosed adoptions who had not changed their openness category from W1 to W2, most did experience some fluctuations in contact within those categories. Fourteen birthmothers (24.1%) experienced no fluctuations in contact within their openness category from W1 to W2. birthmothers in ongoing fully disclosed adoptions experienced the most fluctuations overall, accounting for two thirds of all fluctuations within openness category. Thus, although birthmothers in fully disclosed adoptions cannot technically make many changes in terms of openness category (i.e., they can only move to fully disclosed paused or stopped), they do experience more "action" or movement within their openness category than do birthmothers in mediated adoptions.

Table 12.2 Birthmothers' Nine-Category Openness at Wave 1 and Wave 2

	Confidential	Confidential With Updates	Mediated Stopped With Updates	Mediated Stopped	Mediated Paused	Mediated Ongoing	Fully Disclosed Paused	Fully Disclosed Stopped	Fully Disclosed Ongoing
Wave 1 (N = 127)	23 (18.1%)	11 (8.7%)	14 (11%)	1 (0.8%)	2 (1.6%)	42 (33.1%)	0	0	34 (26.8%)
Wave 2 (N = 127)	8 (6.3%)	23 (18.1%)	22 (17.3%)	7 (5.5%)	6 (4.7%)	17 (13.4%)	0	1 (0.8%)	43 (33.9%)

SOURCE: From B. Neil & D. Howe (Eds.) (2004), *Contact in permanent placements: Research, theory, and practice*. London: British Association for Adoption and Fostering.

Table 12.3   Relationship Between Birthmother's Openness Category and Satisfaction With Openness at Wave 2

Category	Dissatisfied or Very Dissatisfied	Mixed	Satisfied or Very Satisfied
Confidential	16 (51.6%)	5 (16.1%)	10 (32.3%)
Mediated stopped	12 (41.4%)	5 (17.2%)	12 (41.4%)
Mediated ongoing	10 (43.5%)	7 (30.4%)	6 (26.1%)
Fully disclosed	1 (2.3%)	8 (18.6%)	34 (79.1%)

SOURCE: From B. Neil & D. Howe (Eds.) (2004), *Contact in permanent placements: Research, theory, and practice.* London: British Association for Adoption and Fostering.

NOTE: Percentages are by openness category, not as a percentage of total sample.

Overall, most of the birthmothers in this sample had experienced some type of openness change or fluctuation over the course of their adoption. Only 13 birthmothers (10.2%) experienced no changes in openness of any type from the time of placement through W2. Those experiencing changes had an average of 2.4 changes over the history of their adoption.

Satisfaction With Openness

It is clear at W2 that the birthmother's satisfaction with openness is related to her four-category openness (see Table 12.3). Specifically, 52% of birthmothers involved in confidential adoptions were dissatisfied or very dissatisfied with their openness arrangement, and 32% were satisfied or very satisfied. The situation is dramatically different for those in fully disclosed adoptions. Seventy-nine percent of those in a fully disclosed arrangement were satisfied or very satisfied with their openness at W2, and only one fully disclosed birth mother reported being dissatisfied or very dissatisfied.

We also found that W2 satisfaction with openness is related to whether the birthmother's openness category had increased, decreased, or remained the same from W1 to W2. Specifically, those whose openness category had decreased or increased were less satisfied with their current openness than those whose openness category remained stable. Of the 21 birthmothers (42%) who experienced a decrease in openness from W1 to W2, 11 (52%) were dissatisfied or very dissatisfied with their current openness, while only 7 (33%) were satisfied or very satisfied and 3 (14%) reported mixed satisfaction. In contrast, 44 (58%) of birthmothers who remained stable in their openness category from W1 to W2 were satisfied or very satisfied with their current openness. Those who experienced an increase were fairly evenly distributed across the satisfaction continuum.

SATISFACTIONS AND PROBLEMS WITH CURRENT OPENNESS

In an effort to understand which aspects of each openness arrangement were satisfying or dissatisfying to the birthmothers in this sample, we analyzed birth mother responses to the following two questions: "What are some of the satisfactions you've encountered in the current type of adoption you have?" and "What are some of the problems you've encountered in the current type of adoption you have?"

Confidential Adoptions

When asked about satisfying aspects of their openness arrangement, the most frequent response for birthmothers in confidential adoptions was that they experienced no satisfactions in the adoption (35%). When a satisfaction was stated, it was most frequently the belief that the adoptive parents are good people or good parents (19%). birthmothers felt this way for a variety of reasons, including the belief that the agency screened the adoptive parents thoroughly, being told that the parents wanted a baby very badly, or that the agency had chosen the type of family that the birth mother wanted. birthmothers who had received updated information through the agency were pleased with the information they received or happy that if there is an emergency, the parties can contact each other through the agency. Nine birthmothers (29%) felt that confidential adoptions are best for the adoptive parents, the adopted adolescent, or themselves. They believed that the adopted adolescent and the adoptive parents would not experience confusion about who the parent is, that adoptive parents feel safer, and that birthmothers are better able to handle a confidential adoption.

Birthmothers in confidential adoptions considered their primary openness-related problems to be worry about the adopted adolescent (52%) and having no (39%) or not enough (23%) information. Some of the birthmothers worried about the health of the adopted adolescent because their parented children had developed serious medical problems, some of which had been fatal. Others worried that the adopted adolescent would inherit family characteristics that would give him or her trouble, such as being overly sensitive or thrill seeking. However, the majority of the birthmothers had generalized worries about the adopted adolescent's well-being because they had no information rather than having a specific reason to be worried. A common fear was that if the adopted adolescent died or became seriously ill, the birthmother would not be told.

Mediated Stopped

Birthmothers in mediated stopped adoptions most frequently mentioned the letters and information they received in the past as the most satisfying aspect of their adoption (26%). It should be noted that some birthmothers who were thankful for the letters they received in the past were dissatisfied about the letters stopping. The next most frequent satisfactions mentioned were feeling like this type of openness was best for her (23%), feeling that the adoptive parents are good people/parents (20%), knowing the adopted adolescent is alive and thriving (17%), and believing that the agency handled the adoption well (17%). Birthmothers who believed that a mediated stopped adoption was best for them were happy with the information they received in the beginning but felt that they didn't need it anymore. Several used the term *closure*. Only one birth mother felt that she had no satisfactions in this openness arrangement.

As with the birthmothers in confidential adoptions, worrying about the adopted adolescent (23%) was a concern for birthmothers in mediated stopped adoptions. One birth mother expressed her worries: "I think I have the common worries. Every once in a while it'll cross my mind—Is she alive? Did she die of cancer? Has she been in a car accident? Did she die in a car accident?"[1]

Mediated Ongoing

Eighty-two percent of birthmothers in mediated ongoing adoptions most frequently reported satisfaction in knowing about the adopted adolescent's life—what goes on, milestones, interests, and so on. They also expressed satisfaction about receiving letters (76%), in knowing that the adopted adolescent was alive and thriving (71%), and in receiving pictures (71%). Forty-one percent mentioned that mediated ongoing adoption was best for the birth mother. birthmothers described a sense of peace from knowing that the adopted adolescent was developing normally and was happy. Only one birth mother felt that she had no satisfactions in this openness arrangement.

Some birthmothers in mediated ongoing adoptions had problems similar to birthmothers in mediated stopped adoptions. Forty-one percent believed that the adoptive parents had not upheld the contact agreement or wanted to stop the contact. In some cases, the birthmothers were disappointed that the frequency of contact had declined, for example, from receiving one letter per year to receiving one letter every 3 years. Others continued to write to the adoptive parents, even though they had stopped responding. Birthmother responses ranged from acceptance to feelings of betrayal.

Fully Disclosed

The 44 birthmothers in fully disclosed adoptions reported a total of 118 satisfactions in their openness arrangement. The primary satisfaction for birthmothers in fully disclosed adoptions was getting to know the adopted adolescent and developing a relationship with him or her (57%). One birth mother described this as "the sheer happiness at being able to interact with him." Another said, "That I know who she is." Also frequently mentioned was knowing about what is going on in the adopted adolescent's life (45%) and knowing the adopted adolescent is alive and thriving (34%). Thirty-two percent of the birthmothers in fully disclosed adoptions felt that this type of openness was best for them. No birthmothers in fully disclosed adoptions felt they had no satisfactions.

Birthmothers in fully disclosed adoptions also reported that they worry about the adopted adolescent (14%), but their worry stems from issues that they know about, such as difficulties the adolescent is having in school, rather than what isn't known, as is the case in mediated and confidential adoptions. Some similarity can be found in fully disclosed and ongoing mediated adoptions in the interactions they have with the adoptive parents. Eighteen percent of the birthmothers in fully disclosed and paused/ongoing mediated adoptions reported that personality or parenting style differences created some issues for them in the adoption, as compared with 9% in stopped mediated adoptions.

In summary, most birthmothers experienced changes in openness from W1 to W2, with 50% experiencing within-category fluctuations in frequency, person contacted, and mode of contact, and about 40% experiencing a categorical change in openness, with slightly more than half of these changes being increases. The largest increases in openness were from confidential to confidential with updates and from mediated ongoing to fully disclosed. The largest decrease in openness was from mediated ongoing to mediated stopped. Regarding the move from confidential to confidential with updates, this indicates that many birthmothers are either actively seeking or actively providing updated information later in their adoptions—possibly as much as 21 years after the placement. These birthmothers are not necessarily seeking current contact, but rather may be interested in providing the means by which the adopted adolescent could contact them if he or she so desired (i.e., by the birth mother updating her contact information at the agency) or by accessing the files for any updates from the adoptive family that may be available within the confines of confidentiality.

Changes in Openness From the Perspective of
Adoptive Parents and Adopted Children

As noted in the previous discussion about birthmothers, a number of changes in openness occurred between placement and our first wave of data collection. Almost two thirds of the fully disclosed adoptions did not begin that way: 51% began as mediated and 15% began as confidential adoptions. In many of these cases, trust and mutual respect were gradually established between the adoptive parents and birth mother, until they made the decision to share identifying information (Grotevant & McRoy, 1998).

The majority of adoptive families (71.8%) remained within the same major openness level from W1 to W2. Smaller, and roughly equal, proportions of adoptive families increased in openness level (14.7%) or decreased in openness (13.6%). Of those families in fully disclosed arrangements at W1, only 13.2% stopped contact by W2. Among adoptive families with ongoing mediated adoptions, almost equal numbers continued in this category (18), stopped contact (17), and increased to fully disclosed (15). Within the group of adoptive families in confidential arrangements at W1, the majority (89.5%) continued in confidential arrangements at W2.

When there were decreases in openness in adoptive kinship networks, the birthmothers and adoptive parents tended to have both incongruent accounts regarding who initiated discontinuation of contact and divergent understandings about why contact stopped (Dunbar et al., 2006). In addition, adoptive parents were more satisfied when birthmothers respected their family's boundaries and let the adoptive family initiate most of the contact.

Members of adoptive kinship networks involved in ongoing contact found that their relationships were dynamic and had to be renegotiated over time. Early in the adoption, meetings were especially important for the birthmothers, who were very concerned about whether they had made the right decision, whether their child was safe, and whether the adoptive parents were good people. After a while, birthmothers' interest in contact sometimes waned, especially as they were assured that their child was thriving. With the passage of time, many birthmothers became involved in new romantic relationships, sometimes taking attention away from the adoptive relationships. According to the adoptive parents, the ability of birthmothers to provide information when requested was not always in tune with the timing of the request (Wrobel, Grotevant, Berge, Mendenhall, & McRoy, 2003). Adoptive parents tended to become more interested in contact as they became more secure in their role as parents. As the children grew older and understood the meaning of adoption (see Brodzinsky et al., 1984), their questions tended to put pressure on the adoptive parents to seek more information or contact (Wrobel, Kohler, Grotevant, & McRoy, 1998, 1999).

Impact of Openness on the Socioemotional Adjustment of the Child

At W1, there was no relation between level of openness and the children's socioemotional adjustment, as measured by the CABI (Grotevant & McRoy, 1998). However, adjustment was predicted by the quality of relationships between the adoptive parents and child's birth mother, which we have called *collaboration in relationships* (Grotevant, Ross, Marchel, & McRoy, 1999). This emergent property of the adoptive kinship network is characterized by the ability of the child's adoptive and birth parents to work together effectively on behalf of the child's well-being. It involves collaborative control over the way in which contact is handled and is based on mutual respect, empathy, and valuing of the relationship.

We rated collaboration on a 10-point scale for a subsample of 12 adoptive kinship networks. In networks rated low on collaboration, the adults often had very different perceptions about how open the adoption actually was. The needs and fears of the adoptive parents and birth relatives took precedence over their consideration of the children's interests in knowing more about their adoption and background. One adoptive parent wishing to minimize contact stated, "You kind of put up your protection walls. And you think, okay, once I adopt my child, he's mine and I should have the choices." Kinship networks rated high in collaboration were characterized by mutual respect, caring, and affection. The adults were committed to making contact work, because they viewed it as being in their child's best interests in the long run. The adults were sensitive to each other's control needs—who would initiate contact, how communication would be handled—and took these needs into account. Although more collaborative networks were not entirely free of concerns or fears, the adults found ways to deal with their concerns while still valuing the network relationships. We correlated these ratings of collaboration with children's scores on the CABI. Higher ratings on collaboration were associated with lower scores on problematic adjustment (Grotevant et al., 1999).

At W2, adjustment scores for the entire group of adopted adolescents did not differ significantly from gender-specific national norms on the CBCL (mother or father report). Males in the study showed fewer symptoms than the norm group on the BSI. With regard to openness, we compared two groups of adolescents: those who had been in confidential adoptions since placement and those who had been involved in some form of contact since placement or soon thereafter. There were no differences between the groups in child adjustment as reported by parents on the CBCL.

In summary, our data show that this sample of adopted adolescents, on average, is no different in levels of adjustment from the national norms developed on a set of widely used measures. In addition, level of openness by itself was not a major predictor of adjustment outcomes at W1 or W2. However, relationship qualities such as collaboration in relationships were predictive of adjustment across openness levels (Von Korff, Grotevant, & McRoy, 2006).

Satisfaction With Contact

The majority of adoptive family participants reported that they were either satisfied or very satisfied with the level of openness they were experiencing with the child's birth mother: 51.3% of the adopted adolescents, 80.0% of the adoptive mothers, and 82.3% of the adoptive fathers. The teens reported that they hoped their contact with the birth mother either stayed the same (55.8%) or increased (41.9%) in the future. Only one adolescent (2.3%) hoped it would decrease.

Adolescents who had contact with their birthmothers reported greater satisfaction with their level of adoption openness than did adolescents having no contact. Satisfaction with openness was lower during middle adolescence (ages 14–16) than during early or late adolescence (Mendenhall, Berge, Wrobel, Grotevant, & McRoy, 2004). Table 12.4 summarizes rationales for levels of satisfaction held by adolescents having and not having contact. For example, one adolescent who was having contact and was satisfied stated,

> I love her, she's awesome, and she's really supportive, really nice. Oh, it's like having another close older role model, like my parents. Yeah, it's a blessing I think, and it's really nice having an open adoption because you can just interact with her and like, know what she's like instead of wondering throughout your life what your birthmom's like and everything. And I know her personality and so, it's good. It's also like having another family sort of. I get lots of support from both of them. You'd want that, no matter what happens in my life, I'll know I have a lot of support.

In contrast, some adolescents were not satisfied with their level of openness, typically because they wanted more contact and felt unable to bring it about.

> I'm curious to ask my birthmother about, like, if she still cares or thinks about me . . . or is interested in the things I am doing. That's one of the main reasons I want to meet her, I guess.

Other adolescents had no contact but were satisfied with that situation. One adolescent stated, "Birthmothers should not know the location of the children they give up . . . the child is better off not knowing her . . . it would feel funny, you know, to meet her." Another noted, "Information exchange should not occur, it would confuse the kid." And another said, "My birthparents should not even care about, or contact me. It could mess up my life."

In summary, the reasons behind levels of satisfaction coded from the adolescents' interviews provide an important window into how adopted adolescents think about contact. The ways of thinking are very diverse, as are the contact arrangements themselves.

Table 12.4 Adolescents' Satisfaction With Birth Mother Contact: Reasons for Those Having and Not Having Contact

	Contact	No Contact
Satisfied	45.5% of sample • provided an opportunity for a relationship to emerge that would provide additional support for them • positive affect toward birth mother • felt that contact helped them better understand who they are • made them interested in having contact with other members of their birth family, such as siblings	17.1% of sample • felt that adoption was not an important part of their lives • felt it was not necessary to have contact • had generally positive feelings about being adopted • feared contact might be a bad experience for them • felt they were better off where they were than had they been raised by their birth parents
Dissatisfied	16.3% of sample • wanted more intensity in the relationship than they currently had but were not able to bring it about • felt that they could have good relationships with both adoptive and birth family members—did not have to choose one over the other • grateful to birth mother for making adoption plan for them	21.1% of sample • had negative feelings toward birth mother (such as anger, sadness, hurt, disappointment) • desired to have contact to answer identity-related questions about themselves • assumed that birth mother had not made an effort to search for them • worried that adoptive parents or birth mother might feel bad about their pursuing contact • their own efforts to search had been unsuccessful

SOURCE: Berge, Mendenhall, Wrobel, Grotevant, and McRoy (in press).

NOTE: Percentages are based on the 123 participants who indicated that they were either satisfied or dissatisfied with contact; cases indicating "neutral" or "mixed/ambivalent" were not included in this analysis.

SUMMARY AND CONCLUSIONS

These findings regarding openness, 12 to 20 years after the adoption placement, support findings from our earlier study that there is no one type of openness that fits every person's wants and needs. The maintenance of open adoptions is a complex dance in which the roles and needs of the participants change over time, affecting the kinship network as a whole (Grotevant, McRoy, & van Dulmen, 1998). Even though most adoptions that involved fully disclosed contact remained that way, there was no uniform pattern for change or continuity in the details of daily contact—kinship networks have contact by different means, among different people, at varying rates, and with varying degrees of interest. In most adoptions, there is a range of opportunities for parties in the adoption to initiate, decrease, or increase openness over time. However, opportunities for change may be passed by or declined for many reasons, even in adoptions in which changes in openness ultimately do occur. Successful relationships in such complex family situations hinge on participants' flexibility, communication skills, and commitment to the relationships.

Each openness arrangement comes with both high points and issues for all parties to cope with or work through. Most child outcomes that we have studied (e.g., child self-esteem, child adjustment, adolescent adjustment) are not significantly related to the level of openness in the child's adoption. Some birthmothers in this study are satisfied with exactly the amount of contact they currently have—whether confidential, mediated, or fully disclosed. birthmothers who are satisfied with their confidential adoptions tend to be protective of their privacy and do not desire the emotional or relational complications that they perceive would be involved in opening contact with the adoptive family. At the other end of the openness continuum, many birthmothers in fully disclosed adoptions couldn't imagine their lives without fully disclosed contact with the adoptive family, particularly with their birth child, and are committed to maintaining that contact and to working out any problems that might arise.

Implications for Clinical Practice

Contact brings with it additional relationships with their attendant joys and complexities. Deciding what kind of contact to have, how frequently to have it, and with whom requires consideration of the needs and desires of different kinship network members (Grotevant & McRoy, 1997; Grotevant et al., 1998). And because relationships are not static, it means that these considerations must be revisited periodically.

The adolescent period can be the catalyst for both increases and decreases in openness. For some birthmothers in confidential adoptions, the preteen and teen years of the adopted adolescent are a period of renewed interest in establishing contact, updating files with contact or personal information, and/or requesting information about the well-being of the adopted adolescent. For birthmothers in historically mediated adoptions, some have experienced an opening of the adoption to full disclosure, which is indicative of the relationship, trust, and sense of connectedness that was built over the course of the mediated contact. For these women, the preteen and teen years of the adopted adolescent are times of opportunity for increased contact. Their ongoing connection with the adoptive family causes themselves, the adopted adolescent, or the adoptive family to dispense with the barriers of mediated contact and request a more personal, one-on-one relationship.

On the other hand, for birthmothers who have experienced a stop or reduction in their mediated contact, the preteen and teen years of the adopted adolescent can be a time of increased activity and/or turmoil for the adoptive family and for themselves because of family commitments. These stresses may cause either one or all parties to cease or reduce contact. Indeed, many of the birthmothers reported remembering their own adolescence as a turbulent and emotionally difficult time, and they do not want to burden the adopted adolescent or adoptive family with more contact than they can handle. It appears that these critical adolescent years may be turning points in openness, with busy lives, dissatisfaction with openness, family concerns, and other situations for both birthmothers and adoptive parents causing decreases in openness for some. For others, similar circumstances may lead to increased comfort with openness and renewed interest in finding out more about the adopted adolescent. Clinicians who work with birthmothers in either preplacement or postplacement support groups should be aware of these evolving dynamics and their impact on the birth mother over time.

Because there are such wide individual differences in children's and adolescents' adaptation to adoption, school personnel and clinicians should be acquainted with the diversity of ways in which adoptive identity may be explored. Support groups for adolescents exploring identity issues should be normalized and available. Similarly, professionals who work with parents of more than one adopted child (particularly with different openness arrangements) should help them see that their children may not experience identity development in the same way.

Although the agency staff might try to match birthmothers and adoptive parents by their openness preferences at the time of placement, our findings suggest that no one can predict what the parties' preferences will be in the future. Practitioners can educate adoptive kinship network members to expect and prepare for change over the course of the adoption because changes in type, frequency, mode of contact, and relationships seem to be the rule rather than the exception. Agency staff can help kinship members negotiate any difficulties that may derive from changes in openness or in relationships. They can develop appropriate ways to assist the contact process and can offer postadoption services in the event that issues surrounding openness arise. These services should be designed to respond to a diversity of needs. To provide effective services, agency staff need training and knowledge about the issues encountered in different openness arrangements as well as the outcomes most commonly associated with them.

Furthermore, the needs of children themselves—unknowable at placement in the case of infant placements—will also likely differ. At adolescence, for example, some young people desire contact but do not actively seek it for fear they might offend their adoptive parents. In this case, agency staff could facilitate the process by helping the adoptive parents and adopted child talk about their feelings concerning contact with birth relatives. Other adolescents desire no contact with birth family members and are happy with their lives as they are. Agency staff and adoption professionals should be aware that desire for contact can be influenced by many factors, including developmental level, understanding of adoption, prior experiences of the child with birth parents, and current circumstances. Therefore, it should not be assumed that either a desire to search or a desire not to have contact is problematic (Wrobel, Grotevant, & McRoy, 2004). Both are legitimate feelings and highlight the fact that openness arrangements may differ over the life span.

Finally, agency staff serving as the link in mediated adoptions have a very special responsibility, because they serve as information gatekeepers between the adoptive and birthfamily members. Prompt responsiveness to clients' communications is essential, as is communication with kinship network members about impending changes at the agency (e.g., staff or workload) that may affect the information flow in their adoption.

Implications for Research and Policy

Agency policy can be guided by our findings suggesting that openness is not inherently problematic or harmful for children and that many participants in open arrangements consider them to be very positive. We are now in the process of following this sample of adoptive families and birth parents at W3, now that the adolescents have reached young adulthood. This will be the first opportunity to see how these relationships evolve as birth parents are reaching their middle and late adulthood years and youth may be forming families of their own. We will continue to explore family process variables such as the adoptive parents' perceptions of child compatibility as well as empathic understanding, communication, and collaboration in relationships that are related to outcomes for adoptive kinship network members.

With this growing body of scientifically credible findings on outcomes and dynamics of openness, agencies will be able to have more evidence on which to base their pre- and postplacement work with adoptive families and birth parents. The formulation of effective policy requires further ongoing research aimed at revealing how adoption processes play out over time in the lives of adoptive kinship network members. Legal procedures related to initiating and maintaining openness should provide mechanisms for voluntary agreements, for the ability of agreements to be renegotiated, and for the availability of professionals who can assist kinship networks experiencing difficult transitions.

NOTE

1. Birthmothers could list more than one satisfaction so percentages can add up to more than 100%.

BEST PRACTICE IDEAS

1. Adoption professionals should be aware of the importance of matching birthmothers and adoptive parents by their desire for openness, while assisting birthmothers and adoptive parents to recognize, expect, and prepare for both change and stability in openness.

2. The level of openness should be decided on a case-by-case basis.

3. Legal procedures related to initiating and maintaining openness should provide mechanisms for voluntary agreements, for the ability of agreements to be renegotiated, and for the availability of professionals who can assist kinship networks experiencing difficult transition.

4. Through comprehensive education and counseling, birthmothers should be made aware of the prospective challenges and satisfactions that may be experienced in each openness arrangement.

5. Adoption professionals should be available to birthmothers and other adoptive kinship network members over the life course of adoption to assist in renegotiation of contact agreements, resolution of contact-related difficulties, and adoption- and openness-related counseling.

REFLECTION QUESTIONS

1. birthmothers in fully disclosed adoptions were more likely to be satisfied with their openness category than those in any other openness category. Explain possible reasons for this finding.

2. Identify several reasons why contact between birth parents, adoptive parents, and children may change over time.

3. Explain circumstances in which more closed arrangements may be preferred for triad members.

4. List distinctive challenges and opportunities for each member of the kinship network in each type of openness category.

5. In what ways can adoption professionals better prepare families for openness changes?

REFERENCES

Achenbach, T. M., & Edelbrock, C. (1983). *Manual for the child behavior checklist and revised child behavior profile*. Burlington: University of Vermont, Department of Psychiatry.

Achenbach, T. M., & Edelbrock, C. (1987). *Manual for the youth self-report and profile*. Burlington: University of Vermont, Department of Psychiatry.

Berge, J. M., Mendenhall, T. J., Wrobel, G. M., Grotevant, H. D., & McRoy, R. G. (in press). Adolescents' feelings about openness in adoption: Implications for adoption agencies. *Child Welfare*.

Brodzinsky, D. M., Singer, L. M., & Braff, A. M. (1984). Children's understanding of adoption. *Child Development, 55,* 869–878.

Derogatis, L. R. (1993). *Brief symptom inventory: Administration, scoring, and procedures manual.* Minneapolis, MN: National Computer Systems.

Dunbar, N., van Dulmen, M. H. M., Ayers-Lopez, S., Berge, J. M., Christian, C., Gossman, G., Henney, S. M., Mendenhall, T. J., Grotevant, H. D., & McRoy, R. G. (2006). *Processes linked to contact changes in adoptive kinship networks.* Family Process, *45* (4), 449–464.

Frasch, K., Brooks, D., & Barth, R. (2000). Openness and contact in foster care adoptions: An eight-year follow-up. *Family Relations, 49,* 435–446.

Grotevant, H. D., & McRoy, R. G. (1997). The Minnesota/Texas Openness in Adoption Research Project: Evolving policies and practices and their implications for development and relationships. *Applied Developmental Science, 1,* 166–184.

Grotevant, H. D., & McRoy, R. G. (1998). *Openness in adoption: Connecting families of birth and adoption.* Thousand Oaks, CA: Sage.

Grotevant, H. D., McRoy, R. G., & Jenkins, V. Y. (1988). Emotionally disturbed adopted adolescents: Early patterns of family adaptation. *Family Process, 27,* 439–457.

Grotevant, H. D., McRoy, R. G., & van Dulmen, M. H. (1998). The adoptive kinship network: Putting the perspectives together. In H. D. Grotevant & R. G. McRoy (Eds.), *Openness in adoption: Connecting families of birth and adoption* (pp. 173–194). Thousand Oaks, CA: Sage.

Grotevant, H. D., Ross, N. M., Marchel, M. A., & McRoy, R. G. (1999). Adaptive behavior in adopted children: Predictors from early risk, collaboration in relationships within the adoptive kinship network, and openness arrangements. *Journal of Adolescent Research, 14,* 231–247.

Harter, S. (1985). *Manual for the self-perception profile for children.* Denver, CO: University of Denver.

Henney, S., McRoy, R. G., Ayers-Lopez, S., & Grotevant, H. D. (2003). The impact of openness on adoption agency practices: A longitudinal perspective. *Adoption Quarterly, 6*(3), 31–51.

Henney, S. M., Onken, S. J., McRoy, R. G., & Grotevant, H. D. (1998). Changing agency practices toward openness in adoption. *Adoption Quarterly, 1*(3), 45–76.

McRoy, R., Grotevant, H. D., & White, K. (1988). *Openness in adoption: New practices, new issues.* New York: Praeger.

Mendenhall, T. J., Berge, J. M., Wrobel, G. M., Grotevant, H. D., & McRoy, R. G. (2004). Adolescents' satisfaction with contact in adoption. *Child and Adolescent Social Work Journal, 21,* 175–190.

Miller, N. B. (1987). *Scales and factors of the Child Adaptive Behavior Inventory.* Unpublished manuscript, Becoming a Family Project, University of California at Berkeley.

Von Korff, L., Grotevant, H. D., & McRoy, R. G. (2006). Openness arrangements and psychological adjustment in adolescent adoptees. *Journal of Family Psychology, 20,* 531–534.

Wrobel, G. M., Grotevant, H. D., Berge, J. M., Mendenhall, T. J., & McRoy, R. G. (2003). Contact in adoption: The experience of adoptive families in the USA. *Adoption and Fostering, 27*(1), 57–67.

Wrobel, G. M., Grotevant, H. D., & McRoy, R. G. (2004). Adolescent search for birthparents: Who moves forward? *Journal of Adolescent Research, 19,* 132–151.

Wrobel, G. M., Kohler, J. K., Grotevant, H. D., & McRoy, R. G. (1998). Factors related to patterns of information exchange between adoptive parents and children in mediated adoptions. *Journal of Applied Developmental Psychology, 19,* 641–657.

Wrobel, G. M., Kohler, J. K., Grotevant, H. D., & McRoy, R. G. (2003). The family adoption communication model (FAC): Identifying pathways of adoption-related communication. *Adoption Quarterly, 7*(2), 53–84.

Single-Parent Adoptions and Clinical Implications

13

BEHNAZ PAKIZEGI

William Paterson University

S ingle adoptive parenthood, as a social institution, is a relatively new historical phenomenon in the United States. Unless otherwise specified, the term *single* in this chapter will refer to those who at the time of adoption, and at the time they were studied, were not in a coupled relationship. While some may have been married previously, they did not become single parents as a result of divorce, death, or separation. The literature sometimes refers to these parents as "single parents by choice" (Mechanek, Klein, & Kuppersmith, 1987; Miller, 1992; Pakizegi, 1990). The social context of single-parent adoptions will be discussed first, followed by a review of the research on this family form. Finally, the implications of the social context and research findings for clinical work with these families will be discussed.

SOCIAL CONTEXT OF SINGLE-PARENT ADOPTIVE FAMILIES

Two sets of stigma characterize the social context of these families, the adoption stigma and the single-parenthood stigma. Both stigmas have a history in American society. While our society has changed and both stigmas have decreased, they nevertheless continue to influence the experiences of these families. In this section, the stigmas, their history, and some related common assumptions will be explored. In the clinical section of the chapter, alternative views, support for these views, and clinical implications will be presented.

AUTHOR'S NOTE: I would like to thank Jennifer Pineles for assistance in the search for articles.

The Adoption Stigma

What is the historical background for the adoption stigma? At a time when the physical labor of children was necessary in society, couples' infertility affected survival capacities and, therefore, infertility and adoption, by association, were highly negative. Adoption among Caucasians in early America took the form of indentured servitude, and the children were not considered members of their adoptive families. Adoption's instrumental and economic basis rendered babies unwanted and raised the demand for older children (Kressierer & Bryant, 1996). Emotional attachment was more difficult with older children, and problems were thus more common with adoptions.

Industrialization reduced the need for child labor. The economic value of adopted children diminished and the emotional/expressive function of adoption began to develop. Interest in the adoption of infants increased and continues today, along with the historical adoption stigma (Kressierer & Bryant, 1996; March, 1995).

Although a need for physical integrity might also be a contributing factor, the historical background above clarifies, to some extent, why the infertile adoptive mother might feel "barren" and the infertile adoptive father might feel less masculine (Rampage, Eovaldi, Ma, & Weigel-Foy, 2003). Parents' inadequacy in conceiving is perceived as carrying over to their adequacy to raise children. Adoptive parents have to go through an extensive approval process to be considered fit for parenthood. They have to go for preadoptive counseling and a home study, whereas people who want to become pregnant are not evaluated and counseled (Kressierer & Bryant, 1996).

What other forms does the adoption stigma take in the majority culture? Numerous myths about adoption exist, as do common misconceptions of the permanency and authenticity of parental roles. For example, others may try to reassure infertile couples by the comment, "Go ahead and start the adoption process. It will relax you and then you can have one of your own" (Bartholet, 1993, p. 166). Adoptive parents have inevitably been asked about their child's "real" or "natural" parents. In conflicts with their parents, adoptees may tell their parents that they have no authority over them because they are not their "real" parents. The permanence and assurance of having the right to parent may be questioned by society, adoptees, and even the adoptive parent (Caballo, Lansford, Abbey, & Stewart, 2001; Smith, Surrey, & Watkins, 1998).

Underlying these comments are the assumptions that biological ties are best for family members and that adopted children are a cause for concern because of their unknown genetic past. Adoptive parents are warned that "you can't know what you'll get," and the child may be "of bad seed" (Bartholet, 1993; Caballo et al., 2001; Okun, 1996; Smith et al., 1998). Adoptive parents are often told they are wonderful to take in a child or how lucky the child is to be adopted (Rampage et al., 2003). The lack of biological connection often portends impermanence, expressed through concerns about birth parents reclaiming adoptees or adoptive parents dissolving adoptions by giving problematic adoptees back to the state.

Ethical issues are also raised about adoptions. Adoptive parents may be suspected of buying children or taking advantage of economically disadvantaged biological parents and societies (Bartholet, 1993).

The common, accepted view among clinicians and researchers in the adoption field is that all parties involved come to adoption with a profound sense of loss (Bartholet, 1993; Brodzinsky, Schechter, & Henig, 1992; Kirk, 1964; Lifton, 1994). The child has lost the biological parents ("primal wound"; Smith et al., 1998, p. 200). The biological parents have lost their child. The adoptive parents have lost the dream of a biological child, suffering a "narcissistic wound" (p. 208). Some adoptive parents may also have a sense of impending loss, fearing that perhaps if the child finds the birth parents, he or she might reject the adoptive parents. The adoptive family is thus said to have ghosts in the background (Lifton,

1994; Rampage et al., 2003). Clinicians believe that these views permeate the feelings of the members of the adoption triangle about themselves (Bartholet, 1993), that the sense of loss has to be continually renegotiated at different stages of life, and that therefore, there will be lifelong grieving (Grotevant & Kohler, 1999; Smith et al., 1998). The fact that the majority of adoptees are well within the normal range of adjustment (Brodzinsky, 1993; Wierzbicki, 1993) is just one type of finding that raises the possibility of a continuum of degrees of feelings of loss, a finding less attended to in the clinical literature.

There is also a dominant assumption in the field that simple is better and that adoption is complex, and this leads to complexities in the identity development of the children and the parenting of the adults (Shireman & Johnson, 1986; Grotevant & Kohler, 1999). Relatedly, similarity is preferred. Grotevant and Kohler (1999) summarized research suggesting that factors contributing to problems experienced by adopted adolescents included incompatibility between parent and child.

If adoption is second best, it is easy to understand how closed adoptions, secrecy about adoptions, and attempts to pass the adopted child off as a birth child came to be (Grotevant & Kohler, 1999; Kressierer & Bryant, 1996). A few even attribute the motivation to search for biological parents for some adoptees to the adoption stigma (March, 1995). The secrecy of the adoption status of children extends to schools, where the stigma is reflected in the shaming of adopted children by peers and in the shame some adopted children may feel about their adopted status (Smith et al., 1998).

The negative view of adoption is not true for all groups in the society. With slavery decimating many African American families, adoption had a different meaning and value in this group. It often became the glue that held family members together (Smith et al., 1998). To this day, adoption of relatives is more common and accepted among African Americans than among Caucasians (Stolley, 1993).

The Single-Parenthood Stigma

Single-parent led adoptive families also have to deal with the stigma of single parenthood. A woman's second-class citizenship is perceived as being exacerbated by the lack of a man in her life. Historically, without men to hunt or do the hard physical labor that early civilizations required, women, bound to infants and young children, had difficulty surviving. As civilizations evolved and patriarchal attitudes gained strength, more value was assigned to men's labor than to women's. With industrialization, the development of capitalism, and the expulsion of women from the labor force before, and again after World War II, women became economically dependent on men. With the devaluation of women's work at home, they were seen as unable to survive without men. Once women were back in the labor force in increasing numbers, the continuing devaluation of their labor has meant lower wages for their work. With this background, it is easy to understand the skepticism about single women's adoptions. Single men's adoptions also break social stereotypes about men's role in the family. In traditional roles, men are providers, not caregivers (Risman, 1986).

The necessity or importance of men in the lives of women made sex outside of marriage and single motherhood through pregnancy suspect, if not a crime, for a long period in American history (Hawthorne, 1997). The birth mother, often a single woman, was perceived by society as a fallen woman (Kressierer & Bryant, 1996). Children bore the brunt of this through the stigma of illegitimacy. In years past, this stigma was often the reason for placing infants for adoption Simultaneously, the woman was also blamed for being an "abandoning mother" (Smith et al., 1998, p. 212).

The stigma concerning single women is seen through the fact that even through the 1990s, single mothers were thought to be freeloaders off the welfare system, baby machines, incompetent parents who had to be prodded to keep their kids in school, and usually Black and adolescent. The reality is that two thirds of single mothers are White, their median age is 33 years, and most (81%) have only one or two children. Most are single due to divorce or separation, and only one fourth are on welfare (Schnitzer, 1998). Many studies do not differentiate between various forms of single parenthood, despite the evidence that there is much variability in this family form. There are teenage single parents; those who are single through divorce, separation, or death of a partner; and those who choose to be parents, often at a later stage in life, while they are single. The frequent use of the term *intact* for two-parent heterosexual families suggests that other family forms are defective and at high risk.

The single-parent stigma was evident in adoption agencies' historic reluctance to place children with single parents, despite a dearth of adoptive homes for children (Branham, 1970; Shireman & Johnson, 1976). In fact, through the 1960s, many states prohibited single-parent adoptions (Haugaard, Palmer, & Wojslawowicz, 1999). When adoptions did open up to single parents, mostly hard to place children were made available to them (Branham, 1970; Shireman & Johnson, 1976).

This skepticism about placing children with single parents was partly based on the belief in the necessity of male role models, especially for boys (Branham, 1970; Haugaard et al., 1999). There continues to be a belief that a close relationship between mother and son is unhealthy for the son's gender identity and leads to his homosexuality (Schnitzer, 1998). When placing children with single mothers, agencies often required assurance of close contact with male relatives. With some adoption agencies, single mothers also had to explain why they were not married or were divorced (Kadushin, 1970). Even some theorists, researchers, and clinicians have a hard time distinguishing between mother-son physical affection and sexualized contact. Mental health professionals suggest that it is best if fathers or men discuss sexuality with sons (Schnitzer, 1998). These points illustrate the underlying assumption that two heterosexual parents are best for the child (Okun, 1996).

Single parenthood, like adoptive parenthood, has also been assumed to be based on loss. A history of anger, disappointment, and a feeling of failure are often attributed to single parents (Anderson, 2003). Little differentiation is made in the psychological impact of the different paths to single parenthood. Not being married is seen as equivalent to the loss of divorce and widowhood, and single parents by choice are often not differentiated from adolescent single parents in discussions of single parenthood. The possibility that singlehood might be a viable life path and that marriage may be desirable, but not necessary, may be myths that are dying slowly (Straus, 2006).

The single-parent stigma is popularized further in the portrayal primarily of traditional parent and family images in children's books, raising questions in children and parents as to the legitimacy of their family form. While adolescents can intellectually understand their family form, they are familiar with the social stigma and yearn to be like most others (Okun, 1996; Weingarten, Surrey, Coll, & Watkins, 1998).

The internalization of these social phenomena may be observed in the finding that most single parents prefer marriage and the conventional route to parenthood and feel that the traditional way is ideal. Because that has not been possible for them, they choose the second best and "at least have a child" (Okun, 1996).

RESEARCH ON SINGLE-PARENT ADOPTIVE FAMILIES

The earliest systematic single-parent adoptions in the United States took place in 1965. Consistent with the social stigma attached to single parents, the Los Angeles County Bureau of Adoptions cautiously decided to allow single parents to adopt, but only difficult to place children. These children were physically or emotionally disabled, older-aged children, or children of color (Branham, 1970; Shireman & Johnson, 1976).

A few researchers have been responsible for most of the research in this area. Shireman and Johnson (e.g., Shireman, 1996; Shireman and Johnson, 1976, 1985, 1986), Feigelman and Silverman (1977), and Groze (1991; Groze & Rosenthal, 1991) have been responsible for the most systematic work in this area. Others have contributed to the understanding of this family form in less systematic, but still significant ways (e.g., Branham, 1970; Siegel, 1998). In addition to the research specifically on single-parent adoptions, there is an extensive body of research on adoption and on single parenting. The literature review below makes use of the parts of the general literature on adoption and single parenting that are more relevant to this discussion.

The majority of studies on single-parent adoptions were done in the 1970s and 1980s, reflecting the novelty of this family form and questions about its health and viability as a family form at that point in the history of American society. Some research continued into the 1990s. As detailed below, the research to date points to some challenges these families might face. The increasing literature on clinical work with adoption coupled with the methodological shortcomings of past research, the need to fill the gap in information on how adolescent and adult children of single adoptive parents are faring, and changing social conditions influencing stigma make it an important time to revisit the literature in a new light and provide the framework for future research.

Methodology. The research in this area has mostly used interviews or surveys (e.g., Feigelman & Silverman, 1977; Mechanek et al., 1987; Owen, 1997; Shireman & Johnson, 1976; Siegel, 1998), with an occasional use of standardized tests and observations (e.g., Groze & Rosenthal, 1991; Shireman, 1996). Researchers have primarily studied parents (the studies cited above) and occasionally their younger children, but the children have been mainly studied via parent reports (Feigelman & Silverman, 1977; Groze & Rosenthal, 1991). Some studies lack comparison groups (Branham, 1970; Dougherty, 1978). When comparison groups are used, some studies compare single adoptive parents with coupled adoptive parents (Feigelman & Silverman, 1977; Groze & Rosenthal, 1991), some with coupled biological parents (Shireman, 1996), and some with other types of single parents by choice (Siegel, 1998). Where single adoptive fathers have been included, their numbers are very small (Feigelman & Silverman, 1977; Okun, 1996). African American (e.g., Shireman & Johnson, 1976) and Caucasian samples (Dougherty, 1978) are the predominant groups studied. There is some longitudinal work by Shireman and Johnson (1976, 1985, 1986), Shireman (1996), and Feigelman and Silverman (1983) but little work on single-parent family adoptees in adolescence and adulthood. Reliability measures are few, and sources of subjects are diverse. Records (Branham, 1970), national single-parent or adoption support groups (Feigelman & Silverman, 1977), private and public agencies (Dougherty, 1978), and the snowball strategy (Siegel, 1998) are some of the sources used. Small subject pools and loss of subjects over time limit the generalizability of many results (Pakizegi, 1990).

Prevalence. Accurate statistics about the numbers of single-parent adoptive families are difficult to come by, because the U.S. Census Bureau started to gather data on adoptions only in 2000. The census data reveal that in 2000, 2.5% of all children in the United States were adopted into varied forms of households, and 5% of all adopted children less than 18 years of age lived with a never-married mother or father not living with a partner (79,251) (Kreider, 2003). This figure is likely to be an underestimation because it does not include those who adopted children by themselves subsequent to their divorce or widowhood. Although no census data exist before 2000, research suggests that the numbers of single adoptive parents have increased substantially over the past decades (Groze, 1991; Haugaard et al., 1999).

Characteristics of Single Adoptive Parents

Findings on the characteristics of single adoptive parents are highly influenced by the samples used and the historical timing of the study. There are differences as well as similarities between this family form and other single-parent families and coupled adoptive families. Evidence suggests that single adoptive mothers differ significantly from the classic stigmatized portrait of unwed, poor, young, uneducated, minority mothers on welfare (Pakizegi, 1990).

Similar to other single parents, the majority of single adoptive parents are women (Owen, 1997). The 2000 Census revealed that never-married women who adopt outnumber never-married men who adopt by about sixfold (Kreider, 2003). This estimate is consistent with data collected in 1991 by the Survey of Income and Program Participation of the U.S. Department of Commerce (Furukawa, 1994).

Single mothers by choice are those who plan their parenthood (pregnancy or adoption), usually at a later age, when they decide to become a mother without becoming a wife (Miller, 1992). Single adoptive mothers are typically significantly older than coupled adoptive mothers, although single adoptive fathers are not significantly older than coupled adoptive fathers (Feigelman & Silverman, 1977; Groze & Rosenthal, 1991). Single mothers by choice tend to be about 4 years older than married mothers, with adoptive single mothers being the oldest (Siegel, 1998). Dougherty's (1978) predominantly White single adoptive mothers had a mean age of 35 years at the time of adoption, while Shireman and Johnson (1976) found a median age of 34 years among their sample of primarily Black single adoptive parents. Because adoption and single parenthood are nontraditional routes to parenthood, and because the adoption process tends to require more financial resources than a healthy pregnancy, single adoptive parenthood may tend to occur later in the life cycle.

Similar rates of adoption among never-married White and Black women (1.4% and 1.5%, respectively) were reported by Stolley (1993). However, unrelated adoptions were more common among White women, whereas Black women more commonly adopted children of relatives. Hispanic women seemed least likely to adopt. There are relatively more minorities among single adoptive parents than among adoptive couples (14% vs. 2%) (Feigelman & Silverman, 1977).

The classic stigmatized portrait of the single mother was reported in a nationally representative sample of 2,781 mothers, which found that continuously single-mother families lived on about half the income of divorced families and on about one fifth the income of first-time married families (Demo & Acock, 1996b). They were younger, had achieved lower levels of education, and were more likely to be African American than divorced mothers (Demo & Acock, 1996b). Single mothers by choice, however, tended to be educated White women with successful professional or managerial careers (Miller, 1992). The socioeconomic status of single mothers by choice differed depending on the planfulness of their parenthood, with planners (e.g., adoptive parents) having higher earnings than nonplanners (Curto, 1983).

The 2000 Census data supported past research that indicated that adoptive mothers had achieved higher educational levels than biological mothers. In addition, adopted children younger than 18 years of age lived in homes with higher incomes than stepchildren or biological children (Kreider, 2003). Single adoptive parents tended to have higher levels of education than coupled adoptive mothers and higher-status jobs but had lower household incomes (Feigelman & Silverman, 1977; Groze, 1991; Groze & Rosenthal, 1991; Siegel, 1998). The lower incomes of single-parent led adoptive families often reflected the one income of single parents versus the two incomes of couples. While it is not clear how representative of all single adoptive parents they were, 81% of the members of the Committee for Single Adoptive Parents (CSAP) had completed college, 60% had done postgraduate work, and 14% had their doctorates (*CSAP Newsletter*, 1988).

As compared with adoptive couples, single adoptive parents tended to live in urban areas (51% vs. 16%). This could be due to the fact that urban areas are more accepting of nontraditional family forms. Single and coupled adoptive parents are similar in how religious they are (Feigelman & Silverman, 1977).

The majority of single adoptive parents come from two-parent or one-parent stable families of origin. About 20% come from backgrounds of divorced or separated families (Shireman & Johnson, 1976). Phenomenological interviews of 12 single mothers by choice showed similar patterns. In addition, the majority of those who came from coupled families of origin reported tense and conflicted parental marriages (Okun, 1996). Neither of these studies reported comparative data. Thus, it is not clear how these figures compare with the backgrounds of married couples in general and with married couples who adopt.

Studies concerning the past marital history of single adoptive parents themselves are contradictory. The samples on which the studies were based clearly influenced these findings. Most (75%) of Dougherty's (1978) sample of predominantly White single adoptive mothers were never married. Most of Shireman and Johnson's (1976) sample of primarily Black adoptive mothers were previously divorced or widowed, whereas the single adoptive fathers had never been married. Most single adoptive parents do not seem to marry after becoming parents (Owen, 1997).

Single adoptive parents' motivation to adopt was similar to that of couples who adopt or have biological children. They wanted to fulfill their needs to parent, nurture, teach, and guide a child. On the whole, they anticipated enjoying the process (Dougherty, 1978; Shireman & Johnson, 1976).

A substantial number of single adoptive mothers considered pregnancy initially (Curto, 1983; Merritt & Steiner, 1984). Pregnancy is the traditional route to becoming a parent, is less stigmatized in general, and often involves lower fees, less intrusiveness by external agencies, and more control by the mother. However, many single mothers adopted because of their age, infertility, complications of finding a proper male, social acceptability, or moral and ethical considerations (Dougherty, 1978; Pakizegi, 1990). There is, in fact, some evidence that the public reacts more positively to single parents adopting than to their becoming pregnant. Male and female high school students and adults (14–71 years old) rated adoption as the most favorable route to parenthood for single parents (Mechanek et al., 1987).

Earlier studies (e.g., Branham, 1970; Shireman & Johnson, 1976) as well as later ones (e.g., Okun, 1996; Shireman, 1996) described single adoptive parents positively. Researchers described single parents by choice as demonstrating high levels of maturity, high capacities for frustration tolerance, positive self-images, and high expectations for themselves. These parents were described as adaptable and able to follow a course in their lives independently. The older age, greater educational achievements, and financial stability of single adoptive parents seem to contribute to these characteristics. These observations do not support the stigmatized preconceptions of these families.

Characteristics of Children Adopted by Single Parents

The largest group of children adopted by single parents was less than 1 year of age, and the majority of single parents adopted one child (Dougherty, 1978; Shireman & Johnson, 1985; Siegel, 1998). The majority of the children adopted by these parents were of the same sex as the parent (Dougherty, 1978; Feigelman & Silverman, 1977; Shireman & Johnson, 1976; Groze, 1991).

In the early days of single-parent adoptions, the majority of the children adopted by single women were racially different from the adoptive parent or "hard to place" (older, with disabilities, etc.) (Dougherty, 1978). This was not true of Black single adopters (Shireman & Johnson, 1976). Single parents adopted more special-needs children than adoptive couples, and single adoptive fathers were even more open to adopting "hard to place" children than single adoptive mothers (Feigelman & Silverman, 1977). With increasing acceptance of single-parent adoptions, it is likely that these early agency and cultural practices have changed.

Life of the Single Adoptive Parent

Studies indicate that single-parent families, in general, have diminished instrumental and emotional supports (Caballo et al., 2001). Some studies do report lower levels of instrumental but not emotional help (Tilden, 1984). Specifically, middle-class single parents by choice reported exhaustion, low attention to their own personal needs, and concern about unemployment, illness, and death (Okun, 1996). Even more specifically, although single adoptive mothers' financial resources tend to make their lives materially comfortable, and many have the support of extended family (Owen, 1997), they similarly reported a lack of time, exhaustion, around-the-clock demands of the experience, and financial adjustments as sources of concern (Dougherty, 1978). There are some differences between the experiences of single mothers and fathers. Single fathers reported more emotional isolation but seemed to more readily pull on extended family and girlfriends for child care and help (Anderson, 2003). Given their low numbers and the likelihood of their own fathers' traditional behaviors, single fathers have fewer role models for balancing family and work and for socializing (Anderson, 2003).

Single adoptive parents tend to use support groups, and this support was more important for single-parent families than for couples, especially if special-needs children were involved (Shireman, 1996). Most single-parent support groups involved mothers, with fathers feeling like minorities. Some single fathers even reported being perceived suspiciously ("Will I let my child go to a single father's house for a sleepover?") (Anderson, 2003).

There are some data that suggest that life in single-parent families is detrimental to the mental health of the parent (more depression, less global well-being, lower self-esteem), even when controlled for factors such as income, household size, age of youngest child, and years since divorce. However, the differences between one- and two-parent families were not great (Demo & Acock, 1996b) and were not found in all studies. The mixed results indicated by some studies showed less depressive symptoms and better physical health among certain subsets of single parents, such as the more highly educated ones (Caballo et al., 2001), whereas other studies showed no significant differences in depressive symptoms between different kinds of single mothers by choice (adoptive, through intercourse, or through insemination) or between single mothers and married mothers (Siegel, 1998). As for married families (Demo & Acock, 1996b), the variability among single parents contributes to weaker effects.

Single-parent adoptive families of special-needs children were more likely than two-parent adoptive families to evaluate adoption as being very positive (Groze & Rosenthal, 1991). Among different categories of single mothers by choice, adoptive single mothers were most likely to rate themselves as very satisfied with their life (75%), as compared with single mothers through donor insemination (56%) or through intercourse (27%) (Siegel, 1998). Across different family types and for all dimensions of psychological well-being, sociodemographic variables are less significant than family relations, such as enjoyment or difficulty with children (Demo & Acock, 1996b). The structure of the family seems less important than family processes.

Single-parent adoptive families take changes in family life cycle and unforeseen events in stride. In a 3-year follow-up of these parents, Shireman and Johnson (1976) found that none of the changes that had occurred were related to difficulties in the families. In fact, child care plans and parents' employment remained stable and parents were comfortable with their single status (Shireman & Johnson, 1976).

Life of the Child in the Single-Parent Adoptive Family

The primary role of family process (rather than family structure) in affecting outcome is also evident in the literature on children's development in various family forms. Dunn, Deater-Deckard, Pickering, and O'Connor (1998) found higher levels of problems and lower prosocial scores for 4-year-olds and their older siblings in divorced and stepparent families than for those with two biological parents. However, these differences largely disappeared when they took negativity in family relations, maternal age, educational level, depressive symptoms, history of previous live-in relations, mother's support networks, and the families' economic and housing situations into account.

The primacy of process over structure is also seen in families with older children. A comparison of the well-being (internalizing, externalizing, trouble with peers) of 10- to

17-year-olds from married families and divorced single-parent families indicated that parental conflict influenced the children's well-being regardless of family structure (Vandewater & Lansford, 1998). For adolescents, the strongest and most consistent predictors of their well-being, adjustment, and academics were not family structure but instead mother-adolescent disagreement, interaction, aggression, and support (Demo & Acock, 1996a).

What does research show about process specifically in single-parent adoptive families? Okun's (1996) phenomenological investigation of the lives of 12 single mothers by choice suggested that when compared with stressed, dual-career families, the former were more available to their children, less ambivalent, and less conflicted than couples. The literature on single-parent adoptive families reported a similar above-average child orientation in these families (Groze, 1991), especially in the first few years (Shireman & Johnson, 1976). Follow-up studies demonstrated a reduction in this intensity as the child enters school and beyond (Shireman & Johnson, 1985). While a spouse can be a source of support, attention to the child is usually balanced with attention to one's spouse. This can be positive in that the relationship with the child may be less intense and the child can learn to share attention and be part of an intimate triad. However, in coupled families, there may be a greater likelihood for children to feel left out and for triangulations and conflict between adults to occur.

The closeness of single-parent adoptive families might be particularly healing for special-needs children. Groze and Rosenthal (1991) explored special-needs children's characteristics that might better be met by single-parent versus two-parent adoptions. No differences were observed in the adopted children of single- and coupled-parent families when the following variables were examined: foster parent adoptions, sibling placements, relative placements, handicap status, age, gender, out-of-home placement history, and sexual abuse history. Children appeared to do equally well in both kinds of families. However, children who had experienced group homes or psychiatric placements prior to adoption managed especially well in single-parent adoptive homes. Using the Child Behavior Checklist, Groze and Rosenthal found that children experienced fewer problems in emotional and behavioral functioning with single-parent adoptive families than with two-parent adoptive families. Female children with a past history of sexual abuse valued the one-on-one relationship with a caring woman most (Owen, 1997). These findings seem contrary to the findings of Feigelman and Silverman (1977), who reported more adjustment difficulties in single-parent adoptive families than in coupled adoptive families when children were adopted after age 6. This may reflect single parents' acceptance of agency offers of the "hardest to place" children.

In terms of the special-needs adoptees' educational achievements, no differences were observed in the children of single-parent adoptive families and coupled adoptive families when comparing the children's grades, their feelings about schools, and the special education support they received. However, speech and language classes were taken significantly more often by the children from two-parent adoptive homes (Groze & Rosenthal, 1991). Differences in the financial resources of the two kinds of families might account for this observation.

Studies of non-special-needs children's emotional adjustment, developmental progress, and self-concept showed few significant differences related to family structure, especially when age at adoption was controlled (Feigelman & Silverman, 1977; Groze & Rosenthal, 1991; Shireman, 1996; Shireman & Johnson, 1976, 1985, 1986). This is true at various developmental stages of the child and when comparing a variety of family forms such as single adoptive parents, coupled adoptive families, transracial adoptive families, and coupled birth families. Significant correlations were obtained between single adoptive parents' ratings of their children's social adjustment and the support given by extended family and friends (Feigelman & Silverman, 1977).

Research also showed that most single adoptive parents were comfortable telling their children about their adoption. Singles and couples had similar difficulties in talking about adoption. Couples expressed more reservations about discussing birth parents than did single parents (Shireman, 1996; Shireman & Johnson, 1976, 1985). In a more recent study, one third of the 48 children adopted by single parents retained contact with their birth families, the success of the contact being correlated with the adoptive parent's approval of the birth family (Owen, 1997).

When children were studied directly rather than through their parents, a few differences were observed in different family structures. Most children reported that there was no disadvantage with having one adoptive parent, and some even described the situation as more advantageous, because they had to deal with only one parent (Owen, 1997). However, during interviews, themes of security, safety, and loss were more common in responses of children from single-parent adoptive homes, while couples' biological children focused on personal adequacy themes (Shireman, 1996). It is not clear whether adoption, single parenthood, or other variables are responsible for this difference. Most adopted children talked about peers, but a higher proportion of children from single-parent families feared illness or injury to a parent and a higher proportion of these children mentioned outings with parents as a source of joy (Shireman & Johnson, 1985).

The gender identification of children and adolescents from single-parent adoptive homes is clear, unambiguous, and age appropriate (Shireman, 1996; Shireman & Johnson, 1985). The early public and agency concerns about the sex role development of children adopted by single parents and the lack of consistent close interactions with a single important member of the opposite sex (Branham, 1970) have not been supported. Interviews and naturalistic observation of preschoolers from divorced/separated single-mother homes show that these children exhibited more knowledge of sex role stereotypes but tended to be less stereotyped in their use of toys compared with children from two-parent families. However, these two groups did not differ in knowledge of androgynous sex roles or gender-identity concepts. Furthermore, the children's sex role development was not related to how long the children from the single-parent families were separated from the father or the amount of contact they had with males (weekly or daily) (Brenes, Eisenberg, & Helmstadter, 1985).

Although the children's sex role development might not be affected, White, upper-middle-class adoptive single mothers (55%) were significantly more likely than similar single mothers through intercourse (14%) or single mothers through insemination (44%) to mention that a father's absence is hard on the child. The numbers of adoptive mothers (12) and mothers through insemination (9) were small as compared with mothers through intercourse (30) (Siegel, 1998). Relatedly, less than half of the single adoptive parents thought that their children were concerned about their single status (Shireman & Johnson, 1985).

CLINICAL IMPLICATIONS

There is no systematic research on working clinically specifically with single-parent adoptive families. The research studies cited above suggest much similarity between single-parent adoptive families and other families. Where there are differences, empirical evidence does not suggest that inherent psychopathology exists in single-parent adoptive families. While some stressors might be stronger in this family form (e.g., less support, more stigma), there are advantages to this family form over other family forms (e.g., little conflict with another adult in the home). The social stigma and particular stresses of these families and clinical work with adoptive families in general point to issues and areas that clinicians should be mindful of when working with these families. General issues that might reoccur at various points in the life cycle will be reviewed first, followed by an analysis of issues relevant to particular life stages.

Assessment and Intervention in General Issues

Okun's (1996) reminder about adoptive families in therapy seems relevant to single-parent adoptive families. One cannot assume that single-parent adoptive families come into therapy primarily to deal with issues related to adoption or to their single parenthood. This assumption may be informed by the stigma orientation toward these families. Some families come to deal with other issues, whereas others may have already dealt with any family structure issues and some may not be ready yet to deal with the issues they might experience in these arenas.

Stigma

An important responsibility is for clinicians to educate themselves about the subtle and overt manifestations of stigma associated with adoption (Okun, 1996) and single parenthood. Societally and psychologically, "those who cannot remember the past are condemned to repeat it" (Santayana, 1905, p. 284). Knowledge of these issues will allow clinicians to understand their own and others' biases, the marginalization that single adoptive parents and children might feel, and the internalization of this marginalization. This will give a better understanding of how stigma can "hijack lived experience" (Weingarten, 1998, p. 193) and make it difficult for these families to recognize their strengths. By helping clients identify the dominant cultural messages and by helping them critique these messages using existing knowledge and research, their power is diminished.

> Clinicians can therefore avoid . . . replaying in clinical language the social message that single [and adoptive] families are failed social structures. The clinical interchange . . . becomes an opportunity for both client and clinician to develop an alternate vision. (Schnitzer, 1998, p. 168)

Awareness of stigma does not mean that there are no differences between different family forms. Kirk's (1964, 1981) "shared fate" theory about adoption may be useful in working with single adoptive parents and their children. This theory and accompanying research suggests not only that open communication is important in children's adjustment (Brodzinsky, 2005) but also, more specifically, that acknowledgment of the differences between family forms is healthy. It can help remove the stigma and shame, making them different rather than deviant. Brodzinsky's (1987) expanded view of Kirk's theory suggests a curvilinear relationship between acknowledgment of differences and healthy functioning. The mental health of the family is related to a moderate degree of such acknowledgment, while problematic functioning is related to denial of differences or emphasis on differences. This is supported by subsequent research (Kaye, 1990; Kaye & Warren, 1988).

Loss

Loss in single-parent adoptive families is another issue that may need to be addressed at varied points of change in the family (Brodzinsky et al., 1992; Lifton, 1994; Okun, 1996). In this area, the heterogeneity of adoptive (and single-parent) families has not been studied sufficiently (Caballo et al., 2001). The uniform assumption of profound loss and grieving negates the variability of experience common among single adoptive parents and their children. One possible implication of the finding that the majority of adoptees (Brodzinsky, 1993) and children of single adoptive parents (Groze & Rosenthal, 1991; Shireman, 1996) are well-adjusted is that all may not be having difficulties with issues of loss or other issues particular to this family form. Extensive work exists on dealing with loss in adoptive families (Brodzinsky et al., 1992; Kirk, 1964; Lifton, 1994). In addition, if loss is brought up or suspected, clinicians should ask themselves whether feelings of loss may be exacerbated by internalized societal stigma and/or specific unmet needs of single adoptive parents (e.g., parent's need for social support).

Cognitive Restructuring. If loss is exacerbated by internalization of stigma, cognitive restructuring may help address it. Various techniques of cognitive behavioral therapy have been shown to be effective with a variety of populations and disorders (Reinecke & Didie, 2005; Ryan, 2005; Simpson & Liebowitz, 2006). For example, if being single is associated with loss, awareness of the limitations of traditional families may be helpful (Schnitzer, 1998). The assumption that in coupled families partners are consistently sources of instrumental and emotional support for each other and for their children is not supported by the reality that only about 50% of marriages for people less than 45 years of age last (Kreider & Fields, 2002). Even in marriages that last, the "absent father" is common. In many two-parent families, the father is at work for long hours, uninvolved in family matters when present, or so emotionally constricted that he is not a presence in, or support to, his family. Professional and managerial mothers in coupled families report time and energy crunch issues similar to those reported by single-parent adoptive families (Okun, 1996). At other times, the father's absence is a solution for families. The absence of an alcoholic or abusive father might in fact be healing for his family (Schnitzer, 1998).

In addition, cognitive restructuring can include pointing out the many ways in which single-parent adoptions reflect parental strengths. Social conditions associated with previous stigma have changed, and there is increasing societal acceptance of diverse family forms. Research shows that high school students and adults of both sexes see adoption as the optimal route to parenthood for single parents (Mechanek et al., 1987). The socioeconomic status and privilege of many single parents by choice also often insulates them from discrimination (Okun, 1996). The increase in single motherhood by choice might indicate a growing intolerance for problematic or unequal relationships (Schnitzer, 1998). Single adoptive parents' economic condition, advances in technology, and changes in employers' attitudes and societal acceptance allow women to reject dependence on men for economic or self-esteem reasons, giving them new possibilities unavailable to previous generations.

Finally, cognitive restructuring may be helpful if loss is expressed by single adoptive parents through concerns that their adopted children are different from them. These parents can be reminded that biological parents too can have children who are not similar to them. One's biological child can be more similar to one's spouse or show traits not visible in either parent. Differences can add richness in identity development and relationships and enhance more openness to differences, more flexibility, and more imagination. Differences can also help avoid an overidentification with one's children, allowing the children more room to be who they are (Bartholet, 1993).

Support. The experience of loss may also be exacerbated by inadequate emotional and instrumental support in the lives of single-parent adoptive families. Research shows that adequate support is a significant issue in the lives of single adoptive parents (Anderson, 2003; Dougherty, 1978; Shireman, 1996). The clinician should assess the resources in the family. Are there adequate sources of emotional and instrumental support to allow for a quality life, and what is the quality of that support? Is there enough support to allow for parental self-care? Is there enough involvement with family, friends, and community? Is the support network diverse enough to include other nontraditional families? Does the special closeness between parent and child serve primarily a positive function in their lives, or is there enmeshment? The single adoptive parent's community's values and organizations may support or be stressful for these families. If the community is not supportive, risk can be reduced by mobility, if that is a viable choice.

The Internet, chat rooms, blogs, and discussion groups can also provide some support and information, especially for single parents who might be free from child care issues at inconvenient times for social interaction, such as late at night and early mornings. Single- and two-parent adoptive families find support groups of other parents more helpful than individual or family therapy. However, significantly more single-parent adoptive families reported finding these support groups to be very helpful (72% vs. 44%) (Groze & Rosenthal, 1991). If no support groups exist, clinicians might want to suggest and support the formation of such groups.

Brodzinsky's (1987) curvilinear model of adjustment to adoption may have relevance to single parenthood issues as well. If single adoptive parents lack adequate support, it may be because they overemphasize (insist on) or underemphasize (deny) their similarities and differences with other family structures. Overemphasis can result in isolation. Underemphasis can lead to a self-imposed pressure to become two parents in one. The single adoptive parent's tendency toward independence (Miller, 1992), coupled with societal messages about the value of independence (Kim & Markus, 1999), may prevent the parent from seeking help and support. These mothers might, in fact, become even more independent and have difficulty achieving intimacy with others (Miller, 1992). The clinician's ability to normalize the need for help and support that all parents experience can ease some of the pressure on single adoptive parents.

In working with single adoptive fathers, it is important to facilitate the development of support groups that include these men, as they have reported feeling the dearth of male role models and the suspicion of mothers in terms of their parenting adequacy (Anderson, 2003). Women have more experience with balancing work and family, an issue that is particularly new and challenging for men. Men and women can be helped to see the similarity of their situations concerning balancing work and family, with women sharing their experiences and men bringing their new perspectives to bear.

Most single parents by choice would prefer to have a partner (Okun, 1996), so the clinician should be cognizant of the possibility that some single adoptive parents may feel that they cannot be happy and fulfilled without a partner. The clinician can assess whether there are emotional issues to work through toward this goal, especially if there is a history of parental conflicted marriage. Can the single adoptive parent make time to develop an intimate relationship? The clinician can assist the parent in learning better organizational skills and in developing more structure, rituals, and time-management skills. For some, emphasizing the benefits of single parenthood, such as less conflict with an adult in the home, increased closeness to children, and children becoming more independent and mature because of their helping role allows them to reframe their situation (Anderson, 2003).

Concern About Illness and Death. Research reviewed earlier shows that single parents and their adopted children tend to be concerned about loss due to death or injury to the parent (Shireman, 1996). Clinicians should encourage these parents to choose a guardian and an executor for their will shortly after becoming a parent. The cultivation of a close relationship between the guardian(s) and the child can help reduce the parent's and the child's anxiety about parental loss or injury.

Significant and unresolved issues may have to be renegotiated in different stages of the life cycle (Grotevant & Kohler, 1999). It is thus useful to examine the clinical implications of the above issues at each developmental stage of the parent and the child.

CLINICAL IMPLICATIONS DURING THE LIFE CYCLE OF ADOPTEE AND PARENT

Table 13.1 summarizes some of the clinical implications for work with single adoptive parents and their children at different stages in their lives.

Contemplation/Preparation

Making a nontraditional choice to become a single adoptive parent can be anxiety provoking and depressing for some. While supportive of the viability of this choice, clinicians should assess the circumstances of becoming a single adoptive parent, the parent's strengths and risk factors, and what each means for the parent. For example, is loss experienced

Table 13.1   Clinical Implications for Work With Single Adoptive Parents and Adoptees

Life Periods of Child/Parent	Clinical Implications for Work With Single Adoptive Parent and Adoptee
Contemplation/preparation	• Assess circumstances of becoming a single adoptive parent, the degree of sense of loss, sources of sense of loss, parent's strengths and weaknesses, internalization of stigma, support system, expectations, hopes, fears, and information about child (biological, reasons for placement, temperament) • Intervene where risk is noted through grief therapy, supportive therapy, and cognitive behavioral therapy • Cognitive restructuring about stigma issues • Support involvement with family, diverse friends, support groups • Encourage development of a will and choice of a guardian • Assist in the development of a positive and balanced narrative for family structure
Infancy/adulthood	• Assess postadoption depression, attachment progress, sense of legitimacy as a family, views on independence and comfort with seeking support, availability of adequate and consistent positive support, adequacy of child care arrangements and self-care • Dispute irrational beliefs about independence, normalize all parents' need for support • Provide psychoeducation about conditions where multiple caregiving is positive • Provide information and guidance on the development of support groups, participation in online chat and support groups • Encourage and provide information about early intervention, if risk factors exist for the child
Preschool years/adulthood	• Assess parenting style, family narrative being presented to the child • If needed, provide psychoeducation about the importance of limits and challenge any assumptions of "illegitimacy" as "real" parents and a woman's need for a father to set limits, especially for boys • Provide parenting skills training or direct to appropriate resources, if needed • Support the development of a positive and balanced family narrative • Address children's questions about their family form in an age-appropriate way • Encourage maintenance of support systems
School-age years/middle adulthood	• Assess parent's comfort level with single status and with level and quality of support. Do any loss issues surface as the child spends increasing time away from the parent? Assess child's comfort level with family form and any sense of loss or other concerns. Assess child's moodiness or irritability • If marriage dreams are harbored, explore ways that fit the limited time of the single-parent lifestyle for finding a mate (e.g., the Internet) • Encourage parental social life and involvement in other types of close adult relationships • Provide information and guidance on the development of support groups • Be open to and cognizant of child's increasing understanding of the uniqueness of his or her family structure and signs of any internal and external (with others) conflicts that may be experienced in this area (e.g., increased anger or irritability) • Encourage and facilitate an open and empathetic dialogue between parent and child to address any loss, shame, or other concerns • While mindful of the child's feelings and needs, suggest openness with school and community to address any shame, educate, and influence cultural views

(Continued)

Table 13.1 (Continued)

Life Periods of Child/Parent	Clinical Implications for Work With Single Adoptive Parent and Adoptee
Adolescence/middle adulthood	• Assess parent's comfort in dealing with child's independence, identity questions and sexuality, and issues these may raise about the single adoptive parent's and the birth parents' sexuality and the adolescent's identification with birth or adoptive parents in these areas • Assess any loss issues for the parent as adolescents become more nonconformist and peer oriented, especially if parent is not involved in an intimate relationship and is experiencing significant body changes associated with midlife • Support adolescent in verbalizing thoughts and feelings and finding ways of honoring both birth and adoptive parents in constructive ways • Model and role play scenarios and possible questions with parent • Explore parent's feelings about any search issues that may have arisen and support openness to search if interest is expressed • Encourage parent's involvement with close relationships, with other adults, and with other parents of adoptees
Young adulthood/middle to late adulthood	• Support the development of independence for the young adult, while staying connected • Assess any lingering self-doubts as to the legitimacy of their parenthood as the adult child no longer needs them and support their continued caring involvement in a new way in the adult adoptees' lives. Assess any guilt on adoptees' parts for "abandoning" single parents • Assess any loss issues that might surface for the parents and adult adoptees at the time of the adoptees' establishment of intimate relationships and becoming birth parents. Assess any intimacy issues in adoptees
Adulthood/late adulthood	• Support any search efforts on the part of the adoptee • Assess readiness for loss of birth parents and adoptive parent and need for search • Encourage parents to prepare for aging by planning for life structures or communities that allow continued contact with their children, without undue burdens on only children

and/or is adoption an easy choice and a life dream? Parental expectations, fears, and hopes are important to know. Information important to know about the child includes any biological information, reasons for the placement, preadoption experiences, and the child's temperament (Okun, 1996).

Case Study 1

Carla came to see Dr. Boyd when she was 36 years old to discuss her concerns about not finding a mate and wanting to have children. She presented with symptoms of anxiety and depressed mood. A social worker with the state, she had been involved in several relationships, none of which had led to a committed one. She felt that being a mother was more in her control, but she had not planned on being a single mother. To her, "single mothers" were frequently the welfare mothers she worked with who often had disorganized lives, with children who became high school dropouts.

In addition, she had mixed feelings about pregnancy through artificial insemination with sperm from an unknown donor, knew of no man with whom she wanted to have a child, and did not want to deceive any man. With adoption too, she felt that "you don't know what you get" and "it is so complicated," and she was concerned about the costs. Finally, she had concerns about whether she could do it alone and how her child would feel about not having a father. Parenthood without a partner was a major step and not how she had thought it was going to be. She hoped to find a partner after becoming a mother.

Dr. Boyd validated Carla's sense that she was at a major crossroad in life. She underlined the social changes in society that made single adoptive parenthood an acceptable option. She helped Carla identify and assess the major variables that would influence her decision and the route she would choose. Carla was a competent and self-assured person. She had adequate savings and income and owned a condo, where there were other families with young children. Her parents and two married sisters had mixed feelings about her thoughts, especially about her becoming pregnant alone, but she hoped that they "would come around" once the child was a reality. Nevertheless, they had offered occasional child care and support. She had a few close friends who were also supportive. She lived in a major urban center where diverse family forms were common and acceptable. It became clear that there was a potential network of support and diversity in the life of Carla that would alleviate some concerns about her aloneness and her proposed nontraditional family structure. Dr. Boyd validated the viability of the choices Carla was considering.

Dr. Boyd explored with Carla her sense of loss around becoming a parent without a partner. Being nontraditional was uncharted territory and scary. Carla was sad that she had not found a mate, but having witnessed her parents' conflicted marriage, she wondered whether it was better to "have no one than to live like that." Her father was a businessman, who traveled often. Carla had often missed him as a child. Her mother had essentially raised her daughters by herself. Dr. Boyd used Carla's own experiences to reframe her idealization of the traditional family structure and explore some possible advantages of single parenthood.

Dr. Boyd helped Carla articulate what a father and his absence meant to her and her baby. They explored Carla's own early longings for her absent father, the loss she experienced then, and the similarities and differences with the situation in her own life now and in the society. They explored her identification with her mother, who had in effect been a "single parent," and how that identification could support her or limit her, given their different situations. Carla was able to recall friends and relatives whose children had done well despite a lack of a father. They also explored whether a close male friend or a brother-in-law could be involved in their lives in any continuous and close way.

Dr. Boyd also explored with Carla her views on adoption and her concerns that a genetically unrelated child could be problematic and complicated. Carla was clear that she wanted a healthy infant, but she was worried about the unknowns. Her concerns were exacerbated by disturbing stories of problematic adoptions in the media. Dr. Boyd and Carla explored not only the ways of minimizing the unknowns but also the reality that even with one's birth child, there is always the unknown. Dr. Boyd's attempt at normalizing expectant parents' anxiety about the unknowns was helpful in reframing Carla's anxiety and thus reducing it. Dr. Boyd further raised the issue of societal stigma associated with adoption and nontraditional families and the media's role in perpetuating these. She clarified that in fact, the majority of single-parent adoptive families had no major problems.

Dr. Boyd provided Carla with information about Single Mothers by Choice (SMC), an information and support network of mostly professional women in Carla's situation, with chapters in many major metropolitan cities in the United States, and urged her to seek them out. Carla followed through with this suggestion, felt very at home in this group, and realized how important it was to keep in contact with those who were supportive.

Dr. Boyd was aware that by addressing Carla's anxieties early, she was helping her develop her narrative of her nontraditional family in a way that acknowledged the differences as well as the similarities of her family with traditional ones. She was also aware that when the baby arrived, the overwhelming responsibility as well as the excitement of new and single parenthood might influence Carla to tighten the family circle. Carla's competence could also lead her to overburden herself and not to seek help. Dr. Boyd thus urged Carla to maintain her support groups. She emphasized the importance of self-care, especially for single parents. She recommended that Carla develop playgroups with children from diverse family structures. Carla became more cognizant of her neighbors in her apartment building with an eye to finding those interested in such a group. Finally, Dr. Boyd recommended several books for Carla (R. Hertz, 2006, *Single by Chance, Mothers by Choice* and J. Schooler's 1993 book *The Whole Life Adoption Book: Realistic Advice for Building a Healthy Adoptive Family*).

Through the support, guidance, and information provided by Dr. Boyd and her friends at SMC, Carla's anxiety and depression decreased and she felt energized. She decided that she wanted to adopt an infant girl. Carla had kept her significant friends, parents, and siblings abreast of her developing thoughts and feelings; they were quite supportive, and Carla entered the stage of actively looking. She chose an adoption agency which was welcoming to single parents. She became very busy with the paperwork necessary for the adoption and stopped coming to therapy. Fourteen months later, Dr. Boyd received a notice of adoption and the picture of baby Grace in the mail.

Infancy/Adulthood

Postadoption depression has been reported in single adoptive parents (Tarkan, 2006) as well as in adoptive couples (Foli & Thompson, 2004). Although it is not clear how pervasive it is, some single adoptive parents may be surprised by feelings ranging from sadness to despair. Many suffer secretly because of feelings of guilt or shame over negative feelings about a conscious choice that they worked so hard for. Because social support has been found to be a significant correlate of postpartum depression (Wang & Chen, 2006), social support might also be a significant factor in postadoption depression. The nontraditional and stigmatized status of single-parent adoptive families might further contribute to this experience.

During the child's infancy and preschool years, single adoptive parents may have to make arrangements with several caregivers for the care of their children. If these people are constant and caring and if the child continues to feel the caring of the parent, there is no evidence that multiple caregiving per se is damaging (Schnitzer, 1998). The parent needs psychoeducation and support in a society where individual care and the notion of the nuclear family dominate and might concern these parents.

Case Study 2

Grace was a healthy baby whose prenatal care had been good. Her birth mother, Kelly, was 16 and a high school dropout when Grace was born. Kelly had had a one-night stand with Grace's father. She was from a working-class family and could not financially and emotionally take care of a child. Her parents had urged her to relinquish the child and she, very reluctantly, agreed that it was for the best. They had requested a closed adoption, and Carla had agreed.

Even though Carla's job, parenting, and running a household stretched her to her limits, Carla marveled at and enjoyed her baby's development. Grace was a long awaited dream come true. Although Caucasian, Grace was darker in coloring than Carla and her family, something that was a reminder of her adoption for Carla. She worried that lack of similarity would not allow others to treat them like a "real" mother and child. She sometimes wondered herself if they were a real family, given that she was single and her child was adopted. But she steadied herself with Dr. Boyd's remembered words and support. She kept her contacts with her SMC friends for a few years, but eventually, life's demands pulled them all in separate ways. She occasionally thought about dating, but had little time or energy to pursue it. She was content.

Carla was concerned that her patchwork of arrangements for child care, including her parents, a child care center, and two late evenings at a babysitter's, was not good for Grace. She read about societies where multiple caregiving was common and shown not to be detrimental. She also read that the warmth, responsiveness, and consistency of child care were very important. Carla trusted her parents and had in fact chosen the child care center and the babysitter precisely for these qualities. She felt more confident.

Preschool/Adulthood

In the preschool years, parents usually start to share the single-parent adoption narrative, which is taken in by the child without deep comprehension and analysis (Brodzinsky et al., 1992). If any shame is involved with the narrative, it needs to be explored and challenged, and strengths sought after (Weingarten et al., 1998). The parent can be helped to develop a simple presentation of similarities and differences with other family forms, with an emphasis on their family form being different rather than deviant (Brodzinsky, 1987). The story of the family needs to be told in ways that the child does not feel pressured to feel grateful or obligated because of the extra pressures of adoption or single parenthood on the parent (Okun, 1996).

Thus supported, single adoptive parents can be helpful to their children, who in their preschool years begin to notice their differences with peers and feel the stigma attached to their family form (Brodzinsky et al., 1992; Lifton, 1994). Support for the development of children's friendships with diverse families will allow for a more extended social network for parent and child and opens the family system to external influences (Anderson, 2003).

Setting limits is part of the responsibility of parents in the child's preschool years. To do this well, parents need to feel entitled to parenthood, and to feel like the "real" parents they are (Grotevant & Kohler, 1999). The single adoptive parent might feel that he or she cannot set limits for the child without another parent. For women, there has often been a history of "Wait till your father gets home." Mothers have also been told that they can destroy the manliness of sons and feminize them. If they believe this, they could undercontrol their sons. Thus, single parents might need support in limit setting (Schnitzer, 1998). Adoptive parents, who might not feel entitled to parenthood, might also have difficulty in this area (Grotevant & Kohler, 1999). Adoptive single fathers often lack day-to-day experience with children in many areas, including limit setting. They also lack role models of involved fathers (Anderson, 2003). They might need support in the legitimacy of their parenting role and basic parenting skills training.

Case Study 3

Grace was a strong-willed child, but Carla's exhaustion and indulgence meant that Grace did not get the consistent and clear limits that she needed. Carla had waited long to be a mother and she just wanted to enjoy her little girl without conflict. Carla had told Grace that she was born from another woman's tummy, and that she was adopted, but Grace did not seem to understand its significance. Grace's pretend play often involved putting a doll under her shirt, pulling it out and saying the baby was adopted. Once, she had gone for a play date to a friend's house whose father had been home. When she came back, Grace had asked where her daddy was. Carla's male friends and relatives had not been able to keep in regular contact with Grace, and Carla's short discretionary times were spent with other mothers of young children. Carla was not sure how to deal with Grace's attempts at understanding her family structure. She remembered Dr. Boyd suggesting a "balanced" view, emphasizing the similarities as well as differences between family forms and being mindful of societal negative messages about nontraditional families. However, she was never sure what to say or do at the moment.

Carla decided to ask Stephanie, the other single adoptive parent from the diverse playgroup that she had been successful at organizing. Stephanie suggested two books: Watkins and Fisher's (1993) *Talking With Your Young Child About Adoption* for Carla and Zisk's (2001) *The Best Single Mom in the World: How I Was Adopted* for Grace. Carla also took out the books Dr. Boyd had recommended before and found useful guides and suggestions in all of them.

School-Age Years/Adulthood

Past research about the average age of single adoptive parents (Dougherty, 1978; Shireman & Johnson, 1976) and their adoptees (Shireman & Johnson, 1985; Siegel, 1998) suggests that in the child's school-age years, most single adoptive parents are in their midlife. With the child in school, single adoptive parents become freer to attend to their personal needs such as once again considering dating. In addition, as school-age children leave home more than before, separation issues may be heightened for single adoptive parents and their children, who tend to have close and intense relationships (Groze, 1991; Okun, 1996; Shireman & Johnson, 1976).

In the school-age years, children become more cognitively able to understand their nontraditional family structure (Brodzinsky et al., 1992) and the contradictions between their personal experiences and societal messages concerning their family structure. Involvement in school and with peers provides more opportunities for exploration, questions, and possible internal and external conflict (Brodzinsky et al., 1992; Lifton, 1994). If children's concerns and questions are not adequately addressed, they may act them out in anger, silence, or depression (Okun, 1996). Children can be helped to verbalize their thoughts and feelings and to begin to develop their own narratives of the family structure (Weingarten, 1998). Empathetic dialogue between parent and child can be encouraged and facilitated to address any existing shame and concerns (Kirk, 1964). School values and atmosphere need evaluation as well. In order to avoid secrecy which may exacerbate adoptees' shame about their status, clinicians should encourage single adoptive parents to be open with the school about their family structure, within the limits of their children's comfort levels. In some instances, parents can be encouraged to raise the school's level of consciousness through presentations.

Case Study 4

In third grade, Grace came home from school one day and asked "why her real mother didn't want her." Having anticipated this question through her readings and contact with other adoptive families, Carla felt more secure about her legitimacy as Grace's real mother, but also wanted to give Grace the chance to express her concerns. Grace said that children had asked her this question on the playground. It was clear that Grace was very disturbed by it. Carla tried to assure Grace that her birth mother wanted her very much and had been very sad that she was too young and too poor to take care of her. Carla clarified that her birth mother had cared enough to make sure to find someone who could take care of Grace. Carla also explained that real mothers also took care of their children on an everyday basis, and that she was her real mother too. Grace had listened carefully and walked away, still preoccupied.

Grace occasionally wondered aloud about her birth parents, and Carla was comfortable in telling her what she knew. Where there was inadequate information, Grace often filled in with her imagination, vacillating between anger at and idealization of them.

At times Grace wished aloud that she had a dad. Carla would ask her what a dad would mean or do. Grace said he would take her to the park and play ball with her. Carla would suggest they go and play ball or arrange for a ball game with the families she knew.

Carla noticed an increasing moodiness and irritability in Grace. When Carla asked her to pick up her room one day, Grace said, "You aren't even my Mom. You can't tell me what to do." Grace's response was that she would be happy to discuss her adoption if she wanted to, but she needed to pick up her room first. Carla had assumed that Grace, raised with love, support, and openness, would not be struggling with adoption issues. Nevertheless, she showed her openness to discuss Grace's concerns about her adoption. Between her job, helping Grace with homework, taking her to after-school programs, and running a household, there was not time or energy for much else, including herself. Sometimes, Carla would follow through with her limits for Grace. At other times, she was too drained to do so and wished she had someone to share parenting with. She thought she should start dating, but made no effort in that direction.

Adolescence/Middle Adulthood

In adolescence, issues of sexuality, identity, and independence become salient (Arnett, 2004). The adoptee develops more understanding about the biological and adoptive single parent's sexuality and their relations to his or her identity (Okun, 1996). Mothers need support at this time, in their ability and eligibility to discuss all materials, including sexuality, with their children, including their sons (Schnitzer, 1998). If the single parent is romantically involved, given our society's mixed messages about sex and marriage (Arnett, 2004), it may be more difficult for the parent to make distinctions for the adolescent as to when and where sexual involvement is healthy. Adolescents, struggling with coming to terms with their own sexuality, might find it particularly difficult if their single parent starts to date at this time.

A fear and wish to be like the biological parents and the single parent who is involved sexually outside of marriage may also play a part in the adolescent adoptee's sexuality (Okun, 1996). He or she might identify with both sets of parents by acting out sexually. If the adoptee becomes pregnant or impregnates another, he or she may want to keep the baby to "fix the mistake" of the biological parent and his or her adoption. He or she may place the baby for adoption and thereby forgive the birth mother and accept the single parent, or he or she may abort the baby to differentiate from the birth parent.

Distinguishing between thoughts, feelings, and actions is an important aspect of rational emotive behavior therapy (Ellis, 1962). If the clinician can help the adolescent verbalize these feelings and explore how the adolescent can honor both sets of families and the self, the adolescent may not have to act out sexually at this stage.

Lack of genealogical and biological information might make identity questions more difficult for adolescent adoptees (Brodzinsky et al., 1992; Lifton, 1994). It is likely that the stigma of adoption and single parenthood also contribute to this difficulty. A clinician could assist the adolescent in forging a complex identity that is inclusive of the similarities and differences of this family form with other family forms.

The development of independence expected of adolescents in American culture (Arnett, 2004) might be especially hard for the single adoptive parent. The adolescent adoptee's nonconformism might trigger the single parent's own unresolved issues about being nonconformist. If the adolescent raises questions about the birth parents and starts thinking of searching for them, single adoptive parents who have especially close relations with their typically only child might experience a heightened fear of the psychic or physical loss of their child. If the single adoptive parent is not involved in an intimate relationship, the adolescent's increasing independence might trigger fears of abandonment and isolation (Okun, 1996).

Case Study 5

The high school notified Carla that Grace was skipping classes and her grades were plummeting. Carla discovered a joint in Grace's purse and became increasingly uncomfortable with Grace's sexually provocative clothes. She wondered if Grace was sexually active. At home, Grace spent most of her time alone in her room. After school, she would often go with friends and not let Carla know where she was. Her friends were changing from those who were good students to those who found school boring and useless. Grace was increasingly using street language and being critical of her mother. "You dress like an old lady." "Yolanda's Dad is so nice and their house is so full of life. You work too much, Mom. You have no sense of fun." "You embarrassed me when you told them I was adopted." Carla often felt hurt, but did not say anything.

As Grace's involvement with peers increased, Carla was having more dinners by herself and more free time on the weekends. She liked the increasing freedom she had, but also felt lonely and rejected. She wondered how it would feel all by herself when Grace left home. Anxiety about Grace's whereabouts and involvements added to the mix. Having always been an indulgent mother, she felt that talking to Grace and showing her concerns should be sufficient. But that did not seem to help Grace. Carla occasionally wondered if things would have been easier with a biological child and if she had a partner. She remembered her own mother's struggles with her older sister and her complaints that her father was no help. Grace refused to engage her mother in conversations about her concerns and told her not to be such a worrier. There was an occasional conflict, but the distance between them and Grace's risky behaviors concerned Carla.

Grace's turbulent adolescence brought her and Carla back to Dr. Boyd when Grace was 16 years old. Dr. Boyd met with Carla first and pointed out that while Grace seemed to be dealing with the normative adolescent issues of independence, identity seeking, risky behavior, and sexuality, her criticisms of her mother did point to her struggles with her identity as an adopted daughter of a single mom. She agreed with Carla that Grace's behavior was of concern. Dr. Boyd recommended a combination of individual and joint therapy with Grace and Carla.

Dr. Boyd supported Carla in setting consistent limits for Grace. At this confusing time in her life, Grace needed a steadier beacon. Dr. Boyd recommended that Carla use her newfound free time to refuel herself. Carla once again thought about dating but felt it was too complicated a time to start doing so. Dr. Boyd further suggested that Carla create a new parent support group of the parents of Grace's friends and other single adoptive parents from her past SMC group. Dr. Boyd reminded Carla that when adolescents pull away from their families, they feel an even more urgent need to fit in with their peers. Grace's nontraditional family form could then understandably be a source of conflict for her. Carla came to realize that her sense of rejection might reflect her own continuing ambivalence about her single status and adoption choice. Her support group helped her feel less alone and rejected, and she was reminded that some biological children of couples may also go through a difficult adolescence.

Carla's understanding of Grace's need to fit in with her friends from traditional homes helped her become more empathetic with Grace and focus less on her own hurt and rejection. She realized that Grace's friends from working-class backgrounds and her rejection of school might reflect her search for her own identity as coming from working-class birth parents and being raised by a middle-class mother.

Grace was initially suspicious of Dr. Boyd. After seeing that Dr. Boyd was not put off by her street language, Grace felt comfortable with Dr. Boyd, who seemed to understand her and not be hurt and upset by her explorations and confusion. Dr. Boyd encouraged her to find out more about the lifestyles of the families of her working-class friends and to actively think about her choices for the future. Grace felt understood when Dr. Boyd recognized Grace's gravitation toward working-class friends and their values as a possible search for her roots and an honoring of her birth family. Dr. Boyd wondered out loud how else Grace could honor her birth family by the choices she made. It became clear to Grace that doing better in school and not getting pregnant would honor both her single birth and adoptive mothers. She started attending classes more often and her other risky behaviors diminished as well.

Dr. Boyd encouraged Grace to share her thoughts and feelings more openly with her mother. Realizing that Grace's struggles were common among adoptees and children of single mothers, Carla was able to be more empathetic with Grace and to hold back her lectures and her anxieties. Communication between mother and daughter improved and therapy was terminated.

Young Adulthood/Middle to Late Adulthood

With an adult child, single adoptive parents might fear that once their active parenting role is over, the adult child will no longer see them as parents. If the parent has not resolved the issue of his or her legitimacy as a parent, this might be a difficult time, especially if searching for biological parents becomes significant for the adult adoptee (Okun, 1996). Adult adoptees in these families might also have to cope with possible guilt around "abandoning" their single parents when they start to pursue their own independent lives (Brodzinsky et al., 1992; Lifton, 1994).

Adult adoptees' cognitive and social maturity allows for a certain level of independence from family, peers, and social norms (Arnett, 2004), and they are capable of developing a more comfortable narrative about their family structure. Clinicians can aid in this process.

The developmental tasks of forming intimate relationships and making career choices become salient in this period also (Erikson, 1980). The findings of higher socioeconomic status and professional or managerial careers of most single adoptive parents (Curto, 1983; Miller, 1992) suggest that children of single adoptive parents have often had in their parent a model of successful career achievement and successful balancing of career and family affairs. In the realm of intimacy, evidence on the close involvement of external family with many single-parent adoptive families (Shireman, 1996) suggests that clinicians cannot automatically assume that children of single parents have not observed close relationships between adults nor been part of an intimate triad. An assessment needs to be made of whether there were close relationships between the single adoptive parent and extended family members, close friends, or an intimate partner.

For the adult adoptee, expecting a biological child may bring about new questions about one's families and may be profoundly emotional (Brodzinsky et al., 1992; Lifton, 1994; Okun, 1996). It is possible that for single adoptive parents, their child's ability or difficulty in establishing an intimate relationship and having a biological child may raise any previously unresolved issues in these domains.

Case Study 6

Grace recovered enough from her poor grades in her early high school years and was accepted into some colleges. She was excited by the prospect of faraway places and of being completely on her own. But she also did not want to leave her mother alone. She was in tune with Carla's struggles with her anxieties about Grace's leaving home. While Carla wanted Grace to choose the path most right for her, she also wanted her to stay close by. Carla's social life had centered on Grace for almost two decades. Her being single came into sharper focus for her again. The closeness of their relationship over the years was hard to leave for both. Carla acknowledged this to Grace but made it clear that she had a strong support network of friends and that Grace's decision should primarily take into account her interests, the kind of college that suited her needs best, and their financial situation.

Grace decided on a state university a few hours away from home. She studied to become an elementary school teacher. She met John during freshman orientation, dated him for a few months, and broke up. She dated others over time and wondered if she could sustain a relationship. She had experienced the love of her mother, her relatives, and her friends, and she had worked through the ups and downs of these relationships. She had observed close up her closest friend's parents' relationship. Was that enough? She wondered.

Eventually, she and John reestablished a relationship and were engaged. As her wedding date approached, Grace found herself thinking more and more about her two mothers, both unmarried, as she knew them. Carla's joy and involvement with Grace in her wedding plans assured Grace that her mother was able to go beyond herself and be fully there for her. Carla was truly happy for Grace and was aware of letting this be Grace's wedding. Grace wondered if her birth mother ever married and how she would feel if she knew Grace was getting married. Some part of her was sad that she was not going to be there.

Adulthood/Aging

In adulthood and midlife, adoptees are aware that their birth and adoptive parents are aging and will not live forever. If the adoptee has not previously searched for the biological parents, this period is the last chance for it. Health issues in midlife might also serve as a new impetus for a search (Okun, 1996). The possibility of the loss of one's only known parent might similarly be anxiety provoking for children of such families.

Because most single adoptive parents adopt only one child (Dougherty, 1978; Shireman & Johnson, 1985), there will often be no sibling for the adoptee, with whom to share the responsibility of an elderly parent. If the parent has not previously developed close and lasting relationships with other adults, the adoptee will be even more alone in the responsibility for the elderly parent. The intensity and closeness of the younger single adoptive parent and child might make this period more poignant. If the closeness had been healthy and positive, the parent's dependence could be another chance for closeness. If the previous closeness had been problematic, the parent's dependence might create conflict (Okun, 1996).

In late adulthood, if the single-parent adoptive family had been experienced as a loss by the parent, the losses of abilities and people in one's life, typical of this period, may be experienced more intensely. However, if previous losses had been balanced with a sense of gains from their family structure and the issue had been coped with effectively earlier in life, it is likely that this period too will be coped with in a balanced manner (Okun, 1996).

Case Study 7

John and Grace moved out of state and started a family. Grace's complicated pregnancy made her once again think about her birth parents. She wondered about the genetic inheritance of her baby and her lack of knowledge about it. But she didn't dwell on it. The birth of a baby girl brought back thoughts of her birth mother and she became more deeply aware of how wrenching it must have been for her birth mother to relinquish her. John and Grace had invited Carla to stay with them for the first few weeks after the baby was born, and Carla's retirement allowed her to be there. She was overjoyed at being there, but she was surprised at her feelings of jealousy with Grace. Nevertheless, holding Grace's baby brought back memories of baby Grace and Carla glowed inside. It was comforting for Grace to have her mother there. Grace did not want to hurt her feelings by telling her about the ache in her heart for her birth mother. She thought about searching for her birth family, but put it out of her mind. She had too much on her hands with her little one.

Carla's retirement had raised a lot of feelings and questions in her. Should she stay where her home had been and where her circle of friends was or should she move closer to Grace? Mother and daughter were close, but Carla wanted to make sure that she was not a burden on Grace and John when she was old. Grace wanted her mother close for her and her children's sake. Roots meant a lot to her. After much research, Carla found a cohousing group of mixed-age families who shared her values, in a rural center outside of Grace's metropolitan area. She decided to move while she was still young enough to develop relationships with her new community members. Grace never searched for her birth family. While she occasionally wondered about them, she felt "that's the way it was meant to be."

CONCLUSION

If present trends in the increasing numbers of single parents by choice continue and if women continue to delay childbearing, the increasing rate of infertility suggests that single adoptive parenting might also increase. As societal stigma decreases, comfort levels with diverse family forms increase, and sex role stereotypes relax, more single men might consider this option as well.

This trend necessitates more methodologically sound research in this area. More studies are needed, which are observational not only of parents and children individually but also of their interaction, with sound reliability measures and from larger and more representative samples. More studies of different cultural groups who have different extended family supports and place different values on adoption and single parenthood will add perspective to our understanding of this family structure.

In terms of content, there is a dearth of research on adolescents and adults raised in single-parent adoptive homes. How do adolescent adoptees fare in single-parent homes? Because adolescence tends to be a more turbulent time than earlier life stages for American children, and can be difficult for even two parents to cope with, how do single parents manage in positive ways and what are some potential risk factors? Can the experience of witnessing the single parent's close involvements with extended family and friends substitute as a model for establishing intimate relationships for the adoptees of these families?

Because increasing numbers of single men adopt, it is important to learn more about what distinguishes these men from more traditional men. Studies of how the majority of single-parent adoptive families successfully navigate their lives could be quite instructive of how people have resisted stigma or work with it. A minority of single adoptive parents adopt more than one child, a daunting task. How do they and their children fare, compared with those who adopt only one?

For clinicians, a strengths- and resilience-based approach combined with awareness of the common normative stresses in this group of parents seem to hold promise. Those who choose the path of single adoptive parenthood have many strengths and are self-assured enough to embark on this path. Clinicians have to be careful not to imply that there is nothing these parents cannot do, putting undue pressure on them to become superparents and to feel pressured or dismissed and unheard. The clinician also has a role and responsibility to educate the public in the recent research findings and to help reduce the stigma for these families in society (Anderson, 2003).

All families need social-structural supports such as those provided by many European nations. Quality and affordable day care, adequate parental leave policy, universal health coverage, and family centers in each community are some supports that would benefit all family forms (Pakizegi, 1990; Winkler, 2002), especially single adoptive parents.

The words of a single mom might perhaps best summarize the research findings and clinical implications for work with single-parent adoptive families:

With regard to being a single mom, there are definitely some advantages. Yet we don't hear about that. I put a gate up to protect myself from the negative messages. I think I make different choices at different times about filtering them out. But there are times that I don't necessarily want to put a gate up; I want to honor differences. I want to say to my children, "This difference—whatever it may be—is fine. You can be this." (Weingarten, 1998, p. 192)

These alternate family structures, created from a position of strength and choice, change the notions of family, changing conceptions of normality and healthy functioning of families as well. It no longer makes sense to use the nuclear family as the gold standard by which to judge other families (Walsh, 2003).

REFERENCES

Anderson, C. (2003). The diversity, strengths and challenges of single-parent households. In F. Walsh (Ed.), *Normal family processes: Growing diversity and complexity* (pp. 121–152). New York: Guilford Press.

Arnett, J. (2004). *Adolescence and emerging adulthood*. Upper Saddle River, NJ: Pearson.

Bartholet, E. (1993). *Family bonds: Adoption and the politics of parenting*. Boston: Houghton Mifflin.

Branham, E. (1970). One parent adoptions. *Children, 17*(3), 103–107.

Brenes, M., Eisenberg, N., & Helmstadter, G. (1985). Sex role development of preschoolers from two-parent and one-parent families. *Merrill Palmer Quarterly, 31*(1), 33–46.

Brodzinsky, D. (1987). Adjustment to adoption: A psychosocial perspective. *Clinical Psychology Review, 7*, 25–47.

Brodzinsky, D. (1993). Long-term outcomes in adoption. *Future of Children, 3*(1), 153–166.

Brodzinsky, D. (2005). Reconceptualizing openness in adoption: Implications for theory research and practice. In D. Brodzinsky & J. Palacios (Eds.), *Psychological issues in adoption: Research and practice* (pp. 145–166). Westport, CT: Praeger.

Brodzinsky, D., Schechter, M., & Henig, R. (1992). *Being adopted: The lifelong search for self*. New York: Doubleday.

Caballo, R., Lansford, J., Abbey, A., & Stewart, A. (2001). Theoretical perspectives on adoptive families' well-being: Which comparison groups are most appropriate? *Marriage & Family Review, 33*(4), 85–105.

Committee for Single Adoptive Parents Newsletter. (1988, February). Update # 1. Chevy Chase, MD.

Curto, J. J. (1983). *How to become a single parent: A guide for single people considering adoption or natural parenthood alone*. Englewood Cliffs, NJ: Prentice Hall.

Demo, D., & Acock, A. (1996a). Family structure, family process and adolescent well-being. *Journal of Research on Adolescence, 6*(4), 457–488.

Demo, D., & Acock, A. (1996b). Singlehood, marriage and remarriage: The effects of family structure and family relationships on mothers' well-being. *Journal of Family Issues, 17*(3), 388–407.

Dougherty, J. (1978). Single adoptive mothers. *Social Work, 32*, 311–314.

Dunn, J., Deater-Deckard, K., Pickering, K., & O'Connor, T. (1998). Children's adjustment and prosocial behavior in step-, single-parent, and non-stepfamily settings: Findings from a community study. *Journal of Child Psychology & Psychiatry, 39*(8), 1083–1095.

Ellis, A. (1962). *Reason and emotion in psychotherapy*. Oxford, UK: Lyle Stuart.

Erikson, E. (1980). *Identity and the life cycle*. New York: Norton.

Feigelman, W., & Silverman, A. (1977). Single parent adoptions. *Social Casework, 58*, 418–425.

Feigelman, W., & Silverman, A. (1983). *Chosen children: New patterns of adoptive relationships*. New York: Praeger.

Foli, K., & Thompson, J. (2004). *The post-adoption blues*. Emmaus, PA: Rodale.

Furukawa, S. (1994). The diverse living arrangements of children: Summer 1991. *U.S. Bureau of the Census, Current Population Reports*, Series P70, No. 38. Washington, DC: Government Printing Office.

Grotevant, H., & Kohler, J. (1999). Adoptive families. In M. Lamb (Ed.), *Parenting & child development in nontraditional families* (pp. 161–190). Mahwah, NJ: Lawrence Erlbaum.

Groze, V. (1991). Adoption and single parents: A review. *Child Welfare, 70*(3), 321–332.

Groze, V., & Rosenthal, J. (1991). Single parents and their adopted children: A psychosocial analysis. *Families in Society: The Journal of Contemporary Human Services, 72,* 67–77.

Haugaard, J., Palmer, M., & Wojslawowicz, J. (1999). Single-parent adoptions. *Adoption Quarterly, 2*(4), 65–74.

Hawthorne, N. (1997). *The scarlet letter.* Cutchogue, NY: Buccaneer Books.

Hertz, R. (2006). *Single by chance, mothers by choice: How women are choosing parenthood without marriage and creating the new American family.* New York: Oxford University Press.

Kadushin, A. (1970). Single parent adoptions: An overview and some relevant research. *Social Service Review, 44*(1), 263–274.

Kaye, K. (1990). Acknowledgment or rejection of differences? In D. Brodzinsky & M. Schechter (Eds.), *The psychology of adoption* (pp. 121–143). New York: Oxford University Press.

Kaye, K., & Warren, S. (1988). Discourse about adoption in adoptive families. *Journal of Family Psychology, 1,* 406–433.

Kim, H., & Markus, H. (1999). Deviance or uniqueness, harmony or conformity? A cultural analysis. *Journal of Personality and Social Psychology, 77*(4), 785–800.

Kirk, H. (1964). *Shared fate: A theory of adoption & mental health.* New York: Free Press.

Kirk, H. (1981). *Adoptive kinship: A modern institution in need of reforms.* Toronto, Ontario, Canada: Butterworth.

Kreider, R. (2003). Adopted children and stepchildren: 2000. *Census 2000 special reports.* Retrieved November 15, 2005, from www.census.gov/prod/2003pubs/censr-6.pdf

Kreider, R., & Fields, J. (2002). Number, timing and duration of marriages and divorces: 1996. *U.S. Census Bureau Current Population Reports,* Series P70, No. 80. Washington, DC: Government Printing Office.

Kressierer, D., & Bryant, C. (1996). Adoption as deviance: Socially constructed parent-child kinship as a stigmatized and legally burdened relationship. *Deviant Behavior: An Interdisciplinary Journal, 17,* 391–415.

Lifton, B. (1994). *Journey of the adopted self.* New York: Basic Books.

March, K. (1995). Perception of adoption as social stigma: Motivation for search and reunion. *Journal of Marriage and the Family, 57,* 653–660.

Mechanek, R., Klein, E., & Kuppersmith, J. (1987). Single mothers by choice: A family alternative. *Women & Therapy, 6*(1–2), 263–281.

Merritt, S., & Steiner, L. (1984). *And baby makes two.* New York: Franklin Watts.

Miller, N. (1992). *Single parents by choice: A growing trend in family life.* New York: Plenum Press.

Okun, B. (1996). *Understanding diverse families: What practitioners need to know.* New York: Guilford Press.

Owen, M. (1997). Single-person adoption. *Adoption and Fostering, 21*(1), 50–53.

Pakizegi, B. (1990). Emerging family forms: Single mothers by choice: Demographic and psychosocial variables. *Maternal-Child Nursing Journal, 19*(1), 1–19.

Rampage, C., Eovaldi, M., Ma, C., & Weigel-Foy, C. (2003). Adoptive families. In F. Walsh (Ed.), *Normal family processes: Growing diversity and complexity* (pp. 210–232). New York: Guilford Press.

Reinecke, M., & Didie, E. (2005). Cognitive-behavioral therapy with suicidal patients. In R. Yufit & D. Lester (Eds.), *Assessment, treatment and prevention of suicidal behavior* (pp. 205–234). Hoboken, NJ: Wiley.

Risman, B. (1986). Can men "mother"? Life as a single father. *Family Relations Journal of Applied Family and Child Studies, 35*(1), 95–102.

Ryan, N. (2005). Treatment of depression in children and adolescents. *Lancet, 366*(9489), 933–940.

Santayana, G. (1905). *Reason in common sense.* New York: Scribner's.

Schnitzer, P. (1998). He needs his father: The clinical discourse and the politics of single mothering. In C. Coll, J. Surrey, & K. Weingarten (Eds.), *Mothering against the odds: Diverse voices of contemporary mothers* (pp. 151–172). New York: Guilford Press.

Schooler, J. (1993). *The whole life adoption book: Realistic advice for building a healthy adoptive family.* Colorado Springs, CO: Pinon Press.

Shireman, J. (1996). Single parent adoptive homes. *Children & Youth Services Review, 18*(1–2), 23–36.

Shireman, J., & Johnson, P. (1976). Single persons as adoptive parents. *Social Service Review, 50,* 103–116.

Shireman, J., & Johnson, P. (1985). Single parent adoptions: A longitudinal study. *Children & Youth Services Review, 7,* 321–334.

Shireman, J., & Johnson, P. (1986). A longitudinal study of black adoptions: Single parent, transracial, and traditional. *Social Work, 31,* 172–176.

Siegel, J. (1998). Pathways to single motherhood: Sexual intercourse, adoption, and donor insemination. *Families in Society: The Journal of Contemporary Human Services, 79,* 75–82.

Simpson, H., & Liebowitz, M. (2006). Best practices in treating obsessive-compulsive disorder: What the evidence says. In B. Rothbaum (Ed.), *Pathological anxiety: Emotional processing in etiology and treatment* (pp. 132–146). New York: Guilford Press.

Smith, B., Surrey, J., & Watkins, M. (1998). "Real" mothers: Adoptive mothers resisting marginalization and re-creating motherhood. In C. Coll, J. Surrey, & K. Weingarten (Eds.), *Mothering against the odds: Diverse voices of contemporary mothers* (pp. 194–214). New York: Guilford Press.

Stolley, K. (1993). Statistics on adoption in the United States. *Adoption, 3*(1), 26–42.

Straus, J. (2006, May/June). Lone stars. *Psychology Today, 39*(3), 86–92.

Tarkan, L. (2006, April 25). After the adoption, a new child and the blues. *New York Times,* pp. F5, F8.

Tilden, P. (1984). The relation of selected psychosocial variables to single status of adult women during pregnancy. *Nursing Research, 33,* 102–107.

Vandewater, E., & Lansford, J. (1998). Influences of family structure and parental conflict on children's well-being. *Family Relations, 47,* 3223–3230.

Walsh, F. (2003). Changing families in a changing world: Reconstructing family normality. In F. Walsh (Ed.), *Normal family processes: Growing diversity & complexity* (pp. 3–26). New York: Guilford Press.

Wang, S., & Chen, C. (2006). Psychosocial health of Taiwanese postnatal husbands and wives. *Journal of Psychosomatic Research, 60*(3), 303–307.

Watkins, M., & Fisher, S. (1993). *Talking with your young child about adoption.* New Haven, CT: Yale University Press.

Weingarten, K. (1998). Conversation two. In C. Coll, J. Surrey, & K. Weingarten (Eds.), *Mothering against the odds: Diverse voices of contemporary mothers* (pp. 190–193). New York: Guilford Press.

Weingarten, K., Surrey, J., Coll, C., & Watkins, M. (1998). Introduction. In C. Coll, J. Surrey, & K. Weingarten (Eds.), *Mothering against the odds: Diverse voices of contemporary mothers* (pp. 1–14). New York: Guilford Press.

Wierzbicki, M. (1993). Psychological adjustment of adoptees: A meta-analysis. *Journal of Clinical Child Psychology, 22,* 447–454.

Winkler, C. (2002). *Single mothers and the state: The politics of care in Sweden and the United States.* Lanham, MD: Rowan & Littlefield.

Zisk, M. (2001). *The best single mom in the world: How I was adopted.* Morton Grove, IL: Albert Whitman.

The Special Needs of Special-Needs Adoptees and Their Families

14

ELIZABETH J. KEAGY

Montclair State University

BARBARA A. RALL

New Jersey Adoption Resource Clearing House

The nature of adoption has changed over the past several decades due to several social and legal variables. A major factor that affects contemporary adoption is the decline in the number of healthy, White babies being placed for adoption domestically due to a greater societal acceptance of single mothers combined with the increase in White couples and single people interested in adoption (Zamostny, O'Brien, Baden, & Wiley, 2003). There has also been federal and state legislation focused on moving children from foster care to adoption, specifically the passage of the Adoption Assistance and Child Welfare Act of 1980, which focuses on the permanency and continuity of relationships for children rather than multiple foster placements; and the Adoption and Safe Families Act of 1997, which seeks to lessen the amount of time a child stays in foster care and expedite the adoption of children who are in the public welfare system when parental reunification is unlikely. This legislation has greatly influenced the number of children with special needs being placed for adoption. Special-needs children are defined as children who are adopted at older ages, from racial or ethnic minorities, members of sibling groups, or those who have special emotional, behavioral, developmental, or medical problems. These are often children in foster care who seek permanent homes because they cannot be reunited with their birth parents due to neglect or abuse. The shift toward an increasing number of special-needs adoptions "has been accompanied by an increased rate of children and families experiencing post-adoptive problems (i.e., financial, medical, behavioral, legal)" (Reilly & Platz, 2003, p. 782). To assist families who adopt special-needs children, it is essential that specialized pre- and postadoption services designed to address their specific needs are available. We will examine the unique challenges that may be faced by these families and what can be done to support them to ensure positive outcomes.

One of the theoretical perspectives on adoption adjustment that may be particularly relevant for children with special needs is attachment theory. Originally proposed by Bowlby (1969, 1973, 1980), this theory details the parent-child bond that provides a basic sense of security for the infant and is essential for healthy psychological adjustment throughout the life span. The child develops a set of internal expectations about him- or herself, others, relationships, and the world. If the parent or caretaker responds to the child's needs, the child develops trust in the world and is able to develop self-esteem because he or she knows that he or she is important. If the caretaker is unreliable, as with children who suffer neglect or abuse, the child develops a model of the world as untrustworthy, which will affect his or her ability to develop future relationships.

CHALLENGES OF SPECIAL-NEEDS CHILDREN

When an older child is adopted, there may be distinctive problems around developing a bond between the parent and child. "The trauma of the initial separation, impaired ability to trust, fears of repeated abandonment and other experiences typical in relinquishment and adoption can impede the development of healthy attachment" (McGinn, 2000, p. 289). An older child may have memories of his or her birth parents or of previous foster care placements, and there can be a profound sense of grief and loss that can interfere with one's adjustment and attachment when placed with a new family. The child may have suffered neglect and abuse as well that can make the adjustment difficult (Brodzinsky, Schechter, & Henig, 1992). If early parenting was erratic or neglectful, the children may have negative expectations of how others will interact with them (Milan & Pinderhughes, 2000). Children who have histories of abuse also tend to have behavioral problems. These behaviors may previously have helped them cope with and adapt to their abusive home environment, but when these children enter a new home, their behaviors are viewed as challenges. It may be helpful to think of these behaviors as strengths that were vital to the child's survival in a previous situation and use them as a way to better understand the child (Henry, 1999).

For instance, many special-needs children have suffered significant losses and abandonment, and they often exhibit avoidant attachment styles (McWey, 2004). They have learned to depend on themselves and have developed defenses for survival, which may manifest as behavioral problems, such as aggression or withdrawal. They believe that they must control caregivers to remain safe and so they may manipulate or intimidate (Hughes, 2004). These children may view new caretakers with mistrust and often have difficulty forming attachments. Helping foster parents and prospective adoptive parents understand attachment strategies and providing them with therapeutic skills may help them deal with any attachment-related difficulties more effectively. If parents do not understand that behavioral problems are the results of attachment difficulties, they may become alienated from the children and potentially provide less than optimal care (Tyrrell & Dozier, 1999). Attachment difficulties can also lead to disruptions in adoption, as evidenced in the following case of Peter, a 6-year-old boy, who was removed from his birth family at the age of 6 months because of severe neglect and spent most of his young life in foster placements. In fact, by the age of 6, he had already been placed in five foster homes where he did not have the time to develop any meaningful relationships with anyone. He now shows no fear of strangers and often wanders off in public places such as the supermarket. In each placement, Peter's foster parents had hoped to adopt him but became discouraged when Peter refused to be held and cuddled or to differentiate between them and total strangers.

Awareness of the potential for attachment difficulties can inform foster care and adoption agencies when developing services. Individual counseling with these children can help because counselors work to promote a safe therapeutic environment so that the child can begin to develop secure attachments and learn to trust. The behavioral problems may lessen as a result (Hopkins, 2000; Hughes, 2004; McWey, 2004).

IMPORTANT STEPS TO BE CONSIDERED WITH SPECIAL-NEEDS ADOPTION

One of the most important aspects associated with a special-needs adoption is preparation. Some research indicates that families were dissatisfied with the preparation agencies provided (Berry, 1990). This is an area that needs to be a particular focus of preadoption services. There are several components involved in the preparation process once a family has applied to adopt a special-needs child.

Initial Assessment

One of the first is the home study that is necessary for families to qualify. This involves an assessment of various aspects of the applicants' lives such as social, employment, income, and health. They are required to explain their reasons for wanting to adopt and their expectations about life with a special-needs child. The applicant may also be expected to attend a series of group meetings to talk about the process of adoption.

Issues of Having Proper Information

There may also be meetings to share information about the child's background (Sar, 2000). It is important that the adoptive parents have adequate background information on the child so they can realistically and adequately prepare for integrating the child into their lives. If parents are unaware of any abuse or trauma in the child's past, they are unprepared to help the child cope with it and the behavioral difficulties that may arise. Some agencies may fail to provide background information to avoid alarming the parents or to avoid stigmatizing the child as damaged and destined for difficulty (Brodzinsky et al., 1992). Reilly and Platz (2003) found that a majority of families reported not receiving enough information on the child, and several stated that the child's problems were more serious than originally reported. Kirby and Hardesty (1998) recommend comprehensive evaluations of older preadoptive foster children with the findings reported to social workers and potential adoptive parents to facilitate adequate placement, preparation, and intervention. Egbert and LaMont (2004) found that those parents who rated themselves as very prepared for special-needs adoption obtained adequate training and information and had a positive, supportive relationship with the agency. Those who rated themselves as very unprepared indicated that they were not informed of the severity of the children's problems.

Maintaining the Right Expectations

Reilly and Platz (2003) found that parental expectations regarding adopted children had a significant impact on adoption outcomes. Despite their child's reported behavior problems, such as anger, impulsiveness, defiance, and tantrums, the majority of families reported that the quality of their relationship with their child was good to excellent and that the overall impact on the family was positive. The more appropriate the parent's behavioral expectations of the children were, the more likely the parents were to have nurturing, nonabusive attitudes about parenting and the more positive the impact of the adoption on the family. McDonald, Propp, and Murphy (2001) found that appropriate parental expectation was associated with stable placement and a positive assessment of the child's impact on the family. Brodzinsky, Smith, and Brodzinsky (1998) also emphasize the importance of realistic parental expectations in successful special-needs adoption outcomes. Knowing that the risk of a difficult adjustment is a possibility can help parents have more reasonable expectations. This can be addressed in preadoption preparation services, so parents are aware of the challenges they may face. Parents should have access to accurate and comprehensive information about their child's history and behavioral issues before, during, and after the adoption. There should be opportunities for ongoing education and support to help families develop skills to manage and cope with any challenging emotional and behavioral issues (Egbert & LaMont, 2004).

Proper Preparation and Training

One training program that focuses on parental preparation, called PRIDE, an acronym that stands for Parent Resource for Information, Development and Education, was developed by the Illinois Department of Family and Children's Services and the Child Welfare League of America (2005) and is designed to prepare foster and adoptive parents to deal with the specific issues and behaviors of special-needs children. The 27-hour course, taught in nine 3-hour segments, is currently used in New Jersey, Texas, and numerous other states. The first two meetings present prospective parents with an overview of the philosophy of the state child welfare system with a focus on permanence for children. The differences between adoption and foster care are reviewed. Children's connections with their birth families and what the ideal interim caregiver can provide are explored. Session three covers the developmental needs of children, attachment issues, and the effects of abuse and neglect on children. Session four focuses on the issues of loss and separation for all members of the triad. Many foster parents do not understand how a child can remain loyal to those who have abused or neglected him or her. The difficulty birth parents experience in regard to surrendering parental rights despite being unable to care for their child(ren) is also explored. Session five is devoted to strengthening family relationships and to helping children develop self-esteem as well as a personal and cultural identity. Session six covers discipline, and parents are assisted in developing alternatives to corporal punishment. The special issues of disciplining abused and neglected children are covered in this session. Session seven covers the continuation of family relationships. Birth parents can play a real or an imagined role in the child's life. Prospective foster and adoptive parents must learn to speak positively, yet realistically, about the birth parents and the plans for the child's future. Some children may be returning to their families of origin or to a relative. There may be ongoing contact with the birth family whether or not the child ends up living permanently with them. Visitation and ongoing contact can often be very challenging for prospective adoptive parents, particularly when the child returns from visits in a distressed state of mind. Even those children who will have no ongoing contact have fears and fantasies about their birth families. Some children believe it was their behavior that caused their move to foster care. Session eight focuses on planning for change. Unless the child is placed directly in a preadoptive home, a move back home or to another foster or adoptive family is inevitable. Each move causes another bonding break for children. Often, after a number of moves, children begin to feel that they will never find a permanent place. This feeling often leads to acting out early in the placement to get the move "over with" quickly before the child develops another attachment. The issues of sexual abuse, how they may manifest themselves in foster children's behavior, and the risks to other members of the household are also explored in this session. Session nine summarizes the previous sessions and focuses on making the decision to become a foster parent. It can include a live panel of experienced foster parents, adolescents in foster care, and others who can bring personal experience to the prospective foster/adoptive parents. During the course of the training, video clips, role plays, guided imagery, overheads, flip charts, and genograms are used to illustrate various issues. Some states use volunteer foster parents to team teach the course.

As can be seen, there is a great deal of information involved in preparing for a special-needs child, and realistic and adequate preparation involves a series of tasks. A study conducted by Sar (2000) looked at the adoption preparation tasks of mothers who adopted special-needs children with an average age of 10.84 years to determine which tasks were most helpful. The following tasks were covered:

- Learning about the child
- Learning about the process of special-needs adoption
- Learning how the adoption would affect the family system
- Learning how to cope with the special needs of the child
- Learning how to prevent disruption

The mothers focused most frequently on learning about the child and found that participating in training to be an adoptive parent was the most helpful. Those mothers who evaluated their overall preparedness for adoption as high also provided a positive evaluation of life, family life, relationship with the adopted child, and the child's behavior and reported less parental stress. These findings emphasize the importance of preadoptive services providing adequate preparation and education for new adoptive parents.

LET'S NOT FORGET ABOUT STRESS

Stress is another important component when looking at special-needs adoptions and is an area that should be addressed in pre- and postadoptive services for these families. McGlone, Santos, Kazama, Fong, and Mueller (2002) conducted interviews with adoptive parents of special-needs children to determine the nature and extent of parental stress. They identified five categories of stress:

- Child characteristics
- Parent-child interactions
- Family cohesion
- Parental adjustment
- Adoption services issues

The child characteristics reported to be most stressful included behaviors such as lying, stealing, and aggression, both verbal and physical. Rosenthal (1993) also found that behavioral problems were the largest source of stress for families who adopt special-needs children.

Stressors identified by McGlone et al. (2002) related to parent-child interaction included the child lying to them, the child's disobedience, and limit pushing. Family cohesion was also an area of stress. For families with birth children, there was fighting and teasing between the adoptive and birth children, and parents found it difficult to meet everyone's needs. Parents had difficulty adjusting to the extra workload and new routine and had difficulty finding time for themselves. Stressors related to the adoption services were the perceived lack of adequate information about the child and the parents' sense that they were rushed into the adoption placement. These results clearly indicate an elevated level of stress for new adoptive parents of special-needs children. This is a concern because "high levels of parenting stress may be a risk for potential disruption" (McGlone et al., 2002, p. 166). In a review of research findings on adoption disruption Westhues and Cohen (1990) conclude that adoption disruption is higher in special-needs adoptions than in infant adoptions and that the placement is more likely to disrupt if the child is older, if the child has a history of abuse, or if he or she exhibits emotional or psychological problems. Barth, Berry, Yoshikami, Goodfield, and Carson (1988) also report that older children and those with previous adoption placements are at greatest risk of adoption disruption.

Strategies to Reduce Stress

To reduce stress and potential disruption, adoption agencies should pay particular attention to parental stress levels and provide appropriate support. The preadoption assessments should look at the parents' readiness to adopt a special-needs child. Interview questions should be geared toward assessing stress management skills and beliefs and expectations about parenting children who may have emotional and behavioral issues. If there are birth children in the family, it is important to address potential adjustment issues for those children to reduce parental stress. Lipscombe, Moyers, and Farmer (2004) found that difficulties between foster children and birth children were the primary reason for ending placement. Those parents were able to cope with a range of difficult behaviors but found it most challenging when the foster children had a negative impact on the other children in the household. Postadoption services should include ongoing support to monitor stress levels, and agencies must take action to connect families to counseling services for individual or family therapy if parental stress is high due to poor sibling adjustment, emotional or behavioral problems, or low family unity. Respite care can also be an effective strategy to help manage parental stress (McGlone et al., 2002). Active participation by both parents as well as effective communication skills have also been found to sustain a special-needs placement (Westhues & Cohen, 1990). Parents can also be empowered by experiential learning and modeling of effective parenting behavior (Sprang, Clark, Kaak, & Brenzel, 2004).

Many older children who are adopted have come from foster care prior to the adoptive placement. Research done with foster care families can also serve to inform adoption agencies about appropriate areas to focus on in pre- and postadoptive services. O'Neill (2004) found that children in long-term foster care who eventually received permanent placement felt a lack of power and control over their frequent moves, and their challenging behaviors were a way to exert control. They struggled with the effects of past neglect and abuse and found it difficult to learn how to be part of a new family. Some suggestions to help families include creating a structure and setting rules that are clearly explained to the children so that they can gain confidence in their ability to navigate their way in their new family. Consistency and open, honest communication can serve to provide a stable base so that adoptees can develop trust and secure attachments. Kenrick (2000) also stresses the importance of providing therapy for children who have been in foster care as a way to help them learn to cope with the repeated separation and change of multiple placements.

Stress When Placement Is Not a Sure Thing

A unique situation that exists for special-needs children is that they may live with foster-adoptive parents instead of waiting for termination of parental rights if they are victims of abuse or neglect. The foster-adoptive parents hope to adopt these children but the birth parents have not yet terminated their rights and reunification attempts may still be in process. This uncertainty can create a wide range of issues of which prospective parents and social service agency workers must be aware. There can be a great deal of anxiety and uncertainty due to the perceived impermanence of the situation for both child and prospective parent. The child may also feel a great deal of insecurity and a weak sense of belonging (Triseliotis, 2002).

Edelstein, Burge, and Waterman (2002) stress that it is important that the prospective parents are aware of the legal risks associated with this type of placement, so that they can appropriately respond to the needs of the child as well as their own needs. There is the potential for threats to the adoption plan that can cause disappointment and anger or feelings of helplessness. The foster-adoptive parents must be aware of and acknowledge the negative feelings and anger they may have toward the birth parents. If there are continued visitations with the birth parent, the children often experience complex and confusing feelings. They may experience a conflicting sense of loyalty or protectiveness toward the birth as well as the potential adoptive parents and try to meet the needs of both at great emotional cost to themselves. They may fear losing the birth parents with whom they share a history even if it does involve abuse or neglect, but they also acknowledge the security and stability with the foster-adoptive parent. O'Neill (2004) found that despite years of considerable abuse and neglect, children who joined other permanent families expressed a need to maintain contact with their biological families. "Children may feel they are put in the position of making an impossible choice between an old attachment bond and the new experience of safety and consistency in a foster-adoptive home" (Edelstein et al., 2002, p. 116). This stress and worry often results in increased anxiety, acting-out behavior, temper tantrums, or withdrawal around visits. Counseling services for the parents and children should be made available during these times so all parties feel supported. The fact that many older children who are adopted have lived with their birth-family members for several years also raises the issue of open adoption with contact between the adoptive parents, adopted child, and members of the birth family.

Issues Related to Open Adoption

Special-needs adoptees are often older and have developed significant and meaningful relationships in their lives. These bonds could be with birth grandparents, siblings, aunts, uncles, cousins, or previous foster parents, and "openness may be crucial in minimizing further loss in their lives" (Silverstein & Roszia, 1999, p. 645). Open adoption allows the adoptee to maintain these relationships and can even serve to enhance attachment with the adoptive family. If the children feel that the birth family likes the adoptive family and supports the placement, they may feel that permission has been granted by the birth family to attach to the new family. If special-needs adoptees are able to preserve the connections they have already formed with members of their birth family or other significant adults, it can help them feel a sense of continuity and minimize the conflict of loyalty that may come with joining a new family. It is important that families understand that "children . . . are capable of forming multiple, differential, and significant attachments, and that the role one individual plays in another's life cannot be replaced by another person" (p. 643). Maintaining open contact with those the child is close to can ultimately help minimize loss and trauma.

Continued contact with members of the birth family can also help adopted children move through the grief process because they are able to ask questions and obtain accurate information about their birth family. This may help them gain a better understanding of why adoption was necessary and dispel any fantasies they may hold of the birth parents. It can also help "eliminate the secretiveness and fear of the unknown that have proved so debilitating for some adoptees" (Brodzinsky et al., 1992, p. 188). Openness is also important in identity formation for special-needs adoptees. If they have ongoing contact with members of the birth family, they can integrate aspects from that family as well as the adoptive family to create a more complete sense of self (Silverstein & Roszia, 1999).

All members of the adoption triad can benefit from an open adoption. The birth parents may voluntarily relinquish their rights if they know they can maintain a relationship with their child and thus avoid long court proceedings. Adoptive families gain the opportunity to know their child's history and accept their differences (Silverstein & Roszia, 1999). "Although open adoptions may challenge boundary establishment, they also can facilitate a sense of acceptance and belonging" (Elbow, 1986, p. 367). Andersson (2005) found that children in long-term foster care who had a significant relationship with at least one parental figure had good social adjustment and well-being as adults.

It is possible that circumstances exist that could deter openness in adoption, particularly if there was severe abuse and neglect by the birth family. The birth parents or members of the birth family could suffer from substance abuse or serious mental health problems that could lead to uncontrolled violence, which would also limit the contact they have with the adoptee. Court proceedings also have the potential to become adversarial, and the birth parents may be described in negative terms, for example as unfit or undeserving. This may dissuade the adoptive family from allowing contact with the birth parents, and they may disregard attempts of open contact by other members of the birth family because of their negative opinion of the birth parents (Silverstein & Roszia, 1999). It is important that adoption professionals make every effort to increase opportunities for safe contact and open communication between members of the birth and adoptive families for the sake of the child. "Openness can help promote the child's ability to trust, feel optimistic about life, and establish positive relationships" (Silverstein & Roszia, 1999, p. 640).

Programmatic Intervention

If open adoption is the choice for these families, specialized pre- and postadoption services must be considered. Silverstein and Roszia (1999) designed a model for promoting openness in special-needs adoption that combines educational and experiential opportunities. It helps families learn about their personal values, beliefs, biases, and fears and about the adoption process and one another, and it hopes to encourage each to expand the boundaries of their families. Families are provided with adoption-specific information and are taught new skills to learn how to interact with people who may have different lifestyles and ways of relating. There may be a need for both the adoptive- and birth-family members to overcome their prejudices about people who are different from them. This model also suggests that adoption professionals help the families share their views and set clear expectations for contact and communication. "The success of open adoption depends on clear boundaries [and] the participants' respect for each other's roles and responsibilities" (Pavao, 1998, p. 130).

Support groups are also a significant part of this model because they assist families in expanding their concept of kinship. These groups include members of foster and adoptive families that are parenting special-needs children as well as groups with members of adoptive and birth families who maintain open relationships. These support groups provide families with a model of successful open relationships and give people an opportunity to express their fears and learn from others.

EFFECTIVE PRE- AND POSTADOPTION SERVICES

Understanding what adoptive families with special-needs children want can be invaluable when planning appropriate and effective pre- and postadoption programs. Barth and Miller (2000) outline the types of services that adoptive parents seek most often. These parents are looking for educational and informational services that involve topics such as financial costs and special services. They also want clinical services which involve counseling (individual, marital, and family), respite care, and crisis counseling. A final category includes material services such as subsidies and health benefits. McKenzie (1993) also emphasizes financial assistance as an area of focus for postadoption services. Adoptive parents of children with special needs also evaluated support groups and contact with other adoptive parents as very helpful (Rosenthal, 1993). Kramer and Houston (1999) also found that mutual support from other adoptive families and mentoring programs were effective in meeting the needs of adoptive parents. Gray (2002) recommends forming a team of supportive friends and family members in addition to seeking professional help to prevent isolation, obtain help with certain tasks, and enhance the overall system of support. The following case demonstrates the success of support groups and mentoring programs.

Brief Clinical Case

Mr. and Mrs. Jones, the parents of an 8-year-old girl, applied to the local child welfare authority to become foster parents with the long-term goal of adopting two children. A sibling pair, ages 4 and 6, was placed in their care shortly after they finished the home study process. The foster children, Peter and Warren, had been abused and neglected and removed from their birth family 2 weeks before. After a short stay in a temporary foster home, they were placed with the Jones family. From the beginning, it was clear that Peter and Warren had lived in a very chaotic household. They were not used to sitting at the table for dinner, going to bed at a regular time, or complying with the Jones family routines. After a month, Mr. and Mrs. Jones told their caseworker the placement wasn't working out. Their daughter was beginning to misbehave and to resent the behavior of her foster brothers. Mrs. Jones was called to the school because of the boys' behavior. The caseworker recommended that Mr. and Mrs. Jones join an adoptive parent support group, and she arranged for them to have a buddy mentor (ongoing contact with an experienced foster family). Mr. and Mrs. Jones were offered respite care for the boys one weekend per month. They spent extra time then with their daughter, who was feeling very neglected due to the extreme demands of the boys. Over time, the boys settled down and Mr. and Mrs. Jones began to enjoy them more.

Some parents report barriers to obtaining postadoptive services (Reilly & Platz, 2003). The barriers included not knowing where to go for services and a perception that those who were there to help did not comprehend their problems. Parents with children above the age of 14 reported the most difficulty obtaining services. This information is critical for adoption agency programs, because it indicates the agencies must continue to reach out to the adoptive families and provide accessible support after the adoption. It also indicates a need for appropriate training of agency staff so that they can empathize with the unique challenges that can face families who adopt special-needs children. "Specialized training in the competencies needed by foster care and adoption supervisors and workers should have high priority" (McKenzie, 1993, p. 75). Reilly and Platz (2003) also found that the longer the child was in the home, the more the behavior problems that were reported. This highlights the importance of extensive and ongoing postadoption services, because it is possible that behavior problems may not surface until the child has been in the home for some time.

BEST PRACTICES

It is evident from this chapter that professionals in the field of adoption must be educated in the unique challenges present in special-needs adoptions. Agencies should provide adequate training programs for their employees that include information on the challenges faced by special-needs adoptees and their families such as attachment difficulties, behavioral issues, and stressors. They should also be knowledgeable about the ways to effectively deal with these challenges, such as providing individual counseling, respite care, and support groups so that they are prepared to help families adjust and thrive. Families should have adequate access to all pre- and postadoption services through the agency or be referred to an appropriate resource that can provide the help they require.

CONCLUSION

Families who adopt children with special needs have unique challenges related to attachment difficulties and increased levels of stress. Agencies must be aware of this and provide adequate preparation and information about the child so that parents develop appropriate expectations. This will result in less disruption and more positive outcomes. Postadoption services should be easily accessible and provide education, information, and counseling for all members of the family and connect families to support groups so that they can share with others who understand their experiences. This will ensure that the needs of all members of the family are met and that the adoption experience is a positive and satisfying one for all involved.

REFLECTION QUESTIONS

1. Why is it important for adoption professionals to learn why a family is interested in adopting a special-needs child and their expectations about life with that child?

2. What are the potential benefits or risks (short- and long-term) associated with an open special-needs adoption for the adoptee, birth family, and adoptive family?

REFERENCES

Andersson, G. (2005). Family relations, adjustment and well-being in a longitudinal study of children in care. *Child and Family Social Work, 10,* 43–56.

Barth, R. P., Berry, M., Yoshikami, R., Goodfield, R. K., & Carson, M. L. (1988). Predicting adoption disruption. *Social Work, 33*(3), 227–233.

Barth, R. P., & Miller, J. M. (2000). Building effective post-adoption services: What is the empirical foundation? *Family Relations, 49,* 447–455.

Berry, M. (1990). Preparing and supporting special needs adoptive families: A review of the literature. *Child and Adolescent Social Work Journal, 7*(5), 403–418.

Bowlby, J. (1969). *Attachment and loss: Vol. 1. Attachment.* New York: Basic Books.

Bowlby, J. (1973). *Attachment and loss: Vol. 2. Separation.* New York: Basic Books.

Bowlby, J. (1980). *Attachment and loss: Vol. 3. Loss.* New York: Basic Books.

Brodzinsky, D. M., Schechter, M. D., & Henig, R. M. (1992). *Being adopted: The lifelong search for self.* New York: Doubleday.

Brodzinsky, D. M., Smith, D. W., & Brodzinsky, A. B. (1998). *Children's adjustment to adoption: Developmental and clinical issues.* Thousand Oaks, CA: Sage.

Child Welfare League of America. (2005). *The PRIDE program.* Retrieved September 9, 2005, from www.cwla.org/programs/trieschman/pride.htm

Edelstein, S. B., Burge, D., & Waterman, J. (2002). Older children in preadoptive homes: Issues before termination of parental rights. *Child Welfare, 81,* 101–121.

Egbert, S. C., & LaMont, E. C. (2004). Factors contributing to parents' preparation for special-needs adoption. *Child and Adolescent Social Work Journal, 21*(6), 593–609.

Elbow, M. (1986). From caregiving to parenting: Family formation with adopted older children. *Social Work, 27,* 366–370.

Gray, D. D. (2002). *Attaching in adoption: Practical tools for today's parents.* Indianapolis, IN: Perspectives Press.

Henry, D. (1999). Resilience in maltreated children: Implications for special needs adoptions. *Child Welfare, 78*(5), 519–540.

Hopkins, J. (2000). Overcoming a child's resistance to late adoption: How one new attachment can facilitate another. *Journal of Child Psychotherapy, 26*(3), 335–347.

Hughes, D. (2004). An attachment-based treatment of maltreated children and young people. *Attachment and Human Development, 6*(3), 263–278.

Kenrick, J. (2000). "Be a kid": The traumatic impact of repeated separations on children who are fostered and adopted. *Journal of Child Psychotherapy, 26*(3), 393–412.

Kirby, K. M., & Hardesty, P. H. (1998). Evaluating older pre-adoptive foster children. *Professional Psychology: Research and Practice, 29*(5), 428–436.

Kramer, L., & Houston, D. (1999). Hope for the children: A community-based approach to supporting families who adopt children with special needs. *Child Welfare, 78*(5), 611–635.

Lipscombe, J., Moyers, S., & Farmer, E. (2004). What changes in "parenting" approaches occur over the course of foster care placements? *Child and Family Social Work, 9*, 347–357.

McDonald, T. P., Propp, J. R., & Murphy, K. C. (2001). The postadoption experience: Child, parent, and family predictors of family adjustment to adoption. *Child Welfare, 80*(1), 71–92.

McGinn, M. F. (2000). Attachment and separation: Obstacles for adoptees. *Journal of Social Distress and the Homeless, 9*(4), 273–290.

McGlone, K., Santos, L., Kazama, L., Fong, R., & Mueller, C. (2002). Psychological stress in adoptive parents of special-needs children. *Child Welfare, 81*, 151–171.

McKenzie, J. K. (1993). Adoption of children with special needs. *The Future of Children, 3*(1), 63–76.

McWey, L. M. (2004). Predictors of attachment styles of children in foster care: An attachment theory model for working with families. *Journal of Marital and Family Therapy, 30*(4), 439–452.

Milan, S. E., & Pinderhughes, E. E. (2000). Factors influencing maltreated children's early adjustment in foster care. *Development and Psychopathology, 12*, 63–81.

O'Neill, C. (2004). "I remember the first time I went into foster care—it's a long story . . .": Children, permanent parents, and other supportive adults talk about the experience of moving from one family to another. *Journal of Family Studies, 10*(2), 205–219.

Pavao, J. M. (1998). *The family of adoption.* Boston: Beacon Press.

Reilly, T., & Platz, L. (2003). Characteristics and challenges of families who adopt children with special needs: An empirical study. *Children and Youth Services Review, 25*(10), 781–803.

Rosenthal, J. A. (1993). Outcomes of adoption of children with special needs. *The Future of Children, 3*(1), 77–88.

Sar, B. K. (2000). Preparations for adoptive parenthood with a special-needs child: Role of agency preparation tasks. *Adoption Quarterly, 3*(4), 63–80.

Silverstein, D. N., & Roszia, S. K. (1999). Openness: A critical component of special needs adoption. *Child Welfare, 78*(5), 637–651.

Sprang, G., Clark, J., Kaak, O., & Brenzel, A. (2004). Developing and tailoring mental health technologies for child welfare: The comprehensive assessment and training services (CATS) project. *American Journal of Orthopsychiatry, 74*(3), 325–336.

Triseliotis, J. (2002). Long-term foster care of adoption? The evidence examined. *Child and Family Social Work, 7*, 23–33.

Tyrrell, C., & Dozier, M. (1999). Foster parents' understanding of children's problematic attachment strategies: The need for therapeutic responsiveness. *Adoption Quarterly, 2*(4), 49–64.

Westhues, A., & Cohen, J. S. (1990). Preventing disruptions of special-needs adoptions. *Child Welfare, 69*(2), 141–155.

Zamostny, K. P., O'Brien, K. M., Baden, A. L., & Wiley, M. O. (2003). The practice of adoption: History, trends, and social context. *The Counseling Psychologist, 31*(6), 651–678.

Double Stigma

15

The Impact of Adoption Issues
on Lesbian and Gay Adoptive Parents

CAROL ANDERSON BOYER

Montclair State University

L esbian, gay, and bisexual (LGB) people form families in various ways, through stepparenting, adoption, foster parenting, surrogacy, and donor insemination, each of which presents a unique set of issues to be addressed (Crespi, 2001; Matthews & Lease, 2000). For the lesbian or gay adoptive family, the usual challenges of adoption are compounded by the ambivalent attitudes of adoption professionals; the social stigma attached to being gay or lesbian; the legal complexity of forming, maintaining, and protecting nontraditional families; and the internalized homophobia of lesbians and gay men who choose to parent (Crawford, McLeod, Zamboni, & Jordan, 1999; Crespi, 2001; Martin, 1993; Matthews & Lease, 2000; Ossana, 2000; Saffron, 1998; Strickland, 1995).

IMPACT OF PROFESSIONALS' ATTITUDES

Attitude plays an important role in forming a positive working relationship with any client, but for mental health professionals who work with the LGB community, attitude has been shown to be a key factor in client perceptions of counselor helpfulness (Liddle, 1996). For these practitioners, it is not enough to be "neutral" toward their clients' sexual orientation; rather, researchers hold that the most beneficial therapeutic relationships are ones in which the counselor views LGB orientations as normative, thereby avoiding the tendency to judge clients' lives and relationships through a heterosexist lens (Matthews & Lease, 2000; Morrow, 2000; Ossana, 2000).

While a majority of psychologists report positive attitudes toward gay and lesbian parenting (Crawford et al., 1999), adoption by gays and lesbians is still controversial, and

228

adoption professionals themselves seem to be divided. Some professionals continue to express concern over the possibility of sexual or physical abuse of children—particularly by gay men—as well as the general suitability of gay and lesbian parents to serve as role models for children. These attitudes persist despite a considerable body of evidence showing that children of gay and lesbian parents have no increased risk for physical or sexual abuse, no significant differences in psychological development or emotional adjustment, and no greater chance of becoming lesbian or gay than children raised by heterosexual parents (Allen & Burrell, 1996; Bigner, 1999; Golombok & Tasker, 1996; Mallon, 2000; Martin, 1993; Saffron, 1998; Strickland, 1995).

STIGMA AND IDENTITY

There is no question that being gay or lesbian places the individual in a stigmatized group. Lesbians and gay men often have a painful, problematic time growing up due to the hostility of mainstream society toward their sexual orientation (Bozett & Sussman, 1989). As a result of this stigma, they may experience isolation, ostracism, and anger as they internalize their oppression (Richardson, Rayes, & Rabow, 1998). Identity development, therefore, is a central challenge to growing up gay or lesbian as these individuals must develop the tools and coping mechanisms necessary to embark on a conscious, deliberate journey of self-discovery in which they can reconstruct a positive gay or lesbian identity based on self-definition, rather than the negative, stereotyped characteristics assigned to them by mainstream society (Fein & Nuehring, 1981; Martin, 1993). Individuals who come out later in life, after being heterosexually married, may struggle with additional identity issues around giving up a privileged, heterosexual identity to identify with a stigmatized, homosexual one (Matthews & Lease, 2000).

Lesbian and gay individuals or couples who wish to adopt must prepare themselves, and later, their adopted child or children, to face an additional loss of privilege. For lesbians and gay men, who are already stigmatized on the basis of their sexual orientation, becoming an adoptive family creates a second layer of stigma, because adoption is often perceived as an inferior way to form a family (Brodzinsky, Schechter, & Henig, 1992; Brodzinsky, Smith, & Brodzinsky, 1998; Pavao, 1998). The child who is adopted by a same-sex couple, then, must not only struggle with the "differentness" experienced by all adopted children (Mallon, 2000) but also incorporate another layer of identity as the child of lesbian or gay parents.

Balancing multiple identities is a significant source of anxiety and stress for LGB families, and counselors must be sensitive to the possibility of multiple oppressions. To practice ethically with this population, counselors should honestly examine their own biases about how family is defined, including the formation of families of choice, and educate themselves about the availability of appropriate resources and support services for nontraditional families. Likewise, counselors must be aware of the legal status of LGB families in the state in which they practice, and they must familiarize themselves with appropriate resources on which to draw (Matthews & Lease, 2000).

FAMILY OF ORIGIN SUPPORT

Coming out to one's family of origin is a major milestone on the gay or lesbian person's journey of self-discovery and can be complicated by the shame of internalized oppression as well as fear of rejection (Richardson et al., 1998). Families of origin may be split in their willingness to accept a member's orientation, particularly if their negative feelings are rooted in deeply held religious values (Matthews & Lease, 2000). A family that is forced to confront a member's homosexuality may suddenly identify itself as defective and may need to struggle to reidentify itself as healthy (Bozett & Sussman, 1989). However, despite the shock and subsequent necessary adjustment, many families ultimately come to accept a member's gay or lesbian identity and are able to be supportive to some degree (Martin, 1993).

Sharing one's decision to parent, however, is often an entirely different matter and may be met with a wide range of emotions from enthusiasm, reservation, apprehension, or ambivalence to shock, anger, or even shame from family-of-origin members. Negative reactions may be all the more painful for the lesbian or gay family member when contrasted with the unadulterated joy with which the same news is received when it comes from a heterosexual sibling (Martin, 1993; Matthews & Lease, 2000). The family's reaction may depend, in large part, on how fully they processed the initial coming out of the gay or lesbian family member and whether or not that information was subsequently shared with extended family and friends. If the family was accepting but kept the information private, then accepting and acknowledging the grandchild may force the rest of the family to "come out" in a way that simply having a gay or lesbian family member did not. To smooth the process, gay men and lesbians must plan ahead in ways that their heterosexual siblings do not, both by coming out (ideally) several years before announcing their plans to parent and by sharing such plans with their family well in advance of the child's arrival (Martin, 1993).

SOCIAL SUPPORT

Although an individual or couple's desire to parent is not related to sexual orientation (Mallon, 2000), lesbians and gay men encounter a considerable amount of social prejudice as they seek to form families (Crespi, 2001). Gay men, particularly, have a difficult time finding social support for their desire to parent, because the idea of a man in the primary parental role challenges the gender stereotype of women as the primary nurturers and caregivers of children. Furthermore, gay men, who may not be traditionally "masculine" in other ways, will have their ability to parent called into question on the basis of their nonconformity to gender roles at multiple levels (Mallon, 2000; Martin, 1993).

Having a gay or lesbian sexual orientation is often perceived as incompatible with child-rearing, and in fact, the level of internalized homophobia experienced by some gay and lesbian individuals may be so intense that they feel themselves unfit to parent or undeserving of having a child. Because gay men and lesbians still cannot legally marry in most states, the rituals and role models that help legitimize heterosexual family forms are denied to them, leaving them to create these new family forms without the public acknowledgment afforded to their more traditional counterparts (Lynch & Murray, 2000; Matthews & Lease, 2000; Ossana, 2000; Saffron, 1998). They may be further dismayed to find that the gay community, in which they have always found support for their sexual orientation and in which they may have a considerable investment in terms of time, energy, and friendships, is not so supportive of their decision to parent (Bigner, 1999; Martin, 1993; Matthews & Lease, 2000).

For these reasons, gay and lesbian families may find that they need to be more involved with the heterosexual community than they are used to, in order to find the support they need as parents, as well as opportunities for their children to socialize. Yet there is a need for them to stay connected to the gay community and make an effort to find gay and lesbian families so that their children can learn that families come in diverse forms and that their own family is legitimate and normal. This can be particularly difficult for LGB families of color because they are less numerous within the gay community. Ultimately, gay and lesbian families may need to exercise a good deal of creativity in finding adequate support for themselves and their children and may find that they cannot meet all their needs in one place (Martin, 1993).

LEGAL ISSUES

When heterosexual couples marry and start a family, they do so secure in the knowledge that they have the full support of society and the law. For gay and lesbian couples, however, the process is not nearly so straightforward due to their greater legal vulnerability (Lynch & Murray, 2000). Heterosexuals rarely need to obtain legal counsel before bringing children into their families, whether through birth or adoption, because existing family laws were created specifically with them in mind. Gay and lesbian couples, on the other hand, may form their families through adoption, surrogacy, or donor insemination and must have expert legal advice on their rights—or lack of them—in each of these situations (Martin, 1993).

Because adoption laws vary from state to state and most have no legal recognition of same-sex unions, it is often the case that only one partner can be the child's legal parent. This situation creates a "legal limbo" for the nonlegal parent and an extra level of vulnerability, should the union later dissolve (Lynch & Murray, 2000; Mallon, 2000; Martin, 1993; Matthews & Lease, 2000; Ossana, 2000; Zicklin, 1995). Despite the fact that 96% of U.S. counties have at least one gay or lesbian couple with minor children living at home, only seven states and the District of Columbia have enacted laws that support adoption by same-sex couples (Urban Institute, 2003). This means that same-sex couples must execute multiple, complicated legal documents to try to ensure the same legal protections that heterosexual couples can take for granted (Martin, 1993).

For example, if one partner in a married, heterosexual couple becomes incapacitated through illness or injury, the other is automatically authorized to make medical decisions on his or her behalf and to act in the best interests of any children they have together. Partners in a same-sex couple, however, must execute a durable power of attorney—*and be able to produce it on demand*—to be legally empowered to make medical decisions for each other in an emergency. However, these documents are not universally honored, so even with such documentation, equal protection is not guaranteed. Furthermore, if the incapacitated partner is the sole legal parent of any child (or children) the couple has, the remaining partner has no legal status as a parent and may lose custody if the legal parent dies. Coparenting agreements can help ease such situations by demonstrating a couple's intent to parent their children together, but such documents are not legally enforceable and may or may not be honored in a court of law (Martin, 1993).

In most cases, the best way for a same-sex couple to protect their children is through a second-parent adoption, although these are not legal for same-sex couples in every state. As of April 2000, second-parent adoptions by unmarried partners have been granted in only 21 states and the District of Columbia (National Adoption Information Clearinghouse [NAIC], 2000). In some states, the legal definition of a parent is limited to the individual who either is biologically related to the child or performed the initial adoption. However, a second-parent adoption, where available, protects the rights of both parents and allows both of them to claim the child as a dependent for tax purposes, provide health insurance to the child from their employers, take a child to the hospital for emergency care, and share child custody and support, should their union later dissolve. Without a second-parent adoption, none of these rights and protections is available for same-sex families (Martin, 1993).

In addition to the legal issues surrounding primary- and second-parent adoption, two other significant areas of legal concern for same-sex couples are donor insemination and surrogacy. Lesbian couples wishing to conceive by alternative insemination, whether with a known donor or an unknown donor, should seek professional legal advice regarding the pertinent laws in their state. Current laws regarding alternative insemination were written to protect the legal paternity of the husbands in heterosexual marriages, and in a judge's opinion may or may not apply to a lesbian woman and her partner, who most likely will not be legally married to each other. For this reason, a donor agreement is highly advisable; however, it should be noted that such a document is not legally enforceable. In addition, any deviation from the original parameters of the agreement that affords the sperm donor greater involvement in the child's life may change his status, in the eyes of the law, to that of a legal father and may entitle him to visitation or even custody. By the same token, gay men wishing to become fathers through surrogacy must obtain legal counsel beforehand because surrogacy is illegal in some states. In other states, it is only illegal if the woman receives payment, although it may be permissible to cover medical and some other expenses. Surrogacy arrangements, even more than those for alternative insemination, are fraught with extreme legal complexity and confusion and should always include a surrogacy agreement, although, again, these documents are not legally enforceable, should the woman change her mind during the pregnancy or even after the child is born (Martin, 1993).

Gay couples considering surrogacy should also consider the fact that, unlike a sperm donor, a woman acting as a surrogate cannot be anonymous, which could have an impact on the child's sense of identity, as well as his or her wish to search for biological roots. No matter which route a couple takes to parenthood, whether through direct adoption, alternative insemination, or surrogacy, adoption is likely to be involved in one form or another, wherever it is legal, and both prospective parents and counselors would be well-advised to fully consider the implications of each choice before making a final decision.

IMPACT OF INFERTILITY

Perhaps the most profound set of issues to be faced before deciding to adopt are those surrounding infertility (Brodzinsky et al., 1992; Brodzinsky et al., 1998; Crespi, 2001; Pavao, 1998). For lesbians, this is an especially complicated issue and will require sensitivity and patience on the part of the counselor. Many lesbians contemplating motherhood encounter internalized homophobia and have a difficult time feeling "entitled" to a child. Failure to conceive may heighten a woman's feelings of being "defective" and may spark a resurgence of her early awareness of her own differentness as well as the impact of negative sociocultural messages she may have internalized about being lesbian. Furthermore, unlike in heterosexual marriages, a lesbian partner's infertility does not necessarily rule out the possibility of a biological child, so not only must a lesbian who is infertile process the usual feelings of loss, grief, shame, and inadequacy, she may also have to work through the conflict of wanting to support her partner's giving birth when she herself cannot. Grieving one's own infertility under such circumstances can be a lengthy and complicated process. Because of this complex intersection of factors, lesbian couples are just as likely to be divided in their decision to become parents as they are to agree at the outset, and one partner will often persuade the other over a period of time (Crespi, 2001).

Socially, infertile lesbians are not a well-supported group. Even the woman's other lesbian friends may not understand why she continues to struggle to conceive, once she does not do so easily. Extensive, painful fertility testing and surgical procedures can disrupt a woman's professional and home lives to such a degree that she begins to question her desire to become a mother. For the partners of these women, the only available support groups may be heterosexual, and the supportive partner may find herself in a support group for "husbands" that fails to address her particular situation (Martin, 1993).

For some lesbian couples, however, adoption is the first choice. The reasons for this vary from couple to couple but include each parent having an equal connection to the child, providing a loving home to a child in need, having personal experience with adoption, one or both partners having an adverse medical history, and the ability to choose the child's gender. Once the couple has agreed to adopt, there are other choices to be made, including the ethnicity of the child (particularly for interracial couples) and, depending on the state of residence, which partner will be the child's legal parent (Crespi, 2001).

Counselors must be sensitive to the ways in which the sexual orientation and identity development of lesbian clients affect their experience of infertility, as well as their readiness to move toward a decision to adopt. The couples' multicultural identities will be a critical element in the decisions they make as well as their eventual experience of becoming an adoptive family.

ADVANTAGES OF HAVING GAY OR LESBIAN PARENTS

Despite the considerable hostility, prejudice, and discrimination experienced by lesbian and gay individuals and couples who parent, studies involving the children of same-sex parents highlight a number of advantages to having gay or lesbian parents. First, lesbians and gay men tend to do a great deal of soul-searching regarding their desire and aptitude for parenting (Crespi, 2001; Martin, 1993). Many explore these issues in a tangible way by first entering the foster care system to confirm their desire to parent as well as to prove to themselves and others that they are up to the task. Because gay men and lesbians put such forethought into the decision to parent, virtually every child is wanted and planned for (Martin, 1993). Due to the nature of their relationship, gay and lesbian couples are already prepared for one of them not having a biological relationship to any child they may have (Martin, 1993), and children raised by lesbian mothers express a concept of family membership that is earned through quality of relationship rather than by genetic kinship (Saffron, 1998).

Another advantage of having gay or lesbian parents is that they are generally less conforming to traditional gender roles, whereas those modeled by heterosexual parents tend to be more restrictive, affecting children's views of what it means to be male or female and the concomitant potentials for achievement (Bigner, 1999; Ossana, 2000; Saffron, 1998). Divisions of labor in lesbian relationships, where earning income, providing child care, and doing household chores are often shared, offer a more egalitarian relationship model, compared with traditional heterosexual marriages (Saffron, 1998). Children of gay fathers who provide a model of androgyny and healthy self-respect/acceptance are more apt to adopt these same attitudes, helping them transcend traditional gender roles, which are increasingly less functional in an evolving, contemporary society. Furthermore, children with androgynous role models learn to participate in relationships in an egalitarian manner rather than basing their associations on constructs of social or physical superiority (Bigner, 1999). Daughters of lesbian mothers—and heterosexual daughters in particular—expressed a better understanding of how to establish appropriate boundaries, while respecting the needs of others, and displayed a better ability to stand up for themselves in interpersonal relationships (Saffron, 1998).

Gay and lesbian parents who are "out" to their children and have successfully integrated their sexual orientation into a positive self-concept are able to model pride and self-acceptance in a stigmatized identity (Martin, 1993; Saffron, 1998). Although literature on gay fathers is scarce, those who are out to their children tend to have more stable lifestyles, are more likely to be in a committed domestic relationship with a partner, and are perceived by their children as more authentic and trustworthy, whereas nondisclosure has been associated with perceptions of the father as being less authentic, less trustworthy, and less deserving of respect (Bigner, 1999).

Gay and lesbian parents who have struggled with identity formation are uniquely able to teach their children the coping mechanisms that are instrumental in shaping a positive sense of self. Those who have resolved their internal homophobia bring into parenthood the ability to create a positive sense of self in the face of social censure, making them uniquely equipped to value diversity and to pass that value on to their children. Interviews with children of gay and lesbian parents suggest that these children have a greater respect for diversity in others regarding lifestyles, cultures, religions, political views, and values, whereas efforts by heterosexual parents to instill these same progressive values in their children may have a lesser impact because they cannot serve as positive role models of a stigmatized group. Ultimately, personal experience with one kind of oppression can lead to a greater awareness of other forms of oppression in a way that vicarious knowledge cannot (Bigner, 1999; Martin, 1993; Saffron 1998).

Because gay and lesbian parents know firsthand that acceptance from others is unpredictable, they are better able to prepare their children ahead of time that they may encounter hostility and help them benefit from the experience by learning to confront prejudice. Additionally, families that face social censure often develop an openness that more traditional families do not. The coping skills children learn in such families may help them work through their own fears of being different as well as develop greater tolerance for diversity as they mature (Lynch & Murray, 2000; Martin, 1993).

The literature on same-sex families has a number of profound implications for the adopted child. First, having a flexible view of what constitutes a "real" family seems to be inherent in same-sex families, possibly as a result of the primary couple already having learned not to depend on society's validation and support for the legitimacy of their families. Although more research is needed to establish whether or not these findings can be generalized to all same-sex families, this kind of flexible thinking suggests that same-sex couples already possess the mind-set to view adoptive families as "real" families—a critical value for the adopted child to learn. Second, seeing a parent display pride and confidence in an identity that is stigmatized by society can be a powerful example for any child, but particularly for one who must integrate the stigma of adoption into a positive self-concept. Furthermore, the openness found in nontraditional families may foster an atmosphere in which children feel freer to voice their issues and concerns as well as process their negative social experiences. Because adopted children struggle with a wide range of developmental issues as they mature, this kind of openness may offer a more inviting atmosphere in which to raise difficult topics. Finally, while it is obvious that having gay or lesbian parents can be an advantage to children who find that they themselves are LGB, it is equally possible that the resilience and coping skills modeled by lesbian and gay parents can help a child work through the stigma of adoption to form a positive self-concept as an adopted person.

THE "MISSING" PARENT

Same-sex families, by definition, do not have opposite-sex parents. When the children in these families begin to socialize with other children, and certainly once they start school, they will begin to notice that other families are different, and this will inevitably give rise to questions. Martin (1993) offers an excellent discussion of this subject, in which she emphasizes the importance of understanding what the child is asking. "Why don't I have a mommy/daddy?" when asked by a very young child, may simply be an inquiry about why his or her family is different from those of friends. This kind of question presents an opportunity for the parents to initiate a discussion about diversity, which can be expanded as the child matures, helping him or her evolve as an individual (Martin, 1993; NAIC, 2000). Also, such a question illustrates how important it is for children to be exposed to both heterosexual and same-sex families so that the normalcy of their own families can be reinforced (Martin, 1993).

From an older child, however, a question about a "missing" parent may be more complicated. For example, the child may be wondering why his or her biological father (or mother) is not actively involved in his or her life. On the other hand, the child may be expressing a desire for more adult attention or the wish to engage in activities that he or she perceives would happen with the absent parent. It is important for parents to listen closely to the child and to explore his or her questions fully in order to know what is being asked. All children need to have adults of both sexes actively involved in their lives, although they need not necessarily live in the home, so having a large and varied support network can be an enormous asset. As children reach adolescence, it is normal for them to seek same-sex role models, and adopted children of this age may develop a need to connect with another person whom they physically resemble (Martin, 1993).

It is important for counselors to keep in mind that the implications of a missing parent might be different for the adopted children of same-sex couples. For example, if the son of lesbian parents believes that his mothers "rejected" his "father" because he is male, he may believe that they will eventually reject him as well. Martin (1993) stresses the importance of letting adopted children know that they were conceived by an egg and a sperm, just like other children, and were born the same way all children are born. In the case of donor insemination or surrogacy, the story will be a bit more complicated, but Martin says that, just as in heterosexual families, the adoption story—especially when there are difficult or painful details—must be presented in a sensitive, age-appropriate manner. Ultimately, although children may express sadness at not having a father (or mother), or may experience frustration at having to repeatedly explain their family form to others, this does not necessarily imply that there will be psychological damage (Martin, 1993).

CURRENT TRENDS

Although adoption practice has evolved to include a broader range of individuals and couples as potential adoptive parents, adoption agencies often lack a clearly articulated policy regarding gay and lesbian individuals or couples who apply to adopt, creating an ambivalent atmosphere for these candidates (Mallon, 2000). A 2003 survey by the Evan B. Donaldson Adoption Institute found that about 60% of the adoption agencies that responded accept applications from gays and lesbians. However, only about two thirds of these had official policies on gay and lesbian adoption; the rest did not.

Among agencies that had policies, about one third of them were nondiscriminatory. However, gays and lesbians had a better chance of a successful adoption if they were open to adopting an older child, a child with special needs, or a child from another country. More than half of the agencies focusing on special needs and international adoptions reported placing with gay or lesbian parents, while only about one quarter of agencies focusing on domestic infant adoptions did so. However, this should not be taken as indicative that international adoptions are necessarily easy for gays and lesbians. Some countries, such as China, require documentation that prospective parents are not homosexual, while others approach the issue indirectly by requiring all prospective adoptive parents to be legally married. Some countries have no set policy, and more than two thirds of the international adoption agencies in the study reported that they accept gay and lesbian applicants. This suggests a possible ethical dilemma for agencies that place children with gays and lesbians, between honoring the indigenous values of a child's country of birth and placing him or her in a stable, nurturing home (Evan B. Donaldson Adoption Institute, 2003).

The same study also found that agency directors often did not know the law in their own state, where it applies to gay and lesbian applicants. More than 15% of directors surveyed either incorrectly stated that lesbians and gay men were barred from adopting in their state or were unsure of the applicable state law. In addition, trends are difficult to track as only 43% of responding agencies reported collecting information on sexual orientation (Evan B. Donaldson Adoption Institute, 2003).

Whether they are adopting internationally or domestically, gay and lesbian couples may assume that to adopt the child they envision, they will need to keep their sexual orientation private, but this is not always the case. Some state agencies are prohibited from discriminating on the basis of sexual orientation, whereas others simply leave the matter of disclosure to the couple's discretion. Although individuals or couples need not voluntarily disclose their sexual orientation, they should tell the truth if asked directly because withholding such information constitutes fraud and may void the adoption. Whether they adopt as an openly gay or lesbian couple or one of them adopts as an individual, any live-in partner will need to be a part of the home study even if he or she is simply identified as another adult living in the home who will assist with child care (Martin, 1993).

Even in states where adoption by lesbians and gays is protected by law, they may still experience considerable discrimination in the adoption process. In states where the law is less clear, same-sex couples may find themselves in a more ambiguous situation. Because gays and lesbians cannot legally marry in most states, they are not protected by the same laws that govern heterosexual adoption (Martin, 1993). The lack of legal protections and social legitimacy, coupled with the difficulties that lesbian and gay couples encounter at some agencies, creates an atmosphere in which couples are encouraged to hide or misrepresent their relationship to increase their chances of a successful adoption. Often, this means that only one partner receives the preadoption training and counseling that is crucial for a successful adoption, leaving the other partner ill prepared for the experience of adoptive parenthood (Pavao, 1998).

IMPLICATIONS FOR COUNSELING

To competently counsel lesbian and gay clients, counselors must make an active effort to understand the mental health needs of this population and must remain aware of their own attitudes and values as they pertain to homosexuality in general as well as toward gay and lesbian parenting specifically (American Counseling Association [ACA], 2005). Before working with gay and lesbian individuals or families, it is recommended that mental health professionals first have systematic training in sexual diversity, yet only 36% of the psychologists surveyed by Crawford et al. (1999) reported having received such training. It is, therefore, crucial for mental health professionals to educate themselves to gain the necessary competence to serve this population (ACA, 2005).

Theoretical orientation is another area that counselors must carefully consider when working with same-sex adoptive families, to ensure that their approach is flexible enough to allow diverse clients to feel supported and validated (Fukuyama & Ferguson, 2000). At present, there is very little empirical research that evaluates the effectiveness of particular theories or conceptual frameworks with LGB clients. Even interventions that are becoming common practice in working with this population, such as bibliotherapy and referral to support groups, have not been evaluated as to how—or even if—they contribute to the effectiveness of individual therapy alone. LGB clients, in general, present to counselors a unique collection of clinical needs and so may derive the most benefit from an integrated or eclectic therapeutic approach incorporating a wide array of tools and interventions that can be customized by the adept, sensitive counselor into a personalized approach for each client (Fassinger, 2000).

Distinguishing among different kinds of family issues is a critical skill that counselors must develop in working with both LGB clients and adoptive families. Counselors must be able to differentiate among issues that are pertinent to sexual orientation and those that are either irrelevant or merely tangential to it (Martin, 1993; Matthews & Lease, 2000). Likewise, it is important for the counselor to separate issues that are common to all developing families from those that are related to the family's adoptive status (Brodzinsky et al., 1998). For practitioners working with LGB adoptive families, the convergence of sexual orientation, developmental, and adoptive issues will present a unique set of clinical challenges, so continuing education is crucial.

BEST PRACTICES

The literature brings up a number of issues that are unique to practicing individual and couple/family therapy with the LGB population, and some "best practices" may be gleaned that will benefit counselors wishing to work with these clients.

- Lesbians and gay men tend to do a great deal of self-examination before deciding to parent and may seek counseling as part of their decision-making process (Crespi, 2001; Martin, 1993). Counselors should be prepared to assist clients in examining their internalized homophobia, social support system, financial resources, emotional temperament, and desire to parent as well as any other issues the client feels may be pertinent.

- There is not a great deal of empirical research on same-sex couples and even less on multicultural issues within those couples (Ossana, 2000). Counselors should consider not only the impact of multiple oppressions on same-sex couples of color but also how couple *differences* in race, ethnicity, religion, socioeconomic class, age, level of "outness," and so on influence the couple dynamic.

- Same-sex parents tend to adjust their level of outness to accommodate their children's comfort level (Lynch & Murray, 2000). It is possible that such adjustments might bring up old issues of internalized homophobia that the partners thought were resolved, which may need to be addressed through counseling.

- Gay male couples may have a more difficult time building close, intimate relationships due to the fact that men are socialized to be more autonomous and less emotionally expressive and to resolve their differences either through confrontation or separation rather than negotiation. Forging a strong therapeutic bond with these couples is critical. Counselors must honor the men's relationship and point out its strengths to instill the hope that change is possible and, at the same time, must create an environment in which the partners feel safe in trying out new behaviors to replace the ones that no longer work (Tunnell & Greenan, 2004).

- Relationships between gay male couples are often initially based on sexual compatibility and, due to male-based values about sexuality, may not be monogamous. Because family therapy has an intrinsic bias toward monogamy and tends to characterize open relationships as unstable and/or problematic, counselors are advised to examine their personal biases in this area and to educate themselves on open relationships (Bettinger, 2004).

- Counselors should closely examine their personal feelings regarding specific sexual practices of LGB couples and how those feelings affect their ability to work with this population in a nonjudgmental way. Without this critical self-knowledge, clinicians may have a more difficult time identifying and managing countertransference issues of either a negative or positive nature (Bettinger, 2004).

- Same-sex couples in which one partner identifies as bisexual may encounter issues of fear, mistrust, and divisiveness. Counselors may need to help the partners explore and clarify what bisexuality means for them in the context of their relationship and must be prepared to provide educational and/or support resources (Bradford, 2004).

CRITIQUE OF THE LITERATURE

The literature included in this review was, with only a few exceptions, not specific to lesbian and gay adoptive families as such. Rather, most of the articles and studies concentrated either on adoptive couples (with the implied presumption of heterosexuality) or on gay and lesbian families in aggregate, with an acknowledgment that adoption is but one of several ways in which these families are formed. However, it is important to note that, whether same-sex families adopt directly or give birth through donor insemination or surrogacy, adoption is likely to be a part of the picture, wherever it is legal. What was lacking in all the literature, in general, was a consideration of multicultural issues. To be fair, obtaining a sufficient number of participants to perform meaningful studies of the needs and experiences of diverse adoptive families, whether same sex or heterosexual, is likely quite challenging, but there is less sensitivity to multicultural issues in the literature than there could be.

Despite the shortcomings in the literature, some preliminary conclusions are possible. Clearly, being the adopted child of lesbian or gay parents adds one more layer of stigma and oppression than would be present if heterosexual parents had adopted the child. Homonegative social attitudes and discrimination, coupled with the lack of legal recognition of same-sex unions, confers a lower status on these children than would be enjoyed by a child whose parents' decision to adopt was viewed more positively by mainstream society. From this point of view, having same-sex parents could be perceived as simply imposing one more hurdle on a child whose ability to form a positive sense of self is already compromised.

Yet at the same time, lesbian and gay parents seem uniquely able to model a positive self-concept of an otherwise stigmatized identity, and the coping skills they have developed over time can be invaluable to a child learning to cope with multiple levels of differentness. The literature suggests that gay and lesbian parents can instill in their children an awareness of oppression and respect for diversity in an experiential way that is not available to heterosexual parents. So it may be that the very stigmas that make parenthood more difficult for lesbian and gay couples have allowed them to develop the resilience and coping skills necessary to succeed in this difficult task and to teach their children to value themselves for who they are rather than by the judgments of others. The process of self-discovery that lesbians and gay men engage in may also make them more understanding of an adopted child's need to search for his or her roots to form a more complete identity. For this reason, it may be advisable for counselors to explore the level of identity development of lesbian or gay couples wanting to adopt.

Parenting is not an easy task, even under the best of circumstances, and parenting *well* is an even greater challenge. Adoptive parenting brings with it a unique constellation of challenges and issues, but the wise counselor will help each individual or couple identify the particular qualities and strengths they bring to the table when embarking on the adoptive journey.

IMPLICATIONS FOR BIRTH PARENTS

Thus far, this chapter has spoken at length about the impact of social and legal issues on gay and lesbian adoptive parents as well as the implications for the children they adopt. But what of the birth parents of children who may be adopted by LGB individuals or couples? How might social and legal issues that affect gay and lesbian adoptive families affect them?

One way in which these concerns might manifest is in the birth parents' choice of agency. Birth parents whose personal values are incompatible with LGB orientations may be more selective about the adoption agencies to which they relinquish their children, selecting only those that do not accept gay or lesbian applicants. If finding such an agency proves to be too difficult, some birth parents may opt for an open adoption, in which they are able to play a more active role in choosing the adoptive parents of their child rather than leaving the matter to chance.

Some birth parents may object to having a gay or lesbian individual or couple adopt their child, either because of the stigma involved or because they believe their child is more likely to be physically or sexually abused, to have psychological or other developmental problems, or to grow up to be gay or lesbian than if he or she were raised by heterosexual parents. Because a preponderance of the literature refutes these beliefs (Allen & Burrell, 1996; Bigner, 1999; Golombok & Tasker, 1996; Mallon, 2000; Martin, 1993; Saffron, 1998; Strickland, 1995), it is incumbent on counselors and adoption professionals to educate birth parents who may have such concerns.

Birth parents who have no values-based objection to their children being raised by gay men or lesbians may still have other, more practical concerns. Even those who are not well versed in the intricate legal challenges faced by LGB parents may have a general understanding that these alternative families are legally vulnerable in ways that traditional families are not. Hence, they may have concerns about the long-term stability and legal status of the children in a gay or lesbian adoptive family. Birth parents who are aware of these kinds of issues may be reluctant to have their child adopted by a gay or lesbian individual or couple due to their concerns for the child's potential health care needs and financial well-being rather than any objection to the parents' sexual orientation per se.

CONCLUSION

While lesbian and gay individuals or couples wishing to adopt may face considerable challenges with respect to social stigma, it is also possible that those who have integrated a positive sense of self already possess the requisite skills to successfully meet them. As non-traditional family forms become more common, researchers might further explore how our current theories meet—or fail to meet—the needs of these families so that counselors may serve them with competence and sensitivity.

REFLECTION QUESTIONS

1. What responsibility do counselors—as individuals and as a profession—have to advocate for social change on behalf of their lesbian, gay, and bisexual (LGB) clients?

2. How might various theoretical orientations need to be adapted to address the needs of LGB families?

3. How is identity development for LGB individuals and that for adopted persons similar? How is it different?

4. Are there ways in which mainstream culture reinforces the idea that adoptive and other alternative families are not "real" families?

REFERENCES

Allen, M., & Burrell, N. (1996). Comparing the impact of homosexual and heterosexual parents on children: Meta-analysis of existing research. *Journal of Homosexuality, 32,* 19–27.

American Counseling Association. (2005). *ACA code of ethics.* Alexandria, VA: Author.

Bettinger, M. (2004). A systems approach to sex therapy with gay males couples. In J. J. Bigner & J. L. Wetchler (Eds.), *Relationship therapy with same-sex couples* (pp. 65–74). New York: Haworth Press.

Bigner, J. (1999). Raising our sons: Gay men as fathers. *Journal of Gay & Lesbian Studies, 10,* 61–69.

Bozett, F. W., & Sussman, M. B. (1989). Homosexuality and family relations: Views and research issues. *Marriage and Family Review, 14,* 1–5.

Bradford, M. (2004). Bisexual issues in same-sex couple therapy. In J. J. Bigner & J. L. Wetchler (Eds.), *Relationship therapy with same-sex couples* (pp. 43–52). New York: Haworth Press.

Brodzinsky, D. M., Schechter, M. D., & Henig, R. M. (1992). *Being adopted: The lifelong search for self.* New York: Anchor.

Brodzinsky, D. M., Smith, D. W., & Brodzinsky, A. B. (1998). *Children's adjustment to adoption: Developmental and clinical issues.* Thousand Oaks, CA: Sage.

Crawford, I., McLeod, A., Zamboni, B. D., & Jordan, M. B. (1999). Psychologists' attitudes toward gay and lesbian parenting. *Professional Psychology: Research and Practice, 30,* 394–401.

Crespi, L. (2001). And baby makes three: A dynamic look at development and conflict in lesbian families. *Journal of Gay & Lesbian Psychotherapy, 4,* 7–17.

Evan B. Donaldson Adoption Institute. (2003). *Adoption by lesbians and gays: A national survey of adoption agency policies, practice, and attitudes* [Data file]. Available from www.adoptioninstitute.org

Fassinger, R. E. (2000). Applying counseling theories to lesbian, gay, and bisexual clients: Pitfalls and possibilities. In R. M. Perez, K. A. DeBord, & K. J. Bieschke (Eds.), *Handbook of counseling and psychotherapy with lesbian, gay, and bisexual clients* (pp. 107–136). Washington, DC: American Psychological Association.

Fein, S. B., & Nuehring, E. M. (1981). Intrapsychic effects of stigma: A process of breakdown and reconstruction of social reality. *Journal of Homosexuality, 7,* 3–10.

Fukuyama, M. A., & Ferguson, A. D. (2000). Lesbian, gay, and bisexual people of color: Understanding cultural complexity and managing multiple oppressions. In R. M. Perez, K. A. DeBord, & K. J. Bieschke (Eds.), *Handbook of counseling and psychotherapy with lesbian, gay, and bisexual clients* (pp. 81–105). Washington, DC: American Psychological Association.

Golombok, S., & Tasker, F. (1996). Do parents influence the sexual orientation of their children? Findings from a longitudinal study of lesbian families. *Developmental Psychology, 32,* 3–11.

Liddle, B. J. (1996). Therapist sexual orientation, gender, and counseling practices as they relate to ratings of helpfulness by gay and lesbian clients. *Journal of Counseling Psychology, 43,* 394–401.

Lynch, J. M., & Murray, K. (2000). For the love of the children: The coming out process for lesbian and gay parents. *Journal of Homosexuality, 39,* 1–12.

Mallon, G. P. (2000). Gay men and lesbians as adoptive parents. *Journal of Gay & Lesbian Social Services, 11,* 1–12.

Martin, A. (1993). *The lesbian and gay parenting handbook.* New York: HarperCollins.

Matthews, C. R., & Lease, S. H. (2000). Focus on lesbian, gay, and bisexual families. In R. M. Perez, K. A. DeBord, & K. J. Bieschke (Eds.), *Handbook of counseling and psychotherapy with lesbian, gay, and bisexual clients* (pp. 249–273). Washington, DC: American Psychological Association.

Morrow, S. L. (2000). First, do no harm: Therapist issues in psychotherapy with lesbian, gay, and bisexual clients. In R. M. Perez, K. A. DeBord, & K. J. Bieschke (Eds.), *Handbook of counseling and psychotherapy with lesbian, gay, and bisexual clients* (pp. 137–156). Washington, DC: American Psychological Association.

National Adoption Information Clearinghouse. (2000). *Gay and lesbian adoptive parents: Resources for professionals and parents* [Data file]. Available from http://naic.acf.hhs.gov

Ossana, S. M. (2000). Relationship and couples counseling. In R. M. Perez, K. A. DeBord, & K. J. Bieschke (Eds.), *Handbook of counseling and psychotherapy with lesbian, gay, and bisexual clients* (pp. 275–307). Washington, DC: American Psychological Association.

Pavao, J. M. (1998). *The family of adoption.* Boston: Beacon Press.

Richardson, T. A., Rayes, N., & Rabow, J. (1998). Homophobia and the denial of human rights: "It is not my place to find others' relationships agreeable or offensive." *Transformations, 9,* 68–77.

Saffron, L. (1998). Raising children in an age of diversity: Advantages of having a lesbian mother. *Journal of Lesbian Studies, 2,* 35–41.

Strickland, B. R. (1995). Research on sexual orientation and human development: A commentary. *Developmental Psychology, 31,* 137–140.

Tunnell, G., & Greenan, D. E. (2004). Clinical issues with gay male couples. In J. J. Bigner & J. L. Wetchler (Eds.), *Relationship therapy with same-sex couples* (pp. 13–26). New York: Haworth Press.

The Urban Institute. (2003). *Gay and lesbian families in the census: Couples with children* [Data file]. Available from www.urban.org

Zicklin, G. (1995). Deconstructing legal rationality: The case of lesbian and gay family relationships. *Marriage & Family Review, 21,* 55–76.

The Importance of Kinship Relationships for Children in Foster Care

16

KATHLEEN M. DOYLE

Licensed Psychologist, New York

DISTINCTIONS BETWEEN THE NEEDS OF CHILDREN IN FOSTER CARE AND CHILDREN LIVING IN OTHER RELATIONSHIPS

Is there a reason to consider children in foster care separately from children living in the myriad family structures of the 21st century? In this first decade of the century, there are children living in traditional two-parent families, but there are also many children who spend alternate weeks in homes of separated and divorced or remarried parents or who live in homes of grandparents or aunts and uncles (sometimes called "kinship care"), in homes where they have been adopted, in shelters for the homeless, or on the streets (Landauer-Menchik, 2002). Some of these children have been in foster homes, some are in foster care, and some will go into foster care. Are the needs, reactions, and behavior of children in foster care different from those of children living in all other circumstances? Shouldn't the focus be on responding to reactions and behavior of children living in any situation rather than children living in a specific type of place? One answer to this dilemma is that most children living in foster care have at least one fundamental difference from those living in most other situations. Their ties of kinship have been severed, either by parents and relatives or by the state.

How Is Foster Care Defined?

There are many usages of the terms *foster care*, *foster child*, and *foster home*. At one time, the term *foster* was applied to children who were adopted as well as to children who lived with families who were not biological relatives (Herman, 2005). As governments became more involved in the oversight of children, including their rights, or the rights of their biological parents, and the funding for their care, the terms describing the status of children in a home became more uniform and defined in law.

In keeping with the definition in the *Encyclopedia of Adoption (Facts on File Library of Health and Living)* (Adamec & Pierce, 2000), we will refer to foster care as a system that is set up to protect children who are abused, neglected, or abandoned or whose parents or primary caretakers are unable to fulfill their parenting obligations. The reason for this inability could be illness, emotional problems, or a host of other reasons. In most of these types of situations, the placement into foster care by parents may have been voluntary. However, we also see children who are involuntarily removed from their families by the court and placed by the state. These children tend to reside in foster families or in group homes or residential treatment centers. These two situations differ in that in the case of an adoptive family the adoptive parents have the same parental rights and obligations as birth parents, whereas in foster home care the foster parents cannot make many decisions about the child's welfare and have to defer to the state or county social worker (Adamec & Pierce, 2000).

There are, however, a variety of placement relationships and terms to describe them that are found in the laws and regulations of the federal and state governments. For example, *kinship care* is a form of foster care that is used to describe both formal and informal placements of children with persons in the extended birth family (Office of Children and Family Services [OCFS], 2005).

Although they are necessary and basically preserve the rights of parents, children, and society, one of the covert impacts of these legal definitions is that they memorialize the child's status and sense of not belonging to any family. Except in voluntary placement for foster care, the child has been removed from the birth family by the state and yet does not become a legal member of the foster family. The child and others can quickly grasp his or her isolation whether the foster family introduces the child using terms that may appear to be kind and embracing, such as "our little guest," or harsh and distancing, such as "the state kid."

A Fundamental Question

If there is one characteristic of children in foster care that is universally shared, it is their question about their personal identity. Their search for an answer is a persistent, usually covert process that is colored by personal, social, religious, and cultural ideals and beliefs. It is coupled with a sense of emptiness and loss. Such children are often immersed in dialectical thought, even when appearing carefree or nonchalant. Frequently, the mixture of thoughts and emotions are displaced to responses and behavior that anger, perplex, hurt, puzzle, and frustrate those who become their foster parents and caregivers. The essence of this is in a question that a 10-year-old boy quietly and softly asked his caseworker: "Why did my parents give me away?"

This 10-year-old, named Andy, was repeating second grade for the third time. He had repeated first grade once. Outwardly, he was shy, processed information slowly, could follow only one direction at a time, and clung to his elderly foster parents, who considered him a well-behaved and model child. His parents, who had married in their teens, had two sons, who were removed from the home because of severe neglect when they were 3 and 5 years old. The older son, now 12, was enuretic, was disruptive in school, and bullied his brother, Andy, when they visited each other. Their parents had slowly matured and had three small children who lived with them and appeared to be doing well. The parents, however, did not want their older children to return home because they feared that their young children, who were also bullied by their oldest son when he visited, would be disturbed.

When Andy's foster father had a heart attack, the foster family was no longer able to care for Andy and asked that he be placed in another home. Andy's question was actually about his foster parents, not his birth parents. The question, however, began a dialogue with his social worker and another therapist, which revealed a boy who had spent years mulling over the reasons why his birth parents had "abandoned him." He recalled little of the neglect, but remembered the times when his mother would play with him or hold him and the times when his father would scream at him to stop hitting a drum because it made his head hurt. He had seen his birth parents occasionally during his 7 years of foster care, and they had three more children whom they appeared to love and to provide with good care. They went to church. Andy's foster parents had told him that good parents always went to church and that children had a duty to behave so God would love them. Andy had finally decided that he had to be the reason that his birth parents had to give him away. He had been bad, so his father had yelled, and his mother wouldn't want a bad son. Even his brother bullied him, so he must have been the cause of his abandonment. Just prior to his foster father having the heart attack, Andy had scratched the car with his ice skate and his foster father had yelled, and now they were also giving him away.

Andy's mind rarely had been focused on school, chores, and relationships with anyone other than his foster parents. He dwelled on his loss of kinship, his failure as a son, his efforts to be good that did not make his father want him back, and his need to remain a dependent, compliant son to his foster parents so that they would not abandon him as well. He did not learn in school, which strengthened his belief that he was unable to grow up and take care of himself, and he had little energy to play and feared trying to make friends.

A coordinated effort by his social worker and therapist, the foster parents, with whom he continued to live, his teachers, and eventually his parents finally freed Andy from his hidden world of fear, blame, and rage that had prevented him from learning, facing his emotions, and establishing productive relationships (*The Case of Andy*, 1970, personal communication).

Children living in foster care, particularly when custody is taken from parents, appear to have an additional burden beyond that borne by many children in dysfunctional homes or other settings. Their fundamental identity is often shattered when kinship is severed.

HISTORICAL, SOCIOLOGICAL, AND LEGAL BACKGROUNDS

The Evolution of Systems of Foster Care

It is obvious that over the centuries, there have always been children in need of care. The causes for this and society's responses throughout the generations have been explored and reported in many journals and texts (National Advocate, 2005). The impact, however, of caregivers' responses to the biological parents and family has not been studied. It is not only important to understand the factors that enable children in foster care to become independent, well-adjusted, productive adult citizens but also important to understand the history of foster care to avoid its pitfalls and enhance its insights for the future.

The foster care system of the 21st century is generally well regulated by federal, state, and local governments (Herman, 2005). This has evolved partly based on how society has valued children and the religious, cultural, and economic factors of the times. As a generalization, however, children experienced many fates throughout the centuries. While they were often provided shelter and food by individuals or families based on a sense of obligation related to religious belief, they were also abandoned and left to die or survive using their own wiles. In societies based on an extended family structure, they might have been absorbed into various units of the family over time and kept their identity as a family member (Javier, 2006, personal communication; Porter, 2004). The reason that children have needed care has also influenced the kind of care they have received. Children whose biological families sought care due to hardship often were better accepted and cared for and maintained a more integrated and positive sense of self than those who were abandoned or were the children of criminals or other socially distanced groups.

The role of children within cultures also influenced the care they received. In societies that have viewed children as possessions or not fully human beings, small children were usually not seen as a part of the family until they were able to be productive (Carp, 2002). Additionally, in previous centuries, there was a high death rate in infants and children from disease and disability at all levels of society, also lowering the expectation that abandoned or uncared-for children would live and become good citizens (Berebitsky, 2000). This also influenced the personal relationships of parents and children, whether biological or not.

In the 17th century, the "English Poor Law" (2003) permitted poor children to be placed into indentured service until they became legal adults rather than being forced to live in poorhouses where they were often abused and harmed. In the United States, Charles Loring Brace, founder of the New York Children's Aid Society, began the free foster care movement, which is considered the foundation of the current foster care system (National Advocate, 2005).

In 1859, Brace published *The Best Method of Disposing of Our Pauper and Vagrant Children*, in which he described the "orphan trains" that would be used to transport children from the streets of New York to midwestern and western states where they would be offered free homes (Brace, 1872). Children were offered free homes as acts of charity, as part of a mission to instill a religious or value system, or for service in the home or on the farm, similar to the indentured placements in England. Orphan trains continued into the third decade of the 20th century, and the placement of older teenagers for "work in kind" lasted well into the last decades of the century.

There were reactions to Brace's concept of removing children from the bad influences of their environment, including the belief system of their families, by the development of various kinds of service agencies and residential home-school institutions, including orphanages and training schools (Herman, 2005). These were commonly established by churches and religious organizations or by groups attempting to serve families rather than just provide for children. The concept of adoption agencies sprung from reformers who looked for permanent placement of the child in a home where the child would become a legal member of the family, establish a sound personal identity, and be a valued member of the family (Herman, 2005). The issue of permanence was seen as the route to greater self-esteem, high achievement, and the establishment of roots that would provide security for the child and a safety net for society (Harris, 2005).

In the last half of the 19th century, states began to establish laws and regulations regarding the placement of children in foster care (Herman, 2005; National Advocate, 2005). Pennsylvania passed the first law in 1885 that required those who cared for two or more unrelated children to have a license. The movement of government to take charge of the placement and oversight of children in foster care was propelled by the development of public social services and the Social Security Act of 1935, which included "Aid to Dependent Children," later known as "Aid to Families With Dependent Children" (Herman, 2005). In the early 1960s, federal funding for foster care was included in these benefit programs (Herman, 2005).

At the start of the 21st century, most children who require care and services outside of their homes reside in foster care rather than in institutions. Some live with relatives in the extended family, which is usually called kinship care, and others live in homes that have been approved to provide foster care. There are federal and state laws that regulate these placements, but in many cases, the oversight and funding of such care remain with local jurisdictions. In addition to changes in organization and oversight of services to dependent, neglected, abused, abandoned, or orphaned children, there has been a gradual movement from placement solely for maintenance and care to one that seeks permanency in placement through either return to the family or extended family or adoption (Harris, 2005). Although this reduces the cost burden to the government, its primary reason has been described as providing children with stability and a sense of belonging and identity.

Reasons Children Are Placed in Foster Care in the 21st Century

The most frequent reasons that children are placed in foster care today, particularly when this is through a court order where custody is given to the state, are neglect, physical abuse, no available caretaker, and sexual abuse (Adamec & Pierce, 2000). Other reasons for foster placement include mental and physical incapacity of caregivers and economic hardship (Adamec & Pierce, 2000).

Children may be placed in foster care for long periods, but the goal of the state and placement agencies is to seek permanency and, when possible, placement with the child's family or extended family. Most children in foster placement experience a sense of loss, bewilderment, and confusion, although this is less when placement has been voluntary and the children know the true reasons (OCFS, 2005).

When children are abandoned, abused, neglected, or harmed in other ways, they will have to face the mental and emotional burden of these actions as well as the emotional and behavioral overlay from fear, anger, and distrust. For some children, their struggle with these emotions may drive them from one foster home to the other, lengthening their placements, and making it more difficult to return home or find any other permanent home. Other children may enter foster care from institutions where they have been placed due to severe needs and where the foster parents must have experience or special training to handle these physical, emotional, or behavioral needs, offer around-the-clock attention and care, and receive additional funding and resources to provide care. Many of these children remain permanently in foster care (OCFS, 2005).

Regulations Regarding the Approval and Oversight of Foster Care Settings

In addition to various federal laws that authorize funding for foster care and specify certain requirements—such as the need to make reasonable efforts to prevent removal from the home—in 1997, the federal government enacted Public Law No. 105-89, The Adoption and Safe Families Act of 1997. It establishes the policy that our national goals for children in the child welfare system are safety, permanency, and well-being (The Adoption and Safe Families Act [ASFA], Pub. L. No. 105-89, 1997).

The Administration for Children and Families of the U.S. Department of Health and Human Services (2003) describes five principal goals of this legislation as follows: (1) The safety of children is the paramount concern that must guide all child welfare services; (2) foster care is a temporary setting and not a place for children to grow up; (3) permanency planning efforts for children should begin as soon as a child enters foster care and should be expedited by the provision of services to families; (4) the child welfare system must focus on results and accountability; and (5) innovative approaches are needed to achieve the goals of safety, permanency, and well-being. While this law continues to support the need to make reasonable efforts to prevent removal of children from the home, it also identifies exceptions.

States normally establish the legal structure for foster care, and local governments commonly establish payments or other requirements. In addition to regulating foster care, many states, including the states of Alabama, Colorado, Illinois, Georgia, Maryland, Mississippi, Missouri, Oklahoma, Oregon, Tennessee, and Washington, have adopted a Foster Parent Bill of Rights (The National Foster Parents Association, 2005). These statutes address rights extending from general principles related to being treated with dignity to specific rights in regard to receiving training and information from the oversight agency and to a part in making crucial decisions about the child or children in their care. It is interesting to observe the growing awareness of the rights of foster parents, which indirectly support the rights of the child in foster care, but further work is needed to recognize the specific rights of the child in foster care to maintain kinship relationships while also being considered an integral part of the foster home.

In New York State, the Office of Children and Family Services has developed the *New York State Foster Parent Manual* (McBride, 2003), which provides definitions, procedures, and advice for foster parents and those considering offering foster care to a child. This manual reflects the prevailing philosophy and policies that are true not only in New York State but also throughout most of the country. The issues that states must address are captured in the chapter headings of this manual, including

- Being a foster parent
- When a child comes into foster care
- Communication, ongoing, and emergency
- Getting started: the basics
- Daily life
- Teamwork
- Concerns for foster parents
- Adopting a foster child
- Certification and approval of foster homes
- Positive approaches to discipline
- Charts, such as medication logs, developmentally related activities

The manual talks about becoming a foster parent, the rights and obligations of foster parenting, why children are placed in foster care, how placement affects children, cultural factors, health and medications, confidentiality, personal property, and training, among a multitude of issues that arise daily. This state requires a period of training for every foster parent and has an extensive process called Model Approach to Partnerships in Parenting/ Group Preparation and Selection Precertification Training Program. The manual describes this method as encouraging open communication and trust among foster families, adoptive families, birth families, and family services. The oversight and intense training that the states provide for foster families, and often adoptive families, however, emphasize the unique needs of children in foster care.

PSYCHOLOGICAL IMPLICATIONS OF THE FOSTER HOME EXPERIENCE

The Impact of Permanency on the Child's Developing Sense of Security, Self-Esteem, and Identity

When questioned about their identity, people usually respond by providing information about their name, place of residence, occupation, and school and their identification with other persons, such as families, friends, clubs, or associations. Further probing may lead to connections with extended family members, personal interests, hobbies, or personal accomplishments. Yet a deeper inquiry will elicit information on belief systems and philosophies, and if the roots of identity are reached, the person's fears, conflicts, and uncertainties are exposed.

For children in foster care, questions about their identity can create pain and uncertainty. They can also continue to stimulate the underlying struggles that they frequently experience. Children who understand that their families have sought foster care voluntarily due to hardship, loss, or illness may be less prone to the fundamental speculations about who they are or what they believe, but they also face these challenges during periods of separation. Public policy looks at permanency as one solution to the identity struggles of children who have been abused, mistreated, or abandoned by parents and caregivers or left homeless by parental incarceration, illness, or addictions. Permanency, to the extent that it provides stable relationships, consistency, and a safe, long-term home, is viewed as an opportunity for a child to establish a sense of belonging and security and to offer the child the opportunity to become a good citizen.

Private and public agencies that work within the foster care system have begun to recognize the importance of the biological family to the child's successful maturation, no matter what permanency arrangement evolves. Consider the situation of Andy in the first example. He was placed in a foster home during late infancy, where he lived as the only child for 7 years with a couple who were kind, supportive, and generous. His parents rarely met his foster parents and Andy had infrequent visits with them. Even though he was very young, he understood the contradictions between the values and lifestyle of his parents and his foster parents, and although he was living in a home where he was wanted, he feared that if he expressed acceptance of his biological parents and an interest in being with them, he might no longer be the good boy his foster parents praised but might lose that home as well. At another level, he also feared, because he resembled his father and had been compared to him, that any expression of identification with his father would make him unacceptable to any family. Regardless of how well his foster parents provided for his physical care, how constant and stable his daily life was, how much his teachers supported and tried to help him, and how welcome he was in the community, Andy's emotional and mental development were immobilized by his hidden ruminations about the reasons he "was given away."

One of the most important challenges to foster parents and caregivers is to learn to accept the biological parents and family of the children who enter their homes and lives. This acceptance is essentially the recognition that no matter how despicable they think that the child's living situation has been, or how infrequent the child has any contact with his or her parents, the biological bonds remain. "Who am I?" has been one of the fundamental questions of philosophers through the centuries. Finding one's roots became the theme of television series and books in the final quarter of the 20th century (see Margulies, 1977) and can be seen in the upsurge of self-help genealogy resources in libraries and on the Internet. Accepting biological parents and family of the children for whom they provide care does not mean that foster families have to approve of their lifestyles and behavior but, rather, that they recognize that the children for whom they provide homes have a right to know their biological parents and family and to maintain emotional ties with them. This, in fact, provides the opportunity for children to begin their own internal evaluation of not only who they are but also who they want to become.

While the acceptance of biological parents and families may not seem too difficult as an abstraction, its proof to a child in foster care often occurs at the times when the bonds of family life are commonly expressed, such as birthdays and holiday celebrations. Foster caregivers are often dismayed when biological parents or family suddenly ask to visit or take the children when the foster family has organized holiday plans or family celebrations. Children in foster care may want to visit or be with their biological parents, and the grace with which the foster caregivers accept this, even if it disrupts a celebration, can be the sign of acceptance that children need to become free to begin to make their own choices. The acceptance of the parent-child bond does not mean, however, that foster caregivers cannot express their own beliefs and values regarding the actions of biological parents and family. When this is done with respect, it provides the alternatives often needed for children to make personal choices.

The Impact of Social Class and Standing on the Development of a Sense of Self

While it is not unusual for a foster family to be far more economically and socially advantaged than the biological families of the children placed in their home (Herman, 2005), it is more common that foster caregivers are in a similar, or *just* somewhat higher, economic and social class. This has been particularly true in situations where families have taken children into their homes to help in the home or on the farm, or when such child care has been seen as a source of income. Although this situation is declining, it was an outgrowth of the movements of the 19th and 20th centuries and still exists (Herman, 2005).

When children move into homes where there are great distinctions in economic, social, and political status, it is a challenge for both children and foster families. There are gaps in expectations and behavior, as well as the degree of economic comfort that can lead to a wide range of feelings and behavior by both children and the foster caregivers. These can include, among many other things, confusion, resentment, anger, fear, uncertainty, and withdrawal by children and righteousness, indignation, impatience, and ridicule by foster caregivers. It is important for caseworkers to help both children and families to understand these gaps and to assist the transition by reducing its potential to increase alienation, blame, and uncertainty. As in all of the differences between children and their foster caregivers, caregivers have to learn to resist the tendency to say and do things that will cause the child to perceive that he or she comes from what the caregivers see as an inferior class or social group.

It is important to work with families whose principal motivation in providing a foster home is either to save the child from an "inferior" or unacceptable lifestyle, provide additional income for their family, or find extra hands for work in the home or on the farm, to ensure that they recognize clearly that the child in their care requires emotional as well as physical care and is being placed in the home to be a member of the family, and not simply their property or servant. If such foster parents cannot grasp the essential needs of the child being placed in their care, they should not be approved for foster care.

One of the differences in formal kinship care relationships is that the child is a member of the extended family. Children in such homes may have fewer of the conflicts regarding who they are but may also be faced with the displaced resentment or emotions of their caregivers to their biological parents. In many cases, this can put the child in the position of defending his or her parents and, in doing so, clinging to unproductive and self-defeating behavior. Although some research has supported the assumption that children have fewer struggles and mature satisfactorily if they do not have to deal with the harm of severed kinship in placement, more definitive research is currently under way; but it is clear that children in kinship care situations need support, and their caregiver's oversight, to make certain that they have a safe and nurturing environment.

The Effect of Ethnic and Cultural Differences in the Milieu of the Foster Setting

Ethnicity and cultural beliefs are integral elements of a child's personal identity (OCFS, 2005). They must be viewed by placement agencies, providers, foster caregivers, schools, and policymakers with the same importance as that of housing, nourishment, clothing, and education. The attitudes and beliefs of everyone in the child's foster placement system regarding ethnicity will be perceived by the child and will influence his or her capacity to develop and be peaceful in foster care. The facts of ethnicity and cultural status combined with the lifestyle and behaviors of the biological family essentially answer the child's question: "Who am I?" The overt and nonverbal response by persons in the foster care environment as well as the child's own reaction to ethnic and cultural differences will combine to create a climate of success or failure. The impact of ethnic and cultural differences within the foster care placement system permeates all levels of personal, social, educational, and relational interactions and can never be simply dismissed. While it may diminish in one area of life, it can escalate or be intense in others.

The cultural differences that are created by differences in economic class are often less significant to a child's adjustment. Frequently, the economic class distinctions between the foster family and the biological family are not great, so that the child can move relatively smoothly into the foster home. When there are wider distinctions in economic class, the manner in which the foster family embraces the child and provides hospitality will usually have greater importance than the behavioral changes that such differences require.

One aspect of economic class distinctions, however, is the role that they can play in the child's emotional acceptance of the foster home placement. Children in foster care sometimes use the change in economic class as a rationalization to blame or reject one family or the other, and sometimes both. An example of this occurred with Rosie. Rosie was 11 years old when she was removed from a neglectful home, where she had irregular meals, rarely had the opportunity to bathe, had few useful clothes for summer and none for winter, and slept on a soiled mattress with no bedding. The school had brought Rosie's situation to the attention of the local social service agency, which found her to be neglected but not physically abused. She remained in foster care for several months while her single-parent, biological mother struggled to improve her living conditions and hoped that Rosie could return home. Soon after biweekly weekend home visits began, Rosie would eagerly go to her mother's apartment on Saturday mornings and return to the foster home on Sunday nights. Her foster parents encouraged her visits and were generally welcoming and supportive of her biological mother. After three weekend visits, her foster parents discovered that all the hems were cut off Rosie's slacks and dresses. This situation occurred intermittently for the next 3 months. The placement agency's social worker worked with the biological mother, the foster parents, and Rosie, at first in individual meetings and later in joint meetings with everyone where Rosie's behavior was understood as intertwined in the economic class distinctions between her biological and her foster families. Rosie basically was important both to her biological mother and to her foster parents, who had developed a relatively good relationship. The foster parents were concerned about her future and wanted to provide all they could for her to succeed. Her mother had hopes for her child's success, but she had little concern or awareness of the need for a healthy environment that encouraged growth and learning. Rosie had become torn between them. The comforts and support of the foster care home and the availability of food, clothes, books, and toys were symbols that she began to partially destroy as a result of guilt, blame, and shame. On one hand, she wanted to return to her mother but feared what she would lose. By cutting her clothes, she thought that she would not be considered ready to go home. By cutting her clothes, she sent a message to her foster parents that she rejected their lifestyle that emphasized her mother's incompetence and failure as a parent. By cutting her clothes, she punished herself for her anger and resentment toward both families. Cutting her clothes was her loudest cry for help that reflected her kinship dilemma (*The Case of Rosie*, 1988, personal communication).

It is important that those providing service to children in foster care do not ignore the significant, and often subtle, relationship to all aspects of behavior by all persons involved in the foster home placement experience.

The Educational Environment's Contribution to the Mental, Emotional, and Behavioral Maturation of Children in Foster Care

One of the greatest problems for children in foster care is inconsistency in education. In many instances, they have had poor attendance; have had little encouragement or opportunity to do homework; have not been inspired to read outside of the classroom; and, in fact, often may not have paper, pens, or books in their homes prior to their placement in foster care. When placed in foster care, they are often moved to a new school district where they may not be following the same curriculum. In addition to their adjustment to a new home, they may have left a familiar school where they have had good relationships with some adults and children and now are located in a completely new environment where their caseworker may be the person with whom they have had the longest relationship. Some children, who are moved from one foster home to another and experience this series of losses, withdraw, do not learn, become aggressive, or develop other behavior problems.

The school, however, could become a safe haven, where the child's education and social development could both be served. In *The Case of Andy* (1970, personal communication), the school apparently focused on what he appeared to have learned or, rather, not learned and repeatedly retained him in the same situation. The basis of his failure to meet the demands of the classroom was not an inability to learn but the immobilization caused by his internal conflict and fears. While schools are not social agencies, they are becoming more aware of the increasing personal and social problems of their students. Federal and state laws provide mandates and assistance to schools to engage personnel to diagnose and provide educational treatment plans for students who appear to have physical, mental, emotional, and behavioral disorders. Foster parents and caregivers, caseworkers, and other professionals who work with children in foster care should consider the child's progress in school as a barometer of his or her adjustment to foster care as well as the other stresses in the child's life and request that the school provide whatever evaluation and education treatment services that are available to all other students in the school. In addition to determining if there are serious learning disabilities, it is important that the school not also see the child in foster care as their "little guest." As far as can be determined, there is a higher mobility rate in most schools now than in past decades (Fowler-Finn, 2001), so schools should be more prepared to introduce new students to a class, consider them a part of the class, and provide the full range of available services to them. While foster parents of children in foster care do not have the same custodial rights as parents of biological or adopted children, they should be given the opportunities to know the progress and needs of the children. The school should take pains to avoid any sign that the district, individual school, or personnel consider any child as not belonging. Foster parents should be encouraged to attend school functions, serve as class parents, and chaperone trips.

Duration of Foster Care Placements and the Impact on the Child

Although the goal of placement in foster care is spoken of as short term, some children spend a long span of their childhood in foster care placement. Additionally, some children live in kinship care for various periods. In both instances, these can be isolated placements or can be repeated on more than one occasion. It might be reasonable to separate a discussion of the needs of children in kinship care from those of children who live in foster homes with no biological parent. There is little research to support this. A goal of foster care is to provide a safe place where children can learn self-respect, trust, and good coping and decision-making abilities, and develop their knowledge and skills to become self-directed and productive members of the community. There are advantages to kinship care, including maintaining family bonds, but there can also be serious disadvantages, such as the resentment and anger that kin may hold against the biological parents.

This being said, the duration that a child is placed in some form of foster care will influence the intended outcome of the placement. If the placement is principally intended to provide a safe and stable home for the child as he or she awaits a permanent home, then the degree to which the child will be expected or be able to learn the knowledge and skills to become self-directed and productive will vary. If the placement is intended to begin to offer an opportunity for the child to gain greater self-respect, learn to trust, and develop good coping and decision-making abilities, while still anticipating a more permanent home, then no matter how long the child is intended to stay, the atmosphere and attitudes of the home should be the focus of the care and placement.

According to the Child Welfare Information Gateway (2005), there were more than half a million children living in foster care as of September 30, 2003. Approximately half were in nonrelative foster homes, a quarter in relative foster homes, 19% in group homes or institutions, 5% in preadoptive homes, and 7% in other placements. The only significant change between 1998 and 2003 was a drop in the number of children in relative foster homes. In reporting data, the Child Welfare Information Gateway (2005) noted that the duration the child spent in foster care extended from 1 day to several years. Of the estimated 281,000 children who exited foster care during 2003, 18% had been in care for less than 1 month, 32% had been in care from 1 month to 11 months, 20% had been in care from 1 year to

23 months, 11% had been in care from 2 years to 35 months, 10% had been in care from 3 years to 47 months, and 9% had been in care for 5 or more years. At the end of 2003, 50% of all foster children who exited care had been in foster homes from 1 to 5, or more, years. During 2002, a median of 9.9% of children who entered foster care had previously been in care. Also in that year, approximately the same number of children entered foster care as exited. Therefore, the collection and reporting of these data influence the interpretation regarding the use and benefit of foster care placement. There exists little reported data to enable a good analysis of the effects of the foster care because various kinds of settings were identified as foster placements, the duration of placement extended from a day or two in the life of a child to at least 5 or more years of childhood or adolescence, and the discharge from foster care was not solely to a permanent family but could have been to independent living or even incarceration.

To a large extent, the impact of foster care on children will depend on the length of their placement in foster care, their exposure to varying lifestyles, beliefs, and attitudes, including those regarding their biological family, and their acceptance in the foster home, school, and community.

CLINICAL RESEARCH IMPLICATIONS

While there are many sources of statistics about the numbers of children in foster care, the history of how foster care has evolved in this country and in other areas of the world, and the amount of money spent on caring for children in need, there does not appear to be much clinical research that has focused particularly on the significance of children's self-perception, self-esteem, and successful development based on the isolation they find when kinship ties are severed, supposedly "for their own good." It is important to research the many facets of this situation not only to address directly the public policy and budgetary considerations but principally to find the forms of care that enable foster children to have satisfying and productive lives. It is also important that such research be done with safeguards for any children who are involved, so that the possibility for success in their future lives will not be jeopardized.

There are thousands of adults who are currently living in this country, who have experienced all forms of foster placements, and who may be willing to provide factual and recalled information that touches on their kinship ties with their biological families and the most significant factors that influenced the preservation or destruction of such ties. Anecdotal stories do, of course, suffer from distortions of memory, bias, time, and subjectivity, but repetitions of core recollections from multiple persons regarding the severance of kinship ties could provide valid information from which to assess the current movement toward permanency.

The 21st century has opened with a flourish of technological tools that should encourage and enrich the ability of social scientists to unravel the challenging question of the effect and value of severing kinship bonds for the benefits of permanency in family relationships. As health, education, and societal records expand and proliferate, the various factors that influence the lives of children will become more accessible. The ability to gather information at rapid speed from multiple sources will facilitate research that will begin to identify the complex events that interact to enable children, including those in foster care, to achieve satisfying and productive lives as good citizens. A constructive use of advanced research technology, for example, using the data that are already available, would study the concept of permanency as the primary means of ensuring a successful future for a child to determine if it is a clinically sound concept, a subtle way of reducing budgets, or a little of both.

No matter what tools are used, or what kind of data become available, however, the rights of children, their families, and foster families should be protected, because these tools can also be used to violate privacy, reach rapid but not necessarily true generalizations, and establish public policy that is mainly focused on budgetary concerns.

BEST PRACTICE RECOMMENDATIONS

When providing the most effective services to children in foster care, or deciding who potentially will move into a foster home, it is essential to understand the uniqueness of their family relationships. This is different for each child, so the general interviewing, assessment, and treatment skills that a good provider has honed should focus on identifying the elements of uniqueness, as well as similarity, that the child has with other children in placement situations and in general. In particular, however, those serving children in foster care should be aware that the children's responses and behavior may reflect a struggle with personal identity, including and going beyond overt problems in school, home life, and the community. With children who are experiencing daily challenges in relationships, education, and/or behavior, it is often difficult to recognize that the resolution to the problem may occur once the child believes that he or she will not be abandoned by living in foster care.

Roger's struggle and behavior were an excellent example of this. Roger was the child of a farmer who could not read or write. His mother was deceased and he was placed in foster care at age 5 because his father seriously neglected his care and safety. His foster parents were kind and affectionate, and they expected Roger to do well in school. Although they enrolled him in a learning center, provided a tutor, and asked for an evaluation for learning disabilities, and although Roger was cooperative, he could not learn to read. While his foster parents were good to him, they regularly compared his lack of achievement with his father's limitations and worried aloud about his future ability to care for himself. His biological father, whom he saw infrequently, would say he wanted Roger to be a good son but would add that Roger was not like him and he could never provide for him as well as his son's foster family.

The skilled psychologist who began to evaluate Roger listened to Roger tell his personal story about his reading problems. But he also heard within Roger's descriptions of home life and academic disappointments that Roger was torn between loyalty to a father who wanted him as a son, but couldn't cope with raising him, and foster parents who were able to provide for him but were repeatedly disappointed by his failure to learn. The message that Roger got from his father's verbal and nonverbal cues was that if Roger became like his foster parents, there could no longer be a relationship with his father, who felt humiliated. The message that Roger got from his foster family was that he must be limited like his father and would never amount to anything. He was depressed, as might be expected, but that was not the cause of him not learning to read. The psychologist's broad focus and knowledge of the struggles of children in foster care enabled him to determine that Roger could not read because he was afraid that skill in reading would permanently sever the kinship bond with his father, and regardless of the basically good permanent home he had with his foster parents, his greatest need was to maintain the kinship bond (*The Case of Roger*, 1994, personal communication).

Good practices when working with children in foster care include the following:

• Working with the foster parents and family to raise their awareness of the many verbal and nonverbal impressions they give regarding their recognition, respect, and acceptance of the biological family, and helping them recognize that rejecting and disparaging impressions will undo the security that a permanent or long-term foster home may provide

• Helping foster parents learn that respecting the biological family and giving a child in their care the gift of freedom to know and share thoughts and feelings about their biological family to the extent possible will be more important for the child's successful future than most of the other things that they provide

Is the move for permanency, whether in a foster or similar setting or with the biological or extended family, the most important goal for each child? The question that must be considered for each child is whether permanency will lead to a good transition to adulthood and success in community relationships.

REFLECTION QUESTIONS

1. Are verbal or nonverbal cues from other persons more important to a child in determining his or her value to these persons?

2. If foster parents are kind, accepting, supportive, and generous to a child in their care, would that override their angry, rejecting, blaming, or demeaning language or behavior toward the child's biological parents in influencing the child's future accomplishments or behavior?

3. What lessons can be learned from the historical treatment of children regarding foster care that would ensure that children under care in the future will feel that they are part of the community and will want to succeed?

4. Most federal and state policies regarding foster placement and the rights and obligations of biological and foster parents seem focused on establishing permanency in a home for a child. What critical factors should law- and policymakers consider when establishing laws or policies regarding the termination of parental rights, the time period in which a child may remain in foster care, the effect of dispersing the children of one family to more than one home, the kinds of services needed to facilitate positive permanent placements, and their long-range economic impact?

5. Historically, one of the main efforts to care for children who need to live apart from their homes has been to physically remove them, either to other places in the country or to relatively inaccessible residences where they either never or rarely see their biological parents and kin. What message would the child receive by this single reaction to his or her needs or circumstances?

6. What should social service providers, lawmakers, and policymakers learn from the national passion and fascination of the past quarter century in finding one's "roots"?

7. Why would a child whose parents abused, neglected, abandoned, or mistreated him or her not want to find another permanent home?

8. Would a child who is secure in a permanent placement also be likely to have higher self-esteem, achieve well in life tasks, and become a safe and productive citizen?

REFERENCES

Adamec, C., & Pierce, W. (2000). *Foster care*. Retrieved January 22, 2006, from the *Encyclopedia of adoption*, http://encyclopedia.adoption.com/entry/foster-care/144/1.html

The Adoption and Safe Families Act of 1997 (Pub. L. No. 105-89). *Titles IV-B and IV-E, Section 403(b), Section 453, and Section 1130(a) of the Social Security Act*. Retrieved January 22, 2006, from www.ncsl.org/programs/cyf/ASFA97.htm

Berebitsky, J. (2000). *Like our very own: Adoption and the changing culture of motherhood, 1851–1950*. Kansas City: University of Kansas.

Brace, C. L. (1872). *The dangerous classes of New York and twenty years' work among them*. New York: Wynkoop & Hallenbeck.

Carp, E. W. (Ed.). (2002). *Adoption in America*. Ann Arbor: University of Michigan.

Child Welfare Information Gateway. (2005). *Foster care: Numbers and trends*. Retrieved August 19, 2006, from www.childwelfare.gov/pubs/factsheets/foster.cfm

English Poor Law. (2003). In *The Columbia electronic encyclopedia* (6th ed.). New York: Columbia University Press. Retrieved January 22, 2006, from www.bartleby.com/65/po/poorlaw.html

Fowler-Finn, T. (2001, August). *Student stability vs. mobility: The school administrator.* Retrieved February 25, 2006, from www.aasa.org/publications

Harris, T. (2005). *How foster care works.* Retrieved January 22, 2006, from www.brucewillis.com/difference/fostercare.cfm

Herman, E. (2005). *The adoption history project.* Department of History, University of Oregon. Retrieved January 22, 2006, from http://darkwing.uoregon.edu/~adoption/topics/fostering.htm

Landauer-Menchik, B. (2002, March). *With whom do Michigan's children live?* Policy Report #9. East Lansing, MI: The Education Policy Center at Michigan State University.

Margulies, S. (Producer). (1977). *Roots* [Television series]. New York: ABC.

McBride, Rebecca. (Ed.). (2003). *New York State foster parent manual.* New York: New York State Office of Children and Family Services Welfare Research.

National Advocate. (2005). *History of foster care in the United States.* Retrieved September 5, 2005, from www.adopting.org/uni/frame.php?url=http://www.fosterparents.com/articles/index39fchist.html

The National Foster Parents Association. (2005). Retrieved January 22, 2006, from www.nfpainc.org/aboutFP/rights_FP.cfm?page=2

Office of Children and Family Services, Foster Care. (2005). Retrieved January 22, 2006, from www.ocfs.state.ny.us/main/fostercare/requirements.asp

Porter, S. (2004). A good home: Indenture and adoption in nineteenth-century orphanages. In E. W. Carp (Ed.), *Adoption in America* (pp. 27–50). Ann Arbor: University of Michigan.

U.S. Department of Health and Human Services, Administration for Children and Families, Administration of Children, Youth, and Families, Children's Bureau. (2003). Retrieved January 22, 2006, from www.acf.hhs.gov/programs/cb/stats_research/afcars/tar/report8.html

School Issues and Adoption

17

Academic Considerations and Adaptation

FRANCINE FISHMAN

Independent Practice

ELLIOTTE SUE HARRINGTON

Montclair State University

During childhood and adolescence, children and teens spend approximately one third of their day in educational settings. Schools, educators, and researchers have explored the impact of learning styles, disabilities, teacher expectations, and a host of other issues on school-age children. Although they have focused on a number of both internal (e.g., intelligence) and external (e.g., social class) factors that might affect students, relatively little attention has been given to students who were adopted into their families. Thus, although adopted children and teens have been the subjects of research studies addressing heritability issues (e.g., Scarr & Weinberg, 1983), there have been few studies addressing educational and school-related issues pertaining to them. However, given that it is widely acknowledged that adoptees may encounter various challenges and opportunities throughout their lives, such as those related to identity formation and loss (Brodzinsky, Schechter, & Henig, 1992), educational and school issues for this substantial portion of the school-age population need to be discussed. The 2000 U.S. Census (U.S. Bureau of the Census, 2003) found that 2.5% of children below the age of 18 (1.6 million) were adopted, and the U.S. Department of Health and Human Services (2003) estimated that another 542,000 children resided in foster care during 2001. Clearly, this issue deserves greater attention.

Interestingly, the nature of adoption can result in adoptees meeting their greatest challenges during their school years due to the cognitive, emotional, and social development that takes place during that time. Research studies have reported varying results regarding the outcomes for children during these crucial, developmental years. Some studies have suggested that adopted children may be more prone to certain problems when compared with nonadopted children. For example, some traits, including learning disabilities (e.g., Brodzinsky & Steiger,

1991), intelligence (e.g., van Ijzendoorn, Juffer, & Poelhuis, 2005), school performance (e.g., Teasdale, 1984; van Ijzendoorn et al., 2005), adjustment issues (e.g., Benson, Sharma, & Roehlkepartain, 1994; Verhulst, Althaus, & Versluis-den Bieman, 1990), and identity development (e.g., Grotevant, 1997; Miller, Fan, Christensen, Grotevant, & van Dulmen, 2000) reflected differences that might be attributable to adoption. Regardless of the source of the behavioral and emotional issues that may present during the school-age years, children who are adopted may face additional challenges due to the stigma that surrounds adoption (March, 1995; Miall, 1994), and this can lead school personnel, nonadopted children, parents, and society to make faulty attributions for the child's behavior.

In recent years, some researchers have started the complex process of analyzing issues that affect school-age adopted children. For example, meta-analyses were used by van Ijzendoorn et al. (2005) to examine cognitive development, intelligence (in the form of Intellience Quotients), and school performance. This chapter addresses the developmental, educational, and clinical issues that affect school-age children. Using an Eriksonian developmental model, educational issues at each of the relevant stages are reviewed. Case studies and current research are also used to demonstrate some of the issues seen in this population and best practice strategies.

SCHOOL ISSUES VIEWED THROUGH A DEVELOPMENTAL STAGE THEORY

A clear framework through which to view developmental milestones for adopted children is Erik Erikson's (1980) framework for psychosocial development. Using a similar developmental stage model, Brodzinsky et al. (1992), in their seminal work, *Being Adopted: The Lifelong Search for Self*, presented a review of developmental issues that adopted individuals typically face at various ages. Applying their work specifically to educational and school-based issues can further inform school professionals, parents, students, and the community. This section explores the developmental stages across the life span and how they apply to school-based issues for adopted students. These stages and the challenges that accompany each stage can be used as benchmarks for development to illustrate how adoption weaves its way into the fabric of the lives of adopted students at school. Each phase of development represents a set of critical tasks that requires coping skills or adjustment to achieve resolution.

Academic achievement is the universal goal for educational institutions and settings. Students are expected to learn age-appropriate material and to meet educational goals that prepare them for additional educational pursuits as well as for eventual independent living and success. Despite these seemingly reasonable, clear, and attainable expectations, many students struggle in the U.S. educational system. The reasons for their struggle vary, and more contemporary educators recognize the need for emotional and social health to support academic achievement. Emotional and social setbacks can be due to a variety of factors, but when adoption is one of the factors in children's backgrounds, educators, clinicians, parents, and society rightfully question the degree to which adoption may hinder or support educational pursuits. The emotional or psychosocial stages that follow can serve as guidelines for exploring the role of adoption in adopted children's school experiences.

Developmental Ages and Stages

Infancy

Although children may not enter into a formal school setting until they are 3 to 5 years old, the emotional growth during infancy is significant. This phase of life was referred to as the stage of Trust versus Mistrust (Erikson, 1980). Infants adopted at birth seek resolution to this dichotomy, as evidenced, for example, through hurdles they face in bonding and attachment. Attachment theory (Bowlby, 1982) has been used to explain differences that occur at this stage among adopted infants and children, particularly due to the preadoptive circumstances that play a crucial role in the outcome of this task for infants. Age at adoption and preadoptive experiences (e.g., multiple placements, trauma, drug exposure, health concerns) are two factors likely to have significant impacts on attachment. Research suggests that when children are placed for adoption before 6 months, there may be little difference, if any, between the quality of mother-infant attachment in adoptive and nonadoptive families (Singer, Brodzinsky, Ramsay, Steir, & Waters, 1985). In fact, secure attachment (Bowlby, 1982), which results from maternal sensitivity and responsiveness during infancy, was found to predict socioemotional and cognitive achievements in later life (Stams, Juffer, & van Ijzendoorn, 2002). For those adopted later in life, a variety of outcomes may affect their school preparedness and attachment to their families. For example, children who experienced neglect prior to adoption were found to suffer from Posttraumatic Stress Disorder, making early intervention necessary. Early intervention programs allow for children who are experiencing developmental delays to benefit from a combination of state-administered direct services, and children are eligible for these services if they are under 3 years of age and have a disability or developmental delay (Scarborough et al., 2004). A developmental delay is defined as a lag in at least one of the following areas of development: physical development, cognitive development, communication, social-emotional development, or adaptive development. Adoptive families may consider preadoptive circumstances as a predictor of developmental delay; however, if a developmental lag is suspected, a professional evaluation is needed to accurately assess the child. The goal of early intervention is to provide support for the family, while creating opportunities for children with disabilities to participate fully in their communities and their education.

Therefore, the challenge for adoptive families may be to integrate the children into the family and develop a sense of safety, security, and trust, which will become the foundation for healthy psychological development (Brodzinsky, Smith, & Brodzinsky, 1998).

Toddlerhood and Preschool Years

According to Erikson (1980), the toddler and preschool years have to do with the maturation of the muscle system and the consequent ability (or inability) to coordinate a number of highly conflicting action patterns, such as "holding on" and "letting go." Erikson identified this phase as two separate stages: Autonomy versus Shame and Doubt, which lasts from 18 months to 3 years old, and Initiative versus Guilt, which lasts from 3 years old to 6 years old (Erikson, 1980). In addition to new motor skill accomplishments comes the emergence of language and representational thought. The adoption-related tasks at this point involve first learning about birth and reproduction and then incorporating this information into the personal history story. Whereas adoptive families may spend much of the first year mastering the challenge of integrating their children into the family, at this stage they begin the process of *family differentiation* (Brodzinsky et al., 1998). Adoption professionals generally encourage adoptive parents to begin speaking to children about their adoption during toddlerhood (Brodzinsky et al., 1992). Initiating the discussion about adoption can be anxiety producing for some parents. Many adoptive parents seek out support, which helps them get through this task successfully. During this developmental period, adopted children may begin to tell their personal stories of being adopted. Research has shown, however, that although adopted children may identify themselves as *adopted* during this stage, they have relatively little understanding of what that means (Singer, Brodzinsky, & Braff, 1982), and they do not understand the implications of adoption.

Case Study I

Presenting Problem

Deanna, a biracial 5-year-old girl, was adopted at 14 months, and has been attending kindergarten for close to 7 months. Recently, Deanna has not been able to maintain herself at school for the full day. School personnel have had to ask Deanna's mother to pick her daughter up early on numerous occasions. Deanna has been crying inconsolably while asking for her mother and expressing her fear that her mother may not come back.

Preadoptive Background

Deanna was relinquished 6 months after her birth. Deanna's birth mother, Lisa, kept her at home while she made the difficult decision leading to the voluntary relinquishment of her daughter. Lisa was 19 years of age, unwed, unemployed, and living at home with her mother. Just prior to her pregnancy, she spent 6 months in a drug rehabilitation program for cocaine and marijuana. Lisa's parents were divorced, and she had no relationship with her own father. Deanna's biological father, Sean, was African American, and was not accepted into Lisa's family. Lisa loved this man, yet she felt a loyalty to her mother to respect her position and ultimately ended their relationship. Sean moved out of state immediately after Deanna's birth and left no forwarding information. Lisa often wondered if she had masked what was really a fear of her mother's rejection with what she thought of as "loyal."

The few months Lisa spent at home with her daughter were unmanageable. Lisa began using drugs again. She was not able to attend to the needs of a newborn baby. Deanna was a "fussy" baby; she had trouble feeding and was not gaining an acceptable amount of weight, according to the doctors. She cried, it seemed to Lisa, "all day long . . . nonstop." During the pregnancy, Lisa spoke with her mother about possibly making an adoption plan for her child. Lisa's mother was not supportive of this idea. Lisa returned to her drug rehabilitation counselor, who referred her to a family planning counselor.

Adoptive Background

Deanna was relinquished at 6 months; she spent the next 3 months with a foster family and the next 5 months with a second foster family. At 14 months of age, Deanna was placed for adoption with the Fuller family, a middle-class, Caucasian family. The Fullers had two biological sons: Justin, 6 years of age, and David, 4 years of age. Deanna's arrival was a joyous event for the family. This was a closed adoption, facilitated through Social Services; therefore, the information available to the family was limited.

Deanna was "small for her age," the doctor reported to her parents. Her eating habits were poor and she disliked many foods. Dinnertime was always a challenge for the family. The family faced many other challenges as well. Deanna was resistant to affection, and Mrs. Fuller began to feel a sense of disappointment when Deanna stiffened her back and would not embrace her. Deanna's verbal skills were virtually nonexistent. The family was attentive to Deanna's care, both medically and socially. Deanna's adoptive parents were professionals who both worked in the education field. After noticing significant delays in development, the family had Deanna evaluated for early intervention services.

Treatment and Educational Issues: Issues in Education and Treatment

Deanna's early intervention services focused on the family and Deanna. In-home services were provided that involved occupational therapy, speech therapy, physical therapy, nutrition services, health services, family training, and counseling. These early intervention services continued up to 3 years of age and had a significant positive impact on Deanna and her family. Feelings of disappointment, social isolation, stress, frustration, and helplessness were alleviated for the family. Having these services in the home helped to boost the Fullers' self-esteem. The Fullers acquired the skills necessary to help teach Deanna and provide a supportive and nourishing environment. With the help of this early intervention, Deanna was able to start mainstream kindergarten at 5 years of age.

When Deanna began kindergarten, she also began to acknowledge her physical differences as compared with her family and her peers. Just as Deanna began to recognize differences between herself and her parents, so did her classmates. Whether adopted into a traditional two-parent same-race family or by a single parent, older parents, two moms, two dads, or across racial lines, adopted children may be asked innocent yet complex questions by their peers, such as "Where is your dad/mom?" or statements such as "That can't be your mom, she's White." These types of questions and comments were common for Deanna and her family. These remarks were often confusing and hurtful to Deanna and her family.

The adoption agency provided postadoption counseling for the family, which the Fullers participated in on a weekly basis. Their therapist explained that there are no automatic responses since each adoption brings its own set of circumstances. In an effort to be truthful, yet not overbearing, it was important to use simple positive adoption language. Deanna seemed to associate adoption with the concept of "wanted" and "not wanted." Deanna began to question the reasons behind her relinquishment and asked, "Why didn't they want me, why did they give me away?" In anticipation of these types of questions, the Fullers were prepared with the right language and their understanding was able to alleviate some of the confusion. Confusion is common at this age; however, their therapist emphasized that overexplaining may only compound the problem. The opportunity to explain further would come later, as emotional and cognitive development increase readiness and understanding.

While Deanna had been referred to a counselor at school, she was also attending weekly sessions along with her parents at the postadoption counseling center. During Deanna's individual session, the therapist allowed her to use play, dolls, puppets, and storybooks to express her understanding of adoption. On a number of occasions, the play would conclude with the small children in the story being lost or not able to find their way home. As Deanna's therapist assumed the role of the mother in play, it was helpful to be able to use this opportunity to illustrate how "the mother" would search relentlessly for her children and inevitably find them and bring them home. Deanna used play to express her fear of being lost or not belonging anywhere.

Although preschool-age children are not capable of conceptualizing the depth of adoption, presenting it positively and openly is beneficial for adopted children and their peers. Presenting adoption with openness and affection provides a safe environment for children to continue to ask questions about the subject. Deanna and her school counselor read age-appropriate stories of adoption together and spoke about how the stories may have been different or similar to her adoption story. Deanna and her school counselor used the resources available through W.I.S.E. Up (Schoettle, 2001) and FAIR (Wood & Ng, 2001), school-based programs designed to address school-based issues about adoption.

In addition, Deanna's parents needed to decide on how much, when, and if to tell teachers and schools of their child's adoption history. Parents who are reluctant to share adoption-related information with schools may be attempting to avoid potential stereotyping. Whether or not parents choose to inform the school, adopted children must still deal with adoption-related questions. As illustrated in this case, when school personnel are better prepared to deal with questions and peer curiosity in sensitive and supportive ways, schools become a safer place for children to express themselves. Nevertheless, disclosure is a personal decision, and this decision needs to be respected by educators and staff and supported in situations involving other students and their parents (Wood & Ng, 2001).

Middle Childhood

This stage of development encompasses ages 6 through 12 and is identified by Erikson (1980) as the Industry versus Inferiority stage. This stage represents a phase of development characterized by an increase in curiosity, exploration, and children's need to master their environments. It is during this time that children move from the days of play and make-believe to an exploration of their ability and drive to produce. Erikson refers to this as a sense of *industry*. Along with this sense of industry comes its counterpart, *inferiority*. The drive to bring a task to completion may cause children to experience insufficient resolution, thus making them develop a sense of inadequacy or inferiority (Erikson, 1980). They begin to explore, meet new friends, acquire new knowledge in school, and grow physically at a rapid speed. Although adopted children experience this stage just as nonadopted children do, they are also learning to master and make sense of the world of adoption.

The development of cognitive skills at this age enables adopted children to bring adoption into a new focus. As a result of this new understanding, questions may arise that require more concrete answers, which are not always available. As adopted children learn to understand the concept of adoption, they may begin to view adoption as being born out of loss and may stop asking questions aloud. It is important to realize that this is not necessarily an indication that there is no need for discussion. Even though children can verbalize the concept of adoption and retell their adoption stories at this stage, they have not necessarily reached resolution (Brodzinsky et al., 1992). It is important for families to realize that over the next few years children's sensitivity to, and appreciation of the implications of being adopted grow quite rapidly (Brodzinsky et al., 1998). Children's initial understanding of the concept of family is that of a unit represented by individuals who share the same space and provide affection. The development of logical reciprocity allows children to understand that in gaining a family they have also experienced loss. Children may acknowledge familial loss in terms of other significant and related losses, such as loss of culture, language, heritage, birth family, genealogical connections, and identity. These losses can be profound in a child's life and vary for each child.

Implications for School and Social-Based Issues in Middle Childhood. When children begin their academic careers, it is often a time when they will encounter questions from peers. These questions are usually based on innocuous curiosity and not intended to be cruel or impolite; however, they may be interpreted as such. This period represents an opportunity for parents, teachers, and professionals to take on the role of educators about adoptive families. Classroom activities may begin to center on understanding the concept of family. This is an opportunity to include examples of families joined by adoption in the classroom curriculum. A teacher who has knowledge of adoption-related issues is able to introduce the concept of adoption as a means of building a family.

Along with an awareness of being different, adopted children may experience rejection or sometimes an exaggeration of being different. The reactions may manifest themselves in many different ways, which can have an effect on the ability to concentrate at school. Behavioral difficulties that affect academic learning may include the inability to stay on task, the expression of anger, or the display of oppositional attitudes (Brodzinsky et al., 1992). Conversely, adopted children may become consumed with projecting an overly positive image, in an effort to overlook any differences. These may be typical reactions of unresolved grief (Melina, 1998). Whereas the concept of adoption has significantly different meanings for adopted children, their nonadopted peers may categorize adoption as an Achilles' heel. Therefore, adopted children may be teased on the playground by classmates who suppose that adoption represents "bad" or "unwanted" children. The social effects of teasing can result in low self-esteem (Horowitz et al., 2004), thereby affecting school performance. Distractions of this magnitude during such a crucial developmental stage can result in the inability to focus academically. The consequences of these difficulties can be a misdiagnosis of a learning or emotional disability, as will be discussed later in this chapter.

Positive interventions from school professionals can include being supportive and understanding of the fact that some families are joined by adoption, sharing knowledge on a regular basis using positive adoption language, being attentive to teasing and intervening, respecting children's rights to silence or not wanting to share information about their adoption, and a thorough assessment of students' difficulties or behaviors.

Adolescence

This stage of life, categorized here by ages 13 to 19, covers a time of rapid growth and development. The most significant changes come in physical, cognitive, emotional, and social functioning. According to Erikson, due to these rapid changes, the continuities relied on earlier in childhood are questioned. While adolescents experience these physiological changes, they are mostly consumed with what they appear to be in the eyes of others. This stage brings on the dilemma of bridging who or what they feel they *are* with who they feel they are expected *to be* and how to incorporate their earlier roles (Erikson, 1980). This stage of psychological development is referred to by Erikson as Ego Identity versus Ego Confusion. The basics for mastering this task are grounded in establishing a secure sense of the physical self. For adopted adolescents, connecting to the physical self may be more challenging due to the lack of physical similarities with their birth families. In adopted children's quest to identify with another person, this may be a time when they begin to think more about searching for and finding their biological ties.

Along with the emerging physical changes of this stage comes sexual maturation. This can be a very tumultuous time for all teenagers, with added challenges for adopted teens. How adopted adolescents deal with sexual experimentation may be indicative of their identification with either their adoptive parents or their birth parents. The adoptive parents may be symbolic of the responsible choice, and the birth parents may be representative of the "bad seed" (Brodzinsky et al., 1992). Adopted adolescents who are able to move through this period of *identity crisis,* and closer to *identity achievement,* tend to be those whose families allow them to discuss adoption and help them come to a resolution (Brodzinsky et al., 1992).

Academic approaches to the subject of sexual responsibility have changed considerably over the past few decades. Along with these changes have come necessary adjustments in school-based health and family life curricula. The subjects of genetics, sexual responsibility, and human development can have considerable impact on adopted students. A longitudinal research study of the changes in teenage sexual relationships (comparing the high school classes of 1950, 1975, and 2000) suggested a dramatic change in sexual attitudes and experiences. Overall, there has been a steady decline in negative attitudes toward premarital sex, and the percentages of teens that have engaged in sexual behavior have increased steadily over the 50-year period. These findings point to a much more sexually responsible group of teens, who not only engage in sexual intercourse with protection but who also feel comfortable talking about sexuality with others (Caron & Moskey, 2002). Research has indicated that adopted adolescents do not act out sexually more than their nonadopted counterparts (Benson et al., 1994). However, Sorosky's research did suggest that female adopted adolescents may act out sexually more than their nonadopted peers through identification with their birth mothers or out of a desire to become pregnant and create a blood link to a relative (Sorosky, Baran, & Pannor, 1989). These conflicting research studies indicate the need for further research.

Some ways for schools to be supportive in this regard may be to include a lesson about adoption in family life or health classes. Bringing adoption into school discussions about ways of forming a family helps to normalize the adoption experience and sets the stage for open communication. Helping to form a support group for teens from blended families may provide a place for adopted adolescents to share feelings. Group counseling with adolescent adoptees is a particularly potent modality because it mitigates the sense of difference and alienation that they may feel and allows them to identify with others who share their experiences (Cordel, Nathan, & Krymow, 1985).

Adolescence is a time when many changes are considered, such as college, leaving home, and choosing relationships. For example, young adult adoptees who have not dealt with any adoption-related issues may find the prospect of leaving home too disturbing or stressful to even consider. These changes and new choices also represent loss of the familiar and a leap into the unknown. This can be an anxiety-producing time for any young adult, and it may require added considerations for adopted teens. It is often very important to adopted young adults to be in control of their adult life decisions, given that they had no control over the first life-altering decision. It would not be uncommon for young adults to delay or sabotage taking destiny into their own hands with respect to these major decisions. This may require understanding on the part of family, guidance counselors, and other professionals and will involve their continued support. Through a supportive mirror of a counselor or family, adolescent adoptees can tell their stories, integrate the facts of their lives, explore possible journeys, and develop a sense of mastery over themselves and the direction of their lives (Winkler, Brown, van Keppel, & Blanchard, 1988).

Case Study 2

Presenting Problem

Lindsey, now 15, Grade 11, is currently attending her neighborhood high school. Lindsey has recently been suspended for the sixth time this year. The majority of the suspensions were for "cutting class, oppositional/defiant behavior, and insubordination." Currently, Lindsey is out of school on suspension and has started home instruction. The most recent suspension resulted from Lindsey acting sexually inappropriately with a group of her peers. Lindsey's parents anticipate that Lindsey will return to the district school and hope to avoid a referral out of district.

Preadoptive Background

Lindsey was adopted at 6 months and was born with a positive toxicology. Lindsey's birth parents were both 17 years of age at the time of Lindsey's birth and were never married. Lindsey was relinquished at birth, the adoption was closed, and records were sealed. Nonidentifying information was left for Lindsey by her birth parents. This information contained facts about Lindsey's birth mother's bout with drugs and her struggle with drug addiction for most of her teenage years. Lindsey's birth father was a high school graduate. However, Lindsey's birth mother was pregnant during her senior year and dropped out of school. It was reported that Lindsey's birth mother was of Italian descent, her birth father was Colombian. Lindsey spent the first 3 months of her life in foster care and was placed with a family for adoption at 6 months.

Adoptive Background

Lindsey was adopted by the Canes, an affluent, Caucasian couple. Her parents reported that Lindsey's childhood was pleasant and that she did not demonstrate any overt reactions to her adoption. However, the Canes did report that the adoption was very rarely or almost never discussed. Lindsey was aware of the nonidentifying information available to her and viewed it for the first time at age 13. The Canes have always felt that their child was "born from the heart" and admittedly have trouble discussing their child's history or birth family.

Treatment and Educational Issues

Throughout elementary school, Lindsey excelled academically and socially. When Lindsey entered middle school, she began to neglect her studies and separated from her usual group of friends. She drastically changed her look and began to experiment with alcohol and illegal substances. Lindsey's parents sought professional help to address Lindsey's struggle with substance abuse. This course of treatment was specifically designed to deal with Lindsey's drug addiction. During a counseling session, Lindsey revealed that she was not committed to stop using drugs. Lindsey added, "my birth mom used drugs too, it must be inherited." Lindsey also admitted that she felt guilty for causing her birth mother to drop out of school. Family and individual therapy was recommended; however, the Canes did not immediately follow up on these referrals. Mrs. Cane revealed that she had never been in counseling and feared that she would not be able to "deal with the issues which may come up."

During Lindsey's last suspension hearing, the board required that Lindsey get a psychological evaluation. The Canes brought Lindsey for the evaluation. Recommendations from the evaluation included the need for individual therapy along with family therapy, and continued drug counseling. In a desperate attempt to have Lindsey remain in school, the Canes agreed to all recommendations made by the board.

Lindsey's substance abuse continued only for a short time after the start of treatment. Lindsey was able to stop using drugs and continued the treatment while she became sober for close to 1 year. The family began to attend weekly sessions to learn how to support Lindsey in her battle of addiction. During these family sessions, Lindsey began to speak about her biological mother and father for the first time ever in front of her adoptive parents. The Canes presented as defensive and dismissive at first. After weeks of counseling, the family was able to see Lindsey's pain and began to respect her opinions and feelings. Although the Canes were resistant at first, they began to realize that without their love and support, Lindsey would continue to suffer. They also began to consider Lindsey's birth parents as less of a threat to their family's cohesiveness and as more of a common bond.

Lindsey also continued to work hard in her own therapy. She began to understand the connections between some of her behaviors and her feelings about "who she is and where she comes from." Lindsey could understand that her sexual aggressiveness was inappropriate and most likely her way of identifying with her birth mother. Lindsey also worked hard to recognize that failing school may be another way of identifying with her birth mother, who dropped out of high school. Lindsey stated that at times she did not "feel worthy" of living such a privileged life, and she felt selfish and not deserving of a high school diploma.

Lindsey often wondered if there were other students who had not shared their adoption story and who were in pain. With the help of a school guidance counselor, they were able to begin the support group "Here a Different Way," for those students touched by adoption. The group met on Saturday mornings at members' homes, in an effort to consider the confidentiality of students.

As this case illustrates, Lindsey's struggles in school were similar to those of a typical high school student, yet complicated by her adoption. Lindsey's anxiety and pain were exacerbated by her family's avoidance and denial of her feelings. As demonstrated in this case, the support of school and family was instrumental in dealing with issues of adoption and how they may affect a child's behavior and thinking.

CONSIDERING IQ AND ENVIRONMENT

Cognitive Abilities, Genetics, and Environment

The nature versus nurture debate is a controversial topic for many researchers and can generate passionate discussions on both sides. It has been said that heredity and the environment both contribute 50% of the makeup of an entire human being; but much of the existing debate is about specific percentages and the existence of higher percentages of one factor in different age-groups than another (Petrill et al., 2004). The goal of this section is to explore the origins of individual differences in cognitive abilities and the role of genetics and environment. Various studies suggest an increasing role for genetics and a decreasing role for environment. Genetic and environmental influences are found throughout the life span; however, an important issue now is how genetic and environmental factors influence cognitive ability, especially later in adolescence through adulthood (Petrill et al., 2004).

With respect to cognitive ability, various individual skills and abilities can reflect "intelligence." In fact, although one of the most common outcome measures of cognitive ability involves the use of the intelligence quotient, IQ as measured by a variety of instruments reflects one way of looking at intelligence; but other forms of intelligence exist that may not be captured by these measures. Moreover, many of the IQ measures have continually suffered from racial and cultural bias (Suzuki & Valencia, 1997).

Data collected for research studies examining genetic and environmental influences were collected from the Colorado Adoption Project (CAP). The CAP used a longitudinal design, permitting the analysis of the etiology of change and continuity in development. The CAP sample consisted of 245 adoptive families and 245 biological control families matched to the adoptive families (Plomin & DeFries, 1985; Plomin, Fulker, Corley, & DeFries, 1997).

A study to determine genetic and environmental influences on general cognitive ability suggested that there were significant correlations in cognitive ability. Researchers from the CAP found that genetic influence *increases* from infancy to childhood to adolescence. This study indicated that genetic influences are strongest for general cognitive ability and for the specific cognitive development of verbal ability (Plomin et al., 1997). The study concluded that the length of time a family lives together does not influence how similar they will become, unless there is a genetic link.

In a meta-analytical comparison of adopted and nonadopted children's IQ and school performance, researchers found that when compared with siblings or peers who remained in their family or in institutions, the adopted students had higher IQ scores. When adopted children's IQ scores were compared with siblings or peers in the same environment, there was an insignificant difference (van Ijzendoorn et al., 2005).

Transracial IQ Correlations

Transracial adoption studies suggest a genetic contribution to between-group differences. Studies of Korean and Vietnamese children adopted into White American and White Belgian homes reported that, although many had been hospitalized for malnutrition as infants, they excelled in academic achievement and ability with higher IQs than their adoptive nation's norms (Frydman & Lynn, 1989). Researchers concluded that early undernourishment may not cause irreversible damage for children but, instead, can be negated by early, drastic, and stable environmental improvement (Columbo, de la Parra, & Lopez, 1992). However, in a later study by Weinberg, Scarr, and Waldman (1992), results found that at age 17 African American and mixed-race children adopted into White, middle-class families performed at lower academic levels than the White siblings with whom they had been raised.

Literature indicates that environmental differences that exist between races are extremely important in IQ determination. For instance, data from the Minnesota Transracial Adoption Study reported by Scarr and Weinberg (1983) found that when African American children were adopted by White families at an early age, their IQs were more similar to the White IQ average of 110, compared with the average IQ of 90 for African American children reared in the African American community.

Impact of Adoption on School Performance

Research has been conducted in an effort to dispel the myths of the "adopted child syndrome." The "adopted child syndrome" myth supposes that adoptees have higher rates of psychopathology, obtain lower levels of academic achievement, and are overrepresented in psychotherapy. The National Council for Adoption (1989) asserted that adoptees are overrepresented because adoptive parents are familiar with dealing with agencies and are more likely to seek help.

Environmental Influences at School

To determine the effects of the school environment on academic achievement, researchers analyzed data from parents and first graders (adopted and nonadopted) who were from the CAP (Coon, Carey, Fulker, & DeFries, 1993). The question of whether or not school environment influences academic achievement has been a long-standing discussion. It may be supposed that parents who send their children to private school regard education as significantly important in their child's life. With that consideration, it may follow that they themselves are more intelligent and have maintained higher academic standards. Because cognitive ability and IQ are genetically linked, perhaps it may also be assumed that the school environment might be less significant in influencing academic outcomes. The CAP data allowed researchers to separate students for whom the association was entirely environmental and those for whom the association had both genetic and environmental components (Coon et al., 1993).

The design of this study considered the students separately by gender, as compared respectively to both mother and father, in a controlled environment. When the mothers' IQ was compared with boys' academic achievement, there was a negative correlation in adoptive families but not in nonadoptive families. Results for mothers and girls established a positive correlation between IQ and academic achievement (Coon et al., 1993). In addition, results indicated that boys with better reading skills tend to be placed in private schools, whereas results of math achievement were inconclusive regarding private versus public schools. Inconclusive outcomes suggest further research is necessary in evaluating academic achievement and school environment effects. Another mitigating factor was age at adoption. Age at adoption did not influence cognitive IQ as much as it did cognitive performance (school performance). Children adopted within their first year of life did not show any delays in school achievement, whereas children adopted after their first birthday lagged behind in this area (van Ijzendoorn et al., 2005).

School Attitudes and Performance

In an effort to compare adopted students with nonadopted students, a research study was conducted that included a representative sample of adolescents in Grades 7 through 12. Data were collected from adolescents, parents, and school administrators (Miller, Fan, Christensen et al., 2000). As noted in a previous section, across the different developmental stages, adoptees adapted to school and dealt with adoption using individual coping skills. The level of individual resiliency within each child is another significant factor. However, in this research study, certain demographic and background variables were considered, including gender, age, race, family structure, and parental education. Overall, the positive outcomes for adopted students as compared with nonadopted students included higher school grades, a more positive school feeling, and higher participation in academic extracurricular activities. It is interesting to consider the findings regarding a higher rate of adopted students feeling more positive about school and willing to join clubs. Perhaps the need to belong to a group and be accepted by peers is what drives adopted children to seek membership in extracurricular groups. More negative outcomes were associated with issues such as school troubles and skipping school (Miller, Fan, Grotevant et al., 2000).

Data reviewed by the meta-analytic research of van Ijzendoorn et al. (2005) concluded that adopted children outperformed their left-behind siblings or peers in academic achievement.

A major conclusion drawn from this study is that adopted children are able to benefit from a positive change of environment.

SCHOOL INTERVENTIONS AND TEACHER INFLUENCE/SENSITIVITY AND UNDERSTANDING

In discussing school involvement, it is important to consider the fact that some families may choose not to share information about their child's adoption with school personnel. It is essential that anyone involved in the child's education respect the family's decision to share or not to share information. Whether or not to share information with preschools or lower grade teachers remains a controversial issue. Professionals are split as to the necessity of sharing information so early (National Adoption Information Clearinghouse, 1993). However, teachers and school personnel can become more sensitive to adoption issues, use positive adoption language, and help adopted children feel accepted, if parents are not willing to share and affirm their knowledge and feelings about adoption. Increasing the sensitivity of school personnel about adoption should not be interpreted to indicate that adopted students will be treated as "different" or "exceptions."

Restructuring Common Assignments

Baby Pictures

Young students enjoy seeing how much they have grown and changed. Adopted students may not have pictures that show them before the age at which they were adopted. They may have the desire to see themselves as babies, but may never have the opportunity. Although this is an assignment that is intended to be enjoyable, emotions may run high when a teacher suggests bringing in baby photos. The educational goal of this assignment is to assess deductive reasoning ability. As an alternative to this assignment, teachers may request that students bring in facts or childhood pictures of famous people and ask the class to guess who it is.

Family History

Perhaps in the place of asking about family history, teachers can have an "All About Me Day." On this special day, students can create their own individual guidelines for what they will include.

Family Tree

For adopted children the "Family Tree" assignment can be daunting. The educational goal of this assignment varies by age. Younger students learn that there are many loving and caring relationships in their lives. Including all those individuals with whom the students have a loving, caring relationship helps to illustrate the concept of what makes a family. For older elementary school students, this assignment represents learning about societal structures. The family tree can be redesigned to include many different branches and roots. Perhaps a family forest can be used, where there are many different types of trees, yet no two are exactly alike. A family forest is a good representation of diversity in families. Children who may not be prepared to share the details of their history may still consider this assignment overwhelming. Students may not know who to include—the adoptive family or the birth family. If they include the birth family they may feel unfaithful to their adoptive parents. When the family tree assignment is approached with sensitivity, it can become a successful project. Adopted students who have not been able to speak openly about adoption may use the family tree assignment as an opportunity to break ground and discuss details.

Holidays

Children especially enjoy celebrating holidays at school. Holidays and birthdays can be very real reminders of loss or trauma for adopted children. For instance, Mother's Day or Father's Day can elicit many different emotional reactions. These holidays are meant to honor those people who have had an impact on individuals' lives; nonetheless, these special days need to be approached with care and empathetic understanding. Another way to approach Mother's Day or Father's Day is to broaden the assignment to include "Special Persons Day."

Suggestions for Schools

Books. Local school libraries can order age-appropriate books about adoption. Many books include adoption stories and useful information to relay messages of sensitivity about adoption. Books on foreign countries are useful for learning about and introducing other cultures. We suggest some titles to include in the school library:

- *We're Different, We're the Same* by Bobbi Jane Kates (ages 2–6)
- *How I Was Adopted* by Joanna Cole (ages 4–8)
- *Lucy's Family Tree* by Karen Halvorsen Schreck (ages 8–11)
- *The Orphan Train Adventures* by Joan Lowery Nixon (ages 10–14)
- *How It Feels to Be Adopted* by Jill Krementz (ages 12 and up)
- *When You Were Born in Korea: A Memory Book for Children Adopted From Korea* by B. Boyd

Groups/Meetings. Forming an advocate group in schools can be helpful in disseminating information and/or organizing events. Schools can form adoptive parents groups that can be sponsored by the PTA or announced in the school newsletter. These meetings can be facilitated outside the school, or a weekend meeting may be suggested.

A presentation about adoption to students, to faculty, or at a PTA meeting can introduce adoption as a way families are born and will raise awareness. Many of the issues students face about loss or change will be relevant to both adopted and nonadopted students. Moreover, it will help raise the sensitivity level regarding adoption and adoption-related issues. Workshops on adoption may be integrated into parent trainings.

Curriculum. Teachers can integrate adoption into lesson plans. For instance, a history class may reference famous adopted persons who have made contributions in various industries. For example, George Washington Carver and Bill Clinton are two adopted individuals who have contributed to American history. Health or family life cycle classes can include a unit on adoption. The goal is to educate and normalize adoption as a way of forming a family.

Celebrate National Adoption Month. National Adoption Week was first proclaimed by the governor of Massachusetts in 1976. Later that same year, it was officially made a national celebration by President Gerald Ford. More and more states began to celebrate it, and in 1990, the month of November was declared National Adoption Month. Activities, special events, and observances are planned to highlight the needs of foster children who need permanent families. A school hall bulletin board dedicated to National Adoption Month is one suggestion to help students "see" adoption in school.

CONSIDERATIONS OF RACE, CULTURE, AND ETHNIC IDENTITY

❧ Vignette: Jessie's World ❧

Jessie is a 9-year-old boy who loves comic books. They always fit into the duffel bag where he keeps all his stuff. No matter which foster home he was in, he could always pull them out late at night and take a peek at what his favorite superheroes were up to.

Jessie is really excited because next week his foster parents are going to take him along with them to talk to a judge so that they can officially adopt him. He is also a little confused—he has a mom whom he hasn't seen in a few years, but he remembers living with her and his two older stepbrothers in their apartment when he was little. He knows that his mom is sick and can't take care of him, and that his stepbrothers are older and live together with his aunt; but he wonders when he will get to see them all again.

He really likes Judith and Tom; they've told him that he's going to get to stay with them forever and that they'll take care of him and be his parents. But they have a few other kids already and some of them need extra help. He likes playing with his "new" brothers and sister, and they keep saying that they are happy that Judith and Tom are their parents (they even call Judith and Tom "mom" and "dad"). But Jessie keeps wondering what it's going to be like to have White parents. Everyone is going to know right away that he's adopted (and "different") because he's Black. When the kids in his class see Judith drop him off at school, or when Tom comes to watch his baseball games, the other kids might not even know who his parents are, or they might ask stupid questions or make fun of him. Also, he's been wondering if he has to have just White friends now. Will his new parents be disappointed if he keeps his best friend Rafael, who just moved here from Puerto Rico?

Jessie already feels different from everybody else because he's had to move around so much. He was always changing schools because he had lived in so many foster homes before he wound up with Tom and Judith. Now he's going to be different because his parents are White and he is Black. He's heard a lot recently about how Black people are poorer than everybody else. Is the social worker putting him with White parents because she's White too, and she knows that no Black people have enough money to adopt a foster kid? Tom and Judy have told him that he can talk to them about anything, but he's not sure if he should let them know about all the things that he's been wondering about. It would be great if superheroes really did exist—a lot of them have things about them that make them different too. If they did exist, then he could talk to one of them about what it feels like to be so different.

❧ Vignette: Anne's World ❧

Anne is very excited about next week too. Her mom is letting her have a sleepover for her 12th birthday party. It was a little hard to make up the guest list, though. She wasn't sure if she should have her school friends over, or if she should have her girlfriends over from her group for children that were adopted from China. Nobody her age at school belongs to the group, so she felt like it was almost like she was choosing sides when she had to decide who was coming to her party. She remembers that when she first started going to the group for adoptees from China, when she was 6, she was really excited because she got to meet girls who looked just like her. They spoke English really well, without a Chinese accent, and dressed "normally" like she did. Before going to the group, she had only seen Chinese girls in a few books and movies, and most of them were living in China and weren't American like her. She was adopted by her mom and dad when she was less than 2 years old and doesn't remember being in China at all. The orphanage didn't have any record of her real birthday, so her adoptive parents chose a day that was supposed to be "lucky" and that's been her birthday ever since. That's the day she's celebrating next week.

Lately, Anne's been distracted at school. She has a crush on Jason, a boy who is in her class, but she's not sure if he likes her. A girlfriend told her that Jason said he thought that she was pretty, which made her feel good about her looks, which are really important to her lately. She wonders if maybe she'll marry Jason or someone who looks like him one day. If she does, she wonders if her birth mom will be at her wedding. Maybe she has a brother or sister back in China; her mom has talked to her about maybe going back to China in a group tour with other adoptees someday. Maybe she'll meet a brother or sister there and bring them back here to live. Anne knows another girl on her soccer team who is adopted. They talked about it once, but that girl was adopted in the United States and already knew her birth mom and her half brothers. Anne doesn't think that it will be as easy for her to find out about where she came from as it was for that other girl.

❖ Vignette: Nadine and Alek, Through Their Parents' Eyes ❖

Nadine and Alek are siblings who were adopted 1 year ago from the same orphanage in Russia. Nadine is 5 and Alek is 7. Although they are brother and sister, they rarely saw each other in the orphanage since boys and girls were kept in separate areas. They are both relatively small compared with their respective classmates. Beverly and Brian, their parents, were happy to find out recently that the nutritional supplements and diet that the physician recommended have resulted in increasing their children's height and weight, and the children seem healthier than ever these days. However, they had to go through a real trial and error process to find healthy foods that suited Nadine and Alek's already developed preferences for taste and flavor. It also took a while for Beverly to understand why both the children were so unusually anxious around their pediatrician ("Dr. Bob") when they came for checkups. Beverly had mentioned it to another mother who had adopted a child from the same orphanage a few years before. That mother had pointed out that all the caregivers at that orphanage were female, the children there had experienced very little close contact with men, and they almost certainly had never had a man physically touch them before they were adopted.

Nadine and Alek love to play together and share well. When they were first brought to the United States, Beverly was concerned that they seemed to talk only to each other and in a way only they seemed to understand. Beverly had learned some basic Russian words and phrases before she and her husband traveled to meet the children, and none of the words that she heard pass between her children seemed to be any of the ones that she had learned. But that phase seemed to pass quickly, and both children seemed to have picked up on speaking English very quickly. They had learned in the same way Beverly's little niece had—by having to express their needs and desires out of necessity. Early on, there had been a lot of frustration between the kids and their parents as they tried to communicate with each other; the children were old enough to know exactly what they wanted and to expect to be understood. Thankfully, there was a program at the elementary school that worked with students for whom English was a second language.

Socially, the children seem to be doing well; however, they appear to be adjusting to school still, especially Alek. Beverly and Brian were told that there was no formal school day at the orphanage where Alek and Nadine had lived, so, at first, the combination of freedom, structure, and stimulation was perplexing to Alek. He was used to staying either in a very confined place with no specific expectations from grown-ups and only a few toys that were commandeered by the older kids, or being told exactly what to do and when to do it (including activities like going to the bathroom). Although Alek's teachers report that he seeks out his sister on the playground, he is slowly developing friendships in his own class. Nadine is doing well socially, too; she had some extra time at home with Beverly last year, and they were in a music and play group that helped Nadine work on her English and physical coordination through singing and moving to music. Beverly and Nadine also spent a lot of time exploring places that most of Nadine's peers were already familiar with, like the local mall and the grocery store. When Beverly and Brian first brought their children home, they thought that it was great that both Nadine and Alek were so comfortable around other people; the children often put their arms out, wanting to be picked up (even with total strangers). But now, Beverly and Brian have had to work hard on helping them to understand "stranger danger."

Beverly and Brian are very pleased with how their children seem to be progressing physically, mentally, and socially. They know from working with their adoption agency and adoptive parents groups that, should Nadine or Alek need any special counseling or educational assistance, they can go to professionals for help. They continue to look to the teachers and staff at the school for feedback as to how they can continue to raise healthy, happy, and well-adjusted children.

Children of Intercountry/Transracial Adoption and Their Identity

As you can see, Jessie, Anne, Nadine, and Alek are all engaged in the same major developmental tasks as other children in their age-groups, including working on establishing a personal sense of identity. Individual identity is not created in a vacuum but develops through the process of personal exploration, comparison, differentiation, and integration as experienced in relationship to society. Adoptees engage in the additional task of creating an "adoptive identity"—an understanding of the personal meaning of being an adopted person.

Considerations for Children Adopted Into Racially Integrated Families

Jessie and Anne, who were described in the vignettes above, are transracial adoptees in that they were placed with an adoptive family of another race. Nearly 20,000 children were adopted internationally in the United States in 2001, and approximately a quarter of those were adopted from China. It is estimated that transracial adoptions accounted for 15% of the 36,000 adoptions that took place from foster care in 1998 (the most recent year for which comprehensive information is available). The number of transracial adoptions (especially international adoptions) is expected to continue to increase (Evan B. Donaldson Adoption Institute, 2002).

Concurrent with the psychosocial and cognitive development that was described earlier in this chapter, children experience a progression of awareness of race and culture and their meaning in society. Adoptive identity formation can be viewed in multiple contexts, including intrapsychic (a cognitive/affective construct), the family environment, and extrafamilial contexts (community connections, relationships with friends, and culture) (Grotevant, Dunbar, Kohler, & Lash Esau, 2000). This section explores considerations of transracial and international adoption within these three contexts.

When children have been adopted into culturally and/or racially integrated families, cultural and racial identities each play a role in personal identity formation. According to Erikson (1968,

1980), the feeling of belonging to a group both racially and ethnically is an important part of creating a sense of self. The cultural-racial identity model that was developed by Baden and Steward is an especially helpful approach to conceptualizing the complexities of the identity formation of transracial adoptees (Baden & Steward, 2000). Recognizing the limitations of racial identity models that assume a homogeneous family, they created a framework that allows for the multiple dimensions of identity that are encountered by those who are transracially adopted. Their model differentiates between cultural identity and racial identity. It then allows for self-identification within those two areas with either the parents' racial or cultural group, the adoptee's racial or cultural group, or multiple groups (Baden & Steward, 2000). We can see that Anne, represented in the vignette above, is working on figuring out who she is with respect to both her race and her culture; this process may continue throughout adolescence and into early adulthood for Anne. A study of young adults who had been adopted from Korea confirmed that racial and cultural identity development takes place at least into middle adulthood for many transracial adoptees (Meier, 1999).

The complex issues of identity development have long been the basis for the attribution of adjustment disorders to adoptees, especially when observed during adolescence. Findings indicate that the negatively determining factor may be societal racism itself, as opposed to whether children are adopted transracially or intraracially (Feigelman, 2000). Caution is advised when professionals consider the racial and cultural identity formation of children who are members of racially integrated families. The mere presence of additional challenges does not mean that these matters can't or won't be met and mastered. All individuals, including Whites, develop a racial identity (Helms, 1984). However, children who are transracial or international adoptees may need additional support and time as they work through the multiple layers of their personal identity formation.

Domestic Transracial Adoption

Most domestic transracial adoptions involve adoption by White parents. In 1998, although African American children made up only about 15% of the child population in the United States, they constituted 47% of the children in the nation who were awaiting adoption placement in settings such as foster care (Burrow & Finley, 2001). In 2001, African American, Asian American, Hispanic, and Native American children constituted 60% of children waiting to be adopted from foster care (Lee, 2003). In light of the large numbers of children affected by this practice, it is important that educators realize the many challenges that these children face. As in the case of Jessie, most African American adoptees are adopted later in life than other children (Evan B. Donaldson Adoption Institute, 2002). This puts these children at greater risk for certain complications; studies indicate that the older children are at the time of their adoption, the more prone they are to exhibit certain behavioral problems (Smith-McKeever, 2004). Other factors that can result in behavioral problems are a plurality of foster care placements and abuse or neglect. Multiple placements in various foster homes may result in the disruption of the psychological growth of some children as they try to adapt to ever-changing environments. Multiple placements can also necessitate changing schools frequently, making consistent record keeping for purposes of assessment and progress tracking very difficult.

The practice of adoption of African American children by White parents has been a point of controversy for many years; many of the concerns have focused on positive racial identity development and the ability of White families to prepare their children for the experiences of racism that they will encounter in their lives (Grotevant et al., 2000; Park & Green, 2000). A study of transracially adopted African American children revealed that they had more problems with establishing a racial identity than African American children who were intraracially adopted. However, the same study revealed no difference between the first group's overall self-esteem and that of the second group (McRoy, Zurcher, Lauderdale, & Anderson, 1982). African American children who are adopted into families with White parents also appeared to have different patterns and delayed establishment of racial identity (Johnson, Shireman, &

Watson, as cited in Haugaard, Dorman, & Schustack, 1997). Despite concerns about adjustment, the majority of studies indicate that transracial adoptees eventually adjust as successfully as intraracial adoptees (Bagley, 1993). However, every effort should be made to consider these additional stressors that may delay learning and social and emotional growth.

International Adoption/International Transracial Adoption

Nadine, Alek, and Anne were all adopted internationally. Since Alek and Nadine look similar to their White parents, they will probably not have to grapple with the many complex issues of racial identity development that transracially adopted children do. However, they may need to consider their cultural and national heritage and its meaning in each of their lives. As indicated earlier, Anne will also probably develop a sense of how her cultural and racial identities inform her self-concept.

Nadine and Alek were raised in an institution for most of their lives prior to their adoption. Even a short time in an institutional setting can result in delays in social-emotional, cognitive, and motor skills development (Meese, 2005); the longer the time that children spend in institutional settings, the more at risk they are for these delays to continue into later childhood and adolescence (Judge, 2004; Kadlec & Cermak, 2002; Meese, 2005). Many children who have lived in these settings are also at risk for physical complications from malnutrition, limited medical care, fetal alcohol exposure, and the consequences of being exposed to environmental toxins (Meese, 2002). Many of these physical complications can be improved through healthy diets, the administration of nutritional supplements, and the use of therapies that focus on sensory integration, occupational interventions, and speech and language improvement (Meese, 2002). The earliest intervention possible is recommended for the greatest effect (Johnson & Dole, 1999; Meese, 2002).

Reasonable suggestions have been made proposing that the early sensory deprivation and malnutrition that some adoptees experience during institutionalization results in low IQ. However, postadoptive studies show that this may be the case with respect to only those children who have lived in the most extremely depriving of institutions (Rutter, O'Connor, & the English and Romanian Adoptees Study Team, 2004). Research shows that children who have been adopted from overseas institutions may be at an increased risk for Attention Deficit Hyperactivity Disorder (ADHD). This is probably attributable to prenatal, preinstitutional, and institutional environmental factors (Hoksbergen, ter Laak, van Dijkum, Rijk, & Stoutjesdijk, 2003).

A study of children who were adopted from Romania to The Netherlands indicated that some children who had lived in extremely neglectful physical and social conditions exhibited indications of posttraumatic stress disorder (Hoksbergen, ter Laak, van Dijkum, Rijk, Rijk, et al., 2003). Some children from these setting are also prone to indiscriminate friendliness, such as was exhibited by Nadine and Alek. This may be due to a reduced ability to attach to any one caregiver and may be adapted behavior learned in a setting with many caregivers (Haugaard, Palmer, & Wojslawowicz, 1999; Marcovitch et al., 1997). Despite these seemingly overwhelming risks and potential hurdles, a meta-analysis of children who have been adopted through intercountry adoption found that they are well adjusted, have fewer mental health referrals, and have fewer behavior problems than children adopted domestically (Groza, Ryan, & Cash, 2003; Juffer & van Ijzendoorn, 2005). It is important to remember that there is a broad range of care provided to children awaiting adoption from overseas, and that various environmental and psychosocial factors contribute to a child's ability to adapt to postadoption challenges.

Nadine and Alek have faced a challenge that is common to most children who are adopted from another country at an older age—that of acquiring a new language. The most crucial time for language development is from birth to 2 years of age; most American children having acquired a working vocabulary of over 10,000 words before starting school. Children who are adopted from non-English-speaking countries after 2 years of age are at a great disadvantage with respect to school performance as well as making social and emotional connections with others. As we saw in the portrait of Alek and Nadine, children who are raised in neglectful institutional settings may develop their own institutional language. As they transition to American culture and the English language, children of international adoption usually lose what they had learned of their first language, which had served as an important tool for getting their needs met. Children between the ages of 4 and 6 have the greatest difficulty in transitioning. They are expected to rapidly catch up to the level of their peers to function, and yet they may not have enough of a base in their previous language to facilitate an understanding of how language works (Meese, 2002).

Implications for School and School-Based Issues

Educators and school counselors can have a great effect on the racial and cultural identity development of transracial and international adoptees, as well as on all students under their purview. What is of utmost importance is that professionals gain insight into their own thoughts and possible biases regarding adoption-related matters. This might include gaining insight into the following issues: What constitutes a "real" family? Would I anticipate that a particular child was going to have a behavior problem if I found out that he or she was adopted? What about if he or she was adopted from another country or was a different race from most of the students in the class? Research shows that the dominant concept of a "real" family is that of a heterosexual couple and their biological children (Wegar, 2000). A study of preschool and elementary school teachers showed a bias against adopted children, based on preconceptions as to their behavioral and personality attributes (Kessler, 1988). Teachers should consider reframing their perspective on children adopted from institutional settings. Instead of assuming deficits or pathology, they should consider the positive traits that particular children may have, such as resilience or adaptability (Juffer & van Ijzendoorn, 2005). Effective education professionals are those who will challenge their pre-existing opinions and attitudes regarding matters of race, culture, ethnicity, and adoption.

Educators should protect their transracially and internationally adopted students by refusing to tolerate racial slurs, "jokes," or comments in school by students or adults. Keeping a vigilantly high standard sends a message of positive regard and respect for all students.

Encourage early intervention, especially for students who spent time in an institution and for whom assessment reveals additional needs.

Remember that an English-language delay is not necessarily an indication of a learning delay (Meese, 2002) and that there may be differences in language attainment for day-to-day usage and academic usage (Dalen, 2001). Additionally, children who are "losing" one language and "gaining" another may not always make predictably linear progress (Meese, 2002).

Include projects and activities that portray people and places in other countries with respect, and avoid stereotyping. For younger children, this may include making available dolls that reflect various races and cultures. Books and stories about other countries may be used as a springboard to teaching children the similarities and universality between people of different cultures and races.

Recommend and encourage students' participation in adoptive family support and culture groups, or organize a family night for racially integrated families. A study of transracial adoptive families found that participation in such groups increased family stability and functioning (Zabriskie & Freeman, 2004).

SPECIAL EDUCATION ISSUES IN ADOPTION

This section will evaluate the incidence of adopted children in special education. Studies have indicated that adoptees are more likely to have significant learning difficulties. As a prelude to the following research reporting, it is worthwhile keeping in mind that these conclusions are limited because of significant methodological problems. For example, in some studies, only a small sample size was used, and participants were recruited from clinical settings (Brodzinsky & Steiger, 1991). Brodzinsky, Schechter, Braff, and Singer (1984) reported lower teacher and parent ratings of school success among adopted elementary-school-age children. In addition, Kenny, Baldwin, and Mackie (1967) and Silver (1970, 1989) noted that the number of adopted children with learning disabilities was disproportionately high.

A more recent study used a sample population of neurologically impaired, perceptually impaired, and emotionally disturbed students to determine rates of adopted children found in special education. The results of this study concluded that the percentage of adoptees in special education among this group is significantly high (Brodzinsky & Steiger, 1991). The widespread conclusion of the compiled research indicates that adopted children are overrepresented among children having difficulties at school. Therefore, educators and counselors should be compelled to learn about, acknowledge, and address adoption-related issues.

Reasons for Overrepresentation

The reasons for overrepresentation of adopted children in special education are varied. Experts suggest that parents who adopt may be more likely than biological parents to seek help for their children because they are accustomed to using the services of agencies (Deutsch et al., 1982). Adoptive parents are found to have higher education levels than nonadoptive parents and tend to make greater use of counseling and other services than families with less education (Miller, Fan, Grotevant et al., 2000).

Another contributing factor may be the prenatal environment of the child. If a child's birth mother did not have adequate nutrition, or if she drank alcohol, took drugs, or smoked cigarettes during her pregnancy, these environmental influences may have some effect. Abuse or neglect, if it caused physical injury, neurological damage, or emotional distress can also play a role in producing learning disabilities (National Adoption Information Clearinghouse, 1993). The effects may be especially evident in cases of intercountry adoption, particularly in those from institutionalized environments (Meese, 2002).

Intercountry Adoptions

Intercountry and transracially adopted children, who enter school in the United States as students for whom English is a second language, bring to the classroom their own special needs. Children of intercountry adoptions differ from other students who learn English as a Second Language (ESL), such as children who are immigrants and are still exposed to their first language in their home environments. Intercountry adoptees usually lose their first language while learning English. These circumstances make it harder for educators to assess if the difficulties are due to slower but "normal" ESL learning (Pearson, 2001). Just as language is a challenge, so is acculturation into American school systems. Educators who recognize achievements other than academics (i.e., behavioral) will be instrumental in raising the self-esteem of these children (Enge, 1998).

Clinical/Educational Implications

Often, adoption is not the presenting problem with students referred to special education and, therefore, it is disregarded and not included in treatment plans. All too often school counselors who have not had training or who do not understand how adoption can affect students will avoid adoption-related discussions. Without acknowledgment or validation of the impact of adoption, educators and counselors cannot provide a supportive environment in which to work through these issues.

If there is no supportive forum wherein adopted children are able to explore grief and loss, behaviors may emerge that can facilitate a referral to out-of-district special education. Although it is good practice to be aware of the special issues of adoption, educators and counselors should be cautious and avoid overreacting to learning and behavioral difficulties that may be temporary, age-specific responses to adoption issues in children's development (Meese, 1999).

Case Study 3

Special Education Issues in Adoption

Ashley was adopted from Colombia at 6 months of age. Her parents had one biological child who was 13 years old at the time Ashley was adopted. Ashley and her family enjoyed a very affluent lifestyle. Her adoptive mother was a special education elementary school teacher. Ashley struggled in school in the early years, Grades 1 through 5. Although Ashley was very sociable and made friends easily, she would commonly find fault with them and leave them. Ashley's parents divorced when she was 8 years old. At this time, Ashley was living with her adoptive mom and visiting her adoptive father on the weekends. Both parents remained very attentive to Ashley and they continued to enjoy a pleasant lifestyle. Soon after the divorce Ashley's adoptive mother remarried. Her mother's new husband and his two children moved into the home.

Ashley was experiencing failing grades and was refusing to attend school on a regular basis. Her mother was familiar with the required testing for special education and had Ashley tested for special placement. The school district agreed on special education services out of district, stating Ashley's academic testing scored three levels below grade. Remedial classes and an individualized education plan were put into place for Ashley. After close to 2 years of services, an evaluation showed little or no improvement in Ashley's academics.

Ashley's mother then negotiated for special placement in a specialized intensive support program, where the emotional needs of the child were on par with, or perhaps sometimes paramount to, academics. The school district agreed.

Just as Ashley's new school placement was about to begin, Ashley's adoptive mother was diagnosed with cancer. Ashley was displaced from her home once again and moved in with her adoptive father and brother. Ashley's adoptive mother died within 1 year of Ashley's placement in her new school. Her academics showed no improvement at the end-of-year testing. Ashley received intense counseling weekly at school to address the drastic and sad changes in her life. While working with a counselor, Ashley was asked to write about one wish she had. Ashley crossed out the words "one wish" and wrote "three wishes." Ashley wished (1) for her adoptive mom to come back, (2) to find her biological mom, and (3) for money so that she could help her biological mom. Ashley shared with the counselor that these had been her thoughts almost every day for quite some time. After 2 years of intensive work, Ashley was ready to graduate from middle school to high school; triennial testing at the end of the year showed Ashley on grade level for math and above grade level for reading. Ashley was referred to an in-district placement for high school and continued counseling with her family.

REFLECTION QUESTIONS AND DISCUSSION

School Issues Viewed Through a Developmental Stage Theory

1. Adopted preschoolers tend to have very positive feelings about being adopted. At what age does this begin to change for adopted children, and how does this change in thinking manifest itself at school?

2. Which stage of development is considered especially complicated in the search for self? Discuss why.

Considering IQ and Environment

1. During childhood and adolescence, adopted children become increasingly more similar to their biological parents and increasingly less similar to their adoptive parents. Discuss the implications for adoptive parent influence and peer and environmental influence.

2. Age at adoption may influence cognitive IQ and school performance. Are children adopted in their first year of life more apt to excel at school performance or yield a higher cognitive IQ? Discuss the reasons for why this is so.

School Interventions and Teacher Influence/Sensitivity and Understanding

1. In an effort to honor differences in the classroom, discuss an inclusive assignment that a teacher might use.

2. Suggest some activities to acknowledge National Adoption Month.

Considerations of Race, Culture, and Ethnic Identity

1. Discuss concrete and specific ways in which you can or do challenge your students to become more aware and accepting of their own racial, cultural, and ethnic identity and that of others. Discuss concrete and specific ways in which you can or do challenge yourself to become more aware and accepting of your own racial, cultural, and ethnic identity and that of others.

2. Choose one of the vignettes that were presented above and identify specific concerns that you might have if Jessie, Anne, Nadine, or Alek were one of your students. What interventions might you employ to assist that student to develop to his or her fullest potential?

Special Education Issues in Adoption

1. Adoptees were overrepresented in neurologically impaired, perceptually impaired, and emotionally disturbed groups in special education. Discuss reasons why the prevalence of adoptees may actually be overestimated.

2. To support adopted children at school, a counselor or educator should try to provide a supportive environment. Describe examples where professional intervention can be more detrimental than helpful.

REFERENCES

Baden, A. L., & Steward, R. J. (2000). A framework for use with racially and culturally integrated families: The cultural-racial identity model as applied to transracial adoption. *Journal of Social Distress and the Homeless, 9,* 309–337.

Bagley, C. (1993). Transracial adoption in Britain: A follow-up study, with policy considerations. *Child Welfare, 72,* 285–299.

Benson, P. L., Sharma, A. R., & Roehlkepartain, E. C. (1994). *Growing up adopted: A portrait of adolescents and their families.* Minneapolis, MN: Search Institute.

Bowlby, J. (1982). *Attachment and loss* (2nd ed.). New York: Basic Books.

Brodzinsky, D. M., Schechter, D. E., Braff, A. M., & Singer, L. M. (1984). Psychological and academic adjustment in adopted children. *Journal of Consulting and Clinical Psychology, 52,* 582–590.

Brodzinsky, D. M., Schechter, M. D., & Henig, R. M. (1992). *Being adopted: The lifelong search for self.* New York: Doubleday.

Brodzinsky, D. M., Smith, D. W., & Brodzinsky, A. B. (1998). *Children's adjustment to adoption: Developmental and clinical issues.* Thousand Oaks, CA: Sage.

Brodzinsky, D. M., & Steiger, C. (1991). Prevalence of adoptees among special education populations. *Journal of Learning Disabilities, 24,* 484–489.

Burrow, A. L., & Finley, G. E. (2001). Issues in transracial adoption and foster care. *Adoption Quarterly, 5*(2), 1–4.

Caron, S. L., & Moskey, E. G. (2002). Changes over time in teenage sexual relationships: Comparing the high school class of 1950, 1975, and 2000. *Adolescence, 37,* 515–526.

Columbo, M., de la Parra, A., & Lopez, I. (1992). Intellectual and physical outcome of children undernourished in early life is influenced by later environmental conditions. *Developmental Medicine and Child Neurology, 34,* 611–622.

Coon, H., Carey, G., Fulker, D. W., & DeFries, J. C. (1993). Influences of school environment on the academic achievement scores of adopted and nonadopted children. *Intelligence, 17,* 79–104.

Cordel, A. S., Nathan, C., & Krymow, V. P. (1985). Group counseling for children adopted at older ages. *Child Welfare, 64,* 113–124.

Dalen, M. (2001). School performances among internationally adopted children in Norway. *Adoption Quarterly, 5*(2), 39–57.

Deutsch, C. K., Swanson, J. M., Bruell, J. H., Cantwell, D. P., Weinberg, F., & Baren, M. (1982). Overrepresentation of adoptees in children with the attention deficit disorder. *Behavior Genetics, 12,* 231–238.

Enge, N. (1998). "Do I belong here?" Understanding the adopted, language-minority child (Teaching adopted, non-English speaking children). *Childhood Education, 75,* 106–108.

Erikson, E. H. (1968). *Identity: Youth and crisis.* New York: Norton.

Erikson, E. H. (1980). *Identity and the life cycle.* New York: Norton.

Evan B. Donaldson Adoption Institute. (2002). *Facts about adoption.* Retrieved December 1, 2005, from www.adoptioninstitute.org/FactOverview.html

Feigelman, W. (2000). Adjustments of transracially and intraracially adopted young adults. *Child and Adolescent Social Work Journal, 17,* 165–183.

Frydman, M., & Lynn, R. (1989). The intelligence of Korean children adopted in Belgium. *Personality and Individual Differences, 10,* 1323–1325.

Grotevant, H. D. (1997). Family processes, identity development, and behavioral outcomes in adopted adolescents. *Journal of Adolescent Research, 12,* 139–161.

Grotevant, H. D., Dunbar, N., Kohler, J. K., & Lash Esau, A. M. (2000). Adoptive identity: How contexts within and beyond the family shape developmental pathways. *Family Relations, 49,* 379–387.

Groza, V., Ryan, S. D., & Cash, S. J. (2003). Institutionalization, behavior and international adoption: Predictors of behavior problems. *Journal of Immigrant Health, 5,* 5–17.

Haugaard, J. J., Dorman, K., & Schustack, A. (1997). Transracial adoption. *Adoption Quarterly, 1*(2), 87–93.

Haugaard, J. J., Palmer, M., & Wojslawowicz, J. C. (1999). International adoption: Children primarily from Asia and South America. *Adoption Quarterly, 3*(2), 83–93.

Helms, J. E. (1984). Toward a theoretical explanation of the effects of race on counseling: A black and white model. *The Counseling Psychologist, 3–4,* 153–164.

Hoksbergen, R. A. C., ter Laak, J., van Dijkum, C., Rijk, K., & Stoutjesdijk, F. (2003). Attention deficit, hyperactivity disorder in adopted Romanian children living in the Netherlands. *Adoption Quarterly, 6*(4), 59–73.

Hoksbergen, R. A. C., ter Laak, J., van Dijkum, C., Rijk, S., Rijk, K., & Stoutjesdijk, F. (2003). Posttraumatic stress disorder in adopted children from Romania. *American Journal of Orthopsychiatry, 73,* 255–265.

Horowitz, J. A., Vessey, J. A., Carlson, K. L., Bradley, J. F., Montoya, C., McCullough, B., et al. (2004). Teasing and bullying experiences of middle school students. *Journal of the American Psychiatric Nurses Association, 10,* 165–172.

Johnson, D. E., & Dole, K. (1999). International adoptions: Implications for early intervention. *Infants and Young Children, 11*(4), 34–45.

Judge, S. (2004). The impact of early institutionalization on child and family outcomes. *Adoption Quarterly, 7*(3), 31–48.

Juffer, F., & van Ijzendoorn, M. H. (2005). Behavior problems and mental health referrals of international adoptees. *Journal of the American Medical Association, 293,* 2501–2515.

Kadlec, M. B., & Cermak, S. A. (2002). Activity level, organization, and social-emotional behaviors in post-institutionalized children. *Adoption Quarterly, 6*(2), 43–57.

Kenny, T., Baldwin, R., & Mackie, J. B. (1967). Incidence of minimal brain injury in adopted children. *Child Welfare, 46,* 24–29.

Kessler, L. F. (1988). The measurement of teachers' attitudes toward adopted children. *Dissertation Abstracts International, 48*(7), 1710A (UMI No. 8722905).

Lee, R. M. (2003). The transracial adoption paradox: History, research, and counseling implications of cultural socialization. *The Counseling Psychologist, 31,* 711–744.

March, K. (1995). Perception of adoption as social stigma: Motivation for search and reunion. *Journal of Marriage & the Family, 57*(3), 653–660.

Marcovitch, S., Goldberg, S., Gold, A., Washington, J., Wasson, C., Krekewich, K., et al. (1997). Determinants of behavioural problems in Romanian children adopted in Ontario. *International Journal of Behavioral Development, 20,* 17–31.

McRoy, R. G., Zurcher, L. A., Lauderdale, M. L., & Anderson, R. N. (1982). Self-esteem and racial identity in transracial and inracial adoptees. *Social Work, 27,* 522–526.

Meese, R. L. (1999). Teaching adopted students with disabilities: What teachers need to know. *Intervention in School and Clinic, 34,* 232–236.

Meese, R. L. (2002). *Children of intercountry adoptions in school.* Westport, CT: Bergin & Garvey.

Meese, R. L. (2005). A few new children: Postinstitutionalized children of intercountry adoption. *Journal of Special Education, 39,* 157–167.

Meier, D. I. (1999). Cultural identity and place in adult Korean-American intercountry adoptees. *Adoption Quarterly, 3*(1), 15–48.

Melina, L. R. (1998). *Raising adopted children: Practical reassuring advice for every adoptive parent.* New York: HarperCollins.

Miall, C. E. (1994). Community constructs of involuntary childlessness: Sympathy, stigma, and social support. *Canadian Review of Sociology & Anthropology, 31*(4), 392–421.

Miller, B. C., Fan, X., Christensen, M., Grotevant, H. D., & van Dulmen, M. (2000). Comparisons of adopted and non-adopted adolescents in a large, nationally representative sample. *Child Development, 71,* 1458–1473.

Miller, B. C., Fan, X., Grotevant, H. D., Christensen, M., Coyl, D., & van Dulmen, M. (2000). Adopted adolescents' overrepresentation in mental health counseling: Adoptees' problems or parents' lower threshold for referral? *Journal of the American Academy of Child and Adolescent Psychiatry, 39,* 1504–1511.

National Adoption Information Clearinghouse, United States Government. (1993). *Adopting and school issues: Part 1 of 2.* Retrieved November 18, 2005, from http://naic.acf.hhs.gov/pubs/f_devdis.cfm

National Council for Adoption. (1989). *Adoption factbook: United States data, issues, regulations, and resources.* Washington, DC: Author.

Park, S. M., & Green, C. E. (2000). Is transracial adoption in the best interests of ethnic minority children? Questions concerning legal and scientific interpretations of a child's best interests. *Adoption Quarterly, 3*(4), 2–34.

Pearson, C. M. (2001). Internationally adopted children: Issues and challenges. *The ASHA Leader, 6*(19), 4–5, 12–13.

Petrill, S. A., Lipton, P. A., Hewitt, J. K., Plomin, R., Cherby, S. S., Corley, R., et al. (2004). Genetic and environmental contributions to general cognitive ability through the first 16 years of life. *Developmental Psychology, 40,* 805–812.

Plomin, R., & DeFries, J. C. (1985). *Origins of individual differences in infancy: The Colorado adoption project.* Orlando, FL: Academic Press.

Plomin, R., Fulker, D. W., Corley, R., & DeFries, J. C. (1997). Nature, nurture, and cognitive development from 1 to 16 years: A parent-offspring adoption study. *Psychological Science, 8,* 442–447.

Rutter, M., O'Connor, T. G., & the English and Romanian Adoptees (ERA) Study Team. (2004). Are there biological programming effects for psychological development? Findings from a study of Romanian adoptees. *Developmental Psychology, 40,* 81–94.

Scarborough, A. A., Spiker, D., Mallik, S., Hebbeler, K. M., Bailey, D. B., & Simeonsson, R. J. (2004). A national look at children and families entering early intervention. *Exceptional Children, 70*(4), 469–483.

Scarr, S., & Weinberg, R. A. (1983). The Minnesota adoption studies: Genetic differences and malleability. *Child Development, 54,* 260–267.

Schoettle, M. (2001). *W.I.S.E. Up! Powerbook.* Silver Spring, MD: Center for Adoption Support and Education.

Silver, L. B. (1970). Frequency of adoption in children with the neurological learning disability syndrome. *Journal of Learning Disabilities, 3,* 10–14.

Silver, L. B. (1989). Frequency of adoption in children and adolescents with learning disabilities. *Journal of Learning Disabilities, 22,* 325–327.

Singer, L. M., Brodzinsky, D. M., & Braff, A. M. (1982). Children's beliefs about adoption: A developmental study. *Journal of Applied Psychology, 3,* 285–295.

Singer, L. M., Brodzinsky, D. M., Ramsay, D., Steir, M., & Waters, E. (1985). Mother-infant attachment in adoptive families. *Child Development, 56,* 1543–1551.

Smith-McKeever, T. C. (2004). Child behavioral outcomes in African American adoptive families. *Adoption Quarterly, 7*(4), 29–56.

Sorosky, A. D., Baran, A., & Pannor, R. (1989). *The adoption triangle.* San Antonio, TX: Corona.

Stams, G.-J. J. M., Juffer, F., & van Ijzendoorn, M. H. (2002). Maternal sensitivity, infant attachment, and temperament in early childhood predict adjustment in middle childhood: The case of adopted children and their biologically unrelated parents. *Developmental Psychology, 38,* 806–821.

Suzuki, L., & Valencia, R. R. (1997). Race-ethnicity and measured intelligence: Educational implications. *American Psychologist, 52,* 1103–1114.

Teasdale, T. W., & Owen, D. R. (1984). Heredity and familial environment in intelligence and educational level: A sibling study. *Nature, 309*(5969), 620–622.

U.S. Bureau of the Census. (2003). *United States Census 2000. Number and percent of children of the householder by type of relationship for the United States, regions, and states, and for Puerto Rico.* Retrieved December 2005, from www.census.gov/prod/2003pubs/censr-6.pdf

U.S. Department of Health and Human Services. (2003). *Administration on Children, Youth and Families, Child Welfare Outcomes 2000: Annual Report. Safety, permanency, wellbeing.* Washington, DC: Author.

Van Ijzendoorn, M. H., Juffer, F., & Poelhuis, C. W. K. (2005). Adoption and cognitive development: A meta-analytic comparison of adopted and nonadopted children's IQ and school performance. *Psychological Bulletin, 131,* 301–316.

Verhulst, F. C., Althaus, M., & Versluis-den Bieman, H. J. (1990). Problem behavior in international adoptees: I. An epidemiological study. *Journal of the American Academy of Child & Adolescent Psychiatry, 29*(1), 94–103.

Wegar, K. (2000). Adoption, family ideology, and social stigma: Bias in community attitudes, adoption research, and practice. *Family Relations, 49,* 363–370.

Weinberg, R. A., Scarr, S., & Waldman, I. D. (1992). The Minnesota transracial adoption study: A follow-up of IQ test performance at adolescence. *Intelligence, 16,* 117–135.

Winkler, R. C., Brown, D. W., van Keppel, M., & Blanchard, A. (1988). *Clinical practice in adoption.* New York: Paragon Press.

Wood, L., & Ng, N. (Eds.). (2001). *Adoption and the schools: Resources for parents and teachers.* Palo Alto, CA: Families Adopting in Response.

Zabriskie, R. B., & Freeman, P. (2004). Contributions of family leisure to family functioning among transracial adoptive families. *Adoption Quarterly, 7*(3), 49–77.

Training and Education for Adoption Therapy Competence

Preface

RAFAEL A. JAVIER

St. John's University

The greatest obstacles in finding solutions to the basic psychological dilemmas members of the adoption triad often face is the level of awareness the academic and professional communities have about issues of adoption and how it affects these individuals in fundamental ways. In this part, we have included a series of chapters geared at examining issues of training and education in adoption. It starts off with a discussion of a therapy model by Pavao in her chapter "Variations in Clinical Issues for Children Adopted as Infants and Those Adopted as Older Children." It is a "brief long-term therapy model" that allows for all the basic challenges affecting the adoption triad to become essential components of the treatment intervention. It is an inclusive, intergenerational, developmental, and systemic approach that seeks to normalize the stages of development. It includes many extended family members (including birth parents and grandparents) since this model is particularly sensitive to the complexity and multilayer aspects of the kind of influence the adopted child is likely to experience. Finally, the model is based on a comprehensive examination of the adoption experience and the need to maintain an open discussion of issues of relinquishment, loss, grief, search, and reunion, as well as the need to institute psychoeducational interventions to potential adoptive families.

In her chapter "Counseling Adoption Triad Members: Making a Case for Adoption Training for Counselors and Clinical Psychologists," Porch explores the current status of adoption training for counseling professionals and highlights the need for increased training in adoption-related issues to enhance counselor competency for work with adoption triad members. Relevant information regarding adoption is presented, including current rates of adoption in the United States, the proportionately higher occurrence of adoption triad members in therapeutic settings, and the potential significance of adoption factors in understanding client issues. The general lack of adoption training in graduate counseling programs is discussed as well as practicing clinicians' assessments of their adoption knowledge. Similarities between adoptive status and multicultural dimensions of personal identity are examined, in terms of both potential significance to clients and relevance to counselor competencies. A variety of representative adoption training programs are presented for information and comparison.

In Sass and Henderson's chapter "Psychologists' Self-Reported Adoption Knowledge and the Need for More Adoption Education," these authors present a review of a variety of psychological issues related to adoption, which might become the subject matter of therapy. In this context, these authors also assess the level of knowledge psychologists have in dealing with adoption issues and the need for further education in treating triad members. They present the results of a questionnaire completed by a sample of 210 psychologists, all of whom were currently treating clients. Ninety percent reported they needed more education in adoption and 81% reported interest in taking a continuing education course in adoption. They also found that a small percentage reported taking courses as part of their formal education that dealt with adoption, while the majority reported receiving no education in this area.

We contend that only when the academic community takes the issue of adoption as a systematic focus of academic endeavor will more comprehensive treatment and assessment models be possible. A call for a more systematic inclusion of adoption-related issues in the curriculum as an essential part of the training of future professionals is clearly evident in these and other chapters in this volume.

LEARNING GOALS

Among the learning goals for this part, we expect that the readers will be able

- to understand the lifelong nature of adoption and the importance of therapists' knowledge of adoption dynamics;

- to identify several possible areas where adoption could result in the need for therapy for each of the triad positions;

- to develop a habit of routinely inquiring whether a client has any experience with adoption;

- to become familiar with the different ingredients necessary for a comprehensive and adequate treatment model to be used with this population; and finally,

- to encourage those in colleges, universities, and professional training institutes to work closely with academic/professional institutions to include adoption issues as part of their training curricula.

Variations in Clinical Issues for Children Adopted as Infants and Those Adopted as Older Children

18

JOYCE MAGUIRE PAVAO

Center for Family Connections, Inc.,
Cambridge, Massachusetts, and New York

With the media focusing more and more on adoption—and often sensationalizing it—the public's impression is often that an adversarial relationship exists between the birth family and the adoptive family. In many of the contested cases in the media, it looks like *neither* set of parents can do what is in the best interest of the child. Most certainly, in these cases, the professionals (lawyers, judges, therapists) do not seem to understand the systemic problems for the families, and the dysfunction these problems will eventually cause the child who is placed in this adversarial arena. The media's misinformation about adoption often causes continued pain and pathologizing for adoptive parents, birth parents, and adopted people in this country and in the world.

Adoption can be a very positive way to create or expand a family. It is estimated that adoption affects the lives of 40 million Americans (Henderson, 2000). Given these numbers and the fact that adoption is becoming more prevalent in the current era (*Encyclopedia of Adoption*, 2006; Evan B. Donaldson Adoption Institute, 1997), it will be increasingly important for clinicians and other professionals to be skilled in working with the unique issues and challenges that face adoptive family systems. Professionals with a "family systems" perspective can be of particular help to these complex families.[1] The therapist can normalize and demystify the process of adoption, so that the family involved can be treated with respect, and they can be prepared to handle the complex challenges that should be considered normal under the circumstances of adoption. Adoption issues are often magnified in the adoptions of older children and in transracial or international adoptions.

Child welfare professionals should, of course, continue to focus on family preservation, whenever possible. In many instances, some form of open adoption that keeps a child, especially an older child, attached and not cut off from *all* of his or her past is recommended when it is safe and when parents, both birth and adoptive, are aware of their roles and responsibilities. Open adoption is itself a form of family preservation. It provides the legal transfer of the ongoing parenting responsibilities from the birth family to the adoptive family and, thereby, creates a new kinship network, which connects those two families forever through the child or children that they both share. A preventive approach and a normalizing focus to consultation around adoption issues and to the welfare of the children involved is recommended if we, as professionals, are to treat the whole family and community system and take care of the many individuals living in the world of adoption.

PAVAO'S BRIEF LONG-TERM THERAPY MODEL

What do families need? Maybe they need an inclusive, intergenerational, developmental, systemic approach that normalizes the stages of development and includes many extended family members. While the first crisis may be about the decision *to* adopt or the decision *not to* parent, other crises often follow *after* adoption. In Pavao's therapeutic model, called "brief long-term therapy" (Pavao, 1982; Pavao, Groza, & Rosenberg, 1998), a family and various constellations (different family subsystems) are seen during the crisis. The work then involves transforming that crisis into an empowering experience. If families come back for further therapy or consultation at a later stage of development, this return is not seen as a failure. Rather, it is seen as a success in working through yet another stage of development. There is a completion of each stage of therapy, or consultation, but no "termination"; the word *terminate* is too loaded for those who have suffered the losses associated with adoption.

The therapist (or team of therapists) remains available for consultation and for therapy. This avoids the emotional cutoff and loss issues that are primary issues in adoption. Therapists who take a systemic view and encourage empowerment—rather than pathologizing the very normal and complex problems of adoptive families and birth families—are best equipped to help these complex blended families. By complex blended families, we refer to families by adoption, fostering kinship care, remarriage, or alternative reproductive technologies, whereas root families are families where the mother and father who gave birth to the child are also parenting the child together. By working with all the family members, along with the agencies, courts, and schools, the family systems therapist can spread understanding and healing.

The Birth Family

When women and their partners deal with an untimely pregnancy, the decision about whether or not to surrender a child for adoption should be made with *all* options having been presented. When children are removed for abuse or neglect reasons, the birth parents are very often unable to parent, but it does not mean that they do not love their children. The birth parents' psychological and emotional connection is important for the child and can be honored through a careful plan for some level of appropriate openness. (This openness will vary from case to case and, in some cases, will not be appropriate at all for the safety of the child.)

Family preservation and kinship arrangements should be explored prior to any discussion of adoption. The more we work to explore the connections that are safe and in place for a child or children, the more we avoid the possibility of attachment disorders (Hoksberger & Loenen, 1985; Pavao, 2005). Therapists should discuss with potential birth parents the kinds of adoption plans available, the posttraumatic effects that the parents will encounter over time, and the effects that the children will encounter as well. We are using "potential parent" and "birth parent" here, and it is important to remember that until an adoption plan is made and finalized, the birth parents are the parents of the child. It is only after the parental rights are terminated and the adoptive parents are legally and emotionally installed as the "forever" parents of the child, that the term *birth parent* is appropriate.

Preparation Often Leads to Prevention

There are many kinds of adoption, but people think that if they have experience with one kind of adoption, then they understand the whole world of adoption. Potential birth parents need to be educated, as do all people approaching adoption as an option. There are public and private agencies. There are closed and open arrangements for adoption, with many shades between very closed and very open. Birth parents who feel they are being good parents by making a plan that will be best for their child feel more empowered than those who feel like victims. There is not just one kind of adoption option for the birth parents who are either in public or private situations. These options must be clearly defined and presented to the birth parents so that they can make a decision that is, first and foremost, best for their child and, in turn, best for them.

The pain of loss is great, but the reasons for considering adoption indicate that parenting this child might also prove extremely difficult. If possible, birth parents need to speak with a knowledgeable professional at the beginning of their decision-making process, preferably with someone who is *not* connected to a placement agency. Once they have had adequate *psychoeducation* (a term used to describe the education about psychological and developmental issues that are normal under the circumstances in adoption) and counseling, the probability for a good and healthy adoption plan is very high.

Without proper counseling for both birth parents, as well as their extended families, there is a greater chance that there will be ambivalence, contested adoptions, or other problems later. This is most true in older child placements, where the attachment to the birth family is even greater than a psychological and emotional tie; there are *real* memories and *real* relationships in place. In these cases, it is important to explore some options for an open adoption to maintain *healthy* connections in the birth family and, possibly, in fostering families as well.

Open adoption cannot be mandated, as you cannot mandate people's relationships. Families thinking of parenting a child who has had many emotional cutoffs and moves from family to family should consider keeping some of the attachments that have been beneficial to the child, as a way of avoiding potential "attachment disorders," and managing them in the child's best interests. For example, it may not be safe or sane to allow a child to continue a relationship with a birth father who is an abuser and a violent person, but if there is a grandparent or an aunt who has been a safe haven for that child, a supervised clinical visit to keep that relationship—and to develop one between that person and the new family—may be just the thing to keep that child from feeling isolated and cut off once again.

Currently, in this country, many potential birth parents want to be involved in the selection of adoptive parents for their infant child. This is evidenced in the increase in the number of independent adoptions (Evan B. Donaldson Adoption Institute, 1997). Most birth parents want to know something about where the child is going and who will be caretaker and parent to that child. Meeting the preadoptive parents before a decision is made is not uncommon. However, the general trend appears to be toward semiopen adoption rather than toward open adoption.

In *semiopen adoption*, there is usually a one-time meeting of the birth and preadoptive parents. Often, first names are all that is exchanged. The parties make an emotional connection and agree to have the agency or adoption professional act as an intermediary in the yearly (or as otherwise decided by the parties or courts involved) exchange of letters and pictures and updated medical information. Semiopen adoption allows the birth parents to feel more of a sense of connection to the parents who will care for the child that they cannot parent. This is the birth parent's last act of parenting—making a plan that will give their child a safe and secure family for a lifetime. We call this *semiopen* because it is not open to the child. The plan is not necessarily for an open relationship that includes the child and the birth parents, but an open *beginning* with the adoptive and birth parents. This is a fine and trusting way to begin a relationship, but if it is called *open*, the child will eventually protest against this untruth.

Open adoptions can vary a great deal, including arrangements from regular meetings to occasional written contact and picture exchange. In *all* forms of adoption, birth parents terminate parental rights, and the adoptive parents become the only "parenting" parents. Open adoption is *not* joint custody, and it is *not* guardianship.

The permanent plan for parenting of the child is that the adoptive parents *parent* the child, and the birth parents' roles change from parent to extended family. That role should be negotiated early on and clearly defined to ensure that everyone is clear and understands the family relationship. The birth mother and birth father will always be the ones who created this child; but at the time of adoption, their role changes from that of "parent" to that of extended family. A knowledgeable therapist or other professional can help in the mediation process and can help avoid future confusion and inconsistency by having the families discuss roles and responsibilities early on in the adoption proceedings.

Closed adoption has been the traditional form of adoption in the United States since the 1930s. It offers no identifying information, or very little nonidentifying information, and no agreement for future meetings. Closed adoption was created about 80 years ago, and so it is relatively new. Although some people think it guarantees anonymity, it does not. Closed adoption was created to protect children from the public's bias about illegitimacy. It was thought that if a new *birth* certificate were created (rather than an adoption certificate), which had a mother *and* a father, and if the original single parent certificate were sealed away, then the general public would not chastise the "illegitimate" child. This was *not* done to protect the birth parent from the adoptive parent or vice versa. It is outdated at this point in time because we have many single parents, even single fathers: An adoption-altered *birth* certificate can now say that John Brown gave birth! Its a miracle!

Many adult adopted people, adoptive parents, and birth parents are quite upset about the falsified document—the "illegal" legal document that is a false birth certificate, a legal fiction. It is the only situation in this country where an adult does not have access to information about himself or herself. It is a civil right to have that access, and adopted people are somehow still not granted that American right in most states.

It is believed that the secrecy and lies surrounding the system of adoption, more than any other contributing factor, are what have caused many of the problems, issues, and challenges that have evolved in adoptive and birth families over time (Henderson, 2000). The shame and guilt that secrets and lies engender have a negative effect on the lives of the people involved and result in a dysfunctional situation in many cases.

In all of these forms of adoption, it is important to know that the emotional and psychological connections between the birth parents and the child are *never* terminated. To avoid the cutoff that children have experienced in their many moves in and out of foster homes and "relative" or kin placements, it is important to work with families to keep the positive connections that exist, even if they are only the psychological and emotional connections, with no contact. Many older children are separated from their siblings as well, and it is essential that visits between siblings continue after the adoption is finalized.

Relationships between the adopting or foster families and the birth family must often be developed and supervised, in the initial stages, by professionals. The same is true of grandparents who cannot take on the parenting but would like to continue to be the grandparent and have visits. In all these situations, the role of the professional is to develop real and healthy working relationships and to make roles and responsibilities clear to the adults so that they will be clear for the children.

We can help families understand that, while trying to integrate a child with trauma and resulting challenges into the family, even though it is much work to deal with additional people (birth family or foster family), it will pay off in the long run, in that this will integrate the child's sense of self and sense of reality. In some cases, the adults may have to put their egos aside to heal the child.

We often find that especially the oldest, "parentified" children do not have the tendency and need to run to find out how their birth mother/siblings are if they have regular visits and correspondence and know that they are all right. It gives the children "permission to be where they are" and to be healthy and happy as well. Indeed, about 40% of older children have contact with the extended birth family, including siblings in other placements (Evan B. Donaldson Adoption Institute, 1997; also see Chapter 12 in this book). This is a prerequisite for their continued attachment and well-being.

Older child placements, especially domestic, require mediation and discussion among the adults, to give children the understanding that parenting is *more* than just giving birth. In the best of all worlds, a person who gives birth can also parent, but, in many cases and for many reasons, that is not always true or possible.

Childhood is very short. Children cannot wait years for parents to be rehabilitated, to be freed from jail, or to be fit to parent. Children *must* be parented consistently and caringly. It is hoped that this can happen in the extended family or community, but when it cannot, adoption is a very good option, and some open arrangement, with the permission of the birth family for the adoptive parents to be the parents, helps an older child to feel that he or she is not being disloyal.

Preadoptive Parents

Understanding what precedes the adoption, whatever type it may be, is important. A majority of preadoptive couples have struggled with issues of infertility for years. The pain and loss that results from constantly hoping for a child and undergoing invasive medical, pharmacological, and surgical procedures (which can strain a couple's relationship) make the process of adoption seem like additional hoops through which to jump in the process of becoming parents. Like birth parents, adoptive parents feel they are victims of the "process." For them, it is the process of the home study, the scrutiny, and the inclusion or exclusion that is a part of the procedure. They become angry at the "hoops," and they sometimes cut themselves off from the very useful education and supports that might be available to them in the process. Finally, preadoptive parents often suffer from a lack of understanding on the part of some of their own extended family, friends, and community as well. Individuals who adopt confront their own set of prejudices from the world around them.

People sometimes don't understand *why* you would adopt, especially an older child! "Why would you want to deal with all the problems that are inherent in this kind of family?" they ask. This can result in a subtle, but lifelong experience of pain, guilt, shame, and loss, if it is not discussed and normalized. Most adoptive parents become adoption educators and learn that they have to educate all their extended family and community to help them understand what it is that they are doing and why. These parents work to help people in their schools, churches, and communities to understand some of the very common and expected problems that a child—especially an older-placement child—encounters due to early trauma and many moves.

The belief, in days of old, that the panacea for infertility was adoption is one that people may still believe. We know now that adoption does not "fix" infertility. It "fixes" the loss of parenting, and adoption is a wonderful way to *become* a parent and to create a family. However, the issues of never seeing a child of "one's own" continue to exist. These issues exist for extended family members as well, grandparents in particular. Therefore, parents and other extended family members of the adoptive individual or couple can benefit a great deal from being included in psychoeducation and counseling around adoption and its many facets prior to and after the adoption.

Case Study: Louise's Grandmother

Once, in a therapy session that I did many years ago, 30-year-old Louise, who had been adopted as an infant, clearly remembered and recounted a day soon after her eighth birthday. Louise was, and continued to be, very close to her adoptive mom. They were making her room into a "big girl's room" for her eighth birthday. They chose flowered wallpaper, a canopied bed, bright colors for paint, new fabric for curtains, and other new furnishings. They did this whole project together, and had the best of fun. Louise's grandparents came for dinner to celebrate her birthday after the project's completion.

When dessert was done, Louise and her mom took "Grandma" by the hand and led her, with eyes closed, to the door of Louise's newly designed "big girl" bedroom. They gleefully opened the door and told Grandma to open her eyes! Grandma opened her eyes and looked around the room, and looked again, and said, "What a beautiful room for someone else's child."

This was not simply a "wicked" grandmother (although both her daughter-in-law and granddaughter were devastated by her comment). This grandmother was, herself, an aging mother who suffered from the loss of never seeing her very own birth grandchildren. She had no way of processing her own grief and loss about the infertility of her son and daughter-in-law, and it all came out in this one sentence.

Adoptive Families: Ongoing Issues

For adoptive parents who adopt older children—domestically *or* internationally—there is the added issue of trauma and the posttraumatic problems that the family will often encounter. Without the proper preparation and training, and without open discussion prior to placement and during the transition of the child or children to their new home, there is the possibility that these adoptions will become more challenging and complicated. There is also the grave possibility that the child will be considered attachment disordered or reactive attachment disordered. Adoption should provide permanence. When an adoption is not done in the best interests of all included (especially the child), and when there are no post-adoption services available with competent well-trained professionals, many families find it hard to stay together, and the adoption can actually disrupt or dissolve. Adoptions *should* be forever. We should provide all the services that we can to keep families whole and together. Even death does not them part.

Case Study: Trevor/Ricardo

One of the stories that touches my heart most is that of a young man who was adopted at approximately age 5 from an orphanage in Colombia. His adoptive parents went to Colombia and stayed in a hotel while they awaited the processing of papers. They finally got their little boy and brought him back to their home in Dover, Massachusetts. They decided to name him Trevor, a family name. (Names and places have been changed.)

Trevor did quite well. He adapted swiftly and fit in. He did have the expected language problems, which slowed him down in school, and he got extra help for those. He was an athlete and was very busy, and he seemed quite happy during his childhood. However, at approximately age 13, he attempted suicide. On his release from the hospital, the family was referred to me for family therapy. I sat in a room with a severely depressed young man and his very worried parents who were nervous and distraught. I asked them to tell me, first, the story of Trevor's adoption. I then asked what was going on around the time of the suicide attempt. The parents both said "nothing," "everything seemed fine." I probed some more and the dad said that they were in the process of having Trevor become a naturalized citizen, but that, of course, couldn't be the problem! I asked the parents to wait outside while I spent time alone with young Trevor. Trevor was deeply depressed. I asked if he could think about anything that would make him want to live. Would he want to go back to Colombia? Would he fantasize about what would make him have the will to live? He looked at me candidly and said, "Joyce, you do not understand. I do not live. I died when I was 5 years old. I had another name, another language, another family, and I became this person that I am trying to be. I can no longer try." I sat and listened. I asked, "What do you call yourself in your head? When you talk to yourself?" and he answered, "Ricardo."

I asked if we could ask if his parents would give him back his name and he responded, "Joyce, you don't understand. I love my parents. I don't want to hurt them." I suggested then that the suicide attempt had hurt them, but that they would probably be able to withstand a name change! I asked him what else he would like. He said, "I'd like to be around people who look like me . . . I am in a White family, and an all-White school and neighborhood, and there is no one like me." I asked "what else," and he said that he didn't want to be a citizen of the United States. "I lost my country, my language, my people and I don't want to lose anything else. That is all that I have left."

I asked if we could invite his parents back in and tell them what we had talked about and he said, "You tell them," and so I did. When his parents heard about his name, they cried. His mother said, "I wanted you to have our family name so that you would feel that you belonged. . . . I never wanted to make you feel bad." Ricardo then put his arm around his mom's shoulder and told her that it had been hard for him to get used to a new name, and he knew she would slip sometimes and call him Trevor, but that it was okay. He said he would like to keep Trevor as part of his name.

We then talked about the citizenship issue, and his dad explained how important it would be. He suggested that if Trevor got his name back, he could have something from his past and that at age 21 he could choose to be a citizen of anywhere. They extended the discussion. We then talked about Ricardo being the only minority person in his world. I asked if the parents would consider moving to Jamaica Plain, a racially and culturally diverse neighborhood in Boston. (I was stretching things a bit, but just checking it out.) The dad said the market was bad . . . after all they had a huge property in Dover with stables and all. Why would they move to Jamaica Plain? I then suggested that they look into private schools that had a commitment to diversity: not just diversity of students, but with faculty and board that would be "mirrors" for Ricardo as well. I asked Ricardo if this would do. He said, "I guess so."

To make a very long life story short, Ricardo lived. He went on to high school and he had a great experience. He studied and relearned Spanish. His dad took him on a bicycle trip through Colombia when he graduated from high school, and they went back to visit the orphanage where Ricardo had lived and tried to find out if there was any information about his birth family. There was. Ricardo did nothing about this on that trip. He went on to college and he decided to spend his junior year in Colombia; he wanted to be in an American program, but in Colombia. He felt worried that he wouldn't fit in there either.

While in Colombia, Ricardo did find his birth family. He found difficult things. There had been violence and death and poverty. Ricardo had "known" this on some level and had memories that he thought were just "bad thoughts." He thought he was a "bad person," when in fact he had witnessed violence and had been subjected to it. Finding out this very tragic information actually freed him to be in the present. Ricardo went on to law school, and he majored in international law and human rights. He is a champion for the children of the world. Children like him.

I love to tell Ricardo's story because he is an example of the danger and fragility of moving a child without thinking of the long-term consequences. Ricardo felt dead. He was almost dead when I met him, after his suicide attempt. He needed to have his past brought back to him, to integrate with his present, to feel that he might have a future.

Ricardo calls me at intervals. He likes my "brief long-term therapy" model. His most recent call was about commitment. He was in love. The woman is White. He feels that he will be repeating his own life in the lives of his children. He feels the same old divided loyalty. Should he be with a dark-skinned woman? His identity confusion continues. He feels that he loves her and will probably marry her, but he wonders what all this means.

We all want adoption to be forever, and it is. The challenges remain, but they can be diminished over time. We want permanent plans for *all* the children who are in the situation of needing parents other than those who gave birth to them, and we want these children to feel whole, to integrate their past and their present—their birth family and birth culture and their adoptive family and adoptive culture—to be integrated and to be whole.

PSYCHOEDUCATION

Psychoeducation, even many years after the legal act of adoption, can and does help entire families. Psychoeducation and counseling, prior to adoption, for the parents of the couple or individual adopting (the grandparents) and the extended family or community will lead to more support for the adoptive family, along with greater understanding of the participants' own feelings.

A knowledgeable and competent adoption therapist can help families to discuss and make sense of these issues in the preadoptive process. Single parents and gay and lesbian parents who adopt will also benefit from adoptive psychoeducation about the added complexities that their families will face.

The Pavao "normative" model proposes that a systemic approach is needed to work with the adoptive family (which includes the birth family, foster family, and adoptive family). There is no identified patient in this model. The whole system—from the wider context of adoption practices to the intricate relationships in the adoptive and birth families—is regarded as the client. Crises can be normal, and they can even lead to transformation. Clinicians must be familiar with, and empathic toward, each member of the adoption circle, including the birth family—whether they are known or unknown to the adopting parents.

If the professionals who work with these families are not fully trained to understand all aspects of adoption—intergenerational, systemic, and developmental—and if they are not trained to understand that adoption is not just one thing, then they are not providing what the family truly needs. They are not adoption competent.

Adoption is so many things: It is public and private; domestic and international; open, semiopen, and closed. It is inracial and transracial; it involves infants and older children; it is about foster care, kinship, and guardianship. It is a mistake for professionals to think they understand the wider world of adoption because of their own adoption experience; that is a case study of one. If professionals do not have the training and do not understand these complexities, and if they have no experience with trauma work, then they can actually *harm* the family, rather than heal them.

The Adoptive Family: Continued

There are ongoing issues for the whole family: how to tell the child; what to tell the child; when to tell the child; how to deal with extended family members and neighbors; how to work with schools and professionals who have little or no experience with learning disabilities, attention deficit disorder, attachment difficulties, and emotional difficulties in adopted children; and how to discuss adoption in general. Some of these difficulties may be more pronounced with certain kinds of adoptions, such as older-child adoptions, special needs adoptions, international adoptions, and sibling-set adoptions.

Things that birth families take for granted may pose serious dilemmas for adoptive families. One example is medical history. Physicians say that dealing with an adopted person can be like dealing with a coma victim, in the sense that critical and current family history information is often missing (and impossible to get in a closed adoption). The surgeon general has strongly urged that *all* individuals have a full and complete medical history. What about adoptive families? What about adopted people?

For older child adoptions, there are the recurrent posttraumatic symptoms and an ongoing need to understand the early life experiences, cognitive or precognitive. (All children placed at an older age have been involved in removal from their family by authorities if adopted in the United States, and all have suffered some abuse or neglect that led to their removal. Many internationally adopted older children experience similar abuse or neglect prior to adoption.) In adolescence, a variety of issues emerge for the adopted teen and the adoptive family. Adopted teens, like all adolescents, begin to scrutinize themselves more carefully. For the adopted person looking into the mirror, this may lead to the realization that he or she does not know another human being in the world who is genetically related to him or her. The fact of adoption complicates the issues of identity, sexuality, trust, self-esteem, and individuation, to name a few (Pavao, 1998, 2005).

SEARCH

As adolescence includes a search for identity, adoptive parents are often faced with the confusing task of how to help the child to integrate a complete sense of self when pieces of his or her heritage may be elusive, problematic, or even entirely missing.

Simultaneous with the adolescent's search, the adoptive parents are often, subconsciously or consciously, dealing with issues of loss, wondering what their birth children would have been like, and about their preparation for their adopted child's move toward adulthood, along with the intense and very normal but disturbing feelings about the loss of this child who will soon be an adult.

There are also effects on the adopted person and the family when the search for birth parents is undertaken. The search brings up issues of conflicting loyalties for the adopted person between the adoptive and birth parents. It also brings up fears and fantasies that are often difficult to manage for all involved.

It is important to note that although the search brings up difficult and painful issues, it is an integral part of the healing process of identity and intimacy, which is essential to making all these broken connections whole. Clinicians must understand the importance and the intricacies of the search and must recognize that it is a healing journey no matter what is found.

Adoption is an ongoing challenge, throughout the life cycle and beyond, affecting not only the past generations, but the ones to come as well. We are now learning that when adopted people choose not to search, their children—the next generation—often show patterns similar to an adopted person, and they often do the search on their own for their birth grandparents.

CONCLUSION

Let me conclude with a poem I wrote for adoptive parents that I give to them as a token of my love and care for the children in adoption and all their families by birth and by adoption.

> *You cannot change the truth*
> *these are your children*
> *but they came from somewhere else*
> *and they are the children of those places*
> *and of those people as well*
> *Help them to know all about their past*
> *and all about their present*
> *help them to know that they are from extended families*
> *that they only have one parent or set of parents*
> *but that they have more mothers and fathers*

they have grandmothers, godmothers, birthmothers, mother countries, mother earth
they have grandfathers, godfathers, birthfathers and fatherlands
they have family by birth and by adoption
they have family by choice and by chance
Childhood is short
they are our children to raise
they are our children to love
and then they are citizens of the world
What we do to them creates the world that we live in
Give them life
Give them their truth
Give them love
Give them all that they came with
Give them all that they grow with
Your children do not belong to you
but they belong with you
you cannot keep them from what is theirs
but you can keep loving them
You do not own your children
but they are your own
. . . With love to adoptive parents

From Dr. Joyce Maguire Pavao

NOTE

1. What do we mean by "complex blended families?"
   - *Root families* are families where the mother and father who gave birth to the child are also parenting the child together.
   - *Complex families* are every other type of family structure.
   - *Complex blended families* are a blending of many families by adoption, fostering, kinship care, remarriage, or alternative reproductive technologies.

REFERENCES

Encyclopedia of Adoption. (2006). Retrieved May 2, 2006, from http://encyclopedia.adoption.com/intro/introduction/2.html

Evan B. Donaldson Adoption Institute. (1997). *Benchmark adoption survey: Report on the findings.* Washington, DC: Princeton Survey Research Associates. Retrieved May 10, 2006, from http://adoptioninstitute.org/survey/Benchmark Survey 1997

Henderson, D. B. (2000). Adoption issues in perspective: An introduction to the special issue. *Journal of Social Distress and the Homeless, 9,* 261–272.

Hoksberger, R., & Loenen, A. (1985). Adoption and attachment: About problems with attachment with foreign adoptive children. *Kind & Adolescent, 6*(2), 71–83.

Pavao, J. (1998). *The family of adoption.* Boston: Beacon Press.

Pavao, J. (2005). *The family of adoption.* Boston: Beacon Press. (Original work published 1998)

Pavao, J., Groza, V., & Rosenberg, K. F. (1998). Treatment issues in adoption practice from a triad and systemic perspective. In V. Groza & K. F. Rosenberg (Eds.), *Clinical and practice issues in adoption: Bridging the gap between adoptees placed as infants and as older children.* Westport, CT: Praeger.

Counseling Adoption Triad Members

19

Making a Case for Adoption Training for Counselors and Clinical Psychologists

THERESA KENNEDY PORCH

Adoption challenges us to clarify our meaning of family. In doing so, it raises important social and emotional questions: Who constitutes a family? How do we define family roles and family bonds? How important are genetic and phenotypical factors in our family relationships and our identities? Historically, these questions were all but dismissed for adoptive families in furtherance of a mutually beneficial view of adoption in which children got the families they needed and parents got the children they wanted. Over time, it has become clear that the experience of adoption can be a complicated emotional experience for all members of the adoption triad (the adoptee, the birth family, and the adoptive family). Adoption is now understood to be a lifelong process for those involved, which may vary in salience and in the level of satisfaction or distress it creates for individuals at different points in their lives (Brodzinsky, Schechter, & Henig, 1993).

Because it involves deep-rooted emotional issues that may significantly affect individuals throughout their lives, adoption is very likely to be a focal area for triad members who seek counseling. Therefore, adoption issues are relevant for counseling practitioners of both individual and family counseling. Yet despite the potential importance for clients, adoption generally has not been recognized as a significant area of exploration for counseling practitioners, and many counselors are unaware of the potential impact of adoption on clients (Hartman & Laird, 1990; McRoy, Grotevant, & Zurcher, 1988; Sass & Henderson, 2000). Research has shown that adoption issues are rarely taught in graduate counseling programs, and many counselors feel unprepared to deal with adoption-related issues in practice (Post, 2000; Sass & Henderson, 2000). To competently address the needs of this group of clients, it is necessary for counselors and counseling students to receive training in adoption-related issues. To highlight the need for additional counselor training in adoption, this chapter examines research regarding the therapeutic needs of adoption triad members as well as current levels of counselor training and knowledge regarding adoption. In addition, the chapter presents parallels between adoptive status and personal characteristics relevant to diversity and multiculturalism, such as the Dimensions of Personal Identity (Arredondo & Glauner, 1992), and points to the need for adoption sensitivity and competency in light of multicultural counseling competencies. Examples of some recent adoption training programs for counselors are presented. Implications for counseling practice and for counselor education are discussed.

STATISTICS OF ADOPTION

While there is no single comprehensive source of adoption statistics in the United States, estimates are typically drawn from a combination of relevant governmental data sources (Stolley, 1993), which suggest that there are between 1 million (Stolley, 1993) and 5 million (Hollinger, 1993) adoptees in the United States. For the first time in history, the 2000 U.S. Census included a category for adopted children. Based on the reported census results, there were an estimated 2.1 million adopted children in the United States in 2000, with 1.6 million of them being less than 18 years old, meaning that approximately 2.5% of the children in the United States are adopted (U.S. Census Bureau, 2003). Based on data compiled from state courts, about 127,000 children were adopted annually in 2000 and 2001 in the United States (U.S. Department of Health and Human Services [HHS], 2004). The number of adoptions of children in foster care has increased dramatically, from 28,000 in 1996 to 51,000 in 2001 (HHS Adoption and Foster Care Analysis and Reporting System, 2002, 2005). Rates of international adoptions have grown steadily as well, with approximately 23,000 "immigrant orphan visas" issued in 2005, up from 7,000 in 1990 (U.S. Department of State, n.d.). Furthermore, a survey conducted by the Evan B. Donaldson Adoption Institute (E. B. Donaldson) found that 58% of Americans have personal experience with adoption, meaning that they or a close family member or friend is an adoption triad member (E. B. Donaldson, 1997).

The past decade has seen a significant shift toward public adoptions (adoptions of children from foster care or the child welfare system) and toward international adoptions and away from domestic private adoptions. In 1992, 77% of adoptions were private. In 2001, more than half of U.S. adoptions were public or international adoptions. In 2001, public adoptions accounted for about 40% of adoptions, up from 18% in 1992 (Flango & Flango, 1995; HHS, 2004), and international adoptions represented 15% of the adoptions in the United States, up from 5% in 1992 (HHS, 2004; U.S. Department of State, n.d.). The rise in public adoptions has shifted adoptive family demographics as those adopting from foster care are more likely to be single females and on average have lower incomes than private adoptive families or nonadoptive families (Barth, Gibbs, & Siebenaler, 2001; Casey Family Services [Casey], 2003; Howard, Smith, & Oppenheim, 2002). Children adopted from foster care are usually older; many are children of color, and many have spent a significant time in foster care prior to adoption. Most of these children have experienced difficult preadoptive life experiences, including abuse and neglect (Barbell & Freundlich, 2001; Casey, 2003). Approximately half of the children adopted internationally in 2001 were infants (defined as less than 1 year old), and half were more than 1 year old (E. B. Donaldson, n.d.-b), suggesting that many international adoptees have spent time in institutions prior to adoption (Grotevant, 2003). Numerous studies have elaborated on the complex special needs of foster care and institutionalized adoptees, and the levels of postadoption support required by their adoptive families, which can be different or more extensive than the needs of families who adopt healthy infants (Barbell & Freundlich, 2001; Casey, 2003; Dubowitz, 1999; Howard et al., 2002).

ADOPTEES AND ADOPTIVE FAMILIES IN CLINICAL SETTINGS

The question of whether adoptees are more at risk for psychological problems than non-adoptees has generated substantial controversy in the professional literature. Underlying the controversy are valid concerns about how professionals can recognize and acknowledge the very real issues faced by adoptees while not overpathologizing them. As a whole, the body of research suggests that while adoptees may be at increased risk for a variety of behavioral, psychological, and academic problems, the majority of adoptees are well within the normal range of functioning (Brodzinsky, 1987, 1993). Numerous studies have reported that adopted children and adolescents are referred for psychological counseling and residential treatment at a higher rate than that of their nonadopted peers (Brodzinsky, 1987, 1993; Haugaard, 1998; Ingersoll, 1997; Miller et al., 2000; Warren, 1992). While some studies suggest that adopted adolescents may experience more serious problems (e.g., Wierzbicki, 1993) or different types of problems (i.e., more acting-out or externalizing behaviors; Ingersoll, 1997), others have found no significant differences in the psychological problems and outcomes experienced by adoptees and nonadoptees (see O'Brien & Zamostny, 2003, for review), especially when their studies included community or nonclinical populations (Brodzinsky, 1993). In addition, differences found during childhood may not persist into adulthood as no significant adjustment differences were found between adopted and nonadopted adults (Borders, Penny, & Portnoy, 2000; Feigelman, 1997; Irhammar & Bengtsson, 2004). These results have led some researchers to suggest that the overrepresentation of adoptees in therapeutic settings is likely due to professional or parental referral bias, differential use of mental health services by adoptive parents, or other variables in the adoptees' or adoptive families' lives (Brodzinsky, 1993; Haugaard, 1998; Miller et al., 2000; Warren, 1992). These researchers suggested possible reasons for higher rates of parental referral, such as preexisting relationships of adoptive parents with mental health professionals, heightened vigilance for or reactivity to potential problems, likelihood of attributing the problem to adoption, and adoptive families' higher socioeconomic status and/or education levels.

Regardless of the underlying reasons for referral, research consistently suggests that adoptees and adoptive families are seen in therapeutic settings in a greater proportion than their incidence in the general population (see Brodzinsky, 1987; Haugaard, 1998; Warren, 1992; Wierzbicki, 1993, for review). Adoptees make up 5% of the children referred to mental health clinics, and 10% to 15% of the children in residential care and psychiatric inpatient settings (Brodzinsky, 1993). A study of adopted adults noted that more adoptees had sought counseling than their nonadopted friends (Borders et al., 2000). A survey of practicing clinical psychologists found that 5% to 10% of their patients are adoption triad members (Sass & Henderson, 2000). Therefore, most therapists in practice are likely to be working with adoption triad members on a fairly regular basis (Hartman & Laird, 1990; Post, 2000). As Hartman (1991) asserted, "Everyone offering counseling or clinical services under any auspice is faced daily with adoption issues" (p. 149); or, as Smith and Howard (1999) noted, "Every clinician is in post-adoption practice" (p. 26).

Research shows that adoptive parents consistently request that individual and family counseling be included in the array of available postadoption services (Barth & Miller, 2000; Berry, Martens, & Propp, 2005; Casey, 2003; Howard et al., 2002; Smith & Howard, 1999). One study in New York identified counseling as the most frequently requested postadoption service (Avery, 2004). Two studies elaborated further that the most common need identified by adoptive families was for qualified adoption-sensitive therapists and mental health professionals (Franz, 1993, as cited in Smith & Howard, 1999; Frey, 1986, as cited in Casey, 2003). This has caused researchers to identify postadoption counseling as a significant service requirement and to conclude that a critical need exists for trained professionals who are able to provide these services (e.g., Avery, 2004; Casey, 2003). One focus group of adoptive parents "described community providers as lacking in the understanding and skills needed to address the particular issues of adoptive children and families" (Gibbs,

Barth, & Lenerz, 2000, as cited in Barth et al., 2001, Section IV). Another study found that adoptive families sought services from up to 10 practitioners before finding one who understood their unique circumstances, and some families reported never finding such a professional (Frey, 1986, as cited in Casey, 2003). Authors have also expressed concern that too often adoptive families find themselves in the position of teaching therapists about the most basic issues of adoption (Casey, 2003; Sass & Henderson, 2000; Smith & Howard, 1999).

Many studies reported high usage of postadoption counseling services by adoptive families; however, they also noted that many of the families were dissatisfied with the services provided, particularly with the counselors' lack of knowledge regarding unique adoptive family issues (Smith & Howard, 1999). In fact, several postadoption service programs found that few of the adoptive families in their programs actually used the counseling services available even though they had requested clinical services (Barth et al., 2001). This may be due to negative prior clinical experiences such as those described in the foregoing. Another potential explanation was suggested by McRoy et al. (1988), who found that most families sought counseling from a number of clinicians prior to placing their adopted children in residential treatment. However, the families did not seek counseling at the agencies from which the children had been adopted or from other local agencies. The authors suggested possible reasons, including that the families were unaware of available postadoption services, were afraid the agency might take the child away if it became aware of problems, or were afraid that the agency might view them as unfit for adoptive parenthood. These findings suggest that adoptive families may turn more frequently to clinicians in private practice than to agencies, underscoring the need for increased adoption knowledge for all practicing clinicians.

STATUS OF THE COUNSELING PROFESSION: ADOPTION KNOWLEDGE AND COMPETENCE?

Despite the likelihood that adoption triad members will be encountered in clinical practice, many therapists have little real knowledge about adoption or are unprepared to deal with adoption issues when they surface in a clinical setting. While a small number of therapists identify themselves as specialists in adoption counseling, "many clinicians continue to be unaware of and unresponsive to adoption when it emerges in their caseloads" (Hartman & Laird, 1990, p. 223). Because adoption is often regarded as a function of the child welfare system, therapists operating outside the child welfare system may not see adoption as relevant to their practice (Hartman, 1991). However, even among professional social workers, who are often assumed to receive the most training in this area, the lack of adoption knowledge can be significant. As an executive of a child welfare agency noted, "It is amazing how many graduates of Masters Social Work programs have no sense of the importance of adoption to the emotional psyche of a child or adolescent" (Casey, 2003, p. 70).

In a survey of more than 200 practicing psychologists regarding their level of preparedness for dealing with adoption issues, 51% rated themselves as "somewhat prepared," 23% rated themselves as "not very prepared," and 90% reported that they needed more education in adoption (Sass & Henderson, 2000). Furthermore, half of the respondents reported that they did not routinely inquire whether their clients were adopted or were adoption triad members, suggesting that the psychologists did not consider adoption to be a significant factor affecting clients (Post, 2000). This supports previous research indicating that many clinicians in residential treatment centers were not aware of the adoptive status of their residents (McRoy et al., 1988; Miller et al., 2000).

Even when the adoptive status is known, adoption issues are often not raised. Research suggests that family therapists in outpatient settings often do not recognize the potential role of adoption when providing therapy to adoptive family members (McDaniel & Jennings, 1997). Therapists often receive referrals of adopted children who were in long-term inpatient, outpatient, or residential treatment in which adoption issues were never brought up, even though the referring clinician was aware the child was adopted (Rosenberg, 1992). In residential settings, the failure to focus on adoption issues in treatment was found even when staff members were aware of the disproportionately high level of adoptees in treatment (McRoy et al., 1988) and even when staff members identified adoption as an important issue in development and therapy (Dickson, Heffron, & Stephens, 1991). In addition, Dickson et al. (1991) found confusion and disagreement among staff members regarding whether adoption discussions should be initiated by the family or the therapist. The authors concluded that although many staff members viewed adoption as an important issue, adoption was not being addressed in a systemic way in inpatient settings, staff members were not knowledgeable about the impact of adoption on patients, and therapists were uncertain how to approach it in their caseloads.

It seems reasonable to assume that therapists are unlikely to view adoption as a potential issue for their clients if they have not been trained to recognize it as such. The literature is rife with concerns that clinicians are not receiving adequate training regarding the salience of adoption and the nature of issues faced by adoption triad members (Hartman, 1991; Hartman & Laird, 1990; Henderson, 2002; Jones, 1997; Pavao, 1998; Post, 2000; Rosenberg, 1992; Sass & Henderson, 2000). Post (2000) referred to the lack of adoption training for clinical psychologists as "astounding" (p. 370). One study found that 65% of practicing clinical psychologists surveyed reported never taking any courses dealing with adoption in graduate school, and 86% could not recall any courses dealing with adoption in their undergraduate programs (Sass & Henderson, 2000). Researchers have noted that course content is often determined by textbooks (Post, 2000), and several studies have documented the extremely limited coverage of adoption in psychology and family textbooks (Fisher, 2003a; Hall & Stolley, 1997; Stolley & Hall, 1994). A survey of clinical psychology professors (Post, 1999, as cited in Post, 2000) found that while instructors ranked adoption and foster care as relatively important topics for the training of therapists, they reported that these topics were the least taught of all survey topics. These findings suggest that it is highly unlikely that adoption-related issues are being taught in any meaningful degree in the standard curricula of most counseling or clinical psychology graduate school programs.

It is reasonable to assume that without proper professional training, therapists are likely to base their knowledge of adoption on popular media or informal information sources. This may serve to perpetuate misperceptions and stereotypes regarding adoption (Friedlander, 2003). Such a lack of knowledge may also cause therapists to downplay or overemphasize the impact of adoption on triad members (Rosenberg, 1992). Clearly, the literature supports the need for therapists to gain additional knowledge and training in issues that are relevant to adoptive families and the way adoption may affect adoption triad members, to ensure that competent services can be provided to these clients (e.g., Casey, 2003; Dickson, Heffron, & Parker, 1990; Hartman & Laird, 1990; McDaniel & Jennings, 1997; McRoy et al., 1988; Post, 2000; Sass & Henderson, 2000).

CLINICAL ISSUES FACING ADOPTION TRIAD MEMBERS

What are the issues of adoption that counselors need to be aware of to practice adoption-competent counseling? Drawing on the significant volume of research regarding the potential emotional challenges faced by adoption triad members, several themes are briefly mentioned here: loss, identity, variability of experience, acknowledgment of difference, and stigmatization.

Loss. For all members of the triad, adoption may be considered a process of integrating things lost and things found (Lifton, 1979; Rosenberg, 1992). Clinicians suggest that one of the primary challenges for the adoptee is coming to terms with the losses of adoption (Brodzinsky et al., 1993). The adopted child loses a sense of his or her genetic identity, his or her extended biological family, and for internationally adopted children, his or her birth culture. Grief is a common reaction to loss, yet it may be difficult for the adoptee to find an outlet for the grief, since his or her loss is generally not acknowledged by society (Brodzinsky et al., 1993; Jones, 1997; National Adoption Information Clearinghouse [NAIC], 2004). The adoptee's grief may manifest itself in feelings of anger, depression, anxiety, or fear, and these emotions may be experienced during childhood and adolescence and/or later in life, especially during life transitions. In addition, adoptees may feel a loss of control over their lives (Groza & Rosenberg, 1998) as well as powerlessness (Hartman & Laird, 1990).

Adoptive parents also experience loss, especially if they are adopting as a result of infertility: the loss of their hope for a biological child, a genetic legacy, the experience of pregnancy, and childbirth. Adoptive parents often feel defeated and powerless as a result of their struggle with infertility (Pavao, 1998). Issues of infertility may reemerge throughout the life cycle for adoptive parents (Groza & Rosenberg, 1998; Pavao, 1998) and may manifest themselves as generalized anxiety, depression, decreased self-image, difficulties in marital communications, or other forms (Brodzinsky, 1987). Adoptive parents may experience a loss or lack of support and acceptance from family and friends (Brodzinsky, 1987; Kirk, 1964) and may also lack confidence and struggle with issues of entitlement regarding their ability to parent (Brodzinsky, Smith, & Brodzinsky, 1998).

Research on birth mothers suggests that the impact of relinquishing a child may be life-long (Wiley & Baden, 2005). Birth mothers may experience a powerful sense of loss and isolation on relinquishment and have difficulty getting past the relinquishment (Brodzinsky, 1990; Wiley & Baden, 2005). They may experience reactions to unresolved grief throughout their lives (Brodzinsky, 1990), which may manifest as symptoms of depression, anxiety, and posttrauma (Wiley & Baden, 2005). Even when birth mothers report satisfaction with relinquishment and favorable outcomes, they may also experience continuing grief and loss (Wiley & Baden, 2005). Research on birth fathers is extremely limited (Freundlich, 2002), and, therefore, very little is known about the impact of relinquishment on them. Freeark et al. (2005) suggested that the marginalization of birth fathers permeates the adoptive process and may add to their feelings of powerlessness and disenfranchisement.

Identity. Another significant issue that may emerge for the adoptee is identity or the "lifelong search for self" (Brodzinsky et al., 1993, p. 12). Most researchers agree that the task of identity development is more complex for adoptees than for nonadoptees (Brodzinsky et al., 1998; Grotevant, 1997; Lifton, 2002; NAIC, 2004). Adoptees often experience a need for a biological link that can contribute to their sense of identity (Jones, 1997). Lack of information regarding their origins, including the identity of their birth parents and the reasons for their relinquishment, can complicate the formation of a complete and stable identity (Brodzinsky, 1987). Adoptees may struggle with feelings of duality regarding their identity and strive to consolidate a dual identity (Brodzinsky et al., 1993). They often feel a "split in the self" in accepting the identity of the adoptive family and effectively abandoning their birth mother and their "true" self, which may result in feelings of anxiety, isolation, and helplessness (Lifton, 2002). Identity issues also affect self-esteem, and studies have shown that adoptees may score lower on measures of self-esteem and self-confidence (Borders et al., 2000; Sharma, McGue, & Benson, 1996), often related to feelings of being different from their nonadopted peers (NAIC, 2004).

Researchers have defined *adoptive identity* as an individual's sense of identity as an adopted person (Grotevant, Dunbar, Kohler, & Esau, 2000, p. 381). In describing the developmental process of adoptive identity, Grotevant (1997) noted that all identity development "becomes increasingly complex as layers of 'differentness' are added" (p. 4), primarily because the dimensions of differentness usually involve things the person has not chosen. Thus, the adoptee must integrate the adoption into his or her total identity and "come to terms" with himself or herself in the adoptive family and cultural context. Such identity development may be especially complicated for transracial adoptees, compounded by a lack of physical similarity to their parents and their developing racial awareness and experience of discrimination (Brodzinsky et al., 1993). While many researchers describe identity development as a significant challenge for transracial adoptees, studies have found great variability in the racial and ethnic identity development and adjustment of transracial adoptees (Baden, 2002; Lee, 2003).

Variability of experience. Another thematic issue of adoption surrounds the variability of experience of adoptees, due in part to different adoptive and preadoptive experiences, as well as individual differences in temperament, resilience, personality, and perception. In many cases, it is not only the experience of adoption per se that affects children but their preadoption experiences, the nature of the transition from their pre- to postadoption lives, and their ability to integrate themselves into the life and culture of their adoptive families. Therefore, it is important that therapists do not overgeneralize the experience of some adoptees to all adoptees. In addition to individual differences, as in any family, the family structure and dynamics of the adoptive family will contribute to variability in the adjustment of the adoptee (Brodzinsky et al., 1998). Variability of experience is also true for the other members of the adoption triad. Friedlander (2003) notes that the variability of the experience and resulting emotional impact of adoption are as great within each of these three groups as they are among the three triad groups.

Acknowledgment of difference. Kirk (1964) was the first to suggest that adoptive families benefit from maintaining communication styles that acknowledge the differences between adoptive and biological families rather than rejecting or denying the difference. Subsequent research suggested that extreme styles of either "denial of difference" or "insistence of difference" were less likely to promote healthy adjustment (Brodzinsky, 1987, 1993). Brodzinsky (1987) also noted that parental styles may change over time to adapt to the child's developmental stage and family life cycle. Wegar (2000) noted that Kirk's original study found that adoptive parents' communication patterns developed as a means of coping with society's view of them (parents and children) as different; yet this reference to social context was disregarded in the subsequent literature.

Stigmatization. Adoption is generally viewed as a second-best means of forming a family (Bartholet, 1993; Friedlander, 2003; Pavao, 1998; Wegar, 2000). Numerous studies have noted society's ambivalence toward and stigmatization of adoption triad members, which may be rooted in the dual stigma of infertility and illegitimacy (Grotevant et al., 2000; Henderson, 2002; Leon, 2002; Wegar, 2000). For example, Brodzinsky et al. (1998) noted the common assumption that adoptees have less desirable genetic backgrounds. In addition, the structure of closed adoption contributes to a sense of secrecy and shame for those involved (Jones, 1997; Leon, 2002; Lifton, 1994). These societal attitudes affect adoption triad members in profound ways. The literature has described many ways in which adoptive family members experience and internalize social stigmatization in their lives (Leon, 2002; Wegar, 2000). In one study of adoptees, two thirds reported thinking that adoptive families were perceived as different and inferior to biological families; another study found that young adoptees may feel "different" or "bad," based on people's comments or behaviors (Rosenberg & Horner, 1991). Miall (1987) found the following stigmatizing themes: Adoptive families are seen as second-best because biological ties are assumed to be important for bonding and love; adopted children are seen as second-rate because of their unknown genetic past; and adoptive parents are not seen as "real" parents because of the lack of a biological tie. Wegar (2000) stressed the importance of recognizing the potential impact of marginalization and stigmatization of adoption triad members in both research and clinical work with triad members. Similarly, the development of the stress and coping theory of adoption adjustment (Brodzinsky et al., 1998; Smith & Brodzinsky, 1994) recognizes the impact of social stigmatization on adoptive families.

CLINICAL IMPLICATIONS OF THERAPISTS' LACK OF ADOPTION KNOWLEDGE

Missing, neglecting, or misunderstanding a core issue for a client is a highly undesirable outcome for any therapeutic relationship. The clinical and popular literature on adoption contains numerous accounts in which adoptees' underlying issues were not addressed in therapy because of therapists' lack of adoption knowledge (e.g., Andersen, 1993; McDaniel & Jennings, 1997; McRoy et al., 1988). Smith and Howard (1999) noted that when encountering issues related to adoption in their work, many clinicians

> will fail to understand the significance of adoption in the lives of clients . . . and its connection to other aspects of clients' struggles. They will miss the opportunity to help clients come to terms with this fundamental human issue. (p. 26)

In discussing loss, Brodzinsky et al. (1993) stated, "The result of loss is usually grieving, and adoption-sensitive clinicians see much of what has been called pathological in an adoptee's behavior is little more than the unrecognized manifestation of an adaptive grieving process" (p. 11). In discussing practice changes that resulted from increased adoption training at their facility, one agency leader reported, "Now we spend less time on the specific behavioral issues that brought the child into care and more time on the families' sense of loss, guilt about their ambivalence, and fear that they made a mistake" (Christine Gradert, personal communication, in Casey, 2003, p. 70). Gradert added,

> So often we hear adolescents say, "I don't want to be adopted," and we believe it. How different the lives of those children might be if we heard those words, and also heard the unspoken words, "I don't want to ever experience loss again—so I won't let myself get close to anyone." (p. 71)

Sass and Henderson (2000) cautioned that psychologists who do not consider adoption a serious issue may not be able to understand triad members' life experiences, which may hinder the psychologists' ability to competently treat these clients. In addition, they express concern that triad members may undergo inadequate treatment before a therapist recognizes adoption issues. Post (2000) warned, "The apparent lack of therapist training regarding the specific issues of adoption triad members puts these people at risk of being misunderstood and worse, misdiagnosed" (p. 371).

These concerns should give clinicians pause to assess their competence to treat adoption triad members. There are so many client-centered reasons for clinicians to be trained in adoption-related issues that further justification may seem unnecessary. However, there are also significant reasons based on the requirements and standards of the counseling profession that should compel us to seek adoption training. These reasons are related to the profession's commitment to multicultural competence.

MULTICULTURAL COMPETENCIES AND THE RELEVANCE TO ADOPTION

It is somewhat surprising how significantly issues of race, gender, socioeconomic status, ability status, sexual orientation, and so forth are inextricably linked to the adoption process (Bartholet, 1993). These factors affect which children are relinquished for adoption, which families will be allowed to adopt them, and which children may or may not be chosen to be adopted. Because of these links, adoption forces people "to think on a personal level about discrimination" (p. xvii). Given how closely adoption touches on elements of multicultural-ism and diversity, and how some of the salient challenges of adoption such as identity and stigmatization are also multicultural challenges, it seems worthwhile to examine adoption in light of multiculturalism, especially as it relates to clinical practice and counselor competencies.

In general usage, the terms *multiculturalism* and *diversity* are often used interchangeably and in the broadest sense refer to race, ethnicity, culture, language, gender, sexual orientation, age, physical ability status, class, socioeconomic status, education, and religion, all of which are considered critical aspects of an individual's ethnic, racial, and personal identity (American Psychological Association [APA], 2003). In the professional literature of U.S. psychology and counseling practice, the terms have been further clarified. In this context, *multicultural* refers primarily to ethnicity, race, and the culture related to the five primary cultural groups in the United States—African/Black, Asian, Caucasian/European, Hispanic/Latino, and Native American or indigenous peoples (Arredondo et al., 1996)—and the interaction between indi-viduals of these cultural groups and those of the dominant European American culture (APA, 2003). *Diversity* refers to other individual differences, including age, gender, sexual orienta-tion, religion, physical ability status, "or other characteristics by which someone may prefer to self-define" (Arredondo et al., 1996, p. 43). To further explain diversity, the Dimensions of Personal Identity Model (Arredondo & Glauner, 1992) was put forth as a means of describ-ing and discussing the individual differences and shared identity-based affiliations which help provide "a reference point for recognizing the complexity of all persons" (Arredondo et al., 1996, p. 44; see also Baden & Steward in Chapter 7 of this book). Inherent in discussions of the dimensions of personal identity is the recognition that these are characteristics a person is born with or born into, are not in the individual's control, and are fixed or relatively unchange-able. There is also recognition of the individual in context—how external forces affect personal life experiences. The model encourages counselors to acknowledge various dimensions of their own and clients' identity along three categories: *A dimensions*, which are fixed and out of the individual's control, such as race and gender; *C dimensions*, which include the social, histori-cal, political, and economic context of the individual's life; and *B dimensions*, which are more individually determined but which may also be seen as a result of the interactions of A and C, such as educational experience, marital status, and other nonvisible attributes.

The parallels between the Dimensions of Personal Identity and adoptive status are signif-icant. For adoptees, adoption is something that is chosen for them and which is rarely, if ever, in their control. In this respect it can be compared with gender, race, ethnicity, and sex-ual orientation as "an assigned feature of the self that must ultimately be integrated into the person's larger sense of identity" (Grotevant, 1997, p. 16). Research shows that adoptees often feel a lack of control in their lives based on the central fact of their adoption (Hartman & Laird, 1990). Like the Dimensions of Personal Identity, adoption often plays a significant role in identity development and presents specific challenges to individuals as they try to integrate their adoptive identity with other elements of their identity. Research on adoptive identity development (e.g., Brodzinsky et al., 1993; Grotevant, 1997; Grotevant et al., 2000; Lifton, 1998) suggests that for many adoption triad members, adoptive status may play a significant role in how they define themselves and in how they perceive they are defined by others. Adoption triad members experience stigmatization and discrimination based on their adoptive status (Fisher, 2003b; Wegar, 2000). The level of "visibility" of this dimension of identity varies depending on the phenotypical differences between adoptees and adoptive parents and may range from same-race adoptees who do not closely resemble their adoptive parents to transracial adoptees, whose adoptive status is obvious and inescapable. For trans-racial adoptees, the dimensions of racial and adoptive identity interact in complex ways and may vary at different points in an individual's life cycle (Baden, 2002; Freundlich, 2002; Lee, 2003). As with race, gender, physical ability status, sexual orientation, and other dimensions of identity, adoptive status is an aspect of identity that is influenced not only by how indi-viduals feel about their status but by how they are perceived by others. Furthermore, the social, historical, and political context of adoption is interwoven into the experience of adoption throughout the lives of adoption triad members.

It seems clear that the Dimensions of Personal Identity are highly relevant to work with adoption triad members and that this framework can help counselors understand and conceptualize the potential impact of adoption on a client. It also seems clear that the spirit and intent of the Multicultural Counseling Competencies apply to work with adoption triad members. Increasing practitioners' knowledge of adoption by providing additional training in adoption for psychologists and counseling professionals would certainly seem to be in keeping with the Multicultural Counseling Competencies adopted by the American Counseling Association, as well as the *APA Guidelines on Multicultural Education, Training, Research, Practice, and Organizational Change* (APA, 2003). While it is not the purpose of this chapter to urge that adoptive status be formally included in the list of Dimensions of Personal Identity, the strong similarities between adoptive status and the other identity dimensions suggest that adoptive status may be a dimension of personal identity that has thus far been ignored.

Even a cursory review of the counseling literature and counseling graduate programs reveals that the profession has embraced the understanding that competent counselors must be multiculturally competent. Sue (1998) defined *multicultural competence* as "the belief that people should not only appreciate and recognize other cultural groups but also be able to effectively work with them" (p. 440), an aim that seems self-evident for therapists. Given the current consideration in the counseling field for culturally sensitive counseling, it may be helpful for practitioners to consider adoptive status as an aspect of diversity and personal identity. This will provide counselors with a framework for approaching adoption in a way that allows them to be sensitive to the potential impact on their clients. It will also help them examine their own assumptions and biases regarding adoption and to evaluate their level of competency in working with adoption triad members.

Post (2000) noted that providing adoption training for psychologists in graduate psychology programs is in keeping with, and required by, program accreditation guidelines of the American Psychological Association (APA, 1995) under Domain D: Cultural and Individual Diversity. In a separate context, Hall (1997) described how people of color; women; and gay, lesbian, and bisexual individuals historically have been excluded from psychological research, practice, and education and training and called on the profession to rectify this neglect, in part by increasing education and training about diverse populations in graduate psychology curriculums. Post (2000) drew an analogy between the neglect of diverse populations and the neglect of adoption triad members and echoed Hall's (1997) remedy by urging that adoption topics be included in psychological research, practice, and education and training. In addition, Post (2000) and others (e.g., Jones, 1997) suggested that the exclusion of adoption topics in psychology programs and the professional literature parallels the adoptive family and societal fantasy that adoption does not exist and perpetuates unconscious biases against adoptees by maintaining secrecy and silence toward adoption.

ELEMENTS OF ADOPTION TRAINING

While many books have been written about the experiences of adoption triad members, little has been written about specific training for counselors desiring to work with adoption triad members (Janus, 1997). Authors calling for increased adoption training come from many different points of the adoption spectrum, from child welfare workers providing an array of public postadoption services, to adoptive parents of special needs children, to counseling psychologists teaching in graduate programs, to therapists encountering adoption-related issues in their clinical practice, and many others. Despite the variety of perspectives covered, a review of the literature reveals surprising consistency in what professionals and adoptive families believe is necessary for mental health professionals to know to provide adoption-sensitive counseling.

At the most basic level, counselors need to recognize that adoption is another means of forming a family and that the ways in which adoptive families form is different from biological families and has ramifications for adoptive family members. Counselors should understand that adoption is a lifelong process and that the importance of adoption in the life of a triad member may vary for individuals at different stages of their lives. Because of this, adoptive families may need episodic assistance at various points in a child's development or at periods of life transitions (Casey, 2003). Counselors should know that the meaning and importance of adoption will vary greatly from individual to individual. It is most important that counselors understand the role of loss and grief in adoption, and the ways in which unresolved grief may manifest itself for triad members. They should recognize the "normative crises" (Pavao, 1998) that may be experienced by adoption triad members, how adoption losses can reciprocally affect developmental tasks, and how transitions, life events, anniversaries, and so on may trigger a renewed sense of loss. It is important for counselors to approach these issues with the recognition that such reactions are normal and understandable responses to the losses experienced by the triad member and to provide appropriate support (Brodzinsky, 1987, 1993; Pavao, 1998).

Counselors need to understand the ways in which adoption may affect the identity, self-worth, and relationships of each member of the triad. They should acknowledge the impact of societal attitudes on adoption and recognize the ways in which subtle or overt stigmatization can affect adoption triad members (Wegar, 2000). It is very important to be aware of the challenges faced by transracial and international adoptees, who may be subjected to stigmatization on several fronts and whose identity challenges are even more complex (Baden, 2002; Lee, 2003). It is very useful for counselors to understand the legalities of adoption (Grotevant, 2003; Janus, 1997) and the legal choices that are made by triad members as well as to recognize the frustrations, fears, or helplessness that adoption triad members may experience by being exposed to the legal process, including the legal prohibition against adoptees obtaining information regarding their own birth and heritage. Knowledge of closed and open adoption, including varying levels of openness, the impact of secrecy on closed adoption, and potential benefits and detriments of degrees of openness can be significant for a counselor's understanding and guidance of clients. Counselors should also know what postadoption supports are available for adoptive families and be ready to help them access these supports (Barth et al., 2001; Casey, 2003). Counselors should also understand the complex emotions surrounding search and reunion activities for adoptees, birth parents, and adoptive parents to be able to provide appropriate guidance and support (Janus, 1997).

It is important that counselors recognize the overall resilience, strength, and positive coping abilities of adoptees and adoptive families, especially in light of the generally positive outcomes demonstrated through research (Borders et al., 2000; Friedlander, 2003; O'Brien & Zamostny, 2003; Zamostny, O'Brien, Baden, & Wiley, 2003). This will help the counselor to focus on the strengths and potential of adoptive families as the best resource for helping their adopted children (Casey, 2003) and may help mitigate the often sensational and negative media portrayals of adoption (Fisher, 2003b). Counselors should recognize that adoption is a highly successful way of forming a family and that for many children and parents it is the best alternative or solution for their collective circumstances. That recognition will help them focus on strengthening and supporting the adoptive family rather than blaming them for challenging outcomes (Smith & Howard, 1999). Counselors should accept adoptive parents as the people who know their children best and as the experts on their children (Howard et al., 2002). As Friedlander (2003) stated, "A major pitfall in working with children and adolescents is overlooking the need to strengthen the child's emotional bonds with the adoptive family and the community" (p. 747) or to strengthen the adoptive family system (Pavao, Groza, & Rosenberg, 1998). Finally, Rosenberg (1992) and others have cautioned therapists about the danger of either exaggerating or minimizing the relevance of adoption issues. A clinician must be well-informed about the complexities of adoption, yet careful not to "view all feelings and behavior through an adoption lens" (Rosenberg, 1992, p. 147). Rather, the clinician can try to understand the individual personality and lifelong development of each triad member as well as the context of his or her family and social systems.

REPRESENTATIVE TRAINING PROGRAMS AND PARTNERSHIPS

A review of the clinical and popular literature reveals some recent training programs that are attempting to address the critical need for adoption-competent professionals. These programs can be examined as potential models for training curriculum content and delivery. Examples were found through literature and Internet searches, and the list is not intended to be comprehensive. Programs identified range from state-run training programs for employees, training programs offered by adoption-competent agencies, university-based training programs and courses, and collaborations and partnerships between the three groups. While a number of sources are cited, a significant amount of information was found in a publication by Casey Family Services (Casey, 2003), which has contributed greatly to the literature regarding adoption-sensitive training.

Most states offer some form of direct postadoption support services, and some training information can be gleaned from a limited number of studies that examined outcomes and satisfaction levels of adoptive families using state-provided postadoption services. Studies were conducted for programs in Illinois, Iowa, Missouri, New York, and Oregon (Berry et al., 2005). All programs reportedly included some form of adoption training for professionals, but little specific information on that training was provided. One study (Berry et al., 2005) included an analysis of adoption preservation projects using Intensive Family Preservation Services in Illinois and Missouri. In both states, the content of the training programs for adoption preservation workers was said to be significantly enhanced by the inclusion of information relevant to adoptive families, such as grief and loss, attachment, parental expectations, and other topics. In Missouri's program, supplemental training topics were available to practitioners throughout the year, including a 2-day session focusing on the specific strengths, challenges, and issues of adoptive families. Based on positive outcomes of the Missouri and Illinois programs, the study recommended (among other things) that ongoing training should be emphasized for practitioners working on adoption preservation teams.

Colorado's Mental Health Assessment and Services Agencies were tasked with providing adoption-related services to the public, and in response, the agencies instituted a training program funded by an Adoption Opportunities Grant to increase the adoption competence of staff members. Practitioners were trained in issues related to attachment, loss, and grief that were significant for children in the child welfare system. The training model was also shared with the state of Utah. Casey (2003) noted that a valuable aspect of such training programs is that the adoption competence of those traines continues long after the grant has expired and the training program has ended.

In New York, a coordinated postadoption services program was launched in 2000 to serve adoptive families eligible for assistance under Temporary Assistance to Needy Families (TANF). Thirteen community-based agencies were given funding to allow them to provide services and training to adoptive families intended to strengthen the families' coping skills and avoid adoption dissolution and disruption. One of the agencies did not provide direct service to families but received funding specifically to provide training to the other participating agencies (Avery, 2004).

Collaboration among professionals can help advance adoption competence. In addition to providing direct adoption services, some agencies also provide training to other agencies or to state employees through consultation or training partnerships. One example of this is the Center for Adoption Support and Education (CASE) in Silver Spring, Maryland, which provides direct agency services as well as consultation and training to other child welfare and mental health programs to increase the adoption competence of their practitioners. Within the agency, CASE therapists are trained to use interventions with adoptive families to address the grief, loss, abandonment, and identity issues of the adoptive child and family. CASE therapists "are trained to look at child behavioral issues through a developmental lens . . . and to provide an intense therapeutic focus on ways to understand and manage feelings of grief and loss" (Casey, 2003, p. 40). The agency's Adoption-Centered Therapeutic

Approach treatment model is specifically geared for work with adoptive families. CASE training programs for professionals cover a variety of adoption topics, such as children's and adolescents' perceptions about adoption, how to talk to children about adoption, the role of loss in adoption, and providing therapy to adoptive families. Programs range from 2-hour presentations to full-day workshops. CASE also provides consultation and educational programs for school systems and develops materials for publication (CASE, n.d.-a).

Casey Family Services provides comprehensive postadoption services in Connecticut, New Hampshire, Maine, Rhode Island, and Vermont. Each division offers professional adoption training, typically through a collaboration of experienced staff members and adoptive families. Personnel from Casey Family Services Post-Adoption Programs and the Casey Center for Effective Child Welfare Policies serve as consultants to assist public and private agencies in postadoption service policy and practices, including adoption-competent training for professionals (Casey, 2003).

The Center for Family Connections in Cambridge, Massachusetts, offers training programs for adoptive families and professionals through its Family Connections Training Institute, Summer Intensives programs, and customized training programs. Center personnel are involved in adoption-training activities across the country in both public and private settings. In addition, the Center runs periodic training conferences, such as a 2005 full-day training conference in New York in conjunction with the Hunter University School of Social Work (Center for Family Connections, 2005, n.d.).

In Baltimore, Maryland, the Center for Adoptive Families (CAF), a program of Adoptions Together, Inc., developed an interview process to assess the adoption competency of its clinicians and required staff participation in an adoption training program. The training curriculum covers what CAF regards as core elements of adoption-competent practice, including (a) understanding children's reactions to separation, loss, and grief and the relationship to attachment; (b) understanding the individualized emotional issues of the adoptive family; (c) working with community systems to ensure that adoption-related concerns are understood and addressed; (d) sharing knowledge of developmental stages and expectations of children who have a history of neglect or abuse, separation, loss, and grief; (e) providing readings on adoption for adoptive families; (f) using children's and parents' support groups to normalize experiences; (g) shadowing by new staff members at home visits; (h) requiring participation in groups where children share their experiences; and (i) requiring exposure to the language and concepts of postadoption services (Casey, 2003). CAF awards continuing education units to participating Maryland social workers. CAF training materials have been used at Catholic University and the University of Maryland to introduce adoption issues to social work graduate students.

An example of adoption training in a residential care setting is the Nashua Children's Home in Nashua, New Hampshire (Casey, 2003). As the number of adoptees in care increased, the facility recognized the need for additional training in adoption issues. Staff members received training in how loss and grief affect the behavior of adopted children and the reactions of adoptive parents. Staff members began to ask questions at intake regarding the child's adoptive status and the family's perception of how adoption may be affecting current family situations. Staff were trained to address early traumatic experiences and unresolved birth family concerns. Staff members also began to inquire about the family's prior attempts to seek help in an effort to assess the impact of prior adverse experiences with mental health professionals.

Iowa's Family Resources, Inc., program was restructured in an attempt to make the organization better integrated and more adoption sensitive. As a result, "Every program now assesses for the impact of adoption on the behavior of the child and addresses adoptive family issues from a different systemic framework than they assess birth family issues" (Casey, 2003, p. 70). Interdisciplinary teams deliver services, and adoption-sensitive professionals are fully integrated into all aspects of the process.

Some states have also teamed with university graduate programs as a logical venue for professional adoption training programs. In addition, some university graduate adoption training has been initiated independent of state social service agencies. New Jersey's Division of Youth and Family Services' (DYFS) Adoption Program teamed with the School of Social Work at Rutgers University in New Jersey to develop the Adoption Practice Certificate Program for child welfare workers and mental health practitioners. The program includes nine full-day courses that meet once a month. Participants receive 5 continuing education hours per course. Participants earn an Adoption Practice Certificate from Rutgers's Continuing Education Program on completion of the 45-hour coursework. The curriculum is aimed at increasing practitioner knowledge of the core issues facing adoptive families and to "expand their clinical skill regarding attachment-focused, family centered and culturally-sensitive therapeutic interventions" (Casey, 2003, p. 52). The core curriculum courses include the psychology of adoption; issues of adoption with older children; life cycle experience of adoption for children adopted as infants; life cycle experience of adoption for older children; attachment-focused therapy for international or postinstitutionalized children; management of behavior problems and discipline for the traumatized child; individual and group therapy with adopted children, teens, and families; and special clinical issues in adoption (Rutgers University, n.d.).

The Northwest Adoption Exchange and Antioch University in Seattle, Washington, jointly developed a Post-Graduate Certificate in Foster Care and Adoption Therapy. Classes meet once a month for 9 months, for 10 hours on Friday and Saturday. The names of therapists who have completed the certificate program are provided to the Washington State Adoption Support Program for distribution to adoptive families seeking adoption-sensitive professionals. Course topics include foster care and adoption from the child's and parents' perspective; normal versus abnormal child psychological development; child sexual development and impact of sexual abuse; fetal alcohol syndrome/effect and other neurological issues; attachment and the assessment and diagnosis of reactive attachment disorder; trauma and the assessment and diagnosis of posttraumatic stress disorder; childhood disorders and other mental health issues; learning development and attention deficit hyperactive disorder; and adapting theoretical perspectives to work in foster care and adoption therapy (Antioch University, 2002; Casey, 2003). A similar program is offered in Oregon by Portland State University, the Oregon Post Adoption Resource Center, and the Oregon Department of Human Resources, which collaborate to sponsor the Therapy with Adoptive Families Postgraduate Certificate Program (Portland State University, n.d.).

In Maine, a partnership was developed between the state, Casey Family Services, and the University of Southern Maine's Maine Child Welfare Training Institute, which uses adoption-competency training materials from the Adoption Support and Preservation curriculum, developed with a federal Adoption Opportunities Grant by the National Resource Center for Special Needs Adoption at Spaulding for Children in Southfield, Michigan. The 3-day training is team-taught by an adoptive parent, an adoption-competent postadoption clinician, and an adoption caseworker. Practitioners are educated about the normal range of experiences of adopted children and their families as well as ways of helping to strengthen adoptive family relationships (Casey, 2003).

Montclair State University in New Jersey ran a semester-long seminar course in adoption issues titled "Counseling Adoption Triad Members" in spring 2005, as part of its graduate-level counseling course offerings (Montclair State University, 2005). Case Western Reserve University's graduate social work curriculum includes a course titled "Adoption: Practice and Policy" (E. B. Donaldson, n.d.-a). Gallaudet University's department of social work offered a graduate course titled "Adoptive Family Systems" in fall 2005 (CASE, n.d.-b). Antioch University of Los Angeles reportedly offers a graduate-level course on adoption (E. B. Donaldson, n.d.-a). These courses are a welcome and necessary addition to the training opportunities for students and professionals and may be able to serve as models for course offerings at other institutions. It is clear that many more courses of this nature will be necessary for meeting the need for adoption-competent clinicians and therapists.

Finally, some adoptive families have proactively worked to identify and assess the level of adoption competency of counseling professionals. Together as Adoptive Parents in

Harleysville, Pennsylvania, created an interactive Web site that provides data on therapists statewide. The information was obtained from a survey developed by adoptive families and sent to prospective adoption therapists. Questions included how many adoptive families the therapists work with on a regular basis; where they obtained their training; whether they have presented at any training conferences; what they consider to be the most significant issues facing adoptive families; and a description of their most effective intervention strategies. The Web site information is intended to help adoptive parents evaluate the adoption competency of therapists in their area (Casey, 2003) and may be indicative of future questions that clinicians will be asked by informed clients.

CONCLUSION

Even a brief look at the issue of adoption training makes apparent the need for providing better training in adoption to counseling professionals. A sizable population, including significant numbers of children and adolescents, is affected by this lifelong issue, which will not go away, but may change in salience and affect individuals differently at various points in their lives. For a variety of reasons, the members of this population are proportionately more likely to use counseling services than are the general public. If they do receive counseling, they run a significant risk of being misunderstood or misdiagnosed if their core issues are not properly addressed. If their core issues are properly acknowledged and addressed, outcomes for these clients are very good, and the benefits to the individuals and their families are significant. It is hard to imagine why the counseling profession would not choose to take immediate action to enhance counselor training in adoption-related issues, to ensure at least minimal levels of adoption competence across the profession. As Friedlander (2003) states, "As professionals, we should at least be knowledgeable enough to do no harm. At most, we can make a tangible contribution to the lives of this too vulnerable population of children and parents" (p. 751).

REFERENCES

American Psychological Association. (1995). *Guidelines and principles for accreditation of programs in professional psychology.* Washington, DC: Author.

American Psychological Association. (2003). Guidelines on multicultural education, training, research, practice, and organizational change for psychologists. *American Psychologist, 58*(5), 377–402.

Andersen, R. A. (1993). *Second choice: Growing up adopted.* Chesterfield, MO: Badger Hill Press.

Antioch University. (2002). *Journeys: The newsletter for Antioch University Seattle alumni.* Retrieved February 12, 2006, from www.antiochsea.edu/alumni/journeys/02fall.pdf

Arredondo, P., & Glauner, T. (1992). *Personal dimensions of identity model.* Boston: Empowerment Workshops. Retrieved December 1, 2005, from www.counseling.org/Personal+Identity[1].pdf

Arredondo, P., Toporek, R., Brown, S., Jones, J., Locke, D. C., Sanchez, J., et al. (1996). Operationalization of multicultural counseling competencies. *Journal of Multicultural Counseling and Development, 24,* 42–78.

Avery, R. J. (2004). *Strengthening and preserving adoptive families: A study of TANF-funded post adoption services in New York State.* Retrieved December 22, 2004, from www.nysccc .org/Post%20Adoption%20Services/TANFAveryPASrpt.pdf (Web site of New York Citizens' Coalition for Children, Inc.).

Baden, A. L. (2002). The psychological adjustment of transracial adoptees: An application of the cultural-racial identity model. *Journal of Social Distress and the Homeless, 11*(2), 167–191.

Barbell, K., & Freundlich, M. (2001). *Foster care today.* Washington, DC: Casey Family Programs. Retrieved December 26, 2005, from www.casey.org/Resources/Archive/Publications/FosterCare Today.htm

Barth, R. P., Gibbs, D. A., & Siebenaler, K. (2001). *Assessing the field of post-adoption service: Family needs, program models, and evaluation issues.* Chapel Hill and Research Triangle Park: University of North Carolina School of Social Work, Jordan Institute for Families, and Research Triangle Institute. Retrieved December 3, 2005, from http://aspe.hhs.gov/hsp/PASS/lit-rev-01.htm

Barth, R. P., & Miller, J. (2000). Post-adoption services: What are the empirical foundations? *Family Relations, 49,* 447–455.

Bartholet, E. (1993). *Family bonds: Adoption and the politics of parenting.* New York: Houghton Mifflin.

Berry, M., Martens, P., & Propp, J. (2005). *The use of intensive family preservation services with post-adoptive families.* National Family Preservation Network. Retrieved February 1, 2006, from www.nfpn.org/news/2005/files/IFPS-AdoptReport.pdf

Borders, L. D., Penny, J. M., & Portnoy, F. (2000). Adult adoptees and their friends: Current functioning and psychosocial well-being. *Family Relations, 49,* 407–418.

Brodzinsky, A. B. (1990). Surrendering an infant for adoption. In D. M. Brodzinsky & M. D. Schechter (Eds.), *The psychology of adoption.* New York: Oxford University Press.

Brodzinsky, D. M. (1987). Adjustment to adoption: A psychosocial perspective. *Clinical Psychology Review, 7,* 25–47.

Brodzinsky, D. M. (1993). Long term outcomes in adoption. *Future of Children, 3*(1), 153–166.

Brodzinsky, D. M, Schechter, M. D., & Henig, R. M. (1993). *Being adopted: The lifelong search for self.* New York: Anchor Books.

Brodzinsky, D. M., Smith, D. W., & Brodzinsky, A. B. (1998). *Children's adjustment to adoption.* Thousand Oaks, CA: Sage.

Casey Family Services. (2003). *Strengthening families & communities: An approach to post-adoption service.* Retrieved December 22, 2005, from http://161.58.194.157/pdfs/PASwhitepaper2002.pdf

Center for Adoption Support and Education. (n.d.-a). *Training for professionals.* Retrieved January 15, 2006, from www.adoptionsupport.org/train/train_prof.php

Center for Adoption Support and Education. (n.d.-b). *What's new?* Retrieved January 15, 2006, from www.adoptionsupport.org/new/index.php

Center for Family Connections. (2005). *What do families by adoption and complex families need from professionals?* Retrieved January 14, 2005, from www.njarch.org/images/CFFCNYJan2005_training_brochure.pdf

Center for Family Connections. (n.d.). *Training and technical assistance.* Retrieved January 15, 2005, from www.kinnect.org/training.html

Dickson, L. R., Heffron, W. M., & Parker, C. (1990). Children from disrupted and adoptive homes on an inpatient unit. *American Journal of Orthopsychiatry, 60,* 594–602.

Dickson, L. R., Hefron, W. M., & Stephens, S. (1991). Discussing adoption in therapy. *Journal of the American Academy of Child and Adolescent Psychiatry, 30*(1), 155.

Dubowitz, H. (1999). The families of neglected children. In M. E. Lamb (Ed.), *Parenting and child development in "nontraditional" families.* Mahwah, NJ: Lawrence Erlbaum.

Evan B. Donaldson Adoption Institute. (1997). *Benchmark adoption survey: Report on the findings.* Washington, DC: Princeton Survey Research. Retrieved December 29, 2005, from www .adoptioninstitute.org/survey/Benchmark_Survey_1997.pdf

Evan B. Donaldson Adoption Institute. (n.d.-a). *Adoption training curriculum.* Retrieved January 14, 2006, from www.adoptioninstitute.org/proed/procurric.html

Evan B. Donaldson Adoption Institute. (n.d.-b). *International adoption facts.* Retrieved December 30, 2005, from www.adoptioninstitute.org/FactOverview/international.html

Feigelman, W. (1997). Adopted adults: Comparisons with persons raised in conventional families. *Marriage and Family Review, 25,* 199–223.

Fisher, A. P. (2003a). A critique of the portrayal of adoption in college textbooks and readers on families, 1998–2001. *Family Relations, 52,* 154–160.

Fisher, A. P. (2003b). Still "not quite as good as having your own"? Toward a sociology of adoption. *Annual Review of Social Work, 29,* 335–361.

Flango, V., & Flango, C. (1995). How many children were adopted in 1992? *Child Welfare, 74,* 1018–1032.

Freeark, K., Rosenberg, E. B., Bornstein, J., Jozefowicz-Simbeni, D., Linkevich, M., & Lohnes, K. (2005). Gender differences and dynamics shaping the adoption life cycle. *American Journal of Orthopsychiatry, 75*(1), 86–101.

Freundlich, M. (2002). Adoption research: An assessment of empirical contributions to the advancement of adoption practice. *Journal of Social Distress and the Homeless, 11*(2), 143–166.

Friedlander, M. L. (2003). Adoption: Misunderstood, mythologized, marginalized. *The Counseling Psychologist, 31*(6), 745–752.

Grotevant, H. D. (1997). Coming to terms with adoption: The construction of identity from adolescence into adulthood. *Adoption Quarterly, 1*(1), 3–27.

Grotevant, H. D. (2003). Counseling psychology meets the complex world of adoption. *The Counseling Psychologist, 31*(6), 753–762.

Grotevant, H. D., Dunbar, N., Kohler, J. K., & Esau, A. M. (2000). Adoptive identity: How contexts within and beyond the family shape developmental pathways. *Family Relations, 49*(4), 379–387.

Groza, V., & Rosenberg, K. F. (1998). Treatment issues of adoptees placed as infants and as older children: Similarities and differences. In V. Groza & K. F. Rosenberg (Eds.), *Clinical and practice issues in adoption: Bridging the gap between adoptees placed as infants and as older children.* Westport, CT: Praeger.

Hall, C. C. (1997). Cultural malpractice: The growing obsolescence of psychology with the changing U.S. population. *American Psychologist, 52*(6), 642–651.

Hall, K. S., & Stolley, E. J. (1997). A historical analysis of the presentation of abortion and adoption in marriage and family textbooks: 1950–1987. *Family Relations, 46*(1), 73–82.

Hartman, A. (1991). Every clinical social worker is in post-adoption practice. *Journal of Independent Social Work, 5,* 149–163.

Hartman, A., & Laird, J. (1990). Family treatment after adoption: Common themes. In D. M. Brodzinsky & M. D. Schechter (Eds.), *The psychology of adoption.* New York: Oxford University Press.

Haugaard, J. J. (1998). Is adoption a risk factor for the development of adjustment problems? *Clinical Psychology Review, 18,* 47–69.

Henderson, D. B. (2002). Challenging the silence of the mental health community on adoption issues. *Journal of Social Distress and the Homeless, 11*(2), 131–141.

Hollinger, J. H. (1993). Adoption law. *Future of Children, 3*(1), 43–61.

Howard, J. A., Smith, S. L., & Oppenheim, E. (2002). *Sustaining adoptive families: A qualitative study of public post-adoption services.* Washington, DC: American Public Human Services Association.

Ingersoll, B. D. (1997). Psychiatric disorders among adopted children: A review and commentary. *Adoption Quarterly, 1,* 57–73.

Irhammar, M., & Bengtsson, H. (2004). Attachment in a group of adult international adoptees. *Adoption Quarterly, 8*(2), 1–25.

Janus, N. G. (1997). Adoption counseling as a professional specialty area for counselors. *Journal of Counseling & Development, 75,* 266–274.

Jones, A. (1997). Issues relevant to therapy with adoptees. *Psychotherapy, 34*(1), 64–68.

Kirk, H. D. (1964). *Shared fate: A theory of adoption and mental health.* London: Free Press of Glencoe.

Lee, R. M. (2003). The transracial adoption paradox: History, research, and counseling implications of cultural socialization. *The Counseling Psychologist, 31*(6), 711–744.

Leon, I. G. (2002). Adoption losses: Naturally occurring or socially constructed? *Child Development, 73*(2), 652–663.

Lifton, B. J. (1979). *Lost and found: The adoption experience.* New York: Dial.

Lifton, B. J. (1994). *Journey of the adopted self: A quest for wholeness.* New York: Basic Books.

Lifton, B. J. (1998). Shared identity issues. In V. Groza & K. Rosenberg (Eds.), *Clinical and practice issues in adoption: Bridging the gap between adoptees placed as infants and as older children.* Westport, CT: Praeger.

Lifton, B. J. (2002). The adoptee's journey. *Journal of Social Distress and the Homeless, 11*(2), 207–213.

McDaniel, K., & Jennings, G. (1997). Therapists' choice of treatment for adoptive families. *Journal of Family Psychotherapy, 8*(4), 47–68.

McRoy, R. G., Grotevant, H. D., & Zurcher, L. A. (1988). *Emotional disturbance in adopted adolescents: Origins and development.* New York: Praeger.

Miall, C. E. (1987). The stigma of adoptive parent status: Perceptions of community attitudes toward adoption and the experience of informal social sanctioning. *Family Relations, 36,* 34–39.

Miller, B. C., Fan, X., Grotevant, H. D., Christensen, M., Coyl, D., & van Dulamen, M. (2000). Adopted adolescents' overrepresentation in mental health counseling: Adoptees' problems or parents' lower threshold for referral? *Journal of the American Academy of Child and Adolescent Psychiatry, 39*(12), 1504–1511.

Montclair State University. (2005). *Course bulletin.* Montclair Heights, NJ: Author.

National Adoption Information Clearinghouse. (2004). *Impact of adoption on adopted persons: A factsheet for families.* Retrieved December 27, 2005, from http://naic.acf.hhs.gov/pubs/f_ adimpact.cfm

O'Brien, K. M., & Zamostny, K. P. (2003). Understanding adoptive families: An integrative review of empirical research and future directions for counseling psychology. *The Counseling Psychologist, 31*(6), 679–710.

Pavao, J. M. (1998). *The family of adoption.* Boston: Beacon Press.

Pavao, J. M., Groza, V., & Rosenberg, K. F. (1998). Treatment issues in adoption practice from a triad and systemic perspective. In V. Groza & K. F. Rosenberg (Eds.), *Clinical and practice issues in adoption: Bridging the gap between adoptees placed as infants and as older children.* Westport, CT: Praeger.

Portland State University. (n.d.). *Program overview: Therapy with adoptive families: Post-graduate certificate program.* Retrieved February 10, 2006, from www.ceed.pdx.edu/adoption/certificate .shtml

Post, D. E. (2000). Adoption in clinical psychology: A review of the absence, ramifications, and recommendations for change. *Journal of Social Distress and the Homeless, 9*(4), 361–372.

Rosenberg, E. B. (1992). *The adoption life cycle.* New York: Free Press.

Rosenberg, E. B., & Horner, T. M. (1991). Birthparent romances and identity formation in adopted children. *American Journal of Orthopsychiatry, 61,* 70–77.

Rutgers University. (n.d.). *New Jersey adoption certificate program description.* Retrieved December 20, 2005, from www.nrcadoption.org/resources/prac/NewJerseyPostAdoptionProgram.pdf

Sass, D. A., & Henderson, D. B. (2000). Adoption issues: Preparation of psychologists and an evaluation of the need for continuing education. *Journal of Social Distress and the Homeless, 9*(4), 349–359.

Sharma, A. R., McGue, M. A., & Benson, P. L. (1996). The emotional and behavioral adjustment of United States adopted adolescents: Part I. A comparison study. *Children and Youth Services Review, 18,* 77–94.

Smith, D. W., & Brodzinsky, D. M. (1994). Stress and coping in adopted children: A developmental study. *Journal of Clinical Child Psychology, 23*(1), 91–99.

Smith, S. L., & Howard, J. A. (1999). *Promoting successful adoptions: Practice with troubled families.* Thousand Oaks, CA: Sage.

Stolley, K. S. (1993). Statistics on adoption in the United States. *Future of Children: Adoption, 3*(1), 26–42.

Stolley, K. S., & Hall, E. J. (1994). The presentation of abortion and adoption in marriage and family textbooks. *Family Relations, 43*(3), 267–273.

Sue, S. (1998). In search of cultural competence in psychotherapy and counseling. *American Psychologist, 53*(4), 440–448.

U.S. Census Bureau. (2003). *Adopted children and stepchildren: 2000: Census 2000 special reports.* Retrieved January 15, 2006, from www.census.gov/prod/2003pubs/censr-6.pdf

U.S. Department of Health and Human Services. (2004). *How many children were adopted in 2000 and 2001?* Washington, DC: National Adoption Information Clearinghouse. Retrieved December 30, 2005, from http://naic.acf.hhs.gov/pubs/s_adopted/index.cfm

U.S. Department of Health and Human Services Adoption and Foster Care Analysis and Reporting System. (2002). *AFCARS user's guide annual supplement, 1996.* Retrieved December 26, 2005, from www.ndacan.cornell.edu/NDACAN/Datasets/UserGuidePDFs/080_AFCARS_1996_ Supplement.pdf

U.S. Department of Health and Human Services, Adoption and Foster Care Analysis and Reporting System. (2005). *AFCARS user's guide annual supplement, 2003.* Retrieved December 26, 2005, from www.ndacan.cornell.edu/NDACAN/Datasets/UserGuidePDFs/118_AFCARS_2003v1_ Supplement.pdf

U.S. Department of State. (n.d.). *Immigrant visas issued to orphans coming to the U.S.* Retrieved December 26, 2005, from http://travel.state.gov/family/adoption_resources _02.html

Warren, S. B. (1992). Lower threshold for referral for psychiatric treatment for adopted adolescents. *Journal of the American Academy of Child and Adolescent Psychiatry, 31*(3), 512–517.

Wegar, K. (2000). Adoption, family ideology, and social stigma: Bias in community attitudes, adoption research, and practice. *Family Relations, 49*(4), 363–369.

Wierzbicki, M. (1993). Psychological adjustment of adoptees: A metaanalysis. *Journal of Clinical Child Psychology, 22,* 447–454.

Wiley, M. O., & Baden, A. L. (2005). Birth parents in adoption: Research, practice, and counseling psychology. *The Counseling Psychologist, 33*(1), 130–150.

Zamostny, K. P., O'Brien, K. M., Baden, A. L., & Wiley, M. O. (2003). The practice of adoption: History, trends, and social context. *The Counseling Psychologist, 31*(6), 651–678.

Psychologists' Self-Reported Adoption Knowledge and the Need for More Adoption Education

20

DANIEL A. SASS

University of Wisconsin–Milwaukee

DOUGLAS B. HENDERSON

University of Wisconsin–Stevens Point

Those most directly influenced by adoption are members of the adoption triad: the adoptee, adoptive parents, and birth parents. However, the impact extends to birth and adoptive siblings, grandparents, aunts and uncles, and cousins, as well as other members of both the birth and adoptive families. Thus, there may be 25 to 30 people affected in virtually every adoption. Data from 2000 and 2001 (National Adoption Information Clearinghouse, n.d.) indicate that every year in the United States there are more than 127,000 new adoptions, and U.S. Census data in 2000 showed 2,058,915 adopted children living in households in the United States (U.S. Census Bureau, n.d.). It is generally believed that, including adult adoptees, approximately 2% of the U.S. population is adopted (Brodzinsky, 1990). Counting only the census-reported adopted children and their birth and adoptive parents, there are at least 5 million individuals living in the United States today with a direct connection to adoption. Despite the large number of people living with adoption, little is understood about the implications of the adoption experience and about the complications that may occur later in life.

The effects of the adoption process begin long before the birth, or even the conception, of the adoptee. The doll play of young girls is, in a sense, the beginning of their attachment to the babies they hope to have and raise in the future. Both men and women often spend years in anticipation of being parents. For the birthmother, the conception itself may be traumatic, as in cases of rape or incest. At some point after conception, the birthmother realizes that she may be unable to provide the kind of life for her child that she dreamt of during her own childhood. Issues for the adoptive parents often arise with the inability to conceive their own child and the realization that adoption may be their last resort (Daly, 1988, 1990). The adoptive mother faces the fact that the child she will be raising will not have been born to her. For many adoptees, problems often occur as early as the beginning of their prenatal development due to their birthmother's poor prenatal care, depressed mood, or anxiety about giving up her child. After birth, the adoptee is often immediately separated from the birthmother to eliminate any attachment that might occur between the two (Silverman, Campbell, Patti, & Style, 1988).

Earlier studies have indicated that adoptees are overrepresented in therapy. Dickson, Heffron, and Parker (1990) reported that adopted children represent 11.7% of the psychiatric inpatient population and appear at higher risk of returning to a psychiatric hospital after being discharged (13.6% for adoptees vs. 7.2% for nonadoptees) (Dickson et al., 1990; Dickson, Stevens, Heffron, & Parker, 1991). These results may be understood in part by the increased number of difficulties adopted children encounter during their life cycle and their search for answers about their past, as well as by an increased likelihood of adoptive parents to seek help for their children (Miller et al., 2000). According to Brodzinsky (1987, 1990, 1993), few adjustment differences between adoptees and nonadoptees can be found prior to 5 to 7 years of age, because it is at approximately 5 that adoptees begin to develop an understanding of adoption and realize they are different from other children. Following Piaget's cognitive developmental model, Miller (1997) believes the reality of the adoption for adoptees becomes more intense during adolescence. It is at this stage that they develop abstract thoughts, consider multiple possibilities, and make complex logical arguments about their past. These advanced cognitive processes allow adoptees to fully consider issues such as abandonment, loss, rejection, betrayal, self-worth, identity, separation, and trust of other people (Hall, 1997).

Researchers have published limited information that deals with the effects of adoption on birth parents and adoptive parents. Nevertheless, adoption is a lifelong process, which continues to affect both sets of parents (Henderson, 2002). For many adoptive parents, adoption is their last option for having a family; however, they have still not exactly "had" a child (Deutsch, 1945). This implication can have effects on both the child and the adoptive parents. Different phenotypes may constantly remind the adoptive family of their genetic differences, which can create two separate identities inside the family (Deutsch, 1945; Toussieng, 1962).

Nevertheless, the adoptive parents still need to accept their adopted children for who they are and not hold differences against them (Hollingsworth, 1998). Also, adoptive parents should not interpret their child's misbehavior as being innately deviant or become upset when their children enjoy activities different from those of their parents. Instead, adoptive parents need to understand that their children are creating their own identity, which may ultimately bear similarities to that of their birth parents.

Another challenge for adoptive parents is the idea of a birth parent-adoptee reunion. Many adoptive parents fear that a reunion may destroy the closeness of the adoptive family or that the adoptee, finding people who are genetically similar, might prefer the birth parent to them (Daly, 1988). Adoptees often fear that their adoptive parents will be hurt by their desire for a reunion and so do not include their parents in the search and reunion process (Hollingsworth, 1998). Weiss (1984) believes sensing a fear-motivated lack of closeness with the adoptive parents causes harm to the adoptee and may instigate searching. Weiss's notion is supported by previous research that suggests adoptive parents often have psychological conflicts concerning their inability to sexually reproduce. Brown (1959) stated that this conflict is what, in fact, causes intimacy issues and attachment difficulties toward the child. For some adoptive parents, the adoption serves as a constant reminder of their inability to have children, while others view adoption and the adopted child as the savior of their marriage. Still others believe that the child was necessary to prove their femininity or masculinity (Schechter, 1960). None of these potential issues arising within the adoptive family produce a positive situation for child rearing.

The majority of adoptive parents (69%) adopt due to infertility, but more than a quarter of adoptive parents (27%) report they adopt for altruistic reasons (Fisher, 2003). These altruistic parents adopt for the sole reason of sharing their home with a child who otherwise would not have the benefits of an intact family. This is certainly a noble motivation, and in a world without infertility it would be the only ideal reason for adoptions. In fact, in New Zealand, the Children, Young Persons, and Their Families Act of 1989 removed the consideration of the adoptive parents' need or desire for children and made placement with the child's birth kin the preferred choice when a birth parent was unable to keep a child. Adoption in New Zealand is now less about finding children for families, and more about finding families for children. Unfortunately, regardless of the motivation for adoption, adoptees are left in the position of having been done an immense favor by both their adoptive parents and society, and their natural curiosity about their birth families may be seen as an ungrateful response to this favor (Henderson, 2002).

Many adoptees may also act out to test the love and loyalty of the adoptive parents, to determine whether they too will "abandon" them, as they fear was the case with their birth parents (Brinich, 1980). If these tests become too extensive they may actually provoke the outcome the adoptee fears will occur. For this reason, it is important for adoptive families to recognize this self-destructive behavior and get assistance before a disruption occurs. It is important for therapists and counselors to be aware of this testing process, to monitor the situation, and to inform the adoptive parents of this potential problem.

Adoption is also a last resort for many birth parents as well. Few girls dream of bearing a child they will not raise, and few women get pregnant with the intent of giving their child up for adoption. Women who surrender children for adoption often do so because of the lack of financial resources and emotional support from the birth father, family, and social service agencies (Silverman et al., 1988). At least in the past, once the child was surrendered, adoption agencies frequently encouraged birth parents to forget the adoption experience and return to living their prepregnancy life. These same agencies often convinced birth parents that the child would be better off in another home with parents better qualified to raise a child. Many birthmothers report adoption agencies often pushed for adoption even when they preferred to keep their child (Silverman et al., 1988). These authors also found that birth parents whose counselors encouraged adoption were more likely to search later in life than birth parents who voluntarily surrendered their child. Silverman et al. (1988) reported that 79% of birth parents searched for their children and 74% of birth parents were in some type of adoption reform group. It would appear that birth parents do not overcome their feelings of loss. Instead, it is counselors who appear to be misinformed about the effects of adoption on birth parents. For this reason, it is important that birth parents have qualified counselors to prepare them for issues that may arise after the adoption.

Adoptees search for many reasons. They wish to obtain answers to why the birth parents "left them," and also to answer some important questions about themselves. Most adoptees are interested in understanding their genetic characteristics and where certain traits arise from (Jago Krueger & Hanna, 1997). By answering these questions, adoptees are better able to establish a complete and integrated identity, which is a crucial building block for self-esteem (Jones, 1997). More than 60 years ago, Clothier (1943) realized the importance of a relationship with the biological parents and stated that adoption professionals underestimated the repercussions for children who do not know their genetic history and have trouble finding their personal identity.

Delays in placement and problems with the legal system are just some of the other potential problems with the adoption process. The disruption of contact between birthmother and child after birth can produce an early attachment problem, which can be seen in these individuals later in life (Verrier, 1993). Except in some open adoptions, adoptive parents also miss the experience of the birth and lack the early attachment that often begins even before conception.

There have been numerous reports by triad members who have been told by psychologists to "forget about the experience" and "move on with their lives" (Henderson, 2002; Kirschner,

1990). It is now clear that adoption experiences will remain with triad members throughout their lives. A therapist knowledgeable in the dynamics of adoption might better assist triad members in understanding their problems with adoption and assist them in the resolution of the problems. Unfortunately, adoption issues do not seem to be included in the education of many psychologists (Post, 2000) and marriage and family therapists (Fisher, 2003).

Beginning in 1985, the second author became active in local, state, and national adoption search and support groups, in particular in the American Adoption Congress. Conversations over those years with numerous triad members revealed many adoption-related issues that seemed largely unknown to therapists, leading them to make ill-advised statements in therapy.

For example, therapists have suggested that adoptees should "be grateful you were adopted." Many adoptees experience the loss of their birth family, whether they feel the loss of actual contact (the loss of "growing up together") or the loss of knowledge (having unanswered questions such as "why am I the only musician in my adoptive family?" or "why would a parent give up a child?"). Being told to be grateful for a process that produced these losses is not therapeutic. The often-used phrase "your birthmother loved you so much she gave you up," heard by adoptees mostly from their adoptive parents and the general public, but occasionally in therapy, is not only untherapeutic but illogical. Expecting adoptees who may already be experiencing difficulties with the attachment/commitment process to understand that "loving" and "giving away" are in some way related is not a service to them.

Birth parents have been told to "think of your child as having died" to help them to deal with their loss. Far from this, most birth parents hope desperately that their child is alive. Had they not wanted the child to live, they might well have made a very different decision about their pregnancy. And if they think of the adoption process as a death, then who was the cause of that death? For birth parents who are hoping to learn that their surrendered child is alive and happy, such advice is not therapeutic.

Adoptive parents have been told that if they loved their adopted child "well enough" or "as if the child was your own biological child," then all would be well. For adoptive parents whose child is displaying problems, even if these problems have nothing to do with adoption, such advice only adds to their sense of inadequacy, compounding it for infertile adoptive parents. And the fact is that we simply do not know what effect, if any, the adoption process has on attachment and bonding. We do know that for many adopted children, at best, there has been a discontinuity in these processes. Laying the blame for adoptees' problems at the adoptive parents' feet is not therapeutic.

The first steps for an effective therapist are to help triad members recognize the key issues and aid in their resolution by being sympathetic and understanding. Only then can the issues of the triad member be worked out (Russell, 1996). These skills need to be taught before psychologists start treating clients, because too often at present it seems the clients are educating psychologists on the issues triad members encounter.

A very common topic at adoption support group meetings is disappointment with therapists who were either not informed about adoption, or worse, downplayed the importance of adoption in the client's life. Triad members often report having seen multiple therapists before they found one who would even discuss adoption, let alone one who was knowledgeable about adoption issues. Good adoption therapists are few and far between, and when a support group member finds a therapist who "knows adoption," that therapist's name is eagerly sought after and willingly shared. Often, it turns out that the reason a particular therapist is "good with adoption issues" is because the therapist is already an adoption triad member himself or herself, or because the therapist learned about adoption from a previous client. All too often, even clients of knowledgeable therapists report they often felt that as clients they were providing as much help to their therapist with education about adoption issues as they were getting back from their therapist.

It is important that therapists be properly trained in adoption issues, if not before receiving their graduate degree, then as part of the continuing education process. We have presented a summary of many of the issues that arise in adoptions, both as grounds for including adoption in the education of psychologists and as an introduction to their nature.

In this chapter, we report on a survey of licensed psychologists conducted to assess their level of knowledge of adoption issues. Our hypotheses are the following: (1) Psychologists lack sufficient education in adoption issues to treat clients effectively, and (2) many psychologists do not consider adoption to be a serious problem facing triad members.

METHOD

Participants

Data were gathered using a questionnaire mailed to 497 psychologists randomly selected from the 15th edition (1997) of the *National Register of Health Service Providers in Psychology*. This sample represented approximately 50% of the psychologists listed in the *National Register* who had received a doctoral degree between 1990 and 1996. Only data from psychologists currently treating clients were included in the study. Of the 497 psychologists, 221 responded (45.4% of those to whom the questionnaires were distributed), of whom 11 were eliminated because they were not currently treating clients. Participants came from all geographic areas of the United States, and one participant came from Canada. Unfortunately, gender and age were inadvertently omitted from the questionnaire and are not available for the participants who constitute our sample. However, of the 497 psychologists sent questionnaires, 217 (44%) were male and 280 (56%) were female. The respondents are assumed to represent the gender and age distribution found in the sample taken from the *National Register* and therefore likely represent the population of psychologists trained in the early to mid-1990s who are currently treating clients.

Instrument

The questionnaire consisted of seven structured questions and one open-ended question that permitted participants to state any additional comments or information they felt was beneficial to the study (see the appendix). Questions inquired about the amount of education about adoption issues psychologists acquired during the course of their doctoral studies, the number of both total clients and triad members seen per week, and whether the respondents were interested in obtaining more education in adoption. The questionnaires contained no identifying information, and the researchers were unable to identify specific respondents. Further contact occurred with only three participants who gave their name and address to receive the study results.

RESULTS

Data were analyzed using listwise deletion and, therefore, sample sizes varied due to missing data. Of the 210 psychologists in the study, 90% believed psychologists need more education about issues in adoption and 81% indicated an interest in taking an adoption-related continuing education course. Some data were dichotomized to ensure that the test assumptions were met. A significant positive relationship, as indicated by the phi coefficient, existed between whether psychologists treated triad members (i.e., $1 = no$ and $2 = yes$) and whether psychologists indicated an interest in continuing education (i.e., $1 = no$ and $2 = yes$),

$r_p(176) = .304$, $p < .001$. There was also a strong correlation between psychologists who were interested in continuing education and those who felt other psychologists needed more education, as measured by the phi correlation, $r_p(176) = .458$, $p < .001$.

The vast majority of the psychologists (86%) reported having no courses that dealt with adoption during their undergraduate education, and 65% reported having no courses while in graduate school (see Table 20.1). Only 29 respondents (14% of those who responded) took adoption-related courses in their undergraduate education, and 72 respondents (35% of those who responded) received adoption content in their graduate courses. The psychologists who reported having courses that dealt with adoption averaged only 1.3 courses as undergraduates and 1.5 courses as graduate students; however, this study did not evaluate whether the entire course or just a lecture was spent on adoption issues. Thus, the amount of education psychologists received during their studies was extremely low, especially when one considers the percentage of triad members seen clinically.

Psychologists' self-assessment of their preparation to treat adoption issues provided a normal distribution, with the largest group (51%) rating themselves as being "Somewhat prepared," and the second largest group (23%) rating themselves as being "Not very prepared." Only 22% described themselves as either "Very well prepared" or "Well prepared," and 4% reported they had "No knowledge about adoption issues." Of the 4% (8 psychologists) who stated they were "Very well prepared," 6 added in the open-ended portion of the questionnaire that they were either part of the adoption triad themselves, or specialized in adoption or foster care issues. The remaining 2 psychologists did not provide an explanation for their high level of preparation. To examine the relationship between the level of preparation of psychologists in adoption and whether the psychologists treated at least one adoption triad member per week (i.e., this variable was dichotomized), a Kendall's tau coefficient was computed, $r_{kt}(176) = .256$, $p < .001$, and suggested a moderate relationship between the two variables. Preparation of psychologists also correlated positively with psychologists' inquiry about whether their client was part of the adoption triad, $r_{kt}(176) = 297$, $p < .001$.

The mean number of total clients treated per week was 22.6, with a mean of 1.8 triad members per week. Triad members represented 8% of the total clients reported in this study. However, not all psychologists inquired whether their clients were part of the adoption triad, so this likely led to underreporting of the percentage of triad members seen by the non-inquiring psychologists. This was demonstrated by the negative phi correlation between whether the therapist was seeing triad members (i.e., 1 = yes and 2 = no) and whether psychologists inquired (i.e., 1 = no and 2 = yes) about the client's adoption status, $r_p(176) = .304$, $p < .001$. In fact, one half of the respondents reported that they did not routinely inquire whether their clients were part of the adoption triad. In the case of those psychologists who did not routinely inquire, only 5% of their clients were identified as part of the adoption triad. In the case of the half who did inquire, 10% of their clients were identified as triad members.

A positive relationship existed among psychologists who inquired whether their client was part of the adoption triad and those who were interested in continuing education, $r_p(176) = .219$, $p = .002$. Evaluation of this statistic suggests that psychologists who inquire

Table 20.1	Percentage of Courses With Adoption Content					
	Number of Courses					Number of Responses
	0	1	2	3	4	
Undergraduate	86%	11%	2%	0.5%	0.5%	202
Graduate	65%	22%	8%	4%	1%	206

whether the client is part of the adoption triad also realize the importance of adoption and are interested in adoption-related factors that might affect the individual. An analysis of variance indicated a significant difference between the number of adoption triad members seen per week and whether the psychologists inquire ($M = 2.28$, $SD = 2.26$) or not ($M = 1.22$, $SD = 1.90$) if their clients were part of the adoption triad, $F(1, 202) = 13.06$, $p < .001$, $R^2 = .06$, although the overall effect size was relatively small.

DISCUSSION

The results of this study support the authors' hypothesis that psychologists need more education about the effects of adoption on triad members. Due to the number of triad members seen in therapy, it is important that psychologists become more educated about adoption and its consequences. Additionally, the absence of routine inquiry about a relationship to adoption suggests that many psychologists do not consider adoption to be a serious problem facing triad members. This study also suggests that many psychologists themselves feel they are undereducated on this issue and are interested in continuing education.

Psychological problems, their evolution, and systematic procedures for recovery are studied extensively in psychology courses in both undergraduate and graduate programs. However, a lifelong experience such as adoption, which affects a much higher proportion of the population of the United States than many more clearly identified psychological problems, is not given adequate consideration during the education of most psychologists (Post, 2000) and marriage and family therapists (Fisher, 2003). Perhaps a lack of proper education in dealing with the consequences of the adoption process causes the negative reactions psychologists have shown to the difficulties that triad members experience (Kirschner, 1990).

The need for continuing education is further supported by the small amount of adoption-related course work reported. Psychologists completed on average only 0.19 such classes in undergraduate studies and 0.54 classes in graduate school, with most never receiving any formal education in adoption. Psychologists themselves (90%) acknowledged that they lack sufficient education in adoption issues, and 81% stated they needed more education in this area. These points are further supported by the majority (51%) of the psychologists who reported they were only "Somewhat prepared" to deal with adoption issues and the nearly one quarter who reported they were "Not very prepared" or had "No knowledge of adoption issues." These results suggest that adoption needs to be discussed more directly in the education process. Adoption dynamics need to be studied specifically, rather than tangentially in the form of adoption-based studies of the inheritance of psychological traits and disorders, or of heredity-environment issues, which are the most frequently encountered studies of adoption at present (Post, 2000). The educational process needs to address such topics as the impact of the loss of the primary bonding figure, the transition between birth and adoptive parents, the loss of a birth child, the development of a merged identity, the issues of search and reunion, and the other postadoption issues that these triad members experience.

The significant correlation between the number of triad members seen in therapy and the self-reported preparation of psychologists to treat triad members suggests that experience in adoption issues accompanies increases in psychologists' skills in dealing with them. Without further data, it is impossible to tell whether there is a causal relationship present, but it is likely that the relationship is bidirectional in nature. Unfortunately, many triad members may undergo inadequate treatment before psychologists recognize adoption as a serious issue for them. Knowledge of adoption needs to be presented prior to receiving a graduate degree and prior to treating clients. It is important that psychologists become aware of adoption issues prior to initiating treatment rather than during treatment.

Knowledge about adoption issues may prevent false conclusions about the importance and effects of the adoption process.

Attempts to obtain the actual proportion of triad members seen clinically are problematic, because only one half of the psychologists in our sample specifically asked their clients about this. This likely led to a reduction in the number of triad clients reported. Additionally, psychologists presumably did not review all their client records prior to answering our survey to determine the number of triad members, a factor that also likely suppressed the number of triad members reported in therapy. Unfortunately, our data also suffer from our failure to request identification of the specific triad position of the clients treated by the respondents. However, this study likely provides a good approximation of the number of triad members seen clinically if we use only those psychologists who inquired about adoption experience. This group reported 10% of their clients to be part of the triad.

Psychologists who do not consider adoption a serious issue may experience problems when treating triad members, because they are unable to fully understand the triad members' life experiences. This creates a distance between the clients and psychologists and reduces the therapists' ability to treat the core problem. One psychologist who responded to the study wrote, "Adoption does not routinely cause disruption in life development," and another stated, "A good psychotherapist should be capable of handling this kind of issue without specific training." Psychologists such as these possibly do not adequately understand the multiple effects of adoption and thus may not be qualified to treat triad members.

Surveys of instructors and of text, reading, and reference books in graduate programs in mental health fields support the need for increased adoption education (Fisher, 2003; Post, 2000). The present authors have also surveyed triad members to determine how they evaluate their own therapy and what they wish their therapists had known (Sass & Henderson, 2002; Sass, Webster, & Henderson, 2000). These results of studies of the educational process, and of a client population, are consistent with those reported here for psychologists offering treatment services. Further research needs to be conducted to improve our understanding of the adoption process and the effects of adoption that could arise as issues in therapy. However, it is clear that we also need to attend more to sharing the knowledge we already have with therapists.

BEST PRACTICE STRATEGIES

1. Develop a routine for asking clients about whether they have any connection to adoption as part of regular intake procedures.

2. Be familiar with the major developmental issues that may arise in response to having a connection to adoption.

RESEARCH IMPLICATIONS

Better knowledge of adoption issues might contribute to our understanding of human development by suggesting alternative interpretations for data. Consider the potential discovery of a new disorder found to be present in both adopted children and their birth parents. Researchers learn that the disorder is absent in the adoptive parents. The typical interpretation of this pattern of results would be to assume that the disorder was genetic, passed on from the birth parents to the adoptees. However, an adoption-enlightened researcher (or therapist) might at least consider whether the presence of the disorder in both the birth parents and the adoptees might be caused by their common participation in the experiences of loss/separation due to adoption, rather than their common genetics.

REFLECTION QUESTIONS

1. Do you agree or disagree with the response of the psychologist who wrote, "A good psychotherapist should be capable of handling this kind of issue without specific training"? If you disagree, what would you say to try to change this individual's opinion? If you agree, how would you defend this position to a triad member who asked what you knew about adoption?

2. The questionnaire sent to psychologists in this study was intentionally kept very brief to maximize the likelihood of its return. The relatively high return rate (45%) suggests this was successful. Aside from the easy (and obvious!) addition of respondent gender and age to the questionnaire, what additional questions might be added to the questionnaire for future replication/expansion of this research?

APPENDIX

Survey of Licensed Psychologists on Adoption Issues

1. Please circle the number of undergraduate or graduate school <u>courses</u> in which you received information dealing with adoption issues, particularly any emotional or behavioral challenges that members of the adoption triad (adoptee, birth parents, and adoptive parents) might encounter.

Undergraduate	[None]	[One]	[Two]	[Three]	[Four or more]
Graduate school	[None]	[One]	[Two]	[Three]	[Four or more]

2. Please indicate your average number of clients per week. _____

3. Please indicate the average number of clients you treat per week who are part of the adoption triad. _____

4. Do you routinely ask your clients if they are part of the adoption triad?

[Yes] _____   [No] _____

5. Do you feel that more psychologists need education dealing with the problems that members of the adoption triad face?

[Yes] _____   [No] _____

6. How well prepared do you feel to deal with the problems members of the triad experience.

_____	_____	_____	_____	_____
[Very well prepared]	[Well prepared]	[Somewhat prepared]	[Not very prepared]	[No knowledge about adoption issues]

7. Would you be interested in receiving continuing education dealing with the problems of adoption and issues that psychologists need to be aware of while treating members of the triad?

[Yes] _____   [No] _____

8. Any additional comments? (Use reverse if necessary.)

Thanks for your help.

Please return as soon as possible in the enclosed envelope to:

Douglas B. Henderson, Ph.D.
Professor of Psychology
University of Wisconsin-Stevens Point
Stevens Point, WI 54481

REFERENCES

Brinich, P. (1980). Some potential effects of adoption on self and object representations. *Psychoanalytic Study of the Child, 35*, 107–133.

Brodzinsky, D. M. (1987). Adjustment to adoption: A psychosocial perspective. *Clinical Psychology Review, 7*, 25–47.

Brodzinsky, D. M. (1990). A stress and coping model of adoption adjustment. In D. Brodzinsky & M. Schechter (Eds.), *The psychology of adoption.* New York: Oxford University Press.

Brodzinsky, D. M. (1993). Long-term outcomes in adoption. *The Future of Children, 3*, 153–166.

Brown, F. G. (1959). Services to adoptive parents after legal adoption. *Child Welfare, 38*, 16–22.

Clothier, F. (1943). The psychology of the adopted child. *Mental Hygiene, 26*, 257–264.

Daly, K. (1988). Reshaped parenthood identity. *Journal of Contemporary Ethnography, 17*, 40–66.

Daly, K. (1990). Infertility resolution and adoption readiness. *Families in Society, 71*, 483–492.

Deutsch, H. (1945). *The psychology of women* (Vol. 2). New York: Grune & Stratton.

Dickson, L. R., Heffron, W. M., & Parker, C. (1990). Children from disrupted and adoptive homes on an inpatient unit. *American Journal of Orthopsychiatry, 60*, 594–602.

Dickson, L. R., Stevens, S., Heffron, W. M., & Parker, C. (1991). Discussing adoption in therapy. *Journal of the American Academy of Child and Adolescent Psychiatry, 30*, 155.

Fisher, A. P. (2003). Still "Not quite as good as having your own"? Toward a sociology of adoption. *Annual Review of Sociology, 29*, 335–361.

Hall, J. D. (1997). Issues relevant to therapy with adoptees. *Psychotherapy, 34*, 64–75.

Henderson, D. B. (2002). Challenging the silence of the mental health community on adoption issues. *Journal of Social Distress and the Homeless, 11*, 131–142.

Hollingsworth, L. D. (1998). Adoptee dissimilarity from the adoptive family: Clinical practice and research implications. *Child & Adolescent Social Work Journal, 15*, 303–319.

Jago Krueger, M. J., & Hanna, F. J. (1997). Why adoptees search: An existential treatment perspective. *Journal of Counseling and Development, 75,* 195–202.

Jones, A. (1997). Issues relevant to therapy with adoptees. *Psychotherapy, 34,* 64–75.

Kirschner, D. H. (1990). The adopted child syndrome: Considerations for psychotherapy. *Psychotherapy in Private Practice, 8,* 93–100.

Miller, B. C., Fan, X., Grotevant, H. D., Christensen, M., Coyl, D., & van Dulmen, M. (2000). Adopted adolescents' overrepresentation in mental health counseling: Adoptees' problems or parents' lower threshold for referral? *Journal of the American Academy of Child & Adolescent Psychiatry, 39,* 1504–1511.

Miller, P. H. (1997). *Theories of developmental psychology* (3rd ed.). New York: W. H. Freeman.

National Adoption Information Clearinghouse. (n.d.). *How many children were adopted in 2000 and 2001?* Retrieved December 12, 2005, from www.childwelfare.gov/pubs/s_adopted/s_adoptedf.cfm

Post, D. E. (2000). Adoption in clinical psychology: A review of the absence, ramifications and recommendations for change. *Journal of Social Distress and the Homeless, 9,* 361–372.

Russell, M. (1996). *Adoption wisdom.* Santa Monica, CA: Broken Branch.

Sass, D. A., & Henderson, D. B. (2002). Adoptees' and birth parents' therapeutic experiences related to adoption. *Adoption Quarterly, 6,* 25–32.

Sass, D. A., Webster, J., & Henderson, D. B. (2000). *Triad members' experiences in therapy.* Paper presented at the meeting of the American Adoption Congress, Nashville, TN.

Schechter, M. D. (1960). Observations on adopted children. *Archives of General Psychiatry, 3,* 21–32.

Silverman, P. R., Campbell, L., Patti, P., & Style, C. B. (1988). Reunions between adoptees and birth parents: The birth parent's experience. *Social Work, 39,* 523–528.

Toussieng, P. W. (1962). Thoughts regarding the etiology of psychological difficulties in adopted children. *Child Welfare, 41,* 59–71.

U.S. Census Bureau. (n.d.). Retrieved December 12, 2005, from http://factfinder.census.gov/

Verrier, N. N. (1993). *The primal wound.* Baltimore: Gateway Press.

Weiss, A. (1984). Parent-child relationships of adopted adolescents in a psychiatric hospital. *Adolescence, 73,* 77–88.

Research Findings in Adoption Work

Preface

RAFAEL A. JAVIER

St. John's University

Because of the importance of data derived from research findings in adding to our understanding of issues affecting members of the adoption triad, we decided to include a systematic discussion on research issues in this book. With this in mind, we are including contributions by Madelyn Freundlich (Chapter 21), Mary Jo Carr (Chapter 22), Amanda Baden (Chapter 23), and Douglas Henderson, Daniel Sass, and Jeanna Carlson (Chapter 24) to guide our discussion.

Freundlich's critical examination, for instance, of the emerging research contributions thus far, provides important suggestions to guide future researcher initiatives. In her chapter, "Research Contributions: Strengthening Services for Members of the Adoption Triad," she examines the current state of adoption research regarding the impact of adoption on birth parents, adopted persons, and adoptive parents. She explores the nature and scope of the issues on which research has focused and the issues that have received little research attention. With regard to birth parents, she reviews studies on birthmothers' decisions to place their infants for adoption, the longer-term impact of the adoption decision on birthmothers in the United States, and the impact of adoption on birth fathers. She further explores the limited research on the impact of international adoption on birth parents and adoption's impact on parents whose rights are involuntarily terminated. Her chapter then examines the research on the psychological and social well-being of adopted children and adolescents and the limited research on the status of adult adoptees and international adoptees. She next considers the limited research with adoptive parents and reviews the research on the impact of open adoption on all members of the triad. She concludes with an assessment of the contribution of research to adoption practice, with particular focus on the issues that have not been well addressed.

In the next three chapters (Carr's contribution on birth mothers, Baden's contribution, and the work of Henderson, Sass, and Carlson), we see three good examples of the crucial importance that research data have in adding to our understanding of the complexity of the adoption experience. For instance, Carr in her interesting study on "Birthmothers and Subsequent Children," discusses the factors that tend to influence the extent to which Caucasian birthmothers will develop a personally fulfilling life postrelinquishment. Fifty-five women who had surrendered their first child for adoption and went on to have subsequent children, and 32 women who had surrendered their first child for adoption and did not have more children, were given the Revised NEO (Neuroticism, Extraversion, Openness) Personality Inventory (NEO-PI-R) and the Attachment History Questionnaire. According to her findings, women who had more children scored significantly higher on the Extraversion scale of the NEO-PI-R. Women who did not have more children were more apt never to marry and, when there was marriage, more apt to divorce. Women who had more children reported more pressure from family to relinquish their child. Finally, her findings showed that women who did not have more children tended to report "friends" as significant support figures more often than women who did have more children.

Baden focuses her contribution on issues related to identity and psychological adjustment within the context of culture and race. It is an empirical validation study of an early work on the Cultural-Racial Identity Model that she developed earlier with another colleague. The model allows distinctions to be made between racial identity and cultural identity resulting in 16 proposed identities. Identities are based on the degrees to which individuals (1) have knowledge of, awareness of, competence within, and comfort with their own racial group's culture, their parents' racial group's culture, and multiple cultures and (2) are comfortable with their racial group membership and with those belonging to their own racial group, their parents' racial group, and multiple racial groups. Four dimensions of the model were selected for study: the Adoptee Culture Dimension, the Parental Culture Dimension, the Adoptee Race Dimension, and the Parental Race Dimension. In this study, the cultural-racial identity of transracial adoptees was assessed by a modified version of the Multigroup Ethnic Identity Measure. Psychological adjustment was assessed by the Brief Symptom Inventory. The sample consisted of 51 transracial adoptees who completed mail survey questionnaires. According to the author, the exploratory findings supported the Cultural-Racial Identity Model by demonstrating that the modified version of the Multigroup Ethnic Identify Measure successfully yielded variation in the potential cultural-racial identities that the transracial adoptees reported. Findings did not yield support for differences in psychological adjustment among transracial adoptees having different cultural-racial identities. The implications that the results have for counseling practice and social policy are discussed.

Finally, Henderson and his colleagues' study examines the effects of the adoption process on members of the adoption triad (adoptee, birth parents, and adoptive parents), including the experiences of adoptees and birth parents with the adoption caseworker and therapists. Participants consisted of 152 adoptees and 66 birth parents recruited from two adoption search and support groups. According to their findings, 55% of adoptees and 86% of birth parents experienced mental or emotional problems related to adoption. For both groups, problems were related to the quality of information received during placement and the preparation of the caseworker about postadoption experiences. Adoption caseworkers did not provide birthmothers and adoptees with an adequate amount of information concerning their separated birth relatives and did not sufficiently prepare them for postadoption experiences. With regard to therapy, therapists who inquired about adoption or addressed adoption were perceived as being significantly more prepared and helpful compared with therapists who did not inquire about or address adoption issues.

LEARNING GOALS

The following are some of the learning goals that readers are encouraged to consider when reviewing the material included in the chapters listed in this part. Thus, the reader should be able to develop

- a better understanding of the research that has been conducted on the experiences of birth parents, adopted individuals, and adoptive parents;
- a better understanding of the issues related to the experiences of triad members on which research has not focused;
- an appreciation for the need for additional research to enhance the quality of services for triad members;
- a fuller appreciation of the dilemma normally confronting birthmothers throughout their lives;
- a better appreciation of the need for a model for understanding the identity experiences of transracial adoptees;
- an appreciation and the necessary strategy to be able to operationalize the Cultural-Racial Identity Model;
- a realization that adoption has a wide variety of outcomes and that adoption affects virtually all those who participate in it to some extent; and
- an understanding of some of the effects of adoption that can lead triad members to seek out therapy.

Research Contributions

21

Strengthening Services for
Members of the Adoption Triad

MADELYN FREUNDLICH

Child Welfare Consultant

A doption is a complex service designed to meet the needs of a range of individuals. Adoption affects birthmothers and birth fathers who either through their own decisions or through the decisions of others relinquish their children to other families; the children for whom it serves as the path to new families and who, as adolescents and adults, must integrate the adoption experience into their lives; and adoptive mothers and fathers who rely on the adoption system to help them achieve parenthood. The effects of adoption on members of the triad (birth parents, adopted individuals, and adoptive parents) have been the subject of research for many years. The nature and scope of that research, however, have varied significantly, reflecting not only the realities of research interests but social values and professional concerns related to the practice of adoption.

This chapter examines the current state of adoption research with regard to each member of the triad. It outlines the major research interests and identifies the issues that have been the subject of relatively little research. Specifically, it considers the research on birthmothers and birth fathers in both domestic and international adoptions; adopted individuals, with focus both on adopted children and adolescents and on adult adoptees; and adoptive parents. It reviews the research on the issue of openness in adoption, with a focus on the research that has assessed the impact of openness on each triad member. The chapter concludes with an assessment of the contributions that research has made to current adoption practice.

RESEARCH WITH BIRTH PARENTS

Research with birth parents has addressed, to varying degrees, the impact of adoption on birth parents of infants, birth parents who relinquish their children to international adoption, and birth parents whose children are placed for adoption following involuntary termination of their parental rights. The research on birth parents of infants in the United States is far more comprehensive than the research on birth parents in other countries whose children are adopted by families in the United States and the research on birth parents whose rights are involuntarily terminated.

The Birth Parents of Infants

Research has provided some understanding of the impact of relinquishment and adoption on the birthmothers and birth fathers of infants. The decision whether to parent or place for adoption has been explored, although primarily in relation to unmarried teen women's decision making (e.g., Dworkin, Harding, & Schreiber, 1993; Leynes, 1980; Resnick, 1984). Research has considered the psychological impact of relinquishment over the long term, but primarily, the focus has been on birthmothers, and only scant attention has been paid to birth fathers (Deykin, Patti, & Ryan, 1988; Edwards, 1995; Van Keppel & Winkler, 1983).

The decision to parent or to place for adoption. In line with the primary focus on the role of mothers in parenting in general (Rotundo, 1985), research has principally focused on the decision of women to parent their children or relinquish their children for adoption (Clapton, 1997). In the United States and Canada, researchers have been principally interested in the demographic characteristics of unmarried pregnant teen women who relinquish, and the focus has been on the social and psychological factors that influence these young women's decisions (e.g., Chippendale-Bakker & Foster, 1996; Dworkin et al., 1993; Geber & Resnick, 1988). Although it is clear that a small and declining percentage of single pregnant adolescents decide in favor of adoption (Chandra, Abma, Maza, & Bachrach, 1999), those adolescents who make such a decision have been found to conform to a certain demographic and socioeconomic profile. An unmarried adolescent woman who relinquishes is more likely to

- be non-Hispanic White (Bachrach, Abma, Sambrano, & London, 1990; Chippendale-Bakker & Foster, 1996);
- be an older teenager (Bachrach, Stolley, & London, 1992);
- have an intact family (Namerow, Kalmuss, & Cushman, 1993);
- have a family member who is adopted (Resnick, 1984);
- have more years of education (Bachrach et al., 1992);
- have college-educated parents (Cushman, Kalmuss, & Namerow, 1993); and
- enjoy greater economic resources (Chippendale-Bakker & Foster, 1996; Leynes, 1980).

Research has also identified nondemographic influences on decision making by unmarried pregnant teen women. Four factors have emerged from this body of research. First, several studies have found that the mother of the pregnant teenager influences most the decision that she makes (Dworkin et al., 1993; Leynes, 1980; Resnick, 1984). Through the 1980s, the mothers of pregnant teens were most likely to promote a decision in favor of adoption (Resnick, 1984; Leynes, 1980). In more recent research, however, Chippendale-Bakker and Foster (1996) found that when the birthmother's parents had influence in the decision-making process, it was more likely that the woman would choose parenting than adoption. The researchers raised the possibility that with changes in broader social attitudes about single parenting, families may have become more supportive of keeping grandchildren within the family. Second, studies have suggested that the father of the baby influences the consistency of the plan to place or parent the child (Blum, Resnick, & Stark, 1987; Dworkin et al., 1993; Geber & Resnick, 1988). When the father is involved, his values have been found to have significant social, psychological, and economic consequences for the pregnant adolescent woman (Bachrach, 1986).

Third, research has associated the residential environment of a maternity home with an increased likelihood that a teen woman will place her child for adoption. One study, for example, found that pregnant teen women who lived for any time during their pregnancies in a maternity facility were twice as likely to place their children for adoption as those who did not spend time in a residence (Namerow et al., 1993). Fourth, more recent research has found that contact with prospective adoptive parents (a variable not addressed in earlier research) influences young women's decisions to parent or place their infants for adoption. In their study, Chippendale-Bakker and Foster (1996) found that when birthmothers chose and met the prospective adoptive parents, they were more likely to proceed with the adoption plan. birthmothers who participated in the study reported that meeting the prospective adoptive parents provided them with the reassurance that adoption offered a better option for their children than what they themselves could provide and that the particular adoptive parents were the right choice for their children.

The longer-term impact of the adoption decision on birthmothers. Two conflicting themes have emerged from the research on outcomes for unmarried women who choose to parent their children and women who choose adoption. The first theme is that adoption is a traumatic experience for the mother with negative consequences for her future well-being and personal and social functioning. The second theme is that adoption, by providing a positive alternative for an unplanned pregnancy, benefits the unmarried mother on a long-term basis and also significantly benefits her child.

The first theme, suggesting long-term negative effects for birthmothers, is most clearly developed in the empirical research from Australia. This research, which is so homogeneous that it is often characterized as the "Australian" point of view (Curtis, 1990), has consistently found that women who place their children for adoption are at significant risk of long-term physical, emotional, and interpersonal difficulties (Condon, 1986; DeSimone, 1996; McHutchinson, 1986; Van Keppel & Winkler, 1983). These studies suggest that many women who place their children for adoption suffer severe and debilitating grief that continues over time (Van Keppel & Winkler, 1983); have ongoing problems in their relationships with men and difficulties in parenting subsequent children (Condon, 1986); adjust poorly or not at all to placing their children for adoption (Bouchier, Lambert, & Triseliotis, 1991); and often experience symptoms similar to posttraumatic stress disorder (Wells, 1993).

In contrast, research in the United States has tended to highlight the benefits of adoption, emphasizing the risks associated with unmarried parenting and the benefits of adoption for the mother and child (Curtis, 1990). Much of the U.S. research has suggested educational and economic benefits for single women when they choose adoption instead of parenting and important benefits for their children when they are placed with adoptive families. These studies, which primarily focus on teen women, suggest that women who decide to parent their children are at heightened risk of lower educational achievement and lower rates of high school completion (Mott & Marsiglio, 1985); greater dependency on welfare benefits and poorer employment opportunities (Duncan & Hoffman, 1990); and higher divorce rates (Furstenberg, Brooks-Gunn, & Morgan, 1987). Studies have also indicated negative outcomes for children raised by their adolescent mothers: poorer health, higher levels of poverty, lower educational achievement, greater frequency of behavioral problems, and a higher risk of early sexual activity and pregnancy (Hofferth, 1987; Strobino, 1987). The thrust of this research is that mothers benefit from relinquishment in the form of higher socioeconomic status and higher levels of marital stability and that children benefit from the higher socioeconomic status they enjoy in their adoptive homes compared with the likely status of children if they were reared in a single-parent home (Kalmuss, 1992).

Some U.S. research, however, offers a point of departure to the overall positive findings regarding the effects of relinquishment on women. Some research finds mixed outcomes for unmarried teen women who choose parenting or adoption. Namerow et al. (1993), for example, compared unmarried teen women who placed their children for adoption and women who parented their children 4 years after the decision and found that women who chose to place their children had a higher overall satisfaction with life; scored higher on factors such as employment, finances, and the quality of their relationships with their partners; and reported a more positive future outlook. They also found, however, that teen women who placed their children for adoption reported a greater degree of regret about their decision.

Other U.S. studies that are more longitudinal in nature have found decidedly more negative outcomes for women who place their children for adoption (Brodzinsky, 1990). Edwards (1995), for example, found a range of poor psychological outcomes in her study of 56 birthmothers who had relinquished 16 to 51 years previously. The women she studied frequently described the experience of placing their children for adoption as the most traumatic event of their lives; related multiple symptoms of posttraumatic stress; and expressed a desire for search and reunion to fully heal. Similarly, Weintraub and Konstam (1995) found that birthmothers who had placed their infants for adoption during the 1960s and 1970s consistently reported pain associated with secrecy and isolation, a sense of stigmatization and personal disgrace, depression, perceptions of failures in relationships, difficulty "moving on" with their lives, and dissatisfaction with the services they received from helping professionals. More recent studies reach similar conclusions. Carr (2000) found that birthmothers experienced unresolved grief and negative effects on future relationships as well as an increased incidence of secondary infertility. Fravel, McRoy, and Grotevant (2000) found that birthmothers experienced an ongoing psychological presence of the child they relinquished, a finding that they found to empirically discredit the "happy ever after" myth, in which birthmothers supposedly forget their children and move on with their lives.

Research With Birth Fathers

Research has not fully addressed the role of the birth father in adoption or the effects on a birth father of the decision to place his child for adoption (Clapton, 1997; Grotevant, 2003). Mason (1995a) writes that "the birth father continues to be the least represented, least considered and least heard in adoption literature, conferences and advocacy efforts" (p. 29). Although, to some extent, birth fathers have become more involved in adoption decisions (Wiley & Baden, 2005), they have continued to be viewed as uninvolved in and unconcerned about planning for their children (Lightman & Schlesinger, 1982) and as unaffected by decisions related to the adoptive placements of their children (Mason, 1995b).

The current body of research, although extremely limited, suggests that multiple factors bear on birth fathers' involvement in decision making about their children. Deykin et al. (1988), in a nonrepresentative sample of birth fathers identified through postadoption support and advocacy groups, found that a little more than half did not participate in the decision making regarding their children, and most (64%) had no contact with the child prior to the adoptive placement. In examining the factors related to the birth fathers' lack of active involvement in, if not exclusion from, the adoption process, they found that the absence of birth fathers from the process was associated with four major factors: pressures from their families, a poor relationship with the birthmother, financial issues, and the attitudes of adoption agencies.

In another of the few studies with birth fathers, Cicchini (1993) interviewed 30 men in Western Australia who volunteered in response to articles and public appeals. As in the study by Deykin et al. (1988), Cicchini explored the birth fathers' involvement in the decision-making process and found that the majority (66%) had no or only a minimal say in the adoption. He also sought information on the long-term impact of the adoption on the birth fathers and found that they consistently viewed relinquishment as "a most distressing experience." His findings put into question the prevailing assumptions that birth fathers are irresponsible, uncaring, and uninvolved, and they suggest that the experiences and attitudes of these men are far from well-understood.

International Adoption and Birth Parents

Extremely little attention has been given to the birth parents of children who are adopted internationally. The relatively recent growth in international adoption, the diverse cultures in which birth parents live, and the circumstances surrounding many international adoptions have limited the understanding of the adoption experience for birth parents in other countries (Lee, 2003). As a consequence, birth parents of children adopted internationally "are often permanently invisible and silent" (Wiley & Baden, 2005). To the extent that there has been an examination of the impact of adoption on the birth parents of internationally adopted children, the focus has been on birthmothers and has been primarily descriptive in nature.

The limited research suggests that poverty and low social status typify the backgrounds of many women who place their children for adoption internationally. Pilotti's (1993) study of the demographic characteristics of Latin American birthmothers who consented to the international adoptions of their children, for example, found that economic and social disadvantage uniformly characterized their backgrounds. birthmothers were found to be young (between the ages of 14 and 18), poor, unemployed or active in the informal sector as street vendors, beggars, or prostitutes, poorly educated, and from neglectful or abusive home environments. Defence of Children International, an organization that has studied the intercountry adoptions of children from a number of developing countries, has similarly concluded that "the vast majority (of birth parents) part with their children out of despair or with the hope to ensure the child's welfare or survival" (Lücker-Babel, 1990, p. 393).

A study completed by Johnson, Banghan, and Liyao (1998) is one of the few efforts to understand the circumstances under which Chinese parents decide to abandon their children, thus making them available for international adoption. Of the 237 parents that the researchers interviewed, all but 3 were married and in their mid- to late 20s to late 30s. The researchers found that in 50% of the cases, the decision to abandon the baby was made by the child's father, and in 40% of the cases the couple made the decision together. In contrast to Pilotti's findings regarding birthmothers in Latin America, poverty did not appear to play a role in child abandonment in China.

More recently, Roby and Matsumura (2002) studied the factors associated with the decisions of birthmothers in the Marshall Islands to relinquish their children for adoption. As in Pilotti's study, the researchers found that an environment of extreme poverty as well as a breakdown of traditional family support systems and an exploitation of the cultural understanding of adoption characterized the women's experiences. Interviews with 73 Marshallese birthmothers who had placed their children for international adoptions revealed that most birthmothers did not feel financially prepared to care for their children; the great majority experienced considerable pressure from their own extended families to place their children for international adoption; and an astounding 82% believed, based on cultural beliefs that adoption is open and does not terminate parental rights, that their children would return to them at the age of 18 with a good education and material wealth.

No studies have been located on the impact of international adoption on Korean birthmothers despite the long history of international adoptions of Korean children. Wiley and Baden (2005), however, reported based on a visit to Ae Ran Won, a home for unmarried birthmothers in Seoul, that birthmothers expressed deep sorrow, regret, and shame for making the decision to place their children for adoption. These women felt, however, that no other options were available to them given the social stigma associated with unwed parenthood, the social structure of Korean society, and a lack of personal and social support.

Research has not addressed to any extent the effects of international adoption on birth parents in Russia and Eastern Europe. It is assumed that birth parents in these countries, as in Latin America, face dire economic circumstances that make it extremely difficult for them to parent their children and that, unlike in Latin America, alcohol abuse (as suggested by national rates of alcoholism) undermines their ability to parent (Aronson, 2000). Research, however, has not addressed the issues associated with relinquishment and abandonment in Russia and Eastern Europe or the impact of adoption on these birth parents.

Birth Parents Whose Rights Are Involuntarily Terminated

As is the case with birth parents in the international arena, research has not focused to any significant extent on birth parents whose children are in foster care and whose rights are involuntarily terminated through a judicial process (see Edelstein, Burge, & Waterman, 2002). Mason and Selman (1997) note, "The voice of the non-relinquishing parents has not been heard" (p. 22). There has long been consensus that the impact of involuntary termination of parental rights and adoption on parents "is a subject which merits further research" (Hughes & Logan, 1993, p. 33), but the understanding of the experiences of this group of birth parents remains quite limited (Wiley & Baden, 2005).

The few studies that have been conducted in this area (all of which are from Great Britain) are consistent in their findings of long-term psychological distress as a result of involuntary termination of parental rights. Hughes and Logan (1993) identified two major characteristics of parents whose rights were involuntarily terminated: a continuing sense of anger and guilt that persisted long after their children were adopted and significant psychological problems. Mason and Selman (1997), in their study of 21 birth parents whose children were placed with adoptive families after involuntary termination of parental rights, similarly found that adoption "had a devastating and long-term effect on the lives of most of the parents, leaving them with feelings of isolation and emptiness" (p. 25). Birth parents reported adverse effects on their mental and physical health and ongoing concerns about their children's whereabouts and well-being.

Charlton, Crank, Kansara, and Oliver (1998), in their interviews with 65 birth parents whose rights were involuntarily terminated, also found that many birth parents suffered from significant and long-term health problems that many parents related to mourning of their loss. The most commonly reported problems were physical symptoms associated with bereavement and trauma, such as sleeping problems, poor appetite, and dreams either about the loss of the child or about searching and the return of the child to them. The researchers further found that many birth parents described relationship difficulties, particularly with new partners. Some parents were reluctant to enter new relationships, and others felt a sense of isolation within relationships with individuals who had never known the children they lost.

Some, such as Berry, Barth, and Needell (1996), have suggested that because parents whose rights are involuntarily terminated have legal counsel, they are better protected than parents who themselves make an adoption plan, and, consequently, these parents may fare better psychologically. The studies of Mason and Selman (1997) and Charlton et al. (1998), however, found that the presence of legal counsel did not necessarily provide birth parents with a sense of empowerment. Mason and Selman (1997) found that birth parents had difficulties obtaining quality legal representation—that is, attorneys who had experience in working with involuntary termination of parental rights cases and the ability to present such cases effectively to the court. The court experience itself was traumatic for many birth parents who felt that they were being "publicly branded as bad parents" and that no one actually listened to what they had to say (p. 24). Similarly, Charlton et al. (1998) found in their interviews that irrespective of the presence of legal counsel, birth parents experienced the court process with a "sense of despair" because "everything had already been decided" (p. 37). The judicial process for birth parents "involve(d) not only loss of children, but also a loss of self worth and confidence" (p. 35).

There has been considerable research interest in the psychological and behavioral adjustment of adopted children and adolescents as well as some work in the area of identity formation of adoptees. Adult adoptees, however, have largely not been the subject of empirical studies, other than in research on search and reunion. Only a few studies have focused on adult adoptees who were internationally adopted.

Adopted Children and Adolescents

The psychological and behavioral adjustment of adopted children and adolescents has been viewed from two different perspectives, both of which are reflected in the research. The traditional view is that adoption is a highly successful service for children who cannot or will not be raised by their birth parents, and therefore, any challenges associated with loss, rejection, and "differentness" are readily surmountable (Finley, 1999; Wilson, 2004). The other perspective is the epidemiological view that adoptees are more likely to have adjustment problems, as demonstrated by research that shows higher rates of psychopathology among adoptees and adopted individuals' disproportionate representation among those served in mental health settings (Finley, 1999; Wilson, 2004).

The findings of studies on the psychological and behavioral adjustment of adoptees, perhaps the most extensive body of research on any single adoption issue, may be synthesized into three groups:

- Research findings that suggest that there are no significant differences between adoptees and nonadoptees (Carey, Lipton, & Myers, 1974; Irhammar & Cederblad, 2000; Mikawa & Boston, 1968; Norvell & Guy, 1977; Plomin & DeFries, 1985; Stein & Hoopes, 1985; Thompson & Plomin, 1988).

- Research findings that suggest that there are significantly higher rates of maladjustment among adopted individuals as compared with nonadopted persons (Bohman & Von Knorring, 1979; Dalby, Fox, & Haslam, 1982; Dickson, Heffron, & Parker, 1990; Holden, 1991; Lipman, Offord, Boyle, & Racine, 1993; Rogeness, Hoppe, Macedo, Fischer, & Harris, 1988; Schechter, Carlson, Simmons, & Work, 1964; Sharma, McGue, & Benson, 1996a, 1996b; Silver, 1970, 1989; Simon & Senturia, 1966; Slap, Goodman, & Huang, 2001; Verhulst, Althaus, & Versluis-den Bieman, 1990a, 1990b; Verhulst & Versluis-den Bieman, 1995).

- Research findings that suggest that on certain variables related to emotional and behavioral adjustment, adopted children and adolescents function at a higher level than do nonadopted individuals (Marquis & Detweiler, 1985; Sharma, McGue, & Benson, 1998).

These diverse findings may be attributable to differences in the methodologies used (Sharma et al., 1998). These differences, which are not always made entirely clear in analyses of research findings in this area, relate to whether clinical or nonclinical populations are being studied; the types of adopted individuals who are studied (specifically, children adopted as infants versus children adopted at older ages); and the type of comparison group that is used (specifically, children in intact biological families or children in high-risk environments).

Clinical Versus Nonclinical Populations of Adoptees

Research has been conducted with adoptees in both clinical and nonclinical settings, and the results vary accordingly. When clinical populations are studied, adoptees have been found to consistently use mental health services at higher rates than those of nonadoptees (Finley, 1999). Brodzinsky (1993) determined that although children adopted by nonrelatives constitute only about 2% of the child population, they make up about 5% of the children seen in outpatient mental health clinics and between 10% and 15% of the children treated in inpatient psychiatric or residential treatment settings. At the same time, studies suggest higher rates of adjustment difficulties and behavioral problems among adoptees. Studies of clinical populations have suggested that adoptees have higher levels of academic problems (Brodzinsky, Smith, & Brodzinsky, 1998), acting-out behaviors and hyperactivity (Moore & Fombonne, 1999; Rosenberg, 1992), and externalizing behaviors (Cadoret, 1995) and that they score more poorly on measures of self-esteem (Rohner, 1986).

Research findings related to the outcomes of adoptees in nonclinical settings, in contrast, show differences between adopted and nonadopted persons but at a far less dramatic level than is evident in clinical settings (Sharma et al., 1998). One study of adoptees conducted in public schools, for example, revealed that differences in adjustment among adoptees on factors such as drug use, school adjustment, optimism, and antisocial behavior were fairly small when compared with levels of adjustment for nonadoptees (Sharma et al., 1996a).

These differences in the research findings raise methodological issues. Specifically, the research has been criticized because there are no comprehensive data on the number of adoptions or the incidence of referrals of adoptees to mental health services on which to base the estimates that appear in the research; the characteristics of birth parents, adoptees, and adoptive parents have changed over time, which may undermine the validity of comparisons between different cohorts; and researchers may have potential biases when they are aware that the subjects are adopted (Finley, 1999). At the same time, criticism has been directed at conclusions about the level of adoptees' adjustment problems based on their higher usage of mental health services. Warren (1992), for example, maintains that overrepresentation of adoptees in clinical settings is associated more powerfully with factors related to adoptive parents than with the nature or frequency of problems among adoptees: adoptive parents' heightened sensitivity to the risks that adoption poses for their children and their greater readiness to seek mental health services for their children; their perceptions of problems associated with adoption as potentially threatening to the integrity of the family and, as a result, their higher motivation to seek treatment; and the higher socioeconomic status of adoptive families, which gives them greater access to mental health services.

Infant Versus Older Child Adoption

Studies of adoptees' psychological adjustment have not consistently distinguished outcomes for individuals adopted as infants from outcomes for individuals adopted at older ages (Finley, 1999). A lack of clarity regarding the population of adoptees under study may account, to some degree, for the conflicting findings related to adjustment outcomes for adoptees (Groza & Rosenberg, 2001). Although there are findings to the contrary (e.g., Moore & Fombonne, 1999), research has generally supported the belief of many adoption professionals that children adopted at older ages are at greater risk of psychological and behavioral problems (Juffer & van Ijzendoorn, 2005; Sharma et al., 1998; Barth & Berry, 1988). Sharma et al. (1996b), for example, found in their multistate study of 4,682 adopted children that when compared with children adopted as infants, children placed at older ages had greater adjustment difficulties, and children placed with adoptive families after the age of 10 years had the most serious problems, including higher rates of substance abuse and antisocial behavior. Other studies have associated older age at the time of adoptive placement with early disruptive life experiences that may affect adopted children's later adjustment. These studies have found that two factors—a history of multiple placements prior to adoption and a history of abuse or neglect—place an adopted child at increased risk for developing adjustment problems (Barth & Berry, 1988; Groza & Ryan, 2002; McRoy, Grotevant, & Zurcher, 1988; Verhulst & Verslusis-den Bieman, 1992).

Adoptees as Compared With Nonadoptees in
Intact Families and With Children at Risk

A third issue in the research regarding adoptees' overall adjustment relates to the use of different comparison groups and the meaningfulness of the findings depending on the group with which adoptees are compared. A number of studies have compared adoptees with non-adopted persons raised in intact families, and these studies consistently have found lower levels of functioning among adoptees (Bohman & Von Knorring, 1979; Dalby et al., 1982; Holden, 1991; Rogeness et al., 1988; Schechter et al., 1964; Sharma et al., 1996a; Silver, 1970, 1989; Simon & Senturia, 1966; Verhulst et al., 1990a). Another body of research has compared adoptees with children and adolescents in foster care or institutional settings or with children subject to maltreatment by their birth families, and these studies have found that adopted persons function far better (Bohman, 1970; Bohman & Sigvardsson, 1990; Hodges & Tizard, 1989; Triseliotis & Hill, 1990).

The findings have differential applications, an aspect of the research that has not always been acknowledged in discussions of adoptees' adjustment and overall well-being (Sharma et al., 1998). The research that has compared adoptees with children and adolescents in intact families, on the one hand, has sought a better understanding of how well adopted persons fare as compared with nonadopted persons and, with that focus, has provided a basis for assessing the needs of adoptees and their families and developing responsive services. On the other hand, the research that has compared adoptees with children in foster care or institutional care or in abusive or neglectful birth family environments has sought to evaluate the role of adoption as an alternative for children whose birth families cannot or will not care for them. With that focus, the research has provided a basis for understanding the benefits of adoption in relation to nonpermanent, nonfamily, and/or compromised family environments. The contributions of each body of research are distinct and provide an understanding of different aspects of adoption in relation to outcomes for adoptees.

Identity Formation

In contrast to the fairly extensive body of research on adoptee psychological and behavioral adjustment, there has been less attention from a research perspective on adoptees' identity formation. To some extent, the research has considered the question of whether the process by which adoptees form their identities differs from typical patterns of identity development or presents greater challenges for adopted adolescents compared with adolescents who are not adopted. The clinical literature, however, is far more extensive than is the research on this issue (Freundlich & Lieberthal, 2000). The clinical literature suggests that adoptees in adolescence may face a more complex task in resolving identity issues than do nonadoptees because they confront hurdles related to adoption in addition to issues that parallel those faced by nonadopted adolescents (Brodzinsky, 1987; Goebels & Lott, 1986; Rosenberg, 1992). Some clinicians believe that adolescent identity struggles may be intensified by the fact of adoption itself, with early loss exerting significant effects on identity formation (Frisk, 1964; Hoopes, 1990). Other clinicians identify specific aspects of adoption that may have a particular impact on identity: adoptees' physical dissimilarity to adoptive family members; fantasies about birth parents who are not known to them or not present in their lives; and the need, in some cases, to separate from both adoptive and birth families (Schechter, 1960; Sorosky, Baran, & Pannor, 1975).

Research has not provided empirical validation for such postulated psychological phenomena as "family romance" (Hajal & Rosenberg, 1991; Lawton & Gross, 1964; Rosenberg, 1992) or "genealogical bewilderment" (Lifton, 1994; Sants, 1964). It has, however, contributed to a better understanding of the social factors associated with adopted adolescents' identity formation, particularly adoptees' relationships with their adoptive parents (Hoopes, 1990; McWhinnie, 1969; Rickarby & Egan, 1980; Sabalis & Burch, 1980; Stein & Hoopes, 1985) and the impact of adoptive parents' attitudes toward adoption on adolescents' sense of security and sense of identity (Blum, 1976; Schoenberg, 1974; Sorosky, Baran, & Pannor, 1984; Stein & Hoopes, 1985).

Adult Adoptees

There is relatively little research with adult adoptees in which the adoptees themselves (as opposed to their parents) are the primary source of information. To the extent that such research exists, it is primarily in the area of search and reunion and focuses on adoptees' motivations for searching.

Research has provided conflicting findings regarding the extent to which adoptees' interest in search is connected to the quality of their relationships with their adoptive parents. Triseliotis (1973) found that search was associated with high levels of dissatisfaction with the adoption experience; other studies have indicated that most adoptees who search are quite satisfied with their adoptions (Day & Leeding, 1980); and yet other studies have found more or less equal distributions of satisfaction and dissatisfaction among adoptees who search (Kowal & Schilling, 1985; Schechter & Bertocci, 1990). Research also offers conflicting findings on the relationship between adoptees' fantasies of their birth parents and adoptees' interest in searching for their birth parents. Schechter and Bertocci (1990), for example, found that searchers were more likely to have positive images of their birth parents, and Triseliotis (1973) found that searchers were likely to hold negative views. A few studies have explored other possible motivations for search and suggested that searching may be associated with adoptees' perceptions that they are markedly different in physical appearance (Stein & Hoopes, 1985) or in personality (Schechter & Bertocci, 1990) from their adoptive parents and are motivated by a desire to find family members who physically or temperamentally resemble themselves.

As limited as the information is about adult adoptees who search and their search experiences, even less is known about adoptees who do not choose to search. The few studies that have compared nonsearchers with searchers suggest that nonsearchers tend to be more satisfied with the level of their adoptive parents' communications with them about their adoptions (Aumend & Barrett, 1984); score higher on scales measuring self-esteem and self-concept (Sobol & Cardiff, 1983); and score lower on scales measuring self-abasement (Reynolds, Eisnitz, Chiappise, & Walsh, 1976). The research provides little information on the reasons why adoptees choose not to search when they have information regarding their birth parents. The limited research on this issue suggests that the decision not to search is connected to adoptees' fear of not being able to fully integrate the information they might receive (Frisk, 1964); a greater interest in medical and genealogical information than in actual contact with birth family members (Blum, 1976); and a desire to avoid having information about themselves made available to their birth parents (McWhinnie, 1969). It is clear that the understanding of search is partial at best because most adoption research has focused on adoptees who search (Wegar, 1997).

International Adoptees

Research with international adoptees is extremely limited. Much of the research with internationally adopted children and adolescents has focused on issues of racial and cultural identity (Andujo, 1988; McRoy, Zurcher, Lauderdale, & Anderson, 1982; Simon & Alstein, 1992). Few studies have been conducted with adults who were adopted internationally as children, the exceptions being nonrepresentative surveys of adult Korean adoptees (Evan B. Donaldson Adoption Institute, 1999) and adult Vietnamese adoptees (Evan B. Donaldson Adoption Institute, 2000). These surveys reveal that the experiences of adoptees from Korea and Vietnam are highly individualized. Nonetheless, international adoptees in both surveys consistently reported high levels of racism and discrimination as they were growing up in American communities. These adult adoptees also reported that many, if not most, individuals who are adopted internationally seek connections with their birth culture, connections that are often more powerful for them than the possibility of connecting with their birth families.

RESEARCH WITH ADOPTIVE PARENTS

The research with adoptive parents is surprisingly limited, given the emphasis in practice on serving adoptive parents, particularly in the arenas of infant and international adoption. The two areas that have been subject to some study are the psychological and social aspects of adoptive parenthood and the qualifying process through which it is determined whether an individual will be allowed to adopt. More recently, some work has focused on the perceptions of prospective adoptive parents about the adoption process itself (Katz, 2004).

Research regarding the psychological and social implications of becoming an adoptive parent primarily focuses on adoption in relation to infertility. A study by Berry and colleagues (1996) revealed that most adopters have tried to become pregnant before adopting. The researchers found that 83% of those who adopted through private agencies, 80% of those who adopted independently, and 50% of those who adopted through public agencies had unsuccessful attempts at pregnancy. Although significant percentages of adopters reported that they adopted because they were unable to have a biological child, the data also make it clear that slightly more than one half of families who adopted children from the foster care system had biological children of their own (Berry et al., 1996).

Parents who choose to adopt for reasons other than infertility, however, have not been the subject of research to any meaningful extent. Instead, the research has focused on individuals' experiences as they realize that biological parenthood will not be possible and that parenthood can be achieved only through adoption. As one example, Sandelowski (1995) has described the experiential course of infertile couples who, having made the decision to adopt, move toward the point at which a child will be placed with them. She found that this experience involves certain unique psychological processes that distinguish the achievement of social (as opposed to biological) parenthood: creation of "a temporal order" to cope with the unmarked adoption waiting period so that the couple can gain control over the uncertainty and avoid "living only to wait for a child"; the construction of a biography for the child that meshes with the adopters' own biography and emphasizes that the child is "loved" by them; and finally, staking "a claim" to "own" the child as their own. The "claiming" process principally involved adopters' concerns about themselves as "genuine" parents: their anxieties about being "accepted" as the child's "real parents"; their efforts to deemphasize "the importance of the blood tie between parent and child"; and their struggles to establish a "right" to their child "by emphasizing the close biological or biographical match between them and their child" (Sandelowski, 1995, p. 130).

Although the home study process has been dealt with in the practice literature (e.g., Barker, Byrne, Morrison, & Spenser, 1998; Rycus, Hughes, & Goodman, 1998), there is remarkably little research that attempts to validate the processes that are used to accept or reject adoptive applicants. Brown and Brieland (1975), in their early work and one of the few studies on this issue, examined the processes that agencies used in evaluating couples who sought to adopt infants. They reported the results of two nationwide studies of 184 social workers from 27 adoption agencies in which social workers indicated, based on the criteria they generally used in their own practice, whether they would accept or reject certain prospective adoptive couples. The researchers found that there was a statistically significant level of agreement among the social workers in their judgments, but they emphasized that from a practical standpoint, the level of agreement was not "high enough" (p. 293). They found that within many agencies, social workers were evenly split as to whether a particular applicant couple should be accepted or rejected, suggesting that social workers' judgments of the applicants' strengths and weaknesses were based on widely different value systems. The researchers highlighted the need to identify criteria essential to assessment decisions and use standardized procedures to obtain and give weight to the most relevant data.

These recommendations notwithstanding, there have been no outcome studies evaluating different methods of assessing adoptive parents in terms either of their effectiveness in recruiting adoptive families or of achieving optimal outcomes for children (Sellick & Thoburn, 1996). There is some evidence from nonclinical studies that adoptive parents tend to demonstrate good psychological health and levels of marital adjustment at the time of adoption (Levy-Shiff, Bar, & Har-Even, 1990), outcomes that might be associated with the use of effective assessment processes. It is equally possible, however, that the overall health and stability of adoptive parents is the result of self-selection.

OPENNESS IN ADOPTION

One area in which there has been research with regard to all members of the triad is the increasingly common practice of open adoption. Researchers have considered the impact of greater openness on birth parents, adoptive parents, and, to a lesser degree, adopted children (Haugaard, Moed, & West, 2001).

Although concerns have been expressed that openness may prolong birth parents' unresolved grief (Byrd, 1999), several researchers have found that birth parents view greater openness as beneficial (Christian, McRoy, Grotevant, & Bryant, 1997; Fratter, 1991; Grotevant & McRoy, 1997; Hughes, 1995; Lauderdale & Boyle, 1994; McRoy & Grotevant, 2002; Sullivan & Lathrop, 2004). Grotevant and McRoy (1997), in their longitudinal research on the impact of open adoption on all members of the triad, found that birth parents benefited from greater openness. They compared the experiences of birthmothers in fully disclosed adoptions (in which information was shared directly between birth parents and adoptive parents, usually through telephone calls and face-to-face meetings); confidential adoptions (in which no information was shared between birth and adoptive parents after the adoptive placement); and mediated adoptions (in which information was exchanged between birth and adoptive families through an adoption agency staff member acting as an intermediary). The researchers found that birthmothers in fully disclosed adoptions had higher levels of grief resolution regarding the adoption decision than did birthmothers who had no contact with the adoptive family or whose contact with the family had terminated. They also found that birthmothers in fully disclosed adoptions enjoyed levels of self-esteem equivalent to those of birthmothers in closed and mediated adoptions. Similarly, Cushman, Kalmuss, & Namerow (1997), in their study of adolescent birthmothers who resided in maternity homes at the time of relinquishment, found that the receipt of letters and pictures was associated with significantly less worry and slightly higher levels of relief. birthmothers who visited the adoptive family or spoke with them over the telephone reported significantly lower levels of grief, worry, and regret and a greater sense of relief and peace about the adoption.

Concerns have also been expressed that adoptive parents will experience openness as an intrusion into the integrity of their family (Hollinger, 2000). Research suggests that, to the contrary, adoptive parents find greater connections with birth parents to be positive. Siegel (1993), for example, probed the sentiments of 21 adoptive couples in open adoption arrangements. She found that despite initial fears and concerns about openness, most of the respondents identified open adoption with more autonomous parenting and family functioning. They reported that open adoption gave them a sense of control with regard to birth parents; prepared them to effectively fulfill their roles as parents; dissolved fantasies about their child's birth parents; and alleviated guilt and any moral apprehension about "having someone else's child" (p. 18). Interestingly, the adoptive parents reported that openness was "simply not that much of a concern" when weighed against the more difficult issues of infertility: finding a child to adopt; "dealing with unresponsive and obstructive social workers, lawyers, and medical personnel" (p. 20); and coping with the lifelong issues involved in every adoption.

Other research on the impact of open adoption on adoptive families likewise indicates that the "concerns and dire warnings of open adoption critics" have not come to fruition (Brodzinsky et al., 1998, p. 83). Studies have found that adoptive parents in open arrangements report positive benefits for themselves and their families, including a high level of satisfaction with openness and good relationships with birth parents (Belbas, 1987; Etter, 1993; Gross, 1993; Haugaard, West, & Moed, 2000); a greater sense of entitlement to their child (Belbas, 1987; McRoy & Grotevant, 1988); fewer concerns about attachment issues (Silverstein & Demick, 1994); and less concern about efforts by birth parents to reclaim their child (Belbas, 1987).

The research on the impact of openness on adopted children has been limited, largely because the systematic practice of openness is a fairly recent development. It is too early to assess the full impact on young adoptees participating in current research, although the knowledge base is growing (Berry, 1991; Cubito & Brandon, 2000; Gross, 1993; Howe, Feast, & Coster, 2000; Muller & Perry, 2001). In 1998, Grotevant and McRoy, based on their longitudinal study of openness in adoption, reported initial findings on children's perceptions of their open adoptions. They found that the majority of children in their study (all of whom were adopted as infants) were curious about their birth parents and birth siblings. Children with less information about their birth parents were more likely to wonder about their birth parents' physical appearance, health, and well-being. Children with more information tended to wonder about what their birth parents had done since they had contact with them last and when they would meet again, or if they had had no contact with their birth parents, whether they would meet. The researchers found that children did not feel confused or anxious by open adoption arrangements, but instead, openness gave "adoptive parents an opportunity to facilitate their child's understanding of adoption" (pp. 104–105). In the second wave of the study, McRoy and Grotevant (2002) found that adjustment for children with contact with their birthmothers depended on adoptive family relationships and collaboration between the adoptive family and the birthmother. The researchers highlighted the need for more information about the effects of open adoption on adoptees' adjustment as they develop throughout adolescence into adulthood.

The research on the impact of openness on older children in foster care who are adopted also suggests certain benefits to children. Research has shown that, in general, children who maintain ongoing contact with their birth parents have a higher sense of well-being and that contact promotes healthy development (Garrison, 1983). Studies have indicated that the involvement of the birth family and their cooperation with the adoption promote the child's ability to accept the adoptive family (Borgman, 1981); resolve the child's loyalty conflicts after the adoption (Smith & Howard, 1994); and minimize negative behavioral responses to the changes brought about by adoption (Smith & Howard, 1994). There appear to be situations, however, in which ongoing contact between birth parents and their children may not be appropriate for children in foster care who are adopted. Appell (1996), for example, has suggested that these situations may include cases in which there have been multiple unsuccessful placements of the child and the presence of the birth parents presents a risk of future disruption; there is a history of severe child abuse within the birth family; birth parents, as a result of mental health, substance abuse, or other problems, are likely to be unduly disruptive to the adoption; and birth parents continue to present a risk of severe and imminent harm to the child. Research has not addressed the impact of openness on children under such circumstances, suggesting that much more needs to be understood about openness in the adoption of children in foster care.

AN ASSESSMENT OF THE CONTRIBUTION OF RESEARCH TO ADOPTION PRACTICE

Research has made a number of important contributions to adoption practice. It has informed practice with respect to those members of the triad already of great concern to practitioners— unmarried women who may place their newborns for adoption, adopted children, and, to some extent, adoptive parents. Research has addressed the factors associated with women's, and particularly adolescents', decision making regarding adoption and has attempted to assess the longer-term impact of relinquishment on birthmothers. There are marked discrepancies in research findings in this area, however, which raise a number of questions. It is not clear whether the different findings on outcomes for birthmothers are attributable to the degree to which such studies are longitudinal in nature, different samples of birthmothers who participate in the studies, or the overall cultural climate in which the research is conducted. At the same time, it is clear that the psychological and social ramifications of relinquishment on middle-income, White women have been of considerable research interest, whereas the impact of adoption on birthmothers in other countries and women whose parental rights are involuntarily terminated has not garnered equivalent attention.

With regard to the research on adopted children and adolescents, the findings are variable with regard to psychosocial and behavioral functioning, making it difficult to interpret clearly the impact of adoption on adoptees. Nonetheless, the research highlights a number of issues related to psychological well-being and identity formation that require greater attention in both adoption and mental health practice. Primary attention has been given to the impact of adoption on children adopted as infants as opposed to children who are adopted at older ages.

With regard to adoptive parents, the research has primarily been sociological in nature as opposed to practice based, with principal attention given to personal and social definitions of the role of "parent." The findings in relation to the adoption qualification process are limited, and neither practice nor research has made significant contributions to the understanding of who should and who should not be permitted to adopt. It is clear, however, that the level of research interest in infertile individuals who may adopt far exceeds the interest in individuals who adopt children in foster care, despite the growing and pressing need to recruit greater numbers of families for these children.

Research has not focused significantly on the experiences of birth fathers. Similarly, in adoption practice, birth fathers have not been the subject of significant attention and have often been discounted in terms of any "real" role in adoption. Birth fathers continue to be viewed in stereotypic terms. Research has also not extensively focused on adult adoptees. Because they are not involved in the adoption placement decision and process, there has been a tendency to view adopted adults as having no meaningful role in adoption. Adult adoptees are often overlooked altogether or considered only in relation to their interactions with other triad members through search and reunion.

With regard to greater openness in adoption, research thus far has offered limited guidance. Research in this area, however, continues to expand, especially through the work of McRoy and Grotevant, and a more solid knowledge base that addresses the many challenges in this area is developing. Until there is a clearer understanding of the impact of openness across all forms of adoption, however, serious questions remain about the quality of services that are being provided. The failure to address openness in the adoption of children in foster care, in particular, reflects the overarching need for greater research with regard to the adoption of older children with histories of abuse or neglect.

CONCLUSION

Adoption research has focused on infant adoption, with principal interest in birthmothers' decision making, the impact on women when they relinquish their newborns, the psychological and behavioral impact of adoption on children adopted as infants, and the effects of infertility and adoption on infant adopters. It has made important contributions to practice in each of these areas. Far less attention has been given to practice issues in international adoption and the adoption of children in foster care, despite the fact that both these forms of adoption have assumed more prominent roles with the significant increase in the number of children abroad and in the U.S. foster care system who need adoptive families. As future agendas for research are developed, the need for empirical contributions to advance practice in the fields of international adoption and the adoption of children in foster care must be recognized.

REFLECTION QUESTIONS

1. What accounts for the research focus on the birthmothers of infants placed for adoption and the relative lack of research interest in the experiences of birth fathers, the parents of children adopted internationally, and parents whose rights are involuntarily terminated?

2. On which issues should research focus in the future to develop a fuller understanding of the impact of adoption on adopted children, adolescents, and adults?

3. Why might the absence of research on the experiences of adoptive parents be considered "surprising"? Is additional research on their experiences needed?

REFERENCES

Andujo, E. (1988). Ethnic identity of transethnically adopted Hispanic adolescents. *Social Work, 37,* 531–535.

Appell, A. R. (1996). The move toward legally sanctioned cooperative adoption: Can it survive the Uniform Adoption Act? *Family Law Quarterly, 30,* 483–518.

Aronson, J. E. (2000). Alcohol related disorders and children adopted from abroad. In R. P. Barth, M. Freundlich, & D. Brodzinsky (Eds.), *Adoption and prenatal alcohol and drug exposure: Research, policy and practice* (pp. 147–170). Washington, DC: CWLA Press.

Aumend, S., & Barrett, M. (1984). Self-concept and attitudes toward adoption: A comparison of searching and non-searching adult adoptees. *Child Welfare, 63,* 251–259.

Bachrach, C. A. (1986). Adoption plans, adopted children, and adoptive mothers. *Journal of Marriage and the Family, 48,* 243–253.

Bachrach, C. A., Abma, P. F., Sambrano, S., & London, K. A. (1990). *Adoption in the 1980s: No. 181. Advance data from vital and health statistics.* Hyattsville, MD: National Center for Health Statistics.

Bachrach, C. A., Stolley, K. S., & London, K. A. (1992). Relinquishment of premarital births: Evidence from national survey data. *Family Planning Perspectives, 24,* 27–32.

Barker, S., Byrne, S., Morrison, M., & Spenser, M. (1998). *Preparing for permanence: Assessment: Points to consider for those assessing potential adopters and foster carers.* London: British Agencies for Adoption and Fostering.

Barth, R. P., & Berry, M. (1988). *Adoption and disruption: Rates, risks, and responses.* New York: Aldine De Gruyter.

Belbas, N. (1987). Staying in touch: Empathy in open adoptions. *Smith College Studies in Social Work, 57,* 184–198.

Berry, M. (1991). The effects of open adoption on biological and adoptive parents and the children: The arguments and the evidence. *Child Welfare, 70,* 637–651.

Berry, M., Barth, R. P., & Needell, B. (1996). Preparation, support and satisfaction of adoptive families in agency and independent adoptions. *Child and Adolescent Social Work Journal, 13,* 157–183.

Blum, L. H. (1976). When adoptive families ask for help. *Primary Care, 3,* 241–249.

Blum, R. W., Resnick, M. D., & Stark, T. (1987). The impact of a parental notification law on adolescent abortion decision-making. *American Journal of Public Health, 77,* 619–620.

Bohman, M. (1970). *Adopted children and their families: A follow-up study of adopted children, their background environment, and adjustment.* Stockholm: Proprius.

Bohman, M., & Sigvardsson, S. (1990). Outcome in adoption: Lessons from longitudinal studies. In D. M. Brodzinsky & M. D. Schechter (Eds.), *The psychology of adoption* (pp. 93–106). New York: Oxford University Press.

Bohman, M., & Von Knorring, A. L. (1979). Psychiatric illness among adults adopted as infants. *Acta Paediatrica Scandinavica, 60,* 106–112.

Borgman, R. (1981). Antecedents and consequences of parental rights termination for abused and neglected children. *Child Welfare, 60,* 391–404.

Bouchier, P., Lambert, L., & Triseliotis, J. (1991). *Parting with a child for adoption: The mother's perspective.* London: British Association of Adoption and Fostering.

Brodzinsky, A. (1990). Surrendering an infant for adoption: The birthmother experience. In D. Brodzinsky & M. Schechter (Eds.), *The psychology of adoption.* New York: Oxford University Press.

Brodzinsky, D. M. (1987). Adjustment to adoption: A psychosocial perspective. *Clinical Psychology Review, 7,* 25–47.

Brodzinsky, D. M. (1993). Long term outcomes in adoption. *Future of Children, 3,* 153–166.

Brodzinsky, D., Smith, D. W., & Brodzinsky, A. B. (1998). *Children's adjustment to adoption: Developmental and clinical issues.* Thousands Oaks, CA: Sage.

Brown, E. G., & Brieland, D. (1975). Adoptive screening: New data, new dilemmas. *Social Work, 20,* 291–295.

Byrd, D. (1999). Open adoption: Who benefits? In C. Marshner & W. L. Pierce (Eds.), *Adoption factbook III* (pp. 413–416). Washington, DC: National Council for Adoption.

Cadoret, R. J. (1995). Adoption studies. *Alcohol Health and Research World, 19,* 19195–19200.

Carey, W. B., Lipton, W. L., & Myers, R. A. (1974). Temperament in adopted and foster babies. *Child Welfare, 53,* 352–359.

Carr, M. J. (2000). birthmothers and subsequent children: The role of personally traits and attachment history. *Journal of Social Distress and the Homeless, 9,* 339–348.

Chandra, A., Abma, J., Maza, P., & Bachrach, C. (1999). *Adoption, adoption seeking, and relinquishment for adoption in the United States: No. 36. Advance data.* Washington, DC: National Center for Health Statistics.

Charlton, L., Crank, M., Kansara, K., & Oliver, C. (1998). *Still screaming: Birthparents compulsorily separated from their children.* Manchester, UK: After Adoption.

Chippendale-Bakker, V., & Foster, L. (1996). Adoption in the 1990s: Sociodemographic determinants of biological parents choosing adoption. *Child Welfare, 75,* 337–355.

Christian, C., McRoy, R., Grotevant, H., & Bryant, C. (1997). Grief resolution of birthmothers in confidential, time-limited mediated, ongoing mediated, and fully disclosed adoptions. *Adoption Quarterly, 1*(2), 35–58.

Cicchini, M. (1993). *The development of responsibility: The experience of birth fathers in adoption.* Sydney, New South Wales, Australia: Adoption Research and Counseling Services.

Clapton, G. (1997). Birth fathers, the adoption process and fatherhood. *Adoption & Fostering, 21,* 29–36.

Condon, J. T. (1986). Psychological disability in women who relinquish a baby for adoption. *Medical Journal of Australia, 144,* 117–119.

Cubito, D. S., & Brandon, K. O. (2000). Psychological adjustment in adult adoptees: Assessment of distress, depression, and anger. *American Journal of Orthopsychiatry, 70*(3), 408–413.

Curtis, P. A. (1990). An ethnographic study of pregnancy counseling. *Clinical Social Work Journal, 18,* 243–256.

Cushman, L. F., Kalmuss, D., & Namerow, P. B. (1993). Placing an infant for adoption: The experiences of young birthmothers. *Social Work, 38,* 264–272.

Cushman, L. F., Kalmuss, D., & Namerow, P. B. (1997). Openness in adoption: Experiences and social psychological outcomes among birthmothers. *Marriage and Family Review, 25,* 7–18.

Dalby, J. T., Fox, S., & Haslam, R. H. (1982). Adoption and foster care rates in pediatric disorders. *Developmental and Behavioral Pediatrics, 3,* 61–64.

Day, C., & Leeding, A. (1980). *Access to birth records: The impact of section 26 of the Children Act 1975* (Research Series No. 1). London: Association of British Adoption and Fostering Agencies.

DeSimone, M. (1996). birthmother loss: Contributing factors to unresolved grief. *Clinical Social Work Journal, 24,* 65–76.

Deykin, E. Y., Patti, P., & Ryan, J. (1988). Fathers of adopted children: A study on the impact of child surrender on birthfathers. *American Journal of Orthopsychiatry, 58,* 240–248.

Dickson, I. R., Heffron, W. M., & Parker, C. (1990). Children from disrupted and adoptive homes on an inpatient unit. *American Journal of Orthopsychiatry, 60,* 594–602.

Duncan, G. J., & Hoffman, S. D. (1990). Teenage welfare receipt and subsequent dependence among Black adolescent mothers. *Family Planning Perspectives, 22,* 16–20.

Dworkin, R. J., Harding, J. T., & Schreiber, N. B. (1993). Parenting or placing: Decision-making by pregnant teens. *Youth & Society, 25,* 75–92.

Edelstein, S. B., Burge, D., & Waterman, J. (2002). Older children in preadoptive homes: Issues before termination of parental rights. *Child Welfare, 81,* 101–121.

Edwards, D. S. (1995). *Transformation of motherhood in adoption: The experiences of relinquishing mothers.* Unpublished doctoral dissertation, University of North Florida, Jacksonville.

Etter, J. (1993). Levels of cooperation and satisfaction in 56 open adoptions. *Child Welfare, 72,* 257–267.

Evan B. Donaldson Adoption Institute. (1999). *Survey of adult Korean adoptees: Report on the findings.* New York: Author.

Evan B. Donaldson Adoption Institute. (2000). *Survey of adult Vietnamese adoptees.* New York: Author.

Finley, G. E. (1999). Children of adoptive families. In W. K. Silverman & T. H. Ollendick (Eds.), *Developmental issues in clinical treatment of children* (pp. 359–370). Boston: Allyn & Bacon.

Fratter, J. (1991). Parties in the triangle. *Adoption and Fostering, 15,* 91–98.

Fravel, D. L., McRoy, R. G., & Grotevant, H. D. (2000). Birthmother perceptions of the psychologically present adopted child: Adoption openness and boundary ambiguity. *Family Relations, 49,* 425–433.

Freundlich, M., & Lieberthal, J. K. (2000). *The impact of adoption on members of the triad.* Washington, DC: CWLA Press.

Frisk, M. (1964). Identity problems and confused conceptions of the genetic ego in adopted children during adolescence. *Acta Paedo Psychiatrica, 31,* 6–12.

Furstenberg, F., Jr., Brooks-Gunn, J., & Morgan, S. P. (1987). *Adolescent mothers in later life.* Cambridge, MA: Cambridge University Press.

Garrison, M. (1983). Why terminate parental rights? *Stanford Law Review, 35,* 423–437.

Geber, G., & Resnick, M. D. (1988). Family functioning of adolescents who parent and place for adoption. *Adolescence, 23,* 417–428.

Goebels, B., & Lott, S. L. (1986, August 23). *Adoptees' resolution of the adolescent identity crisis: Where are the taproots?* Paper presented at the meeting of the American Psychological Association, Washington, DC.

Gross, H. D. (1993). Open adoption: A research-based literature review and new data. *Child Welfare, 72,* 269–284.

Grotevant, H. D. (2003). Counseling psychology meets the complex world of adoption. *The Counseling Psychologist, 31,* 753–762.

Grotevant, H. D., & McRoy, R. G. (1997). The Minnesota/Texas Adoption Research Project: Implications of openness in adoption for development and relationships. *Applied Developmental Science, 1,* 168–188.

Grotevant, H. D., & McRoy, R. G. (1998). *Openness in adoption: Exploring family connections.* Thousand Oaks, CA: Sage.

Groza, V., & Rosenberg, K. F. (2001). Treatment issues of adoptees placed as infants and as older children: Similarities and differences. In V. Groza & K. F. Rosenberg (Eds.), *Clinical and practice issues in adoption: Bridging the gap between adoptees placed as infants and as older children* (pp. 1–19). Westport, CT: Bergin & Garvey.

Groza, V., & Ryan, S. D. (2002). Pre-adoption stress and its association with child behavior in domestic special needs adoption. *Psychoneuroendocrinology, 27,* 181–197.

Hajal, F., & Rosenberg, E. B. (1991). The family life cycle in adoptive families. *American Journal of Orthopsychiatry, 61,* 78–85.

Haugaard, J. J., Moed, A. M., & West, N. M. (2001). Outcomes of open adoption. *Adoption Quarterly, 4*(3), 63–73.

Haugaard, J. J., West, N. M., & Moed, A. M. (2000). Open adoptions: Attitudes and experiences. *Adoption Quarterly, 4*(2), 89–99.

Hodges, J., & Tizard, B. (1989). IQ and behavioral adjustment of ex-institutional adolescents. *Journal of Psychiatry, 30,* 53–75.

Hofferth, S. L. (1987). Social and economic consequences of teenage childbearing. In S. L. Hofferth & C. D. Hayes (Eds.), *Risking the future: Adolescent sexuality, pregnancy and childbearing* (Vol. 2, pp. 123–144). Washington, DC: National Academy Press.

Holden, N. L. (1991). Adoption and eating disorders: A high-risk group? *British Journal of Psychiatry, 158,* 829–833.

Hollinger, J. H. (2000). Authenticity and identity in contemporary adoptive families. *Journal of Gender Specific Medicine, 18,* 36–42.

Hoopes, J. L. (1990). Adoption and identity formation. In D. Brodzinsky & M. Schechter (Eds.), *The psychology of adoption* (pp. 144–166). New York: Oxford University Press.

Howe, D., Feast, J., & Coster, D. (2000). *Adoption, search, and reunion: The long term experiences of adopted adults.* Norwian, UK: University of East Anglia.

Hughes, B. (1995). Openness and contact in adoption: A child-centered perspective. *British Journal of Social Work, 25,* 729–747.

Hughes, B., & Logan, J. (1993). *Birth parents: The hidden dimension.* Manchester, UK: Department of Social Policy and Social Work, University of Manchester.

Irhammar, M., & Cederblad, M. (2000). Outcome of intercounty adoption in Sweden. In P. Selman (Ed.), *Intercounty adoption: Developments, trends, and perspectives* (pp. 132–146). London: British Agencies for Adoption and Fostering.

Johnson, K., Banghan, H., & Liyao, W. (1998). Infant abandonment and adoption in China. *Population and Development Review, 24,* 469–510.

Juffer, F., & van Ijzendoorn, M. H. (2005). Behavior problems and mental health referrals of international adoptees: A meta-analysis. *Journal of the American Medical Association, 293*(20), 2501–2515.

Kalmuss, D. (1992). Adoption and Black teenagers: The viability of a pregnancy resolution strategy. *Journal of Marriage and the Family, 54,* 485–495.

Katz, J. (2004). How parents really feel about the adoption process. *Adoptalk, 8–9,* 12.

Kowal, K. A., & Schilling, K. M. (1985). Adoption through the eyes of adult adoptees. *American Journal of Orthopsychiatry, 55,* 354–362.

Lauderdale, J., & Boyle, J. (1994). Infant relinquishment through adoption. *Image: Journal of Nursing Scholarship, 26,* 213–217.

Lawton, J., & Gross, S. (1964). Review of the psychiatric literature on adopted children. *Archives of General Psychiatry, 11,* 663–694.

Lee, R. M. (2003). The transracial adoption paradox: History, research, and counseling implications of cultural socialization. *The Counseling Psychologist, 31,* 711–734.

Levy-Shiff, R., Bar, O., & Har-Even, D. (1990). Psychological adjustment of adoptive parents-to-be. *American Journal of Orthopsychiatry, 60,* 258–267.

Leynes, C. (1980). Keep or adopt: A study of factors influencing pregnant adolescents' plans for their babies. *Child Psychiatry and Human Development, 11,* 105–113.

Lifton, B. J. (1994). *Journey of the adopted self: A quest for wholeness.* New York: Basic Books.

Lightman, E., & Schlesinger, B. (1982). Pregnant adolescents in maternity homes: Some professional concerns. In R. R. Stuart & C. F. Wells (Eds.), *Pregnancy in adolescence: Needs, problems, and management* (pp. 363–406). New York: Van Nostrand Reinhold.

Lipman, E. L., Offord, D. R., Boyle, M. H., & Racine, Y. A. (1993). Follow-up of psychiatric and educational morbidity among adopted children. *Journal of the American Academy of Child and Adolescent Psychiatry, 32,* 1007–1012.

Lücker-Babel, L. (1990). The right of the child to express views and be heard: An attempt to interpret Article 12 of the UN Convention on the Rights of the Child. *International Journal of Children's Rights, 3,* 391–420.

Marquis, K. S., & Detweiler, R. A. (1985). Does adoption mean different? An attributional analysis. *Journal of Personality and Social Psychology, 48,* 1054–1066.

Mason, K., & Selman, P. (1997). Birth parents' experiences of contested adoption. *Adoption & Fostering, 21,* 21–28.

Mason, M. M. (1995a, October/November/December). Bringing birthfathers into the adoption loop. *Roots & Wings,* 27–30.

Mason, M. M. (1995b). *Out of the shadows: Birthfathers' stories.* Edina, MN: O. J. Howard.

McHutchinson, J. (1986). *Relinquishing a child: The circumstances and effects of loss.* Unpublished paper, University of New South Wales, Sydney, New South Wales, Australia.

McRoy, R. G., & Grotevant, H. D. (1988). Open adoptions: Practice and policy issues. *Journal of Social Work and Human Sexuality, 6,* 119–132.

McRoy, R. G., & Grotevant, H. D. (2002). *Longitudinal outcomes of openness in adoption: Implications for birthmothers, adoptive parents, and adopted children.* St. Paul: Minnesota University, Department of Family Social Science.

McRoy, R. G., Grotevant, H. D., & Zurcher, L. A. (1988). *The development of emotional disturbance in adopted adolescents: Origins and development.* New York: Praeger.

McRoy, R. G., Zurcher, L. A., Lauderdale, M. L., & Anderson, R. E. (1982). Self-esteem and racial identity in transracial and interracial adoptees. *Social Work, 27,* 522–526.

McWhinnie, A. M. (1969). The adopted child in adolescence. In G. Caplan & S. Lebovici (Eds.), *Psychological perspectives* (pp. 133–142). New York: Basic Books.

Mikawa, J. K., & Boston, J. A. (1968). Psychological characteristics of adopted children. *Psychiatric Quarterly Supplement, 42,* 274–281.

Moore, J., & Fombonne, E. (1999). Psychopathology in adopted and nonadopted children: A clinical sample. *American Journal of Orthopsychiatry, 69,* 403–409.

Mott, F., & Marsiglio, W. (1985). Early childbearing and completion of high school. *Family Planning Perspectives, 17,* 234–237.

Muller, U., & Perry, B. (2001). Adopted persons' search for and contact with their birth parents II: Adoptee-birth parent contact. *Adoption Quarterly, 4*(3), 39–62.

Namerow, P. B., Kalmuss, D. S., & Cushman, L. F. (1993). The determinants of young women's pregnancy-resolution choices. *Journal of Research on Adolescence, 3,* 193–215.

Norvell, M., & Guy, R. F. (1977). A comparison of self-concept in adopted and nonadopted adolescents. *Adolescence, 12,* 274–448.

Pilotti, F. J. (1993). Intercountry adoption: Trends, issues and policy implications for the 1990s. In F. J. Pilotti (Ed.), *Childhood* (Vol. 1, pp. 165–177). Montevideo, Uruguay: Instituto Interamericano del Niño.

Plomin, R., & DeFries, J. C. (1985). *Origins of individual differences in infancy: The Colorado Adoption Project.* New York: Academic Press.

Resnick, M. D. (1984). Studying adolescent mothers' decision making about adoption and parenting. *Social Work, 29,* 5–10.

Reynolds, W. F., Eisnitz, M. F., Chiappise, D., & Walsh, M. (1976). *Personality factors differentiating searching and non-searching adoptees.* Paper presented at the 84th annual convention of the American Psychological Association, Washington, DC.

Rickarby, G. A., & Egan, P. (1980). Issues of preventive work with adopted adolescents. *Medical Journal of Australia, 1,* 470–472.

Roby, J. L., & Matsumura, S. (2002). If I give young child, aren't we family? A study of birthmothers participating in Marshallman Islands: U.S. adoptions. *Adoption Quarterly, 5*(4), 7–31.

Rogeness, G. A., Hoppe, S. K., Macedo, C. A., Fischer, C., & Harris, W. R. (1988). Psychopathology in hospitalized adopted children. *Journal of the American Academy of Child and Adolescent Psychiatry, 27,* 628–631.

Rohner, R. P. (1986). *The warmth dimension: Foundations of parental acceptance-rejection.* Beverly Hills, CA: Sage.

Rosenberg, E. B. (1992). *The adoption life cycle: The children and their families through the years.* New York: Free Press.

Rotundo, E. A. (1985). American fatherhood: A historical perspective. *American Behavioral Scientist, 29,* 7–24.

Rycus, J. S., Hughes, R. C., & Goodman, D. A. (1998). Adoption. In J. S. Rycus & R. C. Hughes (Eds.), *Field guide to child welfare* (Vol. 4, pp. 881–1038). Washington, DC: CWLA Press.

Sabalis, R. F., & Burch, E. A. (1980). Comparisons of psychiatric problems of adopted and non-adopted patients. *Southern Medical Journal, 73*, 867–868.

Sandelowski, M. (1995). A theory of the transition to parenthood of infertile couples. *Research in Nursing & Health, 18*, 123–132.

Sants, H. J. (1964). Genealogical bewilderment in children with substitute parents. *British Journal of Medical Psychology, 37*, 133–141.

Schechter, M. (1960). Observations on adopted children. *Archives of General Psychiatry, 3*, 21–32.

Schechter, M., & Bertocci, D. (1990). The meaning of search. In D. Brodzinsky & M. Schechter (Eds.), *The psychology of adoption* (pp. 62–92). New York: Oxford University Press.

Schechter, M. D., Carlson, P., Simmons, J., & Work, H. (1964). Emotional problems in the adoptee. *Archives in General Psychiatry, 10*, 37–46.

Schoenberg, C. (1974). On adoption and identity. *Child Welfare, 53*, 549.

Sellick, C., & Thoburn, J. (1996). *What works in family placement?* Essex, UK: Barnardo's.

Sharma, A. R., McGue, M. K., & Benson, P. L. (1996a). The emotional and behavioral adjustment of United States adopted adolescents: Part I. A comparison study. *Children and Youth Services Review, 18*, 77–94.

Sharma, A. R., McGue, M. K., & Benson, P. L. (1996b). The emotional and behavioral adjustment of United States adopted adolescents: Part II. Age at adoption. *Children and Youth Services Review, 18*, 95–108.

Sharma, A. R., McGue, M. K., & Benson, P. L. (1998). The psychological adjustment of United States adopted adolescents and their nonadopted siblings. *Child Development, 69*, 791–802.

Siegel, D. H. (1993). Open adoption of infants: Adoptive parents' perceptions of advantages and disadvantages. *Social Work, 38*, 15–23.

Silver, L. B. (1970). Frequency of adoption in children with neurological learning disability syndrome. *Journal of Learning Disabilities, 3*, 10–14.

Silver, L. B. (1989). Frequency of adoption of children and adolescents with learning disabilities. *Journal of Learning Disabilities, 22*, 325–328.

Silverstein, D. R., & Demick, J. (1994). Toward an organizational-relational model of open adoption. *Family Process, 33*, 111–124.

Simon, N. M., & Senturia, A. G. (1966). Adoption and psychiatric illness. *American Journal of Psychiatry, 122*, 858–867.

Simon, R. J., & Alstein, H. (1992). *Adoption, race and identity: From infancy through adolescence.* New York: Praeger.

Slap, G., Goodman, E., & Huang, B. (2001). Adoption as a risk factor for attempted suicide during adolescence. *Pediatrics, 108*(2), 291–299.

Smith, S. L., & Howard, J. A. (1994). *The Adoption Preservation Project.* Normal: Illinois State University Department of Social Work.

Sobol, M. P., & Cardiff, J. (1983). A sociopsychological investigation of adult adoptees' search for birth parents. *Family Relations, 32*, 477–483.

Sorosky, A. D., Baran, A., & Pannor, R. (1975). Identity conflicts in adoptees. *American Journal of Orthopsychiatry, 45*, 18–27.

Sorosky, A. D., Baran, A., & Pannor, R. (1984). *The adoption triangle.* Garden City, NY: Anchor Books.

Stein, L. M., & Hoopes, J. L. (1985). *Identity formation in the adopted adolescent.* New York: Child Welfare League of America.

Strobino, D. M. (1987). The health and medical consequences of adolescent sexuality and pregnancy: A review of the literature. In S. L. Hoffert & C. D. Hayes (Eds.), *Risking the future: Adolescent sexuality, pregnancy and childbearing* (Vol. 2, pp. 93–122). Washington, DC: National Academy Press.

Sullivan, R., & Lathrop, E. (2004). Openness in adoption: Retrospective lessons and prospective choices. *Children and Youth Services Review, 26*(4), 393–411.

Thompson, L. A., & Plomin, R. (1988). The sequenced inventory of communication development: An adoption study of two- and three-year-olds. *International Journal of Behavioral Development, 11*, 219–231.

Triseliotis, J. (1973). *In search of origins: The experience of adopted people.* London: Routledge & Kegan Paul.

Triseliotis, J., & Hill, M. (1990). Contrasting adoption, foster care, and residential rearing. In D. M. Brodzinsky & M. D. Schechter (Eds.), *The psychology of adoption* (pp. 107–120). New York: Oxford University Press.

Van Keppel, M., & Winkler, R. (1983). *The adjustment of relinquishing mothers in adoption: The results of a national study.* Paper presented to the first NSCMC and ARMS conference, Melbourne, Victoria, Australia.

Verhulst, F. C., Althaus, M. S., & Versluis-den Bieman, H. J. M. (1990a). Problem behavior in international adoptees: I. An epidemiological study. *Journal of the American Academy of Child and Adolescent Psychiatry, 29*, 94–103.

Verhulst, F. C., Althaus, M., & Versluis-den Bieman, H. J. M. (1990b). Problem behavior in international adoptees: II. Age at placement. *Journal of the American Academy of Child and Adolescent Psychiatry, 31*, 518–524.

Verhulst, F. C., & Versluis-den Bieman, H. J. M. (1992). Damaging backgrounds: Later adjustment of international adoptees. *Journal of the American Academy of Child and Adolescent Psychiatry, 31*, 518–524.

Verhulst, F. C., & Versluis-den Bieman, H. J. M. (1995). Developmental course of problem behaviors in adolescent adoptees. *Journal of the American Academy of Child and Adolescent Psychiatry, 34*, 151–158.

Warren, S. B. (1992). Lower threshold for referral for psychiatric treatment for adopted adolescents. *Journal of the American Academy of Child and Adolescent Psychiatry, 31*, 512–517.

Wegar, K. (1997). *Adoption, identity, and kinship: The debate over sealed birth records.* New Haven, CT: Yale University Press.

Weintraub, M., & Konstam, V. (1995). Birthmothers: Silent relationships. *Affilia, 10*, 315–327.

Wells, S. (1993). Post-traumatic stress disorder in birthmothers. *Adoption & Fostering, 17*, 22–26.

Wiley, M. O., & Baden, A. L. (2005). Birth parents in adoption: Research, practice, and counseling psychology. *The Counseling Psychologist, 33*(1), 13–50.

Wilson, S. L. (2004). A current review of adoption research: Exploring individual differences in adjustment. *Children and Youth Services Review, 26*(8), 687–696.

Birth Mothers and Subsequent Children

22

The Role of Personality Traits and Attachment Theory

MARY JO CARR

Independent Consultant

HISTORICAL CONTEXT

Much has been written about the adoption triad: the adoptee, the birth parents, and the adoptive parents. One aspect that has often been underrepresented in the professional literature is the birth mother. It is impossible to view studies about unplanned pregnancy and birth mothers without also looking at the social context of the times in which the birth mothers relinquished their children to adoption. In the 1950s and into the late 1960s, most of the articles published on the psychology of the birth mother were based on psychoanalytic theory. Cattell's (1954) study, for instance, found that the unplanned pregnancy of an unmarried woman was a form of sexual acting out of unconscious needs due to unresolved parent-child conflicts. Within that context, it was assumed to indicate significant psychopathology on the part of the unmarried woman. Cattell also found that the unmarried woman who kept and raised her child was more emotionally unstable than the unmarried woman who relinquished her child for adoption.

Deutsch (1945) believed that women who became pregnant out of wedlock did so for several reasons. One was the unconscious acting out of their feelings toward their own mothers of maternal deprivation or abandonment. Another was the ambivalent feelings about dependency and powerlessness within the family. Still another was the need to punish the mother by subjecting her to the social stigma of the illegitimate pregnancy. Deutsch had a good point. An exclamation such as "How could you do this to me?" or "What will the neighbors think?" was probably uttered to almost every birth mother.

Heiman and Levitt's (1960) study had findings that were congruous in at least one aspect with Deutsch's beliefs. They, too, focused on the role of object loss in illegitimate pregnancy and found that many of the unmarried mothers seemed to be unconsciously seeking to reestablish lost relationships with their own mothers. They went on to say that such motivations are not limited to unmarried mothers but were perhaps more frequent in that group because of other multiple losses found so frequently in the histories of unmarried mothers.

Unfortunately, the unconscious seeking to reestablish lost relationships with mothers only served to bring on more loss for most unmarried mothers in the 1950s, 1960s, and 1970s. Not only were they unable to reestablish their lost relationships with their mothers, but they also lost their babies to adoption.

Relinquishment and Pathological Grief

Rynearson (1982) found that relinquishing a child for adoption presented the mothers with a discordant dilemma of separation and loss.

> First, the separation is permanent and was initiated by the relinquishing mother. Second, the loss is irresoluble because the child continues to exist. The timeless and volitional disengagement from her infant, who is alive and developing, inaugurates a significant maternal stress. (p. 338)

Millen and Roll (1985) studied 22 women who had surrendered a child for adoption and who later sought psychotherapy. They found that the women showed many of the elements of the patterns of bereavement described by Bowlby (1963, 1980). The women were told at the time that if they relinquished their child, they would forget about the experience. This was found to be grossly untrue.

Millen and Roll (1985) found instead that the experience of relinquishing a child is similar to pathological mourning, including feelings of intense loss, enduring panic, and unresolved anger; episodes of searching for the lost child in waking life or in dreams; and a sense of incompleteness.

In explaining pathological mourning, Bowlby (1963, 1980) suggested that the more detailed the picture we obtain of healthy mourning, the more clearly are we able to identify the pathological variants as being the result of defensive processes having interfered with and diverted its course.

Bowlby (1963, 1980) looked at four pathological variants of adult mourning and at the tendency for individuals who show these responses to have experienced the loss of a parent during childhood or adolescence. The four variants are

1. unconscious yearning for the lost person;
2. unconscious reproach against the lost person combined with conscious and often unremitting self-reproach;
3. compulsive caring for other persons; and
4. persistent disbelief that the loss is permanent.

As part of Millen and Roll's (1985) study, they took the results of a study by Parkes, Stevenson-Hinde, and Marris (1972) which was done on widows and compared the grief reactions of widows with women who had relinquished children for adoption. The grief reactions of Parkes et al.'s study were

1. Process of realization
2. An alarm reaction

3. An urge to search for and to find the lost person

4. Anger and guilt

5. Feelings of loss and self-mutilation

6. Identification phenomena

7. Pathological variants of grief

In a normal grief reaction, it is through the *process of realization* that the bereaved moves from denial of the loss to acceptance. To come to terms with the loss, the individual must come to realize that the loss is permanent. This proves almost impossible for a birth mother because her child exists in reality.

The *alarm reaction* was defined as the somatic symptoms such as restless anxiety, change in appetite, difficulty sleeping, and so on. Many of the mothers in Millen and Roll's (1985) study faced the same situation, seeing the security of their lives shattered as those around them began to withdraw emotionally. The loss of a child is a situation clearly capable of producing a high state of alarm.

Searching is an expected element in the normal grief reaction. Even though the bereaved can acknowledge that search for the dead person is irrational and futile, the impulse to search is strong. The urge to search is complicated for birth mothers because their searching impulses are not irrational and futile. Birth mothers know their child is alive and the possibility of future contact may be more than a fantasy.

Bowlby (1980) has shown that the *angry* protest seen in grieving is a normal reaction to separation. The anger felt by the bereaved can be directed toward one's self for not preventing the loss, at the lost object for leaving, or at third parties who are perceived as having helped bring about the loss.

Like the grieving person, the birth mother's guilt and anger at herself intensifies with the passage of time as she comprehends her role and the role of others in setting up her loss and the consequent feelings of remorse and grief. The guilt experiences by birth mothers are intensified because they blame themselves and are blamed by others for the loss, because it is they who have actually relinquished their children.

Anger by widows toward third parties (such as medical personnel) in Parkes et al.'s (1972) study diminished over time. Anger by birth mothers toward third parties in Millen and Roll's (1985) study intensified rather than diminished over time.

Birth mothers' experiences with third parties tended to be with family members who withdrew rather than supported, professionals whose words were supposed to provide comfort but whose actions involved manipulation and coercion, and social workers and counselors who offered no options and emphasized instead that others could provide better lives for their children, and insisted that they should leave past mistakes behind them. Clearly, for many birth mothers, bitterness at third parties had a basis in reality, although it was a bitterness that deepened and distorted the bereavement process.

The fifth feature of the grief reaction, *feelings of loss and self-mutilation*, were found exacerbated by the birth mothers by the reality of a child having indeed been a part of them physically as well as emotionally.

The *identification phenomenon*, which is the sixth feature of the grief reaction, is complicated and intensified as a result of the birth mother's carrying the child within her for 9 months.

> The reality of the pregnancy facilitates the mother's sense of a presence of the lost object within her and slows down the letting go which is necessary for the working through of grief and the building of a new identity that is separate from the lost object. (Millen & Roll, 1985, p. 416)

Millen and Roll (1985) found that many of the women in their study showed the signs of pathological grief. They proposed several reasons why birth mothers' grieving was impeded by society and, hence, inhibited and prolonged:

1. The loss was, most likely, socially stigmatized.

2. The external events prevented the expression of feelings of loss. For most birth mothers, once they returned to their families, their pregnancy and the relinquishment of their children were never again discussed.

3. There may have been uncertainty as to whether there was an actual loss—the child was gone, but the child was not dead.

4. There was an absence of mourning at the normal and expected time. Birth mothers were told to forget; they were not told it was expected they would mourn. As a result, the mourning rituals present in most cultures were lacking for birth mothers. There was no wake, there was no shiva, there was no funeral, only silence remained.

Birth Mothers and Subsequent Children

At the time that many birth mothers surrendered their children for adoption they were told by the adoption agencies that they would put the event behind them and go on with their lives. The research overwhelmingly refutes this claim (Anderson, 1987; Deykin, Campbell, & Patti, 1984; Millen & Roll, 1985; Pannor, Baran, & Sorosky, 1978; Rynearson, 1982; Schaefer, 1991; Silverman, Campbell, Patti, & Style, 1988; Sorosky, Baran, & Pannor, 1984; Stiffler, 1991). In fact, most birth parents report that surrendering a child for adoption had a profound negative impact on their lives for many years after the surrender (Anderson, 1987; Deykin et al., 1984; Millen & Roll, 1985; Pannor et al., 1978; Rynearson, 1982; Schaefer, 1991; Silverman et al., 1988; Sorosky et al., 1984; Stiffler, 1991).

When the popular book *The Adoption Triangle* (Sorosky et al., 1984) was written, no follow-up studies of birth parents existed, even though a number of studies had explored the psychological factors involved in illegitimate pregnancies and the relinquishment process. This study was undertaken to provide research on two factors, personality traits and attachment history, which may affect whether or not birth mothers have more children.

Although the professional literature about birth mothers is limited, a number of books written by birth mothers have told their stories. The themes of the birth mothers' stories are almost universal. These include fear of society's or family's reactions, a denial of feelings, guilt for what they were putting their family through, fantasies about the child and the child's future, and shame—profound shame.

Within the adoption movement, there is a belief that a high percentage of birth mothers do not go on to have other children. The reasons for this phenomenon are varied; however, many hypothesize that the shame connected with having relinquished a child for adoption affects a woman's desire to bear more children. Many birth mothers talk about their loss of trust surrounding their pregnancy: Not only trust of other people but also trust of themselves. If she were not a good enough mother to raise her first child, then what would make her believe that she was ever going to be good enough to raise another child?

Components of the Study

This study asked the following questions: (1) What, if any, personality characteristics differ in birth mothers who go on to have more children and birth mothers who do not go on to have more children? (2) What are the differences in attachment history of birth mothers who go on to have other children and birth mothers who do not go on to have more children?

Of the birth mothers who did not have other children, this study addressed those who chose not to have other children and those who did not have other children because of infertility. Birth mothers who never married to avoid subsequent motherhood were also included.

Additional questions included the following: (1) Will the results of the Revised Neuroticism, Extraversion, and Openness to Experience Personality Inventory (NEO PI-R) (Costa & McCrae, 1992) be able to predict birth mothers who are at risk to choose to not become mothers again after relinquishing their first child for adoption? (2) Will the age at which a woman surrendered her first child for adoption be a predictor of whether or not she goes on to have more children? (3) Will early childhood loss, such as the death of a parent, be an indicator in birth mothers who did not go on to have other children?

No other research has examined the existing personality of birth mothers to determine if a certain type of birth-mother profile would suggest predisposition to taking one approach to her childbearing future over another. Additionally, although all birth mothers were traumatized by the act of relinquishing their child for adoption, the study proposed to find if there is an element in birth mothers that may determine who might be so traumatized by that decision (the act of relinquishing a child for adoption) that they were unable to allow themselves to bear another child. Are there differences in early attachment between birth mothers who have more children and birth mothers who do not have more children?

METHOD

The sample consisted of 87 birth mothers: 55 had subsequent children and 32 did not. The ages of the birth mothers ranged from 40 to 76 years. All the birth mothers were Caucasians. The subjects were all members of Concerned United Birthparents and/or the American Adoption Congress. Concerned United Birthparents is a national support organization that serves people whose lives have been affected by adoption. The American Adoption Congress is an international agency whose goal is the reform of current adoption laws.

By limiting the research participants to the above-mentioned organizations, the results of the study were biased. Many birth mothers, however, have not discussed their experiences; hence, recruiting birth mothers from the general population may have been difficult. Birth mothers who join support organizations have shown a willingness to share their experiences and hence were available to participate in this study.

The participants were given three questionnaires to complete. One was a Personal Information Survey, which included questions to elicit information regarding current age, age at relinquishment, marital status, level of education, hospitalization for emotional reasons, medication for emotional problems, marriage to the birth father, and whether the woman had subsequent children after relinquishment and if not, the reason for no subsequent children. The survey also asked whether the pregnancy was a secret from her family, whether there was any family support, whether the birth father knew of the pregnancy, and whether he participated in the decision to relinquish the baby. Participants were also asked who made the decision to relinquish the baby, and if there was any pressure to relinquish the baby.

The Attachment History Questionnaire (AHQ) is a self-report measure developed by Pottharst and Kessler (1986) to identify the quality of a person's early parent-child attachment, the types of discipline or punishment the child received, and the quality of the child's network of social support. The areas addressed in the questionnaire deal with separation and losses in early childhood; parental threats of suicide or of the child being sent away; aversive parental discipline methods; and the extent to which attachment figures were available and responsive, affectionate or rejecting, helpful or critical, and cognizant of the child's accomplishments. The AHQ also contains sections intended to gather information regarding the respondent's psychosocial history and the nature of the family of origin.

The AHQ consists of five parts. Part 1 asks for personal demographic information about the subject, such as marital status, ethnicity, education, and socioeconomic status. Part 2 is designed to gather data about family history involving attachment disruptions. Part 3 elicits information about the quality of the parent-child relationship. Part 4 asks about the types and frequencies of discipline methods used in the home. Part 5 covers the subject's network of social support when living at home and some aspects of present support systems. A total score, representing security of attachment, is derived from scores on Parts 3, 4, and 5. High scores reflect a more secure attachment.

As a measuring instrument, the AHQ was included in this research project for its clinical sensitivity, as well as its internal consistency and external validity, both of which have been established sufficiently to lend confidence to its use in a study of attachment history (Pottharst & Kessler, 1986).

The NEO PI-R (Costa & McCrae, 1992) was designed to measure normal personality traits using the above-mentioned dimensions of neuroticism, extraversion, openness, agreeableness, and conscientiousness. There are two versions of the NEO PI-R (Costa & McCrae, 1992): Form S is for self-reports and Form R is for observer ratings. For this study, Form S was used exclusively. Form S consists of 240 items answered on a 5-point scale. It is self-administered and is appropriate for men and women of all ages. The NEO PI-R has been chosen as a measuring instrument based on its intensive research and factor analytic methods conducted for over 15 years on both clinical and normal adult samples across a wide spectrum of settings.

Procedures

At the annual conferences of the Concerned United Birthparents and the American Adoption Congress, volunteers were recruited and questionnaire packets were distributed.

Results

Of the sample, 37% of the birth mothers who surrendered their first child for adoption did not go on to have other children. Of that 37%, most cited choice as the reason. Specifically, 84% cited choice, 9% cited infertility, 3% cited both, and 3% cited other reasons. The 12% secondary infertility reported by the group of women who did not have subsequent children is greater than the 6% secondary infertility reported in the general population but less than the 17% secondary infertility statistic cited in the study by Deykin et al. (1984).

As can be seen from Table 22.1, those who had more children were more likely to be currently married than those who did not have more children, $\chi^2 = 22.32$, $p < .001$. Table 22.1 also suggests that if married, the women who did not have more children are more likely to be divorced. Although not statistically significant, it is of interest to note that of those who did not have more children, 25% of them never married, whereas all of the women who did have more children married.

Table 22.1   Marital Status of Participants

Demographic Characteristic	Subsequent Children (%)	No Subsequent Children (%)	Chi-Square Test
Never married	0	25	
Married	75	31	22.32*
Separated/divorced	25	44	

*$p < .001$.

The age of relinquishment was 20.24 for women with subsequent children and 20.19 for those who did not have subsequent children, $t(85) = 0.08$, $p < .05$. Of the women who had subsequent children, 13% had been hospitalized for emotional reasons compared with 3% of women who did not have subsequent children, $\chi^2 = 2.23$, $p < .001$. Of the women who had subsequent children, 29% are or were taking medication for emotional problems; 34% of women who did not have more children are or were taking medication for emotional problems.

There was a significant difference between the two groups regarding the pressure to relinquish their child. Of women who had more children, 89% reported pressure to relinquish compared with 67% of women who did not have more children, $t(85) = 5.76$, $p < .05$ (see Table 22.2).

Table 22.2   The Relationship Between Number of Children and Pressure to Relinquish

	Subsequent Children (%)	No Subsequent Children (%)	Chi-Square Test
Pressure to relinquish	89	67	5.76*

*$p < .05$.

Women who did not have more children had significantly more stepmothers than those who had more children, $\chi^2 = 5.81$, $p < .05$.

Six hypotheses were originally presented, testing significance at or beyond .05.
Hypothesis 1 stated that birth mothers who chose not to have more children will score significantly higher on the Neuroticism scale of the NEO PI-R than those who chose to have more children. This hypothesis was not supported ($p > .05$).

Hypothesis 2 stated that there will be no significant difference on the Extraversion scale of the NEO PI-R between birth mothers who chose not to have more children and birth mothers who chose to have more children. This null hypothesis was not supported. The t-test showed significance of $p < .05$.

Hypothesis 3 stated that birth mothers who chose not to have more children will score significantly lower on the Openness to Experience scale of the NEO PI-R than those who chose to have more children. This hypothesis was not supported ($p > .05$).

Hypothesis 4 stated that birth mothers who chose not to have more children will score significantly lower on the Agreeableness scale of the NEO PI-R than those who chose to have more children. This hypothesis was not supported ($p > .05$).

Hypothesis 5 stated that there will be no significant differences between birth mothers who chose not to have more children and birth mothers who chose to have more children on the Conscientiousness scale of the NEO PI-R. This hypothesis was supported ($p < .05$).

Hypothesis 6 stated that birth mothers who chose not to have more children will show significantly more attachment deficits on the AHQ than those who chose to have more children. This hypothesis was not supported ($p > .05$).

Three additional research questions were proposed in this study. The first involves looking at the extent to which the results of the NEO PI-R are able to predict birth mothers who are at risk to choose to not become mothers again after relinquishing their first child for adoption. The results showed that only the Extraversion scale may be able to predict birth mothers at risk for not having more children. Those women who had more children were significantly more extroverted than those who did not have more children.

The second question looked at whether the age at which a woman surrendered her first child for adoption is a predictor of whether or not she goes on to have more children. The age at which a woman surrendered her first child for adoption was not a predictor of whether or not she went on to have more children.

Finally, the third question looked at the extent to which early childhood loss, such as the death of a parent, may be an indicator in birth mothers who did not go on to have other children. There was some indication of early childhood loss affecting whether or not a birth mother would go on to have more children. Women who did not have more children had significantly more stepmothers than those who had more children. Just using the term *stepmother* indicates that at some point there was at least an interruption in the attachment between the birth mother and her mother.

There were no significant differences between the groups on any significant support figure with the exception of "Friends" during the 11- to 15-year-old period where friends were significantly more important to birth mothers who did not have more children.

Although not statistically significant, the data at each age level suggest differences between those women who had more children and those who did not have more children. For example, at ages 0 to 2, women who did not have more children reported less of a relationship with their mothers (75% vs. 84%) and siblings (3% vs. 15%), and a greater relationship with more distant relatives, for example, grandmothers (28% vs. 20%). As the participants matured in age, the relationships appeared to continue migrating away from closer family members and toward more distant relationships. For example, by ages 11 to 15, friends were significantly more important to those women who had no more children (31% vs. 11%).

Turning attention to women who had no more children, 89% reported having lost their fathers compared with 69% of the women who had more children. In addition, 62% of the group with no subsequent children also reported losing their father during their childbearing years compared with only 50% for the women who had subsequent children.

It is possible that the disruption in the relationship with their father may have contributed to the emotional damage suffered by these women. Not only did the birth mothers lose their fathers; they also had to deal with the loss of relinquishing their first child to adoption. This conclusion appears to be supported by Table 22.1. Birth mothers who had no subsequent children were more likely to have never married (25%) or to be divorced (31%).

DISCUSSION

Of the six hypotheses stated, only Hypothesis 5 was supported. Birth mothers who had more children scored no differently on the Conscientiousness scale than birth mothers who did not have more children. It is possible that the methods used were not sensitive enough to measure the other proposed differences between the groups. The author could have added other questions, including "Do you like children?" and "When you were an adolescent did you plan to have children once you reached adulthood?"

It is also possible that the factors surrounding the pregnancy through the adoption process had more significance to later childbearing than attachment history and personality traits. It may have been helpful if more questions were added regarding the relinquishment process for the two groups of women.

Within the adoption reform movement, there is the belief (based mostly on informal surveys) that there is a high occurrence of birth mothers who do not go on to have other children, including a higher incidence of secondary infertility than in the general population. Specifically, in this study participants were encouraged to explain why they may have "chosen" to not have any other children. Responses included the following:

- "I didn't feel I had the right and wasn't sure I wanted children."
- "Choice, but I think it was because I couldn't go thru another pregnancy because of the relinquishment."

Because researching that belief would be difficult (e.g., many birth mothers have never told anyone that they relinquished a child for adoption and would thus be difficult to locate), this study examined whether any other variables might distinguish birth mothers who had more children from birth mothers who did not have more children. The variables selected were personality traits and attachment history.

McCrae and John's (1992) five-factor model of personality, as measured by the NEO PI-R, was appealing on three levels. It integrates a wide array of personality constructs; it is comprehensive, giving a basis for systematic exploration of the relations between personality and other phenomena; and it is efficient, providing at least a global description of personality.

The NEO PI-R does give a global description of personality; however, the global quality of the NEO PI-R may be the reason this study did not get the proposed results. The NEO PI-R is perhaps too global to pick up the nuances of the personality differences between birth mothers who had more children and birth mothers who did not have more children.

Regarding attachment, Holmes (1993) discussed how a child whose mother has provided a secure base will store an internal working model of a responsive, loving, reliable caregiver, and of a self that is worthy of love and attention, and will use these assumptions in all other relationships. Conversely, if a child has an insecure attachment, the child may view the world as a dangerous place in which other people are to be treated with great caution, and see himself or herself as ineffective and unworthy of love. These assumptions remain relatively stable and enduring. They are very persistent and are unlikely to be modified by subsequent experience.

It was expected that the AHQ would show that an insecure attachment with the mother and father would be more prominent in birth mothers who did not have more children. Although it was not statistically proven, the reported results are consistent with weaker attachments with the mother and father in those birth mothers who did not have more children.

As stated earlier, there was a significant difference between birth mothers who did not have more children and birth mothers who did have more children in that birth mothers who did not have more children more often had stepmothers than birth mothers who did have more children. This could suggest disruptions in attachment with the mothers in the group who did not have more children.

One of the most significant findings of the study was that birth mothers who had subsequent children were more likely to have been pressured to relinquish the baby than those who did not. Were birth mothers who felt they were pressured to relinquish and had more children able to have more children because they did not make the decision to relinquish? Did birth mothers who had a more active role in choosing to relinquish feel more shame and guilt and, hence, feel they did not deserve to have more children? Some of the participants elaborated on their answers to the question "Was there pressure to relinquish the baby?" Some responses were as follows:

- "It's not that simple. There was no overt pressure, but lots of subtle pressure just because of time and place, type of family, background, influency [sic] on sibs, inability to become a teacher because of moral turpitude, couldn't rent an apt as a single mom, etc. I believe I'd call that pressure tho' no one ever suggested to me I should relinquish—it was my idea."
- "Societal pressure. Evidence of premarital sex in 1950 was a taboo that only the most brave or most foolish woman would expose themselves and their child to."
- "There was subtle pressure from the social worker I worked with at Children's Home society. . . . I feel this way because other options were not discussed and I definitely got the message that a child needed a mother and father who could provide for this child better than I could. Also, it would have been a stigma attached to this child because of its 'illegitimacy.'"
- "This wasn't a *decision*—A true decision has to be made from a position of *power* with *reasonable alternatives*. I wasn't in a position of power and I don't believe many older birthmom's [sic] were in such a position when they surrendered!"

Although not statistically significant, women who did not have more children reported more of a decline in their relationships with both their mother and their father and a move toward outside relationships (i.e., friends) during their adolescent years. During their late childhood years from age 11 to 15, these women reported having only slightly less of a relationship with their parents and siblings. Even at this age, however, the women who did not have more children had much higher reported relationships with distant relatives (31% vs. 15%) and friends (31% vs. 11%) than did women who had more children.

By the time the women who had no more children reached late adolescence (ages 16 to 20), their relationships with their parents continued to decline, while they reported having much closer relationships with friends than did the women who had more children (38% vs. 27%). Is it possible that when parents played a more significant role for women, they were more apt to have more children? Is it also possible that the converse is also true? Birth mothers who did not have subsequent children may have made this decision in the context of non-supportive or even unpleasant relationships with their parents.

Another finding was that the birth mothers who did not have more children were more likely to be divorced. Does that mean merely that they had more unstable marriages, or did they divorce at the point that their husbands may have started pressuring them to have children?

This study suggests implications for therapists working with women who are considering relinquishing their baby for adoption and with women who have revealed that they have relinquished a baby at some point in their lives. Women who are more extroverted may be at a lower risk for choosing not to have more children. Women with stronger attachments to their mother and father may be at a lower risk for choosing not to have more children. Women who are feeling pressure from their family to relinquish their baby may be at a lower risk for not having more children.

Of the six hypotheses presented, only one, Hypothesis 5, was supported. As predicted, there were no differences in the subscale Conscientiousness of the NEO PI-R between birth mothers who had more children and birth mothers who did not have more children. However, although not statistically significant, there were other interesting trends. For example, birth mothers who had more children were more likely to be currently married than birth mothers who did not have more children.

Clinical/Research Implications

An issue that needs to be addressed is the ability to generalize the findings. All of the birth mothers in the study were Caucasians. All of the birth mothers in the study were members of either the American Adoption Congress or Concerned United Birthparents. With regard to the high percentage of birth mothers who did not have subsequent children, it is entirely possible that birth mothers who never had more children have more of a need to join such organizations as those listed above. It is, however, also possible that birth mothers who had no subsequent children remain closeted and were never included in the sample because they have avoided these support groups.

Professionals working in the field of psychotherapy who are also working with relinquishing mothers should be made aware of these findings. In addition, more research studies should be performed using methods that would measure variables not addressed in this study, such as questions regarding the relinquishment process and regarding whether or not a woman had intentions of having children prior to relinquishing her child for adoption.

The elements of grief and loss cannot be understated in adoption. Adoptive parents have lost the ability to bear their biological child themselves, adopted children have lost their biological ties, and the birth mothers have lost their children.

While adoption can be a vehicle in which the triad members are offered a solution to their needs, it must be remembered that adoption is a second choice for all members of the adoption triad. Therapists' ability to recognize and address the losses suffered will be their most valuable tool in working with all members of the adoption triad.

REFERENCES

Anderson, C. (1987). *Thoughts for birth parents newly considering search*. Des Moines, IA: Concerned United Birthparents.

Bowlby, J. (1963). *Attachment. Vol. 1 of Attachment and loss* (2nd ed., 1982). New York: Basic Books.

Bowlby, J. (1980). *Loss. Vol. 3 of Attachment and loss*. New York: Basic Books.

Cattell, J. P. (1954). Psychodynamic and clinical observations in a group of unmarried mothers. *American Journal of Psychiatry, 111,* 337–342.

Costa, P. T., Jr., & McCrae, R. R. (1992). *NEO PI-R professional manual*. Odessa, FL: Psychological Assessment Resources.

Deutsch, H. (1945). *The psychology of women: A psychoanalytic interpretation* (Vol. 2). New York: Grune & Stratton.

Deykin, E. Y., Campbell, L., & Patti, P. (1984). The postadoption experience of surrendering parents. *American Journal of Orthopsychiatry, 54*(2), 271–280.

Heiman, M., & Levitt, E. G. (1960). The role of separation and depression in out-of-wedlock pregnancy. *American Journal of Orthopsychiatry, 30,* 166–174.

Holmes, J. (1993). *John Bowlby and attachment theory*. New York: Routledge.

McCrae, R. R., & John, O. P. (1992). An introduction to the five-factor model and its applications. *Journal of Personality, 60*(2), 175–215.

Millen, L., & Roll, S. (1985). Solomon's mothers: A special case of pathological bereavement. *Journal of Orthopsychiatry, 55*(3), 411–418.

Pannor, R., Baran, A., & Sorosky, A. D. (1978). Birth parents who relinquished babies for adoption revisited. *Family Process, 17*(3), 329–337.

Parkes, C. M., Stevenson-Hinde, J., & Marris, P. (1972). *Attachment across the life cycle*. New York: Routledge.

Pottharst, K., & Kessler, R. (1986). *Attachment predictors and correlated: Search for measures and methods of information gathering*. Unpublished manuscript, California School of Professional Psychology.

Rynearson, E. K. (1982). Relinquishment and its maternal complications: A preliminary study. *American Journal of Psychiatry, 139*(3), 338–340.

Schaefer, C. (1991). *The other mother*. New York: Soho.

Silverman, P. R., Campbell, L., Patti, P., & Style, C. (1988). Reunions between adoptees and birth parents: The birth parents' experience. *Social Work, 33*(6), 523–528.

Sorosky, A. D., Baran, A., & Pannor, R. (1984). *The adoption triangle* (Rev. ed.). San Antonio, TX: Corona.

Stiffler, L. H. (1991). Adoption's impact on birthmothers: "Can a mother forget her child?" *Journal of Psychology and Christianity, 10*(3), 249–259.

Identity, Psychological Adjustment, Culture, and Race

23

Issues for Transracial Adoptees and the Cultural-Racial Identity Model

AMANDA L. BADEN

Montclair State University

T ransracial adoption, or the joining of racially different parents and children in adoptive families (Zamostny, O'Brien, Baden, & Wiley, 2003), has received a resurgence in attention given the greater frequency with which couples and single parents have been adopting children internationally and domestically. Transracial adoption encompasses both domestic and international adoptions where the children and the parents are racially different. Interestingly, although not all international adoptions are transracial, the vast majority (67.76%) likely fall into this category (Child Welfare League of America, 2003). Estimates of the numbers of transracial adoptees have been difficult to discern. According to the U.S. Department of State (2006), 6,536 children were adopted internationally in 1992, whereas in 2005, that number increased to 21,698. Stolley (1993) found that 8% of all adoptions were transracial, but other estimates have put that percentage at 14% (National Adoption Information Clearinghouse, 1994). However, despite the increased social acceptability of transracial adoption and the continued availability of children for adoption, few studies of transracial adoptees address transracial adoptees' identity and adjustment because studies rarely address clinical practice implications.

Over the past 50 years, the availability of children around the world has shifted based on political, social, and economic events both in the United States and abroad. As White children became less available, as noted in Zamostny et al. (2003), adoptable children from other countries such as China, Korea, Guatemala, and Colombia became the targets of international adoption, but often those children were adopted across racial lines. Thus, transracial adoption was continually practiced in America throughout the past 50 years. However, statements opposing transracial adoptions made by the National Association of Black Social Workers (NABSW; 1972) as well as by other organizations and community leaders in 1972 resulted in fewer domestic transracial adoptions. In particular, placements of African American or Native American children in Caucasian families rarely took place after 1972 until legislation was passed in the mid-1990s.

The first piece of legislation passed was the Howard M. Metzenbaum Multiethnic Placement Act (MEPA) of 1994. MEPA and the 1996 provisions for Removal of Barriers to Interethnic Adoption (IEP) were designed to reduce the practice of race matching in adoptive placements for children (Hollinger & the ABA Center on Children and the Law National Resource Center on Legal and Courts Issues, 1988). Together, these pieces of legislation, commonly referred to as MEPA-IEP, were designed to decrease the amount of time children waited for adoptive placements, to improve and assist in the recruitment and retention of prospective foster and adoptive parents able to meet the distinct needs of these children, and to eliminate discrimination in the practice of adoptive and foster care placements on the basis of race, color, or national origin (Hollinger & the ABA Center on Children and the Law National Resource Center on Legal and Courts Issues, 1988). In effect, this legislation resulted in more transracial adoptive placements. Given this legislation, as well as the large numbers of transracial adoptions that have already occurred, adoption professionals as well as psychologists, counselors, and social workers must be prepared to adequately serve the array of needs that may develop for adoptees.

Criticisms of transracial adoption have primarily targeted both intracountry and intercountry adoptions and have been based primarily on questions regarding identity development and psychological adjustment (Griffith & Duby, 1991; Ryan, 1983; Silverman & Feigelman, 1981; Tizard, 1991). However, criticisms of transracial adoption have not been limited to the NABSW. Economically developing countries (e.g., Asian and South American countries) from which Americans adopted many children as well as organizations representing American Indians and African Americans (Fanshel, 1972; Hollingsworth, 1999; Ryan, 1983; Tizard, 1991) also voiced concerns about the effects of transracial and intercountry adoption. Transracial adoption was referred to as "cultural genocide," as "the ultimate expression of American Imperialism," and as leading to "poor" identity development and psychological maladjustment (Tizard, 1991).

Extreme positions from both proponents and opponents of transracial adoption may frequently forget the children involved in this controversy. Analyses of transracial adoption-related issues primarily focused on disproving the predictions of opponents to transracial adoption. As a result, a substantial amount of research studied the effects of transracial adoption on psychological adjustment, self-esteem, and racial identity. Findings suggested that no differences existed between transracial and intraracial adoptees (e.g., Bagley, 1993a, 1993b; Johnson, Shireman, & Watson, 1987; McRoy, Zurcher, Lauderdale, & Anderson, 1984; Simon & Altstein, 1987). With that "goal" having been essentially "achieved," another area for analysis needed exploration. To adequately meet the developmental, therapeutic, and educational needs of transracial adoptees, professionals still need to determine what differences currently exist among transracial adoptees rather than focusing on their differences from other groups. These differences are not merely demographic but may be of greater importance in explaining the effects of transracial adoption on adoptees.

To better understand the impact and importance of transracial adoption, a guideline for observing and systematizing the study of transracial adoptees was developed called the Cultural-Racial Identity Model (Baden & Steward, 2000; Steward & Baden, 1995). This model proposed varying identity statuses among individuals raised in multiracial families having racial differences between parents and children—it is particularly applicable to transracial adoptees. As described in Chapter 7 by Baden and Steward, the identity statuses postulated by them differed from previous models of racial and ethnic identity with respect to their emphasis on examining the culture and the race of transracial adoptees separately. This model was used for the current study and allowed a new area of analysis to be examined.

By examining transracial adoption from this new perspective, many critical questions are addressed in this chapter. For example, are transracial adoptees a monolithic group in terms of psychological adjustment? Are the predictions of poor psychological adjustment, rejection of transracial adoptees, and identity confusion true? If so, how can we continue to engage in this detrimental practice? Are there some transracial adoptees who fair better than others? All these questions must be answered for a fully informed decision about the practice of transracial adoption.

Because the vast majority of the transracial adoptions that have taken place in the United States have been White couples adopting non-White children and because much of the criticism lodged against the practice of transracial adoption has been directed toward members of the dominant culture as the "socializers" of racial ethnic minority children (Gill & Jackson, 1983), all transracial adoptees who participated in the current study were adopted by White parents. Thus, references made to the "adoptive parents' racial group" or their "racial groups' culture" refer to the White culture.

A Description of the Cultural-Racial Identity Model

Baden and Steward (2000; Chapter 7, this volume) detailed the Cultural-Racial Identity Model in a complete description of the development of the model. To orient the reader to this model, see Chapter 7. In essence, this model combines two axes, the Cultural Identity Axis and the Racial Identity Axis, into a single model and a single graphic representation and consists of 16 potential cultural-racial identities. Using as the definition of culture the set of values, ideals, beliefs, traditions, skills, customs, languages, and institutions into which individuals are born, this model is based on the assumption of a common set of ideals, values, beliefs, traditions, and so on that compose each culture. Although Baden and Steward recognized that there are as many differences within groups as there are between them, any model (especially one looking at cultural and racial identity) that depicts some psychological or psychosocial experience relies on the supposition that a baseline for cultural behaviors and practices exists for a racial ethnic group. Thus, given that the vast majority of transracial adoptions involve White parents adopting children of color, the term "White culture" was used to refer to the dominant, middle-class, White, American culture that can be associated with transracially adopting parents. The very nature of transracial adoption typically involves children of color being adopted by White parents into the White culture and away from the culture into which they were born (hereafter referred to as birth culture). Thus, at least two different racial groups as well as two different cultures are represented within transracially adopting families.

The Cultural Identity Axis of the Cultural-Racial Identity Model accounts for these four possible culture combinations. The Cultural Identity Axis has two dimensions: the *Adoptee Culture Dimension* (the degree to which transracial adoptees identify with their own racial group's culture or birth culture); and the *Parental Culture Dimension* (the degree to which transracial adoptees identify with their adoptive parents' racial group's culture). Identification with a culture or with multiple cultures is determined by levels of knowledge, awareness, competence, and comfort the adoptees have with each of the following: (1) their own birth culture; (2) their adoptive parents' culture; and (3) multiple cultures. Baden and Steward (2000) identified four types of cultural identities (e.g., Bicultural Identity, Pro-Self Cultural Identity, Pro-Parent Cultural Identity, and CulturaDamaging backgrounds: Later adjustment of international adoptees. Journal of the American Academy of Child & Adolescent Psychiatry, 31(3), 518–524.

Yoon, D. P. (2001). Causal modeling predicting psychological adjustment of ptee Culture Dimension; thus, the adoptee would have a Pro-Parent Cultural Identity (see bottom, right box of Figure 23.1). A graphical representation of the Cultural Identity Axis is depicted in Figure 23.1.

The Cultural-Racial Identity Model suggests that racial differences affect racial/ethnic self-identification as well as the allegiances and friendships of transracial adoptees. Using a biosocial definition of race similar to that of Helms (1990) where race is socially constructed, racial groups were designed to be "determined by groups who are distinguished or consider themselves to be distinguished from other people by their physical characteristics and by their social relations with other people" (Baden & Steward, 2000, p. 325). The Racial Identity Axis has two dimensions: the *Adoptee Race Dimension* (the degree to which transracial adoptees identify

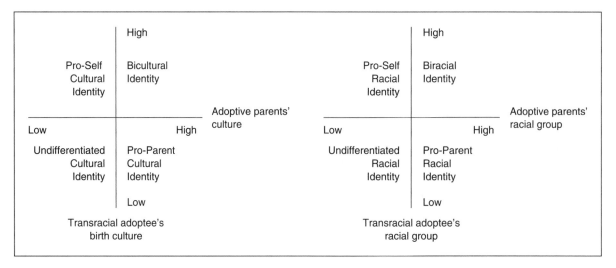

Figure 23.1   Cultural Identity Axis and Racial Identity Axis

SOURCE: Baden, A. L. (2002). The psychological adjustment of transracial adoptees: An application of the Cultural-Racial Identity Model. *Journal of Social Distress and the Homeless, 11,* 167–192. Reprinted with permission of Springer Science and Business Media.

with their own racial group); and the *Parental Race Dimension* (the degree to which transracial adoptees identify with their adoptive parents' racial group). Level of racial identification is assessed by the degree of (1) self-identification with one's own racial group; (2) self-identification with one's adoptive parents' racial group; and (3) comfort one has with people belonging to one's own racial group and one's adoptive parents' racial group. Comfort level also involves allegiances to these racial groups and people belonging to each of the different racial groups. Thus, racial identities are based on the "degree to which transracial adoptees accurately identify and are comfortable with their racial group membership and the degree to which they are comfortable with either or both those belonging to their racial group, their parents' racial group, or multiple racial groups" (Baden & Steward, 2000, p. 327). Four possible racial identities are the Biracial Identity, Pro-Self Racial Identity, Pro-Parent Racial Identity, and Racially Undifferentiated Type Identity (see Figure 23.1).

The final part of the Cultural-Racial Identity Model combines both the Cultural Identity Axis and the Racial Identity Axis into one model. This model pairs each of the four possible cultural identities with each of the four possible racial identities. The resultant 16 cells of the model are presented in Figure 23.2. Baden and Steward (Chapter 7, this volume) described each of these identities but due to measurement limitations delineated later in this chapter, all the cells are not used here.

The two dimensions of the Cultural Identity Axis (i.e., the Adoptee Culture Dimension and the Parental Culture Dimension) and the two dimensions of the Racial Identity Axis (i.e., the Adoptee Race Dimension and the Parental Race Dimension) make up the four dimensions used in this study of the Cultural-Racial Identity Model. Figure 23.3 details the four dimensions, the theoretical criteria that compose each dimension (e.g., knowledge, awareness, competence, and comfort with culture and with those of various racial groups), and the corresponding subscales of the instrument used to operationalize the dimensions. This instrument is a modified version of the Multigroup Ethnic Identity Measure (hereafter referred to as the MEIM-R) (Phinney, 1992). The MEIM-R was chosen to study the Cultural-Racial Identity Model for several key reasons. As Baden and Steward (Chapter 7, this volume) noted, because ethnicity accounts for facets of both race and culture but does not clearly differentiate them and because the construct of race (socially constructed) is more powerful and suited to the experiences of transracial adoptees, modifying a measure of ethnic identity to account for both culture and race was judged to fit the goals of this study.

The MEIM-R was created by building on the Multigroup Ethnic Identity Measure (Phinney, 1992) to appropriately operationalize the four cultural-racial identity dimensions. With these

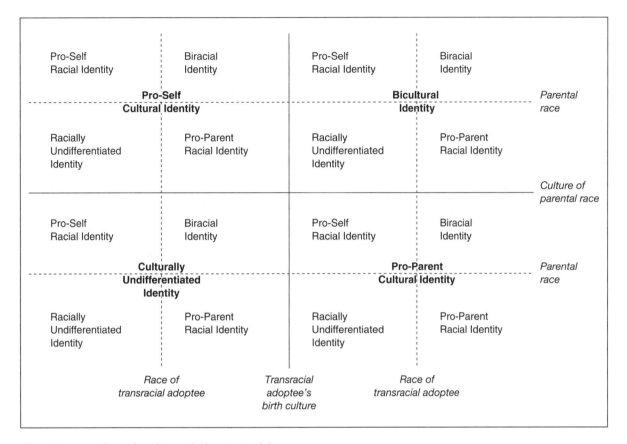

| Pro-Self
Racial Identity | Biracial
Identity | Pro-Self
Racial Identity | Biracial
Identity | |

Figure 23.2   The Cultural-Racial Identity Model

SOURCE: Baden, A. L. (2002). The psychological adjustment of transracial adoptees: An application of the Cultural-Racial Identity Model. *Journal of Social Distress and the Homeless, 11*, 167–192. Reprinted with permission of Springer Science and Business Media.

alterations, the MEIM-R could be used with the transracial adoptee population for the current study. Subscales of the MEIM-R were assigned to each of the four dimensions by matching the "Criteria for Inclusion in the Dimension" to information provided by each of the subscales of the MEIM-R. For example, both the Adoptee Culture Dimension and the Parental Culture Dimension indicated the degree to which the transracial adoptees have knowledge of, awareness of, competence within, and comfort with their birth culture or with their parents' culture. To match a subscale from the MEIM-R to these criteria, an evaluation of the adoptees' participation in cultural practices, traditions, values, and beliefs (e.g., cultural holidays, customs, foods, dress, and music) was done and led to the identification of the Ethnic Behaviors and Practices subscale of the MEIM-R as closely matching these criteria. The four cultural-racial identity dimensions served as the independent variables in the current study.

The dependent variable in this study was a measure of psychological adjustment as determined for the sample of transracial adoptees. To control for preexisting differences in the transracial adoptees and the inability to randomly assign individuals to transracial adoption and preadoptive experiences, several background factors were accounted for in the study. The background variables expected to have an impact were identified in the literature (Andujo, 1988; Bagley, 1993a; Cederblad, Höök, Irhammar, & Mercke, 1999; Feigelman, 1997; McRoy, Zurcher, Lauderdale, & Anderson, 1982; Silverman & Feigelman, 1981; Verhulst, Althaus, & Versluis-den Bieman, 1990a, 1990b, 1992) as accounting for much of the variance in the transracial adoptees' psychological adjustment, particularly when they were compared with intraracial adoptees or nonadopted individuals. Five background variables of the adoptees and their families were controlled for in the study: age at adoption, number of preadoptive placements, preadoptive history/trauma (physical, political, etc.), sex of the adoptees, and socioeconomic status of the adoptive family. The age at adoption (as measured in months), number of preadoptive

Cultural-Racial Identity Dimensions	Criteria for Inclusion in the Dimension	Subscale(s) of the MEIM-R for the Dimension
Adoptee Culture Dimension	Transracial adoptee's level of knowledge, awareness, competence, and comfort with the culture associated with his or her own racial group	• Ethnic Behaviors and Practices for Transracial Adoptee's Ethnic Group
Parental Culture Dimension	Transracial adoptee's level of knowledge, awareness, competence, and comfort with the culture associated with his or her adoptive parents' racial group	• Ethnic Behaviors and Practices for Adoptive Parents' Ethnic Group
Adoptee Race Dimension	Transracial adoptee's level of comfort with his or her own racial group membership and with those belonging to his or her own racial group	• Self-Identication for Transracial Adoptee's Ethnic Group • Ethnic Identity Achievement for Transracial Adoptee's Ethnic Group • Afliation and Belonging for Transracial Adoptee's Ethnic Group
Parental Race Dimension	Transracial adoptee's level of comfort with his or her racial group membership and with those belonging to his or her adoptive parents' racial group	• Self-Identication for Adoptive Parents' Ethnic Group • Ethnic Identity Achievement for Adoptive Parents' Ethnic Group • Afliation and Belonging for Adoptive Parents' Ethnic Group

Figure 23.3   The Four Dimensions in the Cultural-Racial Identity Model

SOURCE: Baden, A. L. (2002). The psychological adjustment of transracial adoptees: An application of the Cultural-Racial Identity Model. *Journal of Social Distress and the Homeless, 11,* 167–192. Reprinted with permission of Springer Science and Business Media.

placements, and preadoptive history/trauma were measured as continuous variables. Preadoptive history/trauma was considered to include abuse, physical health status from birth to adoptive placement, medical history (e.g., predisposition to mental health problems, substance abuse histories), political conditions surrounding the adoption (e.g., war, government sanctions on number of children such as in China), and remembered loss of family members. Preadoptive history/trauma was measured scoring one point for each condition chosen from 11 possible choices. Transracial adoptees were to choose all that applied from eight items describing traumatic physical or social conditions, one item indicating "healthy" (if chosen, this item scored zero), one item for having no information, and one blank item for describing "other" traumatic conditions or events. Socioeconomic status for the adoptive family was measured as a continuous variable with seven levels of socioeconomic status. An additional variable that may have an impact on adjustment is the current age of the adoptees, especially given that adolescence has traditionally been the period during which identity issues are most salient. Because the current study addressed identity as it developed after adolescence, the changes that occur during young adulthood could also potentially have affected adjustment, so was included as a potential confound.

The research questions that were addressed in this study are as follows: (1) Are there differences among transracial adoptees on their level of knowledge, awareness, competence, and comfort with their birth culture (Adoptee Culture Dimension)? (2) Are there differences among transracial adoptees on their level of knowledge, awareness, competence, and comfort with their parents' racial group's culture (Parental Culture Dimension)? (3) Are there differences among transracial adoptees on their level of comfort with their own racial self-identification and with those belonging to their own racial group (Adoptee Race Dimension)? (4) Are there differences among transracial adoptees on their level of comfort with their own racial self-identification and with those belonging to their parents' racial group (Parental Race Dimension)? (5) Controlling for age at adoption, number of preadoptive placements, preadoptive history/trauma, sex of the transracial adoptees, current age of the transracial adoptees, and socioeconomic status of the transracial adoptees, are there differences in psychological adjustment among transracial adoptees having different levels of the four cultural-racial identity dimensions?

METHODOLOGY

Description of the Sample

The subjects who participated in this study were young adult transracial adoptees ranging in age from 19 to 36 years with a mean age of 24.35 years. Thirty-eight of the subjects were females with a mean age of 24.18 years and 13 were males with a mean age of 24.85 years. Subjects were identified as transracial adoptees if they were the biological offspring of at least one person of color and if they were adopted by two White parents. Based on this identification, all the transracial adoptees were racially different from their adoptive parents (i.e., phenotypical differences were not required for inclusion in the sample). These criteria for transracial adoptees were used to ensure external validity. This population includes African Americans and Latino Americans adopted by White American families as well as intercountry adoptees from Asian and South American countries.

Table 23.1 shows the descriptive statistics for the sample of transracial adoptees. The statistics were compiled based on the racial ethnic group with which the adoptees identify and

Table 23.1   Means and Descriptive Statistics for the Sample of Transracial Adoptees

	White American	African American	Asian American	Latino American	Multicultural Mixed Race	Other
Females						
Current age	19	26.50	24.08	—	23.75	20.00
Age at adoption[a]	2	35.17	21.04	—	5.00	6.00
Preadopt Placements	1	.80	2.23	—	.50	2.00
Educational level	4	6.17	4.54	—	4.75	4.00
Adopt family income	6	6.60	6.69	—	6.50	6.00
Males						
Current age	—	—	23.50	31.00	22.00	33.00
Age at adoption[a]	—	—	45.00	0.00	9.00	58.50
Preadopt placements	—	—	1.25	0.00	.83	2.50
Educational level	—	—	4.00	7.00	4.17	6.00
Adopt family income	—	—	6.00	2.00	6.83	8.00

SOURCE: Baden, A. L. (2002). The psychological adjustment of transracial adoptees: An application of the Cultural-Racial Identity Model. *Journal of Social Distress and the Homeless, 11,* 167–192. Reprinted with permission of Springer Science and Business Media.

NOTE: "Educational level" refers to the highest level of education achieved by the transracial adoptees using the following scale: 1 = less than high school; 2 = high school degree (or GED); 3 = post high school; 4 = some college; 5 = completed college; 6 = some graduate or postbachelor's training; 7 = completed graduate or postbachelor's training. "Adopt family income" refers to socioeconomic status of the adoptive family and was measured using the following scale: 1 = $7,499 or below; 2 = $7,500 to $14,999; 3 = $15,000 to $24,999; 4 = $25,000 to $39,999; 5 = $40,000 to $59,999; 6 = $60,000 to $89,000; 7 = $90,000 or more.

a. Age at adoption given in months.

by their gender. Among the 38 females in the sample, 1 identified as White American (2.6%), 6 identified as Black or African American (15.8%), 26 identified as Asian American (68.4%), 4 identified as "multicultural" or "mixed race" (10.5%), and 1 identified as "other" (2.6%). Among the 13 males in the sample, 4 identified as Asian American (30.8%), 1 identified as Latino American (7.7%), 6 identified as "multicultural" or "mixed race" (46.2%), and 2 identified as "other" (15.4%).

Procedure

Transracial adoptees were recruited by advertisements, social service agencies, and special interest adoption groups. Flyers and postcards were distributed via personal contacts and social workers in the field. All respondents to flyers, contacts, and ads were mailed survey packets consisting of the following materials: (1) a letter of introduction to the study, (2) an informed consent form, (3) instructions for the completion of the measures, (4) the measures to be administered (i.e., these are self-report measures only), and (5) a preaddressed and stamped return envelope for their convenience. All survey packets were assigned identification numbers. Subjects who participated signed the informed consent and, if interested in the $200 lottery and/or in receiving a summary of the results, completed a detachable postcard on which they indicated their interest and put their names, addresses, phone numbers, and e-mail addresses (if applicable). On receipt of the completed surveys, the informed consent forms and postcards were separated from the measures and demographic data. The completed surveys were kept confidential, and no identifying data were included on the surveys themselves.

Because of the attrition rate (e.g., those who did not complete the survey) associated with the use of a mail survey for data collection, an increased sample size was desired to maintain power (Heppner, Kivlighan, & Wampold, 1992). To adjust for this procedure, all transracial adoptees identified for the study responded to flyers, advertisements, Web pages, or recruiters prior to mailings to confirm their participation. This initial response consisted of e-mail messages, phone calls, face-to-face contact, or the return of stamped, preaddressed postcards indicating the interested participant's address and phone number. An intensive 9-month data collection period, a Web site designed specifically for the study, and numerous other outreach attempts yielded a sample size of 51 completed surveys.

The self-report measures were presented in the survey packets in the following order: demographics questionnaire (the Cultural-Racial Identity Questionnaire), measures of cultural and racial identity (the MEIM-R), and the measure of psychological adjustment (the Brief Symptom Inventory [BSI]).

MEASURES

Cultural-Racial Identity Measures

The Cultural-Racial Identity Questionnaire (CRIQ) was developed for the current study and consists of 37 items that are open-ended, multiple-choice, or forced-choice. The CRIQ served as a background questionnaire for the study. All items were developed using a rational method of development which used the face validity of the items for inclusion. Demographic information such as age at adoption, trauma/history of the adoption, integration level of the community and schools in which the transracial adoptees were raised, and numbers and adoption status of siblings can be collected on the CRIQ.

The Multigroup Ethnic Identity Measure–Revised (MEIM-R) was administered. This measure was a revised or modified version of the original MEIM developed by Phinney (1992), and permission to modify the instrument for this study was obtained. The original MEIM measure consisted of 20 items that measured seven subscales, and some items were used in more than one subscale. Subscales for the MEIM as described by Phinney (1992) were Ethnic Identity (14 items), Affirmation and Belonging (5 items), Ethnic Identity Achievement (7 items), Ethnic Behaviors and Practices (2 items), Ethnicity (2 items), Other-Group Orientation (6 items), and Self-Identification (open-ended). When modified for use in the current study, 14 items that assessed four aspects of ethnic identity were chosen for use in analyses: Affirmation and Belonging, Ethnic Identity Achievement, Ethnic Behaviors and Practices, and Self-Identification. Items are rated on a 4-point Likert scale from *strongly agree* to *strongly disagree*. High scores indicate high ethnic identity as demonstrated by both exploration and commitment to obtaining information and awareness about one's ethnicity. Low scores indicate low ethnic identity that is evidenced by the absence of exploration and commitment to obtaining awareness and understanding of one's ethnicity. Reported reliability estimates demonstrate adequate internal consistency. For the MEIM, Phinney (1992) reported a Cronbach's alpha of .81 for a high school sample and .90 for a college sample for the whole measure. Individual scales demonstrated alphas of .75 and .86 for Affirmation/Belonging; .69 and .80 for Ethnic Identity Achievement; and .71 and .74 for the Other-Group Orientation.

Due to the racial and other potential differences between adoptive parents and the transracial adoptees themselves, the MEIM was adapted for use with transracial adoptees. Items 1 to 20 were repeated exactly as they appear on the original MEIM. Because the original MEIM included only two items to measure Ethnic Behaviors and Practices, and because the Ethnic Behaviors and Practices subscale was used in the current study to measure the dimensions for the Cultural Identity Axis, six additional items were developed by the author and added to improve the reliability of the scale. For the remaining items, 24 through 46, the wording in items 1 to 20 from the original MEIM and the additional items (21 to 23) were altered so that they referred to the adoptive parents' ethnic group. Reliability for this revised measure can be seen in the results of the reliability analysis shown in Table 23.2.

Psychological Adjustment

The BSI (Derogatis & Cleary, 1977) was used as the dependent measure of the dependent variable assessing the psychological adjustment of the transracial adoptees. This instrument is a brief form of the SCL-90-R, or the Symptom Check List–90, both of which are self-report symptom checklists (Derogatis, 1993). The BSI is appropriate for individuals age 13 and above who are psychiatric patients, medical patients, and nonpatient individuals in the community. It has 45 items on a 5-point Likert scale ranging from "not at all" to "extremely." These items measure three global indices (Global Severity Index [GSI], Positive Symptom Total [PST], and Positive Symptom Distress Index [PSDI]) and nine factors (Somatization, Obsessive-Compulsive, Interpersonal Sensitivity, Depression, Anxiety, Hostility, Phobic Anxiety, Paranoid Ideation, and Psychoticism). Respondents rated items according to "how much that problem has distressed or bothered you during the past 7 days, including today." Reliability estimates for BSI demonstrate good internal consistency and test-retest reliabilities. For the nine factors, Cronbach's alpha coefficients ranged from .71 on Psychoticism to .85 on Depression. Test-retest reliability estimates for a 2-week interval were reported to range from .68 for Somatization to .91 for Phobic Anxiety, whereas the GSI was found to have a stability coefficient of .90. Derogatis (1993) reported validity estimates demonstrating good convergent, discriminant, construct, and predictive validity.

Design

This study was conducted using a correlational field design. No experimental control over or manipulation of independent variables was used. This design was chosen due to the exploratory nature of the study, the inability to make use of randomization in sampling or assignment to groups, and the inability to make the observations of the transracial adoptees in their natural settings. This design does not allow for causal inferences, but it has high external validity given the participation by transracial adoptees throughout the United States. It also enabled the determination of within- and between-group differences.

RESULTS

Descriptive Statistics

Table 23.2 summarizes the means, standard deviations, and reliabilities for the major subscales from the BSI and the MEIM-R. The means and standard deviations for the BSI were standardized using Derogatis and Cleary's (1977) reported factor structure for a sample of nonpatient adults. The means and standard deviations of other relevant variables were also included in Table 23.2.

Table 23.2 also enumerates the items on the MEIM-R used to make up each of the four dimensions of the Cultural-Racial Identity Model and reports standardized item alphas for each subscale as well as their means and standard deviations. The specific items composing each of the four cultural-racial identity dimensions were determined by combining Phinney's factor structure and the additional items generated for the ethnic behaviors and practices subscale. When the items believed to be theoretically related to each of the four cultural-racial identity dimensions were obtained, a reliability analysis of the MEIM-R was conducted to determine those items that, when included in the score for each of the dimensions,

Table 23.2   Descriptive Statistics and Reliabilities

Variable	Actual Range	Mean	Standard Deviation	α
Demographics				—
Age at adoption (in months)	0–144	22.29	31.04	—
Number of preadoptive traumatic incidents reported	0–2	.53	.54	—
Number of preadoptive placements	0–18	1.64	2.67	—
Socioeconomic status of adoptive family	2–9	6.56	1.57	—
Brief Symptom Inventory				
Global Severity Index	36–80	60.65	9.70	.95
Positive Symptom Total	36–76	59.61	8.89	—
Positive Symptom Distress Index	43–78	57.09	8.46	—
Multigroup Ethnic Identity Measure–Revised (MEIM-R)				
Adoptee Culture Dimension (MEIM-R items: 2, 16, 21, 22)	1.00–4.00	2.11	.918	.85
Adoptee Race Dimension (MEIM-R items: 1, 3, 10R, 11, 12,13, 14, 18, 20)	1.22–4.00	2.81	.815	.92
Parental Culture Dimension (MEIM-R items: 39, 44, 45, 46)	2.00–4.00	3.37	.627	.73
Parental Race Dimension (MEIM-R items: 24, 26, 29, 33R, 34, 36, 37, 41, 43)	1.00–4.00	2.84	.680	.84

SOURCE: Baden, A. L. (2002). The psychological adjustment of transracial adoptees: An application of the Cultural-Racial Identity Model. *Journal of Social Distress and the Homeless, 11,* 167–192. Reprinted with permission of Springer Science and Business Media.

resulted in adequate reliability for the dimension. For each of the four cultural-racial identity dimensions, the combination of items that yielded the highest reliability was retained and became the items composing that dimension. Table 23.2 lists those items that were included in each dimension for the analyses to follow. Due to the small number of items making up the Ethnic Behaviors and Practices subscale of the original MEIM, additional items were constructed using a rational methodology.

The Cultural-Racial Identity Model

The first four research questions posed in the current study addressed the degree to which the Cultural-Racial Identity Model is a viable means for representing the unique identity statuses of transracial adoptees. An examination of the data allowed an assessment of the degree to which the measures chosen for this study substantively differentiated between transracial adoptees' cultural-racial identities. As a result, the specific research questions were addressed using three different analyses.

For the first analysis of the Cultural-Racial Identity Model, Figure 23.4 shows two scatterplots of the data points in the Cultural Identity Axis and Racial Identity Axis, respectively. These plots depict the transracial adoptee participants' scores on each of the four cultural-racial identity dimensions. For example, in the Cultural Identity Axis plot, transracial adoptees were plotted on the graph according to the degree to which they reported being knowledgeable of, aware of, competent within, and comfortable with their birth culture (Adoptee Culture Dimension); and by the degree to which they reported being knowledgeable of, aware of, competent within, and comfortable with the culture of their parents' racial group (Parental Culture Dimension). As the two plots illustrate, the transracial adoptee participants reported cultural identities and racial identities that were substantially scattered on the four cultural-racial identity dimensions of interest. In other words, the transracial adoptees reported a wide range of cultural identities or racial identities rather than remaining clustered in a few of the potential cultural-racial identities.

Table 23.3 reports correlations between each of the four cultural-racial identity dimensions and psychological adjustment. Pearson's correlation coefficient is a measure of linear

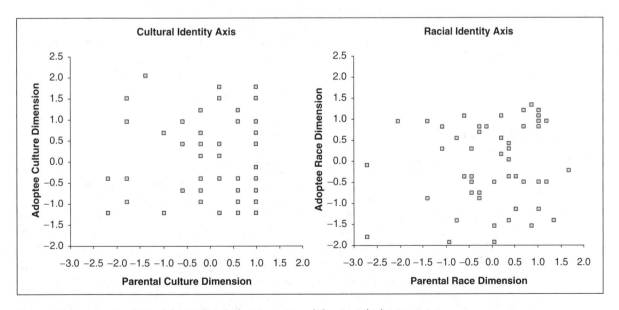

Figure 23.4.   Scatterplots of the Cultural Identity Axis and the Racial Identity Axis

SOURCE: Baden, A. L. (2002). The psychological adjustment of transracial adoptees: An application of the Cultural-Racial Identity Model. *Journal of Social Distress and the Homeless, 11,* 167–192. Reprinted with permission of Springer Science and Business Media.

Table 23.3 Correlations of Variables of Interest

Variable	Adoptee Culture Dimension	Parental Culture Dimension	Adoptee Race Dimension	Parental Race Dimension	Psychological Adjustment
Adoptee culture dimension	—	—	—	—	—
Parental culture dimension	−.118	—	—	—	—
Adoptee race dimension	.804***	−.189	—	—	—
Parental race dimension	.021	.508***	.080	—	—
Psychological adjustment	.046	−.244*	−.023	−.056	—

SOURCE: Baden, A. L. (2002). The psychological adjustment of transracial adoptees: An application of the Cultural-Racial Identity Model. *Journal of Social Distress and the Homeless, 11,* 167–192. Reprinted with permission of Springer Science and Business Media.

NOTE: $N = 51$ for all correlations. "Psychological Adjustment" was measured by the Global Severity Index of the Brief Symptom Inventory.

*Correlation is significant at the 0.10 level (two-tailed).
***Correlation is significant at the 0.01 level (two-tailed).

association and gives an indication of the degree to which a linear relationship exists between two variables. For the Cultural Identity Axis, the Adoptee Culture Dimension was plotted by the Parental Culture Dimension ($r = −.118$, $p = .41$). For the Cultural Identity Axis, a linear relationship was not found between the Adoptee Culture Dimension and the Parental Culture Dimension such that participants reported various cultural identities as measured by the MEIM-R. Similarly, for the Adoptee Race Dimension and the Parental Race Dimension a nonlinear relationship was found ($r = .080$, $p = .57$).

For the third analysis of the Cultural-Racial Identity Model, Table 23.2 reports the reliability estimates for the four dimensions of the Cultural-Racial Identity Model. As seen in Table 23.2, the four dimensions in the Cultural-Racial Identity Model as measured by the MEIM-R had reliabilities ranging from .73 on the Parental Culture Dimension to a high of .92 on Adoptee Race Dimension. Thus, variation in the cultural-racial identities of transracial adoptees in the current study exists.

Model Predicting Psychological Adjustment

Table 23.3 displays a correlation matrix of the variables of interest for this study. These correlations served as guides for examining additional relationships among variables. The correlation between the Adoptee Race Dimension and the Adoptee Culture Dimension ($r = .804$) supports the concern regarding the degree to which race and culture and their respective influences can be separated. This finding demonstrates that these two variables are strongly related. Similarly, the correlation between the Parental Race Dimension and the Parental Culture Dimension ($r = .508$) also shows a relationship of high to moderate strength between these two variables. Another correlation of low strength was between the Parental Culture Dimension and psychological adjustment.

Table 23.4 contains the results of multiple regression analyses used to address the degree to which differences exist in the psychological adjustment of transracial adoptees having different levels of the four cultural-racial identity dimensions. Table 23.4 shows the regression analyses performed to predict psychological adjustment. When all four cultural-racial

Table 23.4   Predicting Psychological Adjustment

Predictor	Partial Regression Weight	
	Raw	Standardized
Regression 1		
Adoptee Culture Dimension	2.254	.232
Parental Culture Dimension		−.339*
Adoptee Race Dimension	−2.762	−.285
Parental Race Dimension	1.304	.134
Intercept	60.647	
Summary statistics:[a] $R = .304$, $R^2 = .093$		
Regression 2		
Parental Culture Dimension	−2.369*	−.244*
Intercept	60.647	
Summary statistics:[b] $R = .244$, $R^2 = .060$		

SOURCE: Baden, A. L. (2002). The psychological adjustment of transracial adoptees: An application of the Cultural-Racial Identity Model. *Journal of Social Distress and the Homeless, 11*, 167–192. Reprinted with permission of Springer Science and Business Media.

NOTE: Psychological adjustment is measured by the Global Symptom Severity Index of the Brief Symptom Inventory.

a. $F(4, 46) = 1.174$, power = .339.
b. $F(1, 49) = 3.110*$, power = .409.
*$p < .10$.

identity dimensions were entered into the regression, the overall model did not reach statistical significance, $F(4, 46) = 1.174$, $p = .335$ but the Parental Culture Dimension was a significant predictor of psychological adjustment ($t = −1.990$, $p = .053$) only when $\alpha = .10$. This indicates that psychological adjustment did not differ based on transracial adoptees' cultural-racial identities as assessed with the MEIM-R.

Further regression analyses on reduced, more parsimonious models indicated that the second regression using the overall model was significant, $F(1, 49) = 3.110$, $p = .084$, at an .10 alpha level of but included only a single predictor, the Parental Culture Dimension.

Confounding Variables

The remaining research questions for this study addressed the psychological adjustment of those having a broad range of cultural-racial identities. To account for potential confounds, six variables were assessed for their impact on psychological adjustment (see Table 23.5). The six variables were age at adoption, number of preadoptive placements, preadoptive history/trauma, sex of the transracial adoptee, current age of the adoptee, and socioeconomic status of the adoptive family. The relationship between these variables serves as an additional source of construct validity. Although these findings did not have implications for the degree to which the variables were confounding, they do substantiate relationships among variables that make intuitive sense.

DISCUSSION

The findings of this study constitute a substantial contribution to the literature on transracial adoption and on racially integrated families. The purpose of this study was to examine

Table 23.5 Correlations of Potential Confounding Variables and Dependent Variables

Variable	Mean	Sex	Age at Adoption	Placements	Trauma	Socioeconomic Status	Current Age	Psychological Adjustment
Sex	1.25	—	—	—	—	—	—	—
(n)		(51)						
Age at adoption	22.29	.090	—	—	—	—	—	—
(n)		(51)	(51)					
Placements	1.64	−.109	−.108	—	—	—	—	—
(n)		(50)	(50)	(50)				
Trauma	0.53	.010	.371**	−.004	—	—	—	—
(n)		(51)	(51)	(50)	(51)			
SES	6.56	−.067	.192	.064	.141	—	—	—
(n)		(50)	(50)	(49)	(50)	(50)		
Current age	24.35	.071	.189	−.044	.130	−.325***	—	—
(n)		(51)	(51)	(50)	(51)	(50)	(51)	
Psychological adjustment	60.65	.134	−.022	.025	.135	.038	−.080	—
(n)		(51)	(51)	(50)	(51)	(50)	(51)	(51)

SOURCE: Baden, A. L. (2002). The psychological adjustment of transracial adoptees: An application of the Cultural-Racial Identity Model. *Journal of Social Distress and the Homeless, 11,* 167–192. Reprinted with permission of Springer Science and Business Media.

NOTE: "Age at adoption" is measured in months. "Placements" refers to the number of preadoptive placements the transracial adoptees reported. "Trauma" refers to the number of traumatic conditions the transracial adoptees reported as composing their preadoptive history. "SES" refers to socioeconomic status of the adoptive family and was measured using the following scale: 1 = $7,499 or below; 2 = $7,500 to $14,999; 3 = $15,000 to $24,999; 4 = $25,000 to $39,999; 5 = $40,000 to $59,999; 6 = $60,000 to $89,000; 7 = $90,000 or more.

**Correlation is significant at the 0.05 level (two-tailed).
***Correlation is significant at the 0.01 level (two-tailed).

the efficacy, applicability, and comprehensiveness of the Cultural-Racial Identity Model by (1) determining the degree to which the model validly describes the cultural-racial identities of transracial adoptees and (2) identifying differences in the psychological adjustment of transracial adoptees having different cultural-racial identities.

The current study was interpreted with the understanding that the significance level chosen for the current study was the traditional alpha level of .05. However, results that were significant at an alpha level of .10 were indicated as well to enable researchers and clinicians to garner as much relevant information as possible. Given that the potential for making a Type I error was substantial enough to force errors on the side of making Type II errors and given the nature of the study and its exploratory nature, the decision was made to adhere to the traditional boundaries for testing the Cultural-Racial Identity Model. Furthermore, the author of the study believes that findings that fail to reach statistical significance are often as important as those that do reach significance. Similarly, the power obtained for the current study was 0.4 for analyses using psychological adjustment as the outcome variable. Thus, the probability of failing to reject the null hypothesis when in fact the null is true is .6 and .4, respectively. Because these are high probabilities, caution must be used when interpreting failures to reject the null hypothesis. Thus, the findings from the current study that approached statistical significance at the .05 level were interpreted and those that were significant at the .10 level were considered in the implications of this research.

SUMMARY

The Cultural-Racial Identity Model

The data obtained for this study was collected from 51 young, adult, transracial adoptees. The transracial adoptees in this study reported a wide range of cultural-racial identities and did not cluster in just a few identity status areas. These findings suggested that the instrument used to measure the cultural-racial identities of transracial adoptees allowed the variation among respondents to be detected and the inference to be made that all 16 cells of the Cultural-Racial Identity Model were represented in the data. However, these findings did not allow the strict validation of the model. To validate the model, a substantially larger sample was needed so that the various cells of the model could be tested. With this limitation in mind and based on the findings of this study, the evidence suggested that the Cultural-Racial Identity Model with the accompanying MEIM-R instrument can be accepted as having been supported. Thus, the four cultural-racial identity dimensions can be used to assess the identity experiences of transracial adoptees and, subsequently, to determine their cultural-racial identity status.

Interestingly, the Adoptee Race Dimension and the Adoptee Culture Dimension were highly correlated (see Table 23.3). Given the positive direction of this correlation, this could indicate that experiences with their culture of origin and people from their own racial group may be very closely related for transracial adoptees. For example, transracial adoptees may become more comfortable with people from their own racial group when they have gained more knowledge, awareness, competence, and comfort with their culture of origin. Another interpretation could be that transracial adoptees make few distinctions between racial and cultural identity experiences or that this measure was limited in its ability to make distinctions between these constructs for these individuals.

Predicting Psychological Adjustment

For the reasons already enumerated, the standard criterion for significance testing (e.g., significance level of $\alpha = .05$ where $p < .05$) was used. Using this criterion, none of the models predicting the psychological adjustment of the young adult transracial adoptees in this sample attained statistical significance. That is, given an alpha level of .05, no single cultural-racial identity dimension nor any combination of the four cultural-racial identity dimensions was found to significantly predict level of psychological adjustment. This means that, for example, a transracial adoptee who identified as Pro-Parent Cultural Identity–Pro-Parent Racial Identity (i.e., an adoptee who highly identifies with the White culture and feels most comfortable associating with White people) was found to be neither better nor worse psychologically adjusted than a transracial adoptee who identified as a Pro-Self Cultural Identity–Pro-Self Racial Identity (i.e., an adoptee who highly identifies with his or her birth culture and feels most comfortable associating with people from his or her own racial group). However, although not found to be within the accepted level of significance, one finding suggested that the Parental Culture Dimension may be predictive of psychological adjustment. This finding could suggest that identification with one's adoptive parents and, therefore, with the White, middle-class American culture, can lead to less psychological distress. That is, given that psychological maladjustment has been measured using the standards set by White, middle-class American culture, individuals who can function effectively in that culture will likely be found to have higher levels of adjustment than those who reject or are disenfranchised from that culture. Furthermore, identification with one's parents may indicate more secure levels of attachment, so that those who share similar values, traditions, beliefs, and practices (i.e., culture) with their adoptive parents may be more likely to report less psychological distress. In essence, psychological distress may be the result of those strained relationships. Perhaps some other construct, such as self-esteem, may better explain the variations in cultural and racial identities. Clearly, these findings of note, although statistically insignificant, need to be further explored and understood.

FIT WITH EXISTING RESEARCH

The exploratory nature of the current study as well as the relatively new development of the Cultural-Racial Identity Model make fitting this model with existing research complicated. This study sought to begin empirically validating the Cultural-Racial Identity Model but was exploratory given limitations in the sampling, data, and design. As noted above, one primary problem with previous studies was the age of the subjects used to examine identity experiences. More recently, researchers have recognized the importance of examining the psychological adjustment of transracial adoptees during adulthood (e.g., Cederblad et al., 1999; Feigelman, 1997, 2000; Freundlich & Lieberthal, 2000; Meier, 1999), but identity has not been centrally explored in a systematic manner in any of the studies. A review of the theoretical bases for identity suggested that identity conflicts and formation occur throughout life but that changes in awareness of race and culture often occur in adolescence. However, the vast majority of studies of identity and adjustment were with preadolescent subjects. Thus, the current study set the important goal of examining identity with older transracial adoptees.

Studies by Andujo (1988) and Vroegh (1997) laid the groundwork for the current study by allowing the focus to be on the differences between the population of transracial adoptees and intraracial adoptees. Because homogeneous experiences of transracial adoptees were not addressed or systematically examined, the current study was able to focus on differences within the population of transracial adoptees. Furthermore, for the current study, the processes of identity crisis and formation were expected to occur at ages later than the ages at which Andujo (1988) and Vroegh (1997) studied transracial adoptees. Therefore, the findings from the current study do not replicate previous findings because there have been no other studies similar in scope.

Limitations

Due to this study's exploratory status, its limitations are fewer than found in studies in which causal inferences are made. The external validity of the current study was high, but the internal validity was a source of limitation. Internal validity was limited because of the inability to apply random selection and random assignment to groups, a small sample size, and the potential problem of selection bias due to the use of survey research. Selection biases may threaten the external validity of the study because of the possibility that those who return the surveys and participate in the very adoption support groups that facilitated their identification as transracial adoptees may be quite different from other transracial adoptees, who are not as amenable to participation in such a study. The small representation of transracial adoptees from non-Asian racial ethnic backgrounds also forced comparisons based on racial groups to be between Asian-identified transracial adoptees and non-Asian transracial adoptees (e.g., Biracial, Black/African American, Latino, and Native American). Moreover, this study was limited to White parents adopting transracially. Another limitation of this study lies in its lack of a comparison group.

Implications of the Study

As the first empirical study of the Cultural-Racial Identity Model, the findings of the current study have several important implications. These implications are in the arenas of future research, clinical practice, and adoption policy. The Cultural-Racial Identity Model serves as the first attempt to conceptualize the unique identity experiences of transracial adoptees. In this role, it has been the first model to make purposeful distinctions between race and culture and their separate influences on identity. The validation of this model by the current study validates the intuitive but yet to be empirically demonstrated belief that heterogeneity exists within the population of transracial adoptees. The demonstration of the scope and nature of that heterogeneity represents a substantial improvement in the understanding of the factors influencing transracial adoptees' identity. As a result, adoption policy and guidelines can be formulated with greater attention to the sources of identity and the impact of identity on such important factors as psychological adjustment.

For example, because a relationship between psychological adjustment and the cultural-racial identity dimensions could not be empirically demonstrated, concerns among adoption policymakers that particular cultural-racial identities may lead to healthier or less healthy adjustment could not be addressed. As the findings of this study suggest, no particular cultural-racial identity or identities were found to lead to better or worse psychological adjustment. This finding should be explored in greater detail, and the cultural socialization practices that adoptive parents use to instill culture knowledge and exposure should be examined (Lee, 2003; Yoon, 2001, 2004).

Moreover, given some indications that the Parental Culture Dimension was approaching but did not attain statistical significance, future researchers should determine if a relationship exists such that when transracial adoptees do not identify with the culture of their adoptive parents (i.e., the White culture), they report more severe psychological symptoms on the BSI. That is, does discomfort within, a lack of knowledge or awareness of, or the perceived incompetence in dominant, middle-class White culture (i.e., the culture of the adoptive parents) have some relationship to psychological distress or maladjustment? The nature of this relationship could suggest that transracial adoptees who function adequately in the White culture and who do not reject White culture may report less psychological distress. If this relationship was substantiated, it could be interpreted to suggest that psychological adjustment would naturally be poorer for those transracial adoptees who did not accept or at least function well within the culture of their parents. Thus, a phenomenon that reinforces common sense and psychological principles may exist such that if children feel disenfranchised from or choose to reject the values, beliefs, traditions, and so on that compose their parents' culture, they are likely to have more difficulty in their adjustment. When an individual endorses values or beliefs that differ from those of their parents, and particularly when they are unable or unwilling to accept these differences, they are likely to have a greater chance of experiencing psychological distress. Although this noteworthy but statistically insignificant finding may be helpful for future clinical practice, it does not suggest that a "healthiest way to identify currently exists."

The failure to find any interpretable, significant relationship between the cultural-racial identity dimensions and psychological adjustment suggests that transracial adoptees' psychological adjustment may be less dependent on their identity experiences than has previously been surmised. However, other facets of transracial adoptees' lives and self-concepts may well be affected by their identity experiences. Perhaps, the psychological adjustment of transracial adoptees may be influenced more by their parental or family relationships, peer relationships, achievement, or a host of other factors than by the racial and often cultural differences that exist in transracially adopting families. Although no empirical evidence was gathered to support this supposition, the findings of the current study suggest that this possibility be explored.

The findings of the study can also greatly inform the view of transracial adoption among opponents and proponents of transracial adoption. First, because heterogeneity exists among transracial adoptees and because a particular way or ways of identifying were not associated with better or worse psychological adjustment, neither proponents nor opponents can purport a "best way" to identify as a transracial adoptee. Second, racial differences between parents and adoptees have been targeted as the primary source of potential problems in transracial adoption. This expectation can be problematic because many other factors (e.g., parenting, reasons for adopting, hardiness, ego strength, and trauma) have been virtually forgotten, and their impact has yet to be examined with respect to transracial adoptees. Although these other factors continue to deserve empirical and theoretical attention, they often do not receive it.

Finally, the results of this study are important to the controversy surrounding transracial adoption. Hollingsworth (1997) found results indicating lower levels of racial identity in transracial adoptees than in intraracial adoptees. Based on the Cultural-Racial Identity Model (Baden & Steward, 2000) and the work on identity presented in this study, more research on transracial adoption is needed to further clarify and delineate the contradictory findings especially in light of the current finding that no form of cultural-racial identity was "better" or "higher" than others. With this contrast in mind, the premise that there are healthier and less healthy racial identities must be revisited.

Implications for Practice

The findings of this study are of substantial importance to the provision of ethical and competent services to transracial adoptees. This study is one of the few studies to specifically focus on young adult transracial adoptees and their unique identity experiences. Unfortunately, no empirical studies of the counseling and psychotherapeutic needs of transracial adoptees exist. Clinicians and researchers have drawn on their experiences to suggest some clinical interventions for adoptees (Clegg & Toll, 1996; Helwig & Ruthven, 1990; Janus, 1997; Jones, 1997; Okun, 1996; Valley, Bass, & Speirs, 1999), but empirical validation or exploration of clinical interventions has been absent from the literature. This study also addresses transracial adoption from a perspective that focuses on assisting those who have already been transracially adopted rather than focusing on whether or not to make transracial adoption placements. As a result, the findings from the present study, in conjunction with the literature on multicultural counseling, can be used to aid psychologists and other clinicians in providing culturally sensitive and culturally competent counseling to existing and future transracial adoptees. To date, clinicians have been without a guide to the unique experiences and influences that affect transracial adoptees' identity statuses. Without this information, clinicians can be prone to errors and assumptions regarding the cultural and racial identities of transracial adoptees.

REFLECTION QUESTIONS

1. What factors affect transracial adoptees' identities? Does the Cultural-Racial Identity Model include those factors?

2. Is there a "healthiest" or most "adaptive" way to identify racially and culturally? If a transracial adoptee does not identify strongly with his or her birth culture and racial group, does that necessarily lead to problems?

3. What clinical issues are likely to accompany the different cultural and racial identities identified in this model?

REFERENCES

Andujo, E. (1988). Ethnic identity of transethnically adopted Hispanic adolescents. *Social Work, 33*(6), 531–535.

Baden, A. L., & Steward, R. J. (2000). A framework for use with racially and culturally integrated families: The cultural-racial identity model as applied to transracial adoption. *Journal of Social Distress & the Homeless, 9*(4), 309–337.

Bagley, C. (1993a). Chinese adoptees in Britain: A twenty-year follow-up of adjustment and social identity. *International Social Work, 36*(2), 143–157.

Bagley, C. (1993b). Transracial adoption in Britain: A follow-up study, with policy considerations. *Child Welfare, 72*(3), 285–299.

Cederblad, M., Höök, B., Irhammar, M., & Mercke, A.-M. (1999). Mental health in international adoptees as teenagers and young adults: An epidemiological study. *Journal of Child Psychology & Psychiatry, 40*(8), 1239–1248.

Child Welfare League of America. (2003). *International adoption: Trends and issues.* Retrieved August 5, 2005, from http://ndas.cwla.org/include/text/IssueBrief_International_Adoption_FINAL.pdf

Clegg, P., & Toll, K. (1996). Videotape and the memory visit: A living lifebook for adopted children. *Child Welfare, 75*(4), 311–319.

Derogatis, L. R. (1993). *Brief Symptom Inventory: Administration, scoring procedures manual.* Minneapolis, MN: National Computer Systems.

Derogatis, L. R., & Cleary, P. A. (1977). Confirmation of the dimensional structure of the SCL-90: A study in construct validation. *Journal of Clinical Psychology, 33*(4), 981–989.

Fanshel, D. (1972). *Far from the reservation: The transracial adoption of American Indian children.* Metuchen, NJ: Scarecrow Press.

Feigelman, W. (1997). Adopted adults: Comparisons with persons raised in conventional families. *Marriage & Family Review, 25*(3), 199–223.

Feigelman, W. (2000). Adjustments of transracially and inracially adopted young adults. *Child & Adolescent Social Work Journal, 17*(3), 165–183.

Freundlich, M., & Lieberthal, J. K. (2000). *The gathering of the first generation of adult Korean adoptees: Adoptees' perceptions of international adoption.* Retrieved April 15, 2005, from www.adoptioninstitute.org

Gill, O., & Jackson, B. (1983). *Adoption and race: Black, Asian and mixed race children in White families.* New York: St. Martin's Press.

Griffith, E. E., & Duby, J. L. (1991). Recent developments in the transracial adoption debate. *Bulletin of the American Academy of Psychiatry & the Law, 19*(4), 339–350.

Helms, J. E. (1990). *Black and White racial identity: Theory, research, and practice.* New York: Greenwood Press.

Helwig, A. A., & Ruthven, D. H. (1990). Psychological ramifications of adoption and implications for counseling. *Journal of Mental Health Counseling, 12*(1), 24–37.

Heppner, P. P., Kivlighan, D. M. J., & Wampold, B. E. (1992). *Research design in counseling.* Belmont, CA: Brooks.

Hollinger, J. H., & the ABA Center on Children and the Law National Resource Center on Legal and Courts Issues. (1988). *A guide to the Multiethnic Placement Act of 1994 as amended by the Interethnic Provisions of 1996.* Retrieved August 16, 2001, from www.acf.hhs.gov/programs/cb/pubs/mepa94/index.htm

Hollingsworth, L. D. (1997). Effect of transracial/transethnic adoption on children's racial and ethnic identity and self-esteem: A meta-analytic review. *Marriage & Family Review, 25*(1), 99–130.

Hollingsworth, L. D. (1999). Symbolic interactionism, African-American families, and the transracial adoption controversy. *Social Work, 44*(5), 443–453.

Janus, N. G. (1997). Adoption counseling as a professional specialty area for counselors. *Journal of Counseling & Development, 75*(4), 266–274.

Johnson, P. R., Shireman, J. F., & Watson, K. W. (1987). Transracial adoption and the development of Black identity at age eight. *Child Welfare, 66*(1), 45–55.

Jones, A. (1997). Issues relevant to therapy with adoptees. *Psychotherapy: Theory, Research, Practice, Training, 34*(1), 64–68.

Lee, R. M. (2003). The transracial adoption paradox: History, research, and counseling implications of cultural socialization. *The Counseling Psychologist, 31*(6), 711–744.

McRoy, R. G., Zurcher, L. A., Lauderdale, M. L., & Anderson, R. E. (1984). The identity of transracial adoptees. *Social Casework, 65*(1), 34–39.

McRoy, R. G., Zurcher, L. A., Lauderdale, M. L., & Anderson, R. N. (1982). Self-esteem and racial identity in transracial and inracial adoptees. *Social Work, 27*(6), 522–526.

Meier, D. I. (1999). Cultural identity and place in adult Korean-American intercountry adoptees. *Adoption Quarterly, 3*(1), 15–48.

National Adoption Information Clearinghouse. (1994). *Transracial and transcultural adoption.* Retrieved August 16, 2006, from http://childwelfare.gov/pubs/f_trans.cfm

National Association of Black Social Workers. (1972). *NABSW opposes transracial adoption* (Report). New York: Author.

Okun, B. F. (1996). *Understanding diverse families: What practitioners need to know.* New York: Guilford Press.

Phinney, J. S. (1992). The multigroup ethnic identity measure: A new scale for use with diverse groups. *Journal of Adolescent Research, 7*(2), 156–176.

Ryan, A. S. (1983). Intercountry adoption and policy issues. *Journal of Children in Contemporary Society, 15*(3), 49–60.

Silverman, A. R., & Feigelman, W. (1981). The adjustment of Black children adopted by White families. *Social Casework: The Journal of Contemporary Social Work, 62,* 529–536.

Simon, R. J., & Altstein, H. (1987). *Transracial adoptees and their families: A study of identity and commitment.* New York: Praeger.

Steward, R. J., & Baden, A. L. (1995). *The cultural-racial identity model: Understanding the racial identity and cultural identity development of transracial adoptees* (Report No. UD030908). East Lansing: Michigan State University (ERIC Document Reproduction Service No. ED 395 076).

Stolley, K. (1993). Statistics on adoption in the United States. *Future of Children: Adoption, 3,* 26–42.

Tizard, B. (1991). Intercountry adoption: A review of the evidence. *Journal of Child Psychology & Psychiatry, 32*(5), 743–756.

U.S. Department of State. (2006). *Immigrant visas issued to orphans coming to the U.S.* Retrieved February 4, 2006, from http://travel.state.gov/family/adoption/stats/stats_451.html

Valley, S., Bass, B., & Speirs, C. C. (1999). A professionally led adoption triad group: An evolving approach to search and reunion. *Child Welfare, 78*(3), 363–379.

Verhulst, F. C., Althaus, M., & Versluis-den Bieman, H. J. (1990a). Problem behavior in international adoptees: I. An epidemiological study. *Journal of the American Academy of Child & Adolescent Psychiatry, 29*(1), 94–103.

Verhulst, F. C., Althaus, M., & Versluis-den Bieman, H. J. (1990b). Problem behavior in international adoptees: II. Age at placement. *Journal of the American Academy of Child & Adolescent Psychiatry, 29*(1), 104–111.

Verhulst, F. C., Althaus, M., & Versluis-den Bieman, H. J. (1992). Damaging backgrounds: Later adjustment of international adoptees. *Journal of the American Academy of Child & Adolescent Psychiatry, 31*(3), 518–524.

Yoon, D. P. (2001). Causal modeling predicting psychological adjustment of Korean-born adolescent adoptees. *Journal of Human Behavior in the Social Environment, 3*(3), 65–82.

Yoon, D. P. (2004). Intercountry adoption: The importance of ethnic socialization and subjective well-being for Korean-born adopted children. *Journal of Ethnic & Cultural Diversity in Social Work, 13*(2), 71–89.

Zamostny, K. P., O'Brien, K. M., Baden, A. L., & Wiley, M. O. (2003). The practice of adoption history, trends, and social context. *The Counseling Psychologist, 31*(6), 651–678.

Adoptees' and Birth Parents' Therapeutic Experiences Related to Adoption

24

DOUGLAS B. HENDERSON

University of Wisconsin–Stevens Point

DANIEL A. SASS

University of Wisconsin–Milwaukee

JEANNA CARLSON (NÉE WEBSTER)

Marshfield, Wisconsin, School District

Relatively little is known regarding the lifelong implications of adoption. This lack of information occurs despite the fact that at any given time 1% to 2% of the U.S. population has been adopted (Brodzinsky, 1990; Jerome, 1986). In an effort to meet the real needs of children and find adoptive families, many adoption agencies and facilitators may have promulgated an overly positive view of the process (Smith & Sherwen, 1988). The success of this promotion may have contributed to the failure to acquire and disseminate adequate information with regard to long-term outcomes for individual members of the adoption triad, which consists of adoptees, birth parents, and adoptive parents. For other reasons for the relative absence of information on adoption in the mental health literature, see Chapter 25 by Henderson in this book.

Between 11% and 25% of all infertile couples in the United States seek to adopt children (Resolve, n.d.), and infertility constitutes the most frequent reason for adoption (Fisher, 2003). Menning (1975) suggested that the presence of unresolved infertility issues was a central source of failure in adoption placements, and Sorosky, Baran, and Pannor (1978) suggested that these issues led to higher rates of emotional disturbances in adoptees. Another possible difficulty for adoptive parents is society's negative response to adoption and the belief that only biology determines a true family, a feeling reported by nearly two thirds of adoptive parents (Miall, 1986).

For most birth mothers, the adoption experience does not end after the relinquishment papers are signed (Russell, 1996). Instead, relinquishment only initiates the development of new questions and issues, such as feelings of loss, guilt, shame, and depression. For this reason, the relinquishment of an infant can be emotionally overwhelming, confusing, and traumatic, especially when birth parent and adoptee never reunite to establish a relationship. In a study by Deykin, Campbell, and Patti (1984), in which the birth mothers' average age at relinquishment was 19.8 years, it was determined that 69% of the birth mothers surrendered their child due to family resistance to the pregnancy, financial reasons, or pressure from the social worker. Years later, however, the birth mothers realized they were unable to forget their past as caseworkers frequently said they would. Young age, pressure to relinquish, and inability to forget may have been causal factors in the development of the birth mothers' negative feelings about their relinquishment.

Deykin et al. (1984) also indicated that surrendering a child created a negative impact on the birth parents. Many of the birth parents who surrendered a child reported feelings of low self-esteem and severe mood disorders. Previous research has found that 40% of birth parents suffer from depression (Burnell & Norfleet, 1979) and 17% chose to remain childless (Deykin et al., 1984). Those birth parents in Deykin and colleagues' (1984) study who later conceived their own infant perceived themselves as more overprotective and compulsive, and they often had more problems allowing child independence than other parents. In addition, they also felt closer to the child and were more active in the child's life.

Birth and adoptive parents also experience distress related to adoption procedures and unanswered questions. They must deal with issues such as guilt, shame, sadness, and fear of unknown information. For these reasons, successful outcomes for adoptive families may be contingent on the accuracy and amount of information provided prior to the adoption process and the contact that occurs between the two families after the adoption (Grotevant, McRoy, Elde, & Fravel, 1994; Mendenhall, Berge, Wrobel, Grotevant, & McRoy, 2000).

For the adopted child, identity issues often arise during adolescence (Dunbar & Grotevant, 2004; Grotevant, Dunbar, Kohler, & Lash Esau, 2000) and may be magnified across the life span, especially if adequate information regarding the adoptee's history is not provided. Dickson, Heffron, and Parker (1990) found that adopted children were more likely than nonadopted children to be treated as inpatients and to return to treatment once discharged; and Jerome (1986) found the same results for adoptees receiving outpatient mental health services. Researchers such as Borders, Black, and Pasley (1998) suggested that reported increases in the incidence of adoptees receiving mental health treatment either were not the case or were due to reasons other than more severe problems in adoptees. Miller et al. (2000) believe that there is an increased likelihood of adoptive parents seeking help but that even controlling for this, adoptees are still overrepresented in therapy. Prevalence rates for birth parents in therapy are even less available than for adoptees. Adoption research may be enhanced by an examination of dyad members' experiences in therapy.

Often adoptees who think about searching are warned about "opening Pandora's box." They are asked, "Why seek out what has to be bad news?" on the assumption that if there was not "bad news," there would not have been an adoption to begin with. Secrecy is seen as protecting the adoptee from this presumably painful truth. Many people believe that a most distressing truth might be to learn one was the product of rape or incest.

In the late 1980s, an adoptee came to the search and support group the first author ran in Stevens Point. "Anne," a single mother and just over 18 years herself, brought her infant daughter to the meeting with her and told us, "I want to find my birth mother." We encouraged her to apply for a search through the Wisconsin Adoption Search Program, even though at the time it was badly run and had a longer than 2-year waiting list for nonemergency searches. Over the next two monthly meetings, we talked about her reasons for searching, the experiences many of the group (adoptees, birth parents, and even an adoptive parent) had in their own searches and reunions, and how she might feel as her own search progressed. Anne, though sincere and earnest in her desire to complete her search, seemed quite emotionally young and fragile. She was living with the father of her daughter, but their relationship did not seem to be a strong one. We were almost glad that the long State waiting list would give us time to help her prepare for whatever challenges her reunion would present.

Phil, one of our members and the husband of a birth mother, was a recently retired Madison police detective, and learning that Anne had been born and adopted in Madison, Phil offered to assist in her search. With the information Anne had, and his connections, it took Phil only a few weeks to locate what he thought was information about Anne's relinquishment. As soon as he found it he called the first author, asking to speak in confidence. He then said he had a pretty strong suspicion that Anne was born of an incestuous relationship between her birth mother and the birth mother's father (Anne's birth grandfather).

This information presented a number of problems. Phil was not 100% certain he was correct, and we did not want to pass on such disturbing news if we were not certain of it. As a support group, we had never faced this issue before; and Phil, his wife, and the first author were all fearful of Anne's ability to deal with this issue. We assumed that she would be as disturbed by it as we were on her behalf. At the same time, as advocates of openness and honesty, we were uncomfortable just "sitting on" this information, keeping it a secret from Anne until the State got around to completing Anne's search. The first author decided to call in a favor with a state adoption social worker, told him about what we thought we knew, and asked him to see if they could expedite Anne's search as an "emergency."

At the very next meeting, Anne clearly had news as she entered the room. She told us she had gotten a call from the State and had just that week gone to our area State social services office to talk with a social worker about her search. She told us that her birth mother had been the victim of incest by her father, and that was why her birth mother had surrendered Anne for adoption. The State was in the process of trying to locate Anne's birth mother to see if she wanted her identity shared with Anne. We held our collective breath to see what Anne would say next, and then she told us,

> Now I really want to find her because I know what she went through. See, getting pregnant with my baby was the only way I figured I could get out of my house and away from my adoptive father, because he was doing the same thing to me. Now my birth mother and I can cry together.

By that time we were almost all in tears.

Anne told us she was offered counseling by the social worker, but we don't know how much she received. Nonetheless, over the next few months the change in Anne was astounding. It seemed that she became stronger, more confident, and more mature at every turn. Perhaps the truth, even unpleasant truth, does not necessarily destroy us and may instead set us free.

To determine prevalence rates of triad members in therapy, it is important that therapists inquire about adoption status. Prior research has revealed that roughly half of a sample of practicing psychologists inquired of their clients about adoption (Sass & Henderson, 2000); however, whether therapists should routinely inquire about adoption remains a controversial topic (Dickson, Stephens, Heffron, & Parker, 1991; Hartman & Laird, 1990; Jago Krueger & Hanna, 1997). Nevertheless, therapists have expressed interest in knowing more about the adoption process (Dickson et al., 1991; Sass & Henderson, 2000).

This present study consisted of a sample of dyad members (adoptees and birth parents) from two adoption search and support organizations to explore how adoption affected their lives and their therapy experiences. We hoped to complement the Sass and Henderson (2000) study, which examined licensed psychologists' self-perceived level of adoption training and their experiences with adoption-related therapy. For the purpose of this study, "inquiring" was operationally defined as whether therapists asked if the participant was a member of the adoption triad. "Addressing" was operationally defined as whether adoption issues were discussed in the participant's therapy. These two variables appear to be of primary importance in obtaining accurate prevalence rates of triad members in therapy. In addition, this study sought to investigate perceived level of therapist helpfulness and preparation related to adoption issues from a dyad member's perspective.

METHOD

Participants

Two hundred and twenty-eight triad members, 190 from the Washington Adoption Reform Movement (WARM) and 38 from the Oregon Adoptive Rights Association (OARA), responded to the study. Three respondents were eliminated due to completion of the questionnaire by a significant other. Respondents included 152 adoptees, 66 birth parents, and 10 adoptive parents. Demographic data are broken down by triad position in Table 24.1. Figures 24.1 and 24.2 provide histograms of the year of birth for adoptees and year of relinquishment for birth parents. Although comparisons between the two support groups were not of primary interest, statistical analyses revealed that the two samples did not differ significantly when evaluating the variables of primary interest.

Procedure

WARM and OARA were responsible for printing, addressing, and mailing the questionnaires to ensure the confidentiality of subjects. Questions were designed to obtain data regarding (1) the degree to which adoption affected triad members' lives, (2) the level of helpfulness and background information provided by the adoption caseworker, (3) adoption triad members' experiences in therapy, and (4) the degree to which therapists were perceived as prepared and helpful. Questions also examined whether therapists inquired about and addressed adoption issues in therapy and whether triad members perceived an adoption

Table 24.1	Gender, Race, and Age by Triad Position			
		Triad Membership		
		Adoptee	Adoptive Parent	Birth Parent
Gender	Male	46	0	3
	Female	106	10	63
Race	African American	0	0	2
	Asian	0	1	1
	Caucasian	144	9	59
	Hispanic	2	0	1
	Native American	3	0	0
	Other	2	0	3
Mean age (SD)		46.03 (11.60)	57.00 (12.37)	52.37 (6.80)

NOTE: *SD* stands for standard deviation of the subject's age, which is provided in parentheses.

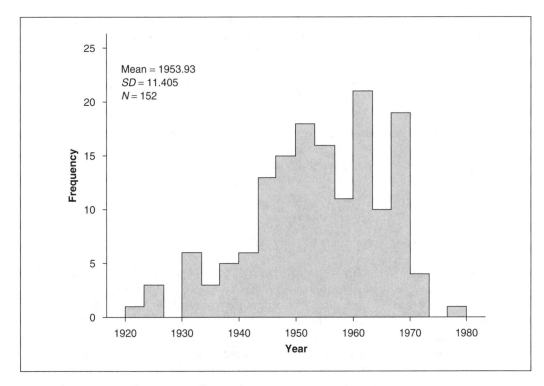

Figure 24.1   Year of Birth for Adoptee Participants

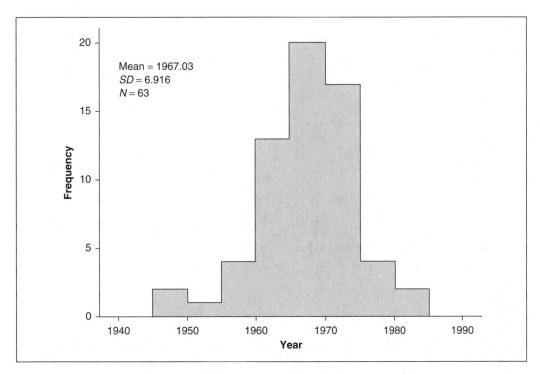

Figure 24.2   Year of Relinquishment for Birth Parent Participants

component of therapy as being needed. The first two pages of the questionnaire are included in the appendix. A third page of the questionnaire repeated the question (#15) about experience in therapy for those who had seen multiple therapists. Because of the low occurrence of adoptive parents ($n = 10$) in our sample, only adoptee and birth-parent data were examined. Furthermore, only numeric results from this study are provided in the results section, whereas the discussion integrates the open-ended responses.

Questionnaires were mailed to 1,397 WARM and 120 OARA members; however, the exact number of various triad members receiving questionnaires was unattainable. Completed questionnaires did not contain identifying information, and no further contact occurred unless the respondent requested a summary of the group results.

Results

Life Effects of Adoption

When adoptees and birth parents were asked whether they experienced mental or emotional problems as a result of the adoption, 55% of adoptees, compared with 86% of birth parents, answered *yes* to this question. This difference was tested with a chi-square and was found to be statistically significant, $\chi^2(1, N = 218) = 18.22$, $p < .0001$, $\phi = -.291$, with the measure of association (ϕ) suggesting a relatively strong relationship between position in the dyad and emotional problems experienced. When adoptees and birth parents were also asked to rate how adoption affected their life and developmental choices on a Likert scale, with 1 and 5 representing *no effect* and *enormous effect*, respectively, birth parents ($M = 3.83$, $SD = 0.93$) tended to have significantly higher ratings on the Likert scale compared with adoptees ($M = 2.99$, $SD = 1.25$), $t(209) = -4.85$, $p < .001$, $d = -0.67$. The frequency and percentage of responses to each question are provided in Table 24.2.

Table 24.2 The Frequency (Percentage) of Adoptee and Birth Parent Responses to This Question: "To What Extent Has Adoption Affected Your Life and Developmental Choices?"

Likert Scale	Adoptee	Birth Parent
No effect	18 (11.8%)	0 (0%)
Minimal effect	41 (27.0%)	7 (10.6%)
Moderate effect	32 (21.1%)	14 (21.2%)
Large effect	35 (23.0%)	27 (40.9%)
Enormous effect	20 (13.2%)	17 (25.8%)
Missing/no response	6 (3.9%)	1 (1.5%)

NOTE: An alternative data analysis approach, which was also statistically significant, would be a chi-square. The test can be calculated from the data provided in this table.

Experience at the Time of Adoption

The descriptive results in Table 24.3 reveal that most of the adoptions were relatively closed, with 85% of adoptees and 89% of birth parents receiving either no information or only demographic information about their separated kin. These results did not appear to change as a result of the year in which the adoption took place. In fact, both adoptees and birth parents (see Table 24.3) indicated that more information would have been beneficial, which may partially explain why the majority of respondents thought that the adoption

Table 24.3 Level of Openness and Adequacy of Background Information Provided at the Time of the Adoption

		Level of Openness	
Likert Scale	Scale #	Adoptee	Birth Parent
Totally closed, no information provided	1	71 (46.7%)	38 (57.6%)
	2	28 (18.4%)	14 (21.2%)
Only nonidentifying demographic information	3	31 (20.4%)	7 (10.6%)
	4	6 (3.9%)	1 (1.5%)
Totally open, all information shared	5	8 (5.3%)	4 (6.1%)
Missing		8 (5.3%)	2 (3%)
		Adequacy of Background Information	
		Adoptee	Birth Parent
Less information would have been beneficial	1	4 (2.6%)	0 (0%)
	2	6 (3.9%)	2 (3.0%)
An adequate amount of information was provided	3	22 (14.5%)	5 (7.6%)
	4	5 (3.3%)	2 (3.0%)
More information would have been beneficial	5	95 (65.5%)	48 (72.7%)
Missing		20 (13.2%)	9 (13.6%)

caseworker did not prepare them for future issues associated with adoption. It should be noted that due to the lack of variability in subject responses, statistical analyses could not be conducted on these data.

The Search Process

Of the adoptees and birth parents sampled, 98% of adoptees and 92% of birth parents thought about searching for the person from whom they were separated. Although this difference in proportions is statistically significant, $\chi^2(1, N = 218) = 4.09$, $p = .043$, $\phi = .137$, the effect size (ϕ) was relatively small. In addition, one cell had an expected count less than 5, which violates the test assumptions, thus producing a potentially biased probability value. Nonetheless, nearly all adoptees and birth parents thought about searching at one point or another. In addition, nearly all adoptees (95%) and birth parents (86%) in our sample actually searched for their separated other. Similarly to those thinking about search, adoptees actually searched significantly more often than birth parents, $\chi^2(1, N = 217) = 5.45$, $p = .020$, $\phi = .158$; however, the effect size (ϕ) was also relatively small, and one cell again had expected counts less than 5. Of the adoptees and birth parents who were reunited, 67% of each group reported reunion to be a positive experience.

Therapy Experience

Results revealed that 35% ($n = 53$) of adoptees and 41% ($n = 26$) of birth parents received therapy at least once, with 155 total therapists seen between 1965 and 1999. Therapy was received from professionals in various fields (psychologists, 47%; social workers, 25%; marriage/family counselors, 21%; psychiatrists, 19%; and those labeled "other," 4%). No meaningful differences were found between therapist professions on inquiring, addressing, helpfulness, or preparation, so these professions were collapsed into a single group. If dyad members saw several therapists, all their therapists' data were used.

To test whether therapists inquired about adoption, addressed adoption issues, and presented increased preparation and helpfulness over time, two logistic regressions and two Kendall's tau correlations were conducted. Logistic regression results indicated that therapist inquiry and addressing of adoption issues both significantly increased from 1965 to 1999, as measured by the Wald chi-square and the Cox and Snell R^2 coefficient, Wald $\chi^2(1, N = 147) = 17.16$, $p = .0001$, $R^2 = .15$, and Wald $\chi^2(1, N = 148) = 18.25$, $p = .0001$, $R^2 = .14$, respectively. Kendall's tau analyses indicated that the perceived level of helpfulness, $r_{kt}(141) = .310$, $p < .001$, and preparation, $r_{kt}(142) = .380$, $p < .001$, both significantly increased from 1965 to 1999.

Adoptees' and birth parents' therapy experiences during only the 1990s were of primary interest for two reasons. The first was to descriptively compare how dyad members perceived their therapists' adoption awareness in comparison with therapists' self-ratings obtained in 1999 by Sass and Henderson (2000). Second, this time frame permits an examination of current therapy practices. Consequently, the remainder of the results section will focus on therapy experiences during the 1990s.

During this decade, therapists inquired about adoption 59% ($n = 27$) and 32% ($n = 6$) for adoptees and birth parents, respectively. Adoption was addressed in therapy slightly more frequently for adoptees than birth parents at 78% ($n = 36$) and 68% ($n = 13$), respectively. However, nearly all adoptees (93%) and birth parents (95%) thought adoption should have been addressed in therapy. From a descriptive standpoint, therapists' level of preparation and helpfulness related to treating adoption issues were relatively uniformly distributed for both adoptees and birth parents (see Table 24.4).

To examine therapists' level of preparation and helpfulness in treating adoption issues more closely, data were examined to determine whether the therapists who addressed adoption issues significantly influenced their rating of therapist preparation and helpfulness. After data were combined to ensure expected counts of greater than 5 for each cell (i.e., ratings 1 and 2 and 4 and 5 were combined; see Table 24.5 for corresponding labels), a statistically significant difference in proportions in relation to whether the therapist addressed adoption was

---

Table 24.4   Adoptees' and Birth Parents' Perceived Level of How Prepared the Case Worker at the Adoption Agency Was in Helping Plan for the Postadoption Process and the Life Changes Encountered as a Result of the Adoption Experience

Likert Scale	Adoptee	Birth Parent
Very prepared	9 (5.9%)	1 (1.5%)
Well prepared	11 (7.2%)	4 (6.1%)
Somewhat prepared	26 (17.1%)	7 (10.6%)
Not very prepared	17 (11.2%)	43 (65.2%)
Did not prepare to deal with adoption issues	52 (34.2%)	55 (83.3%)
Missing/no response	37 (24.3%)	11 (16.7%)

NOTE: The large amount of missing data for adoptees is likely a result of being asked how well the agency helped their adoptive parents. This may be a hard question for adoptees to answer unless they discussed it with their adoptive parents.

revealed for both the preparation, $\chi^2 (2, N = 62) = 35.31$, $p < .0001$, $r_{kt} = .662$, and helpfulness variables, $\chi^2 (2, N = 60) = 33.77$, $p < .0001$, $r_{kt} = .661$. Deviation statistics (not reported here) indicated that those therapists perceived as more prepared and helpful also tended to address adoption issues at a higher rate. In fact, on the preparation measure, all therapists who addressed adoption issues were rated as at least "somewhat prepared" to treat adoption issues. These results make intuitive sense because if adoption was not discussed, then the client might not ever learn whether the therapist was prepared to treat it, and the mere act of addressing adoption suggests at least some level of awareness to deal with it.

Table 24.5   Therapists' Level of Preparation and Helpfulness Related to Adoption Issues in the 1990s

Likert Scale	Rating	Therapists' Level of Preparation	
		Adoptee	Birth Parent
Very prepared	1	11 (23.9%)	3 (15.8%)
Well prepared	2	8 (17.4%)	2 (10.5%)
Somewhat prepared	3	14 (30.4%)	3 (15.8%)
Not very prepared	4	6 (13.0%)	3 (15.8%)
No knowledge about adoption issues	5	6 (13.0%)	6 (31.6%)
Missing		1 (2.2%)	2 (10.5%)
		Therapists' Helpfulness	
		Adoptee	Birth Parent
No help	5	5 (10.9%)	5 (26.3%)
Little help	4	4 (8.7%)	2 (10.5%)
Somewhat helpful	3	10 (21.7%)	3 (15.8%)
Helpful	2	12 (26.1%)	3 (15.8%)
Very helpful	1	12 (26.1%)	4 (21.1%)
Missing		3 (6.5%)	2 (10.5%)

Discussion

Life Effects of Adoption

Birth mothers reported greater levels of problems in comparison with adoptees. This finding is highlighted by the large number of birth-mother respondents who used an open-ended question to comment on feelings of depression, grief, shame, loss, and anger for relinquishing their infant. Related to these issues is the lack of information regarding adoption on later life experiences and improper treatment at relinquishment. Adoption presents two problems for birth mothers. First, they must be comfortable with their decision to relinquish, and second, they must alleviate the loss and pain related to relinquishment. This resolution often involves knowing that their child was adequately cared for and is happy with the birth mother's decision to surrender. Without this knowledge, birth mothers may never truly be comfortable with their decision to surrender their child. Birth mothers' searches are often motivated by the desire to have knowledge about their adoptees' current status.

Although the results of this study indicate that adoption has a relatively large impact on birth mothers' lives, it was determined that these effects were lessened when adequate adoption procedures occurred. The data revealed that the level of preparation displayed by adoption caseworkers was a strong indicator of whether later problems were experienced by the birth mother. Unless they are provided adequate information in an appropriate manner, birth mothers may fail to understand the consequences of their decision to surrender and may regret their decision later.

Experience at Time of Adoption and the Search Process

Some respondents felt angered by caseworkers who pressured them into adoption when they actually thought about caring for their child but were afraid they were not ready for parenthood. This fear is understandable because the average age of adoption finalization for our sample was 20.2, and therefore, the average age of pregnancy was just over 19. It is also important to note that the average year of relinquishment was 1967. During this time period it is reasonable to assume that, consistent with results found by Deykin et al. (1984), many birth mothers were condemned for having an infant out of wedlock and were encouraged to relinquish their infant.

In the present study, 92% of birth mothers thought about searching and 86% actually searched for their child. Similar results were reported by Deykin and colleagues (1984), who reported 96% and 65% in these two categories. The majority of birth mothers in our study (67%) experienced a positive reunion with the adoptee, which was slightly higher than the 60% found by Silverman, Campbell, Patti, and Style (1988). It would appear that birth mothers should be encouraged to seek resolution of relinquishment issues through support groups, reunions, and/or adoption-skilled therapists. Future research, however, is definitely needed to understand why a higher proportion of birth parents did not have a more positive reunion.

Ninety-two percent of adoptees indicated that more information about their birth parents was desired. These results are similar to those of the Sobol and Cardiff (1983) study, which found that 90% of adoptees desired to know more background information concerning their birth parents. Adequacy of background information is as a result believed to play an important role in adoptees' overall adjustment level. Adoptees search for information about their relinquishment and medical history to support healthy identity development (Jago Krueger & Hanna, 1997). Responses to open-ended questions indicated that most adoptees had problems regarding identity, trust in others, intimacy, abandonment, and low self-esteem that were thought to be associated with adoption.

A lack of well-formed identity often causes relationship problems and tends to express itself during early adolescence. These issues compelled many of our adoptees (95%) to search for answers related to their relinquishment, a result comparable with the 97% search rate reported by Sachdev (1992). Additionally, most adoptees search for birth parents when they are in their mid-thirties (Gonyo & Watson, 1988), which may explain why most of our adoptees (mean age 46) had already searched. The current study also indicated that of the adoptee and birth parent reunions, 67% were experienced as positive. These results are slightly lower than Pacheco and Eme's (1993) finding that 86% of reunions were experienced as positive. Again, future research is needed to develop procedures or treatments to increase adoptees' satisfaction with their adoptions or at least determine what facets of the search/reunion process were unpleasant.

It is not even assured that adoptees will reveal to their medical care providers that they are adopted. The first author did not know he was adopted until about 12 years of age, and so it was understandable that during childhood, when asked for health history information, he would give that of his adoptive family. His parents had no health history for his birth family other than the information commonly given in 1946: "They were in good health." Perhaps his parents felt it was better to say something than to say nothing, and giving their health history kept him from learning about his adoption, another common practice of the day. But even after he learned he was adopted, throughout high school and college, and until he was a graduate student, he continued to give his adoptive family's health history whenever asked. As a psychologist looking back at his own history, he might well suggest that he was engaging in some level of denial!

While in therapy as a graduate student in the early 1970s, the first author realized the importance of both the medical and the psychological aspects of adoption in his life. He came to understand that in addition to needing a medical history, he had unanswered questions about who he was, where he came from, and where his future might take him and realized that knowing his biological relatives would help answer these questions. And he realized that he should not give his adoptive family's medical history as his own! When asked for this information, he began to answer, "I was adopted at birth and have no medical history." However, he still made no serious attempts to search for his birth family.

Then in 1981, the first author was diagnosed with testicular cancer. During 3 months of intensive treatment in many different settings, he became increasingly aware of all of the pages of blank information on his history forms. During an early exploratory surgery it was discovered that he had a large number of tiny gallstones, and because he was already under anesthesia it was up to his wife to decide what to do about them. She made the decision for him that the gallbladder should come out. He believes it was the correct decision but had he known his medical history at that time, the decision would have been his to make, before anesthesia.

By the time the first author's hair grew back after chemotherapy, he realized the need to search for his birth family, but it still took him a year to work up the courage to do so. His 1983 reunion with four birth sisters, and several years later with a birth brother, was an incredibly meaningful experience for him and answered many of his medical and psychological questions. In the months after his reunion, a friend who had known him for some 25 years commented on "how much more grounded and relaxed you seem."

By the time of the first author's search, he was in his fifth year of sobriety, and he learned that his birth father had died, 3 months previously, of alcoholism. That knowledge has helped keep the first author sober to the present day. Furthermore, he learned that his birth mother had her gallbladder removed in the late 1970s. Had he known that history in 1981, his physicians would have realized he was at a high risk for gallstones himself, and before going into surgery he would have been the one to decide what to do in case gallstones were found.

Without continuing exchange of updated health information, adoptees (and birth parents also) lack important health care and psychological information. What you don't know just might hurt you. This lack of information drives many dyad members to search and into therapy.

Therapy

While dyad members indicated similar levels of therapists addressing adoption issues and provided equivalent ratings of perceived helpfulness and preparation, adoptees reported increased therapist inquiry regarding adoption compared with birth parents. Additionally, for both dyad positions, adoption was more likely to be addressed in therapy than simply inquired about by therapists. This would suggest that at some point the clients must have disclosed their role in adoption. Although past research, consistent with the present results, indicates that psychologists reported inquiring about adoption approximately 50% of the time (Sass & Henderson, 2000), we know less about the rate at which psychologists address adoption in their practice. Another important implication of our study is that even if adoption is not the focal issue for therapy, adoption might be an associated component or area of concern. Support for this implication is provided by the high percentage of dyad members who reported interest in discussing adoption in therapy.

Limitations

Although the results of this study are in broad agreement with numerous other studies, there are some significant limitations to consider. One limitation is the lack of data from, and information about, adoptive parents. This was not surprising because the source of our participants was the adoption search and support movement, in which regrettably few adoptive parents are active. The small adoptive parent sample size hampered our ability to provide descriptions of their experience and life situation. For this reason, additional research is needed on the long-term reactions of adoptive parents to the adoption process.

As with most adoption research (Warren, 1992), this study failed to obtain a widely representative sample, because participants were sampled from only two adoption search and support groups, both in the northwestern United States. It is unknown if differences exist between adoptees and birth parents taking part in such groups and those uninvolved with support groups. It is plausible that our participants experienced increased problems with adoption, which led them to choose involvement with adoption support groups. Furthermore, the high female to male ratio limits generalizing the results to males and does not permit an examination of how gender may affect either the experience of adoption itself or of therapy. Consequently, future research is needed to explore the effects of gender in adoption. It is feasible that females experience greater, and perhaps different, issues compared with males. If so, such knowledge would be of value when treating dyad members.

It should be noted that a high proportion of female participants have been identified in many adoption search organizations (Gonyo & Watson, 1988; Kowal & Schilling, 1985; Rosenzweig-Smith, 1988). Females may desire more information about biological links between generations, perhaps due to having later children, and may thus be more affected by adoption (Sobol & Cardiff, 1983). The historic absence of both male adoptees and birth fathers in adoption search and support groups has several possible causes but seems to be changing (Henderson, 2000, 2002).

At the very least, the rates of our adoptees (35%) and birth parents (42%) who experienced therapy may provide an indication of incidence rates and perceptions of adoption issues in therapy for those dyad members involved in search and support groups. Given our low response rates, however, sampling issues present a major limitation to our conclusions. Consequently, future research would benefit from using Dillman's (2000) tailored research design method to increase response rates.

Another limitation is participants' retrospective interpretation of their past. An individual's memory of therapy, particularly of experiences from 20 or more years ago, may be inaccurate and, consequently, distort the data. Additionally, reliable and valid measures were not employed to assess initial problem behaviors. Such measures would aid in determining what common problems or themes dyad members present when entering treatment and whether their issues differ from those of the general population.

Our results suggest further research concerning what components of adoption therapists and clients deem significant to discuss. In addition, it would be of interest to evaluate what factors produced the difference in inquiry by therapists for adoptees compared with birth parents. Perhaps, therapists perceive adoption as more detrimental to adoptees than to birth parents, or it is conceivable that the adoptees' status was revealed through history information that resulted in further inquiry by the therapist. Moreover, it would be useful to investigate whether therapists are receptive to discussing adoption in therapy when it is brought up by the client or whether they tend to alter the discussion to address different life issues.

Future research would benefit from measures of therapist preparation and helpfulness that have been psychometrically established. Providing additional questions or indicators that encompass these two constructs may be of value. Asking about therapists' personal history in adoption may be helpful in understanding the relative contributions of adoption training and personal adoption experience to treatment effectiveness for clients associated with adoption (Sass & Henderson, 2000).

Data collected from therapist and client pairs would also enhance adoption research related to therapy practices in adoption. Such data would allow for cross-validation while also determining what aspect of the therapy both the client and the therapist found most useful. One could also determine the therapist's mechanism of inquiry and gain information on a broad range of issues. For example, is the client's association with adoption requested while obtaining preliminary background or intake information? Are common adoption themes or symptoms present that trigger the inquiry? Do the clients mention their experience with adoption, which results in further inquiry by the therapist? This information should aid in the discovery of why adoptees' and birth parents' therapists inquired at different rates and what factors contribute to increased adoption awareness by therapists. In addition, further investigation is needed to establish whether birth parents as well as adoptees are overrepresented in therapy.

Further research should identify therapists' level of acceptance related to adoption issues and whether therapists underestimate adoption's potential importance. Likewise, clients' experiences with adoption should also be assessed to evaluate their level of distress and focus on issues related to adoption that may arise in therapy. Additionally, it would be of interest to determine whether dyad members specifically sought therapists especially trained in adoption, and whether such training significantly benefited these clients.

Clearly, this study uncovers more questions than answers and supports the need to conduct future research in this area. For example, additional research should undertake a more detailed examination of what it means to "address" or "inquire" about adoption in therapy. For example, additional research questions regarding what specific topics or variables were discussed, the length of the discussion, the conclusions related to the significance of adoption that were reached, and the sincerity of the therapists' interest in adoption would be of value.

An important area of adoption that has been largely overlooked both in this study and in general is the effect of adoption on members of the extended birth and adoptive families. If we count just the immediate birth and adoptive families (spouse/partner, parents, grandparents, siblings, aunts and uncles), the typical adoptee may have as many as 25 or more relatives, each of whom experiences some aspects of the adoption.

In over 20 years of attending adoption search and support meetings, the first author has met many relatives of adoptees who have been affected themselves by the adoption. Some, often an adoptee's spouse or partner, come for support because they have seen or experienced the effects of the adoption. Someone they love is hurting or behaving self-destructively, and these significant others may be even more aware of the problem than the adoptee they love.

On occasion, the pain of relinquishment, residual shame, or fear of the unknown will prevent birth parents from acting to gain knowledge of their surrendered child or at least to relieve their guilt or grief. Birth grandparents, siblings, aunts, and uncles are missing kin as well as the birth parent, and often they have not had to experience the same level of shaming and rejection. Sometimes, the birth relatives are the ones wanting resolution and able to seek it.

Search and support groups generally welcome these relatives but have varying policies about conducting a search for the missing kin, particularly if the triad member directly involved does not desire a reunion. State access to record laws or state adoption search programs, if they exist at all, typically do not address the legal rights of anyone but the adoptee, birth parents, and adoptive parents. Left out as they often are, members of the extended family in an adoption are also likely to seek assistance from the mental health community. Therapists should be sensitive to their needs.

One optimistic outcome of this study is that dyad members in the 1990s appeared to receive better treatment and recognition of adoption issues than in prior years. Numerous explanations for this change may be proposed. Changing societal views regarding adoption (Bartholet, 1993; Sorosky et al., 1978) and the development and refinement of child welfare practices in the 1980s (Laird & Hartman, 1985) undoubtedly have contributed to increased recognition of adoption in the mental health community. It is also likely that the rise of adoption search and support groups such as Concerned United Birth Parents, the American Adoption Congress, and the National Council on Adoptable Children and the increased general visibility of adoption search and reunion stories in the media have also played a part. Even with the increase in therapists' understanding of adoption, however, progress may still be needed, given that the average ratings of perceived preparation and helpfulness for therapists were only "somewhat prepared" and "somewhat helpful," respectively.

Reports from members of adoption search and support groups indicate the reluctance of some therapists to discuss adoption issues even when the client is a triad member and brings it up for discussion. It appears that adoption issues are often seen as a "distraction" from the "real" issues or simply not seen as a subject worthy of attention in therapy. Adoptee psychiatrist Bob Andersen (Andersen & Tucker, 2000, p. 18) has noted that he spent "twelve (years) in psychoanalysis, where the issue of adoption never arose." In the early 1990s, Bob and the first author were joined by two other "adoptee shrinks" (another psychologist and psychiatrist, both adopted), and the group spent a weekend talking about how adoption had affected them, both personally and professionally. On the personal side, almost all of them noted that when they observed themselves acting in an unusual or unhealthy manner and began to ask, "What is going on with me?" adoption as an explanation of the behavior had evolved over the years from being the last hypothesis on the list examined to the first. And group members frequently didn't have to go any further down the list.

Perhaps the most important result of this study is that both inquiring about and addressing adoption issues significantly increased the client's perception of therapist's level of helpfulness and preparation. Psychologists also rated themselves as more prepared to deal with adoption when they inquired about adoption issues (Sass & Henderson, 2000). These results demonstrate the importance of inquiring and addressing adoption as a potential therapeutic issue and of recognizing the impact adoption may have on an individual's life. Therefore, we agree with Winkler, Brown, Van Keppel, and Blanchard (1988) that therapists should consider adoption as a potential issue and should inquire about adoption during routine intake procedures.

In conclusion, the results of this study indicate significant life effects of adoption for birth parents and adoptees. It appears that a high proportion of adoption caseworkers do not provide birth mothers and adoptees with an adequate amount of information concerning their separated birth relatives. In addition, adoption caseworkers did not prepare birth mothers and adoptees for postadoption experiences, which resulted in a higher percentage of individuals who searched to help in the resolution of their adoption issues. Therefore, further caseworker education and awareness are needed regarding adoption issues and better procedures are needed to treat postadoption issues. With regard to therapy for adoption-related issues, this study provides insight into how dyad members in adoption organizations experience therapy related to adoption and provides suggestions for future research.

BEST PRACTICE IDEAS

1. Because lack of knowledge is a significant problem for the entire adoption triad, encourage professionals working in adoption to minimize secrecy and maximize the exchange of information between birth and adoptive families.

2. Avoid pressuring pregnant women to relinquish their babies for adoption. Offer support to them to raise the child themselves if at all possible.

3. Recognize adoption as a potential issue in therapy and make inquiry about experience with adoption a routine part of history taking.

4. Realize that adoption affects everyone differently and to different degrees, and, as therapists, evaluate the degree to which the adoption process has affected the life of clients with adoption experience. Adoption effects are even possible in spouses, siblings, parents, and grandparents of members of the triad.

5. Provide more education about pre- and postadoption issues to students in the mental health professions who are contemplating clinical practice or research.

CLINICAL/RESEARCH IMPLICATIONS

1. Investigate the role and experience of birth fathers and male adoptees, two groups currently underrepresented in adoption search and support groups and in adoption research.

2. Replicate the present research with a sample of adoptive parents.

3. This study asked a broad question about how much adoption has affected the life of triad members. Future research should tease out the nature of these effects.

REFLECTION QUESTIONS

1. Nonadoptees take for granted that they "know their place in the world." They form their identity while surrounded by people who are "like them" in a variety of ways, by photos of relatives living and dead, and by family lore and legends. The only "unknown" is whether they share Great Uncle Bill's interest in the bassoon and distaste for broccoli for genetic reasons, for family environment reasons, or for both reasons, or whether the "connection" is nothing but chance. Try to imagine what identity formation is like for adoptees in a closed adoption who know nothing about their genetic background and who have never even seen anyone who looks like them. Can you understand why identity formation may be a challenge for adoptees, and why adoptees might wish to search for their birth family?

2. In the context of your response to Question 1, and given whatever you currently know about identity formation, why do you think some adoptees are reluctant to search for their birth family? How would you evaluate adoptees who state that they have "absolutely no interest in learning anything" about their birth family?

3. What questions should therapists ask triad members? To what degree should these questions focus on the past, present, and future?

4. Should adoption agencies or practice be restructured, especially with regard to what background information those involved with the adoption are given? And if more information is given (particularly if identities are shared), how and when should this be done?

5. What should be the next area of research related to the interaction between triad members and therapists?

6. Will therapists trained in adoption issues be better suited to treat triad members? Or is training to treat general mental health issues (e.g., depression or separation anxiety) sufficient to treat anyone?

APPENDIX: QUESTIONNAIRE SENT TO
MEMBERS OF WARM AND OARA

The following questions refer to "your adoption." Please answer the questions as they apply to YOUR position in the adoption triad. If you hold more than one triad position or have been involved in more than one adoption, please duplicate the questionnaire for each experience if possible.

1. Please indicate your triad position.

   Adoptee _____ Adoptive parent _____ Birth parent _____

2. Your present age _____

3. Your gender _____

4. Your race:

   African American___ Asian___ Caucasian___ Hispanic___ Native American___ Other ___

5. State in which adoption took place (or country of birth if an international adoption) _____

6. Year adoption was finalized: _____ 6a. Age of adoptee at time of finalization: _____

7. Do you feel you have experienced any mental or emotional problems that are related to your adoption experience? Yes _____ No _____

7a. If yes, please provide a brief explanation of the problem(s).

8. To what extent has adoption affected your life and developmental choices?

1	2	3	4	5
[No effect]	[Minimal effect]	[Moderate effect]	[Large effect]	[Enormous effect]

9. Did you *think about searching* for the person(s) from whom adoption separated you? Yes ___ No ___

10. Did you *actually search* for the person(s) from whom adoption separated you? Yes ___ No ___

10a. If yes, please circle the overall experience of your reunion: positive or negative

11. Please circle the number that identifies the level of openness you experienced at the time of your adoption.

1	2	3	4	5
[Totally closed, <u>no</u> information shared]		[Demographic information, but <u>no</u> identifying information]		[Totally open, <u>all</u> information shared]

12. Please circle the number that identifies the adequacy of knowledge and background information about the adoptee, birth parents, or adoptive parents <u>provided by your adoption agency</u>.

1	2	3	4	5
[Less information would have been beneficial]		[An adequate amount of information was provided]		[More information would have been beneficial]

Appendix (continued)

13. From your current perspective, please state how prepared you believe the case workers at your adoption agency were to help you plan for the postadoption process and the life changes you encountered as a result of your adoption experience. (Adoptees please indicate your assessment of how well the agency helped your adoptive parents.)

1	2	3	4	5
[Very well prepared]	[Well prepared]	[Somewhat prepared]	[Not very prepared]	[Did not prepare to deal with adoption issues]

14. Have you participated in therapy after the completion of your adoption?

    Yes ____ No ____ (If no, please go to number 16.)

15. If you *have* been in postadoption therapy (answered YES to number 14) please answer the following questions for EACH course of therapy you have experienced. (If you have been in therapy more than once, please complete the MULTIPLE THERAPISTS section on the last page.)

    Approximate year first therapy began _____

15a. Please indicate the type of therapist:

    Psychologist __ Social Worker __ Marriage/Family counselor __ Psychiatrist __ Other _____

15b. Did your therapist inquire whether you were part of the adoption triad? Yes ____ No____

15c. Were adoption issues addressed in your therapy? Yes ____ No ____

15d. Do you feel adoption issues should have been part of the therapy? Yes ____ No ____

15e. How well prepared do you feel your therapist was in dealing with the problems members of the triad experience?

____	____	____	____	____
[Very well prepared]	[Well prepared]	[Somewhat prepared]	[Not very prepared]	[No knowledge about adoption issues]

15f. Please circle the level of helpfulness your therapist provided in dealing with your adoption issues.

1	2	3	4	5
[No help]	[Little help]	[Somewhat helpful]	[Helpful]	[Very helpful]

16. Please state anything you wish your therapist(s) had known about adoption or any additional comments you feel are appropriate.

Thank you for your assistance. Please return the questionnaire by January 15, 2000.

REFERENCES

Anderson, R., & Tucker, R. (2000). *A bridge less traveled, twice visited.* O'Fallon, MO: Badger Hill Press.

Bartholet, E. (1993). *Family bonds.* New York: Houghton Mifflin.

Borders, L. D., Black, L. K., & Pasley, B. K. (1998). Are adopted children and their parents at greater risk for negative outcomes? *Family Relations: Interdisciplinary Journal of Applied Family Studies, 47,* 237–241.

Brodzinsky, D. M. (1990). A stress and coping model of adoption adjustment. In D. Brodzinsky & M. Schechter (Eds.), *The psychology of adoption* (pp. 3–24). New York: Oxford University Press.

Burnell, R., & Norfleet, M. (1979). Women who place their infant for adoption: A pilot study. *Patient Counseling and Health Education, 1,* 169–172.

Deykin, E. Y., Campbell, L., & Patti, P. (1984). The postadoption experience of surrendering parents. *American Journal of Orthopsychiatry, 54,* 271–280.

Dickson, L. R., Heffron, W. M., & Parker, C. (1990). Children from disrupted and adoptive homes on an impatient unit. *American Journal of Orthopsychiatry, 60,* 594–602.

Dickson, L. R., Stephens, S., Heffron, W. M., & Parker, C. (1991). Discussing adoption in therapy. *Journal of the American Academy of Child & Adolescent Psychiatry, 30,* 155.

Dillman, D. A. (2000). *Mail and internet surveys: The tailored research design* (2nd ed.). New York: Wiley.

Dunbar, N., & Grotevant, H. D. (2004). Adoption narratives: The construction of adoptive identity during adolescence. In W. P. Michael & H. F. Barbara (Eds.), *Family stories and the life course: Across time and generations* (pp. 135–161). Mahwah, NJ: Lawrence Erlbaum.

Fisher, A. P. (2003). Still "Not quite as good as having your own"? Toward a sociology of adoption. *Annual Review of Sociology, 29,* 335–361.

Gonyo, B., & Watson, K. W. (1988). Searching in adoption. *Public Welfare, 46,* 15–22.

Grotevant, H. D., Dunbar, N., Kohler, J. K., & Lash Esau, A. M. (2000). Adoptive identity: How contexts within and beyond the family shape developmental pathways. *Family Relations: Interdisciplinary Journal of Applied Family Studies, 49,* 379–387.

Grotevant, H. D., McRoy, R. G., Elde, C. L., & Fravel, D. L. (1994). Adoptive family system dynamics: Variations by level of openness in the adoption. *Family Process, 33,* 125–146.

Hartman, A., & Laird, J. (1990). Family treatment after adoption: Common themes. In D. M. Brodzinsky & M. D. Schechter (Eds.), *The psychology of adoption* (pp. 221–239). New York: Oxford University Press.

Henderson, D. B. (2000). Adoption issues in perspective: An introduction to the special issue. *Journal of Social Distress and the Homeless, 9,* 261–272.

Henderson, D. B. (2002). *Male adoptees: Issues for adolescent development.* Paper presented at St. John's University Adoption Conference, Queens, NY.

Jago Krueger, M. J., & Hanna, F. J. (1997). Why adoptees search: An existential treatment perspective. *Journal of Counseling and Development, 75,* 195–202.

Jerome, L. (1986). Overrepresentation of adopted children attending a children's mental health center. *Canadian Journal of Psychiatry, 31,* 526–531.

Kowal, K. A., & Schilling, K. M. (1985). Adoption through the eyes of adult adoptees. *American Journal of Orthopsychiatry, 55,* 354–362.

Laird, J., & Hartman, A. (1985). *A handbook of child welfare.* New York: Free Press.

Mendenhall, T. J., Berge, J. M., Wrobel, G. M., Grotevant, H., & McRoy, R. G. (2000). Adolescents' satisfaction with contact in adoption. *Child & Adolescent Social Work Journal, 21,* 175–190.

Menning, B. E. (1975). The infertile couple: A plea for advocacy. *Child Welfare, 65,* 454–460.

Miall, C. E. (1986). The stigma of involuntary childlessness. *Social Problems, 33,* 268–282.

Miller, B. C., Fan, X., Grotevant, H. D., Christensen, M., Coyl, D., & van Dulmen, M. (2000). Adopted adolescents' overrepresentation in mental health counseling: Adoptees' problems or parents' lower threshold for referral? *Journal of the American Academy of Child & Adolescent Psychiatry, 39,* 1504–1511.

Pacheco, F., & Eme, R. (1993). An outcome study of the reunion between adoptees and biological parents. *Child Welfare, 72,* 53–64.

Resolve. (n.d.). *Improving the adoption process.* Retrieved September 25, 2006, from www.resolve .org/site/PageServer?pagename=lrn_adp_opoa

Rosenzweig-Smith, J. (1988). Factors associated with successful adoption reunions of adult adoptees and biological parents. *Child Welfare, 67,* 411–422.

Russell, M. (1996). *Adoption wisdom.* Santa Monica, CA: Broken Branch.

Sachdev, P. (1992). Adoption reunion and after: A study of the search process and experience of adoption. *Child Welfare, 71,* 52–68.

Sass, D. A., & Henderson, D. B. (2000). Adoption issues: Preparation of psychologists and an evaluation of the need for continuing education. *Journal of Social Distress and the Homeless, 9,* 349–359.

Silverman, P. R., Campbell, L., Patti, P., & Style, C. B. (1988). Reunions between adoptees and birth parents: The birth parents' experience. *Social Work, 33,* 523–528.

Smith, D. W., & Sherwen, L. N. (1988). *Mothers and their adopted children: The bonding process* (2nd ed.). New York: Tiresias Press.

Sobol, M. P., & Cardiff, J. (1983). A sociopsychological investigation of adult adoptees' search for parents. *Family Relations, 32,* 477–483.

Sorosky, A. D., Baran, A., & Pannor, R. (1978). *The adoption triangle.* Garden City, NY: Anchor Press.

Warren, S. B. (1992). Lower threshold for referral for psychiatric treatment for adopted adolescents. *Journal of the American Academy of Child and Adolescent Psychiatry, 31,* 512–517.

Winkler, R. C., Brown, D. W., Van Keppel, M., & Blanchard, A. (1988). *Clinical practice in adoption.* Elmsford, NY: Pergamon.

Assessment and Treatment Issues in Adoption

Preface

RAFAEL A. JAVIER

St. John's University

A number of questions have been raised as to whether adoptees and other members of the triad are more prone to mental illnesses and to psychological and behavioral problems because of the inherent challenges in the adoption experience. Are adoptees more likely to suffer from attachment disorders and have difficulty developing relationships? What are the central treatment issues professional should keep in mind in assessing and treating members of the triad? At what point is it appropriate to search and reunite with the birth parents? These are some of the questions addressed by a number of prominent scholars and clinicians over the last few years. Because of the crucial importance of addressing these questions head-on, we have decided to include contributions from several of the scholars who have provided important answers to these questions and enriched our understanding of issues affecting the adoption community.

The contribution by Henderson (Chapter 25) addresses the issue of why mental health professionals have ignored issues of adoption in their practice. He suggests specific reasons for this silence. According to this author, as secrecy surrounding adoption has waned, the mental health community remains largely silent, particularly on postadoption issues. Fear that discussing adoption-related problems will lead to adoption itself being labeled as pathological is addressed as one of the reasons for the silence. Another reason for the silence is privacy issues. This is particularly because sexuality and childbirth have long been difficult to discuss for some, but if one adds the issue of "illegitimacy," common in adoption, it produces even more controversy. According to the author, poverty, powerlessness, social class, and race are difficult issues to face as are the values issues raised by working at the intersection of heredity and environment. Finally, there is great difficulty addressing the business and economic aspects of adoption, and thus, they are often ignored along with the issues surrounding open and closed adoption. The author concludes that acknowledging reasons for the silence may be an important step in addressing it. Other steps, such as continuing education programs and publication of information on postadoption issues, are also suggested.

The chapter by B. J. Lifton (Chapter 26) addresses another important issue in the treatment of the adoption triad. According to this author, many adopted children feel invisible because they are forced to repress their need to know about their origins. They feel that an essential part of them is unacknowledged by their adoptive family and society. In this chapter, the author enters into a description of the specific components of the inner world of the adoptee and the extended community. In this context, she introduces the concept of cumulative adoption trauma and discusses the adoptee's need to dissociate feelings of loss, grief, and anger. According to Lifton, the adoptee's search for the birth mother can be seen as a way to form a coherent sense of self. By integrating the past and the present, the adoptee is able to move on into the future.

The next chapter, by Baden and Wiley (Chapter 27), addresses issues likely to affect birth parents in the adoption triad. In this context, the authors review and integrate data from the clinical and empirical literature and a number of professional disciplines with practice case studies. Included in this review are literature on the decision to relinquish one's child for adoption, the early postrelinquishment period, and the effects on birth parents throughout their life span. Clinical symptoms discussed for birth parents include unresolved grief, isolation, difficulty with future relationships, and trauma. Some recent research reviewed by these authors has found that some birth mothers who relinquish tend to compare comparably with those who do not relinquish on external criteria of well-being (e.g., high school graduation rates). However, there appear to be serious long-term psychological consequences of relinquishment. Limitations of the current literature are presented, and recommendations for practice and research are offered.

Nydam's contribution (Chapter 28) places particular emphasis on the importance of addressing issues of relinquishment in treatment intervention. According to this author, losing one's parents, even moments after birth, may have lifelong reverberations in the psychological development of adoptees that few clinicians, up to the present time, have been aware of, understood, or sufficiently appreciated. This chapter presents clinical considerations that relate to the impact of relinquishment—the necessity of mourning the loss of birth parents; the common struggles that adoptees have with identity; the challenges of bonding when early trust is broken; the challenges in sustaining intimacy as adults; and the resolution of fantasies about birth parents and birth-family stories. Clinicians are strongly encouraged to carefully clarify and resolve the difficulties that sometimes result from being relinquished by one's birth parents and adopted by nonbiological parents. Implications for the roles that both birth parents and adoptive parents play in the lives of adoptees are also reviewed.

Using a psychoanalytic framework, Deeg's (Chapter 29) and Zuckerman and Buchsbaum's (Chapter 31) chapters provide further description of the inner world of the adoptee, including the different parental representations (biological and adoptive parents) that the adoptee needs to reconcile. According to Deeg, psychoanalytic treatment of the adoptee presents the clinician with unique challenges and considerations, which requires an underlying framework for understanding the adoptee. In his chapter, Deeg presents the adoptee's cathexis of the biological parent representation as a fundamental characteristic of the adoptee's inner world and proposes a theoretical model for the genesis of this object relation. He then discusses the various defensive constellations which are centered on this cathexis. In this context, he discusses the relation of adopted self to biological parent as a critical determinant in the development of object relations, and within the formation of identity. He also explores the adoptee's relation to the biological parent as a central issue in treatment and as half of the binary transference, in which the adoptee displaces and projects two sets of self/parent representations onto the therapist. A metapsychological bias in which the therapist discounts the biological parent representation when it is not based on actual contact with a "real" person is discussed. Finally, various transference/countertransferance dyads that echo the adoptee's unique intrapsychic exigencies are discussed in this chapter, as are corresponding technical recommendations.

Zuckerman and Buchsbaum's contribution provides additional understanding of the challenges normally confronting children and adults who have been adopted. These authors contend that transference and countertransference can symbolize adoptees' conflicts and, thereby, can be an essential tool to address such concerns in treatment. Initially, the authors review the literature that contains many descriptions of characterological and behavioral patterns of adoptees but minimal reference to the transferences that give life to these dynamics in treatment. They present portions of a treatment with a 9-year-old adoptee where issues illustrated in the literature are highlighted and new transference-countertransference paradigms are presented as potential conduits to patients' adoption concerns as well as tools to deepen our understanding of the experience of adoption.

Finally, Hoksbergen and Laak's contribution (Chapter 30) provides important empirical data on the extent to which adoptees are more likely to suffer from reactive attachment disorders, including in adulthood. According to these authors, the heterogeneity of adopted children does not allow us to draw general conclusions about the nature and amount of behavioral problems with adopted children. They provided data demonstrating that older foreign adoptees at placement often exhibit complex physical and psychological problems, with many suffering from some kind of behavioral disturbances. They contend that data clearly show that reactive attachment disorder can often be diagnosed and that continuation of this disorder in adulthood can result in feelings of psychic homelessness.

LEARNING GOALS

There are a number of learning goals that we would like readers to consider in reviewing the chapters included in this part. It is expected that the reader will do the following:

- reach a better understanding of the origins of professional secrecy and silence in adoption, including the examination of inherent problems in (a) viewing adoption as successful professional problem solving; (b) looking at adoption as a "favor" done to all involved and reluctance to see the favor "gone bad"; (c) fear that discussing adoption-related problems will lead to adoption being labeled as pathological; (d) freezing of time, locking triad members into the past; (e) privacy issues; (f) stigma attached to sexuality and "illegitimate" childbirth; (g) issues of poverty, powerlessness, social class, and race; (h) social values placed on the roles of heredity and environment; (i) the absence of males from adoption search and support groups; (j) the business aspects of adoption; and (k) resistance to change in adoption;
- have a better understanding of the difference between adoption as a "win-win-win" situation ending with the final adoption (portrayed in the "feelgood" model), and the reality of adoption as involving both gains and losses and lasting throughout the life span;
- evaluate your personal silence on adoption issues by applying the reasons for the professional silence to yourself;
- assist in ending the professional silence through attendance at continuing education programs and sharing of information on postadoption issues;
- have better understanding of the inner world of the adoptee and the extended family;
- review the empirical research on birth parents, an understudied and misunderstood part of the adoption triad. The review of the literature follows the life span and includes pre-relinquishment, early postrelinquishment, and long-term postrelinquishment.
- have a better understanding that birth parents who involuntarily relinquish and international birth parents have unique and qualitatively different experiences of relinquishment;

- have a better understanding that (foreign) adopted children are deeply influenced by the separation from their biological family and country of origin. An important effect of the separation and history of deprivation might be the development of reactive attachment disorder. This disorder is connected with feelings of not completely belonging to the adoptive family. This is called "psychic homelessness." Feelings of psychic homelessness can start early in life or when the adoptee is already an adult.

- offer therapists new avenues to access patients' feelings and conflicts about being adopted;

- increase clinicians' sensitivity to the transferential reactions of adoptees and offer potential links between these reactions and adoption issues;

- increase clinicians' sensitivity to their countertransferential reactions when working with adoptees and offer potential links between these reactions and adoption issues; and

- offer specific examples of a therapist's countertransferential feelings when working with an adopted child, where these feelings yielded insight into the patient's emerging feelings about adoption.

Why Has the Mental Health Community Been Silent on Adoption Issues?

25

DOUGLAS B. HENDERSON

University of Wisconsin–Stevens Point

F or much of the mid-20th century, the process of adoption was shrouded in secrecy, largely based on the assumption of shameful pregnancies and "illegitimate" births. The professed intent of the secrecy was the protection of all those involved in what came to be seen as a private transaction. For detailed reviews of the history of adoption in the United States, see Chapters 2 and 3 in this volume as well as the comprehensive work of Holt (1992), Wegar (1997), O'Brien and Zamostny (2003), and Zamostny, O'Brien, Baden, and Wiley (2003). As societal values changed during the 1980s and 1990s, much of the historic secrecy began to be stripped away. Adoption has now become a topic of public discourse, and in several states adoptees have gained the right to access their adoption records and thus their history. Unfortunately, while society has begun to talk about adoption, particularly about postadoption issues such as search and reunion, the mental health community has remained largely silent. An understanding of the reasons for this silence may assist in ending it.

Recent research has documented what many in the adoption movement have long suspected: Information about a variety of adoption issues is sadly lacking in the education of members of the mental health community. Research on the adoption education of psychologists has been presented at meetings of the American Adoption Congress (AAC) by Post (1999), Sass and Henderson (1999), and Sass, Webster, and Henderson (2000) and appears in the Fall 2000, special adoption issue of the *Journal of Social Distress and the Homeless* (Post, 2000; Sass & Henderson, 2000). In a survey of licensed psychologists listed in the National Register of Health Service Providers in Psychology (Sass & Henderson, 2000), 90% of the respondents thought they needed more education about adoption, and less than a third of the respondents rated themselves as either "very well prepared" or "well prepared" to treat adoption issues. Roughly two thirds of these licensed psychologists reported having had no graduate school courses that dealt with adoption issues, and 81% indicated an interest in taking a continuing education program about adoption.

Fisher (2003) decries the relative absence of adoption in the field of sociology. Adoption received little coverage in text and reading books on marriage and the family from 1998 to 2001. Space devoted to adoption in 21 texts averaged 2.4 pages, and 3.7 pages in 16 books of readings. The information contained about adoption was also likely to emphasize the problems associated with adoption. During the entire 1990s, *The Journal of Marriage and the Family* contained only six articles and four reviews of books related to adoption. That journal's extensive 2000 review of research on the family in the 1990s did not even mention the word adoption in the keyword index (Fisher, 2003).

This silence becomes particularly glaring when one considers the statistical base rate of adoption in comparison with the frequency of occurrence of other issues of interest to the mental health community. Estimates of the number of adopted persons are difficult to obtain, especially given the historic secrecy surrounding the adoption process. Even the U.S. Census did not, until 2000, ask about the number of adopted children. The 2000 census reported that there were 2,058,915 adopted children living in households in the United States (U.S. Census Bureau, 2003), representing about 0.7% of the total U.S. population, and 2.5% of the U.S. population 17 years and under. It is generally believed that, including adult adoptees, approximately 2% of the U.S. population is adopted (Brodzinsky, 1990). Each of these adoptees has two birth parents and (typically) two adoptive parents. After adding in birth and adoptive grandparents, siblings, and other close relatives, the proportion of the public related to an adoptee by birth or adoption rises to between 20% and 30%. The Evan B. Donaldson Institute (1997) asked in a telephone survey whether the respondent, or a close friend or family member, was a member of the adoption triad (consisting of adoptees, birth parents, and adoptive parents). They determined that 58% of all Americans have had personal experience with adoption. It is estimated that adoptees represent some 5 to 6 million Americans, with adoption directly affecting a total of 40 million Americans (Brodzinsky, 1990; Pavao, Groza, & Rosenberg, 1998). Data from 2000 and 2001 (Child Welfare Information Gateway, 2004) indicate that recently there have been over 127,000 new adoptions per year in the United States. According to Fisher (2003), 39% of Americans thought seriously at one time in their life about adopting a child but ultimately changed their mind.

Given that the adoptee base rate is 2% of the American population, consider that the relative frequency of occurrence of schizophrenia in the United States is approximately 0.07% (Kessler et al., 1994), autism affects approximately 0.05% of children, and 1% of the population may suffer from dissociative identity disorder (Ross, 1991). However, despite their lower frequency of occurrence, all these conditions are the subject of much more attention than adoption in the literature of both psychology (Post, 1999, 2000) and sociology (Fisher, 2003).

Although I do not wish by this logic to equate adoption with psychopathology (see below), there would seem to be little doubt that the adoption experience creates at least a risk factor for future developmental and life-adjustment problems. Knowledge about the bonding and attachment process (Crouch & Manderson, 1995; Hoyle, 1995; Smith & Sherwen, 1988a; Watson, 1997) and the importance of prenatal nutrition and health care for the developing fetus (Schroeder, 1988; Streissguth, Barr, Sampson, & Darby, 1989) indicates the potential effect of prenatal and early-life disruptions experienced by many adoptees. Studies of the increased use of mental health services by adoptees (Levy & Orlans, 2000; Miller et al., 2000) suggest that these risk factors result in actual problems for many adoptees.

There are several possible reasons for the underrepresentation of adoption in the mental health literature. These include both cultural and moral values (particularly those related to bad behavior, shame, and privacy) and economic factors (in particular, the social status of many birth parents, the "business" of providing adoptions, and the expense of obtaining a child).

In the view of the general public, as well as the mental health community, the process of adoption as it was practiced for most of the 20th century was seen as a "win-win-win" situation for the three sides of the triad (Henderson, 2000). An adoption was typically portrayed as producing only a happy new family skipping off together through a field of flowers toward a bright future. The birth parents were virtually absent from this pretty image. I would suggest that this image might be called the "feelgood" model of adoption. Smith and

Sherwen (1988b) also point out that much of the literature on adoption has historically made light of the difficulties experienced in the process while overemphasizing the joys of being a "forever" family for both the adoptee and the adoptive parents.

In the "feelgood" model, birth parents, with birth mothers often characterized as "bad girls," were burdened by a challenging, typically unplanned, and frequently illegitimate pregnancy. In this model, birth parents "won" by being freed of parenting responsibilities for which they were (often repeatedly) told they were unprepared. An adoption, especially if the whole process was kept secret, could minimize, or prevent altogether, the "bad" reputation. Birth parents, after a "feelgood" model adoption, were typically told that they could, and should, resume their prepregnancy lives. Because the entire pregnancy was often kept a secret, they could be free of any consequences of their actions, and free to "just have another child" at a better time or under better circumstances.

Adoptees, facing a future in which they were typically "unwanted" and "illegitimate" children, "won" by being placed in a (presumably) better home than the one their birth family could have provided. Adoptees, seen in the "feelgood" model as the "lucky bastards," also "won" by being sheltered from the effects (real or imagined) of the presumed sins of their birth parents. Although this view has softened in the last 30 years, there is still a widespread cultural belief that sex outside marriage is wrong, and that birth parents, particularly birth mothers, are "bad." The adoptee, as the "bad seed" of this "bad behavior," is seen as benefiting from a new start in a "proper" family.

Parents adopt for two main reasons. The majority (69%) adopt due to infertility, while 27% report they adopt for altruistic reasons (Fisher, 2003). The infertile adoptive parents, often in pain from wanting a family they could not create themselves, "won" by being able to raise the child they had long desired. Those parents who adopted for altruistic reasons "won" by basking in the positive light of "saving" a less-than-fortunate child. In most cases, adoptive parents were, and still are, held up by many as "superparents."

The story of a "feelgood" model adoption was believed to end with the phrase "and the baby was adopted," much as other stories were seen to end with the phrase "and they lived happily ever after." And, of course, in the "feelgood" view, adoptions *did* end with everyone involved living happily ever after and never looking back. The adoptee and adoptive parents were supposed to spend their lives as a family indistinguishable from any other family. The birth parents were supposed to return and resume their previous lives again, as if the pregnancy had never happened. Everyone gained something, everyone "won," and nothing was "lost."

Another, and it is hoped unintended, result of the belief that adoption ended with the new family skipping off happily together was that time became frozen at this point. The adopted "child" was never allowed to grow into an adult. Virtually all adoptees, though they may be of parent or grandparent age, have been called an "adopted child." People are likely to say, "Oh, so you *are* an adopted child!" as opposed to "you *were* adopted!" or "you are an *adoptee*!" Many laws concerning adoption refer to the rights of "adopted children" long after the adoption process has been completed. Some states even require adult adoptees to obtain the permission of their adoptive parents before being given information about their adoption or about their birth family. In an American society obsessed with "political correctness," we examine the implications of the language we use to label everything from minorities to sports teams to people displaced by hurricanes, and the persistence of the term "adopted child" is not only interesting, it also suggests some of society's underlying feelings about adoption.

Birth parents also suffer from the same difficulty with time, often remaining forever frozen in the eyes of the public as the "irresponsible boy" who left his pregnant girlfriend, who is perceived as, if not the "bad girl," at least as the "unfortunate girl" who was left with the burden of an illegitimate pregnancy. As with many traumatic experiences, the birth parents themselves sometimes remain frozen in this state at some psychological level. The fact is that the birth parents do continue with their lives and as adults may be very different from what they were at the time of the surrender, and their feelings about the entire adoption and their part in it may be very different from what they once were. The continuing perception of birth parents as a "boy and girl who got in trouble" can prevent the healthy resolution of their past, both inhibiting their sense of entitlement to learn what became of their child and allowing society to continue to "protect" the rights of that unfortunate boy and girl, even when all adult parties to an adoption wish to share information about it. When one is frozen in the past, both a reexamination of one's past in light of one's present experiences and moving forward are silenced.

An early 1990s revision of the Wisconsin Adoption Search Law, specifically designed to apply to rights of access to information about themselves for adoptees over the age of 21, described the process as applying to "the adopted child." The information, which had previously been free, was scheduled to begin to carry a minimum fee of $50. At a hearing of the Joint Finance Committee, I testified against charging adoptees for this information, but I began my testimony by identifying myself as an "adult adoptee" and, after looking around the room, saying pointedly that I saw no "adopted children" present. Before I began talking about the proposed fee, I asked to be given the respect of being addressed in state law as an adult.

While the fee ultimately became part of the budget bill, the bill's language was changed to refer to "adult adoptees." Some weeks later, I received a letter from the Senate Cochair of the Committee, an African American man who undoubtedly knew something himself about labeling, thanking me for calling their attention to the issue and crediting the language change to my testimony.

The more contemporary and realistic view of adoption, of course, is that every adoption represents both gains and losses, that adoption is a multigenerational and ongoing process that permanently affects the lives of all involved, and in which the final adoption is only a midpoint. We know that the story of an adoption does not "end" the day the adoptive parents and their new child walk out of court as a legal family. The adoption does not "end" the day that the birth parent becomes legally childless, or the parent of one less child. The adoption experience for the adoptee only begins with the adoption process itself, and likely never really "ends" (Zamostny, O'Brien, et al., 2003). Because of this knowledge, adoption agencies are now beginning to offer postadoption services in response to the lifelong needs of members of the adoption triad (Brooks, Allen, & Barth, 2002; Fahlberg, 1997; Ryan & Nalavany, 2003).

The "feelgood model" of adoption as a win-win-win solution makes it appear to be a successful social services/mental health intervention. Unfortunately, social services and mental health are fields where failure, or at least the absence of clear success, is all too common, and so an apparent success is a welcome event. Acknowledging that there are problems with the adoption process may be seen as an admission of failure, thus tarnishing the reputation of adoption as a successful social program. Looking the other way when problems arise and ignoring their existence may be seen as a form of (perhaps understandable) professional denial.

Another reason for silence about the issues of adoption is related to professional pride, particularly for social workers. As public- or private-agency adoption has long been practiced in America, before an adoptive family is approved for adoption, the parent(s) must undergo a home study. All manner of questions, some worthwhile, some of doubtful validity, are posed. Character, religion, relationships, income, and home environment are all evaluated, and the family must be "approved" by a social worker. Once this process has been completed, and the child is placed with these "superparents," any evidence of parenting problems suggests the approval process (the home study) may have been faulty. No profession wants to be reminded of its mistakes.

Adoption is widely seen as a favor that society has done for all three sides of the adoption triad, who are often viewed as being in a "one-down" position. To acknowledge that a favor, once it is given, may have some negative consequences is difficult for both the giver and the recipient. The giver of a favor may be more reluctant to give again in the future. The recipients of a favor may be loathe to "look a gift horse in the mouth," and if they do so and find problems they may be equally loathe to complain. Should the recipients of the favor of adoption complain, both society and the mental health professions may perceive them as ungrateful for the favor they have received. It is bad enough to be a bastard. Being an ungrateful bastard is even worse. Complaints from the beneficiaries of adoption might force members of the mental health community to consider whether they have done damage in the name of doing good. Putting it in a simpler way, adoption is supposed to solve problems, not create them.

In fact, reluctance to pathologize adoption by identifying problems in those who have experienced the process is likely another factor behind the silence about adoption. The controversy surrounding Kirschner's (1990, 1992) proposed "adopted child syndrome" may be a case in point (Brodzinsky & Schechter, 1992; Lifton, 1994; Smith, 2001). Even setting the considerable methodological issues aside, those who have intimate connections to the adoption process are understandably reluctant to accept a label suggesting pathology, automatic or otherwise. Adoptee psychiatrist Bob Andersen (Andersen & Tucker, 2000) reports that he sees similarities between being part of the adoption triad and the combat experiences shared by many Vietnam veterans. Andersen suggests that both adoption and combat are unique and challenging experiences that, in and of themselves, are likely not pathological. They are, however, both stressful experiences that can lead some participants to develop pathological adjustment patterns. As noted by Zamostny, OBrien, et al. (2003), there is wide variability both in the levels of stress in the adoption experience and in the resilience to stress. It is probable that both these variabilities contribute to the wide variety of results obtained when the outcome of adoption is examined. We must distinguish between the valid assumption that a stressful process that people have experienced may lead to adjustment difficulties in some of these people and the invalid assumptions that all those who have experienced a stressful process are made pathological by it and that, therefore, the process itself is pathological. And, of course, we need to be open to the undesired possibility that the adoption process might in fact be pathological, which, if true, will not disappear because of our silence or our denial.

Another factor in understanding the silence is also likely related to some level of denial of race and class issues, and of sexuality, or stated less pathologically, to avoiding these sensitive topics. Race and class issues are difficult ones for all of us to discuss. Historically, as the availability of healthy White infants has declined, adoptees have become a much more racially heterogeneous group. Many more recent adoptees do not match the racial background of their adoptive families, and the term *transracial adoption* (TRA) has been used to describe these adoptions. Unfortunately, for many years, far too many of the adoptive parents of these children, and the mental health professionals who served them, have neglected to address the loss of cultural and racial heritage that can occur in these situations. No matter how noble the motivation behind the adoption, children of color adopted into a family of Scandinavian descent are not well served by being named Kristen, Heidi, or Lars and raised as if they were just like the rest of the blond-haired, blue-eyed children in their upper-class White neighborhood. By adhering to the historic belief that adoptive parents needed only to love their children "as if they were their own" to make them their own, the mental health community has been silent too long on the problems of adoptees who do not look like the rest of their adoptive family.

It is beyond the scope of this chapter to present a detailed review of all the issues in TRA, and readers are referred to the comprehensive work of Baden and Steward (2000), Baden (2002), Lee (2003), and Fensbo (2004) for detailed information on this topic. Also see Chapters 7 through 11, 23, and 30 in this book. However, racial identity is one surprising area of silence in many of the studies of TRA. Burrow and Finley (2004) reported that in the widely respected National Longitudinal Study of Adolescent Health, many variables had been studied, including adoption. For TRA, mixed results had been found for measures of academic progress, family relations, psychological adjustment, and physical health. However, a measure of racial identity had not been included in the data set, and it was therefore not addressed. Lee (2003) noted the frequent failure to examine racial identity in other TRA studies. Grotevant (2003) noted that a difficult time for many TRA adolescents is the passage from their home community, where they are well-known, to a college or university, where they initiate a new network of social relationships.

One of the most angry adoptees I have ever encountered, sadly exemplifying this problem, was "Alice," an African American woman in her late 20s who I met in the basement coffee shop of the Wisconsin State Capitol building early one winter morning. We discovered we were both waiting to testify in favor of a bill giving adult adoptees the right to access the records of their adoption. When Alice learned I was the president of the statewide adoption search and support organization that she had recently joined and that I was a clinical child psychologist, she shared with me her feelings about having been adopted by a White family.

Case Study

Growing up in an all-White suburb of Milwaukee, Alice said she was always treated "totally normally, and was always accepted" by her family and those who knew her throughout her childhood and adolescence. But when she left home to go to college, where no one knew about her adoption, she experienced a terrible awakening. African Americans, looking at her, expected her to "be Black" and to know the language and culture of the African American community. Having been raised by a loving and well-meaning White family in a White environment, she knew little of what life was like for the vast majority of African Americans. Because of this, many African Americans did not accept her in their circle of friends. Yet when she met many White people, they looked at her and, seeing that she was "not White," likewise did not expect her to know anything about their language, culture, and background. Thus, she found she was not easily accepted in either the White or African American community.

Her anger (and her sadness) were palpable as she told me she was a person "without a culture, without a home," and that even though she wanted the rights to meet her birth family and to learn about why she had been adopted, she was fearful of encountering the same rejection from her birth kin that she had received from other African Americans.

For a similar perspective on American adoptees of Korean birth, see Fisher (2003). Sexuality is a topic about which there is great ambivalence in society. Despite its ubiquitous presence and despite the lip service we pay to sex education, for many, sexuality is an uncomfortable subject to discuss. Adoptive parents, knowing, or fearing, that their adopted child was conceived by young unmarried birth parents, may become concerned as their children reach puberty that the birth parents' early and uncontrolled sexual activity may be repeated by their child. Birth mothers may also experience sexual and intimacy dysfunctions related to their surrendering a child. These and other issues for adoptive and birth parents were raised in a workshop entitled "Sexuality and Adoption," which I chaired at the American Adoption Congress (AAC) National Convention in April of 1994 (Henderson, 1994).

For adoptees, discussion of sexuality is especially awkward, since they may be aware even as children that the sexual activity that created them was likely "illegitimate" and not part of a natural and socially acceptable sequence of events. When adoptees reach adolescence, their emerging sexuality reminds them of their own particular origins in sexual activity. Potential negative aspects of puberty for the adoptee include awareness that the sexual activity that conceived them may have occurred outside the framework of marriage; fear that sexual activity, and the pregnancy resulting from this activity, may have driven their birth parents apart; and fear that sexuality was what led to their own separation from their birth family. Adolescent adoptees' thoughts or fantasies about each of these issues may lead them to develop feelings about their sexuality that are very different from those of nonadoptees. When adopted adolescents consider their sexuality, they may have questions such as the following: Will I repeat my birth parents' (presumed) active and early sexual activity? How will my adoptive mother react when I become pregnant if she was infertile? What is the relationship between trust, intimacy, and sexuality in my life? Unfortunately, although I raised these questions on behalf of adoptees more than 10 years ago (Henderson, 1994, 1995), the questions seem to have been met with silence.

Privacy of the birth family is another reason for the silence of the mental health community on issues of adoption. The private act of childbearing was, for much of the past century, assumed to take place properly only within the confines of a marriage. Women who were pregnant out of wedlock were expected to hide themselves, and their shame, away. Pregnancy in general, not to mention the pregnancy of a single woman, was not considered a topic for polite conversation. Much of the historic secrecy in adoption was associated with sending pregnant single women away to have their babies where no one could see them or find out about their pregnancy. With their daughter in another town, often under an assumed name, the family could escape the stigma of public knowledge of their daughter's transgression. The pregnancy was to be treated as if it had never existed, and the mental health professions bought into this silence.

The privacy of married couples is another factor in the silence about the adoption process. The decision to have a child and the process of conceiving one are among the most private acts in which a couple can engage. Happily married couples are presumed to be having intercourse. Intercourse, sooner or later, produces children. The option of remaining voluntarily childless was historically unpopular, in addition to being difficult to carry out, especially before the availability of reliable family planning. Society expected that married couples would have a family and voluntarily childless couples were often labeled as selfish. A couple who was married for more than a certain time and remained childless was considered to be experiencing some sort of "problem." They were either not having intercourse (or they would have lost the roulette game with the stork), or their relationship was in difficulty of some sort, or there was a problem with someone's reproductive system. All these explanations for childlessness touch on extremely private matters. In the days when healthy infants were more easily available, adoptees and their families were often matched by adoption agencies for ethnic backgrounds and even physical traits, making it possible to conceal the fact that a child was adopted. Social workers downplayed the importance of adoption and sometimes counseled not telling adopted children of their origin. In particular, if the adoption itself was concealed, a couple who adopted might not have to reveal potentially embarrassing aspects of their most private relationship to others. Mental health professionals likely cooperated in maintaining this privacy by underplaying the importance of adoption both in the parenting process and in the development of the adoptee.

Another reason for denying the importance of problems in adoption lies in the history of the heredity-environment controversy and of the changing acceptance of social Darwinism in the United States. During the early part of the 20th century, social Darwinism became increasingly popular. This model involved the belief that social behaviors, in addition to physical traits, were genetically controlled and differentially heritable, with traits most suitable for survival passed on. The individual defect model, suggesting that causes for mental illness were internal rather than external, was part of this belief system (Albee, 1996). One's genetic background, thus, was of primary importance in the determination of one's future, and eugenics-based laws requiring sterilization of the "unfit" were found even in the United States.

As the influence of the early behavioral psychologists became stronger in the 1920s and 1930s, social Darwinism began to lose popularity. Consistent with the desire to repudiate genetics-based racism and sexism, emphasis began to change from genetic determination of behaviors to environmental or learned determinants (Degler & Byrne, 1991). The Holocaust sped the demise of the eugenics movement and made any reference to the importance of one's genetic background unpopular, if not impossible. Until late in the 20th century, the dominant societal belief, supported by an antiracist, antisexist, and egalitarian value system, was that a child's gender, race, and genetic background (thus the birth family) were of little to no importance. The important determinants of behavior were the love, nurturance, and presumably superior environment provided by the adoptive family. Thus, the advice given to most adoptive parents during this time was to concentrate on providing the best possible environment for their children, to love them intensely, and not to worry about the relatively unimportant role of whatever genetic background their children carried.

Adoption lies at the heart of the confusing intersection between heredity and environment. If an adoptee is having difficulties, and the problems cannot be laid at the door of "bad genes," then the cause of the problem must lie either in a faulty adoptive family child-rearing environment or in a faulty societal de-emphasis of the importance of one's genetic background. Ignoring any problems shown by adoptees is one way of avoiding facing either of these unpleasant possibilities. Although both society and the mental health community now acknowledge that it is an interplay of both heredity and environment that is important, probably no group is more personally aware of this issue than adoptees.

There are also economic reasons why mental health professionals have been silent on the issues of adoption. The almost palpable physical need of many childless couples to raise a child frequently drives them first to increasingly invasive and expensive medical interventions. When these fail, childless couples often look to adoption, and when they do, they find any number of agencies waiting to serve their needs. During the "feelgood" era, before the advent of reliable family planning, and when only "bad girls" got pregnant out of wedlock, there was an ample supply of healthy White infants available. There was, apparently, no shortage of "bad girls." Birth parents, typically in the one-down position financially and socially, as well as psychologically, usually cooperated with whatever demands were imposed on them in releasing their infants for adoption. Paying the birth mother's expenses began as an innocent and humanitarian tradition that has become problematic. As the nature of adoption has changed, so, it seems, has the definition of expenses.

Adoption first began as a charity, "rescuing" children from the streets of eastern U.S. cities. However, particularly in the case of the orphan trains, adoption from the beginning was a charity driven by the economic need for farm workers in the American West (Holt, 1992). For-profit adoption agencies were a later development. A sensitive issue for adoptees and adoptive parents alike is the development in some for-profit agencies of a business model of adoption, where adoptive parents are seen by agency staff less as "clients of a social worker" and more as "customers of a business." Under a business model, the adoptee can be seen as the "product" that is being supplied to the "customer." The word "sold" and the image of adoptive parents "picking out" their child are uncomfortable for many adoptees. As adoption became an increasingly big business, the process also became correspondingly more expensive.

Some of the costs of adoption are certainly legitimate. As the supply of healthy White American infants dwindled, the desires of childless parents for a baby were harder to meet. Agencies had to go first to poor (often minority) American neighborhoods and then overseas to find children to place, and a certain amount of real additional expense was created. In some cases, these legitimate expenses are considerable. Staff salary, office expenses, transportation, and insurance are all legitimate costs of doing business. When agency profits are added into the mix, however, the distressing questions about "buying children" become harder to ignore, and discomfort around these questions may cause them, and other issues of adoption, to be ignored by all involved.

As the nature of adoption changed, children often came from less-than-optimal environments, for example, war or famine zones, or from poor countries where birth mothers had inadequate nutrition and medical care. Adopted children began to have extensive histories in orphanages or other institutions. The risks and expenses of raising these children might well be higher than those associated with raising healthy infants from middle- and upper-class American families. Telling the truth about the history of these children, particularly older, minority, or foreign children, might make them less easily adoptable. Silence about the background of a child, and the consequent underestimating and/or underpublicizing of the nature of the problems that the child might encounter, and of the problems that other children from similar environments have experienced, could be seen as good business practice, increasing agencies' profits if not ennobling their activities.

Another area of silence in both research and clinical literature on adoption involves the roles played by birth fathers (Freundlich, 2002; Zamostny, O'Brien, et al., 2003) and male adoptees (Henderson, 2002). Two recent research papers on birth fathers (Freeark et al., 2005; Miall & March, 2005) begin the investigative process with a confirmation of what many in the adoption movement already knew: Birth fathers are marginalized and generally perceived negatively.

There have likely been many reasons for this particular silence. Perhaps, for reasons of gender role differences, until recently, the adoption support and reform movement has been primarily composed of birth mothers and female adoptees. Birth mothers frequently harbor lingering hostility toward the birth father, who may have deserted them at a time of need, or worse. Adoptees also believe that in many cases had the birth father "done the right thing" there would not have been an adoption, and they would have been raised in their birth family. Male adoptees and birth fathers report that they sense this hostility at search and support meetings and that it is difficult for them to return (Henderson, 2002). Some birth fathers are now making the case that they are no longer the young immature "boys" who surrendered their children.

Male adoptees, sensing the anger at birth fathers, are beginning to ask questions about what it means to be a man and a father themselves. Workshops specifically for male adoptees have been offered annually since the mid-1990s at conventions of the AAC (e.g., Henderson & Hyman, 2001; Henderson & McGowan, 1996; Hyman, 2005). The topics of substance abuse, difficulties with intimacy, and an attraction to dangerous activities seem to be recurring themes in these sessions, but at present these are little more than anecdotal data. Unfortunately, thus far, clinical and research literature on male adoptees and birth fathers, particularly 20 or more years postadoption, is still scarce.

Birth mothers, while they have been significant participants in the adoption search and reunion and adoption reform movements, have until recently also been largely absent in research literature. Silverman, Campbell, Patti, and Style (1988) studied 170 birth mothers in reunion with the adoptee they surrendered. Silverman et al. found that rather than disrupting the birth mother's life, reunion was by and large a positive experience, whether she searched for or was found by the adoptee. Much of other recent research on birth mothers, however, has been in the context of their participation in open adoptions. Recent work by Wiley and Baden (2005) is beginning to shed light on many aspects of the birth parent experience, addressing both birth mothers and birth fathers.

Finally, over the years, the National Committee for Adoption (NCFA), now composed primarily of adoption agencies that still support the role of secrecy in adoption (and make their profits through the adoption process), has long been instrumental in promoting the "feelgood" model of adoption. As part of their model of the ideal adoption, the NCFA advocates closed adoption, in which the adoptive parents and adoptees receive no identifying information about the birth family. In many states, including Ohio (NCFA, 1995b), Tennessee (Pierce, 1997), Maryland (NCFA, 1997a), and Oregon (Learn & Heinz, 1998), the NCFA and/or its member agencies have advised letter-writing campaigns, offered financial assistance, testified in legislative hearings, or gone to court in support of efforts to deny adult adoptees access to information about the identities of their birth kin. At the same time, the NCFA has attempted to marginalize and pathologize anyone who reports that adoption experiences are problematic.

Members of the NCFA have set themselves up as the national experts on adoption, while actually representing not the adoptees and birth parents who have lived adoption but rather, primarily, the agencies making money on adoptions. The NCFA has long characterized anyone who criticized or suggested change in adoption practices as being "antiadoption." Included on their list of antiadoption authors have been a wide variety of widely recognized adoption experts, such as Reuben Pannor (NCFA, 1995a) and Betty Jean Lifton (NCFA, 1997b). The NCFA has also characterized major national adoption reform organizations (the AAC and Concerned United Birthparents) as being antiadoption (NCFA, 1997c, p. 3). The NCFA states that when anyone claiming expertise in adoption "participates in an attack on adoption it is legitimate for others to see him as anti-adoption" (NCFA, 1995a, p. 11). The NCFA statement in opposition to a 2004 access-to-records bill for adult adoptees in New Jersey referred to "a small minority who demand the right for adopted persons to identify and contact their birthparents, with or without birthparents' consent. These activists are not adoption advocates" (NCFA, n.d.). This type of statement is an attempt to silence or discredit those triad members for whom adoption has not been a "feelgood" experience, and likely has also had an effect on members of the mental health community.

Fortunately, the silence on adoption issues has not been complete. A relatively new development in the 1980s was the process known as "open adoption," a term which refers to the sharing of information and, in some cases, contact between birth and adoptive families (Baran & Pannor, 1993). In traditional "closed adoption," no information crosses the boundary of the adoption agency or attorney between the birth and adoptive families, and adoptees grow up with little to no knowledge about their birth family, excepting perhaps the canard "your birth mother loved you so much that she gave you up for adoption" (see Sass & Henderson, Chapter 20 in this book for a discussion of the difficulties with this statement). The concept of open adoption implies the sharing of some information between the birth and adoptive families. The continuum of openness varies widely, sometimes only including one-way passage of information, also known as "nonidentifying information," from the birth family to the adoptive parents. Nonidentifying information might consist of as little as demographics, interest patterns, and health history. In the middle of the continuum is the one-way passage to the adoptive parents of birth-parent identity, and/or social history, including the reasons for surrender. At the more open end is complete two-way information exchange, sometimes including continuing contact with the birth family throughout the developing adoptee's life (Zamostny, O'Brien, et al., 2003). It is beyond the scope of this chapter to present a complete review of open adoption, but the work of Grotevant and McRoy and their colleagues in the longitudinal Minnesota/Texas Adoption Research Project (Grotevant, McRoy, Elde, & Fravel, 1994; Mendenhall, Berge, Wrobel, Grotevant, & McRoy, 2000), and of Siegel (1993, 2003), are representative of this encouraging break in the silence. Grotevant's team is gathering data in the third wave of their study, which follows their sample of adoptees into the decade of their 20s (Chamberlain, 2005).

CONCLUSION

Given the reasons why the mental health community has been historically silent on issues related to adoption, what are the options available to reverse this trend? All those reading this chapter can be part of the solution. Breaking the silence by attending adoption-reform-related conferences is a good start, as is submission of articles about the experiences of adoption triad members to professional journals. The appearance of a special issue on families and adoption of *Marriage & Family Review* (Vol. 25, 1997), two special adoption issues of the *Journal of Social Distress and the Homeless* (Vol. 9, October 2000, and Vol. 11, April 2002), and a series of articles on adoption in *The Counseling Psychologist* (Vol. 9, November 2003) are recent examples of valuable contributions to the literature on adoption and a hopeful sign that the silence is being challenged.

Those with the ability and resources to do research, and those with clinical or personal experience to share, should submit program proposals to their professional organizations. As noted in the work of Sass and Henderson (2000), psychologists believe that they need more information about the effects of adoption, and presenting information on adoption at professional meetings is one way to get this information disseminated. Another avenue is the organization of continuing education programs specifically about adoption for the various mental health professions. Many state licensing boards now require their licensees to attend regular professional development seminars. Encouraging attendance at triad-based adoption conferences (such as those of the AAC) by mental health professionals would also expose them to triad members who are living adoption every day of their lives.

It is clear that actions by one person, in the right place, at the right time, and with the right training, can make a significant difference. As an adoptee in a traditional, closed adoption and a clinical child psychologist, and after surviving testicular cancer in 1981, I realized my need to gain both medical and social history information about my birth family. My search and reunion led me to become active in adoption support groups at the local, state, and national levels in the 1980s and 1990s, speaking and writing primarily for the adoption community about adoption search and reunion issues. Eventually, I became the education director of the AAC and began to involve my undergraduate students in my research on adoption, which we presented at meetings of the AAC.

In the late 1990s, one adoptive parent (Bruce Kellogg) made inquiries as to what his alma mater, St. John's University, was doing to address the problems he had seen in adoption. He was referred to a psychologist on the St. John's faculty (Dr. Rafael Javier), who decided to further investigate the issue. As a result, Dr. Javier attended the AAC annual conference in the spring of 1999. There he listened to many triad members, several of whom were mental health professionals. One of them was me. Based on Dr. Javier's experience at that conference, he and I coedited the first special adoption issue of the *Journal of Social Distress and the Homeless*.

In addition, Dr. Javier spearheaded the St. John's University Fall 2000 adoption conference, where an early version of this chapter was first presented. St. John's University has held additional adoption conferences in 2002, 2004, and 2006, and has committed to holding an ongoing biennial series of conferences on adoption. There has also been a second special adoption issue of the *Journal of Social Distress and the Homeless*, in which a version of the present chapter appeared.

That second special adoption issue was coedited by Dr. Amanda Baden, a psychologist and Chinese adoptee, who completed her doctoral dissertation at Michigan State University on the psychological adjustment of transracial adoptees and whose first academic job was as an assistant professor at St. John's. She was working with Dr. Javier, and when he learned of her interest in adoption he asked her to join the planning committee for the first (2000) St. John's adoption conference. Over the years, Dr. Baden played increasingly larger roles in conference planning, and she now heads the planning committee for the conference series. She also publishes and consults regularly in adoption, has an active private practice specializing in adoption, and is a board member of Families With Children From China in New York City. Perhaps most important, the book you are now reading is a product of discussions between Dr. Baden and Dr. Javier!

Who knows whether all this would have happened had any of these four individuals (Henderson, Kellogg, Javier, and Baden) not taken action.

Another way to challenge the silence is a thus-far underused approach to the study of adoption—the identification of a theoretical issue of development, in general, and the subsequent application of the theory to the adoption process (Grotevant, 2003; Zamostny, O'Brien, et al., 2003). Such a strategy has the advantage of relating adoption to other life span developmental issues, potentially increasing the understanding of both. One example of such an approach is the application of attachment theory to the adoption process (see Chapters 5 and 22 in this book; Edens & Cavell, 1999).

Recently, Powell and Afifi (2005) have applied the theory of ambiguous loss (Boss, 1999) and uncertainty reduction theory (Berger & Calabrese, 1975) to the reaction of adoptees to the ambiguous loss of their birth-family members. Powell and Afifi (2005) found that adoptees' decision to look for their birth family was determined by an interaction between the adoptees' perception of their adoption and the communication and support system in their adoptive families. The application of these two theories to adoption has contributed to the understanding of why some adoptees wish to search for their birth families while others have no such interest, as well as to why and how the level of interest in searching changes over time. This work has also added to the understanding of uncertainty reduction theory, and specifically to the understanding of how uncertainty may at times be a desirable state.

Finally, an interesting way to improve the visibility of adoption issues in psychology has been proposed by Post (2000). She calls attention to the American Psychological Association's (APA) *Guidelines and Principles for the Accreditation of Programs in Professional Psychology*. These principles contain Domain D, "Cultural and Individual Diversity," which states that to qualify for accreditation, graduate programs in psychology must prepare students for practice or research by providing knowledge and experience regarding the importance of cultural and individual diversity in psychological development (APA, 2005). Based on her own work and that of Sass et al. (2000), Post (2000) argues that adoption triad members, as well as those in their immediate families, represent a group of individuals whose diverse needs are not being adequately addressed. Graduate programs in psychology attempting to follow these accrediting guidelines may wish to devote more attention to adoption-related issues.

Post (2000) also supports the importance of understanding the cultural experience of adoption as found in the American Psychiatric Association's *Diagnostic and Statistical Manual of Mental Disorders* (*DSM-IV-TR*; 2000). Information in Appendix I supports the importance of understanding the individual's ethnic and cultural background, family and kinship networks, and social support system, and stresses the importance of making "culturally relevant interpretations" (p. 898). In the introduction to the *DSM-IV-TR*, clinicians are advised that they need to understand an individual's cultural background, lest they "incorrectly judge as psychopathology those normal variations in behavior, belief or experience that are particular to the individual's culture" (p. xxxiv). Individual mental health practitioners attempting to follow these diagnostic and treatment guidelines may wish to increase their attention to adoption-related issues. Grotevant (2003) also suggests the consideration of cultural issues in the treatment of adoptees and families from diverse cultural backgrounds.

Even though much progress has been made in the early part of the 21st century toward ending the silence of the mental health professions on issues related to adoption, the silence still continues. Zamostny, Wiley, O'Brien, Lee, and Baden (2003) call for mental health practitioners and researchers to break the silence on adoption issues. Fensbo (2004) comments on the lack of attention to attachment and identity development in adoptees and concludes that "well-documented research in the adoption field is necessary" (p. 62). It is time for the silence to end. Continuing the silence will serve the interests of no one and will lead to further difficulties for all those touched by the adoption process.

REFERENCES

Albee, G. W. (1996). Introduction to the special issue on social Darwinism. *Journal of Primary Prevention, 17*, 3–16.

American Psychiatric Association. (2000). *Diagnostic and statistical manual of mental disorders* (4th ed., text revision). Washington, DC: Author.

American Psychological Association. (2005). *Guidelines and principles for the accreditation of programs in professional psychology*. Washington, DC: Author.

Andersen, R., & Tucker, R. (2000). *Conflict resolution on the bridge less traveled*. Paper presented at the American Adoption Congress Convention, Nashville, TN.

Baden, A. L. (2002). The psychological adjustment of transracial adoptees: An application of the cultural-racial identity model. *Journal of Social Distress and the Homeless, 9*, 167–192.

Baden, A. L., & Steward, R. J. (2000). A framework for use with racially and culturally integrated families: The cultural-racial identity model as applied to transracial adoption. *Journal of Social Distress and the Homeless, 9*, 309–338.

Baran, A., & Pannor, R. (1993). Perspectives on open adoption. *The Future of Children, 11*, 119–124.

Berger, C. R., & Calabrese, R. J. (1975). Some explorations in initial interaction and beyond: Toward a developmental theory of interpersonal communication. *Human Communication Research, 1*, 99–112.

Boss, P. (1999). *Ambiguous loss*. Cambridge, MA: Harvard University Press.

Brodzinsky, D. M. (1990). A stress and coping model of adoption adjustment. In D. Brodzinsky & M. Schechter (Eds.), *The psychology of adoption* (pp. 3–24). New York: Oxford University Press.

Brodzinsky, D. M., & Schechter, M. (1992). *Being adopted: The lifelong search for self.* New York: Doubleday.

Brooks, D. A., Allen, J., & Barth, R. P. (2002). Adoption services use, helpfulness, and need: A comparison of public and private agency and independent adoptive families. *Children and Youth Services Review, 24,* 213–238.

Burrow, A. L., & Finley, G. E. (2004). Transracial, same-race adoptions, and the need for multiple measures of adolescent adjustment. *American Journal of Orthopsychiatry, 74,* 577–583.

Chamberlain, J. (2005). Adopting a new American family. *Monitor on Psychology, 36,* 70–71.

Child Welfare Information Gateway. (2004). *How many children were adopted in 2000 and 2001?* Retrieved August 17, 2006, from www.childwelfare.gov/pubs/s_adopted/s_adoptedf.cfm

Crouch, M., & Manderson, L. (1995). The social life of bonding theory. *Social Science & Medicine, 41,* 837–844.

Degler, C. N., & Byrne, M. (1991). *In search of human nature: The decline and revival of Darwinism in American social thought.* New York: Oxford University Press.

Edens, J. F., & Cavell, T. A. (1999). A review and reformulation of adoptive relationships from an attachment perspective. *Adoption Quarterly, 3,* 43–70.

Evan B. Donaldson Adoption Institute. (1997). *Benchmark adoption survey: Report on the findings* (Princeton Survey Research Associates). New York: Author.

Fahlberg, V. (1997). Post-adoption services. In S. K. Roszia, A. Baran, & L. Coleman (Eds.), *Creating kinship* (pp. 31–35). Portland, OR: Dougy Center.

Fensbo, C. (2004). Mental and behavioural outcome of inter-ethnic adoptees: A review of the literature. *European Child and Adolescent Psychiatry, 13,* 55–63.

Fisher, A. P. (2003). Still "not quite as good as having your own"? Toward a sociology of adoption. *Annual Review of Sociology, 29,* 335–361.

Freeark, K., Rosenberg, E. B., Bornstein, J., Jozefowicz-Simbeni, D., Linkevich, M., & Lohnes, K. (2005). Gender differences and dynamics shaping the adoption life cycle: Review of the literature and recommendations. *American Journal of Orthopsychiatry, 75,* 86–101.

Freundlich, M. (2002). Adoption research: An assessment of empirical contributions to the advancement of adoption practice. *Journal of Social Distress and the Homeless, 11,* 143–166.

Grotevant, H. D. (2003). Counseling psychology meets the complex world of adoption. *The Counseling Psychologist, 31,* 753–762.

Grotevant, H. D., McRoy, R. G., Elde, C. L., & Fravel, D. L. (1994). Adoptive family system dynamics: Variations by level of openness in the adoption. *Family Process, 33,* 125–146.

Henderson, D. B. (Workshop Chair). (1994). *Sexuality and adoption.* American Adoption Congress National Convention, New Orleans, LA.

Henderson, D. B. (1995). Sexuality and the adoptee. *Adoption Therapist, 6,* 12–19.

Henderson, D. B. (2000). Adoption issues in perspective: An introduction to the special issue. *Journal of Social Distress and the Homeless, 9,* 261–272.

Henderson, D. B. (2002). *Male adoptees: Issues for adolescent development.* Paper presented at St. John's University Adoption Conference, Queens, NY.

Henderson, D. B., & Hyman, C. (2001). *Special issues for male adoptees.* Workshop presented at the American Adoption Congress National Convention, Anaheim, CA.

Henderson, D. B., & McGowan, T. (1996). *Special issues for male adoptees.* Workshop presented at the American Adoption Congress National Convention, Baltimore, MD.

Holt, M. I. (1992). *The orphan trains: Placing out in America.* Lincoln: University of Nebraska Press.

Hoyle, S. G. (1995). Long-term treatment of emotionally disturbed adoptees and their families. *Clinical Social Work Journal, 23,* 429–440.

Hyman, C. (2005). *Special issues for male adoptees.* Workshop presented at the American Adoption Congress National Convention, Las Vegas, NV.

Kessler, R. C., McGonagle, K. A., Zhao, S., Nelson, C., Hughes, M., Eshleman, S., et al. (1994). Lifetime and 12 month prevalence of *DSM-III-R* psychiatric disorders in the United States. *Archives of General Psychiatry, 51,* 8–19.

Kirschner, D. (1990). The adopted child syndrome: Considerations for psychotherapy. *Psychotherapy in Private Practice, 8,* 93–100.

Kirschner, D. (1992). Understanding adoptees who kill: Dissociation, patricide, and the psychodynamics of adoption. *International Journal of Offender Therapy and Comparative Criminology, 36,* 323–333.

Learn, S., & Heinz, S. (1998, December 6). Adoption fight pits diverse groups. *The Oregonian,* p. B09.

Lee, R. M. (2003). The transracial adoption paradox: History, research, and counseling implications of cultural socialization. *The Counseling Psychologist, 31,* 711–744.

Levy, T. M., & Orlans, M. (2000). Attachment disorder and the adoptive family. In T. M. Levy (Ed.), *Handbook of attachment interventions* (pp. 243–259). San Diego: Academic Press.

Lifton, B. J. (1994). *Journey of the adopted self: A quest for wholeness.* New York: Basic Books.

Mendenhall, T. J., Berge, J. M., Wrobel, G. M., Grotevant, H., & McRoy, R. G. (2000). Adolescents' satisfaction with contact in adoption. *Child & Adolescent Social Work Journal, 21,* 175–190.

Miall, C. E., & March, K. (2005). Community attitudes toward birth fathers' motives for adoption placement and single parenting. *Family Relations: Interdisciplinary Journal of Applied Family Studies, 54,* 535–546.

Miller, B. C., Fan, X., Grotevant, H. D., Christensen, M., Coyl, D., & van Dulmen, M. (2000). Adopted adolescents' overrepresentation in mental health counseling: Adoptees' problems or parents' lower threshold for referral? *Journal of the American Academy of Child & Adolescent Psychiatry, 39,* 1504–1511.

National Committee for Adoption. (1995a). Attacks on adoption: More from Reuben Pannor. *National Adoption Reports, 16,* 11.

National Committee for Adoption. (1995b). Ohio Governor misled that there is a consensus on open records. *National Adoption Reports, 16,* 10–11.

National Committee for Adoption. (1997a). MD set to open records. *National Adoption Reports, 18,* 4.

National Committee for Adoption. (1997b). Open records and anti adoption groups hail "secrets and lies." *National Adoption Reports, 18,* 4.

National Committee for Adoption. (1997c). PBS slams confidentiality. *National Adoption Reports, 18,* 3.

National Committee for Adoption (n.d.). *Consent versus coercion: How Senate committee substitute for S1093 and S620 harms adoption.* Retrieved August 17, 2006, from www.ncfa-usa.org/media_News_060704.htm

O'Brien, K. M., & Zamostny, K. P. (2003). Understanding adoptive families: An integrative review of empirical research and future directions for counseling psychology. *The Counseling Psychologist, 31,* 679–710.

Pavao, J. M., Groza, V., & Rosenberg, K. F. (1998). Treatment issues in adoption practice from a triad and systemic perspective. In V. Groza & K. F. Rosenberg (Eds.), *Clinical and practice issues in adoption: Bridging the gap between adoptees placed as infants and as older children* (pp. 157–166). Westport, CT: Praeger.

Pierce, W. (1997). Who stands for adoption? *National Adoption Reports, 18,* 1–2.

Post, D. E. (1999). *Adoption in the college classroom: Who is training clinicians about the particular issues of adoption triad members?* Paper presented at the 1999 meeting of the American Adoption Congress, McLean, VA.

Post, D. E. (2000). Adoption in clinical psychology: A review of the absence, ramifications and recommendations for change. *Journal of Social Distress and the Homeless, 9,* 361–372.

Powell, K. A., & Afifi, T. D. (2005). Uncertainty management and adoptees' ambiguous loss of their birth parents. *Journal of Social and Personal Relationships, 22,* 129–151.

Ross, C. A. (1991). Epidemiology of multiple personality disorder and dissociation. *Psychiatric Clinics of North America, 14,* 503–517.

Ryan, S. D., & Nalavany, B. (2003). Adopted children: Who do they turn to for help and why? *Adoption Quarterly, 7*(2), 29–52.

Sass, D. A., & Henderson, D. B. (1999). *Adoption issues: Preparation of psychologists and an evaluation of the need for continuing education.* Paper presented at the 1999 meeting of the American Adoption Congress, McLean, VA.

Sass, D. A., & Henderson, D. B. (2000). Adoption issues: Preparation of psychologists and an evaluation of the need for continuing education. *Journal of Social Distress and the Homeless, 9,* 349–359.

Sass, D. A., Webster, J. M., & Henderson, D. B. (2000). *An investigation of triad members' therapeutic experiences related to adoption.* Paper presented at the meeting of the American Adoption Congress, Nashville, TN.

Schroeder, S. R. (1988). Prevention of developmental disabilities over the life span. In J. L. Matson & A. Marchetti (Eds.), *Developmental disabilities: A life-span perspective* (pp. 31–46). Philadelphia: Grune & Stratton.

Siegel, D. H. (1993). Open adoption of infants: Adoptive parents' perceptions of advantages and disadvantages. *Social Work, 38,* 15–22.

Siegel, D. H. (2003). Open adoption of infants: Adoptive parents' feelings seven years later. *Social Work, 48,* 409–419.

Silverman, P. R., Campbell, L., Patti, P., & Style, C. B. (1988). Reunions between adoptees and birth parents: The birth parents' experience. *Social Work, 33,* 523–528.

Smith, D. W., & Sherwen, L. N. (1988a). The bonding process between mothers and their adopted children. In E. J. Anthony & C. Chiland (Eds.), *The child in his family: Vol. 8. Perilous development: Child raising and identity formation under stress* (pp. 105–115). Oxford, UK: Wiley.

Smith, D. W., & Sherwen, L. N. (1988b). *Mothers and their adopted children: The bonding process* (2nd ed.). New York: Tiresias Press.

Smith, J. (2001). The adopted child syndrome: A methodological perspective. *Families in Society, 82,* 491–497.

Streissguth, A. P., Barr, H. M., Sampson, P. D., & Darby, B. L. (1989). IQ at age 4 in relation to maternal alcohol use and smoking during pregnancy. *Developmental Psychology, 25,* 3–11.

U.S. Census Bureau. (2003). *Number of children of householder by type of relationship and age: 2000.* Retrieved August 17, 2006, from www.census.gov/prod/2003pubs/censr-6.pdf

Watson, K. W. (1997). Bonding and attachment in adoption: Towards better understanding and useful definitions [Special issue: Families and adoption: Part II]. *Marriage & Family Review, 25,* 159–173.

Wegar, K. (1997). *Adoption, identity, and kinship: The debate over sealed birth records.* New Haven, CT: Yale University Press.

Wiley, M. O., & Baden, A. M. (2005). Birth parents in adoption: Research, practice, and counseling psychology. *The Counseling Psychologist, 33,* 13–50.

Zamostny, K. P., O'Brien, K. M., Baden, A. L., & Wiley, M. O. (2003). The practice of adoption: History, trends, and social context. *The Counseling Psychologist, 31,* 651–678.

Zamostny, K. P., Wiley, M. O., O'Brien, K. M., Lee, R. L., & Baden, A. L. (2003). Breaking the silence: Advancing knowledge about adoption for counseling psychologists. *The Counseling Psychologist, 31,* 647–650.

The Inner Life of the Adopted Child

26

Adoption, Trauma, Loss, Fantasy, Search, and Reunion

BETTY JEAN LIFTON

Private Practice

The time has come to approach the subject of adoption in a new and realistic way: to see where it connects to myth and to plain old life. We have to see the adoptee as a child marked by fate, but not doomed by it. To see birth mothers as women who have lost their children as surely as women lose children to accidents, disease, and war. To see adoptive parents as people who have lost their chance for biological continuity, but who have taken other women's children as their own as surely as parents in biblical and mythical times rescued infants found floating in baskets down the river.

My purpose here is to help mental health and legal professionals, as well as those in the extended community, understand what is specific about the formation of the adoptee's inner world. This means being able to see the adoptee not only as a child who has gained a family, but as a child who has lost one. Because this loss is not usually recognized by society, adoptees often feel alone on their journey, even when surrounded by a loving adoptive family. They also feel invisible because an essential part of them is not acknowledged: The part that was born of other parents whose genetic code is stamped into every cell of their bodies. A Finnish psychiatrist, Max Frisk (1964), called these missing parents "hereditary ghosts."

SEEING THE GHOSTS

We could say that all families have ghosts, but the ghosts in the adoptive family were created in the closed adoption system. As an adopted child, I was haunted by the ghosts of the mother and father I was told were deceased, but who proved to be very much alive. As an adoption therapist, I treat ghost-haunted adoptees, birth parents, and adoptive parents. All of them are accompanied by their own unique ghosts, who are not literally dead, but "as if" dead.

One cannot see adopted children or adults if one is not aware of the ghosts that accompany them. On one side, the adoptee is flanked by the ghost of the child he might have been had he stayed with his birth mother and father. On the other side is the ghost of the child his adoptive parents might have had: the perfect child, his sibling rival with whom he will compete, successfully or not. And just behind the adopted child are the ghosts of the lost birth parents.

So too, the birth mother is surrounded by ghosts: The ghost of the child she surrendered to adoption (the ghost baby); the ghost of the father of that child; and the ghost of the mother she might have been. The adoptive parents are accompanied by the ghost of the perfect child they might have had as well as the ghosts of the birth parents of the child they are raising.

In my book *Journey of the Adopted Self* (Lifton, 1994), I introduced the Ghost Kingdom, where the adopted child keeps the lost birth mother, birth father, and his original self, the eternal ghost baby who was not able to grow up. The Ghost Kingdom is an alternate place, located in one's psychic reality. It is a portable Home that adoptees carry inside them. It is the Land of What Might Have Been. It is the Land of the As If Dead.

After giving up her baby, the birth mother creates her own Ghost Kingdom, where she keeps that lost child. She may try to repress the trauma of her relinquishment, but the ghost baby waits in the Ghost Kingdom, which serves as a ghost nursery. She may visit it there on its birthday, when she is pregnant with her next child, and at unexpected moments over the years.

The adoptive parents have their Ghost Kingdom, where they hold on to their unborn or stillborn baby, or the child who died. They may visit it when they are disappointed in the child they are raising as their own—the child who does not live up to the high standards of the ghost child who might have been.

Until recently, the Ghost Kingdom was an inaccessible place that adoptees never expected to visit, except in their dreams or fantasies. But now with society's fascination with roots and the increasing openness in adoption, many adoptees are setting out to find their ghosts. It is known as The Search. And crossing over into the Ghost Kingdom is known as Reunion.

Acknowledging the Trauma

Every adopted child has experienced the trauma of being separated from his or her blood kin under some kind of legal arrangement. Social workers feel it is politically correct to say that the birth mother has made an "adoption plan." Birth mothers call it "surrendering" the child. Nancy Verrier (1993), an adoptive mother, calls it the "primal wound." Whatever language one uses, adoptees feel the trauma of the mother's disappearance as an abandonment.

I speak of the adoptee as having not one but "cumulative adoption trauma." What do I mean by this?

The first trauma is the baby's separation from the mother with whom nature intended it to be. Not too long ago, the baby was placed in foster care for 3 to 6 months while the agency studied its fitness for adoption and chose its adoptive parents. The baby then experienced another separation—this time from the foster mother when it was placed with the adoptive mother.

The next trauma comes with the child's awareness that he did not grow in his mommy's tummy, but in some other woman's. He realizes that he is not a natural part of the family. He is unnatural. He is not normal like other kids.

And yet another trauma is the adoptee's realization that he is not going to know the mother who gave birth to him. He is not going to understand the reason why she gave him up. He is not going to learn her name or what she looks like. And she is not going to come back for him. He must have been a bad baby.

Inside every adopted person is that abandoned baby. Adoptees carry that ghost baby through life, and their developmental task is to become adults who can hold and comfort it. They have to accept their adopted fate. But here is the paradox: Adoptees can love their adoptive parents and not love being adopted. For being adopted means being different, living an "as if" life—as if you were born into your adoptive family. It means being biologically disconnected; being disempowered because you have no right to your original birth certificate, which has been sealed away.

The Self as Double

An adopted teenager once told me, "I feel there are two me's. The me that was born, but didn't live. And the me who was not born, but lived the life I have today."

Without understanding it, she was expressing the split in the self that so many adoptees make in order to survive. Early on they get the message that they cannot grieve for their lost kin, that they must commit themselves to the adoptive clan if they are to keep their adoptive parents' love. Already abandoned by the birth mother, the child feels no choice but to abandon her. By doing so, he abandons his real self. This early potential self that is still attached to the birth mother is often unacceptable to the adoptive parents and, therefore, must become unacceptable to the child.

Karen Horney (1950) stressed that there is no more consequential step than abandoning the real self. The child forced to give up the real self cannot develop feelings of belonging. There is instead a feeling of basic anxiety, of being isolated and helpless. For this reason, adopted children often try to shut out the subject of adoption. This means that they are separating one part of the self from the rest of the self—a pattern known as dissociation, disavowal, numbing, or splitting.

D. W. Winnicott (1965) and R. D. Laing (1960) both used the terms *true self* and *false self* to describe the split in the human psyche that many children make. I call the split in the adopted child the *artificial self* and the *forbidden self*, neither of which is completely true or completely false.

The artificial self looks like the perfect child because he or she is so eager to please. These children are compliant, put everyone's needs before their own, and suppress their anger. But deep inside they feel like a fake and an imposter, feelings that may overwhelm them as an adult. Having cut off a vital part of themselves, they sometimes feel dead. The forbidden self is oppositional. Refusing to please, these children often act out antisocially as a way of feeling alive.

An adoptee often switches from one self to the other during various stages of the life cycle. The artificial self may express his or her anger in adulthood. And the forbidden self may eventually become a dutiful son or daughter.

Escape Into Fantasy

For people who know little or nothing about their antecedents, there may be no place to go except into fantasy. It makes sense that adopted children would spend a great deal of psychic time there. They may seem to be sitting quietly in their room or just looking out the window at school when they are really deep in the Ghost Kingdom, imagining scenarios that might have been or still might be. These fantasies often alternate between the positive and negative. Sometimes the birth mother emerges as a famous movie star or a favorite teacher, or she morphs into the local bag woman, a prostitute, or a drug dealer.

Adoptee fantasies must be taken seriously, for they are the fragile center beam around which the edifice of the adopted self is being built. They are a kind of umbilical cord, enabling the child to stay connected to the lost mother. They are an attempt to fill in the missing part of their narrative with real people. But the very anonymity of the birth parents devalues their status and suggests that it is beneath that of the adoptive parents. Some adoptees have been known to drop to a lower level of society than the one they were raised in because they imagine that it is like the one they came from.

The Search

Most adoptees do not search until their twenties or thirties or after their adoptive parents have died. But we could say that they have been searching from the moment they learn they are adopted. He is searching when he fantasizes what his mother might look like; she is searching when she looks for women who resemble her on the street or in a bus. The adolescent who asks, "Who am I?" is already on the search. But the adult adoptee literally searches when life seems at a dead end: when she has a child of her own, or when he is immobilized by some loss in his life.

We can see the search as a quest for the missing parts of one's narrative, for origins, for meaning, and for a coherent sense of self. We can understand it as a rite of passage, as a chance to take control of one's destiny, as a way of finding oneself.

Still, many years may pass from the moment one knows one will search and the moment one begins this part of the journey. There are no safe parameters. No way of staying in control or knowing what one will find. One is moving not only toward the original mother but toward the original trauma. There is the peril of being rejected or disappointed, of losing the fantasy ghost mother, of losing the adoptive parents, of losing one's magical self that set one off from ordinary people, and of losing the self that grew up adopted. But perhaps most terrifying, the search can uncover one's psychic split, beneath which lies the threat of fragmentation and disintegration, which one has spent a lifetime trying to ward off.

Lack of control of the outcome is the major reason why many adoptees either do not begin the search or turn back in the middle of it. Yet there are ways one can take control— I call them "control points." One can control how fast one searches: Either one does it oneself, which takes time because the records are sealed in most states, or pays a professional searcher, which can hurry the process. One can control how to make contact once one gets the information: by phoning or writing or using an intermediary. And one can decide when to take the plunge: in a few days, a few weeks, or even a few years.

But although adoptees can control the externals of the search, they may still be overwhelmed by the inner experience: the unexpected highs and lows they feel as they get in touch with formerly repressed grief and anger. This is because adoptees who search not only go forward to unite with the lost birth mother but also regress back to the past, to the moment of separation. They are both the adult trying to recover the past and the baby trying to recover from the trauma of separation.

Reunion

While the search is the longing for the retrievable, reunion, no matter how successful, brings with it the painful knowledge that what has been lost cannot be found in its original form. The young mother who surrendered her baby has changed with time. An unfamiliar older woman—married or unmarried, with or without other children—has taken her place. And no matter how well the relationship goes in the beginning, at some point the adoptee realizes that this woman is not the fantasy ghost mother that he or she was seeking, the mother who would give unconditional love and make him or her whole. Whatever gain there is, perhaps the greatest loss in reunion is the fantasy ghost mother.

The birth mother and adoptive parents experience their own kind of loss. The birth mother is catapulted back to the trauma of that period when she gave up her baby and is usually overwhelmed with unresolved grief. No matter how close she might feel to the son or daughter who has returned in adult form, she has lost the ghost baby she carried all those years. And adoptive parents, no matter how understanding they are of their child's reunion, have lost their role as exclusive parents.

Reunion, like adoption, can be seen as a lifelong process. One's first meeting with the birth mother may be exhilarating, but it is only the beginning of the journey. Adoptees must live with ambiguities where they were seeking certainties. They must accept that there are parts of their narrative that they may never know. They must find a way to keep their adult self in charge during the reunion and not let what I call the "mad/sad baby" inside control their emotions with temper tantrums expressing their grief and anger over their perceived abandonment. They must somehow persuade their spouses, partners, and friends not to feel threatened by their mood swings and irrational behavior. And they must continue on with their adult lives and careers, with the parenting of their own children, rather than staying stuck in the past trying to relive what might have been.

Whether they have exorcised their ghosts, invited them into the Adoption Kingdom, or carved out an alternative place that one adoptee calls the "New Territories," reunion usually proves to be a positive experience. One has taken control of one's life, one is empowered, grounded in history, and feels real.

THERAPEUTIC STRATEGIES WITH THE ADOPTED CHILD

Parents may bring their adopted child to therapy because he or she seems depressed or is acting out. The child is the identified patient, as if it is only his or her problem and not that of a family system built on secrecy. Even if the adoption is semi-open, which means that the adoptive parents have met the birth mother and have sent pictures the first 2 years through their lawyer or agency, it must be remembered that the child has not seen the birth mother. She remains as much of a mystery and ghost as the birth mothers in the closed system.

Therapists must see the ghosts that accompany the adoptive parents as well as those of the child. They must see the trauma everyone has suffered and the dissociation all of them have done. Only then will they understand that it is the dissociation that causes the resistant adoptee to say, "Adoption is no big deal."

Therapists who have treated young adoptees, especially adolescents, know how difficult it is to get them to talk—especially about adoption. How do you talk about a subject you have split off from your conscious mind and no longer have access to? How do you talk about a set of parents that you don't know and have no shared experiences with? Therapists may have to do most of the talking in the beginning. If they can win the adoptee's trust, they may even become part of his or her fantasy life—an ideal birth parent. They may even be invited into the Ghost Kingdom.

Therapists can earn that invitation by telling the adoptee that they have some idea of what it feels like not to know your birth mother or father or anything about how you came into the world. When adoptees realize that therapists are speaking their language, they begin to share the private thoughts that they keep hidden from their adoptive parents.

At the same time, a therapist must be careful not to exclude the adoptive parents. It is a good idea to see them in separate sessions and sometimes with the child, so that everyone can express their feelings and their fears to each other. Often it is the only time they have communicated like this. The parents are usually taken by surprise at their child's interest in his birth family. They were not told that there can be identity problems when adopted children are kept in ignorance about their origins. Some adoptive parents are eager to learn and do everything they can that will help their child. Others may become jealous of the close tie the child has formed with the therapist and end the relationship. Or they may resist a therapist's suggestion that they try to get updated information about the birth mother and make her a real person. They may fear opening up their closed adoption. The therapist has the task of helping the adoptive parents understand that their child's need to know about his heritage does not reflect on their parenting skills. They cannot lose their child. On the contrary, their child will feel even closer to them if they can take part of this adoption journey together rather than leave the adoptee to take it alone at a later time.

STRATEGIES WITH ADOPTEES IN SEARCH AND REUNION

Adoptees do not go into therapy saying they want to search. They usually go to understand why they have problems with intimacy, why they cannot get married or stay married, why they cannot hold a job, why they are depressed. Only after the therapist helps them become aware of the defenses they have used from an early age do they get some insight into the importance that adoption has played in their lives. Gradually, the dissociation begins to wear off, like a fog lifting, and they see clearly that they need to find the answers to the questions that they buried long before. Only the birth mother has those answers: Only she knows who the birth father is.

Therapists who are knowledgeable about the adoptees' journey can guide them through the uncharted terrain that comes with reunion. They can explore with them what their expectations are. They can prepare them for the various scenarios that are possible: finding that the mother has died; that she doesn't want to meet them; that she will meet, but doesn't want to tell the rest of her family; that she wants more of a relationship than the adoptee does; that she has married the birth father; that she will not tell them who the birth father is; and that she is in an institution.

Even in the best scenarios, there is eventually a letdown. Adoptees must accept that they cannot have the inflated ghost mother in human form. She doesn't come in that size. They have to be careful not to let the "mad/sad baby" express their disappointment but keep the adult self in charge. They have to accept the actual mother for who and what she is and forgive her.

Strategies With Birth Mothers

Birth mothers often go into therapy after reunion because they are overwhelmed with sadness, guilt, and anger. Therapists can help them understand that they are in touch with the emotions they had split off after the relinquishment. They should be encouraged to let go of the ghost baby they have held on to and accept the adult the baby has become. They should be prepared for the "mad/sad baby" to emerge from time to time. And they should be helped to understand that the adoptee may not want to introduce them to the adoptive parents. Loyalty to the adoptive parents may account for the adoptee's ambivalence in the relationship and the need to withdraw once in a while.

Strategies With the Adoptive Parents

Adoptive parents are often threatened by the adoptee's reunion and growing friendship with the birth mother. They may be hurt that they have not been asked to meet the birth mother. They should be helped to understand that their child needs to fill in this part of his or her narrative and that the adoptee's relationship to his or her adoptive parents often becomes stronger after reunion because there are no more secrets cutting off communication.

CONCLUSION

Many adopted children feel invisible because they are forced to repress their need to know about their origins. They feel that an essential part of them is unacknowledged by their adoptive family and society. The purpose of this chapter is to help mental health and legal professionals, as well as those in the extended community, see what is specific about the formation of the adoptee's inner world. It introduces the concept of cumulative adoption trauma and discusses the adoptees' need to dissociate feelings of loss, grief, and anger. It explains the adoptee's search for the birth mother as a way to form a coherent sense of self. By integrating the past and the present, the adoptee is able to move on into the future.

REFERENCES

Frisk, M. (1964). Identity problems and confused conceptions of the genetic ego in adopted children during adolescence. *Acta Paedopsychiatrica, 31*, 6–12.

Horney, K. (1950). *Neurosis and human growth*. New York: W. W. Norton.

Laing, R. (1960). *The divided self: An existential study in sanity and madness*. Harmondsworth, UK: Penguin Books.

Lifton, B. J. (1994). *Journey of the adopted self: A quest for wholeness*. New York: Basic Books.

Verrier, N. N. (1993). *The primal wound: Understanding the adopted child*. Baltimore: Gateway Press.

Winnicott, D. W. (1965). *The maturational processes and the facilitating environment*. London: Hogath Press.

Birth Parents in Adoption

27

Using Research to Inform Practice

AMANDA L. BADEN

Montclair State University

MARY O'LEARY WILEY

Independent Practice

For Monica, From Her Birth Mother

We've grown together for two years.
We've shared together your laughter and tears.
Since your first moments in this world
So many, many things have unfurled.
Once a child, you're grown now,
The time has come to pass.
Know I'll always love you.
That's all I'll ever ask.
You've had the time to live and grow.
How was I to ever, ever know
I couldn't give the care that you would need.
Mine wouldn't be the voice that you would heed.
When I had to say good-bye to you
I didn't know how much that I'd go through
Wanting to be with you all the while.
I pray you have someone to care
And friends that always, always will be there
A family to support you all the time
Who give the love I long to give a child of mine.

(Imelda Buckley, as cited in Roles, 1989, p. 7; reprinted
by permission from the Child Welfare League of America.)

Note: Portions of this chapter are reproduced from the following paper: Wiley, M. O., & Baden, A. L. (2005). Birth Parents in Adoption: Research, Practice, and Counseling Psychology. *The Counseling Psychologist, 33*, 13-50. Copyrighted 2005 by Sage Publications, 2455 Teller Road, Thousand Oaks, CA 91320. Reprinted by permission.

Although the feelings expressed in Imelda Buckley's poem are widely understood, birth parents are the least studied, least understood, and least served members of the adoption triad (Freundlich, 2002; Reitz & Watson, 1992; Zamostny, O'Brien, Baden, & Wiley, 2003). Birth parents are often the invisible members of the adoption triad. For some, this is by choice; for some, this is an artifact of the adoption system and its historical legal requirements of full relinquishment, secrecy, and anonymity (Winkler, Brown, van Keppel, & Blanchard, 1988). In international adoptions, birth parents are often permanently invisible and silent due to the cultural norms and structures related to relinquishing their children (Lee, 2003; Steinberg & Hall, 2000).

Between 1 and 5 million Americans are adopted (Hollinger, 1998; Stolley, 1993), leading to the inference that up to 10 million people are birth parents of adoptees reared in America. These birth parents are from numerous countries, including the United States, making this group a global population. Terminology related to this group has changed over the years and has included *natural parent*, *biological parent*, *genetic parent*, and *real parent*. However, the terms *birth parent*, *birth mother*, and *birth father* have become accepted nomenclature for referring to the mother and father who gave birth to a child that was placed for adoption (A. Brodzinsky, 1990).

Historically, research has been more limited on this hard-to-access population than on other members of the adoption triad (Freundlich, 2002; Zamostny et al., 2003), although the theory and clinical observations related to the experience of birth parents have a longer history (A. Brodzinsky, 1990; Winkler & van Keppel, 1984). Both the clinical and empirical research literature related to birth parents originate within a wide variety of professional/academic disciplines and in a number of Western countries, but integration of this literature has been limited in part because of the paradigmatic differences in research and practice among disciplines. This lack of integration has slowed both the development of empirical research and the clinical treatment of birth parents. The purposes of this chapter are to provide a scientist-practitioner review of the interdisciplinary clinical and empirical literature on birth parents; to incorporate this literature with actual case studies; and to make recommendations for practice and research based on this literature.

Woven into this literature are several clinical case studies that have been derived from the authors' combined 33 years of counseling experience and one author's extensive experience with international adoption practice. Clinical interventions and issues are drawn from the literature, the authors' experience, and model programs for birth parents (e.g., Barker Foundation, 2004; Center for Family Connections, 2004; Spence-Chapin, 2004).

This chapter first includes a review of the clinical and research literature for three periods in the life of a birth parent: (a) the pre-relinquishment period, including both voluntary and involuntary relinquishment, (b) the early post-relinquishment period, and (c) long-term post-relinquishment, including search and reunion. Each of these sections contains a case study of a birth mother in counseling, including presenting issues, background factors, assessment concerns, treatment issues, and effective treatment strategies. Following these are reviews of the clinical and research literature on birth fathers, international birth parents, and openness in adoption for birth parents. Finally, there are sections on structuring research and practice, and practice and research implications and future directions are discussed.

PRE-RELINQUISHMENT PERIOD

Voluntary Relinquishment

The decision about whether to voluntarily relinquish one's child for adoption is likely the most difficult decision a prospective parent will ever have to make (Winkler et al., 1988).

Typically, it is the pregnant woman who seeks professional services, but increasingly the experience is shared by the father of the unborn child. The conflicting feelings of shame, pride, desolation, excitement, fear, terror, and denial can be overwhelming and disruptive. Women and men facing the possibility of relinquishing their children for adoption consistently report not talking about their feelings because they believe their feelings are abnormal or disproportionate to their crisis.

Different theoretical models have offered varied clinical interpretations of the issues that birth mothers face. Early psychodynamic models (Deutsch, 1945) viewed the unwed mother as using her pregnancy to regressively act out unconscious unmet needs toward her own mother. Jung (1989) used early family systems theory to describe the unplanned pregnancy as a statement of ambivalent feelings and powerlessness in the family. Less psychodynamic but no less influential was the description of adoption that Silverstein and Kaplan (1988) proposed, where they depicted adoption as a lifelong, intergenerational process that unites the triad of birth families, adoptees, and adoptive families forever. They proposed seven core issues in adoption that can assist triad members and professionals working in adoption better to understand each other and the residual effects of the adoption experience. These seven issues are (a) loss, (b) rejection, (c) guilt and shame, (d) grief, (e) identity, (f) intimacy, and (g) mastery/control. Shortly thereafter, D. M. Brodzinsky's stress and coping model (1987, 1990) described the cognitive adjustments and adaptations undergone by the birth parents in adjusting to the pregnancy and making complex decisions regarding relinquishment. Most recently, attachment theory combined with developmental neurobiology was used to hypothesize that stress hormones and neurotransmitters of the birth mother affect the developing fetus differentially, depending on the level of attachment that the birth mother experiences toward her child (Axness, 2001; Maret, 1997; Rini, Dunkel-Schetter, Wadhwa, & Sandman, 1999).

Nine empirical studies were identified that compared samples of pregnant adolescents and young adults who relinquished with control groups who chose to parent, making pre-relinquishment the largest category of birth-parent research. These studies were all conducted in the United States or Canada, were primarily done in maternity homes or adoption agencies, and focused almost exclusively on predictive external variables such as age, race, educational level, socioeconomic status (SES), family situation, and attitudes. Several variables were consistently related to relinquishment, including race, age, socioeconomic level, educational level, preference of birth grandmother, vocational goals, and living arrangements (Chippindale-Bakker & Foster, 1996; Cocozzelli, 1989; Dworkin, Harding, & Schreiber, 1993; Herr, 1989; Low, Moely, & Willis, 1989; McLaughlin, Pearce, Manninen, & Winges, 1988; Resnick, Blum, Bose, Smith, & Toogood, 1990; Warren & Johnson, 1989; Weinman, Robinson, Simmons, Schreiber, & Stafford, 1989).

The literature consistently documented that White women relinquished their infants for adoption at higher rates than did women of color, including African American, Mexican American, and Filipino American women (Chippindale-Bakker & Foster, 1996; Cocozzelli, 1989; Dworkin et al., 1993; Herr, 1989; Warren & Johnson, 1989; Weinman et al., 1989). These studies found race to be a predictive variable of relinquishment, with White women being most likely to relinquish and African American (or African Canadian) women least likely to relinquish.

Moreover, the literature suggested that single mothers in African American communities were less likely to make adoption plans for their infants and more likely to use what has been termed informal adoption (Sandven & Resnick, 1990). An explanation offered for the lower rates of adoption among birth mothers of color is based on both cultural norms from African ancestors and survival norms from postslavery America, where family boundaries include the extended family and are not limited to the nuclear family. One legacy of the forced separations of families during slavery was the strong need reported by many African Americans to retain children of African heritage to be raised within their culture and among their community. Thus, the various forms of informal adoption arrangements included both shared parenting with extended family and "gifting" a child to an extended family member without legally relinquishing parental rights. Historically, this practice was unrelated to social class (Landrine & Klonoff, 1996). Other explanations for lower rates of relinquishment to adoption point to the lack of economic opportunity for birth mothers of color due to issues of oppression and privilege. Authors have not focused, however, on the possibility that birth mothers of color do not relinquish as often because children of color are less likely to be adopted (Lee, 2003).

Recent trends in adoption plans (i.e., decisions made to relinquish children for adoption) were also delineated in the research literature. Adoption plans tended to be made by single mothers who were of higher socioeconomic and educational groups than those who chose to parent (Chippindale-Bakker & Foster, 1996; McLaughlin et al., 1988; Resnick et al., 1990). Adolescent mothers who chose to parent tended to be younger (early to midteens) and of a lower SES, whereas those who made an adoption plan tended to be older (late teens) and of a higher SES (Dworkin et al., 1993; Warren & Johnson, 1989). Mothers who made adoption plans were also found to have higher vocational aspirations and more goal-directed life plans than those who parented (Cocozzelli, 1989; Low et al., 1989).

Family attitudes and dynamics were found to predict the likelihood of a woman making an adoption plan versus choosing to parent. Several studies found that one of the strongest predictors of relinquishment was the preference of the pregnant woman's mother (Chippindale-Bakker & Foster, 1996; Dworkin et al., 1993; Herr, 1989; Low et al., 1989). The relationship between the mother and father was also found to be predictive of relinquishment, particularly when the mother changes from an adoption to a parenting plan (Dworkin et al., 1993).

In summarizing the reasons given by birth mothers for making an adoption plan, Chippindale-Bakker and Foster (1996) stated that most "do so out of a belief that it will offer a better life for their child than they are able to provide" (p. 341). Resnick et al. (1990) added an additional factor in their summary and reported that both the baby's best interests and the birth mother's own school plans were primary motivators for making an adoption plan.

Case Study I

Presenting Issues: Kathleen, a 17-year-old Caucasian from a middle-class family, was 6 months pregnant and was experiencing symptoms of panic, depression, and anxiety.

Background Factors: Kathleen is the elder of two children. Her parents have been married for 18 years, and she is a senior in high school. Kathleen had been dating her boyfriend, Tommy, for more than a year but did not want to marry him and did not want to "wreck my [her] life" by becoming a mother at this stage. After she contacted a private attorney to make an adoption plan for her child, Kathleen's school counselor referred her for more comprehensive therapy.

Assessment Concerns: Kathleen's judgment and insight appeared to be good, but she was experiencing ambivalence and fear about making what she called a "popular" choice for her baby. Kathleen's parents were encouraging relinquishment and adoption although Kathleen heard negative comments about her plan from numerous friends, teachers, and relatives. Even the nurse in her obstetrician's office had said that she didn't know how she could "do such a thing." Kathleen was preparing to review histories of prospective adoptive parents for her baby and knew she wanted this for herself and her baby, but she felt alone, isolated, and sad.

Treatment Issues: Kathleen was trying to avoid internalizing the judgments of others and repeatedly stated the need to do what is right for her baby and herself, but her limited social support was a vital area to address in treatment. Kathleen's fears resulted in multiple changes to her adoption plan (i.e., wavering between keeping and relinquishing the baby) and thereby limited her ability to feel comfortable and safe in her choice. These fears also hindered her progress through the grieving and relinquishment process.

Effective Treatment Strategies: Her therapist validated all options as potential choices (either relinquishment or parenting) and also provided her a nonjudgmental place in which to talk about her ambivalent feelings. Using knowledge of the adoption system and the lifelong impact of relinquishment, Kathleen's therapist urged her to join a support group for relinquishing mothers at a local private adoption agency and to explore placement through an adoption agency with a strong birth-parent support program. The therapist knew that working with such an agency would enable Kathleen to receive support for the relinquishment issues she would experience throughout her lifetime (support a private attorney could not provide). The agency Kathleen chose to work with had an ongoing birth-parent support program that she could work with at any time throughout her lifetime. This agency sent materials to Kathleen's physician and to the obstetrics unit where Kathleen would deliver her baby so that they would understand the unique needs of a mother planning to relinquish her child for adoption (Melina & Melina, 1988). Kathleen worked with her social worker at the agency, chose a mediated contact adoption for her baby (one with limited exchange of information between birth parents and adoptive parents), and participated in choosing the adoptive parents. With her therapist's support, during her eighth month, Kathleen met the adoptive parents and wrote a letter to her baby that included photographs. Kathleen wavered on her adoption plan a few times toward the end of her pregnancy but followed through with her decision to allow the adopting parents to be with the baby immediately after delivery. Her widened support system of her parents, therapist, agency, and birth mother support group was invaluable to her both before and after relinquishment.

As the case above illustrates, Kathleen's experience of the pre-relinquishment period is a typical one in many ways. Her symptoms of depression and anxiety are common. Background factors in Kathleen's life as well as her personal feelings are reflected in the literature's findings regarding her likelihood of making an adoption plan (i.e., her mother preferred that she make an adoption plan, she was a Caucasian teen from a middle-class family, and she did not feel ready for the responsibility of a baby). However, given the pressure and negative judgments that she received from others regarding her choice to relinquish her baby, Kathleen clearly needed structured pre-relinquishment support that could come in the form of therapy, support groups, or other supportive resources. Her therapist provided this adoption-sensitive support (Janus, 1997) for her decision making and assisted Kathleen in three crucial ways: (a) by providing referrals to a support group of other pregnant women making choices about adoption plans and to an adoption agency with a strong and sensitive birth-parent program, (b) by demonstrating competence regarding the issues for relinquishing birth mothers and being nonjudgmental and supportive of Kathleen's decisions, and (c) by creating an atmosphere where Kathleen could prepare for the relinquishment and provide a link (by choosing the adoptive parents and by writing a letter and sharing photographs) for her child following the relinquishment. Adoption specialists report that pre-relinquishment counseling for the prospective birth mother is best for her and may prevent disrupted adoptions. This case study illustrates several aspects of the specific and crucial knowledge for effective therapy during the pre-relinquishment period and is reflective of the points elucidated for adoption-sensitive counselors (Janus, 1997).

Relinquishment Continuum and Coerced Relinquishment

It is important to note that the distinction between voluntary and involuntary relinquishments is actually a continuum rather than a dichotomy. Whereas some parents who sign voluntary relinquishment papers actually feel coerced by loved ones, spouses, parents, or even their culture (i.e., cultural norms against childbearing out of wedlock) to relinquish their children (DeSimone, 1996), other parents who formally have their rights terminated by the court system can be in agreement with that plan. This continuum and the issue of coercion have not been addressed in the birth-parent literature and have only been addressed as an ethical issue more recently in the adoption literature (Post, 1996). Although no literature currently exists that documents this phenomenon, the personal stories and communications of many birth parents coping with relinquishment, particularly birth mothers, strongly support this concept of a continuum. Such a distinction between the legal category of relinquishment (voluntary vs. involuntary) and the emotional experience of the parent(s) dealing with relinquishment (totally voluntary vs. coerced) is important to make in both practice and research.

Involuntary Relinquishment

When parents do not *choose* to relinquish their children voluntarily, the experiences of parents during the pre-relinquishment period differ greatly. Involuntary relinquishment is accompanied by legal processes and court decisions that culminate in a process known as the termination of parental rights (Edelstein, Burge, & Waterman, 2002; Wattenberg, Kelley, & Kim, 2001). Likened to the "death penalty" for parents due to its finality and gravity (Hewett, 1983), the termination of parental rights is a path that leads to distress and a unique and different set of issues for parents who become birth parents.

Prior to relinquishment via the termination of parental rights, parents whose children were removed due to findings of neglect or maltreatment were given visitation rights, and the children entered foster care. But who are these parents who no longer have the legal right to parent their children? Although they have been briefly described in the literature, national statistics on these individuals, developmental histories, and outcomes are difficult to determine (Freundlich, 2002). What is known about these parents are reported reasons for the termination of rights (e.g., mental illness, abusive domestic relationships, substance abuse, limited intellectual functioning, legal problems or incarceration, or inability to maintain stable housing; Wattenberg et al., 2001) and background histories of the women whose rights were terminated (e.g., little formal education, unemployment, abuse, out-of-home placement as children, birth of first child at young ages, children by multiple fathers, chaotic home environments; Wattenberg et al., 2001). Statistics on the numbers of children whose parents have had their rights terminated can be readily accessed (e.g., in 2001, parents of 65,000 children in the United States had their parental rights terminated; Administration for Children and Families, Administration on Children, Youth and Families, Children's Bureau, U.S. Department of Health and Human Services, 2003), but statistics on the actual numbers of parents whose rights were terminated are not available. Despite this lack of reported statistics, recent trends in family preservation supported the rehabilitation of parents who were deemed neglectful or maltreating, and attempts at family reunification are now built into the system (Wattenberg et al., 2001). However, increasing concerns about the length of time spent in foster care without permanency planning incited movement toward legislation that speeds the process of parental rights termination for parents who fail to make substantial progress in their rehabilitation efforts (Festinger & Pratt, 2002).

Also missing from the statistics on these parents whose rights were terminated are data on their racial/ethnic backgrounds. Extrapolating from the available 2001 data (Administration for Children and Families, Administration on Children, Youth and Families, Children's Bureau, U.S. Department of Health and Human Services, 2003) and assuming a similar distribution among children in foster care and their parents, the racial ethnic backgrounds of parents whose rights were terminated may generally fit the following categorization: (a) 2% American Indian non-Hispanic; (b) 1% Asian non-Hispanic; (c) 38% Black non-Hispanic; (d) 17% Hispanic; (e) 37% White; (f) 3% unknown; and (g) 2% two or more races non-Hispanic. However, the racial ethnic distribution of people in the United States reflects very different proportions of racial ethnic minorities, as follows: (a) 75.1% White; (b) 12.3% African American; (c) 13% Hispanic or Latino; (d) 0.9% American Indian non-Hispanic; (e) 3.7% Asian Pacific Islander non-Hispanic; and (f) 5.5% other race (Grieco & Cassidy, 2001). Thus, disparity in the figures between the proportion of racial ethnic minorities in the population and the proportion of racial ethnic minorities whose parental rights were terminated suggests some degree of inequity in several systems that affect involuntary relinquishment. This bias can be attributed to institutions (e.g., the judicial system and children's welfare agencies) and can be a reflection of the system of disadvantage (e.g., racism) and oppression all too commonly found in these institutions. Although these disparate figures may also reflect bias and oppression related to social class, the degree to which social class affects the likelihood of involuntary termination of parental rights is not fully explained in the literature.

A clear determination of the experiences of parents whose rights were terminated is difficult to discern. Research on the impact of rights terminations reflects little attention to the impact of involuntary relinquishment on parents and focuses more on the adoption or placement outcomes for the children. The only research to address outcomes for parents who lost their rights has repeatedly found long-term psychological distress (Freundlich, 2002). Some outcomes commonly found among these parents are (a) ongoing anger and guilt; (b) substantial psychological problems; (c) health problems usually associated with bereavement (e.g., sleep and appetite disruption, dreams about loss and search); and (d) relationship problems (Charlton, Crank, Kansara, & Oliver, 1998; Hughes & Logan, 1993; Mason & Selman, 1997). Other deficits in the research literature and in practice with parents whose rights were involuntarily terminated include the lack of attention to posttermination issues for parents (e.g., no counseling programs after termination of rights). Although a single study was found that discussed group therapy issues for birth parents whose children were in foster care (Charbonneau & Kaplan, 1989), no literature addressed treatment following involuntary relinquishment.

EARLY POST-RELINQUISHMENT PERIOD

During the early post-relinquishment period (defined broadly as the first 2 years following relinquishment), the reported impact of relinquishment on birth parents, but especially birth mothers, varies greatly, depending on their coping skills, support system, and degree of involvement in the adoption plan (e.g., extent to which they chose and met the adoptive parents).

Clinically, birth mothers frequently reported that relinquishment involves a powerful sense of loss and isolation (A. Brodzinsky, 1990) and that these feelings accompany both closed adoptions (i.e., traditional adoptions where no contact or information transfer occurs between birth and adoptive families either before or after placement) and open adoptions (i.e., adoptions where information and/or contact between birth families and adoptive families is shared directly or via a mediator along a continuum of contact) (Zamostny et al., 2003). Birth mothers in more open arrangements may become childlike in their dependence on the adopting parents, only to feel discarded and betrayed by them on the births of their babies. Birth mothers in more traditional, closed arrangements reported more traumatic dreams, sleep disruption, and experiences of surrealism. Physical, hormonal, and relationship changes brought disruption to the birth mothers' lives, yet their hope that they would be able to "get on with their lives" did not reach fruition (A. Brodzinsky, 1990; Sorosky, Baran, & Pannor, 1976).

Three empirical studies were identified that studied birth mothers during the initial period following relinquishment (Cushman, Kalmuss, & Namerow, 1993; Donnelly & Voydanoff, 1996; McLaughlin et al., 1988). The findings indicated a complex combination of differences and similarities in the outcomes between mothers who placed their children for adoption (placers) and those who chose to parent (parenters). There were no differences between the groups in school enrollment at 6 months, high school graduation rate, and perceived quality of life (McLaughlin et al., 1988), and there were no differences in self-reports on SES, religion, depression, and self-efficacy. Both groups reported satisfaction with their decisions 2 years later (Donnelly & Voydanoff, 1996). However, Cushman et al. (1993), in the only multistate sample with interview data, found higher levels of grief at 6 months than at post-partum and the highest levels of grief in birth mothers whose babies went to foster placement prior to adoptive placement. They also reported that 55% of birth mothers found signing the adoption papers to be one of the most difficult parts of the adoption process, and 9% reported that they felt pressure from their agency to sign the papers. At 6 months after they gave birth, 38% of the placer sample reported feeling "a lot" and 27% reported feeling "some" grief. Kalmuss, Namerow, and Bauer (1992), using the same longitudinal data set, found that placers fared somewhat better than parenters on a set of sociodemographic outcomes assessed at 6 months postbirth. However, they also found that even when controlling for preplacement variables, placers were less comfortable with the pregnancy resolution decision than were parenters.

Case Study 1 (Continued)

Course of Treatment: Kathleen found herself alternating between numbness and grief both in the hospital and after returning home. She spent time with her baby girl in the hospital, and her mother took a few photographs of the baby with Kathleen and with her adoptive parents before they left the hospital with their newly adoptive daughter. Others wanted her to "get on with her life," but she sensed that a change had occurred in her that wouldn't go away. She tried to remember details of her baby's birth and the hours after she was born, but she found herself unable to, as is common for birth mothers. Kathleen found that both physical and emotional changes were overwhelming and that her feelings would erupt at unpredictable times.

Effective Treatment Strategies: Kathleen worked with both her therapist and her birth mother support group to express her feelings. She also worked at accepting and owning her decision, getting past blaming others for her circumstances, and becoming able to share her story and defend her decision. Kathleen realized that it was normal to think about her child and discussed her fantasies with her therapist. She learned through continued reading that living with the unknown has been identified by birth parents as the most difficult part to cope with throughout life, and she worked to become more comfortable with this unknown. Kathleen's counselor became more didactic during this period of treatment, teaching her about the stages of grief, and she found comfort in hearing her feelings echoed in the stories of other birth mothers, both in her group and from her therapist's experience.

This case study demonstrates how Kathleen's counselor allowed her to face her grief and also avoid the factors suggested by Roles (1989) to block, delay, or prolong mourning. These factors, which were based on clinical experience, are (a) lack of acknowledgment of the loss by society, family, friends, and professionals; (b) lack of expression of intense feelings; (c) not having a mental image of the baby due to lack of information or never seeing the baby; (d) preoccupation with the fantasy of reunion to avoid dealing with loss; (e) preoccupation with searching for something to fill the gap and to avoid facing painful feelings; (f) belief that having a choice takes away the right to grieve; (g) self-deprecation and self-blame; (h) pressure from others to decide on adoption making ownership of the decision to relinquish difficult; (i) lack of support; (j) numbing through abuse of alcohol or drugs; and (k) maintaining secrecy and not acknowledging the loss to yourself or others. The adoption-sensitive counselor's knowledge about these factors, provision of psychoeducation regarding the grief reactions common for birth parents, and assistance in normalizing her anger, loss, and sadness were crucial in effectively treating Kathleen during the post-relinquishment period (Janus, 1997).

Because relinquishment of one's parental role for one's children is lifelong, counselors must recognize that many of these post-relinquishment reactions can revisit birth parents at any point during their lives. Counselors should also be prepared to address these issues during important transitions in the birth parents' and the adoptee's lives such as birthdays, holidays, Mother's Day, and other events that mark the relationship.

LONG-TERM POST-RELINQUISHMENT

Long-term effects of relinquishment on birth mothers fill the clinical literature, with *long-term* defined broadly (i.e., more than 2 years post-relinquishment). The clinical literature includes many different personal accounts of birth mothers who experience lifelong symptoms of depression, anxiety, and posttrauma (A. Brodzinsky, 1990; Gediman & Brown, 1991; Guttman, 1999; Jones, 2000; Robinson, 2000; Schaefer, 1991). Birth mothers detail ongoing symptoms of grief, isolation, and difficulty setting aside the experience of relinquishment. They describe what Fravel, McRoy, and Grotevant (2000) termed the "psychological presence" of the relinquished child by the birth mother. At the same time, some research found reports of satisfaction with the relinquishment decision and favorable outcomes on some sociodemographic and social psychological outcomes 4 years after giving birth, in addition to continuing grief and loss (Namerow, Kalmuss, & Cushman, 1997).

Clinicians reported that the birth mothers they see in therapy alternate between denial of the relinquishment of their child and feelings of continuing shame, depression, and negative self-image. They felt they carried a serious secret and are unacceptable and unlovable. They reported difficulty attaching to romantic partners and, sometimes, future children. If the birth mother had an open support system, one in which she could honestly communicate, then these intense emotional sequelae were reduced. Those in closed adoptions worried about the safety and lives of their birth children, reported recurring dreams about their children, and wondered more intensely about their children near birthdays and holidays. If they had maintained secrecy, they often feared that others would reject them if the adoption placement were disclosed. Many reported losing their sense of faith and spirituality during this stage.

When viewing both the clinical and research literature on long-term outcomes, it is essential to remember that research has heavily focused on the birth mothers who continue to struggle with the loss of their child for years following the relinquishment. This is likely due to a sample bias in which research participants became participants in the studies because they were already seeking clinical treatment and they were open to and involved in exploring relinquishment. Thus, their preparedness and willingness to address their psychological needs and their adoption exploration may already make them different from those who do not seek treatment and who might not acknowledge their desire to understand their own adoption. No data were found in either the clinical or empirical literature on birth parents that suggested that birth parents cope well with their decision to relinquish, although Namerow et al. (1997) found some positive outcomes on both sociodemographic and social psychological variables.

Empirical studies implied that, at least for a percentage of birth mothers, the experience of relinquishment was a trauma in their lives due to unresolved grief (Carr, 2000; DeSimone, 1996; Deykin, Campbell, & Patti, 1984; Namerow et al., 1997; Rynearson, 1982; Winkler & van Keppel, 1984). Findings indicated a negative impact on future relationships and an increased incidence of secondary infertility (Carr, 2000; Condon, 1986; DeSimone, 1996; Deykin et al., 1984). In fact, even 30 years after relinquishment, birth mothers reported no decrease in feelings of sadness, anger, and guilt and told of ongoing dysfunctional relationships with subsequent children and with men. Birth mothers who were White and in their teens when they relinquished also reported feeling pressured by parents and by social and altruistic ideals to make an adoption plan (Rynearson, 1982). They described (a) dreading delivery, (b) remembering labor as a time of loneliness and painful panic, (c) feeling traumatized by signing the adoption papers, (d) having questions about the future of their children after leaving the hospital, and (e) experiencing recurring traumatic dreams about relinquishment and episodes of seeing strangers with babies and wondering if one was their child. In other research, DeSimone (1996) found that higher grief levels were related to (a) feelings of guilt/shame about the decision to relinquish, (b) the perception of coercion by others into relinquishment, (c) the lack of opportunity to express feelings about the relinquishment, and (d) involvement in searching for the relinquished child. Although grief levels were not related to the lack of social support, lower grief levels were related to high satisfaction with current marriage, more personal achievements, and having gained information about the children since placement. Carr (2000) found that 37% of the 87 birth mother participants had secondary infertility (higher than the national average) and that emotional pain, including grief, was a consistent long-term outcome in each of these studies of birth mothers. In spite of this grief, Namerow et al. (1997) reported that after 4 years postbirth, their longitudinal sample of adolescent placers from maternity homes fared better on external outcomes (e.g., high school graduation, employment outside the home) than did parenters. Moreover, 4 years after making their pregnancy resolution decision, more than 90% of the parenters versus 66% of the placers reported no regret and 3% of the parenters versus 10% of the placers reported high regret. Thus, a more complicated picture emerges as the sample becomes less clinical.

Using a somewhat different outcome measure of "psychological presence of the relinquished child," Fravel et al. (2000) found that the adopted child remained psychologically present for relinquishers both on special occasions and as they went about their daily lives. Fravel et al. discussed these findings as an empirical discrediting of the "happily ever after" myth, in which birth mothers are to forget their children and get on with their lives. The adopted child, in their study, was psychologically present to some degree in every case.

Case Study 2

Presenting Issues: Donna is a 62-year-old African American woman who came to therapy for depression and anxiety.

Background Factors: Donna was raised in an orphanage along with her brother from age 9 because her mother was alcoholic and her father was out of the country in the military. Evidently, this was common practice at that point in history in this locale because Donna knew that others at the orphanage weren't "orphans" either but were brought there due to various family circumstances by their parents. Older boys at the orphanage sexually molested Donna when she was 11 years old and continued to do so until she ran away at age 16. Donna married a 25-year-old when she was 18 and had four children in 5 years. Her husband drank heavily and soon left her. Donna became despondent, unable to support herself or her children, and developed pneumonia. She had no car, no income, and no social services or other social support. A cousin gave her food, which she gave to her children and not herself. She finally sought medical care for herself (she believed she was going to die) and went along with the suggestion of the physician to relinquish her children (ages 3, 2, 1, and newborn) for adoption because she feared they would end up in the orphanage as she had (and she refused to allow that for her children). Donna knew the adoptive families of each of her children and kept track of two of the three silently throughout their lives. The third left the area with his adoptive family when he was a toddler, and Donna always feared they moved to get far away from her. She backed out of relinquishing her youngest child and only daughter before it happened because she was afraid her daughter would be victimized as she had been. Donna married again, adopted another daughter herself through social services, and went on to live a healthy and productive life. However, the sexual abuse and trauma from relinquishing her sons tormented her most of her life, and her psychologist diagnosed her with posttraumatic stress disorder (PTSD).

Assessment Concerns: Donna's insight and judgment appear to be strong despite her experience of multiple traumas. The accumulation of many years since the sexual abuse and the relinquishment have allowed her to feel buffered from their effects, but the PTSD symptoms suggest a 40- to 50-year history of trauma. Furthermore, Donna's tracking of her sons' movements suggests some fixation on the trauma without any apparent resolution to this point.

Treatment Issues: Donna had several major losses that complicated her PTSD issues—the abandonment by her parents, sexual abuse as a child, the abandonment by her husband, poverty and feeling powerless, her illness, the relinquishment of three children, and secrecy. Treatment included attention to Donna's PTSD symptoms and issues but also recognized the close relationship between the losses and trauma. Donna's actions suggested an interest in search and reunion. This required careful planning and support.

Effective Treatment Strategies: Treatment consisted of appropriate protocols for PTSD and special attention to the loss she experienced as a relinquishing birth mother. Donna was extremely harsh on herself for this relinquishment, yet her repetitive reviews of her pre-relinquishment situation always resulted in her reaching the conclusion that relinquishment had been "best" for her sons. She wished, however, that she could have placed them together. Nevertheless, she found it very hard to forgive herself. Her therapist used journaling, photo reviews, bibliotherapy, and psychoeducation as strategies for facing this loss. They also used grief strategies such as writing letters to each of her sons on numerous occasions. Her therapist used her own knowledge of adoptee development to reassure Donna that the vast majority of adoptees do quite well (Zamostny et al., 2003) and gave her reading material on the birth-parent experience (e.g., Jones, 2000) to decrease her feelings of isolation. Donna eventually decided to contact each birth son and established caring relationships with two of them; the third preferred no contact, but she made it clear that she was open to contact should he ever desire it. Her birth sons met her daughter and other family members and continually reassured Donna that they had had good lives and did not harbor resentment toward her. On the suggestion of Donna's therapist, Donna's two birth sons and her daughters entered family therapy for three sessions where family dynamics were addressed via family sculpting and other experiential techniques. Donna's PTSD symptoms diminished (but did not disappear), but even with good treatment and appropriate medication, she continued to find it hard to forgive herself for relinquishing her children. She has, however, improved in her ability to speak about her traumas and has developed a group of supportive friends for the first time in her life.

Donna's case illustrates the lifelong effects that relinquishment can have on a birth mother. However, in Donna's case, her own traumatic history combined with the closed adoptions of her sons created additional stress reactions, grief, loss, intense guilt, and remorse. Donna's psychological treatment was designed to address the multiple layers of trauma she experienced and to begin the grieving and self-forgiveness processes she needed (Janus, 1997). The treatment provided by Donna's psychologist reflects the need to understand the powerful effects that relinquishment can have on birth parents when both diagnosing and treating them. Had the treating psychologist minimized the relinquishment of her three sons, Donna's history of trauma prior to the relinquishment could have been the focus of treatment, with poor overall results. The effective use of techniques such as journaling, bibliotherapy, and letter writing required sensitivity to the grief, loss, guilt, anger, and trauma that often continue for many years following relinquishment. The use of family therapy following the search and reunion helped Donna better understand the role relinquishment had in her family (Reitz & Watson, 1992).

Search and Reunion

Feast, Marwood, Seabrook, and Webb (1994) noted recent increases in birth relatives initiating searches for children relinquished for adoption many years ago, but research has only addressed adoptee-initiated searches. Feast et al. (1994) reported that "some birthmothers [search because they] need to feel reassured that they did the right thing and want to make certain that their child knows they were very much loved and why they were adopted" (p. 9).

Research addressing search and reunions described and categorized the ensuing relationships that do or do not develop between birth parents and their relinquished children. Howe and Feast (2001) surveyed adoptees who were in reunion with their birth parent(s) an average of 10.6 years (63% women, 37% men; 93% in matched White same-race placements, 7% of mixed race and adopted transracially). They found that reunions were characterized by (a) continued contact and positive evaluation (30%), (b) ceased contact and positive evaluation (30%), (c) continued contact and mixed or negative evaluation (30%), and (d) ceased contact and mixed or negative evaluation (10%). Gladstone and Westhues (1998) surveyed 67 Canadian adoptees in reunion (mean age 42.5 years, 81% female, 19% male) and identified seven categories of postreunion relationships that can occur: close (35%), close but not too close (10%), distant (22%), tense (6%), ambivalent (14%), searching (8%), and no contact (6%). Factors found to affect the types of relationships developed included structural factors (geographic distance and time), interactive factors (boundaries of the relationships, adoptive family's support, and birth family's perceived level of responsiveness), motivating factors (sense of involvement or pleasure from contact), and the outlook of birth relatives (close matching on lifestyle, values, and desire regarding intensity of relationship). Feast et al. (1994) noted that "for the most part, though, birth parents are very pleased to see their children again" (p. 104).

Birth Fathers

Birth fathers are underrepresented in both the clinical and the research literature. Perhaps this is because they tend to be less involved in the pregnancy and less involved in the decision to relinquish compared with the birth mother. Perhaps it is because many birth fathers do not see the child prior to relinquishment. Very little clinical literature addresses birth fathers, although it is routine to decry their absence in the literature (Freundlich, 2002; Grotevant, 2003; Zamostny et al., 2003). Only two studies were located that specifically examined birth fathers. Deykin, Patti, and Ryan (1988) surveyed 125 American birth fathers and found that the birth fathers' relationships with the birth mothers often continued beyond the relinquishment—44% of these birth fathers reported marrying the child's birth mother at some point during their lives, and 25% reported that they were currently married to the birth mother. They also reported that the relinquishment had an effect on their relationship with the birth mother: 22% negative, 34% positive, and 44% mixed or none. Most did not see or hold the child prior to relinquishment, and half were not involved in the adoption process. Birth fathers who were older and who identified external pressure as a primary reason behind the adoption were almost five times as likely to be presently opposed to adoption compared with those who cited their unpreparedness for fatherhood or the best interest of the child as a reason for relinquishment.

Similarly, Cicchini (1993) did a study of 30 Australian birth fathers and found that the majority (66%) had no or minimal say in the adoption. Most remember it as "a most distressing experience," and only 17% of the men reported feeling positive about the experience. A majority of the birth fathers in this sample took active steps to locate their child; however, most had not yet had reunions. The most frequently cited reason for searching was to ensure that their child was doing well. The authors concluded that the fathers retained an emotional and psychological feeling of responsibility for the child and challenged prevailing assumptions that birth fathers are irresponsible, uncaring, and uninvolved. Perhaps as the literature expands to include birth fathers, including those who have had contact with their birth children, our understanding of their experiences will increase. In any case, based on the current literature, while birth fathers may seem to be less affected by the relinquishment and adoption of their children than are birth mothers, an accurate assessment of the impact of relinquishment on birth fathers is difficult to determine, given the paucity of empirical investigation with this population.

INTERNATIONAL BIRTH PARENTS

Research on international birth parents is exceptionally limited despite the increased visibility of international adoption in America. The advent of media portrayals of transracial families that adopted internationally (e.g., celebrity international adoptions, print and television commercials, newspaper and magazine articles, Web-based adoption sites), an older population of "waiting parents," increased acceptance of single-parent adoptions, and greater availability of healthy infants internationally have all led to a growing population of adoptive families who have power, influence, financial resources, and a thirst for information about the nations from which their children were adopted. Despite this growing population of internationally adopting families, very little is actually known about the birth parents from these countries. The perception of greater permanency related to non-U.S. relinquishments and the implications of relinquishing children to an entirely different culture are just a few of the issues that arise when considering treating birth parents who have relinquished internationally.

Johnson, Banghan, and Liyao (1998), in their descriptive work on infant abandonment in China, found that almost all the birth parents ($n = 237$) were married and that the abandonments were related to government birth regulations. Relinquishment decisions were most often made by the birth father (50%), although 40% were made by both birth parents. Relinquishing families (88%) came from rural areas, with their primary occupation being agriculture. Reasons given for relinquishment were the children's gender (90% female), health (86% healthy), birth order (82% of females not firstborn; no data on males), and gender composition of siblings (88% of females had no brothers, 93% of females had older sister(s); no data on males). Relinquished male children were those having disabilities and those born to widowed or unwed mothers.

In Korea, 85% of unwed mothers in a maternity home relinquished their children (Dorow, 1999). Freundlich (2001) described the typical Korean birth mother as being very poor, coming from a large family in which she is the youngest, and lacking family and social support.

These data, although very limited, represent the infancy of research on two countries that place children for adoption in the United States. Research on birth parents in many other countries (e.g., Latin America and Eastern Europe) is not yet found in the literature at all. Clearly, research that leads to an increased understanding of international birth parents in many countries needs to be done.

OPENNESS IN ADOPTION FOR BIRTH PARENTS

Over the past 10 years, birth mothers making adoption plans for their children increasingly chose alternatives that included some degree of openness between themselves and the adopting family. Three studies were identified as assessing openness and its effect on birth parents (Christian, McRoy, Grotevant, & Bryant, 1997; Cushman, Kalmuss, & Namerow, 1997; Lauderdale & Boyle, 1994). In their interviews with 12 birth mothers planning open adoption compared with those planning closed adoption, Lauderdale and Boyle (1994) reported that those who planned open adoptions showed more attachment to their fetuses and were more likely to seek support and prenatal care although they experienced more grief in the immediate postadoption period than did mothers with closed adoption plans or bereaved parents. Birth mothers who planned closed adoption reported nonattachment to their fetuses, hid their pregnancies, were less likely to receive prenatal care, and reported more difficulty accepting the loss of the child after relinquishment. Four to 12 years after placing their children in open adoptions, birth mothers having ongoing contact with the adoptive family through either mediated or fully disclosed adoptions showed better resolution of grief than did birth mothers whose contact stopped (Christian et al., 1997). Furthermore, they found that those with fully disclosed adoptions also showed better grief resolution than those who never had contact (confidential adoptions).

In a study of the relationship between openness in adoption and social psychological outcomes for birth mothers, Cushman et al. (1997) interviewed 171 adolescent birth mothers who were maternity home residents at relinquishment and who were reinterviewed 4 years after relinquishment. They found that 69% helped choose the couple who ultimately adopted their babies, 28% met the adoptive couple, 62% had received letters or pictures since the adoption, and 12% had visited or talked on the phone with the adoptive parents since placement. The most notable pattern was the association between helping to choose the adoptive couple prior to relinquishment and positive social psychological outcomes for birth mothers 4 years later. Those who received letters or pictures reported significantly lower levels of worry and slightly higher levels of relief. Having ever visited or talked on the phone after relinquishment was strongly associated with lower levels of grief, regret, and worry, and greater feelings of relief and peace regarding the adoption. Continuing research is needed to assess the specific variants of openness in adoption and their effects on outcomes for birth parents. Early research suggested that open adoption might be a process that decreases the emergence of negative symptoms for birth parents. Given how serious and long term the psychological effects of relinquishment can be, a model that ameliorates these effects is greatly needed.

PRACTICE IMPLICATIONS FOR COUNSELING BIRTH PARENTS

The case studies, the empirical findings regarding the lifelong trauma associated with relinquishment, and the sizable numbers of birth parents who currently exist both in the United States and abroad suggest that helping professionals should be well prepared to counsel birth parents. However, despite the recognition of the impact of relinquishment on birth parents and some identification of who relinquishes, for what reasons, and how that may affect these clients, clinicians have virtually no empirically validated guidelines for practice with birth parents.

Clinical practice with birth parents, therefore, has relied on best practices that were generated from the case studies, theoretical guidelines, and a few treatment programs developed with sensitivity to adoption-related and relinquishment issues. The literature reviewed and the cases analyzed above suggest several techniques and sensitivities to the unique and complex issues that birth parents face when relinquishing either voluntarily or involuntarily.

Janus (1997) proposed the term *adoption-sensitive counseling* and proposed that counselors are in an excellent position to become adoption counseling specialists. A review of the clinical and research literature on birth parents led to the following suggestions for counseling psychologists working with birth parents:

• Adoption-sensitive counselors and psychologists are attuned to their own attitudes and biases about birth parents, including their own feelings about giving birth, raising children, relinquishing children, the openness continuum in adoption, and the concept of an adoption kinship network. They are keenly sensitive to issues of ethics—both professional and adoption-related ethical practices (such as coerced relinquishments) (Post, 1996).

- Adoption-sensitive counselors and psychologists are always conscious of the social and cultural factors involved in the lives of birth parents and in the lives of all adoption triad members (Lee, 2003). These factors include race, culture (including religious and spiritual beliefs), family dynamics, and SES for birth parents and can be expanded to include civil unrest, cultural norms, and legal regulation of family size for international birth parents. Adoption-sensitive counselors and psychologists practice using the American Psychological Association's (2003) multicultural guidelines (www.apa.org) and are aware of all adoptions as multicultural, broadly defined.

- Adoption-sensitive counselors and psychologists are aware of the political and economic aspects of adoption and their effects on birth parents. Zamostny et al. (2003) pointed to the increasing role of commercialization in the adoption process, and these economic forces have a significant impact on birth parents both prior to relinquishment and after. Grotevant (2003) described advocacy groups that are calling for reform within the birth-parent community such as Concerned United Birthparents (2004) and the American Adoption Congress (2004). Counselors must be aware of the wide range of political awareness and activism among birth parents.

- Adoption-sensitive counselors and psychologists are familiar with community and national resources for birth parents, including support groups, agencies that have birth-parent support programs, online resources (e.g., www.kinnect.org, http://forums.adoption .com), reading material, and search assistance. Some birth-parent specialists believe that adoption agency services present an inherent conflict of interest since they are also placing children for adoption. It is incumbent on the counselor to be familiar with agencies in their communities and refer birth parents carefully to services and organizations that will advocate for them.

- Adoption-sensitive counselors and psychologists allow birth parents to experience their loss, without minimizing it. They are aware of the seven core issues of adoption (Silverstein & Kaplan, 1988) and how they affect birth parents as described in the foregoing.

- Adoption-sensitive counselors and psychologists allow birth parents to experience their own resiliency and strength, increase their self-esteem, and plan for their own future. They are aware that not all birth parents share the same experience and that satisfaction with their relinquishment experience may be positive, having led to positive outcomes in their own lives.

- Finally, adoption-sensitive counselors and psychologists are aware of the complexity of each birth parent's story. Grotevant (2003) pointed out that adoption refers to a surprisingly diverse set of family circumstances, which is certainly true for birth parents. To avoid overgeneralizing to this heterogeneous population, counselors and psychologists working with birth parents must respect the individuality of birth parents, regardless of their life circumstances.

Clinically Driven Research: Future Directions

Research has been more limited on birth parents than on other members of the adoption triad (Freundlich, 2002; Zamostny et al., 2003). Empirical research on birth parents would benefit from greater attention to make it both methodologically sound and clinically informed. First, the use of broad nonclinical samples, standardized instruments, process-outcome studies, and individual surveys or interview data with less reliance on retrospective reports and/or self-reports would increase the generalizability of birth-parent research. Because of methodological and sampling problems, much of the existing literature has limitations in its applicability to current-day relinquishing populations, so validity and reliability have suffered. Both short-term and long-term outcome studies can be improved by controlling for age at relinquishment and the pre-relinquishment adjustment level of birth parents, given that the developmental stage and psychological history at relinquishment could affect outcomes.

Birth-parent research would also benefit from greater attention to the complexity of the birth-parent experience. Rather than focus solely on self-reported indices of adjustment, outcomes for birth parents would be more informative if the inclusion of both internal (e.g., measures of grief, depression, self-esteem, coping skills, satisfaction) and external variables (e.g., SES, educational level, income, vocational level) is sought. More detailed and richer depictions of birth parents can also be obtained from the use of advanced statistical analysis to determine the interaction effects of these variables. With greater knowledge of the complexity of the experience of birth parents, more effective treatment interventions, counseling skills, therapeutic techniques, counseling process concerns, and treatment models can be proposed, empirically validated, and implemented in counseling and psychology preparation programs. This research could be built on further by comparing the effectiveness of treatment using adoption-sensitive therapy (via training) versus therapy without adoption training versus some other support or intervention.

Another major area for future research includes the background, clinical, and outcome issues for birth parents of color. A greater understanding of the factors leading to relinquishment for birth parents of color, of the inequities found in the racial ethnic distribution of involuntary relinquishment, of effective treatment strategies for assisting those coping with relinquishment (voluntary or involuntary), and of their post-relinquishment experiences would provide very useful treatment and research information. Furthermore, more research is needed on the experiences of birth parents whose parental rights have been terminated through the legal system.

Reasons for relinquishment by international birth parents also need to be assessed, including poverty, civil unrest, financial incentives, and urban migration. To serve the needs of international birth parents better, the profoundly intricate and often difficult circumstances, factors, treatment issues (e.g., stigma of therapy), and outcomes for international birth parents must be understood. The lifelong effects and outcomes need to be assessed for international birth parents with no less consideration than for domestic birth parents.

An area yet to be explored in the birth-parent literature involves attention to relinquishment coercion as an important variable. Specifically, in both voluntary and involuntary relinquishments, the phenomenological experience of birth parents on the relinquishment continuum (voluntary to coerced) should be considered in the design of future research. Empirical designs that account for this continuum may assist in elucidating possible differential outcomes based on the degree to which the birth parents felt empowered to make their own adoption plan.

More research needs to be conducted assessing both the short- and long-term effects of relinquishment and any subsequent treatment on nonclinical samples of birth parents. Longitudinal cohort studies of both birth mothers and birth fathers, including studies of openness and search, would be powerful additions to the outcome literature. Longitudinal studies of birth parents would also allow clinicians and researchers to make substantial progress in their knowledge of the developmental effects of relinquishing. Developmental issues could also be identified by additional research incorporating health psychology models about stress and pregnancy outcomes (e.g., Rini et al., 1999) that would elucidate the effect of the prenatal experience on both birth mothers and their children. This research would substantially aid our ability to choose or design effective and appropriate treatment models that account for the effects of these various dimensions of development.

Multicultural models must be used in the design and implementation of research with this global population. Models used for understanding oppression, privilege, identity, and awareness of difference experienced by many birth parents can be of assistance when considering the unique life circumstances that lead to relinquishment for birth parents.

CONCLUSION

Both the research and clinical literature reviewed on birth parents have shown that relinquishing a child for adoption is a traumatic experience for many birth parents, in spite of some positive outcomes shown in more recent research. The development of research and practice that explicitly use trauma as a framework for the study of the birth-parent experience could also add to our understanding. Moving beyond a trauma paradigm, however, to incorporate an epidemiological stress and coping model for the study of the birth-parent experience and the incorporation of a multicultural perspective in all research and practice with birth parents would allow counseling psychologists to set a powerful agenda for research and practice in the field of adoption in the 21st century.

REFLECTION QUESTIONS

1. If you could design a pre- and post-relinquishment birth-parent counseling program, what structures, goals, and clinical skills would be advisable for the most positive outcomes?

2. What are other potential issues that birth parents who relinquish to either international or domestic transracial placements might experience? What clinical needs are they likely to report?

3. What similarities and differences are likely to exist between voluntary and involuntary relinquishing parents? What might be additional or unexplored problems for involuntary relinquishers, and how can clinicians help them?

REFERENCES

Administration for Children and Families, Administration on Children, Youth and Families, Children's Bureau, U.S. Department of Health and Human Services. (2003). *The AFCARS report: Preliminary estimates for FY 2001 as of March 2003*. Retrieved August 18, 2006, from the Administration for Children and Families Web site: www.acf.hhs.gov/programs/cb/stats_research/afcars/tar/report8.htm

American Adoption Congress. (2004). *American Adoption Congress: Families rooted in truth*. Retrieved March 10, 2004, from www.americanadoptioncongress.org

American Psychological Association. (2003). Guidelines on multicultural education, training, research, practice, and organizational change for psychologists. *American Psychologist, 58*, 377–402.

Axness, M. W. (2001). When does adoption begin? *Decree, 18*, 8–9.

Barker Foundation. (2004). *The Barker Foundation lifelong services*. Retrieved March 13, 2004, from www.barkerfoundation.org

Brodzinsky, A. (1990). Surrendering an infant for adoption: The birthmother experience. In D. Brodzinsky & M. Schechter (Eds.), *The psychology of adoption*. New York: Oxford University Press.

Brodzinsky, D. M. (1987). Adjustment to adoption: A psychosocial perspective. *Clinical Psychology Review, 7*, 25–47.

Brodzinsky, D. M. (1990). A stress and coping model of adoption adjustment. In D. M. Brodzinsky & M. D. Schechter (Eds.), *The psychology of adoption* (pp. 3–24). New York: Oxford University Press.

Carr, M. J. (2000). Birthmothers and subsequent children: The role of personality traits and attachment history. *Journal of Social Distress and the Homeless, 9,* 339–348.

Center for Family Connections. (2004). *Pre/Post Adoption Consulting Team (PACT) services.* Retrieved March 13, 2004, from www.kinnect.org/services_pact.html

Charbonneau, B., & Kaplan, Z. (1989). Group therapy for birth parents of children in foster care. *Child & Youth Services, 12,* 177–185.

Charlton, L., Crank, M., Kansara, K., & Oliver, C. (1998). *Still screaming: Birth parents compulsorily separated from their children.* Manchester, UK: After Adoption.

Chippindale-Bakker, V., & Foster, L. (1996). Adoption in the 1990s: Sociodemographic determinants of biological parents choosing adoption. *Child Welfare, 75,* 337–355.

Christian, C. L., McRoy, R. G., Grotevant, H. D., & Bryant, C. M. (1997). Grief resolution of birthmothers in confidential, time-limited mediated, ongoing mediated, and fully disclosed adoptions. *Adoption Quarterly, 1,* 35–58.

Cicchini, M. (1993). *The development of responsibility: The experience of birthfathers in adoption.* Mount Lawley, Western Australia, Australia: Adoption Research and Counselling Service.

Cocozzelli, C. (1989). Predicting the decision of biological mothers to retain or relinquish their babies for adoption: Implications for open placement. *Child Welfare, 68,* 33–44.

Concerned United Birthparents. (2004). *What is CUB?* Retrieved March 13, 2004, from www.cubirth parents.org

Condon, J. T. (1986). Psychological disability in women who relinquish a baby for adoption. *Medical Journal of Australia, 144,* 117–119.

Cushman, L. F., Kalmuss, D., & Namerow, P. B. (1993). Placing an infant for adoption: The experiences of young birthmothers. *Social Work, 38,* 264–272.

Cushman, L. F., Kalmuss, D., & Namerow, P. B. (1997). Openness in adoption: Experiences and social psychological outcomes among birth mothers. *Marriage and Family Review, 25,* 7–18.

DeSimone, M. (1996). Birth mother loss: Contributing factors to unresolved grief. *Clinical Social Work Journal, 24,* 65–76.

Deutsch, H. (1945). *The psychology of women: A psychoanalytic interpretation* (Vol. 2). New York: Grune & Stratton.

Deykin, E. Y., Campbell, L., & Patti, P. (1984). The postadoption experience of surrendering parents. *American Journal of Orthopsychiatry, 54,* 271–280.

Deykin, E. Y., Patti, P., & Ryan, J. (1988). Fathers of adopted children: A study of the impact of child surrender of birthfathers. *American Journal of Orthopsychiatry, 58,* 240–248.

Donnelly, B. W., & Voydanoff, P. (1996). Parenting versus placing for adoption. *Family Relations, 45,* 427–443.

Dorow, S. (Ed.). (1999). *I wish for you a beautiful life: Letters from the Korean birth mothers of Ae Ran Won to their children.* St. Paul, MN: Yeong & Yeong.

Dworkin, R. J., Harding, J. T., & Schreiber, N. B. (1993). Parenting or placing: Decision making by pregnant teens. *Youth and Society, 25,* 75–92.

Edelstein, S. B., Burge, D., & Waterman, J. (2002). Older children in preadoptive homes: Issues before termination of parental rights. *Child Welfare, 81,* 101–121.

Feast, J., Marwood, M., Seabrook, S., & Webb, E. (1994). *Preparing for reunion: Experiences from the adoption circle.* London: The Children's Society.

Festinger, T., & Pratt, R. (2002). Speeding adoptions: An evaluation of the effects of judicial continuity. *Social Work Research, 26,* 217–224.

Fravel, D. L., McRoy, R. G., & Grotevant, H. D. (2000). Birthmother perceptions of the psychologically present adopted child: Adoption openness and boundary ambiguity. *Family Relations, 49,* 425–433.

Freundlich, M. (2001, July). *Access to information and reunion in Korean American adoptions: A discussion paper.* Paper presented at the Korean American Adoptee Adoptive Family Network, Seattle, WA.

Freundlich, M. (2002). Adoption research: An assessment of empirical contributions to the advancement of adoption practice. *Journal of Social Distress and the Homeless, 11,* 143–166.

Gediman, J. S., & Brown, L. P. (1991). *Birth bond: Reunions between birth parents and adoptees.* Far Hills, NJ: New Horizon Press.

Gladstone, J., & Westhues, A. (1998). Adoption reunions: A new side to intergenerational family relationships. *Family Relations, 47,* 177–184.

Grieco, E. M., & Cassidy, R. C. (2001). *Overview of race and Hispanic origin: Census 2000 brief* (U.S. Department of Commerce, Economics and Statistics Administration, U.S. Census Bureau). Retrieved March 10, 2004, from www.census.gov/prod/2001pubs/c2kbr01-1.pdf

Grotevant, H. D. (2003). Counseling psychology meets the complex world of adoption. *The Counseling Psychologist, 31,* 753–762.

Guttman, J. (1999). *The gift wrapped in sorrow.* Palm Springs, CA: JMJ.

Herr, K. M. (1989). Adoption vs. parenting decisions among pregnant adolescents. *Adolescence, 24,* 795–799.

Hewett, C. (1983). Defending a termination of parental rights case. In M. Hardin (Ed.), *Foster children in the courts* (pp. 229–263). Boston: Butterworth Legal.

Hollinger, J. H. (1998). *Adoption law and practice: Vol. 1. 1998 Supplement.* New York: Matthew Bender.

Howe, D., & Feast, J. (2001). The long-term outcome of reunions between adult adopted people and their birth mothers. *British Journal of Social Work, 31,* 351–368.

Hughes, B., & Logan, J. (1993). *Birth parents: The hidden dimension.* Manchester, UK: University of Manchester, Department of Social Policy and Social Work.

Janus, N. G. (1997). Adoption counseling as a professional specialty area for counselors. *Journal of Counseling and Development, 75,* 266–274.

Johnson, K., Banghan, H., & Liyao, W. (1998). Infant abandonment and adoption in China [Electronic version]. *Population & Development Review, 24,* 469–510.

Jones, M. B. (2000). *Birthmothers: Women who have relinquished babies for adoption tell their stories.* Chicago: Chicago Review Press.

Jung, C. G. (1989). *Memories, dreams, reflections.* New York: Vintage Books.

Kalmuss, D., Namerow, P. B., & Bauer, U. (1992). Short-term consequences of parenting versus adoption among young unmarried women. *Journal of Marriage and the Family, 54,* 80–90.

Landrine, H., & Klonoff, E. A. (1996). Traditional African-American family practices: Prevalence and correlates. *Western Journal of Black Studies, 20,* 59–62.

Lauderdale, J. L., & Boyle, J. S. (1994). Infant relinquishment through adoption. *Journal of Nursing Scholarship, 26,* 213–217.

Lee, R. M. (2003). The transracial adoption paradox: History, research, and counseling implications of cultural socialization. *The Counseling Psychologist, 31,* 711–734.

Low, J. M., Moely, B. E., & Willis, A. S. (1989). The effects of perceived parental preferences and vocational goals on adoption decisions: Unmarried pregnant adolescents. *Youth and Society, 20,* 342–354.

Maret, S. (1997). *The prenatal person: Frank Lake's maternal-fetal distress syndrome.* Lanham, MD: University Press of America.

Mason, K., & Selman, P. (1997). Birth parents' experiences of contested adoption. *Adoption & Fostering, 21,* 21–28.

McLaughlin, S. D., Pearce, S. E., Manninen, D. L., & Winges, L. D. (1988). To parent or relinquish: Consequences for adolescent mothers. *Social Work, 33,* 320–324.

Melina, C. M., & Melina, L. (1988). The physician's responsibility in adoption: Part I. Caring for the birthmother. *Journal of the American Board of Family Practice, 1,* 50–54.

Namerow, P. B., Kalmuss, D., & Cushman, L. F. (1997). The consequences of placing versus parenting among young unmarried women [Special issue: Families and adoption: Part II]. *Marriage & Family Review, 25,* 175–197.

Post, S. P. (1996). Reflections of adoption ethics. *Cambridge Quarterly of Healthcare Ethics, 5,* 430–439.

Reitz, M., & Watson, K. W. (1992). *Adoption and the family system: Strategies for treatment.* New York: Guilford Press.

Resnick, M. D., Blum, R. W., Bose, J., Smith, M., & Toogood, R. (1990). Characteristics of unmarried adolescent mothers: Determinants of child rearing versus adoption. *American Journal of Orthopsychiatry, 60,* 577–584.

Rini, C., Dunkel-Schetter, C., Wadhwa, P., & Sandman, C. (1999). Psychological adaptation and birth outcomes: The role of personal resources, stress, and sociocultural context in pregnancy. *Health Psychology, 18,* 333–345.

Robinson, E. B. (2000). *Adoption and loss: The hidden grief.* Christies Beach, South Australia, Australia: Clova.

Roles, P. (1989). *Saying goodbye to a baby.* Washington, DC: Child Welfare League of America.

Rynearson, E. K. (1982). Relinquishment and its maternal complications: A preliminary study. *American Journal of Psychiatry, 139,* 338–340.

Sandven, K., & Resnick, M. D. (1990). Informal adoption among black adolescent mothers. *American Journal of Orthopsychiatry, 60,* 210–224.

Schaefer, C. (1991). *The other mother.* New York: Soho Press.

Silverstein, D. N., & Kaplan, S. (1988). Lifelong issues in adoption. In L. Coleman, K. Tilbor, H. Hornby, & C. Boggis (Eds.), *Working with older adoptees: A source book of innovative models* (pp. 45–53). Portland: University of Southern Maine.

Sorosky, A. D., Baran, A., & Pannor, R. (1976). The effects of the sealed record in adoption. *American Journal of Psychiatry, 133,* 900–904.

Spence-Chapin. (2004). *Spence-Chapin post adoption services.* Retrieved March 13, 2004, from www.spence-chapin.org

Steinberg, G., & Hall, B. (2000). *Inside transracial adoption.* Indianapolis, IN: Perspectives Press.

Stolley, K. S. (1993). Statistics on adoption in the United States: The future of children. *Adoption, 3,* 26–42.

Warren, K. C., & Johnson, R. W. (1989). Family environment, affect, ambivalence and decisions about unplanned adolescent pregnancy. *Adolescence, 24,* 505–522.

Wattenberg, E., Kelley, M., & Kim, H. (2001). When the rehabilitation ideal fails: A study of parental rights termination. *Child Welfare, 80,* 405–431.

Weinman, M. L., Robinson, M., Simmons, J. T., Schreiber, N. B., & Stafford, B. (1989). Pregnant teens: Differential pregnancy resolution and treatment implications. *Child Welfare, 68,* 45–55.

Wiley, M. O., & Baden, A. L. (2005). Birth Parents in Adoption: Research, Practice, and Counseling Psychology. *The Counseling Psychologist, 33,* 13–50.

Winkler, R. C., Brown, D. W., van Keppel, M., & Blanchard, A. (1988). *Clinical practice in adoption.* New York: Paragon Press.

Winkler, R. C., & van Keppel, M. (1984). *Relinquishing mothers in adoption: Their long-term adjustment.* Melbourne, Victoria, Australia: Institute of Family Studies.

Zamostny, K. P., O'Brien, K. M., Baden, A., & Wiley, M. O. (2003). The practice of adoption: History, trends, and social context. *The Counseling Psychologist, 31,* 651–678.

Relinquishment as a Critical Variable in the Treatment of Adoptees

28

RONALD J. NYDAM

Calvin Theological Seminary, Grand Rapids, Michigan

Strictly speaking, this chapter is *not* about adoption. If we take adoption in a narrower sense to refer specifically to the formation of a nurturing relationship between a relinquished infant or young child and (new) adoptive parents, then the focus of this chapter is not on the subject of adoption. Rather, the concern of these pages has to do with relinquishment—the break in the primary bond between an infant or child and his or her parents of birth and the manner in which this rupture in first attachments informs and sometimes influences psychological development. The first point to be made here is that relinquishment and adoption are different; each needs its own focus for us to understand adoptive development. To properly appreciate each, they must be carefully separated in theory and language. Furthermore, they are not only judicial moments in time when legal transactions occur with regard to ending parenting with one couple and beginning parenting with another; they are also wisely thought of as lifelong processes of development that inform and sometimes affect each other in a complicated fashion. The early narcissistic injury of relinquishment, if indeed it is that, may set in motion a variety of defenses that adoptees may use to protect themselves (Lifton, 1979, chap. 9)—dynamics that this chapter intends to explore. To the extent that language both explains and hides things from our awareness, it is interesting to note that today relinquishment is subsumed under the term *adoption*. For example, it is sometimes said that "adopted children have problems" when it might better be stated that "relinquished children have problems," bringing light to bear on the real issue at hand for most adoptees, namely, the injury of beginning life by way of separation from one's parents of birth. Accordingly, in this chapter, as awkward as the language may appear, adoptees will always be referenced as *relinquished and adopted* persons.

Historically, in American culture, relinquishment has been accompanied by secrecy, deceit, and shame. It might be said that one of the major problems with the manner in which society has dealt with relinquishment is that relinquishment is related so directly with sexual shame. Unplanned pregnancy has, until recent times, been accompanied by significant guilt about illicit behavior and shame about oneself. For most of the 20th century, the punishment for getting pregnant in Anglo-America was relinquishment, that is, giving "up" the child to adoption. Many birth mothers who relinquished their infants within the closed adoption system of the past 50 to 60 years report that they in fact "surrendered" their children to a social system that demanded relinquishment to avoid the guilt and shame of unplanned pregnancy. Single White mothers were seldom given the opportunity or the family and social support needed to parent their children. Relinquishment was seen as the wisest way to deal with unplanned births. Such "shame-based" decision making served to protect birth mothers (and birth fathers too, although they were seldom seen as participants in anything beyond conception) as well as their families from the stigma of illegitimacy. Accordingly, pregnant young women were "sent away" to maternity homes with names like "The Home of Redeeming Love," which most often fell far short of the meaning of their names (Solinger, 1992). In some instances, pseudonyms were given to these women to maintain secrecy of identity. Birth mothers who resisted signing relinquishment papers were sometimes drugged into doing so. When children were adopted they were given "new" amended birth certificates that (dishonestly) recorded adoptive parents as parents of birth and, in so doing, in some communities removed the ink of judgment, the words "bastard child" stamped on the original birth certificate. The secrets of conception needed to be kept.

Although such behavior may appear unprofessional and unethical today, it must be understood that in a different historical era, these practices were seen as helpful and, therefore, useful things to do. The *stigma* attached to the illicit sexual behavior resulting in pregnancy was so great that secrecy and dishonesty were seen as necessary to avoid the shame of illicit sexual behavior. Within the last 15 to 20 years, the tide has turned with regard to the degree of guilt and shame about sexual behavior in American culture. With regard to domestic adoptions, varying degrees of openness in adoption practice are now the rule. Birth parents make the choices about placement in terms of selecting new parents for their children. Whereas infants and young children were once "put up" for adoption (on railroad crates when the orphan trains of 100 years ago arrived in town), today, adoptive parents are "put up" for adopting in portfolios that birth parents review (Graham & Gray, 1995). Because decisions about relinquishment are no longer primarily shame-based decisions, secrecy and deceit play much less of a role in current adoption practice. Nevertheless, for many adoptees, societal attitudes toward their conceptions have set in motion dynamics that diminish or deny the reality and the importance of the loss of the first two people in their lives. This chapter attends to this: You can't fix a problem if you say it's not there!

NECESSARY MOURNING

Adoptive families are usually formed out of loss. All the triad members may be dealing with the injury of losing people of importance. Birth parents obviously lose their children, which sometimes leads to a paralyzing lifelong grieving for birth mothers who never "get on with their lives." Adoptive parents who have struggled with infertility face very directly the loss of the children-by-birth for whom they wished for several years. Although adoption is *not* a solution to infertility in that a couple remains nonconceptive, adoption does build a family. But it is usually a family of people who are at times grieving, and they are sometimes sad and angry, especially the adoptees themselves.

A case illustration may make the point.

Case Study 1

June sat in my office with photos from a recent trip to Seoul, South Korea. There, at the offices of Holt Children's Services, she met her birth mother and half sister as well as others in her extended birth family. For the first time in 19 years since her relinquishment by parents unable to care for her,

June was held by her weeping birth mother who could not help but express a litany of "I am sorry"s to her in reference to the decision to leave her at an orphanage. As June presented her album of digital photos to me, tears flowed freely, because now that she was back in the United States she missed these people. Two weeks of reunion were not enough. June had come for psychotherapeutic treatment some months before this trip to her homeland, complaining of low-grade depression, a dysthymic condition that had plagued her since leaving for college, which was a break in the good attachment that she had to her adoptive parents. (Another 22-year-old adoptee reported, "I was sad all my life; I just didn't know why.") Once in college, she had felt the freedom to pursue this melancholy more directly, arranging a brief internship assignment in Seoul, hoping to search for her birth family. Her search was successful; reunion was a rich and painful experience.

But what were these tears shed months later in my office? How might we understand them? Do these tears betray a less than healthy relation to her adoptive parents? Are they to be seen as evidence of nostalgic imagination of another life in Korea that should best be forgotten? Simply put, are they healthy or pathologic?

The question of grieving, even prenatally, has been in discussion for some time. The first sound that each of us as human beings ever heard was the sound of our mother's heartbeat, at about 24 weeks of prenatal life. Bonding of the fetus and attachment of the parent is thought by some (Verny, 1981) to occur before birth as the fetus hears the voices of others and responds to both calm and distress. It is argued that the emotional and physical well-being of the mother facilitates attachment to the baby *before* birth as well as after. The question has to do with the capacity of the "fetus-becoming-child" to be an "experiencing self," who would then take note not only of a pleasing environment, but also react to distress and disengagement on the part of the birth mother. At birth and immediately afterward comes the possibility of a significant injury in terms of parental loss, to the degree that a neonate is bonded to heartbeat, voice, and person. The self of the infant is now thought to be in place much earlier in life than previously thought by people such as Mahler, Pine, and Bergman (1975) and Ainsworth and Wittig (1969). Daniel Stern (1985), for example, demonstrates how at as early as 3 days of age infants respond specifically to the scent of their own mother's breast milk (Stern, 1985, p. 39). How might relinquishment at such a tender age affect an infant? Nancy Verrier (1993) refers to this loss as a "primal wound," and even the very young must manage to cohere in the face of such loss. She writes,

> When the natural evolution [of birth mother and fetus bonding] is interrupted by a postnatal separation, the resultant experience of abandonment and loss is indelibly imprinted upon the unconscious mind of these children, causing that which I call the "primal wound." (p. 1.)

Object-relations theorist Donald W. Winnicott (1957) calls this early loss and exchange of parents a certain "muddling" in the intersubjective space between mother and child, a developmental challenge that may be difficult for infants to negotiate. And again, you can't fix a problem if you say it's not there!

A second wave of grieving may occur when cognitive development moves beyond so-called concrete thinking to the capacity to conceptualize. A 3-year-old relinquished and adopted little girl was offered her first understanding of relinquishment when informed by her adoptive mother that she was grown in "another mummy's tummy" and then brought to her adoptive parents and that the other mother's name was Molly. After hearing this thoughtful explanation of her beginnings, she responded simply with, "Mom, Molly is the name of Gramma's horse!" The concept of a birth parent had not yet taken hold at age 3. But soon it would. Around ages 6 or 7 (for girls earlier than boys), relinquished and adopted children begin to figure out their birth stories, asking questions of interest, wanting to know more. Their curiosity is sometimes accompanied by sadness. With international adoptions, where "matching" with adoptive parents is obviously not a reality, curiosity and bewilderment may run higher.

Absorbing one's birth and relinquishment story, a tale sometimes told with moderate anxiety, is challenging, especially when adoptive parents communicate their own possible discomfort with the painful meanings of relinquishment and adoption. If conversation about relinquishment is laden with anxiety because of unresolved grief around infertility or of possible fear of birth parents returning and reclaiming a child, then children learn not to talk about these things, not to ask questions, and not to be innocently curious. And then the emotions of sadness and anger and fear and shame that surround such an important personal and developmental loss may submerge into less-than-conscious depths, outside the awareness of the relinquished child.

In adolescence, more grieving may occur; it often presents itself more as anger than sadness, but usually it has to do with further negotiations with self about loss. In what sometimes looks like an angry protest, a fiery demand that life be different, relinquished and adopted teens may register their struggle with the alternate, but so real, reality of adoption. To the degree that adolescence is about clarifying one's identity (Erikson, 1980), when pieces of the human puzzle of self are missing, there comes an understandable protest against the injustice and unfairness of relinquishment. The difficulty of constructing a clear sense of self is obviously more problematic when many unknowns about birth family, birth history, medical history, and cultural history remain hidden. In today's more open adoptions, certainly less is lost to view in terms of these histories, but losses, nevertheless, remain in terms of both fantasy and quiet attachment to birth parents. At some level, relinquishment exacts a price in the formation of self and, in a corresponding fashion, may elicit more mourning of the losses that occur. Relinquished teens may be lacking in the necessary healthy levels of self-esteem and sturdy sense of self required for continuing development. And "underneath" lingering depression or behavioral protest there may be tears of sadness yet to be cried, the tears that June cried when faced with the reality of parent loss.

With adulthood and its usual challenges, there may be yet another wave of mourning the loss of birth parents when certain experiences trigger grieving yet to be done. Medical histories that are absent or incomplete may remind the adult adoptee once again of both the difficulties and the injustices of relinquishment. With today's more open adoptions, less information and less of relation are lost, so less may need to be grieved, but many in the closed adoption system as well as the newer sizable population of international adoptees face significant lacunae in their medical histories. Some adoptees report that in the act of giving birth they have experienced a surprising wave of grieving the loss of their birth mothers. As aging continues and medical problems develop, relinquished persons are at a real disadvantage. With over 4,000 genetically related conditions existent, many adoptees are at considerable risk of knowing less than is necessary for early detection and adequate treatment of what may be life-threatening disorders. But more directly akin to the experience of mourning may be the exquisite sensitivity to rejection, what might be called "relinquishment sensitivity," that adoptees sometimes face in the context of intimate relationships. For example, one 41-year-old client, relinquished and adopted at birth, found increasing difficulty maintaining closeness to his wife, especially when a new attraction turned his head toward a much younger colleague. In the course of his own psychotherapy, he came to the painful realization that he was truly seeking the love of his life that he had lost, some 40 years ago, the birth mother of his fantasies and dreams. With tears that had been carefully repressed for so many years, he cried, "Why didn't she love me?" in a therapeutic moment of the dawning of awareness of his grief.

Mourning the loss of loved ones, even ones lost at birth, may be one of the most important developmental challenges that relinquished persons face. It may be a lifelong echo, a song of sadness and irritation that needs careful management for an adoptee to become a healthy individual. Again, you can't fix a problem if you say it's not there. Up until the present time North American society has carefully hidden the injury of relinquishment from careful review. One thoughtful adult adoptee, after clarifying her own grief about the loss of her birth parents (who she searched for and found), made this comment: "I love my adoption, but I hate my relinquishment!" Because she was able to see the injury of losing her birth parents, she was able to grieve their loss. Teasing relinquishment and adoption apart from each other, and helping relinquished and adopted persons grieve the losses of relinquishment, helps them become well.

COMPLICATED IDENTITY

Personal identity, one's inner sense of self, is initially a fluid psychological construct that solidifies with time and experience in a manner such that persons come to some clarity about the "me" that they have come to be. Identity formation is an ongoing process of self-definition and self-presentation that has to do with the ebb and flow of many variables, some that are relatively constant and some that are always changing. Relinquishment at birth, or as a young child, affects identity formation in a variety of ways. First of all, an adoptee must usually draw on four psychic representations of parents, not two, because indeed there are at least four people involved in the story of relinquishment and adoption. (When single parents adopt, the number is three.) Early adoption theorist Paul Brinich (1980) writes,

> Every child uses a combination of personal experiences, cultural materials, and constitutional givens to create mental representations of himself and of people around him. These mental representations are organized into a "representational world" used by the child to predict the outcome of his interactions with people and with his world. Thus, the child's mental representations of himself and others influence his object relationships. The adopted child must include two sets of parents within his representational world. He must also integrate into his representation of himself the fact that he was born to one set of parents but has been raised by another set of parents. (p. 108)

An adoptee's sense of self develops out of this "split-life" experience of living betwixt and between what may be two different families, sometimes quite unknown to each other.

Identity formation usually has to do with the internalizations of primary caregivers that flow from attachment to those persons. For example, consider the delightful comment of the 3-year-old in Osh Kosh B'Gosh overalls who startled his father with an opened quart of oil held sideways in his hands. As he observed his father changing oil in an old Ford Maverick, he reported with great confidence, "I want to be an oilman like you, Dad." We develop our sense of self by taking in the qualities and values and styles of those to whom we are most deeply attached in early development. For adoptees, it is sometimes the case that this is an especially difficult task.

Although identity formation may become a primary task in adolescence, as Erik Erikson (who learned at age 16 that he was adopted by his father . . . and renamed himself the son of himself) suggests (1980), the development of identity is an ongoing constructive process from the earliest days of life. A sense of belonging to parents is foundational for a sense of self. Some adoptees report that belonging has been a nearly lifelong struggle and that, within their adoptive families, they never experienced themselves fully as one of the family. When awareness dawns that there are other parents, "ghost parents," who are both real and unreal in the experience of the child, then identity formation becomes more challenging. Relinquishment impinges as adoptees are usually left without the necessary building blocks of identity, especially when information is legally locked away in closed adoption files, or when relinquishment occurs in other countries where no records are available, or when infants are left at police stations or fire stations without record of parents. (In the past few years, nearly all the states in the United States have passed legislation in support of baby abandonment laws, which allow such practice.) How does one construct a sense of self when pieces of the puzzle of self are simply missing?

Constructing an identity is, for some adoptees, as much a matter of inventing oneself from creative imagination as of deep internalizations from caregivers. It should be no wonder that over the past several decades adolescent adoptees have been overrepresented in clinical populations (Fullerton, Goodrich, & Berman, 1986; Senior & Hamadi, 1985; Simon & Senturia, 1966; Tec, 1967; Toussieng, 1962; Weiss, 1985). They are often registering their angry protest against the injustices of relinquishment and its unfortunate results, specifically in terms of not knowing their birth parents and not knowing about them. Again, with today's more open domestic adoptions, the losses of personal relation and birth parent information may be lessening, but nevertheless the loss of closeness to birth parents extracts a price. (Identity formation is more difficult for the relinquished child. It is heartening to note that adoptees are *not* overrepresented in adult clinical populations, wherein the percentage of adoptees is exactly consistent with their presence in the general population, namely, an incidence of 2% [Brinich & Brinich, 1982].) Adoptees' struggles with identity in adolescence are best interpreted as an understandable reaction to one of the overwhelming challenges of their development.

However, adoptees not only often face gaps in their own birth narratives and birth parent history but also sometimes deal with information they do have or hold in fantasy that is negative. Brinich (1980) writes,

> The tragedies, inabilities, and failures of both the biological and the adoptive parents are reflected in the adopted child and his psychological development. For the "realities" of the adult world mean little to the young child; the sudden death of loving biological parents may be experienced as a malicious abandonment; his adoptive parents may tell him that he is "chosen," but he may choose to believe he was stolen. No matter how often the adopted child is told that his adoptive parents are now his "real" parents, he may never completely ignore his first parents and the fact that they gave him up. (p. 107)

This "twoness" of adoption is a fundamental reality that informs the way in which adoptees experience and think of themselves. For example, one relinquished and adopted adolescent who knew something of her beginnings reported in treatment that "I am just a broken condom," giving voice to a negative sense of self as a child of accident of time, not intended, an unwished-for child, only optional at best. This negative internalization served to guide her own self-abusive behavior in word and in deed. When relinquished adolescents reflect on their birth parents in fantasy they sometimes create negative images of these abandoning figures—greasy-spoon waitresses, even prostitutes on unknown streets—in some attempt to explain to themselves why relinquishment or even termination of parental rights occurred. When such tragic fantasies are held in mind and heart by adoptees, their sense of self, their foundational identity, is experienced painfully. For example, one teenage adoptee took to the streets, rejecting the care and resources of his adoptive parents, smoking marijuana, and living with friends on the fly. In conversation about these choices, images came to mind of his own birth parents, wondering if that's exactly where and how they lived. When such negative, broken pictures of birth parents play a role in identity formation, it should be no wonder that constructing a positive identity with good self-regard becomes a difficult challenge. When, intentionally or inadvertently, birth parents are described by others in negative terms within the earshot of adoptees, those comments may serve in the unfortunate construction of a poor sense of self, a less-than-worthy human being. Again, relinquishment has its price.

As Brodzinsky, Schechter, and Henig (1992) suggest, "All adoptees engage in a search process" (p. 79), if only in their minds. Every adoptee does something with the reality of "ghost parents" out there somewhere. Efforts at search and reunion with one's birth parents within the closed or international adoption systems were at one time seen as indicative of poor attachment to one's adoptive parents, as if to suggest that were these parental connections stronger there would be no need for such curiosity. This is thought about differently today. For example, in the case of June, although search and reunion in Seoul led to tears of sadness with regard to loss, she also achieved something useful in terms of identity. She knew more about "who she was." Her sense of "me" became more clearly defined. Adoptees consistently report that they feel "more complete" when reunion occurs, even if the reunion is a conflicted experience. They relate that as their curiosity about their birth narratives is satisfied, and the puzzle of their identities is better resolved, they have a stronger sense of who they are.

Identity is of interest in that once one's self-definition is firmly in place, it can be more or less "forgotten" as matters of intimacy, of empathic closeness to others, come to the fore. With one's identity established, the focus of living usually turns to others things, especially relationships. (Consider Erikson's stage development from "identity vs. role confusion" to "intimacy vs. isolation" [Erikson, 1980].) Unselfconsciousness might be seen as a mark of human maturity. However, with a sense of self not firmly in place, nagging self-doubt and insecurity may leave an adoptee more fearful of intimacy and less capable of the empathy that is the bedrock of healthy human relations. Accordingly, relinquished persons, whose identities may have been, in part, kept from them, or internalized with negative value, or else held in fantasy, may be at risk in terms of adequate self-definition. Naming, for example, is a very important concern for many adoptees. A Korean American adoptee named "Elizabeth Chin Chin" is given the opportunity to claim both parts of her international identity—more adequate self-definition. There's so much in a name!

COMPROMISED BONDING AND LIMITED ATTACHMENT

There is a part of every adoptee that can never be adopted. This has to do with what is forever connected to birth parents, namely one's genetic line and blueprint, one's birth narrative, one's birth culture, and what some might call one's spiritual bond (Nydam, 1999) with one's birth family. Accordingly, these losses from the experience of relinquishment of necessity compromise adoption, if by adoption we intend comprehensive substitute parenting. In this sense, adoption can never be complete. There is always a part of an adoptee that is connected in some way to his or her primal family; this is the "twoness," the split-life nature of adoptive experience.

Strictly speaking, *bonding* is the term used to describe what a child does initially in forming a relationship with caregivers, and *attachment* is the term used to describe the activity of parents in connecting to their children—hence the phrase "bonding and attachment." Today, *attachment* usually refers to the relationship between child and caregiver including both directions of care. In this mix of relational negotiations, adoptees sometime face a particular difficulty. The Catch-22 of adoptive development has to do with the manner in which managing the narcissistic injury of such loss and abandonment, even prenatally or at birth, may make comprehensive bonding to adoptive parents a formidable task. If relinquishment, as this chapter argues, is a primal wound to be reckoned with, then the infant's first environment is experienced as arbitrary, as less than trustworthy. The psychic energy needed to facilitate connection to (new) adoptive parents may be tied up in defense against further loss, less available for the needed nurture of parental affection. The heart of the adoptee, bruised by relinquishment, may not be entirely available for the emotional attachment that adoptive parents may very much seek to offer. That is to say, the disruption of relinquishment may result in a child's being less available to the very care needed for maturation. Put differently, the mirroring of adoptive parents that serves as the fuel for emotional development may not be readily accessible to the relinquished child; it may be constricted, compromised, by narcissistic injury and fear of further abandonment. The child, even at an early age, may be too fearful to take the risk of closeness. If the early experience of a child's world is less than trustworthy, that child's capacity for connection may then be compromised in such a way that adoptive parents may never be able to reach the heart of their adopted child with the care they offer. The Catch-22 is that adoptive parent care, so necessary for healthy emotional development, may not be sufficiently accessed by the relinquished child. As a result, the emotional strength needed to become a healthy person—needed to *do* the grieving of parent loss and the construction of identity—may be in short supply. How much adoptive parents adopt a child may be one question; how much the child adopts the adoptive parents may be another.

It is interesting to note that the beginnings of attachment theory are first presented in the work of theorists like Renè Spitz (1946), John Bowlby (1969, 1973, 1980), and Donald W. Winnicott (1957), who observed young children who had been separated early in life from their parents by incarceration or by the ravages of World War II (Karen, 1994). The settings for their observations, the clinics outside London, where children managing loss were housed, are not unlike many of the orphanages found today in Eastern Europe, where children lose their parents for other reasons. Children adopted from these countries (e.g., Russia, Ukraine, Romania) may demonstrate behaviors quite consistent with those described by these early attachment theorists.

Case Study 2

Lilly, for example, came to the United States at age 20 months, adopted by parents who had made the required visit to the orphanage and then appeared in Russian court, assuring the judge that she would not be sold. Whenever she was stressed, Lilly would bang her head against the wall, creating significant anxiety in her newly adoptive parents. This head-banging behavior is associated with significant neglect in early life; it serves the purpose of psychic cohesion through the experience of pain. In the orphanage, Lilly had to somehow manage the neglect and isolation and discovered this pain-inducing behavior to be useful in terms of warding off the agony of abandonment. Her adoptive parents worked to hold her close and rub her head whenever she started banging it against a chair or a wall. The behavior subsided in about 6 months, after which bonding with her adoptive parents was able to occur.

Lilly's presentation, like that of many adoptees from difficult circumstances, exists on the right end of a continuum of attachment described by Bowlby (1969, pp. 27–28) as secure attachment on one end with anxious attachment or detachment (disengagement) at the other. The critical questions along this continuum with regard to maturational progress have to do with the depth of injury that an infant or child endures in relinquishment or abandonment and the manner in which the child negotiates the suffering resulting from these injuries.

When the intensity of suffering moves beyond a certain threshold, "psychic nerves" may be cut to avoid fragmentation. An infant or child can only protest so long (as Bowlby suggests) before new psychological defenses are arranged to cohere mentally. (Here may be the beginnings of characterological formation.) Anxious attachment or detachment inevitably results if adequate relations with a caregiver are not restored. For example, behavior described as "indiscriminate friendliness" is sometimes observed in children for whom the losses and neglect and possible abuse have been too much to manage. Such children may appear playful and well-adjusted at first view, but it is quickly noticed that they behave so with anyone and everyone, exhibiting no significant attachment to another person. They have learned to survive by operating more than by bonding to any caregiver.

Case Study 3

A very distraught adoptive mother called to report her deep frustration with a newly adopted Chinese daughter. At 3 months of age, this infant had been retrieved from China by her adoptive parents. Now, after 3 weeks of time together, this child continued to be inconsolable, crying constantly, arching her back when the adoptive mother tried to bring comfort. At such a young age, this was a powerful protest against the new arrangement in her life, and this was a form of resistance to these parents' care. The mother was advised to partially unclothe and gently hold her naked child, skin to skin, for 20 minutes at least 3 times a day. Five days later in another phone conversion this mother reported, with tears in her eyes, the good news that the child was beginning to bond, allowing herself to be held in times of distress. This infant had negotiated the transition to new parents enough to seek security in the arms of a new mother, a very critical first step toward healthy development. The injury of her relinquishment was becoming more manageable.

But what if the injury was too massive to manage? What if this child had been adopted a year later? What if, in addition to parent loss, neglect and abuse had been a significant part of the story? Further along on the continuum of limited attachment, this child may have become of necessity less available for the care of parental attachment, less available for the very nurturance needed to become a person (the Catch-22 of adoptive development). Expressions of affection may, at times, not "get through" to the heart of the child. Efforts at cognitive treatment later in life may have little effect. In such cases, parents are left with few resources beyond structure and behavior influence by reward and consequence to assist a child in taking the risk of vulnerability to form an attachment. They may of necessity default to very firm regiments of care, whereby they learn to be both clever and objective in the interventions that they create to promote bonding and manage oppositional behavior (Gray, 2002; Hughes, 1998, 2000; Keck, 1998). Otherwise, at times, adoptive parents may be held hostage by the acting-out impulses of relinquished and unattached children, a very difficult challenge for parents to endure.

With relinquished children who are adequately bonded to adoptive parents, this closeness becomes the necessary emotional supply for healthy development. They are then equipped to face the challenges of adoptive development. They can seek comfort in the midst of their necessary mourning; they can construct a sense of self bolstered by adequate self-esteem; they can enjoy the pleasure of this critical connection, the vital foundation for intimate relations in their future. All this is to say that adoption can go well; families formed out of the losses of relinquishment or abandonment and the possible tragedy of infertility can be the sources of nurture that facilitate growth and maturation, *if* they are families that honestly address the given realities of relinquishment.

PATTERNS OF INTIMACY

Probably no other emotional phenomenon demonstrates so clearly the profound impact of relinquishment on adoptees as the experience of *genetic attraction*. This relatively unknown and puzzling sexual impulse (of which clinicians and adoption specialists must be aware) often occurs in the midst of reunion with sought-after birth parents or birth children or birth siblings (Lifton, 1994, chap. 15). At first called *genetic sexual attraction*, this is a reference to the eroticization of the newly experienced connection between birth parents and birth children or between birth siblings, whereby strong feelings of sexual attraction emerge out of reunion. Those involved are often blindsided by this incestuous impulse and understandably frightened by the wish for a sexual relationship with their own mother or father, son or daughter, brother or sister. It is an emotional tempest that usually subsides after the excitement of reunion has abated, but nevertheless it is powerful and puzzling and a challenge to manage. But genetic attraction also testifies to the reality and psychic significance of connection to one's birth parents. Relinquishment of a child inhibits (disallows the development of) the "incest taboo" common in human experience. In search and successful reunion, along with the "discovery" of long-lost parents, children, or siblings, may come this powerful sexual interest. What may have been repressed, put away from consciousness, blocked from awareness now erupts into profound hunger for that lost person. This experience may begin with looking, then staring at one's birth mother, attending to common physical features, then touching, holding hands, and walking arm in arm; and then a sexual wish emerges. Yet it is not so much about sexual experience as it is about primal connection to someone lost. One telling comment by a birth mother who erotically kissed her birth son and narrowly avoided intercourse with him was this: "Yes, I wanted to have sex with him but I also wanted to count his fingers and his toes." The point to be made with regard to genetic attraction is that relinquishment turns development on its head and, when reunion occurs, the wrong of relinquishment is temporarily righted in a powerful cry for deep connection.

If the impingements of relinquishment are adequately managed in terms of mourning, identity formation, and bonding in the first years of adoptive life, then the challenge of creating and sustaining intimacy in adult life may proceed in good fashion. If children are relinquished and adopted at a later age, these challenges are more significant and at times overwhelming because later breaks in attachment or, worse, a series of breaks in attachment may disallow trust in the formation of new relationships. (Much of the earlier research on adoption outcomes did not attend to the age at which relinquishment and adoption occurred.) Understandably, for some adoptees, dealing with one's relinquishment in an ongoing way may be the organizing principle around which adoptees arrange their relationships of love. When this is the case, a variety of patterns of relating may develop.

Some who are relinquished and adopted may make the less-than-conscious choice to be alone, to avoid intimate relations, to carefully manage the possibility of being rejected again. The safety of being alone then carries the price of isolation, usually experienced with some sadness. Other adoptees who are more bruised by relinquishment or abandonment and/or abuse may be indifferent to the need for closeness to another human being. For these persons, life is more about survival than it is about connection. These were the relinquished and adopted children for whom their adoptive parents were never able to connect to their hearts—hearts damaged and hidden by too much human suffering. And for them, the need to stay distant from their adoptive parents plays itself out in the need to stay distant from others as adults.

Usually, however, the human spirit seeks its own healing by responding to suffering by living within the tension between psychological defense and relational risk. Inevitably, this dance of relating leads to intrapsychic struggle and interpersonal conflict, but it may also open the way to the restoration of the relinquished and adopted self. Sometimes, powerfully so in adolescence, physical intimacy is taken for love and connection. Skin-to-skin warmth is experienced as opposite to the coldness of parent loss and, at least for the moment, satisfies the human need for deep connection to another. As relinquishment interferes with the most powerful of human relations, the bonding of a child and the attachment of its mother to the child, it is understandable that correctives to this disruption may take on their own fierce intensity, especially in terms of sexual experience. The wish to restore the lost relationship may overpower and overshadow a more informed, careful approach to intimacy.

Case Study 4

Leslie, for example, a 22-year-old adoptee (adopted at 3 months of age), entered psychotherapeutic treatment to learn ways to manage her romantic relationships. She reported a series of short-term very physical relationships, which she found to be both important and meaningless at the very same time. Efforts at search and reunion had succeeded in locating and meeting both of her birth parents but without their sincere interest in her. She felt the subtle sting of a "second rejection" from both and, more alone than ever, she found physical intimacy a useful antidote to the inner emptiness of not being wanted. The men in her life, in her own words, "want me." Only when this interpretation opened the way to more grieving did her sexual behavior change. Relinquishment has its price in relationships.

Another pattern of relating that adoptees sometimes choose is that of arranging a relationship around concerns for security. Again, if dealing with relinquishment serves as a guiding principle in relating, one way to make one's life successful is to guarantee one's safety, secure from being relinquished again. One method to accomplish this is to relate from a posture of control. In so doing, that is by choosing a passive, adaptive partner and being very much in charge of the relationship, an adoptee can gain a sense of security, free from the fear of rejection. Whereas in his or her relinquishment an adoptee obviously has no say, in relating in a controlling fashion, an adoptee has all the say. Passion is sacrificed for safety, as being married to a "pet rock," but the value of security is paramount. An opposite approach with the same goal of security is that of arranging relationships wherein one is very much controlled, the passive, adaptive partner, the "pet rock," who carefully adapts, never creating conflict, so as to be assured of the safety of acceptance. Reminiscent of the "good adoptee" who keeps his or her true self carefully hidden, but self-assured that one will not be relinquished again, this method of relating sacrifices real passion for a sense of security, leaving the adoptee without a true voice in the relationship. The tragedy of these safety-net approaches to intimate relationships is that real and unguarded closeness is never achieved. To the degree that awareness of these dynamics dawns in the mind and heart of the adoptee, low-grade depression or mild anxiety may be the price that is paid.

The most dramatic presentation, however, of relinquishment-guided relationships occurs when adoptees less than consciously recapitulate their early-in-life relinquishments by recreating them in the context of romantic love. This scenario sets the stage for conflict in an intimate relationship of the adult adoptee in such a way that adversarial behavior rises to the point where the relationship becomes impossible for one's partner to tolerate and a second rejection results. The "primal wound" of the adoptee is then reexperienced in the context of one's current relationship, bringing the adoptee "back to the scene of the crime" for further review and possible repair. But the compulsion to repeat the injury of relinquishment seldom accomplishes healing, and more human suffering results.

Case Study 5

Anne, a stunningly beautiful 22-year-old adoptee, had the regular attention of many of her college co-eds, although courtships rarely lasted very long, despite her best efforts to be loving. After some reflection about failed attempts at sustaining intimacy, she noticed her own attempts to sabotage these relationships, and then added the words, "I know that they will reject me, so I give them a reason to." The cloud of relinquishment sometimes casts a long shadow over love.

FANTASY RESOLUTION

Although the current practice of more open adoption may mitigate some of the need to fantasize about one's birth parents, as more of the "picture" of them may be known and experienced in visitation and ongoing relating, it is nevertheless the case that adoptees sometimes struggle to feel "fully real" because of the unknowns about themselves set in place by relinquishment. Adoptees in more open adoption arrangements still wonder about their birth parents and birth siblings—what they are doing, whom they love, what they are like. These gaps in knowing and relating become a complicating variable because the construction of a self, a personal identity as discussed above, can only be built on the foundation of reality, on a real assessment of human experience. In this sense, even bad news is good news because it is real news. Adoptees need to know their stories. (Although this chapter focuses on clinical practice and therapeutic benefit and does not attend to the ethics of adoption practice, at some point, it ought to be noted that adoptees have a civil human right to their stories. No other citizens have such unjust restraining orders against them without crime.) Depending on the degree to which adoptees must invent themselves, as opposed to discovering themselves, there remains a lingering sense of unreality. Imagine hearing an ethnic joke without known reference to your own ethnic identity and "inventing" your laughter, pretending hilarity to be part of a group. This simple illustration demonstrates the "unreality" of adoptive experience that must somehow be managed. Relinquishment has its price in terms of lived reality.

Adoptees within the closed adoption system report an unusually rich fantasy life, a world of imagination that they are seldom asked about (Nydam, 1994). Fantasies about birth parents range from the very positive, even glorified images of royal birth parent splendor, to very negative images of prostitute birth mothers and one-night-stand sailor birth fathers who always leave. Many adoptees report fantasies of rescue wherein a birth parent returns to reclaim the once lost birth child/adoptee. One relinquished and adopted adult remembers the following as a child:

> We had a summer cabin up north and I always fantasized about being able to stay there (at the cabin) by myself and live in Wisconsin because I, for some reason [*take note*], felt that was where this person, this perfect person, was going to drive down the street and take me away.

This fantasy of rescue may have served the purpose of keeping the adoptee connected to his or her birth parents, that is to say, kept them alive in fantasy so as to keep the relationship in place despite the estrangement of relinquishment. In Winnicottian object-relations terms, these birth parent fantasies may serve as transitional objects that assist the adoptee in transitioning from the one reality of birth story to the other reality of adoptive existence (Nydam, 1994; Sugarman & Jaffee, 1989; Winnicott, 1971). But they are stuck in place precisely because the real presence of the missing object (the parent) is needed on occasion to facilitate movement out of intersubjective space into clear visions of one's given reality. The missing objects—birth parents—remain missing, so progress toward a more focused reality is interrupted. In this sense, adoptees are stuck in time in a way that does not allow for further self-construction as far as one's self relates to being relinquished.

Without full grounding in reality, relinquished and adopted persons are left to fend in life without a complete sense of self. Not knowing one's whole story leaves an adoptee at a disadvantage, not only in terms of grieving and identity and intimacy concerns but also in terms of a foundational sense of being real. It should be no wonder that adoptees who experience reunion with birth parents make comments like, "Finally, I feel real as a human being." Accordingly, the more that is known about birth parents and birth family, the less that is left to fantasy, the greater the chance for the adoptee to make successful adjustments in his or her own reality as a human being with a full sense of self. Even when the real "news" about birth parents is sad or tragic, even when they are finally met by touching the cold granite of a gravestone, the truth about these important people can set the adoptee free. One adoptee reported the painful disappointment of finally meeting his birth mother in a state hospital, a schizophrenic woman who showed no recognition of him or his story. As painful as it was, he stated that he finally had his truth, a truth with which he could live. Other stories are less dramatic. Another adoptee, age 29, finally boarded an airplane to visit his birth mother and birth siblings. As pleased as he was to meet them, he expressed sincere disappointment that "they all listened to Rush Limbaugh!" In this regard they were not "like him." Time and different adoptive circumstances had had their way. Nevertheless, he was pleased to know his story and his first family. He was able now to more clearly define himself. Again, even bad news is good news because it is real news. To whatever degree fantasy can be resolved into reality—through curious inquiry, open conversations with adoptive parents, efforts at search and reunion—the adoptee stands on firmer ground, because this gives him or her the opportunity to develop a stronger sense of self as comprehensively real. In so doing, the impingements of relinquishment are mitigated by a new reality. We all need our truths to be truly free.

IMPLICATIONS FOR PARENTS OF ADOPTEES

All parents of a relinquished and adopted child will respond with greater wisdom and empathy to that child if they more deeply appreciate the challenges of adoptive development. If, simply stated, parenting is about being a resource to one's children in a way that maximizes development, then both birth and adoptive parents have much to contribute to the lives of their children. As said in the outline of this chapter, this begins with adoptees' parents understanding the necessity and the importance of grieving. Birth parents are called on, as difficult as it may be, to acknowledge the injury that adoptees sustain in relinquishment. Certainly, there is a resiliency in the human spirit that helps us face the pain of loss, but the loss must be addressed and grieved in some way. For some birth parents, this means moving beyond personal guilt and corresponding shame to an empathic stretch toward the heart of the relinquished child. They may choose not to parent, but they may not choose not to care. As they attend to their own experience of loss, they can become people who appreciate the grief of their children. Care from birth parents takes the form of interest in the child, acknowledging birthdays and holidays if allowed to do so, regular reporting on health concerns so that medical history is continuously updated, and patience with birth children as they clarify their relinquished and adoptive experience. Adoptive parents will parent well to the degree that they understand their children. Parenting by guessing as to what a child is facing is much less effective than parenting with confidence because one knows what a child may be communicating by his or her behavior. For adoptive parents who have dealt with infertility, that grief must, to some degree, be behind them, otherwise it will negatively affect their attachment to an adopted child. Adoption is not a solution to infertility; no adoptee can ever replace a wished-for child-by-birth. Nor is it fair to the adoptee to be asked to make such an effort. Part of effective adoptive parenting is at times helping a child be sad, to touch the heart of an infant or child grieving relinquishment.

With regard to identity formation as well as the challenges of fantasy resolution, all parents of a relinquished child need to play their roles in helping the adoptee become a self-defined person. Birth parents do well to provide their own personal and medical histories and stories, as well as the specific birth and relinquishment narrative that informs adoptees of their own stories. Even if one's history has significant suffering in it, these building blocks of identity are to be honored and explained so that adoptees can ground their identities in truth and reality. Adoptive parents are challenged to acknowledge birth narratives honestly. (Adoption specialists no longer tell adoptive parents that a child's birth parents were killed in a car accident.) Furthermore, adoptive parents assist in a child's positive maturation by honoring the reality and the voice of birth parents by initiating conversations about them and concern for them. Denying their reality, "making believe" as it were that they do not exist, or casting them in a negative light (e.g., years ago adoptees were called children of "bad seed"), sets adoptees up for lifelong struggles with healthy self-regard. All parents of adoptees can assist in providing a solid foundation for adoptive development by bringing truth to the conversation in a caring way and empathically appreciating how an adoptee must draw on all four parents to construct a solid identity.

Finally, with regard to the importance of strong attachments, all the parents of adoptees can contribute to their strength in sustaining intimacy with others by acknowledging the difficulties in doing so. Birth parents can be seen as partners in the formation of families who support the efforts of adoptive parents for attachment. For example, one birth mother wrote her son a note in response to his interest in her style of discipline, and she said, "Carl, if you lived with me you would have to do your homework too!" That simple acknowledgment sent Carl on his way to stronger connection with his adoptive parents. Birth parents who are honest with themselves about their issues with trust (sometimes in a society that punished them for illicit sex) can ironically be empowered to lend a supportive ear to the struggles adoptees face in trusting the family they live within. Adoptive parents who appreciate the Catch-22 of adoptive development can assist their children in the formation of attachment to them, first of all, by understanding their fears of closeness, by providing the security of structure in family life, and by learning methods that build relationships with sometimes fearful relinquished and adopted children. It is at times a struggle to find the hearts of their children; understanding the inner experience of their children can guide them toward useful approaches to care.

BEST CLINICAL PRACTICES

Adopted children are first of all relinquished. Specialists in adoption counseling and practice will, first of all, take care not to collude with societal interest in denying the reality and the impingements of relinquishment. When children lose their parents, at whatever age, good clinical practice dictates that this loss be acknowledged and reviewed in a careful fashion. As stated before, to treat a problem one must first acknowledge its reality.

1. Interpret intrapsychic and interpersonal difficulties that an adoptee might present in the light of the necessary mourning of early losses in life. The process of grieving includes not only the tears of sadness but also the fist of anger and the wince of fear, all part of coming to terms with loss and facing an uncertain future.

2. Solicit information along with all its emotional weight with regard to an adoptee's birth parents and birth narrative as well as past and present fantasies about these birth parents and birth stories. Asking questions about birth parents and the birth narrative is *not* to be thought of as "leading the client." Conversely, not bringing these figures into review is colluding with societal denial of painful reality, which only serves to heighten the difficulties of adoptive development.

3. Consider struggles with bonding and attachment as *normal* responses to parent loss (as well as possible neglect and abuse). This means avoiding pathologizing adoptees in terms of attachment disorders until a clearer picture of emotional relating takes shape. (Relinquishment itself must be seen, to some degree, as the behavior of [pathological] shame-based decisions in society. Systemically, adoptees are not to be seen and treated as scapegoats for societal anxiety about sexual behavior.)

4. Observe problematic patterns of intimate relating for adoptees in the light of central struggles with the ongoing impact of relinquishment on development. To whatever degree relational difficulties in adult adoptee life emerge, they may best be understood by way of reference not so much to adoptive parent relations as to birth parent relations, that is, seeking the lost objects.

CLOSING COMMENT

Adoption must be honest, attending to all the verities of what life is like when one begins with one set of parents and is raised by another. Certainly, relinquishment is the "dark side of adoption," needing to be balanced by the positive value of creating families for relinquished children. From a clinical perspective, however, it is expedient, in contrast to recent societal practices of secrecy and deceit, to see the challenges of adoptive development in the light of daytime reality. Places that are dark keep fear alive and inhibit the necessary trust that is critical to strong, healthy human relations for adoptees. This chapter is very partial; it has only examined the relationship between adoptees and their birth parents, paying special attention to the event and ongoing implications of being relinquished. It has *not* taken note of the very important role that bonding to adoptive parents plays in adoptive development. Further research needs to be done to carefully examine the manner in which relinquishment informs and affects the bonding relationships adoptees create with their adoptive parents. In such inquiry, clinicians and adoption specialists may gain a new and deeper appreciation for the hard work that adoptees do in becoming persons.

REFLECTION QUESTIONS

1. How has managing the societal stigma of adoption informed adoption philosophy and affected adoption practice in the past 100 years?

2. What are some of the difficulties in accurately assessing the experience of the infant or young child in terms of parent loss?

3. How might the historical societal instruction that "relinquishment does not matter" affect adoptive development?

4. What is involved in developing the strength to sustain intimacy in human relationships?

REFERENCES

Ainsworth, M. D. S., & Wittig, B. (1969). Attachment and exploratory behavior in one-year-olds in a stranger situation. In B. M. Foss (Ed.), *Determinants of infant behavior*. New York: Wiley.

Bowlby, J. (1969). *Attachment*. New York: Basic Books.

Bowlby, J. (1973). *Separation: Anxiety and fear*. New York: Basic Books.

Bowlby, J. (1980). *Loss: Sadness, and depression (attachment and loss)*. New York: Basic Books.

Brinich, P. M. (1980). Some potential effects of adoption on self and object representations. *Psychoanalytic Study of the Child, 35*, 107–133.

Brinich, P. M., & Brinich, E. (1982). Adoption and adaption. *Journal of Nervous and Mental Diseases, 170*(8), 147–165.

Brodzinsky, D. M., Schechter, M. D., & Henig, R. M. (1992). *Being adopted: The lifelong search for self*. New York: Doubleday.

Erikson, E. H. (1980). *Identity and the life cycle*. Scranton, PA: W. W. Norton.

Fullerton, C. S., Goodrich, W., & Berman, L. B. (1986). Adoption predicts psychiatric resistances in hospitalized adolescents. *Journal of the American Academy of Child Psychiatry, 25*(4), 542–551.

Graham, J., & Gray, E. (Producers and Directors). (1995). *The orphan trains*. New York: PBS Home Video.

Gray, D. D. (2002). *Attaching in adoption*. Indianapolis, IN: Perspectives Press.

Hughes, D. A. (1998). *Building the bonds of attachment: Awakening love in deeply troubled children: A guide for parents and professionals*. Lanham, MD: Jason Aronson.

Hughes, D. A. (2000). *Facilitating developmental attachment: The road to emotional recovery and behavioral change in foster and adopted children*. Lanham, MD: Jason Aronson.

Keck, G. C., & Kupecky, R. M. (1998). *Adopting the hurt child: Hope for adoptive families with special needs kids.* Colorado Springs: Navpress.

Karen, R. (1994). *Becoming attached: First relationships and how they shape our capacity to love.* Oxford: Oxford University Press.

Lifton, B. J. (1979). *Lost and found: The adoption experience.* New York: Harper & Row.

Lifton, B. J. (1994). *Journey of the adopted self: A quest for wholeness.* New York: Basic Books.

Mahler, M., Pine, F., & Bergman, A. (1975). *The psychological birth of the human infant.* New York: Basic Books.

Nydam, R. J. (1994). *Hope and fantasy in the lives of searching adopted adults: A qualitative study.* Doctoral dissertation, University of Denver and the Iliff School of Theology, UMI Dissertation Services, Ann Arbor, Michigan. (UMI No. 9429764)

Nydam, R. J. (1999). *Adoptees come of age: Living within two families.* Louisville, KY: Westminster Press.

Senior, N., & Hamadi, E. (1985). Emotionally disturbed, adopted, inpatient adolescents. *Child Psychiatry and Human Development, 15*(3), 189–197.

Simon, N. M., & Senturia, A. G. (1966). Adoption and psychiatric illness. *American Journal of Psychiatry, 122,* 858–868.

Solinger, R. (1992). *Wake up little Suzie.* New York: Routledge, Chapman, & Hall.

Spitz, R. A. (1946). Anaclitic depression: An inquiry into the genesis of psychiatric conditions in early childhood. *Psychoanalytic Study of the Child, 2,* 313–342.

Stern, D. N. (1985). *The interpersonal world of the human infant.* New York: Basic Books.

Sugarman, A., & Jaffee, L. S. (1989). A developmental line of transitional phenomena. In M.G. Fromm & B. L. Smith (Eds.), *Facilitating environment: Clinical applications of Winnicott's theory* (pp. 88–129). Madison, CT: International Universities Press.

Tec, L. (1967). The adopted child's adaptation to adolescence. *Journal of Orthopsychiatry, 37,* 402.

Toussieng, R. W. (1962). Thoughts regarding the difficulties in adopted children. *Child Welfare, 41,* 59–71.

Verny, T. (1981). *The secret life of the unborn child.* New York: Bantam Books.

Verrier, N. (1993). *The primal wound: Understanding the adopted child.* Baltimore: Gateway Press.

Weiss, A. (1985). Symptomology of adopted and non-adopted adolescents in a psychiatric hospital. *Adolescence, 20*(8), 763–764.

Winnicott, D. W. (1957). Two adopted children. In *The child and the outside world: Studies in developing relationships.* London: Tavistock.

Winnicott, D. W. (1971). Transitional objects and transitional phenomena. In *Playing and reality.* New York: Basic Books.

Psychoanalytic Understanding and Treatment of the Adoptee

29

CHRISTOPHER DEEG

Independent Practice, Dix Hills, New York

Historically, the adopted person has always been faced with a lifelong dilemma. The adoptee is the central figure in a triad, enveloped within various social strictures, customs, and legal structures that deny a historical and psychological reality—namely, connection to the biological parent. Social and legal attempts to sever the connection of adoptee to biological parent have ostensibly striven to ensure that the machinery of adoption is functional; nonetheless, they portend the underlying negative collective attitudes toward the biological parents and, by extension, the adoptee (Feigelman & Silverman, 1986).

Given the prevailing moralistic sexual attitudes, the institution of adoption has attempted to "protect" the adoptee from the perceived prurience of the biological mother, who is typically unwed. On a deeper level, the practice of permanently separating adoptee from biological parent and legally ensuring that this schism is never forded—by sealing adoption records and falsifying identifying information such as the adoptee's original name—appears to betray a shared perception and fear of the lifelong connection between adoptee and biological parent (Lifton, 1994).

THE ADOPTEE'S CATHEXIS OF THE LOST OBJECT

More recent literature on the psychological challenges to the adoptee (Colarusso, 1987; Lifton, 1994; Verrier, 1993) more explicitly identifies the relationship of adoptee to biological parent as a central feature of the adoptee's experience. In previous contributions to this subject (Deeg, 1989, 1990, 1991, 2002), I have proposed a psychoanalytic model for representing the inner world and experience of the adoptee. In short, the connection or cathexis of the biological parent representation to the adoptee is the central feature of this model. The question of the origin of the representation challenges the rigors of psychoanalytic theory as well as common sense. How does an individual develop an internal representation without external extrauterine experience? From a drive model perspective, the object is first cathected for a number of reasons: (1) because of its direct drive-gratifying function; (2) because once it is gradually internalized, it provides temporary gratification when the environment fails to do so; and (3) because it directs the organism back to the external source of gratification. Following initial cathexis, libido can be withdrawn from a particular object and become available for new attachments (Greenberg & Mitchell, 1983). This second process corresponds to Freud's description (1923) of the ego as the aggregate of abandoned object cathexes.

Most object relations theories posit the object as an inherent aspect of drive from the start. Either there are no drives without objects or the drives are inherently object directed and only secondarily libidinal or aggressive (Fairbairn, 1952). Klein (1932) posited inborn, inherent universal "phantasies" of objects, a concept that has been challenged by modern paradigms of cognitive development and in the present discussion is too general to adequately account for the specificity of the adoptee's fantasy of the biological parent and its related affect.

I proposed that the biological parent is an amalgam of both forerunners of drive derivatives, possibly originating during the uterine period, and displaced or projected aspects of the adoptive parents (Deeg, 1989). In this model, the biological mother enjoys a physiologically elite relationship with her fetus by virtue of the prepatterned "eurthymy" of the neonate's responses to the mother's vocal and physiological sounds and overall biological presence. The "prepatterning" would therefore occur in utero and create a prepsychological bond and "dialogue" between neonate and mother. Research findings, such as those of DeCasper and Fifer (1980) and Stern (1985), in which neonates were able to recognize the voices of their biological mothers are not contradictory to this supposition. In psychoanalytic terms, the biological mother may be in a superior position to provide the newborn with drive-neutralizing, auxiliary ego functions necessary for its survival and growth.

This physiological "advantage" does not ensure optimal symbiosis, nor does its absence—in the case of a competent and empathic adoptive parent—denote certain pathology. It does, however, imply that the bond between biological mother and infant predates, at least as a forerunner, the surrender of the infant for adoption. The surrender, then, registers a loss, a disruption, even if this is "experienced" prepsychologically, by virtue of an interference with physiological forerunners of enteroceptive and proprioceptive perception. In short, this model supports the view that the adoptee, in some manner, records the experience of surrender as a loss, and thus it provides a theoretical underpinning for many other works on adoption that describe the adoptee as having suffered a trauma.

Early work on adoption typically focused on perduring negative or traumatic effects for the adoptee (Barnes, 1953; Hodges, 1984; Schechter, 1960). More recent literature (Lifton, 1988, 1994) has detailed the journey of the adoptee vis-à-vis the "trace" of the biological parent. In the model that I have proposed, the connection of the adoptee to the biological parent is.given a definite historical referent. Even under optimal conditions, the adoptee's surrender is registered as disruptive, since the cathexis of the biological parent essentially begins in utero. Trauma, in psychoanalytic terms, refers to an event that overwhelms the ego's ability to manage the flood of instinctual cathexis in response to a stimulus. From this perspective, the adoptee's surrender can be understood as traumatic, and the adoptee's inner connection to the "lost object" (Deeg, 1989) would be presumed to exist in every case.

The adoptee's cathexis of the biological parent evolves, as do all internalized object relations, under the influence of psychological maturation and interpersonal and environmental events. The relation of adoptee to biological parent is conceptualized in traditional object relational terms (i.e., as consisting of a self representation and an object representation, and an affective link between the two) (Kernberg, 1976). A multiplicity of adopted self/biological parent units can be conceptualized corresponding to the various fantasy and thematic materials that the adoptee presents. Since the original "layer" of the representation is thought to be developmentally primitive, splitting mechanisms typically regulate the quality of these early representations. Thus, an "all-good" biological parent is linked to an "all-good" adoptive self representation and obversely, an "all-bad" self representation is linked to an "all-bad" object representation. Since the surrender of the adoptee has been registered within as a structural forerunner, the earliest representations of the mother and the corresponding self are often imbued with aggression.

One of the earliest psychological challenges for the adoptee is to contain the aggression attached to the biological parent representation so that the corresponding self representation is preserved and separation is supported (Deeg, 1989). Splitting mechanisms corresponding to nascent ego processes (Jacobson, 1964) are mobilized to facilitate this process. The adoptee's earliest internal representation of her relation to the biological parent then consists of groupings of good objects and self representations kept separate from bad objects and self representations. As aggressive drive derivatives are contained or metabolized, further integration of internalized object relations become possible, that is, an all-good object representation can be "related to" a bad self representation and vice versa. Certain fantasies are commonly observed during treatment that illustrate and textualize the adoptee's struggle with this relationship.

The biological parent can be presented as an evil or negligent abandoner of the vulnerable adopted self. In the obverse of this fantasy, the idealized, potentially all-giving biological parent abandons the hated, deformed, or worthless adopted self. Both fantasies are based on splitting mechanisms; they are not mutually exclusive and can, in fact, be seen to oscillate within the clinical material. Their emergence is not restricted to the therapy of adoptees with borderline personality organization. Often, an adoptee with more traditionally neurotic adaptation splits off this particular object relation, thereby removing it from the realm of integration and maturation within which the remainder of the personality functions.

An adult adoptee with a severely strained marriage and a highly ambivalent relationship with his adoptive mother, but generally positive relations with others, initially reported only a vague emptiness when he thought of his biological mother. Eventually, his associations revealed that he imagined her to be narcissistic, cold, and completely unable to love him or anyone else. He appeared to transfer this fantasy to his adoptive mother and wife but not to the men in his life or to women with whom he enjoyed less intimate relationships.

Another fantasy predicated on the idealization of the biological parent presents the all-good birth mother as a *lost* object, with whom reunion promises the ineffable fulfillment that is only gleaned through merger with a perfect other. In treatment, intensely negative connections to the biological parent representation are more heavily defended and often kept from consciousness. Often, an underlying wish for reunion can be detected even within fantasies of a dreaded birth mother.

A preadolescent adoptee reported a story and caveat that particularly terrified him despite his age-appropriate awareness that there were no ghosts or monsters living in his house. He reported with great trepidation that his friends had told him that if he stood in his bathroom and said the name "Bloody Mary" three times, a ghostly woman would appear in the mirror and demand to know the location of her lost baby. He would only spell the moniker and was too frightened to actually utter it.

DEFENSIVE FUNCTIONS OF THE INTERNALIZED RELATION BETWEEN ADOPTED SELF AND BIOLOGICAL PARENT

The internalized relationship between adoptive self and biological parent is a dynamic factor within the personality and is both influenced by, and a determinant of, the adoptee's development (Deeg, 1990). Although beyond the scope of the current exposition, I have previously detailed some of the possible ways in which the connection to the biological parent is used as a defensive function for the adoptee. In general, the object relation is used to maintain psychic equilibrium: Objectionable impulses are warded off, or missing gratifications are provided in fantasy. Six defensive functions that I have described earlier are the biological parent representation as (1) a receptacle for warded-off negative aspects of the adoptive parents, (2) a primitive narcissistic regulator, (3) a fantasy source of libidinal gratification, (4) a defense against (conscious) disruptive aggressive discharge toward the adoptive parents, (5) a defense against disruptive libidinal discharge toward the adoptive parents, and (6) a means of masochistic defense. In general, the biological parent either is projected or displaced onto difficult aspects of the adoptive parents or substitutes for absent gratifications in the environment. In the former function, the biological parent representation becomes more defined and, through projective/introjective processes, acquires content. In either case, the need of the adoptee for increased form and content in the sphere of the biological parent is emphasized.

An adolescent adoptee described his fantasized biological mother as warm, nurturing, and possessing the ability to quell his anxiety. He experienced his adoptive mother as relatively cold and unaffectionate. Analysis of this latter fantasy suggested that when he was younger, the adoptive mother was better able to "fit" with him physically and thereby provide less ambivalent affection and warmth. The fantasy of the biological parent contained the lost contact with the adoptive mother. Obversely, the exaggerated portrayal of the adoptive mother as "cold as ice" was a projection of a defended representation of a depriving biological mother who cruelly had left her infant and had abandoned a baby defenseless to the elements.

As the internal biological parent imago becomes layered with nonmetabolized, idealized, and devalued aspects of the adoptive parents, the adoptive self also evolves and becomes more "knowable" by virtue of increased content. This idea is brought into relief when one conceives the concept of "identity" as always involving the relationship of internalized "selves" to objects. The overall experience of a continuous, relatively seamless "self-feeling" is based on the gradual intrapsychic separation and differentiation of self and object representations, initially through the process of splitting. Eventually, these representations are reintegrated into larger, more inclusive, depersonalized self and object representations. This lends to one's overall feelings about one's place among other people. In general, an overall but not exclusively positive or libidinal cathexis of the representations helps to support this cognitive/emotional process. Kernberg (1976), borrowing from Erikson (1950), designated the product of this process "ego identity."

The splitting off, disassociation, disavowal, or repression of the biological parent/adoptive self dyadic representation, even in cases where overall object relations and ego functioning are not severely impaired, interferes with the consolidation of identity (Deeg, 1991). The central significance of the issue of identity and identity consolidation in exploring the experience of the adoptee is generally obvious in treatment work with adoptees. The questions "Who is my mother?" and "Who am I?" are critical in the psychotherapy of adoptees (Hodges, 1984). This can be explained from the vantage point of the centrality of the underlying cathexis of the biological parent (Deeg, 1991).

From an object relational perspective, questions pertaining to personal identity are always in relation to object representations. "Who am I?" is thus reframed as "Who am I in relation to whom?" The experience of identity is therefore not uniform across relationships. Nonadopted patients frequently report feeling a regressive shift in their identity as adults when visiting a parent. A patient may report, "I always feel like I'm a little kid again when I stay with my mother." For the adoptee, the relation to the biological parent is often the least integrated sector of personal identity. Since external experience with this figure has been prevented, typical drive-neutralizing, affective, and cognitive maturational processes do not have an opportunity to bring this relation into the evolved level of maturity and adaptation of the rest of the personality. The adoptee's focus on the issue of identity can also be seen as a feature of the adaptational pull to correct this disunity.

THE ADOPTEE IN PSYCHOANALYTIC THERAPY

The adoptee brings to treatment a specific dynamic that represents all the vicissitudes and iterations that having an internal relation with biological parents with whom one has had little or no extrauterine contact engenders. This circumstance requires a clinical sensitivity to specific treatment configurations that arise under these conditions. This, however, is not a substitute for diagnosis. The adoptee's ego functioning, general quality of internalized object relations, and degree of adaptation still require study and some attempt at initial formulation. The relationship of diagnosis to treatment is somewhat theory bound, but in classical psychoanalytic therapy, generally, parameters of technique (Eissler, 1953) that modify one's emphasis, and perhaps therapeutic goal, are determined by one's conception of the patient's functioning. It is not enough to identify a patient as "adopted," nor can this fact be ignored. The adoption of the patient can be seen as vital idiographic data; the question of the patient's diagnosis, however, remains.

By first addressing diagnosis, the issue of technique in treating the adoptee raises questions such as "Are the conflicts generally neurotic within the context of generally stable good inner object relations?" and "Is the adoptee's personality organization borderline?" and "Has reality testing been permanently impaired or merely compromised as a result of ongoing external crisis or intersystemic conflict?" (Deeg, 2002). Second, the therapist must attend to the specific manifestation of the issue of adoption as it unfurls within the treatment matrix. In my view, the leitmotif of the adoptee's experience—namely, the relation of adopted self to biological parent—will be displayed both within and outside of the transference. The issue of identity and the particular ambiguity regarding inner and outer reality (as expressed by Hodges's [1984] report of two central questions of the adoptee, viz., "Who am I?" and "Who is my mother?") are brought into relief by both technical adjustment and emphasis—a point to which I will return below.

One is immediately confronted with countertransferential difficulties. As with any patient who is "identified" with a prominent idiographic issue, in this case adoption, one must remain open to allowing therapeutic attention to evenly drift into areas that may not be a part of these narratives. Derrida's (1974) notion of "interiority" is relevant here. Material that does not appear to be derivative of the adoption can be seen as secondary, not as relevant, or "exterior" and therefore given reduced therapeutic concentration. This is particularly likely in cases where a patient seeks treatment with a therapist who is known to have expertise in the area of adoption. A tacit collusion can evolve in which the patient is "adopted" as "special" because of his or her adoptive status by an idealized adoptive parent/therapist. Conversely, the therapist's unacknowledged narcissistic or dependency needs can be gratified by a patient who specifically sought the therapist out for his or her specific prowess. If the collusive fantasy comes into analytic focus, the patient may experience re-abandonment, while the therapist may worry that he or she has been emotionally unavailable or unnecessarily depriving (Deeg, 2002).

The fact of the patient's adoption can be seen as vitally important and uniquely relevant idiographic information that will place the treatment in a specific context and increase the likelihood of specific dynamic configurations. This approach does not, however, demand a radical departure, either in diagnosis or in treatment, from broad ego psychological or object relational parameters.

The Binary Transference

The very existence, let alone its analysis, of transference in the treatment setting is confusing. The patient's reality testing is challenged by the interpretation that feelings experienced as connected to one person are also reflections of currently nonexperienced feelings for a person from the past. Transference interpretation is an immediate assault on the patient's construction of reality that provides the means for the ultimate acquisition of increased insight and for an opportunity to experience and work through in vivo conflicts. Part of the analytic work consists of a reconstruction of the patient's reality testing with an improved differentiation between inner and outer reality.

For the adoptee in treatment, the situation is strikingly complex. The adoptee's transference to the therapist typically consists of affects connected to both sets of parents. The existence of two sets of internalized parental representations (in addition to attendant self representations) creates a transference situation that ranges from multilayered amalgams of biological/adoptive parental representations to chaotically undifferentiated representations, where differentiation between biological and adoptive is largely absent.

To some extent, "complete" differentiation of the biological from the adoptive parent representation is impossible; the biological parent representation is already an amalgam of prepsychological forerunners of affect, fantasy contents, *and* aspects of the adoptive parents that have been incorporated through the defenses noted above (Deeg, 2002). In cases where the relationship with the adoptive parents is ongoing, the representation of the adoptive parent that emerges in treatment can be checked against current experience. Questions about the past can be asked, and narratives can be gathered. Ultimately, some degree of differentiation can be achieved. The analyst in effect offers this observation:

> The image of your adoptive parent appears to differ from the way you currently experience him or her, or is quite different from the information you now have about your childhood. It is possible that your image is at least in part, a reflection of your feelings about the image you have of your biological parent.

The analysis of the binary transference inevitably brings to the fore the real limitation that adoption, particularly closed adoption, has for the adopted patient. The nonadopted patient can legitimately ask, "Which parent from my past do these particular set of feelings appear to identify, on the basis of my recollection of that parent's personality and behavior?" (Deeg, 2002). Furthermore, an ongoing relationship with the parent or someone who knew the parent permits further cross-checking and exploration. In the typical adoptive case, the analysis of transference brings into relief the absence of these avenues of interaction; the adoptee is once again faced with the presence of a relationship to a mother and father who are absent in the everyday world. Sometimes, this exploration may serve as an impetus for a search for the biological parent. Regardless, the unfolding of the binary transference confronts the adoptee with real loss and is typically met with any of a full spectrum of affect and affect-infused object relational derivatives.

> A female adolescent adoptee in treatment continually complained about the excessive regulations imposed on her by her adoptive mother whom she regarded as distrustful, rigid, and repressive. The patient frequently referred to her as "not my real mother." She described a preferred mother who was more physically attractive than her adoptive mother (the patient herself was quite attractive), tolerant, and able to weather the patient's desire for increased contact with her male peers. The adoptive mother in consultation revealed considerable anxiety that the patient would become sexually active and impregnated or afflicted with venereal disease. These fears appeared to have originated as reactions to the daughter's evolving feminine beauty and sexuality, and represented compromise formations that suppressed her own sexual conflicts as expressed by the fear and wish that the patient would emulate her birth mother's sexual history. Earlier in the life of the patient, the adoptive mother seemed less anxious and less conflicted in her emotional and tactile interchanges with her daughter. The likelihood, therefore, was that the fantasy of the desired mother was based in part on actual childhood experiences with the adoptive mother, and on a cathexis of intrauterine forerunners. The therapeutic work then focused on the patient's gamut of reactions and defenses to her recognition that this ambiguity could not be fully resolved, and the resulting feeling that another bit of full adult access and privilege had been denied to her. (Deeg, 2002, p. 197)

As the adoptee encounters a more complex and ambiguous lost object both within and beyond the treatment setting, the wish for reunion with and love from an idealized birth parent, as represented by the attainment of actual knowledge or reunion, becomes frustrated. In nonadoptive cases, the patient often experiences the pleasure of experiencing a renewed relationship with a parent following transference exploration or the satisfaction of acquiring the ability to experience an old memory differently. The patient's increased tolerance for ambiguity is often suggested as a central element in these new experiences. Without actual knowledge, or eidetic memory of the birth parent, the adoptee's representation of the lost object retains an impermeable degree of ambiguity and tentativeness. This outcome, despite the best of attempts to discern the adoptive from the biological parents, illuminates the real loss and permanent disadvantage that is inherently part of being adopted. The provision of empathy in working with this situation, along with the working through of the transference, is critical.

On occasions where treatment is permitted to run a long-term course and is not abbreviated, evidence of displacement from the adoptive parent onto the representation of the biological parent can be discerned. It is here that the various "defensive mechanisms" that use the adoptee's cathexis of the biological parent (Deeg, 1990) are typically clarified. The portrait of the adoptive parent may reflect warded off, fantasized elements of the biological parent, or more often, the "content" of the biological parent representation may represent projected or displaced aspects of the adoptive parent. As reconstruction of the adoptive parent proceeds, the various "borrowed" aspects of the adoptee's fantasy of the biological parent may become less nebulous and more available. Initially, the displacement satisfied two needs at once: (1) the relationship to the adoptive parent was protected by sanitizing the representation's undesirable aspects and (2) the representation of the biological parent acquired real, although often negative, content. That the adoptee unconsciously prefers negative content to a contentless, inchoate, shadowy figure is the typical clinical situation.

An adult male adoptee was surprised by the nurturing and supportive portrait of his adoptive mother that emerged in his treatment. He had perceived her as "off in her own world" and indifferent to his needs and sensibilities. This perception screened an early childhood fantasy of his biological mother as a self-absorbed, although talented and attractive, woman who had been circumstantially unable to love him and with whom he had symbolically sought reunion in the various relationships he endured with emotionally unavailable women. This insight enabled him to experience less ambivalent loving feelings for his adoptive mother. (Deeg, 2002)

As will be discussed below, the revelation of this mechanism does not reverse the trend of accruing content and making the biological parent more discernable. The therapeutic goal is to increase the availability of numerous, well-developed, and affectively enriched fantasies, thus enabling the adoptee to enjoy a widening laterality of emotional discharge and enlivened interchange with the biological parent representation.

The ambiguity that is confronted in the treatment through the emergence of the binary transference extends to the question of identity. For the nonadoptee, real eidetic and visceral memories of self interacting with the birth parent reference, imbue, and demarcate the self representation with cognitively and affectively processed content. In many ways, the absence of the birth parent in memory signals an experience of the absence of self. Therapeutic focus on the reflection of the adopted self and birth parent in the here and now of current exchanges between patient and therapist and patient and contemporaries can provide some succor to the patient who feels condemned to bear a permanently nebulous self representation under the shadow of a lost birth parent. The analyst must declare to the patient,

Although you cannot see yourself through memories of interaction with your birth mother, let us not focus on the revelation of your self vis-à-vis others and here with me.

Let us also encounter you in deciphering your fantasies of the birth mother you wish for, and the birth mother you dread. (Deeg, 2002, p. 198)

The self representation in toto of the adoptee is under construction, as it would be in any analysis. The absence of early experience with the birth parent, or the denial of access to information about the birth parents, and all vicissitudes of loss that accompany these facts, are recognized and empathized with by the therapist but not accepted as an impermeable block to full identity consolidation. The therapist brings to the adoptive patient the message that "the uniqueness and completeness of your self can be reclaimed in our work here."

If the adoptive self is retrievable, what of the biological parent representation? In attempting to differentiate birth mother from adoptive mother, the adoptee often reveals a tacit metapsychological bias: that the "self" of the self-object dyad is present and evident, while the object is only represented or signified. The adoptee's analyst may share in this bias as well by perceiving that the lost maternal or paternal biological object is not as available to reformulation and reconstruction as the adopted self; the *object* may then, more or less, be left out of the treatment endeavor. This bias probably derives from the traditional Western metaphysical axiom that the presence of the self is both constant and evident. In psychoanalytic treatment, an unexamined assertion may be discerned: The self representation somehow stands closer to the *thing-in-itself*, the self, and is therefore more central or real than the object representation. When the historical confusion between the terms *self* and *self representation* is added, the analyst may well foster an assumption that the self is more knowable, experience-near, and therefore malleable than the object. For the adoptee, this reinforces the fear that the biological parent will remain alien and nonmetabolized within the psychic system.

Derrida's (1974) contention that the linguistic form, "the signified," which in traditional Western metaphysical thought is granted axiomatic self-evident *presence*, is merely a signifier—referring not to actual presence, but instead to a web of other linguistic signifiers—is relevant to this issue. In this view, the analyst and patient are always dealing in the currency of signifiers. There is no "real" self that underlies and supplants all self representations. The self is yet another narrative contrivance, a metaphor, signifying another link in the web of signification. This web is not discovered as being out there; it is written and edited by human beings struggling to express meaning. A multitude of selves and objects are deconstructed and constructed as the "text" of the analysis is written and rewritten—selves as equally substitutive as objects. This perspective yields a particular freedom with which the patient's texts can be decoded and new, mutually constructed selves and objects are coalesced and integrated, all of which better contextualizes and codifies the patient's history and experience. The internalized representation of the *other*, in this case the biological parent representation, is rendered no less real or present than the representation of the abandoned self or any variation on the adoptive theme. In fact, the biological parent representation can enjoy equal analytic status with any other representation or content and therefore fully participate in the treatment. For the adoptive patient in particular, this affords critical therapeutic advantages.

While fully validating the register that the visceral, tactile, sexual, and interpersonal absence of the birth parent has left on the patient, the sense that the psychic world of the adoptee must perforce sustain an experiential sense of unreality can be metapsychologically and clinically rejected by the analyst and interpreted to the patient in drive/defense, interpersonal, or transferential terms. In essence, the patient is given the hope of a more complete and integrated phenomenology. Second, the tacit assumption that therapeutic construction and reconstruction of the birth mother representation cannot take place because the exterior "signified," *real* origin of the imago is absent can be dismissed, for the adoptee's sake and often for the therapist as well. Frequently, the adoptee enters treatment with a silent hopelessness regarding the prospects of inner exploration and change because the real object "was never there."

Although the analyst may support the work of mourning the absence of the birth parent, particularly when the patient's ego is temporarily overwhelmed with the burden of deprivation and frustration of drives not gratified by the birth parent, tacit collusion with the patient's resistance to examining the representation of the biological parent is reinforced by sharing the patient's perception that the representation is infused with a shadowy unreality and immutability. When both patient and therapist consciously or unconsciously believe that the distance of the birth mother representation from the "actual" mother renders it clinically irretrievable, the therapeutic work is necessarily limited and goals corrupted. By conceptually creating a level playing field in which all intrapsychic objects are considered constructions, object representations can be regarded as highly condensed narrative residues subject to process, modification, fantasy, enactment, and interpretation. The metaphysical bias deconstructed places the representation of the biological parent squarely back into the therapeutic field, its shadowy unreality and immutability viewed as only one possible narrative theme. In short, a central figure in the adoptee's inner world becomes valid grist for the mill.

> An adopted woman in psychoanalytic treatment presented a scarcity of associations or other manifest material relating to her adoption. She clearly stated that fantasies regarding her birth parents were "pointless" because she had no actual contact with them. She presented a sharp dichotomy between inner and outer reality and only valued the former if it accurately represented the "real" objects of her environment. This was part of a deeper distrust and rejection of fantasy in general. Her rejection of fantasy portrayed an enactment of her need to reject her unreliable biological mother and simultaneously gratified a desire for revenge that expressed her pained representation of the abandoned infant self. (Deeg, 2002, p. 200)

The Adoptee's Need for Content

As defenses are analyzed and countertransferential issues resolved or consciously integrated into the treatment, the adoptee's need to fill the vacuous image of the birth parent with content often takes center stage. Borderline or severely regressed adoptive patients often construct a rigidly idealized representation designed to permanently restrict the emergence of overwhelming sadistic or annihilation fantasies. Adoptive patients with greater ego strength will also frequently offer up an initially idealized image of the birth parent as a tentative first step in allowing hitherto inaccessible fantasy elements a free rein. In the latter case, the need to "keep things positive" is less draconian and more susceptible to interpretation.

For the therapist, it is important to regard the biological parent as a representation *in statu nascendi* and to convey this attitude to the patient. To patients who regard their image of the birth parent as an empty, psychic "black hole," this may seem farcical, counterintuitive, and on a deeper level, frightening—a possible symbol for uncontrolled or irreversible regression. Sometimes, the patient's insistence that a "real," knowable person stand behind the fantasy person discussed in therapy may be discerned as a demand that the lost object return and nurture the abandoned self. The adoptee in essence states, "No, I will not entertain an examination of my feelings and ideas about an inner person, unless that person is also external, and reciprocates by considering me as well" (Deeg, 2002, p. 200).

The adoptee's fear of regression in doing this work is understandable. By fantasizing about a person he has never met, the adoptee's hard-won differentiation between inner and outer reality is blurred. As the adoptee is asked to report his feelings about the biological parent as though engaged with an external object with the promise that reality testing will in the end be fortified, he may report that he feels "strange" or "silly," like children entertaining conversation with an imaginary friend or toy. These affects signal the emergence of conflicts with the biological parent.

Just as the biological parent is ultimately contemporized within the level of the patient's overall relationships to others both internal and external, the representation of the adopted self is also revisited and revised. The patient's question "Who am I?" is therefore addressed as identity formation is supported. The patient gains access to the various aspects of the adopted self as narrative texts regarding the biological parent are explored and tolerated.

A *Specific Resistance to Exploration* *of the Biological Parent Representation*

No patient wants to lose something valuable by virtue of analytic treatment. In the most general terms, this can apply to intrapsychic objects, symptoms, or contents of any sort. The fear of loss can be one motivation for resistance, defined by Fenichel (1945) as "everything that prevents the patient from producing material derived from the unconscious." The fear of losing the experience of love of the analyst through interpretation was described by Greenson (1967). The fear that treatment generally or interpretation specifically "takes away" can have various meanings, including anal (the robbing of valued internal contents) or oedipal (as a reaction formation to the wish to be penetrated by interpretation). When the adoptee fears that treatment will take away or ruin the love experienced as flowing from the good biological parent, themes of abandonment or a reliving of the surrender of self by the mother may be remobilized. The adoptee essentially pleads, "Please do not violate the security I experience from the image of my all-good birth mother loving my infant self." Conversely, the counterwish—to abandon the mother in retaliation—is supported by this resistance. The patient basically states, "Now that I have filled this representation with good content, let's just let it be and talk about something else."

The patient's fear of mourning or re-abandonment can be assuaged by the eventual realization that the fantasy of the "good" birth parent does not have to be destroyed. The rewriting and cocreating of various internal scripts acquires increasing latitude as more affects are tolerated linking self to biological parent. The "good birth parent" becomes one among possibly many alternatives. No one true fantasy becomes enshrined as the "real" relationship to the birth parent. As a result, the patient's store of fantasy, means of interior discharge, and overall inner life become more vibrant. As affects and fantasies regarding the birth parent become more easily expressed in the treatment, both the biological parent representation *and* the adopted self become enriched, less threatening, and better integrated into the adoptee's identity.

The Adoptees's *Overall Gestalt of the Analysis*

Given a treatment situation that is not prematurely interrupted, the adoptee integrates the various thematic and affective transference elements into a superordinate gestalt roughly corresponding to the transference neurosis (Fenichel, 1945). Despite the variations in the ebb and flow of the treatment, the patient often reports that the therapy experience as a whole tends toward a particular theme. The patient reports feeling abandoned, surrendered, or reunited with the therapist or reverses the roles. The superordinate theme generally, at least in part, retells important historical elements as well.

The therapist, once again, works with the overall transference not as an absolute truth, but as a signified, co-constructed interplay, which allows for increased insight, emotional availability, and reparation. The choreography of interaction is observed by both participants. The therapist's invitation to "join me in this endeavor" mobilizes an ego that is interested in overcoming passivity, repression, or splitting as a means of coping. The experience of becoming active modifies the adoptee's inner experience of passive abandonment.

An adopted male patient feared that his ridicule and scorn of his analyst would undermine the latter's confidence in himself as a professional and as a person. The patient's adoptive father was a passive, schizoid man whose frequent verbal excoriation by the patient's mother occurred nakedly within the center arena of the family. The father would then scornfully criticize his son when the mother was away. Mirroring his reluctance to retaliate against a castrated adoptive father, the patient also feared that he would unwittingly participate in his biological father's emasculation and humiliation (also in the person of the analyst). Together, these binary transference elements comprised the central dynamic of the treatment and also explained the patient's general inhibition of masculine aggression toward his peers. (Deeg, 2002, pp. 200–201)

Termination

For the adoptive and nonadoptive patient alike, termination typically symbolizes loss; active libidinal ties are severed, self and object representations are separated, fantasies that connote an act of aggression inflicted on either patient or analyst are common. For the adoptee, the universal meanings of loss are necessarily colored and imbued with particular meanings and affects. Thus, the impatient adoptive analyst re-abandons the patient because the latter cannot elicit love, the biological parent analyst abandons the patient because of the latter's inherent badness, or the adoptive self is punished by the adoptive analyst in retaliation for the autonomy and independence that has been gleaned through the treatment but now threatens the latter's belief that emotional ties to the birth parents are dead.

> A late-adolescent adoptive patient unconsciously feared termination and began missing sessions in an attempt to postpone the event. The patient eventually recalled a similar childhood fear that his proficiency in art would cause his adoptive mother to say, "You think you're so talented and better than us, why don't you go and live with your biological mother?"

Specific ideographic elements of each case will largely determine the heuristic context that the termination mobilizes, but in general the ending of the therapy bespeaks the resurgence of fantasies of loss, abandonment, salvation, or reunion.

Resistance to termination often is expressed by a resurgence of symptomology (Dewald, 1966; Firestein, 1969; Kernberg, Selzer, Koenisberg, Carr, & Appelbaum, 1989). Langs (1974) described the specific fantasies regarding birth and death that are often generated in all terminations. For the adoptee, it is prudent to expect a pronounced reaction to termination, as one would with any patient whose unconscious leitmotif is inextricably linked to experiences of irrevocable separation or loss (Deeg, 2002). Resistance to termination does not alter the therapeutic goal: to facilitate a verbal expression of the associated affects, drive derivatives, and internalized object relations that emerge through associations, enactments, fantasy, or symptom. The reemergence of symptoms should not be automatically considered a failure of treatment but, again, as a resistance to full conscious experience and expression.

A resistance specific to the adoptee who is ending treatment while simultaneously beginning a search for birth parents may emerge. The patient may tacitly equate the search with activity, mastery, and control while devaluing the treatment as a passive "spinning of the wheels," unconsciously equated with the original abandonment. The adoptee frequently becomes impatient with the passivity of talking and yearns for the reality of a search. The therapist may be seen as helpful and kindly but incontrovertibly substitutive for the real world, for the birth parent. The patient is saying yet one more time, "I've had enough substitution (adoption), give me the real thing" (Deeg, 2002). In this fantasy, the intolerable passivity of the infant self is irrevocably undone by the motility and activity of the search for the birth parent.

SUMMARY

An outline of a psychoanalytic approach (Deeg, 1989, 1990, 1991, 2002) to understanding and treating the adoptee has been presented. At the heart of this model lies the identification of the adoptee's internal relationship to the psychic representation of the birth parent. This relationship is presented as a leitmotif for the adoptee, determining and influencing in various ways many subsequent internal and external object relations. The origin of this relation is presented within hypothetical parameters, since treatment and observational data cannot be accessed so early in development. Nevertheless, an explanation for the identification of surrender/adoption is postulated. The reciprocal relation to fantasy is described in which the relation of adopted self to biological parent both determines and is determined by fantasy. Specific defensive uses of the relation are described, documenting the manner in which the object relation operates as a personality determinant throughout the life cycle. The relationship of the object relation to the issue of identity formation is described. Finally, the technique of psychoanalytic psychotherapy with the adoptee is described—diagnostic issues, treatment parameters, and specific modes of transference and countertransference are described. A radical deviation from technique is not prescribed.

The adoptee in psychoanalytic treatment is adopted, surrendered, abandoned, and reunited as the protean, nonlinear affective flow of internal object-relational dynamics demand. The therapist is called upon to acknowledge the particular thematic and textual idiosyncrasies of the adopted patient, while avoiding the temptation to perceive an abandoned infantile self as "special," and therefore requiring perduring "empathic" departure from the analytic position. This caveat heeded, the analyst avoids a promise that cannot be fulfilled, and thus paves the way for reacceptance by the patient of the abandoned self whose object is irretrievably lost–beyond the love, but not the understanding that empathy can offer. (Deeg, 2002, p. 204)

REFERENCES

Barnes, M. F. (1953). The working through process in dealing with anxiety around adoption. *American Journal of Orthopsychiatry, 23*, 605–621.

Colarusso, C. A. (1987). Mother, is that you? *Psychoanalytic Study of the Child, 42*, 223–237.

DeCasper, A. J., & Fifer, W. P. (1980). Of human bonding: Newborns prefer their mother's voices. *Science, 208*, 1174–1176.

Deeg, C. F. (1989). On the adoptee's cathexis of the lost object. *Psychoanalysis and Psychotherapy, 7*, 152–161.

Deeg, C. F. (1990). Defensive functions of the adoptee's cathexis of the lost object. *Psychoanalysis and Psychotherapy, 8*, 35–46.

Deeg, C. F. (1991). On the adoptee's search for identity. *Psychoanalysis and Psychotherapy, 9*, 128–133.

Deeg, C. F. (2002). Issues of psychoanalytic technique with adoptees. *Journal of Social Distress and the Homeless, 11*(2), 193–205.

Derrida, J. (1974). *Of grammatology*. Baltimore: Johns Hopkins University Press.

Dewald, P. (1966). Forced termination of psychoanalysis. *Bulletin of the Menniger Clinic, 30*, 98–110.

Eissler, K. (1953). The effects of the structure of the ego on psychoanalytic technique. *Journal of the American Psychoanalytic Association, 1*, 104–143.

Erikson, E. (1950). *Childhood and society*. New York: Norton.

Fairbairn, W. R. D. (1952). *An object-relations theory of the personality*. New York: Basic Books.

Feigelman, W., & Silverman, A. R. (1986). Adoptive parents, adoptees, and the sealed record controversy. *Social Casework, 106*, 219–226.

Fenichel, O. (1945). *The psychoanalytic theory of neurosis*. New York: Norton.

Firestein, S. (1969). Panel report. Problems of termination in the analysis of adults. *Journal of the American Psychoanalytic Association, 17*, 222–237.

Freud, S. (1923). The ego and the id. *Standard Edition, 19*, 29.

Greenberg, J., & Mitchell, S. (1983). *Object relations in psychoanalytic theory*. Cambridge, MA: Harvard University Press.

Greenson, R. (1967). *The technique and practice of psychoanalysis*. New York: International Universities Press.

Hodges, J. (1984). Two crucial questions: Adopted children in psychoanalytic treatment. *Journal of Child Psychotherapy, 10*, 47–56.

Jacobson, E. (1964). *The self and the object world*. New York: International Universities Press.

Kernberg, O. (1976). *Object relations theory and clinical psychoanalysis*. New York: Jason Aronson.

Kernberg, O., Selzer, M., Koenisberg, H., Carr, A., & Appelbaum, A. (1989). *Psychodynamic psychotherapy of borderline patients*. New York: Basic Books.

Klein, M. (1932). *The psychoanalysis of children*. London: Hogarth Press.

Langs, R. (1974). *The technique of psychoanalytic psychotherapy* (Vol. 2). Northvale, NJ: Jason Aronson.

Lifton, B. J. (1988). *Lost and found: The adoption experience*. New York: HarperCollins.

Lifton, B. J. (1994). *Journey of the adopted self*. New York: Basic Books.

Schechter, M. D. (1960). Observations on adopted children. *Archives of General Psychiatry, 3*, 21–32.

Stern, D. N. (1985). *The interpersonal world of the infant*. New York: Basic Books.

Verrier, N. (1993). *The primal wound: Understanding the adopted child*. Baltimore: Gateway Press.

Psychic Homelessness Related to Reactive Attachment Disorder

30

Dutch Adult Foreign Adoptees
Struggling With Their Identity

RENÉ HOKSBERGEN

Faculty of Social Sciences, Utrecht University

JAN TER LAAK

Faculty of Social Sciences, Utrecht University

FOREIGN ADOPTION IN CONTEXT: AN INTRODUCTION

The first Dutch adoption legislation was introduced in 1956, which opened the way for international adoption. An interesting phenomenon is that after 1974, mainly children with a different racial background were adopted and domestic adoption became more a thing of the past. Since 1980, only 50 to 70 children are domestically adopted each year in a population of 16.5 million inhabitants. By the end of 2005, there were 32,000 foreign adopted children in the Netherlands from 50 countries (Hoksbergen, 2001; Ministry of Justice, 2005).

These children were placed with parents who did not have their first biological children: The adoptive parents were on an average 8 years older, predominantly from a higher socioeconomic background, and made great efforts to get their adopted child (Hoksbergen, 1979; Verhulst & Versluis-den Bieman, 1989). Since 1987, about 600 to 800 foreign adopted children per year have been placed in Dutch families, almost half the number that was placed yearly between 1974 and 1986. Increasing awareness among prospective adoptive parents of the children that adoption is often accompanied by complex problems has caused this halving. Particularly, adoptive parents realize now, more than in the past, that it is not a for-gone conclusion that the child will attach itself to them (van Egmond, 1987; Storm, 1985).

The average age at arrival of the children has risen since 2001, and since 1997, fewer children below 1 year of age are arriving (Table 30.1). This increasing age of foreign adopted children represents an important change because several international and Dutch studies indicate a relationship between the nature and the intensity of child-rearing problems and their age at arrival (Goodman, 1993; Hoksbergen, Spaan, & Waardenburg, 1988; Verhulst & Versluis-den Bieman, 1989). In older children, the process of attachment to the new parents and the process of feeling "at home" is likely to develop at a slower pace (Geerars,'t Hart, & Hoksbergen, 1991; Grotevant & McRoy, 1990; Hersov, 1994).

Table 30.1 Age of Foreign Adopted Children at Time of Placement, 1997 to 2004 (in Percentages)

Age	1997	1999	2001	2002	2003	2004
0–1	41	41	41	37	32	25
1–2	24	25	35	32	33	42
2–3	13	15	13	16	18	16
3–5	14	14	8	11	12	12
>5	8	5	3	4	5	5
Total	100	100	100	100	100	100
Average age	1.9	1.8	1.6	1.7	1.9	1.9

SOURCE: Ministry of Justice (1997–2004).

HEALTH AND BEHAVIORAL PROBLEMS IN FOREIGN ADOPTED CHILDREN

Typically, the first psychological problem in adoptive families is often reactive attachment disorder (RAD; Hoksbergen, 1998; Howe, 1995). A second problem of adoptive adolescents in particular is the feeling of being between two cultures and being between two families, the adoptive parents and the biological parents (Lifton, 1975). This is called *psychic homeless-ness* and refers to the experience of not completely belonging to the family in which one is growing up. This results in insufficient bonding and feelings of rootlessness.

The Case of Kim

Kim was born in South Korea in 1978 and adopted into a Dutch family when she was 3 years old. After her adoption, her parents had two daughters. She had a good relationship with her parents and her two younger sisters. Kim is very intelligent and has completed master's degrees in two subjects. She has a healthy relationship with a young Dutch boy, 2 years her junior.

When recently asked about how her adoption experience may be influencing her current situation, she responded,

Instinctively, I have always searched for a sort of recognition. I am able to connect to people very vastly, and I am also very understanding of people in general. A part of me continuously strives for mutual understanding. I am not able to find it, but as some sort of compensation I try to get close emotional connections with as many people as possible. The social part of my personality is extremely well developed. Thus, I have a large number of good friends and I am able to live with all sorts of people, independent of their race, religion, and cultural background.

However, the part of me that looks for instinctive, almost bestial sort of recognition by other people feels itself very isolated from people living around it. That part of me exists deeply in myself without anybody knowing it or being able to know and understand anybody else. It seems as if this almost bestial-human-like part of me only exists in myself and has no grip on the world around. That feels very lonely.

Psychic Homelessness and Attachment

When someone says "I have a home" or speaks of "my home," the person means that he or she feels secure under a certain roof, feels safe, and exhibits an emotional bond with that home and the people who live there. Many (foreign) adoptees do not feel that way (Lifton, 1979, 1994; Sorosky, Baran, & Pannor, 1975). Verrier (1993) cites a number of examples of this in her book titled *The Primal Wound*. The author related in her book how many adoptees feel that a part of them is missing. Many adoptees told Verrier that no matter how close they are to their adoptive parents, there is a special space reserved for the mother who gave birth to them. When these children grow older, they run the risk of developing feelings of psychic homelessness.

The relationship with the adopted child, feelings of bonding, and attachment are the central focus in adoptive families (Hoksbergen & Loenen, 1985; Howe, 1995; Keck & Kupecky, 1995). Adoptive parents always expect that the adopted child will attach safely to them as its new parents. Research and clinical practice make clear that the attachment is established relatively well for children who arrive in the family before 6 months of age (Juffer, Rosenboom, Hoksbergen, Riksen-Walraven, & Kohnstamm, 1995; Karen, 1998). Children who arrive at a later age run the risk of insecure attachment, and a diagnosis of RAD is often appropriate. With children younger than 2.5 years on arrival, however, the first important problems—difficulties with attachment and relationships in the family and acting-out behavior—appear around the age of 9 years.

In the *Diagnostic and Statistical Manual of Mental Disorders*, fourth edition (*DSM–IV*; American Psychiatric Association, 1994), RAD is described as follows:

Children with this disorder have either excessively inhibited, hyper vigilant, or ambivalent and contradictory responses to most social interactions or diffuse, indiscriminate attachments to other people. The presumed cause is pathogenic care evidenced by at least the following three events:

(a) Disregard for the child's emotional needs

(b) Disregard for the child's physical needs

(c) Repeated change of primary caregiver. (p. 30)

According to Bowlby (1983), the internal working model about relationships and the expectations about the attention and availability of a caretaker (usually the mother) that a child builds up in the first few years of its life are severely distorted. In situations where other children may experience security, care, and love, children with RAD experience danger, evoking a sense of uncertainty (Archer, 1996). There are so far no indications that there is a genetic factor involved in RAD. However, it cannot be ruled out that there exists a predisposition for RAD. Bowlby (1969, 1973, 1980) suggests that a genetic anchoring of the tendency toward an attachment disorder exists.

RAD emerges in various ways and in various phases of a child's life (Goodfriend, 1993; Richters & Volkmar, 1994). The most serious form of RAD occurs when a newborn has not been able to build any attachment with a specific adult in the first 2 or 3 years of life. The child will be hurt because it has to adapt several times to new persons in conjunction with physical and psychological neglect or extreme lack of stimulation (Minnis, Ramsay, & Campbell, 1996). In addition to RAD, these children also develop antisocial behavior, such as a lack of conscience, low levels of impulse control, aggression, apathy, and irresponsibility. The sense of psychic homelessness and self-destructive behavior may occur as well. This fits the characteristic behaviors that children with attachment disorder display according to the *DSM-IV* (American Psychiatric Association, 1995, pp. 110–112) and Archer (1996, p. 56). They refer to the following eight disturbed types and behaviors:

1. The inhibited types avoid all intimacy. They are the so-called frozen children (Jewett, 1982), who are not able to respond to efforts to get close to them, especially by adults. They display an avoiding and often clearly rejecting behavior.

2. The uninhibited types are often easygoing in direct contact and relate very superficially with strangers. These children can sometimes make a very charming impression. They tend to make friends with just about everyone but often can't develop stable relationships within their own age-group.

3. There are expressions of both extremely resistant deviant behavior and extremely passive behavior.

4. There are tendencies toward self-destructive as well as aggressive and cruel behavior toward people and animals.

5. There is a lack of conscience formation that is manifested in, among other ways, stealing and excessive lying.

6. There is chronic attention seeking in a negative way.

7. There is hypervigilance.

8. There is avoidance of eye contact.

Medical and Behavioral Problems in Foreign Adopted Children in the Netherlands

Epidemiological studies show that adopted children exhibit more behavioral and medical problems than do children in general (Bohman & Sigvardsson, 1990; Brodzinsky & Schechter, 1990; Brodzinsky, Schechter, & Henig, 1992; Finley, 1999; Haugaard, 1998; Hoksbergen, 1979; Hoksbergen et al., 1988; Verhulst & Versluis-den Bieman, 1989; Warren, 1992; Wierzbicki, 1993). This implies that adoptive parents and health professionals are confronted with medical and/or behavioral disturbances after the adoptive placements. This has recently been confirmed in Romanian and Russian adoptive children and adolescents (Groza, 1998; Hoksbergen, 1999; Hoksbergen et al., 2003; Jenista & Chapman, 1987; Johnson et al., 1992; Rutter, 1998). There is much controversy, however, about adoption, as such, causing the behavioral and psychosocial problems of adopted children. Comparisons of adopted children with children who are living in families of the same socioeconomic level as the birth family suggests that adoptees fare significantly better (Brodzinsky, Smith, & Brodzinsky, 1998; Feigelman, Barth, & Brooks, 1997). The consequences of being reared and educated in an adoptive family are obvious (Bharat, 1997; Moore & Fombonne, 1999; Tizard & Hodges, 1977).

Health and Behavioral Problems in
Dutch Foreign Adopted Children

Many foreign adopted children display serious health problems. Sorgedrager (1988), a pediatrician, examined 1,003 children who arrived in 1984 and 1985. He assessed that almost all children arrived with physical abnormalities or in a poor medical condition. Twenty-five percent had been seriously physically neglected. The data of Hoksbergen (1979) and Verhulst and Versluis-den Bieman (1989) support these results. In addition to this early deprivation and one or more separations from the biological parents and caretakers, some children also witnessed traumatic events. This refers to the murder of relatives, natural disasters, and acts of violence (Hoksbergen, 1996; Terr, 1991). Wolters (1989) investigated a clinical group and found that 9 out of the 25 children witnessed traumatic events, such as the killing of a family member, sexual abuse of children or of others in the child's presence, sadistic abuse, torture, or abduction of a child. Such experiences lead to anxiety attacks, unexplained panic behavior, and internalized or externalized aggressive-destructive behavior (Rutter, 1972). The child may display acting-out behavior or show suicidal tendencies.

A first consequence of serious early deprivation up to 3 or 4 years may be "pseudoadaptation behavior," which can deceive therapists as well as parents (Wolters, 1989). The adopted child is seemingly securely attached to the parents and feeling at home. Growing up, particularly during adolescence, this pseudoadaptation can turn into an acting-out or avoidance behavior, which can be damaging for the child and its environment (Hoksbergen, 1997). A second consequence of early childhood neglect, abuse, and traumatic experiences might be the occurrence of RAD. Several studies and clinical experience support this (Goldstone, 1999; Goodfriend, 1993; Grotevant & McRoy, 1990; Johnson & Fein, 1991; Kim, 1980; Rutter, 1972; Verrier, 1993; Zeanah & Emde, 1994).

A REVIEW OF EMPIRICAL DATA ON
RAD IN ADOPTED CHILDREN

There is no specific research available that gives clear indications of RAD in adopted children. However, already available data may be useful in providing some sense as to the extent to which RAD may be more prevalent in adopted children. We know, for instance, that relationship formation is problematic in many adoptive families (Hoksbergen & Bakker-van Zeil, 1983). We could also use a number of items of the Child Behavior Checklist (CBCL; Achenbach & Edelbrock, 1983) to assess levels of attachment. Thus, we can see if the previously listed characteristic behaviors displayed by children with attachment disorder are more often found in adopted children in general and specifically in the adopted children placed in residential care compared with nonadopted children. Especially important are items that mark socially deviant behavior. According to Zeanah and Emde (1994), this is an important diagnostic criterion for the diagnosis of RAD. The CBCL consists of 18 questions about behavioral and/or emotional problems and 20 questions about social competence.

Hence, to answer the question of the extent of RAD in adopted children, we administered the CBCL to the parents of adopted Dutch children who had been placed in residential care ($n = 30$). The control group consisted of adoptive parents without children in residential care. Second, we asked a group of 40 boys and girls between 15 and 20 years of age staying in residential care to fill out a youth self-report, following the CBCL. The control group consisted of adolescents not placed in residential care. Matching on the following child variables was used for the control groups: gender, country of origin, age at arrival, and age at date of the study (Geerars et al., 1991). The CBCL was then administered to a large group of 10- to 15-year-old adopted children (Verhulst & Versluis-den Bieman, 1989). In total, 2,148 adoptive parents (response rate 65%) completed the questionnaire. It was found that compared with nonadopted children, adopted boys aged 12 to 15 years displayed more antisocial behavior such as stealing, lying, cheating, vandalism, and another eight behavioral problems than did the control group. The group of 12- to 15-year-old adopted girls obtained much higher scores on questions that point at cruel and aggressive behavior against people and objects, and other antisocial behavior, compared with the control group.

The first two studies concerning adopted children in care reported comparable results. We see significant differences ($p < .01$) on seven CBCL items (Verhulst, 1985) that refer to the previously listed (Items 1 to 8) *DSM-IV* indicators. It needs to be kept in mind that these indicated CBCL items are not intended to operationalize the *DSM-IV* indicators concerned. The seven items are as follows:

1. Withdrawn, does not achieve contact with others; closed, others don't quite know what goes on inside him or her; complains about feeling lonely or left abandoned

2. Other children don't like him or her

3. Contradicts or argues a lot

4. Injures himself or herself deliberately or makes suicide attempts; talks about wanting to commit suicide; has tantrums or volatile temper; fights a lot, attacks others; destroys things belonging to others; vandalism; cruel to animals; cruel to others

5. Does not feel guilty after misbehavior, lies or cheats, steals from home, steals from outside the home

6. Destroys own property

7. Suspicious

According to Karen (1998), 10% of all children who were adopted at later ages are diagnosed with RAD. Karen summarized studies that concerned mainly intracountry adopted children. A higher incidence of RAD can be expected with intercountry adopted children. In particular, the experience of sudden radical changes in care at a point between the ages of 14 and 18 months often leads to RAD (Kim, 1980).

Research on Homeless People: Behavioral and Situational Similarities With Adopted Children

Research in the Netherlands shows that the homeless were often neglected in their youth, were unwanted, and rejected in the first years of their lives. Seventy percent of the homeless have spent periods of their lives in children's homes (Tavecchio, 1991). They experienced too little safety, love, and security with their biological parents. They grow into people who are, due to psychological reasons, not able to live and function independently in society (Kessler Stichting, 1992). They have a fundamental distrust of themselves and consequently do not easily develop normal relationships.

Homeless persons perceive intimate emotional bonds to be threatening and are not able to deal properly with emotional experiences. They show a lack of sense of identity, evidenced by limited insight into their own capabilities; muddling of fantasy and reality; insufficient impulse control; great need for attention; amoral behavior; fear of failure, sometimes combined with high demands of self. They are very often manipulative and show externalized problem behaviors, such as stealing, sexual provocation, and vandalism. Their limited planning abilities lead them to live from day to day. They often have a high measure of animosity toward their environment (Kessler Stichting, 1992; Tavecchio, 1991). This picture is similar to that in the United States (Wright, 1993).

When we compare the early home-life circumstances of foreign adopted children placed for adoption at an older age, there is a great deal of similarity with the homeless. Many foreign adopted children have, like the homeless, experienced abuse and neglect in their first period of life in their country of origin. These experiences will influence them negatively even though the circumstances in the adopted family are favorable. In addition, foreign (and interracially) adopted children show the feeling of being between two cultures, of having two ethnic identities, and of being between people (Tahk, 1986). A consequence of this experience is that the nearest microreference group (the adoptive family) has a weak and ambivalent identification function for the foreign adoptee, resulting in feelings of psychic homelessness. The following case illustrates the behavior involved in RAD and psychic homelessness.

The case of Antal. Antal is the daughter of an unmarried 19-year-old German girl. For 1.5 years, the young mother attempted to care properly for Antal. She then tried to arrange care with a local child's home, with poor results. Antal reacted negatively to her new situation and woke up screaming every night. She could barely go back to sleep afterward. Antal then began to avoid any form of contact. Soon, it was suggested that Antal should be given up for adoption. When Antal was about 2 years of age, she left for the Netherlands to a childless couple who received her lovingly. Antal reacted, however, in an avoiding manner, sometimes explicitly rejecting the adoptive mother. The mother, in turn, wanted to approach Antal with much love and attention. Although the relation between Antal and the adoptive father seems more normal, she was somewhat distant. Antal was prone to difficult moods, and the frequency increased as she grew older. She became unreasonable, screamed, and reacted with tantrums when people asked her simple things, especially her adoptive mother. Toward outsiders, she usually showed no emotional problems. They noticed nothing special about her; perhaps only that she tended to remain at a distance. Antal has only had one close friend. During puberty, Antal's unreasonableness, egocentricity, and being unapproachable became too much at times for her parents, and they frequently needed a place Antal could use as alternative accommodation.

Antal's most important problem remained the fact that she was unapproachable and closed off. She seldom displayed emotional reactions. She did not like anyone showing her affection. Sometimes it almost seemed as if she led a double life: at home where she was closed off and moody, and elsewhere where she was cool, somewhat distant, but functioning well on a cognitive level. She sometimes sought contacts with young men for a one-night stand. However, as soon as the young man tried to start an emotional relationship, he was rejected.

Although she thought about her adoption often, she did not talk about it. When she turned 20 years old, she went to a psychologist for assistance in finding her birth mother. The psychologist also talked to her parents. It was clear that it could be a liberating experience for Antal if she could meet her birth mother. After some difficulties, the birth mother was found. Antal met her and literally fell into her arms. She showed a behavior toward her birth mother completely different from that toward her adoptive mother. She did not have problems at all in showing affection. Yet in her diary she wrote that she loved her adoptive parents but in a different way. However, 3 years later, when Antal had met with her birth mother many times, the relationship became less emotional and, perhaps, more realistic.

The birth mother herself never found a stable socioeconomic place in her country. She was rather positively surprised about the new relationship with her daughter and became increasingly dependent on Antal, sometimes even claiming her as if she had never surrendered her for adoption. In the beginning, Antal really wanted to help her, but soon she realized that this relationship created extra emotional problems for her. In addition, the reactions of her adoptive parents started to trouble her. She truly felt between two families. The result was that Antal began to struggle more intensely with her own feelings and identity. Her emotional problems became so severe that she required psychotherapy for many years. One important issue was her feeling of loneliness. She hardly had any contacts with friends, and she neglected her studies.

Having been involved with Antal for a long period, we get the impression that this 26-year-old woman still has a long way to go. She has been diagnosed as having a border-line personality. Antal is able to care adequately for herself, but she is still struggling with relationships, and she does not really feel at home in the Netherlands. However, the relationship with her adoptive parents is stable and good although she does not visit them often.

The feelings of psychic homelessness are closely connected with the motives for searching for a birth mother. Sometimes, the intended effects of searching are therapeutic. Sometimes, when one wants to meet a blood relation, as is the case with Antal, one is searching for one's own identity. The need can be great, and the satisfaction can bring certain calmness. However, when the search is only partially successful or if the encounter is filled with negative information, new psychological problems, such as confusion and perhaps feelings of abandonment, can emerge.

Other cases from the literature. Keilson (1979) investigated 204 Jewish foster children. In 71 children who were 0 to 4 years old at the time they were separated from their parents, Keilson frequently observed neurotic effects on the character—a nonmalicious, mild form of a psychosocial disorder that is deeply anchored in the person and, therefore, difficult to cure. The symptoms were great insecurity, attachment disorders, a paranoid attitude, and conduct disorders. These behaviors bother the child and disturb the social environment. The micro-reference group (parents) can also belong to this environment. Likewise, Keilson saw in his Jewish group significant loyalty and identity problems that can lead to serious crises, especially during adolescence. These Jewish children had problems with bonding and feeling attached. If they display these at all, they often do so in a neurotic fashion. Emmy Kolodny is an example.

Kolodny was a Jewish girl born in 1939 who went into hiding in several households between 1943 and 1945 and then returned to her mother (her father had been murdered). When she was an adult, she first moved to Israel and then to the United States. She later wrote an article titled "Who am I?" She ends her story with the following:

> I do not feel as if I ever found a home. When we were children we were always told that we had to be grateful, because we had others to thank for our lives. "You are lucky to be alive" was something we heard often. Ever since 1945, when we came "home," I have lived with feelings of guilt that I survived the persecution. To this day I feel the pressure of the yoke on my shoulders of the unwanted responsibility for the fact that I am alive. (ICODO INFO, 1992)

Emmy resembles many adopted children coping with the oft-repeated phrase, "You are lucky you were adopted."

Another example is a 21-year-old Indian girl. As a 6-year-old, she came from a children's home in Bombay [now Mumbai] to a young Swedish couple. Her answer to the question whether she sees herself as Swedish or Indian is, "I am not Swedish, I am not Indian, I am nothing."

General Treatment and Evaluation Issues in Foreign Adoption

Research and practice show that adopted children form a heterogeneous group. Consequently, general statements about effects of adoption on the behavior of adopted children are difficult to make.

First, it is necessary to distinguish categories of adopted children and determine differences in behavioral problems. Each group of adopted children shows a different prevalence of behavioral problems. These groups differ because of the following: (a) *Different ages at placement of the adopted child*: Adoptive children who are older at the time of placement show more behavioral problems than do adopted children who are younger at the time of placement (Hoksbergen et al., 1988; Verhulst & Versluis-den Bieman, 1989). (b) *Different prenatal and postnatal circumstances*: Prenatal circumstances are often unknown but can be expected to differ between adopted children. Risk factors in postnatal circumstances also differ (e.g., the number of different caretakers, the level of psychological and/or physical deprivation, and the presence or absence of trauma; late adopted children are more likely to have experienced traumas and physical abuse) (Moore & Fombonne, 1999; Wolters, 1989). (c) *Intra- or interracial adoptions*: Backgrounds of racially distinct adopted children are less favorable than backgrounds of racially equal adoptees. (d) *Composition of adoptive family*: Families with biological children, born before or after the adoption, experience more psychosocial and rearing problems than do full adoptive families (Hoksbergen et al., 1988; Schneider, 1995).

Second, one must take into account the group of subjects with which the adoptees or the adoptive parents are compared. The comparison group is crucial to the outcome of the comparison and, hence, to the success of the adoption. The comparison will never be perfect because randomization is impossible. There are at least three possible comparison groups: (a) the general population of nonadoptive parents; (b) the general population of nonadoptive parents with the same socioeconomic background and family composition as the adoptive parents; and (c) parents with socioeconomic backgrounds similar to that of the biological parents of the adopted children.

Bohman (1970), Hoksbergen, Juffer, and Waardenburg (1987), Verhulst and Versluis-den Bieman (1989), Wierzbicki (1993), Versluis-den Bieman (1994), and Triseliotis, Shireman, and Hundleby (1997) compared adopted children with the general population of nonadoptive parents and found that the well-being of the adopted children was higher than that of the children from the general population if the adopted children were placed before 6 months of age (see also Brodzinsky et al., 1998). The second comparison group listed above is not yet used as a comparison group. If this group had been used in adoption studies, the results could have been expected to be more negative for the success of adoption than for the comparison with the first comparison group. The third comparison group favors the outcome of adoption (Tizard & Hodges, 1977). The psychosocial and economic background of adoptive parents is more favorable and higher than that of biological parents. This is even more valid for biological parents of adopted children from the Third World or eastern European countries.

Third, in addition to the use of comparison groups, it is necessary to refer explicitly to various situations in which the children of the comparison groups live. Three situations can be distinguished (Howe, 1998): (a) children in residential care with the same socioeconomic background as the adoptees; (b) children in foster care; and (c) domestically or foreign adopted children.

Finally, it is relevant to compare different groups of foreign adopted children regarding country of origin and various demographic and background variables.

Dutch research showed that parents of foreign adopted children require four to five times more frequent professional assistance or even residential care for their adoptive children compared with parents of nonadopted children (Geerars et al., 1991; Hoksbergen and Bakker-van Zeil, 1983; Verhulst & Versluis-den Bieman, 1989). Both research and clinical experience have led to conclusions that many parents with a foreign adopted child encounter many emotional and relational problems with their adoptee. The outcome of a study of 670 organizations, with a response rate of 93% (Hoksbergen et al., 1988), showed that 6% of the foreign adopted children needed residential care. Regardless of the age on arrival, the highest rate of residential placement of foreign adopted children is reached when adolescence starts (i.e., about 12 years of age). The disruption starts, on an average, 9 months earlier with boys than with girls.

If the children are older when they arrive in the adoptive family, they more often need residential care. One percent of the group younger than 6 months of age on arrival needed residential care, as compared with 20% of the group that was 6.5 years old on arrival. Children from Asia or South America are 3 to 4 years younger at the time of entering residential care compared with adopted children born in Europe (Greece, Austria, Germany), on an average.

Supporting Adopted Children With
Reactive Attachment Disorder and Their Parents

Having children with RAD is extremely stressful for adoptive parents (van Egmond, 1987; Grasvelt, 1989). They are faced with seemingly impossible child-rearing tasks. Additionally, the experiences of these adoptive parents with social agencies and caretakers are not positive. They are aware that the behavior disorder is extremely difficult to treat. Much discussion exists about ways in which children with RAD should be treated. A standard approach of a counseling session one or more times per week does not prove very effective. Two other methods are suggested: holding therapy (Keck & Kupecky, 1995; Welch, 1988) and creative therapy (Wrobel, 1991). Holding therapy works with close physical proximity. Holding the child is accomplished by having him lie across the laps of two therapists and/or his parents. Eye contact is critical. Although the effectiveness of these approaches has not yet been sufficiently proved by empirical research, the data of the first study (Parents to Parent Information on Adoption Services, 1994) and the case histories are promising. Furthermore, there is empirical research in which intervention techniques were used to improve the attachment between mother and child (Speltz, 1990). These behaviorally focused interventions were carried out in families with adopted children and are based on the premise that improving the level of responsiveness of the mother is supposed to improve the attachment between mother and child. However, Zeanah and Emde (1994) point out that an evaluation of the effectiveness of this approach does not exist yet: "Again, research to aid in selecting appropriate treatment is lacking, even though clinical activity and intervention in problems of disturbed parent-child relationships are considerable" (pp. 500–501).

Psychic Homelessness and Intercountry Adoption

As stated previously, it is suggested that foreign adopted children with RAD will develop feelings of psychic homelessness. In the Netherlands, as in other West European countries and the United States, foreign adoption and mostly interracial adoption have existed for three or more decades. Thousands of these foreign adoptees have become adults. So it is possible to study the long-term effects of RAD, other behavior disorders due to abuse/maltreatment/ deprivation, and the long-term consequences of one of the three categories of insecure attachment—avoidant, resistant/ambivalent, and anxious/disorganized/disoriented (Colin, 1996). Facts and constructs from neurology, neurobiology, and social psychology are helpful in explaining this relationship.

The neurologist Perry (1995) shows that the young child's midbrain and limbic system are involved in emotional reactions, affiliation, and attachment. Perry suggests that there is a critical period early in life for adequate attachment and that at a later age the child will be much less receptive to attachment. Schore's (1994) neurobiological research supports Perry's conclusions. He suggests that the quality of the initial attachment relationship affects the neurological development of significant areas of the brain. The infant who experiences a lack of attunement perceives the preverbal self as being basically flawed, thus feeling empty, helpless, and hopeless (Hughes, 1997; Schore, 1994). Federici's (2003) work on adopted children supports these conclusions. Lieberman and Pawl's (1988) conclusions, in summarizing the clinical work of Fraiberg, are relevant here as well. Nonattached children show impairment in interpersonal relationships, cognitive functioning, impulse control, and the regulation of aggression (Hughes, 1997).

Various Dutch empirical studies (Geerars et al., 1991; Verhulst & Versluis-den Bieman, 1989) lead to the same conclusions about the nature of the often-occurring behavioral problems in foreign adopted children. Considering cognitive functioning, adoptive parents of these children, however, may gain courage from the outcome of a recent French adoption research project. The researchers in this study concluded that a stimulating environment will have a positive effect of 14 points on the IQ of young children with an IQ between 60 and 85.

Besides neurology and neurobiology, social psychology does help clarify psychic homelessness in the adoptee. Krech, Crutchfield, and Ballachey (1962) define the reference group as follows:

> Any group with which an individual identifies himself such that he tends to use the group as a standard for self-evaluation and as a source of his personal values and goals. The reference groups of the individual may include both membership groups and groups to which he aspires to belong. (p. 102)

The adoptive and biological families are microreference groups from the perspective of the adoptee. For an extensive period, the adoptive family is the most important microreference group for the adoptee. As the adoptee grows up, the biological family turns out to have an important "reference" function as well. Sometimes, this is the reference group "to which one aspires to belong." This can become apparent from concrete actions and fantasies.

For instance, we asked a group of 56 Dutch/Greek adoptees to rate the extent of membership to their Dutch or Greek reference group. We present the data in Table 30.2. The adoptees were on an average 6 months old at placement and 29 years of age when interviewed.

Table 30.2   Adult Adoptees: The Intensity of Feeling Dutch or Greek, Percentages (*n* = 56)

Score	Male	Female	Total
Low (strong Dutch feelings), 0–4	53	65	59
Moderate, 5–9	37	27	32
High (strong Greek feelings), 10–14	10	8	9

SOURCE: Storsbergen (1995).

Eighty percent of these Dutch/Greek adoptees have searched for information regarding their background. Half of this group of adult foreign adoptees feel being both Greek and Dutch, and feel between two countries and cultures (Tahk, 1986). Adoptees have to cope with these confusing feelings often. Further corroboration of these findings is found by De Pauw (1997), who studied 57 adult foreign adoptees born in India and adopted in Belgium. They were on an average 4.5 years old at the time of placement and 26 years old when interviewed. A quarter of the respondents report that they don't feel completely Belgian. Of even more importance for our theorizing is the outcome that 49% feel between two countries and two cultures (see Table 30.3).

Table 30.3 Do Foreign Adopted Children Feel Themselves at Home in Belgium? (21 Males, 36 Females)

	True	Untrue
I see myself completely as Belgian	75	25
I feel myself at home in Belgium	93	7
I feel myself a foreigner in Belgium	20	80
My character is more Indian	48	52
Being born in India is very important in my life	46	54
I feel both Belgian and a foreigner	51	49

SOURCE: De Pauw (1997, p. 121).

CONCLUSION

The reactions of some foreign adopted children may seem extreme but are at the heart of the matter. Adoptive children, and particularly those with symptoms of RAD, can run into significant problems with their feeling at home, their identity, and receiving a satisfying and quieting answer to questions such as, "Who am I actually?" "Who am I in your eyes?" and "Am I still the same person I was before the adoption?" When these adoptees struggle with RAD and other problem behaviors due to experiences of deprivation, problems with obtaining a stable identity might be much more intense, and feelings of psychic homelessness are the result.

For many children, adoption seems to be the only solution. These children, however, do not remain children. As adolescents and later on as adults, they confront us with new problems, of which the solution or improvement is again of vital importance. The responsibilities for adoption agencies and adoptive parents are obvious. Longitudinal research may help us find proper ways of preventing the long-term negative effects of RAD.

PRACTICAL CONSEQUENCES AND SOME IMPLICATIONS FOR ADOPTIVE PARENTS AND ADULT ADOPTEES

Consequences for Adoptive Parents, Agencies, and Social Workers

Aspirant adoptive families have to be prepared properly. Basic information about problem behavior that young adopted children might exhibit should be given by the adoption agency involved. Adoption agencies placing an adoptive child into a family should give proper information about the physical and psychic health situation of the child. This means that social workers of the agency should check properly all the information about the adoptive child they get from the (foreign) mediator. Important topics include confirmation of the following: the child's date of birth, the reported history of the child, facts about the child's health, and descriptions of caretaking by the caretakers in the children's home or elsewhere.

Especially when the adopted child is 5 months or older and is institutionalized during the first months or years, the adoptive parents need to have books and articles available and to have access to practical advice concerning problems with attachment. One important aspect of experiencing feelings of psychic homelessness is the experience of not completely belonging to the family in which one is growing up. These feelings can start early in life as an important effect of deprivation. Advice for adoptive parents on how to deal with this behavior may prevent the growing of these feelings of insufficient bonding.

In this respect, it will be of great help for adoptive parents to be taught to look critically at their own behavior toward their child. One way of improving their critical view is using video interaction training. Some of the parents' upbringing and educational activities in the family are recorded on video (about 30 minutes) and are discussed later with professionals. One of the problems of quite a few adoptive parents is their overprotectiveness. This means not leaving enough space for their child, space to explore and experiment with normal situations of life.

Dealing with adopted children demands special knowledge from all the social workers involved. They should have basic knowledge about the effects of deprivation on the behavior of young children and of adolescents.

They should also realize that adoptive families in need of professional help are not fully comparable with other families needing help from social workers. Well-prepared adoptive parents have more knowledge about important issues of education. They might also be more involved in the challenges of raising their children and be more active in that process. Adoptive parents have a strong wish to start a family with children. Their feelings of responsibility for and belonging to the family will mean that they definitely want to know what social workers intend to do with their child who shows some problem behavior. Their attitude toward social workers might even be rather critical. These social workers often need to involve the adoptive parents in their therapy with the child.

Placing an adoptive child in residential care has special risks. Again, the child might feel rejected and abandoned. Feelings of not belonging, or psychic homelessness, might be reinforced. Social workers must take extra care when making this decision. For instance, if out-of-house placement of the adoptee is absolutely necessary for some period of time, contacts between the adoptive family should be arranged and may benefit from the social worker's guidance of these contacts.

Implications for Adult Adoptees

Adult adoptees should be given all the information of the past. Self-insight will help them deal in a healthy way with issues from the past. Discussions about effects of separation and effects of deprivation on the behavior of children, adolescents, and young adults will promote the growing of this self-insight. Well-prepared and -educated adoptive parents are the primary persons with whom to start the discussions. However, if the effects are strongly influential for the adoptee, specially trained social workers may have to be brought in as well.

REFLECTION QUESTIONS

1. Try to describe why adopted children form a heterogeneous group of people.

2. Argue why reactive attachment disorder (RAD) can result in psychic homelessness in adulthood.

3. Why is the problem of adoptees called an RAD?

4. Why do adoptees have problems with their identity?

5. Why do children adopted at a later age have a greater chance of developing RAD?

6. Describe in behavioral terms the behavior of an adopted child exhibiting RAD.

7. Why can we expect a higher incidence of RAD in intercountry versus domestically adopted children?

8. Describe some similarities and differences in behaviors and situational circumstances between adoptees and homeless people not adopted.

9. Describe an experiment to prove that one of the therapies for RAD is effective (or not).

10. Three groups of explanations to understand psychic homelessness are reported. Which of the three offers a possibility for a psychologically based therapy, and why?

REFERENCES

Achenbach, T. M., & Edelbrock, C. S. (1983). *Manual for the child behavior checklist and revised child behavior profile*. Burlington: University of Vermont Department of Psychiatry.

American Psychiatric Association. (1994). *Diagnostic and statistical manual of mental disorders* (4th ed.). Washington, DC: Author.

American Psychiatric Association. (1995). *Diagnostische Criteria van de DSM-IV*. Lisse, The Netherlands: Swets & Zeitlinger.

Archer, C. (1996). Attachment disordered children. In R. Philips & E. McWilliam (Eds.), *After adoption: Working with adoptive families* (pp. 55–65). London: British Agency for Adoption and Fostering.

Bharat, S. (1997). *Intellectual and psychosocial development of adopted children*. Mumbai, India: Tata Institute of Social Sciences.

Bohman, M. (1970). *Adopted children and their families*. Stockholm: Proprius.

Bohman, M., & Sigvardsson, S. (1990). Outcome in adoption: Lessons from longitudinal studies. In D. Brodzinsky & M. Schechter (Eds.), *The psychology of adoption* (pp. 93–106). New York: Oxford University Press.

Bowlby, J. (1969). *Attachment and loss* (Vol. 1). Harmondsworth, UK: Penguin Books.

Bowlby, J. (1973). *Attachment and loss* (Vol. 2). Harmondsworth, UK: Penguin Books.

Bowlby, J. (1980). *Attachment and loss* (Vol. 3). Harmondsworth, UK: Penguin Books.

Bowlby, J. (1983). *Verbondenheid* [Connection]. Deventer, The Netherlands: Van Loghum Slaterus.

Brodzinsky, D. M., & Schechter, M. D. (Eds.). (1990). *The psychology of adoption*. New York: Oxford University Press.

Brodzinsky, D. M., Schechter, M. D., & Henig, R. M. (1992). *Being adopted: The lifelong search for self*. New York: Doubleday.

Brodzinsky, D. M., Smith, W. D., & Brodzinsky, A. B. (1998). *Children's adjustment to adoption: Developmental and clinical issues*. London: Sage.

Colin, V. L. (1996). *Human attachment*. New York: McGraw-Hill.

De Pauw, A. (1997). *Evaluatie van interculturele en interraciale adoptie in Vlaanderen* [Evaluation of intercultural and interracial adoption in Flanders]. Leuven, Belgium: Onderzoekscentrum Mens, Maatschappij en Marginaliteit.

Federici, R. S. (2003). *Help for the hopeless child: A guide for families: With special discussion for assessing and treating the post-institutionalized child*. Alexandria, VA: Federici.

Feigelman, W., Barth, R., & Brooks, D. (1997). *Comparing the adjustments of transracially adopted young adults with their interracially adopted peers*. New York: Nassau Community College.

Finley, G. E. (1999). Children of adoptive families. In W. K. Silverman & T. H. Ollendick (Eds.), *Developmental issues in the clinical treatment of children and adolescents* (pp. 358–370). Boston: Allyn & Bacon.

Geerars, H., 't Hart, H., & Hoksbergen, R. A. C. (1991). *Waar ben ik thuis? Geadopteerde adolescenten over adoptie, hun familie, problemen, uithuisplaatsing en toekomstvisie* [Where am I at home? Adopted adolescents about adoption, their family, problems, out-of-house placement and vision of the future]. Utrecht, The Netherlands: Adoption Center.

Goldstone, C. (1999). *Come to the window: Life with Daniel: Our child from Romania: The story of a post-institutionalized child.* Euclid, OH: William Custom.

Goodfriend, M. S. (1993). Experience and reason briefly recorded: Treatment of attachment disorder of infancy in a neonatal intensive care unit. *Pediatrics, 91*(1), 139–142.

Goodman, D. A. (1993). *Here today, gone tomorrow: An investigation of the factors that impact adoption disruption.* Ann Arbor, MI: UMI Dissertation Services.

Grasvelt, C. (1989). *Justo, een gekwetst kind: Ervaringen van een moeder met een ernstig erwaarloosd adoptiekind* [Justo, a hurt child: Experiences of a mother with a seriously deprived adoptive child]. Haarlem, The Netherlands: De Toorts.

Grotevant, H., & McRoy, R. (1990). Adopted adolescents in residential treatment: The role of the family. In D. M. Brodzinsky & M. D. Schechter (Eds.), *The psychology of adoption* (pp. 167–186). New York: Oxford University Press.

Groza, V. (1998). Adopted children from Rumania: Special focus on Roma (gypsy) children. *International Journal of Child & Family Welfare, 1*, 6–25.

Haugaard, J. J. (1998). Is adoption a risk factor for the development of adjustment problems? *Clinical Psychological Review, 18*(1), 47–69.

Hersov, L. (1994). Adoption. In M. Rutter, E. Taylor, & L. Hersov (Eds.), *Child and adolescent psychiatry, modern approaches* (pp. 267–282). Oxford, UK: Blackwell Science.

Hoksbergen, R. A. C. (Ed.) (with Baarda, B., Bunjes, L. A., & Nota, J. C.). (1979). *Adoptie van kinderen uit verre landen* [Adoption of children from far countries]. Deventer, The Netherlands: Van Loghum Slaterus.

Hoksbergen, R. A. C. (1996). *Child adoption: A guidebook for adoptive parents and their advisors.* London: Jessica Kingsley.

Hoksbergen, R. A. C. (1997). Turmoil for adoptees during their adolescence? *International Journal of Behavioral Development, 20*(1), 33–46.

Hoksbergen, R. A. C. (1998). Reactieve hechtingsstoornis bij adoptiekinderen [Reactive attachment disorder with adoptive children]. *Nederlands Tijdschrift voor Opvoeding, Vorming en Onderwijs, 14*(6), 303–322.

Hoksbergen, R. A. C. (with the coworkers of the Romania project). (1999). *Adoptie van Roemeense kinderen: Ervaringen van ouders die tussen 1990 en medio 1997 een kind uit Roemenië adopteerden* [Adoption of Romanian children: Experiences of parents who adopted a child from Romania, between 1990 and mid-1997]. Utrecht, The Netherlands: Universiteit Utrecht, Adoption Department.

Hoksbergen, R. A. C. (2001). *Vijftig jaar adoptie in Nederland: Een historisch-statistische beschouwing* [Fifty years of adoption in the Netherlands: A historical-statistical essay]. Utrecht, The Netherlands: Utrecht University, Adoption Department.

Hoksbergen, R. A. C., & Bakker-van Zeil, T. (1983). Adoptiekinderen bij Medisch OpvoedkundigeBureaus en Jeugd Psychiatrische Diensten. In R. Hoksbergen & H. Walenkamp (Eds.), *Adoptie uit de kinderschoenen* [Adoption coming of age] (pp. 223–241). Deventer, The Netherlands: Van Loghum Slaterus.

Hoksbergen, R. A. C., Juffer, F. A., & Waardenburg, B. (1987). *Adoptive children at home and at school.* Lisse, The Netherlands: Swets & Zeitlinger.

Hoksbergen, R. A. C., & Loenen, A. (1985). Adoptie en attachment: Over hechtingsproblemen bij buitenlandse adoptiekinderen [Adoption and attachment: About problems with attachment with foreign adoptive children]. *Kind & Adolescent, 6*(2), 71–83.

Hoksbergen, R. A. C., Spaan, J. J. T. M., & Waardenburg, B. C. (1988). *Bittere ervaringen: Uithuisplaatsing van buitenlandse adoptiekinderen* [Bitter experiences: Out-of-house placement of foreign adoptive children]. Utrecht, The Netherlands: Adoptie Centrum.

Hoksbergen, R. A. C., Ter Laak, J., Van Dijkum, C., Rijk, S., Rijk, K., & Stoutjesdijk, F. (2003). Posttraumatic stress disorder in adopted children from Romania. *American Journal of Orthopsychiatry, 73*(3), 255–265.

Howe, D. (1995). Adoption and attachment. *Adoption and Fostering, 19*(4), 7–15.

Howe, D. (1998). Adoption outcome research and practical judgment. *Adoption & Fostering, 22*(2), 6–15.

Hughes, D. A. (1997). *Facilitating developmental attachment: The road to emotional recovery and behavioral change in foster and adopted children.* London: Jason Aronson.

ICODO INFO. (1992). *Themanummer: Joodse onderduikkinderen van toen* [Jewish hidden children in those days]. Utrecht, The Netherlands: Stichting ICODO.

Jenista, J. A., & Chapman, D. (1987). Medical problems of foreign-born adopted children. *American Journal of Diseases of Children, 141,* 298–302.

Jewett, C. L. (1982). *Helping children cope with separation and loss.* Harvard, MA: Harvard Common Press.

Johnson, D., & Fein, E. (1991). The concept of attachment: Applications to adoption. *Children and Youth Services Review, 13,* 397–412.

Johnson, D. E., Miller, L. C., Iverson, S., Thomas, W., Franchino, B., Dole, K., et al. (1992). The health of children adopted from Romania. *Journal of the American Medical Association, 268*(24), 3446–3451.

Juffer, F. A., Rosenboom, L., Hoksbergen, R. A. C., Riksen-Walraven, M., & Kohnstamm, G. A. (1995). Attachment and intervention in adoptive families with and without biological children. In W. Koops, J. B. Hoeksma, & D. V. Van den Boom (Eds.), *Development of interaction and attachment: Traditional and non-traditional approaches* (pp. 93–108). Amsterdam: North-Holland.

Karen, R. (1998). *Becoming attached: First relationships and how they shape our capacity to love.* New York: Oxford University Press.

Keck, G. C., & Kupecky, R. M. (1995). *Adopting the hurt child.* Colorado Springs, CO: Piñon Press.

Keilson, H. (1979). *Sequentielle traumatisierung bei kindern: Deskriptiv-klinische und quantifizierend-statistische follow-up untersuchung zum schicksal der jüdischen kriegs waisen in den Niederlanden.* Stuttgart, Germany: Ferdinand Enke Verlag.

Kessler Stichting. (1992). *Huis voor thuislozen* [Home for the homeless]. The Hague, The Netherlands: Author.

Kim, P. S. (1980). Behavior symptoms in three transracially adopted Asian children: Diagnosis dilemma. *Child Welfare, 59*(4), 213–223.

Krech, D., Crutchfield, R. S., & Ballachey, E. L. (1962). *Individual in society: A textbook of social psychology.* New York: McGraw-Hill.

Lieberman, A., & Pawl, J. (1988). *Clinical applications of attachment theory.* Hillsdale, NJ: Lawrence Erlbaum.

Lifton, B. J. (1975). *Twice born: Memoirs of an adopted daughter.* New York: McGraw-Hill.

Lifton, B. J. (1979). *Lost and found: The adoption experience.* New York: Dial Press.

Lifton, B. J. (1994). *Journey of the adopted self: A quest for wholeness.* New York: Basic Books.

Ministry of Justice. (2005). *Statistische gegevens betreffende de opneming in gezinnen van buitenlandse adoptiekinderen in de jaren 1992–2004* [Statistical data regarding foreign adoption in the years 1992–2004]. The Hague, The Netherlands: Ministerie van Justitie.

Minnis, H., Ramsay, R., & Campbell, L. (1996). Reactive attachment disorder: Usefulness of a new clinical category. *Journal of Nervous Mental Disorders, 184*(7), 440.

Moore, J., & Fombonne, E. (1999). Psychopathology in adopted and non-adopted children: A clinical sample. *American Journal of Orthopsychiatry, 69*(3), 403–409.

Parents to Parent Information on Adoption Services. (1994). *A resource pack for professionals supporting families who have a child with an attachment disorder.* Derby, UK: Bookstall Services.

Perry, B. (1995). *Maltreated children: Experience, brain development and the next generation.* New York: W. W. Norton.

Richters, M. M., & Volkmar, F. R. (1994). Reactive attachment disorder of infancy or early childhood. *Journal of the American Academy of Child and Adolescent Psychiatry, 33*(3), 328–332.

Rutter, M. (1972). *Maternal deprivation reassessed.* Harmondsworth, UK: Penguin Books.

Rutter, M. (with the English and Romanian Adoptees study team). (1998). Developmental catch-up, and deficit, following adoption after severe global early privation. *Journal of Child Psychology and Psychiatry, 39*(4), 465–476.

Schneider, S. (1995). Adoption and ordinal position. *Adoption and Fostering, 19,* 21–23.

Schore, A. (1994). *Affect regulation and the origin of the self.* Hillsdale, NJ: Lawrence Erlbaum.

Sorgedrager, N. (1988). *Oriënterend medisch onderzoek en groeistudie van buitenlandse Adoptiekinderen* [Medical examination and growth of foreign born adoptive children]. Haren, The Netherlands: Cicero.

Sorosky, A., Baran, A., & Pannor, R. (1975). Identity conflicts in adoptees. *American Journal of Orthopsychiatry, 45*, 18–27.

Speltz, M. (1990). The treatment of preschool conduct problems: An integration of behavioral and attachments concepts. In M. T. Greenberg, D. Cicchetti, & E. M. Cummings (Eds.), *Attachment in the preschool years* (pp. 399–426). Chicago: University of Chicago Press.

Storm, M. (1985, January 10). Het drama van de mislukte adoptie [The tragedy of the failed adoption]. *De Tijd*, p. 7.

Storsbergen, H. E. (1995). Geadopteerd zijn is . . . . In R. A. C. Hoksbergen, H. E. Storsbergen, & C. Brouwer-van Dalen, *Het begon in Griekenland: Een verkenning van de achtergrond van in Griekenland geboren, geadopteerde jongvolwassenen en de betekenis van de adoptiestatus* [It started in Greece: An exploration of the background of Greek adoptive young adult children and the significance of the adoption status]. Utrecht, The Netherlands: Adoptie Centrum.

Tahk, Y. T. (1986). Intercountry adoption program in Korea. In R. A. C. Hoksbergen & S. D. Gokhale (Eds.), *Adoption in worldwide perspective: A review of programs, policies and legislation in 14 countries.* Lisse, The Netherlands: Swets & Zeitlinger.

Tavecchio, L. W. C. (1991). *Affectieve verwaarlozing en thuisloosheid: Een haalbaarheidsstudie naar thuisloosheid vanuit het perspectief van de gehechtheidstheorie* [Emotional deprivation and homelessness: A study of homelessness in the context of attachment theory]. Leiden, The Netherlands: Vakgroep Algemene Pedagogiek.

Terr, L. C. (1991). Childhood traumas: An outline and overview. *American Journal of Psychiatry, 148*, 10–20.

Tizard, B., & Hodges, J. (1977). The effect of early institutional rearing on the development of eight year old children. *Journal of Child Psychology and Psychiatry, 19*, 99–118.

Triseliotis, J., Shireman, J., & Hundleby, M. (1997). *Adoption: Theory, policy and practice.* London: Cassell.

van Egmond, G. (1987). *Bodemloos bestaan: Problemen met adoptiekinderen* [Bottomless existence: Problems with adopted children]. Baarn, The Netherlands: AMBO.

Verhulst, F. C. (1985). *Mental health in Dutch children, an epidemiological study.* Meppel, The Netherlands: Kris Repro.

Verhulst, F. C., & Versluis-den Bieman, H. J. M. (1989). *Vaardigheden en Probleemgedrag* [Skills and problem behavior]. Assen, The Netherlands: Van Gorcum.

Verrier, N. N. (1993). *The primal wound.* Baltimore: Gateway Press.

Versluis-den Bieman, H. (1994). *Interlandelijk geadopteerden in de adolescentie: Vervolgonderzoek naar gedragsproblemen en vaardigheden* [Foreign adoptive children in adolescence: Continuation of research in problem behavior and skills]. Unpublished PhD dissertation, Rotterdam Erasmus University, Rotterdam, The Netherlands.

Warren, S. B. (1992). Lower threshold for referral for psychiatric treatment for adopted adolescents. *Journal of the American Academy of Child and Adolescent Psychiatry, 31*, 512–527.

Welch, M. G. (1988). *Holding time.* New York: Fireside.

Wierzbicki, M. (1993). Psychological adjustment of adoptees: A meta-analysis. *Journal of Clinical Child Psychology, 22*(4), 447–454.

Wolters, W. (1989). Uithuisplaatsing van buitenlandse adoptiekinderen: te vroeg of te laat? In R. A. C. Hoksbergen & W. Wolters (Eds.), *Verstoorde Relaties, adoptie en Hulpverlening* [Disturbed relations, adoption and care] (pp. 52–63). Baarn, The Netherlands: AMBO.

Wright, J. D. (1993). Downward mobility in contemporary American society: "Address unknown: Homelessness in Contemporary America." In B. Feigelman (Ed.), *Sociology full circle: Contemporary readings on society.* New York: Harcourt Brace Jovanvich.

Wrobel, J. (1991). Story-making/story-telling als therapeutisch middel bij problematische Adoptiekinderen [Story-making/story-telling as therapeutic instrument for problematic adoptive children]. *Tijdschrift Voor Creatieve Therapie, 91*, 95–100.

Zeanah, C. H., & Emde, R. N. (1994). Attachment disorders in infancy and childhood. In M. Rutter, E. Taylor, & L. Hersov (Eds.), *Child and adolescent psychiatry: Modern approaches* (pp. 490–504). Oxford: Blackwell Science.

"I Don't Know You"

31

Transference and Countertransference Paradigms With Adoptees

JANET RIVKIN ZUCKERMAN

Center for Preventive Psychiatry, White Plains, New York

BETTY BUCHSBAUM

Center for Preventive Psychiatry, White Plains, New York

P atients who are adopted are often highly resistant to exploring their adoptive status as well as the experience of adoption itself in psychotherapy. The mores of our culture typically discourage the openness required to help members of adoptive families work through their difficulties (Nickman, 1996a). Clinicians who work with such patients are well aware of this phenomenon, and the literature on psychotherapy with adoptees documents the difficulty in exploring patients' conflicts about adoption (Kernberg, 1985–1986; Sherick, 1983; Soll, 2000). The subject of adoption is not uncommonly brought up by the patient at the beginning of treatment, prematurely closed by patient and parent, and never discussed again (Kernberg, 1985–1986). Though therapists are aware that adoption exerts profound effects on identity formation (Glenn, 1974), object and self-representations (Brinich, 1980, 1995; Glenn, 1985–1986), superego formation (Kernberg, 1985–1986), and sexual identity (Kernberg, 1985–1986), finding a foothold to apply such knowledge clinically can be daunting.

This overall difficulty in accessing adoption concerns is often intensified where (a) a child manifests acute symptoms that significantly interfere with effective functioning (Deering & Scahill, 1989); (b) the adoptive family is invested in maintaining the child's insecurity about her adoptive status as a smoke screen for other family pathology (Deering & Scahill, 1989;

Authors' Note: The authors acknowledge the generous contributions of Drs. Neil Altman, Lewis Aron, and Ruth Lesser in reviewing this manuscript.

Kirschner, 1990); (c) couples have struggled with the psychological sequelae of infertility (Nickman, 1985; Nickman et al., 2005); (d) adoption is treated as a nonevent by parents lacking psychological insight (Kirschner, 1990); and (e) therapists' negative attitudes toward adoption preclude or interfere with an empathic therapeutic connection (Nickman et al., 2005).

We contend that a pivotal way to traverse the patient's resistance to speaking about adoption is to understand and explore the transference-countertransference relationship as it brings to life the patient's internal experience of adoption. The literature reviews proto-typical dynamics and behaviors of the adoptee in therapy (Jones, 1997; McDaniel & Jennings, 1997); however, few articles highlight the unique role of transference in the treatment, leaving both the relational dimension and the specific meanings of the adoptee's behavior largely unelaborated.

We will review the literature on psychotherapy with adoptees, describing the few trans-ferential patterns discussed, and propose a variety of transferences that could accompany the behavioral trends illustrated. We will thereafter describe the treatment of a 9-year-old adopted girl, where transferences discussed in the literature are highlighted and new transference-countertransference constellations are proposed. Our hope is to provide addi-tional channels to access patients' conflicts about adoption.

LITERATURE REVIEW

We have organized this overview around three categories of transference found in the clini-cal literature with adoptees: negative, positive, and unstable.

Negative Transference

Many authors have observed different aspects of one of the most pervasive phenomena observed in adoptees—namely, their intense belief that they are unwanted and defective and their repeated efforts to prove it (Brinich, 1990, 1995; Derdeyn & Graves, 1998; Kernberg, 1985–1986; Nickman, 1985; Nickman et al., 2005; Parkhill, 2004; Sherick, 1983; Wieder, 1978). Such feelings of defectiveness in the adoptee derive initially and most profoundly from having been relinquished by one's biological parents. Feelings of defectiveness can thereafter be compounded by (a) unconscious identifications with defective biological parents (Nickman, 1985); (b) self-blaming to excuse the actions of rejecting biological parents (Kernberg, 1985–1986; Parkhill, 2004); and (c) projections onto adoptees of their adoptive parents' neg-ative fantasies about biological parents (Derdeyn & Graves, 1998; Glenn, 1974; Nickman, 1996b; Nickman et al., 2005; Samuels, 1990).

The adoptee's intense feelings of defectiveness are described in the literature; however, descriptions of the transferences enacted around such feelings are few. Kernberg (1985–1986) provides one notable exception when she observes in passing that patients may come to view the therapist as a monster since it is too much of a burden to view themselves as one. The authors propose that chronic feelings of unworthiness can result in a variety of negative trans-ferences to the therapist, including the patient's belief that the therapist (a) is disapproving and critical of her assumed defectiveness; (b) is as unworthy and defective as she believes she is; and (c) lacks vision because the therapist sees the patient as a person of value.

Several authors discuss another common dynamic among adoptees, their intense anger at both biological and adoptive parents, which can be projected (Brinich, 1995; Hughes, 1997; Kernberg, 1985–1986; Nickman et al., 2005) and displaced (Sherick, 1983) onto the thera-pist. Driven by this dynamic, the patient might come to transferentially view the therapist as angry and rejecting, reflecting her own projected self-states as well as her expectation that others will resemble her biological and adoptive parents. In a related dynamic, the patient may allow herself to experience rather than project such intense affects. In this case, the patient may fear that due to her rage, (a) the therapist may become dangerous and retaliate with harm as she may fantasize her biological parents did in rejecting her (Sherick, 1983; Silverman, 1985–1986); (b) she herself will drive the therapist away or annihilate her, as she may believe occurred with her biological parents (Silverman, 1985–1986); or (c) the therapist is weak in contrast to her own overpowering affects.

Other authors cite the adoptee's desire to reject her adoptive parents (Kernberg, 1985–1986) as part of her effort to put into active form the loss she was forced to endure passively (Novak, 2004). We would extrapolate that where such a dynamic is at play, the adoptee may enact the rejecting parent to the therapist's helpless child, seeking to master her rejection and heal profound feelings of vulnerability (Kernberg, 1985–1986). Transferentially, the therapist would be viewed as the helpless and passive victim whom the patient is repeatedly able to coerce and denounce despite genuine effort by the therapist to connect and stay alive.

Glenn (1985–1986) and others (Derdeyn & Graves, 1998; Jones, 1997; Parkhill, 2004; Treacher, 2000) observe another prototypical challenge for adoptees, their incomplete identificatory picture. Associated feelings of anonymity may result from having had to live in a "virtual witness protection program" (Homes, 1996) as a result of having been adopted. Applying these observations, we might envision a transference, where the patient feels intense envy toward the therapist, who seems to possess a complete life story and clear social and familial status. Adoptees may also view the therapist transferentially as an omniscient and withholding object who possesses answers to the vital question of who she really is but sadistically retains them. In this regard, Glenn (1974) notes that adoptees sometimes explore the therapist's records fantasizing that they contain vital identifying information.

Other authors (Derdeyn & Graves, 1998; Parkhill, 2004; Sherick, 1983) note the tendency of adoptees to chronically lie or play with the truth, leaving the therapist uncertain about actual data. The adoptee may do this (a) to deny or ease the pain of her rejection by birth parents, for example, by pretending that the adoptive parents are her birth parents or that she is the biological child of her adoptive parents; (b) as a consequence of the pressure to disavow reality and live as if adoptive parents are biological parents, repressing yearnings for the latter (Lifton, 1990; Samuel, 2003); and (c) as an enactment with the therapist where the lie can reveal as much as it conceals (Wilkinson & Hough, 1996). We propose that, transferentially, a patient prone to such a dynamic may doubt the therapist's credibility and mistrust her. That is, where adoptees themselves alter reality, they will expect others to act in kind, yielding the experience of an untrustworthy therapist. In addition, the patient may view the therapist as puzzled or helpless in the face of the uncertain reality that has been presented. This may afford secondary gratification to patients, who can (a) taunt the confused therapist or (b) convince themselves that the therapist is useless due to the failure to understand the patient.

Positive Transference

In addition to the negative transferences discussed, the adoptee may enact a variety of positive idealizing transferences. One such variation reflects the adoptee's defensive mission to preserve her biological parents as good objects and avoid the greater pain of knowing their limitations. Fairbairn (1943/1990, chap. 3) and others thereafter (Kernberg, 1985–1986) elucidate this dynamic where abused children idealize their parents, unconsciously assuming all responsibility for familial trauma in a dissociated fragment of self to avoid the more painful experience of acknowledging parental limitations. Owing to this dynamic, the patient may come to view the therapist as a perfect and idealized object who makes no mistakes and is never hurtful. Patients may protect the therapist by rushing to take the blame for inevitable errors that arise in treatment or deny being hurt by suboptimal actions of the therapist.

In another variation of an idealizing transference, patients may come to view the therapist as the lost biological parent who can finally provide the love and comfort of which they have been deprived (Brinich, 1990, 1995; Jones, 1997; Lush, Boston, Morgan, & Kolvin, 1998; Nickman et al., 2005). This idealization is often magnified further by the possibility that given the anonymity of the adoptee's biological parents, the patient may think the therapist actually is the lost parent. In a related dynamic, Nickman (1985) notes that adoptees' reality-fantasy distinction is often muddied by the fact that anyone in their life might actually be a biological parent. Seeing the therapist as the lost biological parent is also enhanced by the family romance dynamic (Freud, 1908; Derdeyn & Graves, 1998) in which all children sometimes imagine the parents they live with are lowly, adoptive parents as against their original parents seen as regal, exalted people. This is an easy leap for the adoptee, who actually has two sets of parents and may develop powerfully fueled ideas that the therapist is this idealized, biological parent (Nickman, 1985).

Unstable Transference

The adoptee's reactions to the therapist are typically intense and conflicting. They often alternate between extremes such as idealization and devaluation and/or a desire to attach and a need to distance for fear of abandonment (Samuel, 2003). The adoptee's therapeutic connection is therefore likely to become wildly fluctuating and unstable (Nickman et al., 2005). While such upheaval is an opportunity to enter into and therapeutically survive inevitable enactments in the work, its intensity can also dangerously erode the minimum levels of safety and security required for a viable therapeutic relationship. Reeves (1971) describes one such transferential pattern among adoptees that originates in empathy and engagement on a deep unconscious level with the therapist but is inevitably interrupted by a negative reaction that consistently disintegrates into disillusionment and alienation. Reeves views this pattern as an enactment of the adoptee's original experience of attachment followed by rejection, which leads to subsequent fragile connections that reenact this original experience.

Other qualities of the adoptee described in the literature can translate into an unstable transference to the therapist. Some authors point to the adoptee's chronic fear of abandonment and compromised sense of safety deriving from the experience of losing one's original parents (Glenn, 1974; Jones, 1997; Lanyado, 2003; Nickman et al., 2005; Samuels, 1990; Silverman, 1985–1986). This dynamic coexists with the adoptee's intense desire to attach (Lanyado, 2003; Novack, 2004). We propose that such fears could result in the patient's view of the therapist as untrustworthy and thereby difficult to embrace as a potentially soothing object. We would expect the adoptee's fear of abandonment and danger to intensify as loving, intimate, or dependent feelings emerge in treatment and the therapist becomes a more essential figure. These collective anxieties pose a serious threat to the patient's growing ability and motivation to connect to the therapist on an ever-deepening level.

An unstable therapeutic attachment may also result from the adoptee's often-noted difficulty in achieving the developmental task of integrating good and bad parts of self and others (Bartram, 2003; Glenn, 1985–1986; Kernberg, 1985–1986; Samuel, 2003). This challenge can be burdened for the adoptee by having two sets of parents (Riley & Meeks, 2005), since each can be conveniently thought of as all good or all bad. To the extent this integrative task is unfinished for adoptees, it may manifest in gross fluctuations in their view of the therapist, potentially weakening the therapeutic support structure. Sudden reversals in the patient's view of the therapist may also reflect the struggle with conflicting loyalties noted by Nickman (1985). He and others (Quinodoz, 1996; Samuel, 2003) discuss the often divergent representations that adoptees have of their two sets of parents (typically, bad biological, good adoptive). This conflict can manifest in therapy as a "double" transference characterized by opposing and shifting views of the therapist that further destabilize the therapeutic relationship.

Background

Lisa is a Black child of Caribbean descent reportedly born to a teenage mother residing in a group home. Lisa was given up at birth to a foster agency and soon thereafter taken in by a foster family with whom she lived for the first 3 years of her life. Little is known about these early years. We know only that Lisa had foster siblings in this home but experienced the loss of most of them as they were chosen "over her" for adoption by other families. Additionally, she was reportedly in a special needs nursery during this time. Since so little is known about Lisa's early years in foster care, we are unsure of their impact on her life. We do know, however, that having been in foster care compounded Lisa's experience of loss as she was forced to sever ties with foster parents and siblings when she was adopted at age three.

Lisa's adoptive mother, Adele, is also of Caribbean descent. She became interested in adopting a child to provide companionship for her biological son, Steven, given many unsuccessful attempts to bear a second child. In addition to losing multiple pregnancies to miscarriage, Adele also lost her second husband of 7 years, the father of her biological child, 5 years prior to Lisa's arrival. Adele divorced her first husband in her country of origin, reportedly over physical abuse.

During early visits to her home, Adele remembers Lisa as quiet, clingy, disinterested in play, and cloaked in a blank stare. At times, she destroyed Adele's things. Although she believed Lisa would be difficult, Adele proceeded with adoption 6 months after visitation began. Lisa was then three, and Steven was six. While Adele was in the process of adopting Lisa, Lisa's maternal grandparents were attempting to do the same. The court reportedly granted adoption rights to Adele, representing yet another loss for Lisa. They reasoned that Lisa's biological grandparents had difficulty raising their own daughter, Lisa's biological mother, and thus might not be reliable parents.

Lisa began attending regular nursery school on arrival at Adele's home, where school personnel were quick to report, "She's no Steven." By the time she reached kindergarten, Lisa had already stolen snack money from other children as well as from the teacher. Adele recalls feeling she was unable to discipline and set consequences for Lisa as she "cared about nothing." In first grade, Lisa was recommended to see a school psychologist, which she did through the time of referral to our clinic.

Treatment

The following presents aspects of Lisa's treatment emphasizing transference and countertransference developments that have been raised or implied in the literature as well as those newly observed in our clinical work. It is of note that descriptions of countertransferential reactions with adoptees are infrequent in the literature (Kernberg, 1978) and even where raised are usually not elaborated. Countertransferential reactions in the work with Lisa are understood to reflect potential problem areas for the therapist as well as possible parallels to Lisa's internal states and those of her primary objects (Racker, 1968).

We wish to clarify that when transferences and countertransferences are described in this chapter, either as companions to common behavioral patterns of adoptees or arising anew out of our clinical material, we do not mean to suggest a one-to-one relationship between a given transference-countertransference constellation and a complementary adoption issue. This would be particularly illusory in discussing treatment with adoptees, where isolating conflicts around adoption is always questionable since they are typically unacknowledged by the patient (as in our case). In addition, particular transferential patterns may represent conflicts not only about adoption but also about issues related to the specific therapeutic pair. Thus, descriptions of transference and countertransference are offered and analyzed in this chapter to suggest clues rather than answers to the way adoption issues have been psychologically incorporated. By proposing connections between particular transference-countertransference developments and specific adoption issues, clinicians can work "backward" to access warded-off adoption concerns.

Lisa was almost nine when Adele brought her to therapy at our clinic, where she remained in a once-a-week psychoanalytically-oriented treatment for one year. At the outset, Adele had a lengthy list of complaints about Lisa, including her constant attention-seeking behavior, difficulty in getting along with others, and disruptiveness and disobedience at home and in school. Adele's laundry list of complaints mirrored the tendency of adoptive parents to experience and express significant distress about the adoptee's behavior (Derdeyn & Graves, 1998; Leiberman, 2003). Lisa reportedly destroyed and stole objects from teachers and peers, denied responsibility for her actions, and acted in sexually provocative ways with boys. She also reportedly attached to people indiscriminately with inappropriate intensity. Adele described her bitter disappointment that things were not working out as she had hoped with Lisa. She did not see herself as contributing to such problems, however, reasoning that her biological child seemed well-adjusted. During Adele's first visit with the therapist, she reported that Lisa had announced she intended to search for her birth mother when she grew up. Adele explained that she did not pursue this topic with Lisa, believing "the past was better left alone."

Lisa began therapy with a decided air of excitement and hope. As her feelings of safety steadily grew during these early months, Lisa began to reveal more and more of her secrets, including the way she stole money and food from schoolchildren and teachers and stashed food from her home refrigerator in her room until it would rot. She quickly developed idealized notions about the therapist (Janet Rivkin Zuckerman), which soon escalated into a full-blown idealizing transference as Lisa basked in the warm glow of the therapist's sustained attention and interest. There was a strong sense that Lisa needed to view me as perfect and unerring (Kernberg, 1985–1986) and worked hard to uphold this vision by forgiving me or turning a blind eye to mistakes or omissions I made. When Christmas approached still early in treatment, Lisa announced that she had asked her mother for a red coat just like mine. Our interactions were soaked in the feeling that Lisa wanted to be like me and belong to me, as if I might be her long-lost parent (Brinich, 1990, 1995; Nickman, 1985) offering love and comfort she had never before known. My countertransference at such times involved both a desire to rescue Lisa (Treacher, 2000) and the fear that I would abandon her and fail to satisfy her intense and poignant longings (Lanyado, 2003). Kernberg (1985–1986) alludes to this experience, noting that when the family romance dynamic is actualized in the transference, "this in turn exerts inordinate pressure on the analyst not to let down the abandoned child for a second time" (p. 297). We would expand this observation to say that fears of failing the adoptee exist in a broader scope across the countertransferential field. Given the adoptee's painful early history, along with intense pressure on the therapist to be the good restorative object, there is a potent and persistent countertransferential fear of repeating the patient's traumatic past particularly given the therapist's circumscribed role in the patient's life. This countertransferential fear also reflects the often fragile quality of adoptees' relationships with the therapist as well as with others in their lives. At other times, countertransferentially, I felt the desire to reject Lisa owing to my extreme discomfort at her efforts to get inside of me, physically and emotionally, and to idealize me. Reeves (1971) similarly discusses his tendency to feel a fusion with adoptees, experienced as so intolerable that on more than one occasion he unconsciously disengaged from its hold by calling the patient the wrong name.

Where the therapist experiences such an idealizing transference with an adoptee and its accompanying countertransferential anxieties, it can be useful to consider and, where appropriate, introduce potentially relevant adoption issues. These can include feelings of loss toward unknown biological parents as well as a need to protect imagined defective biological parents.

Lisa's idealization was short-lived, as she quickly bumped into the reality that I was not always available to her and that our relationship had palpable limitations. She also began to realize that our emerging alliance posed new and uncomfortable threats to her connection with her adoptive mother. Following one session where both Lisa and Adele had been present in the room, Lisa collapsed into panic and despair after I declined Adele's request to have Lisa's adoptive brother Steven join our session. Witnessing the tension between such important figures in her life was terrifying for Lisa and jeopardized her sense of connection to each of us. Devaluation, rage, and disappointment emerged in Lisa as she felt betrayed by my behavior in her mother's presence. But as she hated me, she also worried that I would reject her as a consequence of her fury. Adding further to these already complex and intense affects were Lisa's fears of abandonment and diminished sense of object constancy. At the end of our sessions, she would sometimes ask, "Will we ever see each other again?" Such concerns are typical for adoptees who suffered the loss of their original parents (Glenn, 1974; Lush et al., 1998; Samuels, 1990; Silverman, 1985–1986).

Given this multiplicity of intense and shifting feeling states, the seeds were sown for a fundamental instability and mistrust in our relationship. These sudden affective shifts mimicked Lisa's overall tendency to experience herself and others in extreme and unmodulated ways. This dynamic emanated from a home environment that tolerated few mistakes and failed to provide models of soothing or modulation of affect. On one occasion, Lisa tentatively disclosed some of her misdeeds but became anxious about her revelation, commenting, "I don't tell these things to anyone. . . . I tell only the Devil or the angels." For Lisa, these were the only choices, and transferentially we each oscillated repeatedly between them. Lisa's intense and shifting emotional states resemble those typically ascribed to adoptees, including (a) Reeves's description of a transference that originates in deep affective engagement but inevitably deteriorates into disillusionment and alienation, recapitulating the original traumatic loss, and (b) the clashing of ego ideals described by Nickman (1985), where extreme and rapidly shifting views of the therapist may symbolize a struggle to reconcile widely divergent views of biological and of adoptive parents. Such a conflict was suggested when Lisa would address me as Dr. Zuckerman in the midst of a fitful rage, explaining that her adoptive mother would disapprove if she called me by my first name.

When faced with a rapidly shifting transference in work with adoptees, the therapist can consider and potentially introduce dialogue about adoption themes. Key issues include reenactment of the adoptee's journey from attachment to loss as well as symbolic efforts to reconcile conflicting parental representations.

Well into the middle phase of treatment, my sessions with Lisa became heavily punctuated by Lisa's anger, oppositionality, and disillusionment. Hatred of me, as well as hatred of herself, were now more fully present in the therapy room. At times, Lisa became so filled with fury that she would turn and face the wall, speechless for most of the session. On other occasions, she provoked me continually with outbursts and attacks, such as "You look disgusting . . . you disgust me," as though committed to enacting the rejection that was so familiar to her. Provocations could include manipulation and demand ("Hurry up and move, I don't have all day!"), assigning me the role of helpless victim that she more typically inhabited. Transferentially, I was seen as disapproving and rejecting or pitifully helpless. Countertransferentially, anxiety along with a strong sense of rejection and anger arose in me as intense affects were projected and displaced onto me, triggered by my own personal vulnerabilities (Wilkinson & Hough, 1996). At such times, I could experience the anger of the abuser that Lisa feared but at the same time provoked. This created extreme discomfort in me and also hinted at the quality of Adele's internal states. When immersed in rejection, I could feel the profound internal disruption that resulted from the other's rage and insensitivity, as Lisa presumably did.

These provocations served many possible masters, including Lisa's need to (a) recapitulate her own rejection by birth parents, (b) assure herself that she was the damaged object rather than her parents or the therapist, (c) unconsciously maintain an identification with her devalued biological parents through her unacceptable behavior, (d) test the therapist with outrageous behavior to see if the latter would reject her (Hopkins, 2000), and (e) lock herself into a destructive but predictable sense of worthlessness and confirmation of her fundamental defectiveness. Any of these dynamics, intimately connected to the patient's adoptive identity, may be considered and explored when experiencing such a critical, rejection-tainted transference along with the accompanying countertransferential feelings of rejection, anger, and abusiveness.

Adding to this already difficult phase was the fact that Lisa's initial and noteworthy symptomatic improvements were regularly and readily dismissed by her mother as nonexistent. Setbacks were viewed as a hopeless return to an irreparably damaged core: "How else can you explain why someone who had to eat out of the garbage all her life but now doesn't have to, would continue eating out of the garbage?" Adele's reactions dampened the positive feelings gained in treatment and fueled Lisa's feelings of self-loathing. Powerful cultural, racial, and ethnic differences between Lisa, Adele, and me created intense countertransferential challenges at these junctures. Clashing values regarding education, discipline, religion, and work ethic were painfully at play. Adele's mistrust of therapy, my competence, and my values, along with her unconscious sabotage of the treatment (missed appointments, late arrivals, criticism of me to Lisa) due to its profound threats (Bartram, 2003), seriously strained the therapeutic relationship. Adele's tendency to undermine the treatment in these ways eroded Lisa's confidence in me, communicated that it was not safe to make a real connection, and eventuated in my doubting my own efficacy. Countertransferentially, I struggled to control my anger and frustration, which I did by hiding behind a pleasant affect or distancing myself emotionally. Maintaining a neutral stance, if ever possible, was all the more impossible. Adele's anger and my resulting anxieties caused me to avoid addressing critical issues such as our racial and social status differences. Ultimately, these forces further burdened the already difficult task of understanding the impact of adoption on Lisa and Adele.

Lisa was also growing notably uncomfortable with my attention, nonjudgmental attitude, and commitment to repair empathic failures. At times, she angrily asked, "Why are you so nice to me?" or "Why are you smiling at me?" and stated, "Don't look at me that way, with that smile." Kind treatment was destabilizing as it challenged Lisa's fundamental assumptions about who she was and how the world operated. Though tempted to engage more fully with my invitation to become close, Lisa usually withdrew in favor of the more familiar position of mistrust and distance. At times, she sat for entire sessions in her buttoned-up coat, determined to keep me at bay. Countertransferentially, I felt impotent as Lisa seemed stubbornly committed to rejecting the only tools I had to offer.

Lisa was also suspicious of me, doubting my acceptance of her, my credibility and smile. In part, this view may have derived from her own tendency to lie (Sherick, 1983) and blur reality (e.g., she often referred to her adoptive mother's boyfriend as "daddy"), to soften or deny the traumas of her life. This pattern often evoked countertransferential confusion and mistrust about what was and was not real. Was Lisa's household in fact emotionally and physically abusive as she sometimes suggested it was but usually later denied? Was Lisa perpetrator, fabricator, or victim? A fuzzy reality, puzzlement, and doubt ensued, echoing Lisa's experience of not being solidly anchored in what was and was not real, and the disorientation resulting from such a state. When presented with the adoptee's lies and suspiciousness and the therapist's concordant confusion and mistrust, it can be valuable to consider and perhaps introduce the idea that the adoptee may engage in this behavior as a way to stave off the pain related to her adoptive identity.

Hints of shame and curiosity about Lisa's unknown origins began to emerge in treatment. This was contrasted with Lisa's view of me as possessing all the fundamentals she lacked. In one session, she spoke of Edgar, Adele's first husband. Momentarily confused, I asked, "Do you mean your biological father?" Lisa responded, "Oh, I don't have one of those. My mother never married." On another occasion, she commented that I had three names. I answered that she also had three names, referring to her biological name and adoptive name; however, Lisa refused to further engage around this topic. She sometimes expressed interest in my files (Glenn, 1976), pretending she was the omniscient therapist equipped with knowledge of her identity and making entries into her records. Transferences that incorporate such identity themes provide a potentially useful way to engage adoptees' conflicts about their unknown origins.

New Faces of the Transference

As discussed, we observed new transference-countertransference patterns in this case not yet described in the clinical literature. One salient new piece of transference emerged from a theme Lisa introduced in the earliest stages of treatment and returned to throughout. She would beseechingly ask me, "Who are you?" and "What is your name, I don't remember?" She repeatedly insisted, "I don't even know you." In this powerful repetitive enactment, Lisa seemed to view me as a stranger who had inexplicably entered her life. Once, as I touched her shoulder while we walked together to another room, she recoiled and ordered, "Don't touch me, only people in my family touch me, you're a stranger!" (see Hughes, 1997, where the adoptee insisted that the therapist ask permission before touching him). This confusion about my identity continued throughout Lisa's treatment, when she continued to insist, "I don't even know you!" In such moments, we were truly "strangers in a strange room," with all traces of our relational history momentarily erased.

Countertransferential feelings of rejection and abandonment sometimes followed Lisa's retreats, informing me of the kind of loneliness and disconnectedness that must accompany the experience of being handed over at a pivotal point in life with no tools to comprehend the experience. On other occasions, I could also feel invisible as a result of Lisa's repeated insistences that I was a stranger who was having no impact on her. Reeves (1971) briefly describes a similar experience of remoteness in working with adoptees, which is "like the feeling of being engulfed with another person in a blanket of fog" (p. 160). I felt lacking in identity and presence, as if my words were falling on deaf ears.

We may consider this transference-countertransference pattern as a projection of Lisa's fundamental anxiety and ungroundedness about who she is in the world and how she arrived. Her insistence that I am a stranger may also reenact her ignorance of her unknown mother, her belief that her mother could be anyone, including me, and her tentativeness about everyone in her world.

Lisa's insistence that I was a stranger also served to deny a growing closeness between us. Maintaining a relational gulf posed less of a threat to her relationship with her mother, minimized fears of my retaliation, maintained her identity as an outsider, and helped Lisa maintain the status quo. How could she be expected to discuss an issue as profoundly intimate and disturbing as her adoption with someone she didn't really know? Countertransferentially, even when experiencing myself as having a deep connection with Lisa, it was inevitably interrupted so abruptly and profoundly that I often doubted its initial efficacy. This was dramatically experienced in one session, when Lisa initiated the game of Hangman. Coded game messages began as mundane references to daily life but quickly evolved into communications about deep feelings of what had been missing from her life and what she needed to be healed: "I love you." "Do you love me?" "You make me happy." "Love is what I need from you." I responded with messages that confirmed our mutually special feelings for one another, deeply touched by what was evolving. However, in one vignette, I unwittingly guessed Lisa's Hangman code too quickly. She became instantly infuriated and withdrew into isolation, refusing to communicate for the remainder of the session. I was caught by surprise and unsettled by Lisa's reaction as it was not at all apparent to me how I had triggered it. Although I had several broad hypotheses about what precipitated this rupture (poor timing on my part, Lisa's fear of intimacy and intense feelings for me), I could not use any of them as Lisa shut down completely, refusing to meet any of my efforts to understand and repair this rift (see Bartram, 2003, where the adoptee was unable to tolerate any comment by the analyst that reflected on what was occurring in the room). Weeks later, she could only broadly allude to how I had hurt her. The tenuousness and variability of my connection with Lisa caused me to doubt my continuing viability in her eyes and, ultimately, to feel like an ineffectual failure. This state helped me better understand Lisa's experiences of powerlessness and ineffectualness in her world, where all efforts to establish herself as a viable agent remained unrealized.

Such persistent characterizations by the patient of estrangement in the therapeutic relationship, and the ensuing countertransferential feelings of invisibleness and ineffectiveness, provide a potentially useful entrée into the adoptee's world. We propose that relevant issues associated with feelings of ungroundedness, powerlessness, and ineffectualness in therapist or patient include the fact that the adoptee was uprooted and shifted from adult to adult as a near-anonymous object.

In a related transference, Lisa sometimes revealed her view of me as someone who was different and alien from herself. She would enumerate many areas of our differences, neglecting other things we had in common. "You don't celebrate Christmas like I do," "You're Jewish, I'm not," and "You're white, unlike me." Countertransferentially, I felt helpless in bridging the gulf she felt compelled to inject between us. Her preoccupation with uncovering our differences is reminiscent of Nickman's (1985) assertion that adoptees who are of different origins are unconsciously directed toward distinguishing themselves particularly from their adoptive parents in an intense pursuit of their own identity. Persistent attempts by adoptees to focus on differences between themselves and the therapist, and the accompanying feelings of distance and resignation in the therapist, may provide a useful therapeutic springboard to adoptees' concerns and discomfort about their unknown origins.

Another new transferential pattern involved Lisa's perception that I was the mother of myriad children whom I actively favored over her (see Goldberg, 2000, discussing how the adoptee may feel tortured by exclusion from the therapist's real family to a degree never felt by the nonadoptee). Lisa's anxieties about sibling competition were deepened by her loss of multiple foster siblings selected "over her" for adoption and the presence of an adoptive brother who was a favored biological child. Lisa's concerns were reflected in a persistent return to references, questions, and comparisons with other children's drawings on my office walls, along with intense curiosity about the identity of those children and of my biological children. Her preoccupation with sibling rivalry and her rejected child status surpassed that usually seen among children in treatment. Such a transferential stance may encapsulate Lisa's anxiety about (a) being a second-class citizen because she is adopted and (b) the impending rejection owing to such second-class status. It may thus be useful to explore the adoptee's preoccupation with sibling issues in treatment against the backdrop of her insecure identity within and beyond her adoptive family.

Lisa's hypervigilance was another new dynamic in this case. Lisa often studied my expression from moment to moment and came within inches of my face to inspect me, creating extreme countertransferential self-consciousness and discomfort at this intrusion into what I considered my personal space. She searched my expression for signs of my real feelings, asking, "Are you mad?" or "Why are you always smiling?" Lisa might have been worried that I could disappear at a moment's notice (like her biological mother) and was working overtime to "keep an eye on me." As stated elsewhere, she also believed that I stood in constant judgment of her. Her hypervigilance can thus be thought of as her early warning system against impending rejection. Finally, Lisa's searching stare seemed to embody her experience of me (and potentially herself) as not completely whole, real, or graspable. She seemed to stare and study in an effort to put me all together. Thus, hypervigilance and its accompanying transference-countertransference manifestations may provide a gateway to the adoptee's unresolved issues of early abandonment and rejection along with related difficulties in seeing self and others in an integrated way.

Another new pattern observed in the work with Lisa was her tendency to offer and then retract salient pieces of information about her life. She communicated information about her adoptive mother's emotional abuse and Adele's boyfriend's dysfunctionality, only to deny and withdraw it. She explained that I was not part of the family and should not be told. She fluctuated about whether I could discuss this disturbing information with Adele, initially giving permission but inevitably retracting it for fear of betrayal by me and revenge from her mother. At some level, she desperately wanted to share her secrets with someone safe but ultimately found it too terrifying to complete the process.

This pattern seemed to contain a transferential view of me as someone who (a) threatened her relationship with her mother, (b) could undo the safety of the status quo, and (c) could betray or reject her with this inflammatory information. This perspective was intensified by Lisa's mother, who was visibly unsettled by our developing alliance and preached values such as independence and impenetrability, which conflicted with Lisa's experience of the therapeutic relationship. Accordingly, Lisa withdrew her disclosures about family pathology, realigned with her mother to avoid internal conflict, and commanded, "Don't say anything about what we talked about, look happy!" Countertransferentially, I felt paralyzed at such times between the temptation to ignore crucial data to ensure Lisa's safety and the therapeutic mission of unearthing these deeply disturbing developments. Thus, the adoptee's patterns of offering and retracting affectively rich information paired with countertransferential feelings of confusion and paralysis are noteworthy. They may provide a signal to explore the adoptee's fear that therapy might further jeopardize her already tentative position within the adoptive family.

Another new trend emerging in this case was Lisa's pattern of enacting conflicts around death and dying. In treatment, Lisa elaborately described her grandmother's funeral in the Caribbean, which she would soon be attending, only to later tell me that this was all a ruse. After expressing deep affection for me on another occasion, she asked whether I would bother to attend her funeral should she die. In newly developing projective play, Lisa was eating food with her family at a fun-filled party that suddenly and shockingly turned into a funeral.

In these moments, when Lisa seemed to be working through some of the most fundamental losses of her life, she was successfully using me as a new and safe object in her life to accompany her through this painstaking process. Greenberg (1991) discusses the idea of the therapist as a new and safe transferential object, stating, "First, the analyst works to facilitate the feeling of safety that allows the observing self to tolerate more . . . of early experience that has been warded off" (p. 209). The analyst thus differentiates herself from the patient's dangerous objects of early experience and establishes herself as someone new, though the analyst should not be too safe, as this can inhibit the emergence of negative transference. Greenberg advocates "a kind of balance between the patient's experience of the analyst as a safe and as a dangerous presence" (p. 217). A similar portrayal of the therapist is offered in Frankiel (1993), where the therapist positions herself as an "ally" (p. 353) reliably present through the patient's pain without attacking or interfering with her ability to work through her history of early separation or traumatic loss (see also Downey, 2002, discussing the analyst who sits with the patient as when one "sits shiva," thereby reactivating the patient's mourning process).

As this working through began to take hold for Lisa, a new feeling was palpable in the treatment room. She seemed more and more tolerable to herself, even when experiencing intense affects. She began to view me differently as well. Phrases like "I'm scared of you," "I think I'm beginning to like you," and "I want to come back and see you" slowly emerged, evoking parallel countertransferential feelings of therapeutic efficacy and overall goodness. At this time, Lisa also began to engage in projective play for the first time, whereas previously, she was rarely, if ever, able to leave the safety and structure of board games. Nickman (1996b) and others (Derdeyn & Graves, 1998; Treacher, 2000) remind us of the importance of helping adoptees experience in consciousness their sadness and grief about absent birth parents and relationships that never were and never will be. Moments when the adoptee is able to experience the therapist as new and safe, and the therapist feels aligned with the fundamental therapeutic task, are essential steps in the adoptee's journey of mourning a family that was never known and uncovering a new self in the process.

CONCLUSION

Adoptees who seek psychotherapy typically have difficulty acknowledging and discussing issues related to adoption in an elaborated way (Nickman, 1996a). As such, any tools that might further the clinician's ability to stimulate dialogue about adoption would be quite valuable. In this chapter, we contend that transference and countertransference enactments provide such a tool since they often incorporate adoption-related conflicts, providing a rich means of accessing these otherwise warded-off issues. We have discussed transference and countertransference developments with adoptees from several angles. Initially, we discussed transferential patterns presented in the literature, noting that while adoptees' behavior/characterological patterns have been extensively described, this kind of elaboration has not extended to transferential patterns. Where only behavioral descriptions exist, we have proposed ways in which they may manifest within the therapeutic relationship.

Thereafter, we presented portions of a treatment with a 9-year-old adopted girl, incorporating patterns discussed in the literature and proposing new transference-countertransference constellations. We recognize that it would be oversimplifying the complexities of the clinical picture to suggest that a given transference-countertransference development would always signify a specific adoption conflict. On the contrary, we mean to posit potential relationships between particular transference-countertransference events and possible adoption concerns.

Given that transference and countertransference configurations are invaluable aids in accessing patients' warded-off feelings about adoption, we recommend continuing research into (a) transference-countertransference manifestations that arise during psychotherapy with adopted patients; (b) the frequency with which these manifestations appear; (c) the particular circumstances of the adoption situations in which these manifestations arise; (d) the adoptee's dynamics and conflicts that are potentially symbolized by particular transference and countertransference patterns; and (e) whether accessing and exploring adoption issues are consistently enhanced through a focus on transference and countertransference issues. The inventory presented in this chapter can help clinicians begin to experience transference and countertransference within an adoption context, thereby enhancing their ability to generate dialogue about an otherwise unmentioned and unmentionable subject.

BEST PRACTICE IDEAS

It is essential that the therapist who works with adoptees (a) closely monitor the patient's transferential reactions as they yield invaluable clues to access and understand her feelings about being adopted; (b) closely monitor his or her own countertransference reactions as they too yield invaluable clues to access and understand the patient's feelings about being adopted; and (c) have a detailed understanding of the core issues with which adoptees typically struggle, to help the therapist view transference and countertransference reactions through the lens of the adoptee's central concerns.

REFLECTION QUESTIONS

1. Did the therapist's awareness of this patient's transferential reactions facilitate the exploration of her adoption issues? What aspects of the adoption experience were exposed? How else might these issues be uncovered?

2. What additional clues might there have been in the transference and countertransference patterns of this therapeutic dyad that might have furthered the work on adoption in this case?

3. How did you feel about the way problems with the patient's mother were managed by the therapist, and how might you have handled them differently?

4. How successful was the therapy in helping the patient contact her feelings about having been adopted?

5. What are some of the common themes that emerge during psychotherapy with adoptees?

REFERENCES

Bartram, P. (2003). Some oedipal problems in work with adopted children and their parents. *Journal of Child Psychotherapy, 1,* 21–36.

Brinich, P. M. (1980). Some potential effects of adoption on self and object representations. *Psychoanalytic Study of the Child, 35,* 107–133.

Brinich, P. M. (1990). Adoption from the inside out: A psychoanalytic perspective. In D. Brodzinsky & M. Schechter (Eds.), *The psychology of adoption* (pp. 42–61). New York: Oxford University Press.

Brinich, P. M. (1995). Psychoanalytic perspectives on adoption and ambivalence. *Psychoanalytic Psychology, 12*(2), 181–199.

Deering, C. D., & Scahill, L. (1989). Adopted children in psychotherapy. *Archives of Psychiatric Nursing, 3*(2), 79–85.

Derdeyn, A., & Graves, C. (1998). Clinical vicissitude of adoption. *Child and Adolescent Psychiatric Clinics of North America, 7*(2), 373–388.

Downey, W. (2002). Little orphan Anastasia, Part 2: Developmental growth, love, and therapeutic change. *The Psychoanalytic Study of the Child, 57,* 218–244.

Fairbairn, W. R. D. (1990). The repression and return of bad objects. In P. Buckley (Ed.), *Psychoanalytic studies of the personality* (pp. 59–81). London: Routledge. (Original work published 1943)

Frankiel, R. (1993). Hide-and-seek in the playroom: An object loss and transference in child treatment. *Psychoanalytic Review, 80*(3), 341–359.

Freud, S. (1908). Family romance. In J. Strachey (Ed. & Trans.), *The standard edition of the complete psychological works of Sigmund Freud* (Vol. 9, pp. 237–241). London: Hogarth Press.

Glenn, J. (1974). The adoption theme in Edward Albee's "Tiny Alice" and "The American Dream." *Psychoanalytic Study of the Child, 29,* 413–429.

Glenn, J. (1985–1986). The adopted child's self and object representations. *International Journal of Psychoanalytic Psychotherapy, 11,* 309–313.

Goldberg, R. (2000). Clinical work with adults who have been adopted. In A. Treacher & I. Katz (Eds.), *The dynamics of adoption* (pp. 199–212). London: Jessica Kingsley.

Greenberg, J. (1991). *Oedipus and beyond: A clinical theory.* Cambridge, MA: Harvard University Press.

Homes, A. M. (1996, March 27). The birth mother who found me. *New York Times,* p. A21.

Hopkins, J. (2000). Overcoming a child's resistance to late adoption: How one new attachment can facilitate another. *Journal of Child Psychotherapy, 26*(3), 335–347.

Hughes, D. A. (1997). *Facilitating developmental attachment: The road to emotional recovery and behavioral change in foster and adopted children.* Northvale, NJ: Jacob Aronson.

Jones, A. (1997). Issues relevant to therapy with adoptees. *Psychotherapy, 34*(1), 64–68.

Kernberg, P. (1978). Algumas reacoes contratransferencias no tratamento de criancas e pais adoptivos [Countertransference reaction in work with adoptive children and their families]. *Revista Brasileira Psicanalise, 12,* 439–448.

Kernberg, P. F. (1985–1986). Child analysis with a severely disturbed adopted child. *International Journal of Psychoanalytic Psychotherapy, 11,* 277–299.

Kirschner, D. (1990). The adopted child syndrome: Considerations for psychotherapy. *Psychotherapy in Private Practice, 8*(3), 93–100.

Lanyado, M. (2003). The emotional tasks of moving from fostering to adoption: Transitions, attachment, separation and loss. *Clinical Child Psychology and Psychiatry, 8*(3), 337–349.

Lieberman, A. (2003). The treatment of attachment disorder in infancy and early childhood: Reflections from clinical interventions with later-adopted foster care children. *Attachment & Human Development, 5*(3), 279–282.

Lifton, B. (1990). The formation of the adopted self. *Psychotherapy in Private Practice, 9*, 85–91.

Lush, D., Boston, M., Morgan, J., & Kolvin, I. (1998). Psychoanalytic psychotherapy with disturbed adopted and foster children: A single case follow-up study. *Clinical Child Psychology and Psychiatry, 3*(1), 51–69.

McDaniel, K., & Jennings, G. (1997). Therapists' choice of treatment for adoptive families. *Journal of Family Psychotherapy, 8*(4), 47–68.

Nickman, S. L. (1985). Losses in adoption: The need for dialogue. *Psychoanalytic Study of the Child, 40*, 365–398.

Nickman, S. (1996a). Challenges of adoption. *The Harvard Mental Health Letter, 12*(7), 5–7.

Nickman, S. (1996b). Retroactive loss in adopted persons. In D. Klass, P. Silverman, & S. Nickman (Eds.), *Continuing bonds: New understandings of grief* (pp. 257–272). Washington, DC: Taylor & Francis.

Nickman, S., Rosenfeld, A., Fine, P., Macintyre, J., Pilowsky, D., Howe, R. A., et al. (2005). Children in adoptive families: Overview and update. *Journal of the American Academy of Child and Adolescent Psychiatry, 44*(10), 987–995.

Novak, B. (2004). From chaos to developmental growth: Working through trauma to achieve adolescence in the analysis of an adopted Russian orphan. *The Psychoanalytic Study of the Child, 59*, 74–99.

Parkhill, N. (2004). *Healing the adoption experience.* Martinsville, IN: Bookman.

Parsons, M. (1992). Problems of self esteem in the analysis of a seven-year-old adopted girl. *Journal of Child Psychotherapy, 18*(2), 19–40.

Quinodoz, D. (1996). The adopted analysand's transference of a "hole" object. *International Journal of Psychoanalysis, 77*, 323–336.

Racker, H. (1968). *Transference and countertransference.* Madison, CT: International Universities Press.

Reeves, A. C. (1971). Children with surrogate parents: Cases seen in analytic therapy and an aetiological hypothesis. *British Journal of Medical Psychology, 44*(2), 155–176.

Riley, D., & Meeks, J. (2005). *Beneath the mask: Understanding adopted teens.* Silver Springs, MD: CASE.

Samuel, H. (2003). Adoption: Some clinical features of adults who have been adopted and the difficulties of helping them in NHS psychotherapy. *Psychoanalytic Psychotherapy, 17*(3), 206–218.

Samuels, S. (1990). *Ideal adoption: A comprehensive guide to forming an adoptive family.* New York: Plenum Press.

Schechter, M. D. (1973). A case study of an adopted child. *International Journal of Child Psychotherapy, 2*, 202–223.

Sherick, I. (1983). Adoption and disturbed narcissism: A case illustration of a latency aged boy. *Journal of the American Psychoanalytic Association, 31*(2), 487–513.

Silverman, M. A. (1985–1986). Adoptive anxiety, adoptive rage and adoptive guilt. *International Journal of Psychoanalytical Psychotherapy, 11*, 301–307.

Soll, J. (2000). *Adoption healing: A path to recovery.* Baltimore: Gateway Press.

Treacher, A. (2000). Narrative and fantasy in adoption: Towards a different theoretical understanding. In A. Treacher & I. Katz (Eds.), *The dynamics of adoption* (pp. 20–28). London: Jessica Kingsley.

Wieder, H. (1978). On when and whether to disclose about adoption. *Journal of the American Psychoanalytic Association, 26*, 793–811.

Wilkinson, S., & Hough, G. (1996). Lie as narrative truth in abused adopted adolescents. *The Psychoanalytic Study of the Child, 51*, 580–596.

Poetic Reflections and Other Creative Processes From Adoptees

Preface

ALINA CAMACHO-GINGERICH

St. John's University

There is a large body of literature on adoption; some of this literature is artistic, creative, or nonscientific. Poetry or prose, or a combination of both, this literature provides an important window on the issues the members of the triad face and how they attempt to cope and/or resolve them. Perhaps predictably so, there is more known literature from the perspective of adoptees and adoptive parents than birth parents.

We have gathered here poems and other creative writings by three of the best known authors who write about adoption from a personal perspective: Penny Callan Partridge, Christian Langworthy, and Sarah Saffian. Partridge, both an adoptee and an adoptive parent, is the cofounder of Adoption Forum, a Philadelphia-based organization for all the adoption community. She has published widely, including *Pandora's Hope: Poems and Prose About Being Adopted* and *An Adoptee's Dreams*; she continues to be invited to talk and read from her own work in numerous symposia on adoption. We have included in this chapter a generous selection of Partridge's poems on adoption; for the benefit of brevity, we will refer only to some of them in this preface.

Christian Langworthy was born in Vietnam in 1967 and came to the United States as an adopted child in 1975. He has an MFA from Columbia University and is the recipient of several prestigious literary awards and recognitions, including a Pushcart Prize Nomination, a Pulitzer Prize Nomination, an Academy of American Poets Prize, and a Grand Prize National Poetry Chapbook Contest for his book of poems, *The Geography of War*. His poems have appeared in various anthologies and publications, including *Poet Magazine, Viet Nam Forum,* and *The Asian-American Experience*. He is also the author of a novel, *War Child*.

Sarah Saffian is a journalist and an author, most significantly of the highly-acclaimed *Ithaka: A Daughter's Memoir of Being Found* (1998). She has worked as a staff writer for the *New York Daily News,* a senior writer for *US Weekly,* and a senior editor at *Entertainment Weekly,* and is currently a writing professor at the New School in New York City. An adopted child who as an adult was contacted out of the blue by her birth family—both parents and three full siblings. Saffian is active on issues pertaining to adoption, including being on the board of directors of an adoption agency and leading a book club for members of the adoption triad.

The selected pieces are beautiful, insightful reflections on the experience of adoption. Adoption is the common thread that unites these reflections; however, as the readers will immediately notice, there is a diversity of styles and approaches to this theme. And that, of course, is what good art should be: a reflection of the soul, of your own unique sensitivity and experience.

In "Portrait in Five Parts of a Daughter of Four Parents," Penny Partridge examines her own identity as an adopted child in a sensitive, lyrical five-part poem. Being adopted is seen as a plus, not a minus. It means you have two sets of parents from which to draw your talents, inclinations, physical appearance. The birth parents and adoptive parents are seen as four different mirrors to the poet's self-identity. The poet's face, which resembles her birth father's, makes her brother think of that father, Billy Duckett, whom she never met. An adopted child's face like hers can become a bridge and mirror to others' in the universe. It does that, the poet says, without her "lifting a finger."

The poet's body and sense of humor are her birth mother's; she actually discovered she had a sense of humor in the first phone call with her birth mother. She knows she inherited her artistic talent from her adoptive mother, an actress turned housewife, who liked and recited poetry to her (T. S. Eliot's, Gerald Manley Hopkins's, and Basho's *haiku*). The poet sees her adoptive mother as the person who helped her to overcome and accomplish; her own life is a tribute to hers.

The poet had a troubled relationship with her adoptive father, whom she rejected. He never really wanted to have children, dropped most or all of the parental responsibilities on her adoptive mother; a Republican full of stereotypes. The poet, not surprisingly, dismissed and moved away from him. But she appreciated his humble heart and his love of classical music; those qualities became the connection between the two of them and his legacy to her. The poet concludes that she is the product of all those people that formed and nurtured her: the daughter of two fathers, a junkman and an accountant (she counts with "words rather than numbers"), and also of two mothers, a teacher and an actress/housewife. She is from all those places they were from: Arkansas, Philadelphia, South Dakota, and Pasadena, Palo Alto and Shehawken, San Gabriel and Massachusetts. She will leave the same kind of legacy to her own two adoptive children.

"An International Story" is a beautiful poem/prayer that deals with international adoption as a connection to other places and cultures and as an opportunity to be more of a part of their children's lives. Through their adopted children adoptive parents can establish bridges, amplify their world. Partridge's friend Anna, by establishing contact with her Russian adopted daughter's world and culture, becomes even more connected to her adopted daughter's life. The poet expresses her desire and intent to include all of her adopted children's history (people, places, words, feelings) in their lives.

"Oregon" is a bonding poem among adoptees in their desire, need, and right to know about their birth parents. It is a passionate free-verse poem that carries the title of the state that passed the law in 1998 which allowed adoptees to seek and get such information. Those records were now open to them. The alliteration of the verses "imagine not knowing" and "it's *little* enough to learn" drives the point across very powerfully.

In her long poem *The Adopted Woman Reads an Obituary*, Partridge establishes a connection between poets and all adoptees. They are bonded by similar needs that transcend language and culture: "And who more than the adopted / would want poetry want / things put together want / words pushed together into music / so they can hear things they / can't in ordinary language?" She finds the symbol of poetry and poets in Czeslaw Milosz, the Polish poet and winner of the 1980 Nobel Prize in Literature, with whom, as an adopted person who happens to also be a poet, she clearly identifies. Milosz, who left his homeland ("a world no longer existing") and adopted and was adopted by a new one (he lived and taught in the United States for many years), symbolizes for her the need not only to express things and feelings in words in an original way, creating "music," but also to translate from other languages and cultures as well as to mix them ("The adopted can surely appreciate this / mixing of two mother tongues / more than anyone."). Partridge begins eight of nine stanzas of this poem with "I can't even read the Times"; the second verse of each stanza plays with the word "adopted": "being adopted," "reading it adopted," "musing adopted," "arguing adopted," "remembering adopted," and so on. This technique gives the poem not only a certain rhythm but also continuity of thought from one stanza to the next.

In Christian Langworthy's poetry there is no explicit desire to search for the identity of his biological parents. Adopted as a child from Vietnam, old enough to remember, he already knows about his past: "a prostitute's son in a Vietnamese / city bristling with rifles / and as a result of my mother's truancy / from motherhood, I was given / to nuns and locked within the confines of missionary walls." In this poem of free verse and three stanzas *How I Could Interpret the Events of My Youth—Events I Do Not Remember Except in My Dreams*, marked often by explanatory expositions in parentheses, he tells about his transition from a violence-ridden country to a childhood of "firsts" in America: first time to flush toilets, first time to see snow, first time to see cartoons on Saturday. Those events seem so far away to him, however, that the memories are perceived like dreams. During the years as an adopted child, his "second life" as he calls it, his adopted parents did everything possible to be good parents to him, including going to the cinema and reading him fairy tales like *Rumpelstiltskin*. He learned about "the false beauty of the wicked witch, / the castle besieged by thorns / the terror of the kidnapped son." The last two verses of the poem clearly indicate that the child remembered scenes from his prior life but was unable to explain them or separate them from the fiction of fairy tales. This poem attempts to reconstruct those memories, validating his childhood, prior and after adoption.

The Fourth of July is a poem in prose or poetic prose about, at a first level, a family Fourth of July picnic. It is, however, much more than that. The poem starts with the following lines: "I have killed the butterflies in my stomach, and my mother sits by the kitchen counter and stares at a tub of unsalted butter. She prepares an afternoon picnic for the Fourth of July." With exquisite attention to detail and the sounds of words, Langworthy describes the preparation of that picnic from its first stages till the family (minus the father) finally sits down to eat. The story is told from the child's perspective; with a very observant eye, the child describes everything surrounding him and the events that are taking place. Central to the story are the butterflies ("White butterflies. Yellow butterflies. Green butterflies"), present from the beginning until almost the end of the poem. As the mother is preparing for the picnic, flies and butterflies are everywhere: on the food, on the table, on the child. The butterflies become the central thread of the poem and the child's life: "I look at the butterflies in my life." It is not coincidental that the line "I have killed the butterflies in my stomach" is repeated twice, at the beginning and again toward the end with both its literal and symbolic meanings. This poem about a Fourth of July picnic, then, is also a poem of relationships, emotions, roles in the family. It reveals the relationship between the child and his parents, and between the parents, a loving woman who finds her identity in her family, especially in her children, and a somewhat distant and absentee father.

The Burned Walls is a poem of six stanzas; five of three verses each, and the sixth of four. It is a lullaby (the poem achieves its musicality through the repetition of certain verses, words, and endings of words) sung by the mother to her children. The lullaby serves as a contrast and a protection against the burned walls that surround them ("We sleep in the shadow of burned walls") and the bugs that crawl all over their bodies. The mother provides the necessary comfort and feelings of safety to her children: The verse "Mother will be here before night falls" is in the first stanza as well as in the last.

In Sarah Saffian's "Origin," a chapter from *Ithaka*, the protagonist is a fetus. Like in the internationally renowned Mexican novelist Carlos Fuentes' *Christopher Unborn*, the embryo-fetus-and-finally-baby expresses her emotions at different stages and moments of her development. In beautifully revealing prose ("I feel dragged along, like a piece of lint on the back of a sweater that lingers unnoticed"), this omniscient fetus shares with the readers, in an intimate, innocent but wise tone, her birth mother's uncertainty and anguish about this pregnancy.

The fetus, although at first ignored as an embryo, eventually gets to feel tenderness and love from the birth mother. She can even feel the close presence of her birth father, Adam. Like a poet, or any other artist, the fetus feels the void of knowledge about what is happening outside the womb with images of possibilities. Her imagination begins to create or re-create reality. Very soon after her birth, however, the newborn baby girl feels the detachment process from the birth mother ("her love, while unconditional, is mingled with despair, turning furtive unconfident") until, after her disappearance, the baby feels completely alone, "motherless," "nameless."

Reflections

32

PENNY CALLAN PARTRIDGE

CHRISTIAN LANGWORTHY

SARAH SAFFIAN

PORTRAIT IN FIVE PARTS OF
A DAUGHTER OF FOUR PARENTS

*PENNY CALLAN PARTRIDGE**

I. My Face

It turns out my face
is from my birthfather.

My fifty year old face
a mirror image
of the portrait
of our father
on the wall
in my brother's study.

My brother says
the older I get,
the more I bring him
our father,
Billy Duckett,
whom I never knew.

And I tell you
what is either
a sad commentary
on my *life*
or else inevitable
in *my* life;

This bringing someone
to someone else

without lifting
a finger
is one of the
thrills of my life.

It is also what has made me
really like my face.

II. My Sense of Humor

It turns out my body
is my birthmother's.
My sense of humor, too,
if you are willing to grant
that either of us had one.

I've rarely told a joke
(or told one right) and I cried
at Abbott and Costello movies,
they were so mean
to the fat one.

Catharine and I
liked coming out
with things bluntly
and being amused
by this privately.

Oh, I know this doesn't
leave you rolling in the
aisles (ho ho),
but our first phone
call told me that I do so

have a sense of humor.

III. My Art

It turns out my art
is from the mother
who adopted me.
She liked poetry.

She liked T. S. Eliot
("Do I dare . . . ?") and to
read aloud while she
brushed my hair.

She liked Gerard Manley
Hopkins "dappled things"
and Basho's haiku.
So wouldn't you?

My mother was
an actress turned
fifties housewife.
And I see my life

in so many ways
as improvement,
overcoming,
but also praise

of hers.

IV. My Heart

Does my heart
belong to Daddy?
Who'd thought it fine
not to have any children?

Who let my mother
do all the parenting?
Who had such
stereotypes?

Who was Republican?
Whom I dismissed,
I detached from,
moved away from?

But he had
this humble
heart this
appreciative heart.

He said a certain
symphony
was as close as we get
to heaven on earth.

I was glad
he'd come close
to heaven
on earth.

He would sigh in the shower it
felt so good.
Now I sigh in the shower
can feel that good.

If my heart is his
it's that he
let me see
his heart.

If my heart is like his,
I'm glad
I have
his heart

V. My Conclusion

I am a junk man's daughter.
I have some pipe from his junk yard.
I can see my face in it.
I have his face.

I am an accountant's daughter.
I have a ledger he kept.
I can account with words.
I have his name.

I am a teacher's daughter.
She encouraged her husband to paint.
I have his prize winning painting.
I have her hands.

I am an actress slash housewife's daughter.
I replay her scenes.
I have her mother's pearls.
I have her dreams.

I am from Arkansas and Philadelphia,
South Dakota and Pasadena,
Palo Alto and Shehawken,
San Gabriel and Massachusetts.

I will leave on Earth
two adopted children.
And I will be part
of them.

THE ADOPTED WOMAN READS AN OBITUARY

*PENNY CALLAN PARTRIDGE**

I can't even read the Times
without being adopted.
Like the death of Czeslaw Milosz.*
Who wasn't adopted
but he was a poet.
And who more than the adopted
would want poetry want
things put together want
words pushed together into music
so they can hear things they
can't in ordinary language?

I can't even read the Times
without reading it adopted.
Like the death of Czeslaw Milosz.
Who wasn't adopted
but was a translator.
You become a translator
with Poles, Lithuanians,
Jews, Russians and others
all sharing the area
but speaking their
separate languages.
Or you grow up knowing
that most people's
meaning of *mother*
doesn't mean *your* mother.
So who more than the adopted
would want to go back
and forth between languages?

I can't even read the Times
without musing adopted.
Like the death of Czeslaw Milosz
who did tranlsation but
thought you could write *true* poems
only in your mother tongue.
So where does that leave
the adopted who come from Korea
but grow up in English?
Can your mother tongue be your
adoptive mother's tongue?
Isn't Mi Ok Bruining a
powerful poet in English?
But look how she in-
corporates Korean. The adopted
can surely appreciate this
mixing of two mother tongues
more than anyone.

I can't even read the Times
without registering adopted.
Like the death of Czeslaw Milosz
who wasn't adopted
but was "from a world
no longer existing."
Who more than the adopted
can be from a place
no longer existing? A
nuclear family that didn't
stay stabile for a second.
Maybe not even atom for a
day before splitting. Or if
from a world still there
then not for us to know about.

I can't even read the Times
without spinning adopted.
Like the death of Czeslaw Milosz.
Who wasn't adopted
but he couldn't stand lying.
Which is how he explained his
defection from Communist Poland:
rejecting "the New Faith" with its
"practice of the lie as one of its
principal commandments."
Now who more than the adopted
could appreciate this problem
with lying? But can we agree
it is different to hate
secrecy, lies and corruption
than it is to hate the
original institution?

I can't even read the Times
without doing it adopted.
Like the death of Czeslaw Milosz
who decided to defect after
being told by no less
than Albert Einstein
to go back to Poland,
not to choose the West
"and the sad fate of the exiles."
What was Einstein thinking?
I bet no one but the adopted
can completely appreciate
this paradox of Einstein
in the paradise of Princeton
the world's prince at the time
feeling sadness of exile
from a slaughterhouse.

I can't even read the Times
without arguing adopted.

Like the death of Czeslaw Milosz
who didn't go back for thirty years
til "all Poland had fallen." I didn't
go back for thirty years myself
and it was only by the good grace
of my second mother that I
did get back to the first one.
No thanks to the law in California
that still hasn't fallen
as all Oregon *has* fallen
or their closed record
adoption law has finally fallen
as all New Hampshire has fallen
or their closed record adoption
law has just fallen. Who but
the adopted could appreciate
this juxtaposition of Oregon and
New Hampshire with Poland?

I can't even read the Times
not remembering adopted.
Like the death of Czeslaw Milosz
with his Nobel Prize as poet
"of memory and witness."
Who more than the adopted
want a witness? Can we get one?
When asked to remember those
shipyard workers shot by the
Soviets in the Seventies,
He wrote, "Ye who harmed a
simple man, do not feel secure:
for a poet remembers."
Oh can I translate that
to the situation of the
adopted who die not knowing
where they come from?
Oh let me be like Milosz
and help people remember
so more of us go to our
graves with the right to
remember where we came from.

I can't even read of the
death of Czeslaw Miloz
without feeling adopted.
Near the bottom
righthand corner
of this full page
spread with picture
in the Sunday Times
the fifteenth of August
the same summer we lost
Ray Charles, Marlon Brando,
and way too many
on all sides in Iraq:

"Mr. Milosz
was a man of
quiet manner
but strong opinions
and he expressed them."
Oh let me be like Milosz.

*Pronounced CHEZlav MEEwoesh (and all manner of other ways)

ADOPTION RESEARCH: A POET'S RESPONSE

*PENNY CALLAN PARTRIDGE**

So I'm reading the *Adoption Quarterly*
at the Center for the Study of Adoption
when I come across this sentence.
And write down this sentence:

Even though a study relying on PARENTAL
reports has found that adopted children
rarely want to meet their birthparents
(Feigelman & Silverman, 1983),

another study (Benson et al, 1994)
using adopted adolescents' SELF reports
has shown that the majority of adopted adolescents
do want to meet their birthparents.

What an example of how slippery the
truth is: how much depends on
who's asking whom and when
and with what hopes for answers.

So now I'm thinking that before we are part of any study,
we should interview the researchers:
Just how did they come to be interested
in adoption in the first place?

Who's funding them?
Who'll review their findings?
Who'll choose which
ones will be reported?

(We had some experience with this after the parents of a suicide
gave money to learn how to keep this from happening to others.
And somebody didn't like all they found and had it reported that
everything is fine; adopted children are better adjusted than their
counterparts. So nothing we can do to make it better for anybody.)

Meanwhile have the researchers read
Joyce Maguire Pavao or seen Edward Albee?

Have they been to any meetings of an adopted
people's support group AND JUST LISTENED?

From whom have they LEARNED
about adoption and what do they
think this research they are
doing now will be good for?

Why do they think some parents
(and some researchers) have to
ASK why their children would
want to know their birthparents?

Why a parent might THINK
a twelve year old too
young to know her
name before adoption?

Why an experienced family therapist
would say the ONLY families that ever
made her want to reach for a cigarette
were the adoptive ones?

Why they think Bill Pierce
who quotes old Scottish studies
about only two percent of us
wanting to know our birthparents

and calls those of us who do
anti-adoption just got six
million dollars to help Americans
understand adoption better?

We hope you will be comfortable with our
questions, researchers. If you answer them,
we are likely to keep being in your studies.
We do
                    really
                              appreciate

                                        your time.

AN INTERNATIONAL STORY

PENNY CALLAN PARTRIDGE*

My friend Anna is Italian,
her daughter Dasha Russian.
Recently my friend Anna
took Dasha back to Russia
where they had gotten her
as we so
inelegantly
say in English.

And Dasha met people who remembered her at the orphanage.
And went with her mother
to her other mother's grave.
And Anna e-mailed that while
she had done this trip for Dasha,
what it gave her Anna
was more of her daughter.

One thing Anna did in Russia
was to order a new headstone
(una nuova pietra tombale in Italian),
(novee pomm yaht neek in Russian)
for her daughter Dasha's
Russian mother's gravesite.
Someone named Jeanne
was going to place this headstone
and they were going to pray
together from Russia and from Italy.

I join them now from the USA
(ooza in Italian, *sah sheh ah* in Russian)
already joined by e-mail and
in not wanting our children
to have any part of their history–
people places words feelings
(which are parts of themselves)–
either purposely
or thoughtlessly
removed.
Let us pray.

ATTACHMENT

PENNY CALLAN PARTRIDGE*

For Joyce Maguire Pavao
(Provincetown, July 2002)

The movie is
Second Best.
Which is not
how I rate it.
It has
(after all)
William Hurt
who seems to me
like me only male:
that slow speaking
stab
at making sense
of what may not.
I am right
behind his face
when he does this.

And then
in this film
he's becoming
a parent
which I'm doing
all the time
reaching out
of myself
toward my kids.
For my kids.

But the way
Second Best
almost had me
on the floor
was not
with William Hurt
on the screen
though Hurt
is the name
of what is happening
in the scene
and what is soothed
by the child
William Hurt
wants to parent.

Is soothed
in the child
himself
and in Hurt's
angry
stroke victim
father
when the child
places
in the hand
of the man
a pin
he has taken
from his birthmother's
family:
this laying
of the child
of himself
in the hands
of new family.

I cry here
seeing
how tricky
all this is
how deep
all this is
how far
we must reach
how far
we must come
but also
how much
we give
when we place
our *selves*
in others'
hands.

OREGON

PENNY CALLAN PARTRIDGE*

the day of the
new law in Oregon
I had to call
Jim in Michigan
Pam in New Jersey
Tom in New York
and Mary Ann
in Pennsylvania

to be with them
as this new thing
flew up the flagpole
and the colony
we had been
became the Independent
Republic of the Adopted

we were now
legitimate
at least to the
people of Oregon
whether we were born
in Oregon or not

we were now
full citizens
at least to the
people of Oregon
whether we lived
in Oregon or not

is how it seemed to me
who lived in Massachusetts
had been born in California
and who'd been told the
summer before by
Susan Soon-Keum Cox

that I could at least
learn how to pronounce
the name of her state
not Ore-reh-gone like origami
but Orrigun like Milligan

imagine not knowing
imagine not knowing
how to say the
name of that state
imagine not knowing
imagine not knowing
how to say the name
of the woman
you were born to

it's *little* enough to learn
it's little *enough* to learn

FOR ALL THE LITTLE GIRLS FROM CHINA

PENNY CALLAN PARTRIDGE*

Whenever I see one
I know there will someday be
this incredible sorority
of women brought here
as babies from China.

And their Great Wall
will always go all the
way through them to
split what happened in China/
what's happened here.

But they will help each other
over this wall all their lives
until those walls at their
centers are merely their
strong and flexible spines.

Maybe on the basis of
collective cultural hybrid
strength which they'll
find many ways to cultivate
(the strength of their stories!)

these women of the world's
first international
female diaspora
will inherit the earth.
And do something good with it.

THE WOMAN WHO WAS ADOPTED HAS FIVE MIRRORS IN HER BEDROOM

PENNY CALLAN PARTRIDGE*

She can't recall
seeing her face
in a mirror
as a child.

She can't recall
finding her face
in her mind
as a child.

She can't recall
her parents
mentioning
her appearance.

She can't recall
feeling
she had
an appearance.

A roommate
in college
saw how she
stared into mirrors.

A man she married
would scare her
with how
he saw her.

Another man
she married
barely saw her
would walk into her.

She knows now
her birthmother
couldn't bear to see
what she looked like.

She knows now
her parents
couldn't bear to see
whom she looked like.

She knows now
any sibling
would have told her
what she looked like.

She knows now
that photographs
on the wall
would have helped.

She doesn't mind
looking older now
so much like
her birthfather.

She doesn't mind
looking older now
so much like
one grandmother.

She doesn't mind
sounding
so much now
like her parents.

The woman
who was adopted
has five mirrors
in her bedroom

and sometimes
whispers
into one of them
I see you.

* Poems are reprinted with permission from Penny Partridge.

HOW I COULD INTERPRET THE EVENTS OF MY YOUTH—EVENTS I DO NOT REMEMBER EXCEPT IN DREAMS

CHRISTIAN LANGWORTHY

Because I was a newly adopted
    child from another country
(a prostitute's son in a Vietnamese
    city bristling with rifles
and, as a result of my mother's truancy
    from motherhood, I was given
to nuns and locked within the confines
    of missionary walls)
I crossed the South China Sea
    and Pacific in three days
(barely surviving anti-aircraft fire)
    aboard an eight prop-engine plane.
I came to this country
    to a nine-inch carpet of snow
and a sure welcome by strangers
    engaged with the possibilities of parenthood.

My new beginning consisted of firsts:
    first experienced snowfall in America—
(how it was magic in a fairy tale land)
    first toilet flushings,
(at the airport, when I flushed every
    toilet in the men's room to my new
father's delight)
    and another notable first—
the first cartoon I ever saw on Saturday
    morning: Bugs Bunny and Elmer Fudd,
and how there were no wounded or dead
    from the flying bullets,
and I laughed so hard I cried
    though I did not understand their language then.

As the years of my second life progressed,
    My adopted parents tried to be
a good father and mother and to the cinema
    we went, and I saw the children's epics:
Snow White and the Seven Dwarves
    and Sleeping Beauty; at home my mother read
fairy tales to me, tales like Rumpelstiltskin,
        and I learned
the false beauty of the wicked witch,
        the castle besieged by thorns,
the terror of the kidnapped son.
        I could have told them I'd seen these tales
before, but I was too young to know the difference.

SOURCE: "How I Could Interpret the Events of My Youth, Events I Do Not Remember Except in Dreams" was first published in *Premonitions,* Kaya Productions (1995).

THE FOURTH OF JULY

CHRISTIAN LANGWORTHY

I have killed the butterflies in my stomach, and my mother sits by the kitchen counter and stares at a tub of unsalted butter. She prepares an afternoon picnic for the Fourth of July.

I imagine my father down in the cellar, tinkering with the lawnmower engine. I hear his ratchet wrench biting on the engine's bolt heads. He will come up, as he usually did on a Saturday, to shoot at the blackbirds which drop shit on our pool. His shotgun still leans against the wicker chair on the patio. At the edge of the woods, four blackbirds candle the branches of an elm.

My mother carries a Tupperware tub of macaroni salad out to the mahogany picnic table. She does not look at the shotgun. In the hot, humid air, I hear a swarm of flies buzzing over the potato salad, the hot dogs and the pickled beets. My mother swats away the flies. I open the screen door and walk to the table. A shadow streaks across the bottom of the pool. "Gary, they're at it again," my mother mumbles as she puts seasoning on the salad. "Mom, you're putting sugar on the macaroni instead of salt. Mom!" She stops, suddenly aware of what she is doing. "I don't know where my mind is these days," she says as she looks up. "Here, we'll blend it in."

All the butterflies I have killed lie on the cement patio. White butterflies. Yellow butterflies. Green butterflies. The picnic table is set with plastic forks, knives, and spoons. A slight wind licks the corners of the tablecloth, folding the cartoon faces of several Hanna-Barbera characters. The wind picks up a bit and stirs the butterflies around my feet. I swat away more flies. My mother has already gone back into the house. I feel her gaze on the back of my neck. A gust of wind blows the butterflies onto the table. I pick them off the table and flick them down to the cement. My mother says something through the kitchen window, but I can only see her lips move.

My father is back again from his long absence. He walks around on the patio, patrolling the edges of the swimming pool. An inner tube drags its shadow across the blue pool liner. My father takes his false teeth out and sets them on the table. He starts scooping leaves out of the pool with a fishnet. "Gary!" My mother shouts. "Put those back in your mouth. You're setting a bad example for the kids!" My father laughs as he always laughed, gumming a few words as he scoops up soggy maple leaves.

I pull at my own teeth with my fingers, but they don't budge. I sit down at the table to inspect the food that has been laid out. I move the butter so that it is next to the sourdough bread. I put the salt and pepper shakers together. Next are the hot dogs and rolls. I place the potato salad at one end of the table, the macaroni on the other. The butterflies are now swirling around. One lands on the back of my hand for an instant and is blown off by the wind. My hand has a smudge of yellow powder on it.

The wind suddenly dies down, and the butterflies drop onto the patio cement. The buzzing of the flies gets louder and louder. I look at the butterflies in my life—the white butterflies that flew among the rows of tomato plants in the weedy garden and flew among the clotheslines—the green butterflies bobbling erratically in the summer breeze—the yellow butterflies clinging to the windowsills. I inspect the smudge of yellow dust on my hand and go into the kitchen to wash it off, remembering an old superstition that the powder of butterflies can crack dishes and pottery. The water from the faucet is cool and washes the yellow smudge off quickly. My mother has gone back out onto the patio again.

I look out the window, past the wind chimes dangling from the top of the window, and I see flies swarming around the unsalted butter. My mother looks old. She does not say much anymore. All of her energy is spent on preparing for the picnic. The tub of butter has a deep hole in it from the huge chunk she has gouged out for the table setting. Soon, her other sons and daughters will arrive, and she will feel that her life has meaning.

My father returns. He sits in the wicker chair, cradling the shotgun as he guards the pool. Two blackbirds sit perched on the elm's branches. He gets up, shotgun in hand, and walks down the path through the rose garden. My father shoots. A branch snaps and collapses, but the blackbirds fly off unharmed.

My mother stands across from me at the counter. She looks down into the tub of unsalted butter. Sunlight filters in through the screen door and brightens the butter. It is difficult to hear anything but the buzzing of the flies around the picnic table and an occasional wind brushing against the house. The picnic table is covered with butterflies. Their wings are in the pickled beets, the unsalted butter, the hot dogs and the potato salad. Some are trapped by the strong wind against the flapping tablecloth and, when the wind dies, the flies rush back to claim the food again.

I have killed the butterflies in my stomach and my mother smiles; her teeth showing above the butter, her lips quivering for an instant as if she will say something before the flies finish off her sentences. She told me once that she could hear the butterflies, that she could hear them in the breeze in the night, in the woods along the creek. All the white, green, and yellow butterflies on the mahogany picnic table.

The table is set, and I go out and stretch in the sunlight before sitting on the bench. I swat the flies off the unsalted butter and pick butterflies off the food. The wind scatters the butterflies and tumbles them along the patio and pretty soon, the butterflies are gone.

The sun is hot on my back. My mother sits down at the picnic table, and I half expect my father to walk up the path through the rose garden, but he doesn't. The butterflies are no longer in my stomach, so I pick up the false teeth from the table and hand them to my mother, and she takes them into the house. Only when she comes back after the teeth have been put away, do we eat.

SOURCE: "The Fourth of July" was first published under the title "Sestina" in *Watermark*, Temple University Press (2000).

THE BURNED WALLS

CHRISTIAN LANGWORTHY

We sleep in the shadow of burned walls
That comfort and shade us where we nap.
Mother will be here before night falls,

And on our shoulders she will tap
A lullaby under cherry trees
That comfort and shade us where we nap.

The charred walls resist the breeze
Above our heads, and breezes bring
A lullaby under cherry trees.

In the night, mother remains to sing—
To ease the buzzing of the bugs
Above our heads and breezes bring

The smell of scorched wood and rugs
Hidden from us who hope the sun will rise
To ease the buzzing of the bugs

Which crawl on our bodies, our thighs.
We sleep in the shadow of burned walls
Hidden from us who hope the sun will rise.
Mother will be here before night falls.

SOURCE: "The Burned Walls" was first published in a chapbook titled *The Geography of War*, Cooper House Publishers (1995).

ORIGIN

SARAH SAFFIAN

Excerpt from *Ithaka: A Daughter's Memoir of Being Found*

I'm in the womb, a mere embryo, and it's warm and orange, with sloshing sounds and vibrating. In these first three months it's peaceful, but lonely. Although I sense Hannah, my birth mother, physically, I don't have any emotional connection to her, because she doesn't even know that I'm here. She's in motion, traveling around Europe with me inside her, and I can feel and hear her there. Chatting with friends, eating rich foods and drinking wine, sightseeing, walking, walking. I feel dragged along, like a piece of lint on the back of a sweater that lingers, unnoticed. It's a carefree but detached feeling.

It is only when we return to New York that I feel any response from Hannah. But rather than being welcomed, I now suspect that she is aware of me, but ignoring me, denying me, not wanting to believe in my existence. So there is still the loneliness, but more acute than before, because I feel deliberately left alone. The womb that had moved so easily and naturally with her rhythm is now seizing up, and I feel crowded within it. My translucent tadpole fingers are up by my face as I bend my arms and legs until they are folded in half, to take up as little room as possible. I feel guilty, sensing Hannah's unease in the tightness of the womb, the coldness of the fluid, and knowing it is because of me.

When we move to the hideout, the tension gradually subsides and the sounds outside become muted, gentler. I hear my birth father Adam frequently along with Hannah, but rarely any other people, and even my birth parents' voices come through only as murmurs. This is a period of retreat: Hannah seems placid, resting, and I picture the apartment to be a sunny little place, quiet, removed. Occasionally, I feel Adam's or Hannah's hands on her abdomen, a firm but tender pressure. Through the veiny red womb walls I can see the darker handprints as though they are of paint on canvas, or of water on stone, or making an impression in sand. I lean my face against the hands, and close my fish eyes, and hum to my birth parents.

One evening, there is the serenity of a snowstorm. The night city is blanketed white, muffling sound, no cars or people out except for us. I imagine sheets of snow falling steadily but landing lightly, silently. I can feel the love growing between Hannah and Adam as they walk. She is taking deep, full breaths, and the amniotic fluid undulates in time with her motion. Over these months, the womb has expanded and become warm again, as I feel embraced by her. I move around slowly, participating in the walk, fully present, recognized and accepted by my birth parents.

When we go to the unwed mothers' home and then, a week later, to the hospital, the womb turns tight again, but is still warm. This time, I feel like my birth mother's ally, that her tension is directed outward. I sense that I am still the reason for her distress, but that she no longer resents me, rather, that she wants to protect me. Just as before I felt that she was wishing me away, now I feel that she's trying to draw me ever closer to her, so passionately that her embrace is painful. I am afraid now, because she is afraid. She feels helpless and I feel helpless, too—I want to aid her somehow.

As scared as I am of the situation around us, I don't feel safe where I am anymore. I decide to come out, even though I'm not quite ready. The womb is smaller all the time, as if I'm being squeezed out by Hannah's anxiety. I rotate so that I am upside down, dizzy and disoriented, and begin pushing out. As I leave it, the womb shrinks behind me, like a deflating balloon, clinging to my stomach, my legs. The canal is pitch dark, not glowing like the womb was, and very narrow. As my head emerges, I am struck by the chill of the outside for the first time. I finally slide out, slimy and terribly cold. I am washed and wrapped in a blanket swiftly, perfunctorily, by someone in white whom I don't know, and whisked away. Later, I am brought to my birth mother. I know that it is she, recognizing her warmth, her smell, her soft voice. She holds me, and it is familiar, yet strange, because I am outside of her now. This moment seems fleeting—her love, while unconditional, is mingled with despair, turning furtive, unconfident.

Then one day I am not brought to Hannah. I look around for her, but everyone is a stranger. The hospital nursery is antiseptic, chilly, the crisp white sheet in my glass crib rough on my new, raw skin. I see other parents of other babies, peering through the window at their children, pointing, smiling, and holding them, cooing, doting. I am cared for by the people in white, but I don't feel any love from them—the love that I felt from my birth mother, eventually while inside her, and briefly after being born. But now she is gone, and I am motherless, nameless. Alone.

Conclusion

The Future of Adoption 33

A Call to Action

FRANK A. BIAFORA

St. John's University

RAFAEL A. JAVIER

St. John's University

AMANDA L. BADEN

Montclair State University

ALINA CAMACHO-GINGERICH

St. John's University

> *It's tough to make predictions, especially about the future.*
>
> —Yogi Berra

To claim that adoption in the United States is in the midst of change may be an understatement. In his recent influential book *Adoption Nation*, Adam Pertman (2000) suggests that America is experiencing nothing short of an "adoption revolution." Drawing on a volcanic analogy, Pertman maintains that the simmering evolution of adoption over the past quarter century has quickened to a boil into what many observers would consider a full-blown eruption. "Before our eyes," he concludes, "in our homes and schools and media and workplaces, America is forever changing adoption even as adoption is forever changing America" (p. 5).

To be sure, traditional adoption laws at the local, state, national, and international levels are being reviewed and updated or cast aside so quickly that it is difficult to keep pace with regulations much less track their intended or latent effects (see Chapter 4 by Madelyn Freundlich, "A Legal History of Adoption and Ongoing Legal Challenges," in Part I). Similarly, our norms, perceptions, and collective attitudes toward the family are being challenged and are slowly adapting in an effort to play catch-up with new social realities. In the midst of recent legal challenges to acknowledge, for example, domestic partnerships and formal kinship care, America has also just entered the unexplored world of opportunity, and by extension corruption, by means of an Internet technology that brings together infertile couples and adoptable children, and formerly adopted children and their birth parents, all with the click of a mouse. The expediency with which information can now be obtained through these technological advances has its own consequences, as was the case when information was not available. For instance, it may be more possible for members of the triad interested in searching for birth parents to find information of their whereabouts and attempt to contact the birth parents without proper preparation for the reunion, with the initial euphoria and the period of deflation that are part of that experience. Fantasies are shattered, anger may emerge, and perceptions have to be realigned before a more realistic sense of the experience is developed.

In speaking about broader concepts of social change, William Ogburn (1964), a noted sociologist, defined the process of "cultural lag," a term he coined to describe those elongated periods of uncertainty in which societies tend to be ill prepared and ill equipped to keep up with rapid change and innovation. Ogburn predicted that as a result of this lag, conflict and confusion would be unavoidable. As an example, it was not long ago when a young pregnant woman, typically White, not wanting to endure the stigma of an "illegitimate" child, would depart for an extended visit away from home only to return months later ready to continue, apparently unabated, with her normal routine. The birth mother, not wanting to "ruin" her life, listened to the advice of others who argued that her baby deserved the best in life, that is, a two-parent family. Parallel in time and waiting anxiously in the wings was a married woman of similar racial features carefully stuffing her maternity clothes in gradual weekly increments, trying desperately not to disclose the fact that she was incapable of pregnancy and natural childbirth. The shame, guilt, and feelings of loss by both women were to be discussed in private, if at all, and were expected to be forgotten. Although stories such as these have become less common in recent years for a variety of reasons, not the least of which is a broader social acceptance of single motherhood, whether unplanned or planned, we are still witnessing children being left at the doorsteps of fire departments, police stations, and churches or in dumpsters by mothers who have tried desperately to deny their pregnancy because of their young age or special circumstances.

As discussed in various chapters of this book, the mental health community informs us that despite greater social awareness and acceptance, adoption wounds never really heal—from the older woman who years ago put up her child for adoption (see, e.g., www.keepyourbaby.com), to the middle-aged couple who never stopped wondering about their baby that never was, to the adoptive parent(s) trying to understand and overcome their "postadoption blues," a syndrome only recently recognized (Foli & Thompson, 2004). Nevertheless, mental health professionals are pretty clear that honest discussion about such matters, however painful and awkward it may seem, is far better for all parties than simplistic views that trivialize or ignore the truth. When the adopted person is not given the information about his or her adoption experience or is outright lied to, the growing adopted child who learns about the world and how to trust in the context of his immediate environment is now left with having to come to terms with an environment that he or she now feels is fraught with secrecy and lies, leaving him or her feeling betrayed and not knowing whom to trust. This is an area amply discussed in Chapters 12 (by McRoy, Grotevant, Ayers-Lopez, & Henney) and 28 (by Nydam) of this volume.

It may be a stretch to claim that America as a whole is in the midst of adoption enlightenment or that citizens across the board support recent changes in domestic and international adoption policy and practice. For the foreseeable future, there will surely remain a gaggle of critics who will hold to the view that open adoption contracts between triad members are bizarre and unthinkable or that adoption should remain an alternative for married hetero-sexual couples only, not single parents by choice, much less gay and lesbian singles or cou-ples. And while some would rather turn back the clock, it appears that the train has already left the station. We hold that the future of adoption *is* upon us already and is unfolding before our eyes at an unprecedented pace. We also believe that change is being fueled not only by the recent Internet phenomenon and free-trade global opportunities but also by con-cerned professionals, hopeful would-be parents, educators, clinicians, and a slew of public and private agencies articulating for more acceptance of familial diversity and more toler-ance of difference, all the while remaining focused on what is in the "best interest of the child." The difficulty, of course, is garnering agreement on whose definition of best interest we should be following. It is on this cultural battleground that much of the adoption story is currently being written.

Changes unfolding within public foster care provide a prime example of recent debate. One of the guiding principles within the public foster care community had been for many decades "family reunification" at almost any cost. Pertman (2000) recounts that such a view was a wonderful ideal in theory as it would provide the much needed temporary time-out for parents to obtain professional assistance for their alcohol, violence, and drug problems before returning to child care responsibilities (p. 32). The reality, of course, was too often a different story, in which children were shuffled back and forth between foster parents, bio-logical parents, and emergency shelters. The long-term impact of such instability on the physical and mental well-being of a generation of foster care children is, as one can imagine, incalculable, as discussed by Doyle in Chapter 16 in this volume. In response to what was described as a national crisis, throughout the 1980s, lawmakers in Washington pushed for a new formula for "best interest" standards, ultimately coming up with time limits and a financial incentive framework to encourage "early permanency" (the rapid legal termination of parental rights and simultaneous eligibility for adoption) and the placement of special-needs children. In the first few years of existence of the Adoption and Safe Families Act, since its passage in 1997, the numbers of finalized adoptions from foster care have skyrocketed, nearly catching up with the percentage of private adoptions. The professional and research community is still trying to absorb the overall impact of this important policy shift. And while this may appear to be the beginning of a curative measure for a national problem, society has yet to come up with a proactive vaccination to address the source of much of the problem—generational poverty, drugs, crime, and violence.

Related to this is a story, not without controversy, of child exports that is just beginning to raise questions about America's foster care system. Each year, a small number (perhaps less than 100) of special-needs children, mostly African American, are being adopted by our North American neighbors (mostly White) in Canada. Unlike international adoptions to the United States from foreign countries, where the exact numbers of orphan visas are kept by the State Department, the numbers of children exiting the United States in this manner are not recorded. That the world's only "superpower" nation is now engaged in exporting children has not gone unnoticed, argues Glaser (2004). "For many, it raises questions about identity, race and the tangled legacy of American Slavery," and for some, it is the "last stop on the historic Underground Railroad." The size of the Black population in Canada is only 2%, but it has apparently not gone unnoticed by some placement officers and birth parents that Canada may ultimately provide an intriguing alternative, both for its proximity and because skin color has less of a legacy in determining the social order and personal oppor-tunities. This is one story worth watching as it seems to touch on so many emotions and at the same time exploits America's inability to take care of its own social concerns. This is an issue that emerged recently more poignantly in the case of those affected by Katrina, when the African American population in New Orleans, by and large, felt that the way govern-mental agencies were dealing with them in terms of their response to their needs to evacuate and rebuild was de facto encouraging them to go elsewhere to settle.

History has already demonstrated that societal change inevitably brings with it early adapters at one end, critics at the other, and a large silent middle who sit idly by to see what the future will hold. With respect to adoption, those blazing new trails may at times feel that they are going it alone. The White couple from Allentown, Pennsylvania, who decide to adopt a special-needs African American boy from foster care and the single woman from Houston, Texas, who flies off to Guatemala on her own and returns with a teenage girl remain two out of any number of stories unfolding each day that still may raise (or lower) more than just a few eyebrows.

Television shows in the United States depicting the perfect nuclear family, such as *Ozzie and Harriet* and *Leave It to Beaver*, were popular in their day, and they were, interestingly enough, presented to American audiences in black and white. With the advent of color TV and what seems to be limitless channels, many family portraits today represent a tapestry of possibilities. Lest we forget, just a few short years ago, social workers enforced the common policy designed to "match" babies on physical and other features with their take-home parents so as not to draw attention to the "artificial" family. Today, there is no hiding the multiethnic and multiracial patterns in planned families. One needs only to visit the increasingly popular Web sites such as Bi-Racial Families Network (www.bfnchicago.org) or the Association of Multiethnic Americans (www.ameasite.org) to get a glimpse of the future. From movie stars to our next-door neighbors, new family formations are being created by individual actors, many no longer being pressured into the expectations of others but instead marching onward with courage, love, and respect for the dignity of others.

It may have taken American society the aches and pains of a civil rights movement and a gender revolution to get to where it is today. And some social commentators may claim that it was inevitable at this epochal moment in history that members of American society would engage in framing a new discourse about things such as the nature of the family and the sociological boundaries of adoption. Who can forget the transforming role that a generation of vocal Baby Boomers had in helping to define, for example, the Vietnam War and debates about equity in the workplace or how their sheer size alone (80 million born between 1945 and 1964) was able to move the business community to cater to everything from disposable diapers to fast food to 1-800-DIVORCE? It makes sense that once the boomers reached adulthood and reflected on parenting and family construction, somehow any authoritarian attempt, cultural or legal, to coerce the status quo would also be challenged.

Adoption experts believe that if recent trends continue, the impact of adoption will significantly alter the demography of the family for many years to come (Pertman, 2002). There is no reason to believe that the exponential growth in domestic foster care and international adoption will diminish anytime soon (see Chapter 3 by Biafora and Esposito, "Adoption Data and Statistical Trends," and Chapters 8 through 11 in this volume on transracial adoption), so we can expect far more diverse and transracial families to enter the mainstream. Likewise, because of open (as opposed to traditionally closed) adoption arrangements and increased support for formal kinship arrangements, don't be surprised if at your next children's party, you happen to be introduced by a young girl to "my adoptive mother and my birth mother" all in the same breath.

Yogi Berra, of baseball's lore, reminds us in the opening quote that looking too far ahead can sometimes be foolish. And while it may come to pass that the discussion outlined on these pages may be better suited to wrapping tomorrow's fish than making predictions about the future, no one can question that adoption discourse is far different from just a few short years ago and will most likely be different in a few years from now. The current adoption research literature, while minimal in size and scope compared with related research topics in the sociological and psychological literatures, was an indispensable resource for helping frame our look ahead. But it was insights from semistructured personal interviews that brought these texts alive. The purpose here was not to conduct a full-scale research project or follow any specific methodology, and there was no attempt to randomize the interview subjects. Rather, the main purpose was to carefully listen to the unrehearsed stories of selected individuals who have direct and extensive exposure to adoption from different angles. One need not go very far to find an adoptive parent enthusiastic to tell his or her story. Each of us is surrounded by individuals who have some exposure to adoption, whether directly or indirectly.

The profile and story of Kate are not uncommon. Like many single women who adopt, Kate, a well-established and highly respected professional, started her adoption journey in her 40s. A White female, Kate began to seriously explore adoption once her career was at a comfortable plateau and she could focus on the next important phase of her life. Her decision to go forward with the adoption process came only after a great deal of introspection, extensive discussion with family members, and, ultimately, drawing on even more determination and patience than even she thought she had. Her journey, for purposes of this story, begins with a plan to adopt a school-age girl, 4-8 years old, from foster care. She was aware of the demographics of the foster care system in her area and that this would likely be a transracial adoption. Kate worked with an agency that provided required training about parenting and adoption and assigned a social worker who provided her with support and completed her home study. After 2 years of searching public listings of foster children and requesting several times to be considered as an adoptive parent, only two possibilities emerged. Both were girls nearing adolescence with significant emotional and psychological needs. Kate realized her own limitations to begin parenting an adolescent girl with these challenges. In struggling to clarify whether to continue to pursue adoption from foster care, she was surprised when the social worker indicated that, as a single white female, it would be unlikely that a young black child would be placed with her as the preference would be to place the child with a young black couple.

Kate then decided to pursue international adoption, but her first experience there did not go as planned either. After doing another home study, preparing the required dossier and obtaining clearances from INS, she waited for the review of her papers in Ecuador. After a year of postponements and waiting, she was informed that international adoptions were indefinitely delayed since the government had initiated a review and restructuring of its adoption procedures. Her journey ends about a year later in Siberia where she adopted a 10-year-old girl she met through a summer program in the U.S. which hosted children from Russia. These programs have been largely discontinued at present and have an uncertain future.

Kate says "I have no regrets and would do it all over again. In retrospect, it seems each step was necessary to learn something and to test the sincerity of my intent to adopt, strengthen my resolve and bring my daughter and I together." Her daughter, ten years old at the time of the adoption, was included in the adoption decision, as were some of her extended family. They agreed to continue communication between the adoptive and birth family. Meanwhile, back in the States, in just a few short months, Kate's daughter is adjusting to her new surroundings, learning English, making friends and keeping in touch with several other adopted children from the summer program. One of Kate's anxieties, she claims with a smile, is figuring out how best to navigate through their first discussion of the "birds and the bees" without a translator! Her major concern, however, is providing a secure, supportive and loving home where her daughter may thrive, heal, and come to integrate the reality of her two families and grow to accept herself as a whole, valued, and loveable person despite the disruption, grief, loss and separation she has already experienced in her young life.

From just one conversation, Kate story had touched on so many issues and themes relevant to a discussion of the changing nature of adoption in America. Among these were the preadoption highs and lows of a single woman who is blazing her own trail, the use of Internet technology to explore adoption alternatives, the "cultural lag" within the foster care community as it relates to placing Black and African American children in non-Black and non–African American homes, the uncertainties in planning for international adoption, open adoption contracts, postadoption services for triad members and the availability of support networks, integration into the public schools, and the financial costs of adoption. But, more than any of these, Carol's story is ultimately a story about love, trust, and hope among and between individuals in an adoption triad.

LETTING GO OF STEREOTYPES

Among the greatest obstacles members of the adoption triad must overcome is the at times subtle and at times obvious stigma and stereotyping. This is shown in some of the language we have heard used to refer to the adoption experience: "discarded," "unwanted," "illegitimate," "bastard," "abandoned," and "crack" babies; "real or natural parents," to distinguish them from the adopted parents; "saving" the child by removing him or her from an unhealthy family environment; "giving the child a better chance for life"; "the child will begin a new life" with a new birth certificate and name as if "nothing prior to that should now matter"; the birth parents were "drug addicts, alcoholics, and irresponsible"; or "she was a loose and sexually depraved woman," to refer to the birth mother, to name a few. Such statements trigger pejorative and prejudicial images of members of the triad that are reflective of the discomfort and anxiety members of our society continue to harbor. That such comments increase misperceptions and perpetuate stereotyping can be seen from the results of a study exploring the impact of adoption on the formation of attitudes toward students among schoolteachers. Research by Freidman-Kessler (1987) determined that knowledge of adoption may be connected with views of student attractiveness, aggressiveness, callousness, or disagreeableness and the intensity of punishment required to address perceived problems. We know from this research that adoption challenges core beliefs and existing notions about the nature of the human condition, nurture versus nature, family, and individuals' versus society's responsibilities. It challenges our view of what we believe *should* be the nature of human relationships, the importance of blood relationships in human interaction, the role of sexuality in our lives, and the like. It challenges the notion of morality and the nature of race and international relationships. Finally, it challenges our educational and religious institutions.

While the positive benefits of adoption on members of the triad are undeniable, we might, nevertheless, ask whether we have failed to date as a society to address adoption issues at the level required by its complexity. We argue that empirical knowledge addressing the challenges that each member of the triad faces throughout the adoption experience is in its infancy. And one can only hope that once institutions, at all levels, in our society come to terms with adoption and see it as a true human endeavor that benefits the lives of many, we will witness a corresponding realignment and allocation of resources and research interest to address the complex issues, many of which have been outlined in this text.

It is the increasing number of individuals who are directly influenced by adoption that makes our call for research into the theory, practice, intervention, and experience of adoption all the more urgent. When we consider that about 500,000 people turn to adoption each year and 140,000 children find permanent homes with American families each year in domestic and international adoptions, not counting those American children who find permanent homes in countries outside the United States, and that between 40 million and 100 million Americans are directly affected by adoption in very fundamental ways (Henderson, 2002; United States Bureau of the Census, 2000), it is clear that our society is much more intricately involved with adoption than ever before. We expect this number to increase even more as political and socioeconomic changes in the world continue to create situations where children are left with international adoptions as their only option.

GOOD SIGNS FOR THE FUTURE OF ADOPTION

Our decision to create this book was guided by the recognizable need for one comprehensive resource that presents the current state of empirically tested and derived information regarding adoption. It is meant to be a reference, source, or textbook for those interested in gaining a more complete understanding of the multiple challenges members of the triad face throughout their lives. The book is unique because it offers opportunities for academics, professionals, students, members of the triad, and legislators to enter into a shared dialogue on adoption issues from their respective disciplines and perspectives.

The fact that 45 members of the U.S. Senate and 128 members of the U.S. House of Representatives signed on as members of the Congressional Coalition on Adoption, cochaired by Senator Larry Craig of Idoho and Mary Landrieu of Louisiana, reflects the growing importance adoption has attained in the U.S. legislators' conscience. The coalition was originally founded by Rep. Thomas Bliley of Virginia and Rep. Jim Oberstar of Minnesota (also cochairs of the Coalition); the former senator from Texas, Lloyd Bentsen; and the former senator from New Hampshire, Gordon Humphrey, four adoptive parents. These members of Congress have been actively involved in drafting important adoption and foster care legislations that would effectively eliminate barriers to adoption domestically and internationally, promote understanding of infant adoption, and support the adoption of children in foster care waiting for adoption (Encyclopedia of Adoption, 2006). The Angels in Adoption Program, organized by the coalition and held in the U.S. capital (Washington, D.C.) every fall, helps keep adoption issues in the mind of policymakers and the public. This program officially recognizes individuals all over the nation who are nominated by elected officials for their work on adoption. It also has an international program to increase positive dialogue with other countries. Finally, national awareness is greatly helped by the recent declaration of November as the National Adoption Awareness Month by President George W. Bush (Holt International Children's Services, 2006).

Other positive trends are seen in some academic institutions that are beginning to take on a more active leadership role by establishing forums where adoption issues are systematically and regularly addressed. One such institution is St. John's University in Queens, New York, which since the early 1990s has organized a biannual conference on issues affecting the adoption community, prepared training tapes and special journal issues dedicated to adoption (see *Journal of Social Distress and Homeless*, 2000, Vol. 9, No. 4, and 2002, Vol. 11 No. 2), and, most recently, developed an ongoing consultation group for professionals working with members of the adoption triad. Similarly, Rutgers University has begun to offer a certificate program in adoption, and training programs are being organized by other independent institutes (e.g., Family Connections in Boston, Casey Family Programs).

We are also witnessing some forward movement in the area of treatment and training centers designed to address adoption-related issues with members of the triad. A few universities have created specialty clinics on adoption, such as the International Adoption Clinic at the University of Minnesota and the International Adoption Clinic at Yale. The Internet has also served as a platform for national and global awareness (see, e.g., the North American Council of Adoptable Children, The American Adoption Congress, The National Adoption Information Clearinghouse, The Evan B. Donaldson Adoption Institute, The Child Welfare League of America, Eastern European Adoption Coalition, The Joint Council on International Children's Services, New Jersey Adoption Resource Registry, and Maine Department of Human Resources Task Force on Adoption). Some organizations maintain a pulse on adoption as it is being played out in the realm of race, ethnicity, and culture (e.g., National Association of Black Social Workers, Latin American Parents Association, Korean American Adoptee/Adoptive Family Network, and the China Connection), while others engage in a common mission to provide legal information/services to members of the triad (e.g., American Academy of Adoption Attorneys, National Center for Adoption Law & Policy, and Adoption Consumer Assistance and Protection).

OUR CHALLENGE TO THE ACADEMIC
AND PROFESSIONAL COMMUNITY

Notwithstanding our progress so far, there remain fundamental areas that are still in need of systematic and concerted attention by the academic and professional community. We have discussed evidence in this book that the majority of adopted children are not more vulnerable to mental and behavioral problems than the regular population and that the children adopted as infants primarily do as well as nonadopted children in terms of these factors. But we also acknowledge that there is a clear subset of adopted children who struggle with adoption issues, early-life trauma, identity concerns, psychological adjustment, self-esteem, and a host of other factors that must be served appropriately and competently. There is also empirical evidence to suggest that most children adopted transracially do, indeed, mature with a healthy psychological constitution in the long run, but as suggested by Roorda in Chapter 9, some children of color raised in White suburban neighborhoods face identity issues similar to those faced by children of color being raised by White families in that they identify more with the majority culture than with their own ethnic culture (as discussed in www.adoptioninformation institute.org/JGuide.html). Finally, a report by the American Academy of Pediatrics (2003) presented evidence that children raised by gay and lesbian families are not different from children raised by heterosexual couples (http://pediatrics.aappublications.org). The problem is that many of these findings are based on surveys and observations or doctoral dissertations, and we still lack a more systematic mechanism that would allow for the exploration of these issues from multiple sources and under more controlled conditions, hence our fervent call to the scientific and professional communities to bring these issues to bear as central components of their scientific and professional endeavors. Governmental agencies are also called to set up the necessary structure and mechanisms and to allocate resources to encourage more systematic investigation of these issues. Considering the many questions that continue to be raised about adoption at every level of our society, it is clear that our health care professionals, school personnel, mental health providers, legal system, and religious institutions will all benefit from a concerted effort to explore issues related to adoption.

Hence, we have identified a series of crucial topics/issues derived from our careful and extensive review of the literature that are still in need of attention if we are to arrive at a better place in our understanding of the adoption experience. Because children in foster care may also end up in adoption, we have also included this population of children in our exploration. To the extent that academics, graduate students, professionals, governmental officials, and our society at large become actively involved in pursuing these questions, we will be successful in our effort toward the normalization of the adoption experience. We have organized our challenge around eight primary adoption issues:

1. *The need for a systematic examination of the early stage of the adoption experience:*
   - The short- and long-term effects of relinquishing on the birth mother and the birth father as well as the extended birth family
   - How, and the extent to which, the manner of the adoption situation (forcefully vs. voluntarily surrendering and relinquishing the child or the adoptive parents' reasons for their decision to adopt) affects the future adjustment of the adopted child and the birth parents
   - The extent to which the birth mother's decision to give up the child for adoption during pregnancy affects the manner in which the child interacts with the birth mother in the womb, the experience of separation from the birth mother, and the early adjustment to the postnatal environment

2. *The need for a careful examination of developmental challenges likely to have an impact on adoption triad members:*
   - Identification of adoptee-specific challenges to bonding and attachment formation in early versus late adoption
   - Identification of adoptee-specific challenges to identity formation, self-definition, worldview, and the like in early and late adoption
   - Identification of specific challenges to identity formation, self-definition, worldview, and the like for children in foster care and how these children compare with adopted children
   - Identification of the essential ingredients that could help adoptive parents foster bonding in early and late adoption and in foster care situations

- Identification of specific developmental challenges likely to emerge in adoption and foster care situations involving single parents
- Identification of specific developmental challenges likely to emerge in adoption and foster care situations involving lesbian and gay individuals and couples
- Identification of the specific factors (i.e., individual, situational, family, etc.) that make it possible for many adoptees and foster care children to adjust well
- Identification of specific risk factor characteristics in adoptees and foster care children that are related to serious problems during adolescence
- Identification of specific risk factor characteristics in adoptees and foster care children that are related to problems with intimacy and in developing meaningful adult relationships and how they compare with the general population
- Identification of specific developmental challenges faced by single adoptees compared with those faced by multi-adoption families and an examination of these challenges in foster care arrangements
- Examination of the specific impacts the gender of the adopted child may have in single versus multiple adoptions

3. *The need for a serious examination of the birth and adoptive parents'/family's situation:*

- Identification of the essential qualities that adoptive individuals/parents/foster parents should possess to be successful in the adoption and foster care endeavor
- Examination of how (in terms of adjustment and general mental health) adopted/foster care children in a traditional family situation fare when compared with children in a nontraditional family situation (i.e., single parents)
- Identification of the specific ways adoption affects the adoptive parents and extended adoptive families; similarly, an examination of the ways foster care affects foster care parents and the extended foster care family
- Examination of the impact the socioeconomic, sociopolitical, and religious differences of birth and adoptive parents may have on the adopted/foster care child's identity development and ultimate adjustment

4. *The need for a more careful examination of issues pertaining to international and interracial/transracial adoption:*

- Identification of the specific issues likely to emerge in interracial and international adoptions with regard to basic developmental challenges when the adoptive/foster care parents are from different races and ethnicities
- Examination of how transracial adoptees/foster care children raised in same-race adoptive/foster care family situations fare as compared with transracial adoptees and foster care children raised in different-race adoptive/foster care family situations
- Examination of how African American children who are adopted internationally fare when compared with those domestically adopted with regard to ethnic identity formation and general adjustment
- Examination of the experiences of birth parents who relinquished and whose birth children were adopted internationally or transracially
- Examination of the benefits and risks of international and transracial placements

5. *The need to examine more carefully different-level interventions and different programs to determine their levels of effectiveness for members of the triad:*

- Identification of the specific factors that determine when closed versus open/open versus closed adoption is advisable
- Examination of the extent to which the pre- and postintervention programs for the birth and the adoptive parents are beneficial
- Determination of the specific and crucial ingredients to be covered in these programs (i.e., issues of loss and grief, search, reunion, the importance of bonding development, and the specific way to encourage such a development, etc.)

- Examination of the specific factors to consider in determining when these programs are most useful and when they may be counterproductive
- Examination of the determining factors in pursuing search and reunion and who should initiate the search and reunion and when

6. *The need for a systematic examination of school-related issues in what pertains to education and learning in general:*
- Determination of when and how much information should be given to the school about the factors surrounding the adoption/foster care situation of the child
- Determination of specific ways the primary and secondary school curricula could be changed so as to be more responsive to adoption/foster care issues
- Delineation of the specific content of training programs for school personnel to help them with specific ways to address adoption and foster care issues in counseling and in dealing with students at large and parents

7. *A careful look at what should be the response of colleges and universities:*
- Identification of specific ways adoption and foster care issues can be included in training modules within the college and university curricula
- Identification of specific ways that colleges and universities could encourage open discussion and systematic research among faculty and students on specific aspects of adoption/foster care

8. *Consideration of specific regulation/legislation proposals by federal, state, and city government agencies to address the need for adoption:*
- Development of practice regulations to guide the professional practice of those involved in the evaluation and treatment of members of the adoption triad and children in foster care and their families
- Establishment of a mechanism to regulate adoption expenses to reflect the best interests of children and the Hague Convention so child trafficking and financial limitations do not limit the placement options for children
- Establishment of federal government requirements to consider including adopted children and adoptive parents as part of research with human subjects

That is, we are calling for a comprehensive analysis of all aspects of the adoption and foster care situation. We are calling for an examination of descriptive and explanatory factors and for a careful examination of intervention and treatment models used to address health, mental health, and educational issues in members of the triad so that more sophisticated and effective interventions may be possible. For this to work, it will require the involvement of major governmental and private institutions and the media and political support, as well as the active involvement of you, the readers.

We invite you to be part of this journey!

REFERENCES

American Academy of Pediatrics. (2003, June). Report of the task force on the family. *Pediatrics, 111*(6), 1541–1571. Retrieved August 22, 2006, from http://pediatrics.aappublications.org

Encyclopedia of Adoption. (2006). *A brief history of adoption.* Retrieved May 2, 2006, from http://encyclopedia.adoption.com/intro/introduction/lhtml

Foli, K., & Thompson, J. (2004). *The post adoption blues: Overcoming the unforeseen challenges of adoption.* Emmaus, PA: Rodale Books.

Freidman-Kessler, L. (1987). *The measurement of teachers' attitudes toward adopted children.* Doctoral dissertation, Fielding Institute, Santa Barbara, CA. Retrieved April 24, 2006, from http://www.adoptioninformationinstitute.org/JGuide.html

Glaser, G. (2004). *While U.S. couples spend tens of thousands to adopt children from abroad, more and more U.S. birth mothers choose to place their infants with Canadian families: Issues of race, money and culture raise questions about adoption, Canada USA, U.S. children.* Retrieved August 22, 2006, from www.Canadiancrc.com/articles/the_Oregonian_US-adoption Canada/04jul04.htm

Henderson, D. (2002). Challenging the science of the mental health community in adoption issues. *Journal of Social Distress and the Homeless, 11,* 131–141.

Holt International Children's Services. (2006).*Congressional coalition on adoption.* Retrieved May 2, 2006, from www.holtintl.org/coalition.shtml

Ogburn, W. (1964). *On culture and social change: Selected papers.* Chicago: University of Chicago Press.

Pertman, A. (2000). *Adoption nation: How the adoption revolution is transforming America.* New York: Basic Books.

Pertman, A. (2002, January 28). *Adoption in America.* Paper presented at The Future of Family and Tribe Seminar. Retrieved January 30, 2006, from www.clal.org/csa56.html

United States Bureau of the Census. (2000). *Facts for features-adoption.* Retrieved January 30, 2006, from www.adoptioninformationinstitute.org/JGuide.html

Resource Guide

R eaders are encouraged to review the reference list below for further details on the subjects touched upon in the different parts listed in the book. Several of the resources are not referenced in the chapters.

PART I: FOUNDATION

Adoption History Project of the University of Oregon at http://darkwing.uoregon.edu/~adoption

Adoption Information Clearinghouse at http://naic.acf.hhs.gov

AFCARS Reports of the Administration on Children, Youth and Families, Children's Bureau at www.acf.hhs.gov/programs/cb

Child Welfare League of America at http://cwla.org

Dave Thomas Foundation at www.davethomasfoundationforadoption.org

Evan B. Donaldson Adoption Institute at www.adoptioninstitute.org

National Adoption Center at www.adopt.org

National Center for State Courts Adoption Project at http://ncsconline.org

National Data Archive on Child Abuse and Neglect at www.ndacan.cornell.edu

U.S. Census Bureau at www.census.gov

U.S. Department of State at http://travel.state.gov/family

PART II: THEORETICAL ISSUES IN ADOPTION

The Adoption Institute is to "improve the quality of information about adoption, to enhance the understanding and perception of adoption, and to advance adoption policy and practice." The Institute Web site includes a great deal of research-based information about adoption as well as a fully searchable database of adoption research studies.

Adoption Learning Partners at www.adoptionlearningpartners.org

The Adoptive Parents' Committee at www.adoptiveparents.org

Brodzinsky, D. M., & Palacios, J. (2005). *Psychological issues in adoption: Theory, research, and practice*. Westport, CT: Greenwood.

The Center for Adoption Support and Education at www.adoptionsupport.org

The Center for Family Connections at www.kinnect.org

Evan B. Donaldson Adoption Institute at www.adoptioninstitute.org

Gray, D. D. (2002). *Attaching in adoption: Practical tools for today's parents*. Indianapolis, IN: Perspectives Press.

The National Adoption Information Clearinghouse (naic.acf.hhs.gov) is a service of the Children's Bureau, Administration for Children and Families, U.S. Department of Health and Human Services. "The mission of the Clearinghouse is to connect professionals and concerned citizens to timely and well-balanced information on programs, research, legislation, and statistics regarding the safety, permanency, and well-being of children and families."

Wrobel, G. M., Hendrickson, Z., & Grotevant, H. D. (2006). Adoption. In K. Minke & G. Bear (Eds.), *Children's needs: Vol. 3. Development, problems, and alternatives*. Washington, DC: National Association of School Psychologists.

PART III: TRANSRACIAL AND INTERNATIONAL ADOPTION

The American Adoption Congress at www.americanadoptioncongress.org

The Asian Society at www.asiasociety.org

Chinese Cultural Center of San Francisco at www.c-c-c.org

Comer, J. P., & Poussaint, A. F. (1975). *Black child care*. New York: Simon & Schuster.

Crumbley, J. (1999). *Transracial adoption and foster care*. Washington, DC: Child Welfare League of America.

The Cultivation of a Political Asian Consciousness at www.yellowworld.org

Evan B. Donaldson Adoption Institute at www.adoptioninstitute.org

Families with children from China at www.fccny.org

John, J. (2002). *Black baby White hands: A view from the crib*. Silver Spring, MD: Soul Water.

Kennedy, R. (2003). *Interracial intimacies: Sex, marriage, identity, and adoption*. New York: Pantheon Books.

Lukas, J. A. (1985). *Common ground*. New York: Knopf.

McBride, J. (1997). *The color of water: A Black man's tribute to his White mother*. New York: Riverhead Books.

National Adoption Information Clearinghouse at http://naic.acf.hhs.gov

The North American Council on adoptable children at www.nacac.org/pas_database.html

Simon, R. J., & Roorda, R. M. (2000). *In their own voices: Transracial adoptees tell their stories*. New York: Columbia University Press.

Steinberg, G., & Hall, B. (2000). *Inside transracial adoption*. Indianapolis, IN: Perspectives Press.

Tatum, B. D. (2003). *Why are all the Black kids sitting together in the cafeteria?* New York: Basic Books.

West, C. (1993). *Race matters*. New York: Vintage Books.

For regional-specific information, visit the following sites:

1. PACT: An Adoption Alliance in Oakland, CA, at www.pactadopt.org
2. The Center for Adoption Support and Education in Maryland at www .adoptionsupport.org
3. The Center for Family Connections in Cambridge, MA, at www.kinnect.org
4. The New Jersey Adoption Resource Clearing House, a program of Children's Aid and Family Services, Inc., in New Jersey at www.njarch.org
5. The New York Council on Adoptable Children in New York City at www.coac.org/support/support_groups.shtml

PART IV: SPECIAL ISSUES IN ADOPTION

Adoption History Project (Charles Loring Brace, 1826–1890). Retrieved January, 2006, from http://darkwing.uoregon.edu/~adoption

COLAGE: Children of Lesbians and Gay Everywhere at www.colage.org

Dunbar, N., & Grotevant, H. D. (2004). Adoption narratives: The construction of adoptive identity during adolescence. In M. W. Pratt & B. H. Fiese (Eds.), *Family stories and the life course: Across time and generations*. Mahwah, NJ: Lawrence Erlbaum.

Family Matters, 1010 University Ave., Suite C-209, San Diego, CA 92103, Tel. 619-497-2279, ext. 102.

Family Pride of the South, P.O. Box 177, Decatur, GA 30031-0177, Tel. 404-786-9711.

GAY.COM: The "families" link points to www.gay.com/families. Provides search by state for LGB family support organizations.

GLAD: Gay and Lesbian Advocates and Defenders at www.glad.org. Strives for equal treatment under the law for GLBT individuals.

GLSEN: The Gay, Lesbian and Straight Education Network at www.glsen.org. Promotes the respect of all members of every school community, regardless of sexual orientation.

Grotevant, H. D. (1997). Coming to terms with adoption: The construction of identity from adolescence into adulthood. *Adoption Quarterly, 1*(1), 3–27.

Grotevant, H. D., Dunbar, N., Kohler, J. K., & Esau, A. L. (2000). Adoptive identity: How contexts within and beyond the family shape developmental pathways. *Family Relations, 49,* 379–387.

Grotevant, H. D., & McRoy, R. G. (1998). *Openness in adoption: Connecting families of birth and adoption*. Thousand Oaks, CA: Sage.

Henney, S., McRoy, R. G., Ayers-Lopez, S., & Grotevant, H. D. (2003). The impact of openness on adoption agency practices: A longitudinal perspective. *Adoption Quarterly, 6*(3), 31–51.

The Lesbian, Gay, Bisexual & Transgender Community Center, 208 W. 13th Street, New York, NY 10011, Tel. 212-620-7310.

McBride, R. (Ed.). (2003). *New York State foster parent manual*. New York: New York State Office of Children and Family Services Welfare Research.

Miall, C., & March, K. (2005). Open adoption as a family form: Community assessments and social support. *Journal of Family Issues, 26*(3), 380–410.

Minnesota/Texas Adoption Research Project (MTARP) Web site at http://fsos.che.umn.edu/projects/mtarp.html

National Adoption Information Clearinghouse at http://naic.acf.hhs.gov

National Child Welfare Resource Center for Adoption at www.nrcadoption.org

National Conference of State Legislatures. The Adoption and Safe Families Act of 1997 (Public Law 105–89), Titles IV-B and IV-E, Section 403(b), Section 453, and Section 1130(a) of the Social Security Act. Retrieved January, 2006, from www.ncsl.org/programs/cyf/ASFA97.htm

The National Foster Parents Association. Retrieved January 2006 from www.nfpainc.org

National Gay and Lesbian Task Force at www.thetaskforce.org. LGB political advocacy site, with links to state and local resources.

Neil, B., & Howe, D. (Eds.). (2004). *Contact in permanent placements: Research, theory, and practice*. London: British Association for Adoption and Fostering.

Office of Children and Family Services, Foster Care. Retrieved January 2006 from www.ocfs.state.ny.us/main/fostercare/requirements.asp

One Little, West 12th Street, New York, NY 10014, Tel. 212-620-7310.

OutProud: The National Coalition for Gay, Lesbian, Bisexual & Transgendered Youth at www.outproud.org. Support, advocacy and resources for LGB youth.

PFLAG: Parents and Friends of Lesbians and Gays at www.pflag.org. Provides education and advocacy for the health and wellbeing of LGB people and their families and friends.

Proud Parenting at www.proudparenting.com. Provides information on reproduction, surrogacy, adoption/fostering, and other gay parenting issues.

Rainbow Families of Illinois, 961 W. Montana Street, Chicago, IL 60614, 773-472-6469, ext. 464

SNAP: Society of Special Needs Adoptive Parents at www.snap.bc.ca

Sobol, M. P., Daly, K. J., & Kelloway, E. K. (2000). Paths to the facilitation of open adoption. *Family Relations, 49*(4), 419–424.

Wrobel, G. M., Kohler, J. K., Grotevant, H. D., & McRoy, R. G. (1998). Factors related to patterns of information exchange between adoptive parents and children in mediated adoptions. *Journal of Applied Developmental Psychology, 19,* 641–657.

PART V: TRAINING AND EDUCATION
FOR ADOPTION THERAPY COMPETENCE

Andersen, R. (1993). *Second choice: Growing up adopted.* Chesterfield, MO: Badger Hill Press.

Andersen, R., & Tucker, R. (2000). *A bridge less traveled twice visited.* Chesterfield, MO: Badger Hill Press.

Brodzinsky, D. M., & Schechter, M. D. (Eds.). (1994). *The psychology of adoption.* Oxford, UK: Oxford University Press.

Lifton, B. J. (1994). *Journey of the adopted self.* New York: Basic Books.

Pavao, J. M. (1980). *Mothers and daughters.* Paper presented at the Wellesley College Center on Research, Massachusetts.

Pavao, J. M. (1996). Post adoption services model. In Casey Family Services, *Post adoption proceedings* (pp. 75–82). Green Cove Springs, FL: Hartford Press.

Pavao, J. M. (1997). Adoption and healing. In *Conference on adoption trust* (pp. 32–36, 196–201). Wellington, New Zealand: New Zealand Education and Healing Trust.

Pavao, J. M. (1998/2005). *The family of adoption.* Boston: Beacon Press.

Pavao, J. M. (2001). Older child open adoption. In V. Groze & K. Rosenberg (Eds.), *Clinical and practice issues in adoption: Bridging the gap between placed as infants and as older children.* Westport, CT: Bergen & Garvey.

Pavao, J. M. (1980). Adoption. In Boston Women's Health Collective, *Our bodies, ourselves.* New York: Simon & Schuster.

Pavao, J. M. Secrecy in adoption. In J. Shlien (Ed.), *The psychology of secrecy.*[AU: Please provide year and page range.]

Pavao, J. M. In A. Baran, L. Coleman, & S. K. Roszia (Eds.), *Creating kinship.* Child Welfare Resource Center for Organizational Development.[AU: Please provide year, chapter title and page range.]

Verrier, N. (1997). *The primal wound: Understanding the adopted child.* Baltimore: Gateway Press.

PART VI: RESEARCH FINDINGS IN ADOPTION WORK

Andersen, R. (1993). *Second choice: Growing up adopted.* Chesterfield, MO: Badger Hill Press.

Andersen, R., & Tucker, R. (2000). *A bridge less traveled twice visited.* Chesterfield, MO: Badger Hill Press.

Lifton, B. J. (1994). *Journey of the adopted self.* New York: Basic Books.

Maxtone-Graham, K. (1983). *An adopted woman.* New York: Remi Books.

Russell, M. (2000). *Adoption wisdom.* Santa Monica, CA: Broken Branch.

PART VII: ASSESSMENT AND
TREATMENT ISSUES IN ADOPTION

Abbarno, G. J. M. (Ed.). (1999). *The ethics of homelessness: Philosophical perspectives.* Amsterdam: Rodopi.

Brodzinsky, D. M., Schechter, M. D., & Henig, R. M. (1992). *Being adopted: The lifelong search for self.* New York: Doubleday.

Federici, R. S. (2003). *Help for the hopeless child: A guide for families.* With special discussion for assessing and treating the post-institutionalized child. Washington, DC: Federici Associates.

Hughes, D. A. (1998). *Building the bonds of attachment: Awakening love in deeply troubled children. A guide for parents and professionals*. Lanham, MD: Jason Aronson.

Hughes, D. A. (2000). *Facilitating developmental attachment: The road to emotional recovery and behavioral change in foster and adopted children*. Lanham, MD: Jason Aronson.

John, J. (2002). *Black baby White hands: A view from the crib*. Silver Spring, MD: Soul Water.

Karen, R. (1994). *Becoming attached: First relationships and how they shape our capacity to love*. Oxford, UK: Oxford University Press.

Keck, G. C., & Kupecky, R. M. (1998). *Adopting the hurt child: Hope for adoptive families with special needs kids*. Colorado Springs, CO: Navpress.

Lifton, B. J. (1994). *Journey of the adopted self*. New York: Basic Books.

Nydam, R. J. (1999). *Adoptees come of age: Living within two families*. Louisville, KY: John Knox/Westminster Press.

Pertman, A. (2000). *Adoption nation: How the adoption revolution is changing America*. New York: Basic Books.

Russell, M. (2000). *Adoption wisdom*. Santa Monica, CA: Broken Branch.

Verrier, N. N. (1993). *The primal wound: Understanding the adopted child*. Baltimore: Gateway Press.

Wadia-Ellis, S. (1995). *The adoption reader: Birth mothers, adoptive mothers, and adopted daughters tell their stories*. New York: Avalon.

Index

About the Editors

Amanda L. Baden, PhD, is currently Assistant Professor in the Department of Counseling, Human Development, and Educational Leadership at Montclair State University in Montclair, New Jersey, where she is on the faculty in the counseling graduate program. Her research interests focus on adoption triad members, transracial/international adoption issues, racial and cultural identity, and multicultural counseling competence. She received the honor of being chosen as an Angel in Adoption in 2005 by Congressional Representative Jerold Nadler. She has also written and spoken extensively on adoption-related issues. In 2003 and 2005, she and her colleagues published several papers in *The Counseling Psychologist* on adoption and birth parents. A related article on adult adoptees is in press in the same journal. She has served as the cochair since 2002 for the national conferences on adoption hosted by St. John's University, and was the keynote speaker for the fourth conference held in 2006 which focused on transracial adoption. She is a licensed psychologist in New York City and has a clinical practice in Manhattan. She received her PhD in counseling psychology from Michigan State University. More information about her is available on her Web site at www.transracialadoption.net.

Frank A. Biafora, PhD, is Associate Professor of Sociology in the Department of Sociology and Anthropology at St. John's University, New York. His ongoing research addresses a range of issues that affect the psychosocial development of youth and adolescence, with a special focus on risk factors for substance use, delinquency, and victimization. His most recent research and scholarly publications explore topics such as the perpetuation of school tracking on student learning, the impact of adolescent stress on alcohol and tobacco experimentation, the relationships between racial mistrust and delinquent behaviors, and the protective influences of Latino ethnic enclaves on street crime victimization. In addition to his scholarly achievements, since 1999 he has served as Associate Dean in the College of Liberal Arts and Sciences and as the codirector of the Ronald McNair Post-Baccalaureate Achievement Program. He graduated from the University of Florida (BA and MA) and received his PhD from the University of Miami.

Alina Camacho-Gingerich, PhD, a renowned literary critic and writer, is Chair of the Committee on Latin American and Caribbean Studies (CLACS) and Professor in the Department of Languages and Literatures at St. John's University, New York. A leading scholar on Latin American and Latino studies, she is the author of numerous multidisciplinary studies, including the books *La cosmovisión poética de José Lezama Lima en Paradiso y Oppiano Licario*, *Coping in America: The Case of Caribbean East Indians*, and *Mexico in the Twenty-First Century: Selected Essays*, and more than 65 scholarly articles, chapters, and reviews on Latin American and Caribbean studies, published in peer-reviewed academic journals, books, and anthologies. In addition, she has presented more than 80 papers in international and national symposia of scholarly and learned societies and is on the editorial board of various academic journals. She is frequently interviewed by the media for her expertise on Latin American and Caribbean issues and has been the recipient of many professional awards and recognitions. She has been involved in adoption-related issues as one of the organizers and cosponsors of St. John's University's biannual adoption conference.

Rafael A. Javier, PhD, ABPP, is Professor of Psychology and Director of Interagencies Training and Research Initiatives and the Postgraduate Professional Development Programs at St. John's University. He is on the faculty and a supervisor at New York University Medical Center, Department of Psychiatry, and the Object Relations Institute. Prior to joining St. John's University, he was the head of psychology at Kingsboro Psychiatric Center and on the faculty at Downstate Medical Center. He has been working extensively on issues of adoption, including creating and co-organizing a biannual conference structure to address issues affecting the members of the adoption triad. He has edited several special journal issues on adoption published by the *Journal of Social Distress and the Homeless*. In 2004, he was given the special honor of Angel in Adoption by the Congressional Adoption Coalition in Washington, D.C., in recognition of the work he has done to advance the cause of adoption in the academic and professional communities. He holds a PhD in clinical psychology and Postdoctoral Certificate from New York University. He holds diplomates in Clinical Psychology and in Psychoanalysis from the American Board of Professional Psychology. He also holds a diplomate in Psychological Assessment, Evaluation and Testing from the American College of Forensic Examiners.

About the Contributors

Susan Ayers-Lopez, MEd, is Research Project Coordinator with the Center for Social Work Research at the University of Texas at Austin School of Social Work. She, Harold Grotevant, and Ruth McRoy have collaborated for more than 20 years.

Carol Anderson Boyer has worked in the information technology sector for the past 10 years. She is currently pursuing a master's degree in counseling at Montclair State University and holds a bachelor's degree in music education. She is interested in how identity development for adopted persons parallels that of other multicultural minorities. She plans to become an individual and couples counselor and has a particular interest in serving the lesbian, gay, bisexual, and transgender community.

Susan Branco-Rodriguez is a licensed professional counselor in Virginia. She maintains a clinical practice serving families created through adoption. She completed postgraduate research and training in the field of adoption, incorporating both her knowledge of mental health services and her experiences as an adopted person from Colombia, South America.

Betty Buchsbaum is on the faculty and a supervisor at the Andrus Children's Center (formerly the Center for Preventive Psychiatry) in White Plains, New York, and is in private practice. She was formerly Assistant Clinical Professor in the Psychiatry Department, Albert Einstein College of Medicine, Bronx, New York, and at New York Presbyterian Hospital, Westchester Division. From 1986 to 1999, she was the Director of the Psychology Internship Program at the Center for Preventive Psychiatry. She has written several articles dealing with the developmental aspects of bereavement, with a focus on children's memories of a deceased parent. She received her master's degree in psychology from the University of Pennsylvania and her PhD from Yeshiva University.

Jeanna Carlson (née Webster) is a School Counselor with the School District of Marshfield (Wisconsin). She participated in this research as an undergraduate student while attending the University of Wisconsin–Stevens Point and presented an early version of this chapter at the American Adoption Congress Annual Convention in Nashville, Tennessee. She received her master's degree in guidance and counseling from the University of Wisconsin–Stout.

Mary Jo Carr has been involved for over 12 years with adoption issues through her involvement with Concerned United Birth Parents and the American Adoption Congress. The chapter in this book contains research findings from her doctoral dissertation. As a birth mother who never had other children, she was interested in learning whether there were characteristics in women that would inhibit them from having additional children after relinquishing a child for adoption. She also wanted to contribute to the literature about birth mothers, a subject which is still in great need of attention. She received her doctorate in psychology from the California Graduate Institute in Westwood, California.

Christopher Deeg, PhD, is a licensed psychologist who maintains a private practice in Dix Hills, New York. He specializes in the treatment of adoptees and in all aspects of adoption.

He regularly consults with adoption agencies and is involved in adoption evaluations and consultation for adopting parents, partners, and single-parent adoptions. He is the author of the following previously published papers: "On the Adoptee's Cathexis of the Lost Object," "Defensive Functions of the Adoptee's Cathexis of the Lost Object," "On the Adoptee's Search for Identity," and "Issues of Psychoanalytic Technique With Adoptees."

Kathleen M. Doyle has worked as an adoptive and foster care home finder and supervisor of foster children, a school psychologist, and a licensed psychologist. During her career, she has provided services to children and families in widely diverse family structures. During the past decade, among other functions, she has been the Executive Secretary for the State Board for Psychology in New York State. She received a BA in sociology from the college of St. Rose, a master's degree in clinical psychology, and a doctoral degree in professional child psychology from St. John's University.

Nora Dunbar writes in the area of adolescent development with a focus on identity formation. She lives in Flagstaff, Arizona, with her husband and two sons. She received her MS in developmental psychology from the University of California at Santa Cruz and her PhD in family social science from the University of Minnesota.

Amy M. Lash Esau currently teaches marriage and family courses at Northwestern College in St. Paul, Minnesota, and other colleges in the Minneapolis-St. Paul area. She also provides community-based marriage and family education through her business, Family Points. She received her doctorate in family social science from the University of Minnesota in 2000. Her dissertation research focused on identity and intimacy development of birth mothers following placement of infants for adoption.

Dawn Esposito, PhD, is Associate Professor of Sociology and the Chair of the Sociology and Anthropology Department at St. John's University. She is currently researching the migration of Eastern European women's labor to Greece and Italy and its impact on southern Mediterranean family structure. Her most recent articles on popular culture have appeared in *MELUS,* the *Journal of the Society for the Study of Multi-Ethnic Literature,* and *VIA.*

Francine Fishman works with members of the adoption triad in a special education setting as an LMSW. She is a reunited adoptee, in reunion for 9 years. She and her husband are busy raising three daughters in New York. She earned her master's in business administration while working as a pension administrator for 10 years. She has since earned her master's in social work from Stony Brook University.

Madelyn Freundlich, MSW, JD, LLM, has worked in the field of child welfare for almost 20 years. She is a social worker with training in public health and law. Her publications include four volumes on ethics in adoption, articles on legal issues in adoption, and guides on best practices in adoption.

Harold D. Grotevant, PhD, is Distinguished University Teaching Professor of Family Social Science at the University of Minnesota. His research focuses on relationships in adoptive families and on identity development in adolescents and young adults. He is a Senior Research Fellow of the Evan B. Donaldson Adoption Institute, Fellow of the American Psychological Association and the National Council on Family Relations, and former Board President of Adoptive Families of America.

Elliotte Sue Harrington is currently pursuing a master's degree in counseling at Montclair State University. She worked for 17 years in the financial industry. Now, she plans to become a family and marriage counselor and specialize in working with members of the adoption triad. She and her husband Ron are new parents to their daughter, who joined their family through domestic adoption. She has a bachelor's degree in music.

Douglas B. Henderson, PhD, is an adoptee who found his birth families in 1983. He retired in the spring of 2001 as Professor of Psychology at the University of Wisconsin–Stevens Point, and was a licensed Wisconsin psychologist, specializing in behavior problems in children and adolescents. Since the mid-1980s, he has been a presenter of a variety of workshop sessions at national and regional American Adoption Congress conferences. He was a copresenter of programs on special issues for male adoptees, and for many years he led the Stevens Point chapter of Adoption Information and Direction, a triad-based search and support group. He served for 3 years as State President of this group. He was a member of the American Adoption Congress Board of Directors and served as Director of Professional Relations and Continuing Education, as the Midwest Regional Director, and as Chairperson of the Nominations and Elections Committee.

Susan M. Henney, PhD, is Assistant Professor at the University of Houston, Downtown. Her research focuses on the experiences of birthfamily members and on volunteerism across the lifespan. She received her PhD in Child Development and Family Relationships from the University of Texas at Austin. While at the University of Texas, she also worked as a Post-Doctoral Fellow on the openness in adoption research project.

René Hoksbergen, PhD, is on the faculty of Social Sciences at Utrecht University. He has been a professor in the field of adoption since 1984. He has held various posts in the fields of education and adoption. He has written 30 books on adoption, adult education, modern procreation, and adolescence, some of which have been translated into English and German. He has authored hundreds of articles in several journals in different countries. He has his own practice counseling adoptees and adoptive parents. He studied social psychology, pedagogics, and mathematical statistics at the University of Amsterdam (1962–1969).

Elizabeth J. Keagy volunteers her time at Shelter Our Sisters, a shelter for battered women and their children, and teaches part-time at a local community college. She earned her master's degree in clinical psychology from Loyola College in Baltimore and her master's degree in counseling from Montclair State University. She holds a bachelor's degree in psychology and religion from Muhlenberg College, where she met her husband, Seth Fischer. She is currently staying home to raise their new son, Ben.

Julie K. Kohler is the Director of Evaluation and Program Assessment/Manager for the Fund for Education Organizing at Public Interest Projects (PIPs) in New York City. Prior to joining PIPs, she worked for the Miami-based John S. and James L. Knight Foundation, where she directed the foundation's National Venture Fund, and the University of Maryland's Department of Family Studies, where she taught and conducted research on a variety of child and family policy topics. She received bachelor's degrees in psychology and human development/family studies from the University of Wisconsin–Stout and a master's degree and doctorate in family social science from the University of Minnesota.

Jan ter Laak, PhD, is Associate Professor in Developmental Psychology at Utrecht University. He is the author of a book on psychological assessment, among others. He has published many articles with the participants of the Dutch Rumanian Adoptee project. He is the chairman of the Child and Youth Section of the Dutch Psychological Association and chairman of the Dutch committee for judging tests and questionnaires according to APA standards. He studied psychology and philosophy.

Christian Langworthy is the author of *The Geography of War*, which won Poet Magazine's Grand Prize National Poetry Chapbook Award in 1994. Among awards and honors he has received are a Columbia University Writing Arts Fellowship and Pulitzer Prize and Pushcart Nominations in 1995 for *The Geography of War*. His poetry and fiction have been selected for numerous anthologies such as *Isn't It Romantic: 100 Love Poems by Younger American Poets, Charlie Chan Is Dead II, Watermark, From Both Sides Now, Bold Words, Premonitions, Poetry Nation, Music, Pictures, & Stories, A Poetry Anthology, Tilting the Continent, Muae,* and *Asian American Literature Anthology*. Various poems and fiction have been published in the *Michigan Quarterly Review, Fence Magazine, The Recorder, PBS American Experience, Salon.com, Manoa, Failbetter.com, Can We Have Our Ball Back?, Mudfish, Brooklyn Rail Literary Magazine, Vietnam Forum,* and the *Asian Pacific American Journal*. In 2003, several of his poems were performed in libretto at the National Gallery of

Art and at the Glimmerglass Opera Festival. In 2002, dance choreographer Tai Dang incorporated his poem *Mango* into performance: "Fragile. Family. Structures." at the Danspace Project in St. Mark's Church.

Betty Jean Lifton is a writer and adoption counselor. She is the author of *Twice Born: Memoirs of an Adopted Daughter, Journey of the Adopted Self: A Quest for Wholeness, Lost and Found: The Adoption Experience,* and the children's book *Tell Me a Real Adoption Story.* Her books also include *The King of Children,* a biography of Janusz Korczak, one of the world's first children's rights advocates. During the years she lived in the Far East, she wrote *The Children of Vietnam* and *A Place Called Hiroshima.* Dr. Lifton has conducted workshops here and abroad on the psychology of the adopted child, the birth parents, and the adoptive parents. She has been a lecturer at Harvard Medical School, as as at numerous colleges, hospitals, and adoption agencies, and spoken on radio and television. She was a board member of the American Adoption Congress and on the ethics committee of Evan B. Donaldson Adoption Institute. She has a clinical practice in Cambridge and in Manhattan and does telephone counseling across the country. Her Web site is at www.bjlifton.com.

Michael F. McGinn became active in adoption issues while undertaking a research project to complete his doctoral degree in child clinical psychology at Pace University (New York). Subsequently, he has attended and made presentations at numerous adoption-themed conferences and has authored a previous contribution to the literature. He is currently employed as a psychologist in the Freeport, New York, public schools. His personal adoption journey began with his relinquishment for adoption at birth, at which time he was named Joseph by his birth family. He was subsequently adopted as Michael F. McGinn, at the age of 10 weeks.

Hollee A. McGinnis is currently the Policy and Operations Director at the Evan B. Donaldson Adoption Institute, a national organization dedicated to improving adoption policy and practice. She is a prominent educator, speaker, and community organizer on international and transracial adoptions. In 1996, she founded Also-Known-As, Inc., a nonprofit, adult, intercountry adoptee organization providing postadoption services. McGinnis, also known as Lee Hwa Yeong, was adopted from South Korea and has united with her birth family. McGinnis received her master's degree in science from Columbia University School of Social Work and a post-master's clinical social work fellowship at the Yale University Child Study Center.

Ruth G. McRoy, PhD, is Research Professor and the Ruby Lee Piester Centennial Professor Emerita at the University of Texas at Austin School of Social Work. She has coauthored *Openness in Adoption: New Practices, New Issues* (with H. Grotevant and K. White, 1988) and *Openness in Adoption: Exploring Family Connections* (with H. Grotevant, 1998). She and Harold D. Grotevant are currently writing a third book based on their research on longitudinal outcomes of openness in adoption for members of the adoption triad.

Ronald J. Nydam is the Executive Director of Adoption Dynamics, an agency providing counseling for triad members, community education, and legislative support for adoption reform. He also serves as Professor of Pastoral Care at Calvin Seminary in Grand Rapids, Michigan. In 1994, he coproduced *More Than Love,* a 55-minute video presentation on healthy adoptive development, which includes a guidebook on the issues and impact of relinquishment and adoption. He is a frequent speaker and presenter at conferences of the American Adoption Congress. Most recently, he wrote a book, *Adoptees Come of Age: Living Within Two Families,* on the emotional and spiritual dimensions of adoptive development. He holds a PhD from the University of Denver and the Iliff School of Theology, where he wrote a dissertation titled *Hope and Fantasy in the Lives of Searching Adopted Adults.*

Behnaz Pakizegi is Professor of Psychology at Wm. Paterson University, her professional home for the past 29 years. She was Director of the MA Program in Clinical and Counseling Psychology at the University for 6 years. She is also a licensed psychologist in New Jersey and is in private practice. She received her PhD from Cornell University in 1974.

Penny Callan Partridge was an activist in the adoption community, beginning in the early 1970s. She co-founded Adoption Forum, in Philadelphia, one of the earliest groups to bring together adoption triad members and others "for more mutual respect." Partridge was the first elected President of the American Adoption Congress and a member of the Advisory Board of the National Child Welfare Training Center.

She wrote the article on self-help groups for *A Handbook of Child Welfare* (Laird & Hartman, 1985) and three articles about adopted people that were published in *Smith College Studies in Social Work.* Her collections of poems are titled *An Adoptee's Dreams, Pandora's Hope,* and *New Legs.* Her next book, *Bridge of Words,* will pair 13 poems with essays tracing each poem's evolution with the poet to its reception by a particular listener or reader in the adoption community. An adopted person and a parent of two, both by open adoption, Partridge has a degree in English from Stanford and one in social work from Smith.

Joyce Maguire Pavao, EdD, LCSW, LMFT, is the Founder and CEO of Center for Family Connections, Inc. (CFFC; established in 1995) in Cambridge and New York; Adoption Resource Center (ARC; established in 1973) in Cambridge; Pre/Post Adoption Consulting Team (PACT; established in 1978) in Cambridge; and Family Connections Training Institute (FaCT; established in 1995) in Cambridge. She is a Clinical Member and Approved Supervisor of the American Association of Marriage and Family Therapy, Clinical Member of the American Orthopsychiatric Association (Ortho), and Clinical Member of the American Family Therapy Association. She is a member and past director of the American Adoption Congress, former Board member of the Open Door Society of Massachusetts, of Kinship Alliance in Monterey, California, of the Education and Policy Board of Adoptive Families of America in Minneapolis and the Practice Board of the Evan B. Donaldson Adoption Institute in New York, and currently on the Editorial Boards of *Adoptive Families* magazine and *Foster Families Today* magazine, on the Board of Directors of the Home for Little Wanderers in Boston, on the Adoption Advisory Board of the Child Welfare League of America, and on the Library Board of the Oregon Post Adoption Resource Center. She has done extensive training, both nationally and internationally. She is an adjunct faculty member and Lecturer in Psychiatry at Harvard Medical School and has served as a consultant to various public and private child welfare agencies, adoption agencies, schools, and community groups, as well as probate and family court judges, lawyers, and clergy. Additionally, she has worked closely with individuals, families created by adoption and foster care, and other complex blended family constructions. She has developed models for treatment and for training using her systemic, intergenerational, and developmental framework "The Normative Crises in the Development of the Adoptive Family," and her book *The Family of Adoption* has received high acclaim. She has received many awards and honors, including the Children's Bureau/U.S. Department of Health and Human Services "Adoption Excellence Award for Family Contribution" (2003) and the Congressional Coalition on Adoption award for "Angels in Adoption" (2000), for which she was nominated by Senator Edward Kennedy and Congressman Mike Capuano.

Raúl Ernesto Pitteri, Lic., is a psychologist. He was on the staff at José T. Borda Neuropsychiatric Hospital in Buenos Aires (1991–1993), Resident Psychologist at Perrando Hospital in Chaco (1994–1999), Assistant Professor in Adolescence Evolutive Psychology at La Cuenca del Plata University (1997–1999) in Corrientes, Argentina, and Professor in Forensic Psychology (2000 till the present) in the Departments of Law and Psychology, also at La Cuenca del Plata University, Corrientes. He has given lectures at national and international congresses. He is an expert psychologist at Family Court in Chaco, Argentina, and Researcher on domestic violence and adoption at La Cuenca del Plata University, Corrientes, Argentina. He graduated from the Rosario National University, Argentina, in 1991.

Theresa Kennedy Porch holds a bachelor's degree from Cornell University, and has worked as a private investigator for over 20 years. She recently completed her master's degree in counseling at Montclair State University. Her extended family includes many adopted family members. She is married and has two adult daughters.

Barbara A. Rall, LCSW, is currently the Assistant Director at Children's Aid and Family Services, Inc., where she manages the New Jersey Adoption Resource Clearing House, a federally funded program to disseminate information and assistance to people whose lives have been touched by adoption. She is married and the parent of four children, two by birth and two adopted, as well as the grandmother of three. She has a master's in social work from New York University and is a licensed clinical social worker who has worked in the adoption field since 1983.

Rhonda M. Roorda was born in Rochester, New York, in 1969. She was adopted 2 years later into a White family and was raised in the Washington, D.C., metropolitan area with her brother, Christopher, and sister, Jean, both biologically related to the Roordas. She has served as program associate to the Council for Christian Colleges and Universities in Washington, D.C., where she concentrated on racial and ethnic issues in higher education. She has worked on several community and media relation projects through Michigan State University and at local TV and radio stations in the Midwest. She coauthored *In Their Own Voices: Transracial Adoptees Tell Their Stories* (with Rita J. Simon), which was published in the spring of 2000. She has written featured articles for *Fostering Families TODAY* magazine and continues to speak across the country on issues facing Black and Biracial adoptees in White families. Currently, she is working as Coordinator of Financial and Support Services at an educational advocacy organization in Lansing, Michigan. She lives in Brighton, Michigan, with her husband. She earned her bachelor's degree in telecommunications from Calvin College in 1992 and her master's degree in communication-urban studies from Michigan State University in 1996.

Sarah Saffian, an adoptee, is the author of *Ithaka: A Daughter's Memoir of Being Found*; a new edition of the book with a current Afterword has recently been published. She is on the Board of Directors of Spence-Chapin Services and on the Advisory Board of *Adoptive Families Magazine*, which featured an excerpt from *Ithaka* in its 2005 roundup of best adoption literature. She has spoken on national television and radio programs and at conferences including the American Adoption Congress, Concerned United Birth Parents, Also Known As, Bastard Nation, and St. John's University. She holds a BA from Brown University and an MFA in creative writing from Columbia.

Daniel A. Sass was an advisee of Doug Henderson at the University of Wisconsin–Stevens Point, where he worked toward his undergraduate degree in psychology. He recently received a doctorate in educational psychology with an emphasis on research and evaluation from the University of Wisconsin–Milwaukee, where he studies various issues related to measurement and statistics.

Robbie J. Steward, PhD, is Professor, Director of the Michigan State University Master's Counseling Program and an APA Division 45 Fellow. She received a doctorate in counseling psychology from the University of Oklahoma in 1984. Her research areas include issues of race/ethnicity in training, service delivery, and academic persistence.

Mary O'Leary Wiley is an adoptee who specializes in the adoption kinship network in her independent practice as a licensed psychologist in Altoona, Pennsylvania. She has spoken widely on growing up adopted and on psychotherapy and clinical issues for those whose lives are touched by adoption. She has also published on adoption issues in psychology journals. She was Director of the Counseling Center at Ithaca College (New York) and in independent practice in both Ithaca and Gaithersburg, Maryland, prior to Altoona. She is also cofounder of the Center for Adoption Education of Central Pennsylvania (www.caecp.org). She received her PhD from the University of Maryland in 1982.

Janet Rivkin Zuckerman is Visiting Instructor at the Westchester Center for the Study of Psychoanalysis and Psychotherapy, White Plains, New York. She is Adjunct Clinical Supervisor of doctoral students at the Derner Institute of Advanced Psychological Studies, Adelphi

University, and the Ferkauf Graduate School, Yeshiva University, and a faculty member and supervisor at the Andrus Children's Center (formerly the Center for Preventive Psychiatry), White Plains, New York. She maintains a private practice in psychoanalysis and psychotherapy in White Plains, New York. She received her PhD in clinical psychology from the Derner Institute of Advanced Psychological Studies, Adelphi University, and her Certificate in psychoanalysis from the New York University Postdoctoral Program in Psychotherapy and Psychoanalysis.